Landscape, Community and Colonisation: the North Somerset Levels during the 1st to 2nd millennia AD

best wishes
Steve

Landscape, Community and Colonisation: the North Somerset Levels during the 1st to 2nd millennia AD

by Stephen Rippon

with contributions by

Nigel Cameron, Paul Davies, Simon Dobinson, Rowena Gale, Alejandra Gutiérrez, Sheila Hamilton-Dyer, Jen Heathcote, Colin Humphreys, Julie Jones, Amanda Kear, Annette Kreiser, Alan Outram, Richard Parker, the late David Richards, Jane Timby, Heather Tinsley, and Ciorstaidh Trevarthen

CBA Research Report 152
Council for British Archaeology
2006

Published 2006 by the Council for British Archaeology
St Mary's House, 66 Bootham, York YO30 7BZ

ISBN 978-1-902771-67-0

British Library Cataloguing in Publication Data
A catalogue for this book is available from the British Library

Cover designed by BP Design, York

Typeset by Archetype IT Ltd, www.archetype-it.com

Printed by the Charlesworth Group

Front cover illustration: The Banwell River, looking south from ST 398 608

Back cover illustration: Puxton, looking north across the North Someset Levels towards Clevedon and the Severn Estuary

Contents

List of abbreviations

BaTM	field number in Banwell tithe map/apportionment
BCA	Birmingham City Archives
BL	British Library
BodL	Bodleian Library
BRO	Bristol Records Office
CoTM	field number in Congresbury tithe map/apportionment
DRO	Devon Records Office
GRO	Gloucestershire Records Office
LPL	Lambeth Palace Library
MC	Merton College
MHWST	Mean High Water Spring Tide
PxTM	field number in Puxton tithe map/apportionment
OS	Ordnance Survey
PRO	Public Records Office
SMR	Sites and Monuments Record
SRO	Somerset Records Office
SRS	Somerset Records Society
WCA	Wells Cathedral Archives
WCL	Weston-super-Mare Central Library
WiTM	field number in Wick St Lawrence tithe map/apportionment
WRO	Wiltshire Records Office
YaTM	field number in Yatton tithe map/apportionment

List of illustrations

List of tables

Acknowledgements

The North Somerset Levels Project was very much a collaborative venture in which many people contributed. Firstly this project could not have been carried out without the generous funding from the British Academy, the Arts and Humanities Research Board, the Society of Antiquaries, the Roman Research Trust, Royal Archaeological Institute, the Maltwood Fund, and the Haverfield Bequest. I must thank all the landowners and householders who gave permission for the archaeological fieldwork and standing building recording, most notably Mr and Mrs David James, Mr Derek Mead, and the Avon Wildlife Trust. The Project benefited from the involvement of an excellent team of specialists who have contributed to this volume, and in particular I must thank Gill Bedingfield and Martin Ecclestone for their work on the documentary sources. Keith Gardner and Linda Jenkins were also an invaluable source of local intelligence, and Dick Broomhead kindly supplied a copy of his unpublished survey of Congresbury parish. Sue Shaw kindly discussed the results of her standing buildings survey in Barton and other research in the Winscombe area. I must also thank the many staff and students at the Universities of Exeter and Reading who have provided help, encouragement, and contributed to the fieldwork, notably Mike Rouillard for his supervision in the field and assistance in preparing illustrations. Martin Gillard, Charlotte Hawkins, and Colin Humphreys also supervised various aspects of the fieldwork. Alan Lambourne transcribed the Wick St Lawrence tithe survey and Ralph Fyfe carried out the coring transect. John Allan and Roger Taylor identified green-glazed ridge tile and worked Dundry stone respectively from 'Courts'. I would also like to thank the following for their assistance with other aspects of the project: Michael Costen (University of Bristol), Simon Cox and Ed McSloy (Cotswold Archaeology), Charles and Nancy Hollinrake, Jane Hill and Chris Richards (North Somerset Museum), Andrew Jackson (University of Bristol), Steve Minnitt (Somerset County Museum), Vince Russett (County Archaeologist), Andrew Young (Avon Archaeological Unit), and staff at the local studies libraries and records office in Bristol, Taunton, Weston-super-Mare, and Trowbridge. The RAF air photographs are reproduced with the permission of the National Monuments Record, English Heritage, while the others were taken by the author from planes flown by Alan James and Philip Pearce.

Alejandra Gutiérrez thanks Alan Vince and Christopher Gerrard for their help with the identification of the medieval wares, Jane Timby and Paul Tyers for their comments on the medieval puncheon of Roman style, and Jane Young for her comments on the Stamford ware sherd. Sheila Hamilton-Dyer thanks P Saddler for checking the *Ciconia* material at Tring. Julie Jones thanks Mary Wood of the Avon Wildlife Trust and Karren Pollack of English Nature for information supplied on the contemporary flora and fauna of the Puxton Dolemoor Nature Reserve. Amanda Kear wishes to acknowledge the help given by Vanessa Straker, Julie Jones, and Prof Derek Briggs; Dr Liz Cook of the University of Bristol; Sam Hallett of the Natural History Department, Bristol City Museum, for access to the reference collections, and Jim Williams of the University of Sheffield for providing a list of avian taphonomy references and advice on identifying barn owl assemblages. Terry Green and Robert Waterhouse are thanked for their comments on the standing building survey and for assisting in the survey of Hodders Farm, and Richard Parker thanks the foreman and staff of Layzell Building Conservation and the Churches Conservation Trust for allowing access to Puxton church during conservation work in 2004.

Finally, many friends and colleagues helped with this project through discussions and encouragement at various conferences, seminars, field visits, and of courses pubs, most notably Mick Aston and Chris Gerrard of the Shapwick Project, and Chris Dyer, Mark Gardner, Richard Jones, and Mark Page of the Whittlewood Project.

List of contributors

Nigel Cameron
Environmental Change Research Centre, Department of Geography, University College London, 26 Bedford Way, LONDON, WC1H 0AP

Paul Davies
Geography Department, Bath Spa University College, Newton Park, BATH, BA2 9BN

Simon Dobinson
Environmental Change Research Centre, Department of Geography, University College London, 26 Bedford Way, LONDON, WC1H 0AP

Rowena Gale
Bachfield House, Kimbolton, LEOMINSTER, HR6 0EP

Alejandra Gutiérrez
Swale Cottage, Low Swainby Farm, Burneston, BEDALE, North Yorkshire, DL8 2JH

Sheila Hamilton-Dyer
5 Suffolk Avenue, Shirley, SOUTHAMPTON, SO15 5EF

Jen Heathcote
Centre for Archaeology, English Heritage, Fort Cumberland, Fort Cumberland Road, Eastney, PORTSMOUTH, PO4 9LD

Colin Humphreys
The Thornes, Kentisbury, BARNSTAPLE, North Devon, EX31 4NQ

Julie Jones
22 Beaconsfield Road, Knowle, BRISTOL, BS4 2JF

Amanda Kear
BBC Natural History Unit, Whiteladies Road, BRISTOL, BS8 ILR

Annette Kreiser
260 Gertrude Road, NORWICH, NR3 4YR

Alan Outram
Department of Archaeology, University of Exeter, Laver Building, North Park Road, EXETER, EX4 4QE

Richard Parker
Exeter Archaeology, Bradninch Place, Gandy Street, EXETER, EX4 3LS

Stephen Rippon
Department of Archaeology, University of Exeter, Laver Building, North Park Road, EXETER, EX4 4QE

Jane Timby
Sister Mary Cottage, High Street, CHALFORD, Gloucestershire, GL6 8DH

Heather Tinsley
112 Weston Road, Long Ashton, BRISTOL, BS41 9B2

Ciorstaidh Trevarthen
Somerset County Museum, Taunton Castle, Castle Green, TAUNTON, Somerset TA1 4AA

Summary

Britain's historic landscape provides a remarkably detailed record of past human endeavour over many millennia that has created the networks of fields, settlements, communication systems, and patterns of land use and resource exploitation that make up the countryside and townscapes of today. Local and regional variation in the character of this landscape also forms an important part of our modern sense of place and community: the compact, nucleated villages of the Northamptonshire, for example, are very different from the scattered farmsteads and hamlets of Devon. Between 1993 and 2004 the North Somerset Levels Project (NSLP) set out to explore how such local and regional variation in landscape character came into being, with a time frame extending from the late Iron Age through to the 19th century. A series of nested study areas are focused on some one hundred square kilometres of reclaimed marshland beside the Severn Estuary in south-west England. This study shows both how the origins and development of an individual landscape can only be understood in its wider context, and equally how the study of individual landscapes can be used to address issues of far wider significance. A highly interdisciplinary approach is adopted, with archaeological, palaeoenvironmental, documentary and field- and place-name evidence being integrated within the context of an analysis of the historic landscape as it survived into the 19th century. Various techniques of survey and excavation are in turn used to test hypotheses derived from historic landscape analysis, leading to a series of maps reconstructing how the landscape changed over the 1st and 2nd millennia AD.

The NSLP has examined how successive marshland communities have created the historic landscape of today through first exploiting the area's rich natural resources, then modifying their environment to make it more amenable to settled agriculture, and ultimately transforming what was an intertidal salt marsh into a freshwater reclaimed landscape. This sequence of exploitation, modification, and transformation occurred on two occasions: during the Roman and medieval periods. The first of these reclaimed landscapes is mostly buried under later alluvium, although in a few places it survives as earthworks. One such location is Puxton Dolemoor where a programme of survey and excavation has revealed early Romano-British salt production that was followed by a ditched enclosure system dug into the surface of what remained a high intertidal salt marsh. As these ditches silted up, a marked change in environment was brought about following the cessation of tidal flooding which is interpreted as resulting from reclamation in the 3rd century AD. Lower relative sea level during the Roman period means that this need not have entailed the construction of flood defences on the scale of those of today, but would still have required low embankments along the coast and major tidal rivers along with dams and sluices across former tidal creeks. This investment in wetland reclamation is part of a wider pattern of agricultural wealth, investment, and innovation seen across the *civitas* of the Durotriges and the Dobunni that also saw some of the most opulent villas in later Roman Britain.

During the early medieval period the North Somerset Levels were flooded and the landscape reverted to an intertidal salt marsh. An analysis of the historic landscape, along with survey, excavation, and palaeoenvironmental analysis, has revealed that the earliest phase in the area's recolonisation was the construction of a series of localised ring dikes protecting small areas of marsh from summer flooding. By the mid-11th century these had been replaced by more substantial embankments running along the coast and major tidal rivers that protected the landscape all year round. The integration of archaeological survey, excavation, palaeoenvironmental analysis, documentary sources, place- and field-names, and standing building recording has allowed the story of how the historic landscape was created to be told, through both thematic discussion of its individual components (such as its settlements, fields, and drainage systems) and a series of maps reconstructing the landscape at different points in time. The excellent preservation afforded by the wetland conditions led to the recovery of important assemblages of plant macrofossils and bird and animal bones.

Of particular interest is the way in which the character of the medieval landscape varied so significantly, both physically and tenurially, with at least one area having a relatively nucleated village, communally managed open fields, and very scattered landholdings, while adjacent areas had a pattern of isolated farmsteads associated with compact landholdings comprising enclosed fields held in severalty. Such differences cannot be due to variations in the natural environment (as a reclaimed coastal marshland this was physically an almost homogeneous area) or to the effect of earlier antecedent landscapes (as the earlier Romano-British land surface is largely buried under later alluvium). Clearly, this local variation in historic landscape character was due to cultural factors, and as the study area was for the most part held by the same landowners during the crucial centuries either side of the Norman Conquest (alternately the king and the bishops of Bath and Wells), it would appear that different sub-tenants and local communities were responsible for creating and managing their landscape in different ways.

Résumé

Le paysage historique de la Grande-Bretagne atteste de manière remarquablement détaillée des efforts passés faits par les êtres humains au cours de nombreux millénaires, efforts qui ont créé les réseaux de champs, de peuplements, de systèmes de communication, et de modèles d'occupation des terres et d'exploitation des ressources qui forment les campagnes et les villes d'aujourd'hui. Les variations locales et régionales au niveau du caractère de ce paysage forment également une importante partie de notre sens moderne de lieu et de communauté : les villages compacts et centrés du Northamptonshire, par exemple, sont très différents des hameaux et des fermes dispersées du Devon. Entre 1993 et 2004, le North Somerset Levels Project (NSLP) [Projet des niveaux du Nord du Somerset] s'est donné pour tâche de découvrir comment sont apparues de telles variations locales et régionales au niveau du caractère du paysage, avec un calendrier allant de la fin de l'âge de fer au 19ème siècle. Une série de zones d'études imbriquées sont concentrées sur environ cent kilomètres carrés de régions marécageuses asséchées près de l'estuaire de la Severn, au Sud-Ouest de l'Angleterre. Cette étude montre à la fois comment les origines et le développement d'un paysage individuel ne peuvent être compris que dans son contexte plus large, et aussi comment l'étude de paysages individuels peut être utilisée pour aborder des questions de bien plus générale importance. Une approche hautement interdisciplinaire est adoptée, avec l'intégration d'indices archéologiques, paléo environnementaux et documentaires, et d'indices relevant des noms de lieux et de champs, dans le contexte d'une analyse du paysage historique, tel qu'il a survécu jusqu'au 19ème siècle. Diverses techniques de relevés et de fouilles sont à leur tour utilisées pour mettre à l'épreuve des hypothèses dérivées d'une analyse du paysage historique, menant à une série de cartes retraçant l'évolution du paysage pendant le 1er et le 2ème millénaire.

Le NSLP a examiné la manière dont les communautés successives des terres marécageuses ont créé le paysage historique d'aujourd'hui par le biais, en premier lieu, de l'exploitation des riches ressources naturelles de la région, ensuite par la modification de leur environnement pour le rendre plus propice à une agriculture stable et établie, et finalement par la transformation de ce qui était un marais salant intertidal en un paysage bonifié d'eau douce. Cette séquence d'exploitation, de modification et de transformation s'est produite à deux reprises : pendant l'époque romaine et l'époque médiévale. Le premier de ces paysages bonifiés est, pour la plupart, enseveli sous des alluvions déposées par la suite, bien qu'il survive encore dans quelques endroits sous la forme d'ouvrages en terre. Un de ces endroits est Puxton Dolemoor, où un programme de relevés et de fouilles a révélé qu'il y avait eu, au début de la période romano britannique, une production de sel, laquelle fut suivie d'un système d'enceintes à fossé creusées dans la surface de ce qui restait un marais salant intertidal élevé. Avec l'envasement progressif de ces fossés, un changement marqué de l'environnement se produisit à la suite de la cessation de l'inondation par les marées, que l'on interprète comme le résultat de l'assèchement du 3ème siècle. Le niveau relativement plus bas de la mer pendant la période romaine signifie que ceci n'a pas forcément entraîné la construction de défenses contre l'inondation à l'échelle de celles qui existent à l'heure actuelle, mais il aurait quand même fallu avoir des levées de bas niveau le long de la côte et des grandes rivières qui avaient des marées, ainsi que des digues et des écluses au travers des anciennes criques soumises aux marées. Cet investissement dans la bonification des terres humides fait partie d'un plus large modèle de richesse agricole, d'investissement et d'innovation dont on voit l'existence dans les *civitas* des Durotriges et des Dobunni, lesquelles ont également vu certaines des villas les plus opulentes de la fin de la Grande-Bretagne romaine.

Au début de la période médiévale, les North Somerset Levels avaient été inondés et le paysage était revenu à l'état d'un marais salant intertidal. Une analyse du paysage historique, accompagnée de relevés, de fouilles et d'une analyse paléo environnementale, a révélé que la phase la plus ancienne de la recolonisation de la région fut la construction d'une série de digues annulaires localisées protégeant de petites zones de marécages contre les inondations estivales. Dès le milieu du 11ème siècle, elles avaient été remplacées par des levées plus solides qui s'étendaient le long de la côte et des grandes rivières soumises aux marées, et qui protégeaient le paysage toute l'année. L'intégration des fouilles et des relevés archéologiques, de l'analyse paléo environnementale, des sources documentaires, des noms de lieux et de champs, et du relevé des bâtiments restant encore, a permis de raconter l'histoire de la manière dont avait été créé le paysage historique, à travers à la fois une discussion thématique de ses éléments individuels (tels que ses peuplements, ses champs et ses systèmes de drainage) et une série de cartes qui retracent le paysage à différents moments dans le temps. L'excellente préservation permise par les conditions des terres humides a mené à recouvrir d'importants ensembles de macro fossiles végétaux ainsi que d'os d'oiseaux et d'animaux.

Ce qui est particulièrement intéressant est la

manière dont le caractère du paysage médiéval variait si considérablement, tant sur le plan physique que par ses habitants, une région ayant un village relativement centré, des champs ouverts gérés en commun, et des propriétés agricoles très dispersées, alors que des régions adjacentes avaient un modèle de fermes isolées associées à des propriétés agricoles compactes, composées de champs clos tenus individuellement. De telles différences ne peuvent pas être dues uniquement à des variations de l'environnement naturel (en tant que terres marécageuses côtières asséchées, c'était une région presque homogène au niveau physique) ou à l'effet de paysages précédents plus anciens (comme la surface du terrain romano britannique est en grande partie ensevelie sous les alluvions ultérieures. Il est clair que cette variation locale du caractère du paysage historique était due à des facteurs culturels et que, étant donné que la région étudiée avait été, pour la plupart, tenue par les mêmes propriétaires terriens au cours des siècles cruciaux de part et d'autre de la conquête normande (tour à tour, le roi et les évêques de Bath et Wells), il semblerait que les différents sous-locataires et communautés locales étaient responsables de la création et de la gestion de leur paysage de différentes manières.

Übersicht

Das heutige Landschaftsbild in Großbritannien verkörpert eine bemerkenswerte Chronik menschlichen Strebens, dass über Jahrtausende ein Geflecht von Feldern, Siedlungen, Verkehrsverbindungen und ein Mosaik aus verschiedener landwirtschaftlicher Nutzung geschaffen hat. Variationen im örtlichen und regionalen Charakter dieser Landschaft geben uns in der heutigen Zeit ein besonderes Heimatgefühl: Die kompakten Kerndörfer in Northamptonshire sind zum Beispiel ein Kontrast zu den zerstreuten Gehöften und kleinen Dörfern in Devon.

Wie diese besonderen regionalen Eigenarten historisch zustande gekommen sind, hat sich das North Somerset Levels Projekt (NSLP) im Zeitraum von 1993-2004 zum Ziel gesetzt und spannt die späte Eisenzeit bis zum 19. Jahrhundert. Eine Reihe von miteinander verbundenen Forschungsgebieten befindet sich in einem einhundert Quadratkilometer großen Marschgebiet an der Mündung des Severn in Südwest England, dass durch Entwässerung urbar gemacht wurde. In dieser Studie wird aufgezeigt, wie der Ursprung und die Entwicklung einer typischen Landschaft nur im Rahmen ihres Umfeldes verstanden werden kann, und auch, wie individuelle Landschaftsstudien Sachverhalte von allgemeiner Bedeutung veranschaulichen können. Es wird hier eine Multidisziplinäre Forschungsmethode angewandt, bei der die Forschungsergebnisse aus der Archäologie, Archäobotanik, Archäozoologie, Quellenforschung, und die Untersuchung von Felder- und Ortsnamen integriert werden und es werden Vergleiche angestellt mit der historischen Landschaft, wie sie bis ins 19. Jahrhundert überliefert ist. Ergebnisse von verschiedenen Geländestudien und Ausgrabungen werden herangezogen, um Hypothesen zu testen, die sich aus der Analyse des historischen Landschaftsbildes herausgebildet haben. Das Resultat ist eine Atlas von Karten, die landschaftliche Veränderungen in den letzen beiden Jahrtausenden veranschaulichen.

Das NSLP hat untersucht, wie Generationen von Marschbewohnern die heutige Landschaft geschaffen haben, ursprünglich durch die Ausbeutung der natürlichen Rohstoffe und später durch bewusste Veränderungen an der Umwelt, die einen sesshaften Lebensstil möglich machten, und zuletzt durch die Transformation des ehemaligem Salzmarschs in eine von Süßwasser geprägten und trockengelegten Landschaft. Diese Folge von Ausbeutung, Veränderung und Neuerschaffung wurde zweimal vollzogen: in der Römerzeit und im Mittelalter. Die erste dieser neuerschlossenen Landschaften ist fasst ausschließlich unter Sedimentablagerungen verborgen, nur an einigen Stellen sind Erdwälle sichtbar. Einer der Orte, wo dies zu sehen ist, befindet sich in Puxton Dolemoor, wo ein intensives Programm von Geländevermessungen und Ausgrabungen ein frühes Beispiel Romano-Britischer Salzgewinnung ermittelt haben. Später wurde an dieser Stelle ein Gefüge von Erdwällen und Gräben angelegt, das sich auf einem höhergelegenen Salzmarsch befand. Als diese Gräben verschlammten, trat eine grundlegende Umweltveränderung ein, die zur Folge hatte, dass sich die Gegend ausserhalb der Gezeiteneinwirkung befand. Dieser Prozess wird als eine Konsequenz von Landerschliessung durch Entwässerung im 3. Jahrhundert interpretiert. Eine niedrigerer Meeresspiegel während der Römerzeit hatte zu Folge, daß die Flutwälle nicht dieselben Ausmaße wie heutzutage haben brauchten, es war jedoch trotzdem notwendig niedrige Erdwälle entlang der Küste und größeren Flüssen zu errichten, sowie Dämme und Schleusen über die gezeitlichen Entwässerungsbäche. Die Erschließung dieser Feuchtgebiete wird in einen breiteren Zusammenhang gesetzt, in dem Investitionen und Neuerungen in den *civitas* der Durotriges und Dobunni einen landwirtschaftlichen Wohlstand schufen, aus dem auch die wohlhabenden Villen der späten Römerzeit hervor gingen.

Während des frühen Mittelalters wurden die North Somerset Levels erneut überflutet und in einen Salzmarsch verwandelt. Die multidisziplinäre Untersuchung der historischen Landschaft mit Beiträgen von Geländeuntersuchungen und Ausgrabungen, hat gezeigt, dass in der frühen Phase der Neuansiedlung eine Reihe von kreisförmigen Deichen angelegt wurde, um kleinere Marschgebiete vor Überflutungen während der Sommermonate zu schützen. Im 11. Jahrhundert waren diese Deiche durch größere Wälle ersetzt, die entlang den Küstenstreifen und grösseren Flussmündungen die Landschaft das ganze Jahr über vor Flut schützen sollten. Die Integration von Geländeuntersuchungen, Ausgrabungen archäobotanischen und archäozoologischen Analysen, Quellenstudien, Analyse von Ortsnamen und architektonische Untersuchungen hat dazu beigetragen, die Entstehung der historischen Landschaft zu verstehen und thematische Diskussionen über die einzelnen Komponenten der Landschaft (wie zum Beispiel Siedlungen, Felder und Entwässerungssysteme) anzuregen und der Atlas illustriert die Entwicklungsphase der Landschaft zu einem bestimmten geschichtlichen Zeitpunkt. Die hervorragenden Bedingungen im Feuchtgebiet haben dazu beigetragen, dass wichtige und guterhaltene Sammlungen von Pflanzenresten, Tierknochen und insbesondere Vogelknochen zu Tage kamen.

Von besonderem Interesse sind die Unterschiede in der Struktur der mittelalterlichen Landschaft im Zusammenhang mit Besitzverhältnissen. In einem Gebiet befindet sich ein Kerndorf umgeben mit Gemeindeland und sehr verstreuten Besitztümern. Im Gegensatz dazu war die Nachbargemeinde von verstreuten Gehöften, kleineren Besitztümern und eingefriedeten, im Eigenbesitz befindlichen, Feldern geprägt. Solche Unterschiede können nicht nur durch Variationen der natürlichen Umweltbedingungen erklärt werden, (der durch Entwässerung neuerschlossene Küstenmarsch war physisch eine fast homogene Landschaft), und auch nicht durch den Einfluss von vorhergehenden Landschaften (die frühere Romano-Britische Landoberfläche ist fast ausschliesslich durch spätere Sedimentablagerungen verdeckt). Solche örtlichen Strukturunterschiede waren offensichtlich von kulturellen Faktoren bestimmt. In den Jahrhunderten vor und nach der Normannischen Eroberung wurde das Studiengebiet von denselben Grundbesitzern verwaltet (abwechselnd von dem König und Bischof von Bath und Wells) und es scheint, dass die Pächter und Dorfgemeinschaften die Landschaft auf verschiedene Weise schufen und nutzten.

Glossary

bow	local term for bridge
clyce	sluice gate to allow the discharge of water from a major ditch into tidal rivers/estuaries
dolemoor	local term for a common meadow
ear (or year)	local term for a sluice gate controlling the flow of water within major ditches or through sea walls
gout	local term for a sluice gate controlling the flow of water within major ditches or through sea walls
gripe	local term for a spade-dug gully in the surface of a field to aid drainage
lugg	local term for a strip within a common meadow
mead	field-name indicative of meadow
moor	field-name indicative of rough and/or common pasture
pill	local term for a tidal creek; also used as a field-name possibly indicating a droveway
rhyne	local term for canalised natural streams and wholly artificial watercourses that form part of the drainage system
wall	local term for an earthen embankment designed to control flooding
year (or ear)	local term for a sluice gate to control the flow or water within major ditches, and allow the discharge of water from a major ditch into tidal rivers
yeo	local term for a river

Part 1:
Understanding the history of a landscape

1 Introduction: a marshland community and its landscape

Understanding regional variation in landscape character

Our rich and varied countryside

Anyone who travels around the countryside of Britain cannot fail to appreciate its rich and varied character. In a midland county, for example, substantial nucleated villages surrounded by vast expanses of large straight-sided fields are linked by roads that run in a more-or-less straight line for many miles. Such landscapes display a degree of regularity and planning not seen in areas beyond this 'central province' and in the south-west of England, for example, isolated farmsteads and small hamlets are scattered across the countryside, set amongst a complex pattern of irregularly shaped fields and lanes that twist and turn in a seemingly inexplicable fashion. Such local and regional variation in the character of our countryside makes an important contribution to our sense of place and community, but why are these landscapes so different? How old are these different patterns of fields, roads, and settlements, and can we tell the story of how our countryside came to have its distinctive character-defining features?

Through the example of one rural community – the people living in an area of reclaimed coastal marshland beside the Severn Estuary in north-west Somerset – this highly interdisciplinary study hopes to demonstrate how the complex history of a landscape can be untangled through the careful integration of archaeological, palaeoenvironmental, architectural, cartographic, and documentary evidence with perhaps the richest source of all: the historic landscape itself. The term historic landscape refers to the physical fabric of our present countryside – the patterns of roads, fields, settlements, industry, communications, woodland, and parkland – and its cultural associations with paintings (eg Constable country'), literature (eg Hardy's Wessex), and legend (eg Robin Hood's Sherwood Forest). The term 'historic landscape' is a relatively recent one and is designed to emphasise the time-depth present within our countryside, which in most places contains elements that date back to the medieval period or beyond (Fairclough and Rippon 2002; Rippon 2004a). Though Crawford (1953, 51) said 'the surface of England is a palimpsest, a document that has been written on and erased over and over again; it is the business of the field archaeologist to decipher it', and Hoskins (1955, 14) described the landscape as 'the richest historical record we possess', there was little systematic research into the origins and development of the historic landscape as a whole until the 1990s when techniques such as 'historic landscape characterisation' emerged (eg Rippon 1996a; 1996b; Fairclough 1998; Foard and Rippon 1998; Herring 1998). These techniques were designed to inform planners and countryside managers of the time-depth present within our countryside, but they were all too often based primarily upon a morphological classification of field boundary patterns. These techniques of historic landscape characterisation were kept relatively simple as they had to cover large areas in a relatively short space of time, and this has led to some criticism on the basis that they place too much emphasis on the form of fields, roads, and settlements as mapped in the 19th century, with too little testing of these morphology-based hypotheses with regards to historic landscape origins using archaeological and documentary data. This study hopes to take historic landscape analysis one step further by showing that a strongly interdisciplinary programme of research can be used to validate hypotheses derived from historic landscape analysis, and reveal how a combination of local, regional, natural, and cultural factors have shaped the character of our countryside.

Villages, hamlets, and farmsteads

One of the key issues that this study will address is the development of local and regional variation in the physical fabric of the medieval countryside and the way that it was managed, though there has been a marked bias in previous research towards landscapes characterised by villages and open fields (eg Wharram Percy, Raunds, Whittlewood and Shapwick). It was traditionally assumed that villages were the typical form of medieval settlement in England, with a community's land laid out in two or three open fields that covered most of the parish. Increasingly, however, it is now recognised that landscapes characterised by villages and open fields were not found throughout Britain but were restricted to an area extending from central southern England, into the midlands and south Wales, and up to the north-east of England and south-east Scotland, an area that Rackham (1986) describes as having 'planned countryside' and which Roberts and Wrathmell (2000; 2002) describe as England's 'central province' (Fig 1.1). Topographical writers from the 16th century describe these areas as having 'champion' landscape, characterised by huge open fields and occasional nucleated villages, and whose appearance was in sharp

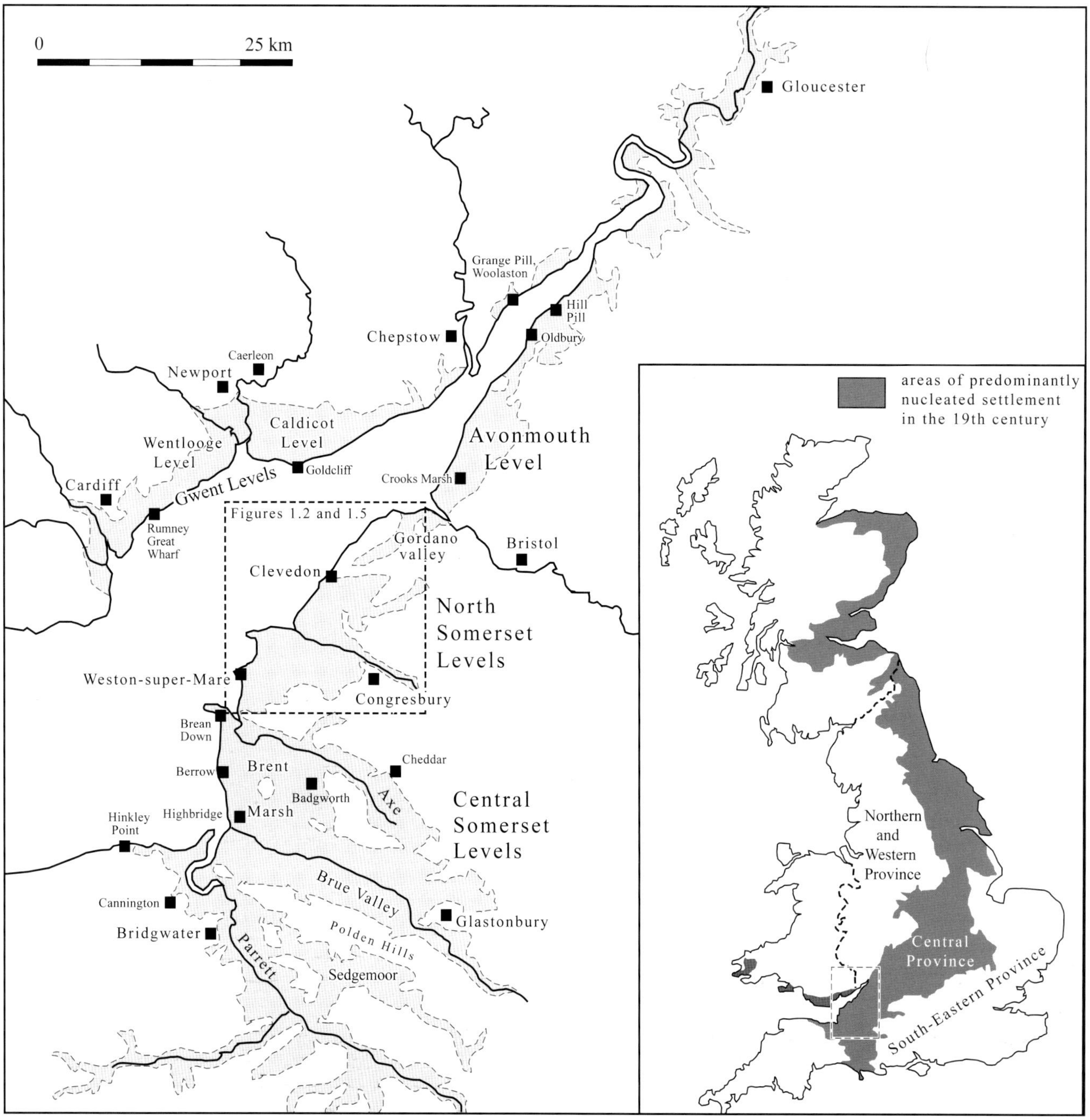

Figure 1.1 The Severn Estuary and its wetlands with the major historic landscape provinces of England (after Roberts 1987, fig 1.1, and Roberts and Wrathmell 2002, fig 1.4)

contrast to the 'bosky' landscapes of the south-east, west, and north-west of England where the view was dominated by trees, in hedgerows and woodland, and more dispersed settlement patterns (Rackham's 'ancient countryside', and Roberts and Wrathmell's south-eastern, and northern and western provinces).

Villages are, however, relative latecomers to the British countryside as predominantly dispersed settlement patterns are known to have characterised the prehistoric, Romano-British, and early medieval periods. Both spatially and temporally the villages of midland England are an aberration, but where did they come from? Only in a very few places are the origins of villages recorded, most notably during the Anglo-Norman conquest and colonisation of south Wales and northern England in the late 11th–early 12th centuries (Richter 1976, 18–21; and see Rowlands 1980; Harten and Schuyf 1983, 54–5; Toorians 1990; 1996; 2000; Rippon 1996a; 1997c; 2001a, 149–50; Kissock 1997), and the way that these village-based landscapes were created in such a similar way to central England suggests that this approach towards managing the countryside was well established by that date: but where did it come from?

Archaeological work in the east midlands has shown that nucleated villages replaced a more dispersed settlement pattern during the later 1st millennium AD in what Roberts and Wrathmell (2002, figs 1.6 and 3.12a) have termed 'landscapes of cataclysm' (and see Foard 1978; Hall and Martin 1979; Hall 1988; Shaw 1993/4; Lewis *et al* 1997, 81; Brown and Foard 1998). There has been some debate over the relative roles of landlords and the community in this reshaping of landscape character (eg Dyer 1985; Harvey 1989), and in recent decades a view has emerged that 'this adaptation [villages and open fields], once introduced and established, probably spread by emulation: the nucleated settlements and regular open fields in so many communities across the east midlands show so many similarities as to suggest that, as the success of the nucleated open-field village became evident, the idea spread following a standard model' (Lewis *et al* 1997, 200). This idea, that the concept of settlement nucleation and the reorganisation of agricultural land into open fields spread out from the midlands like the ripples generated by a pebble thrown into a pond, suggests that landscapes beyond the 'central province' (Roberts and Wrathmell's 'landscapes of continuity') simply failed to follow this lead. Lewis *et al* (1997, 200), for example, suggest that 'in other regions . . . this adaptive evolution of fields, boundaries and settlements was not followed. Where the arable contribution to the economy was less dominant, the pressure on the land never reached the point at which a transformation of the landscape seemed either necessary or desirable. Although areas of continued dispersed settlement were subject to the same factors, such as increased population or the emergence of markets, nonetheless the availability of additional land for cultivation, their pastoral interests, or opportunities to make a living from the woods and wastes, insulated them from radical change' (and see Roberts and Wrathmell 2002, fig 5.11).

This midland-centric view can be challenged on a number of grounds. The idea that the 'active' concept of settlement nucleation and the reorganisation of agricultural land into open fields spread out from the midlands but failed to reach 'passive' areas such as the south-east and the south-west of England, and that in these 'peripheral' areas things carried on much as they had for centuries before, may not do justice to indigenous developments within these other regions. In the south-west of England, for example, the 7th–8th centuries see a marked change in agricultural practices that may be related to the replacement of an essentially prehistoric countryside with the historic landscape of today whose essential components were certainly in place by the 10th–11th centuries (Fyfe *et al* 2003; 2004; Rippon *et al* in press). In East Anglia a similar intensification in agriculture occurs at the same time as settlement nucleation begins around what became parish churches, though within a few centuries settlement had started to drift away, towards the greens and commons that were such a characteristic feature of the East Anglian landscape (Wade-Martins 1980a; Silvester 1988; 1993; Davison 1990; Rogerson *et al* 1997; West and McLaughlin 1998). Could it be that midland-style villages and open fields failed to reach areas such as East Anglia and south-west England because the communities living there were developing their own very successful approaches towards landscape management?

In the discussion so far socio-economic factors have been the most prominent, though this has recently been challenged by Williamson (2003), who has argued for a strong link between soil conditions and the development of open field farming in the midlands. Roberts and Wrathmell (2002, 72–7) have added another possible factor, in arguing that in some places there is a correlation between areas that went on to see the creation of villages and open fields and the character of the landscape that went before (what they term 'antecedent landscapes'), notably areas where woodland had already been most extensively cleared. It is certainly the case that individual boundaries within some medieval settlements and field systems followed earlier features (eg Wharram Percy: Beresford and Hurst 1990, 73; Shapwick: Aston and Gerrard forthcoming; and the east midlands: Jones and Page forthcoming; Taylor and Fowler 1978; Upex 2002), though whether the same is true of landscape character on a local or even regional scale remains to be seen.

The major problem in trying to understand why the medieval period saw such marked local and regional variations in landscape character is untangling this series of possible causal factors. In areas such as Somerset, that straddle the 'central' and 'western' provinces (with nucleated and dispersed settlement patterns respectively), there is certainly no simple correlation between areas of high population and the creation of villages and open fields. Some parts of western Somerset (around Bridgwater and Taunton), for example, which had a landscape characterised by fairly dispersed settlement, were as populous at the time of Domesday as central and south-eastern Somerset that had a classic midland-style landscape of villages and open fields (Darby 1967, figs 84–6; Rippon 2004a, fig 27.9). The same is found in the east of England where areas such as East Anglia had an even higher population density than village-dominated areas to the west (Darby 1973, fig 11). Similarly, in Somerset, there is no simple correlation between settlement pattern, soil type, or farming practice: from the 16th to the 19th centuries at least there was far more arable in the lowlands of western Somerset (around Bridgwater) than in the village-dominated east (Williams 1969, fig 1; Rippon 2004a, figs 27.3–5). Rather than simple deterministic interpretations, such as villages being created as a response to high population, certain soil types, or a dominance of arable cultivation, it must have been the complex interaction of socio-economic factors that led to some lords and communities adopting this new form of landscape management, while others did not.

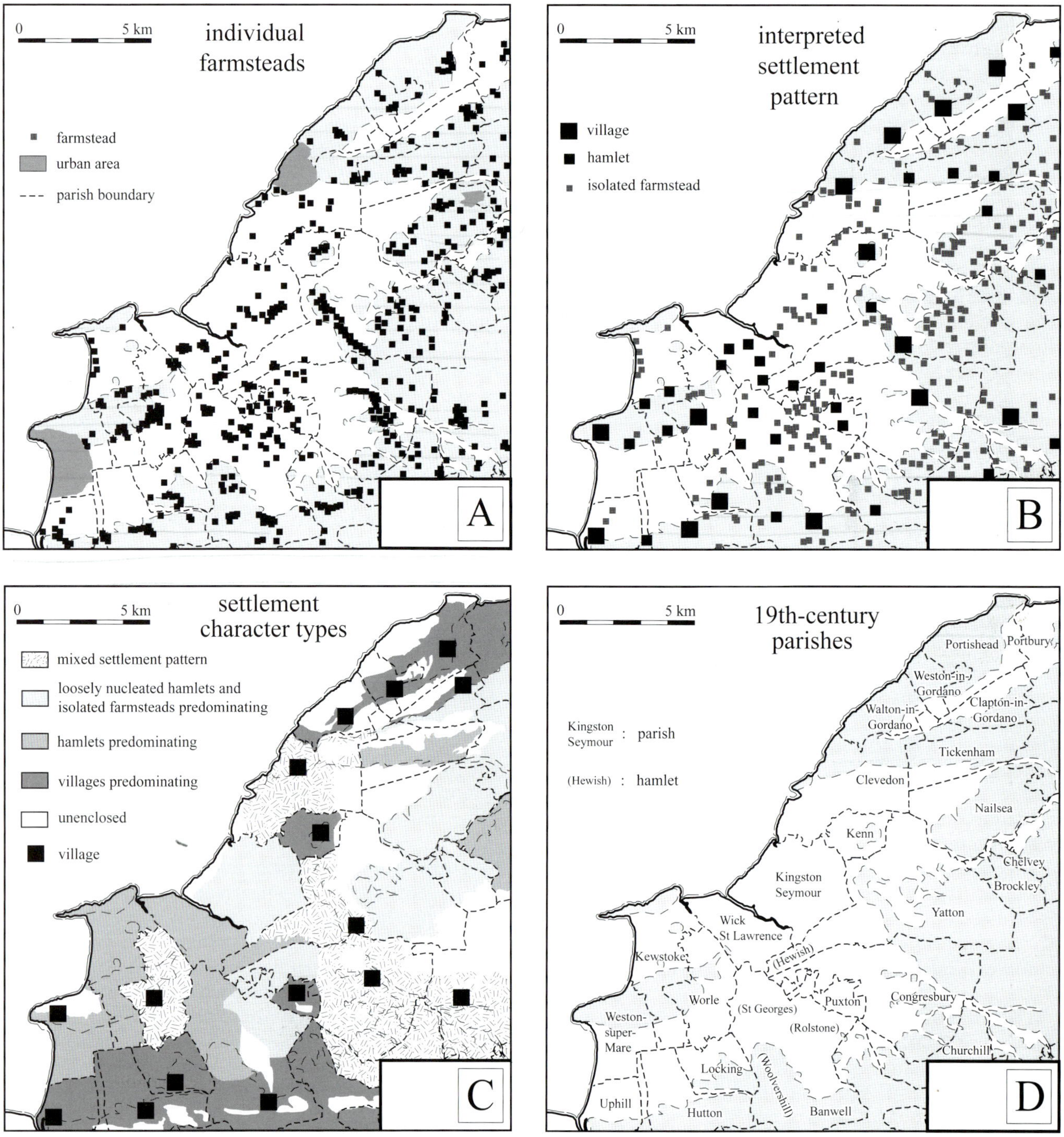

Figure 1.2 North-west Somerset: a characterisation of the 19th-century settlement pattern based on the First Edition Ordnance Survey Six Inch maps of the 1880s

With this series of recent, stimulating, but sometimes contradictory studies, the NSLP occurred at an exciting time to be thinking about the origins and development of historic landscape character. One problem has been that most major studies into medieval landscape have been carried out within the 'central province', notably at Wharram Percy in Yorkshire (Beresford and Hurst 1990), Shapwick in Somerset (Aston and Gerrard 1999), and Whittlewood (Jones and Page 2003; forthcoming), Milton Keynes (Croft and Mynard 1993), Raunds (Selkirk 1987), and Yarnton (Hey 2004) in the midlands. There is an increasing awareness, however, that we also need to study landscapes characterised by dispersed settlement patterns (MSRG 1996, 6), as these will reflect landscape evolution in areas that had not experienced the causes of nucleation. North-west Somerset is, therefore, of particular interest as it lies at the interface of England's central and the south-west provinces, with landscapes characterised by both nucleated and dispersed settlement patterns in close proximity (Fig 1.1). Figure 1.2.A shows every individ-

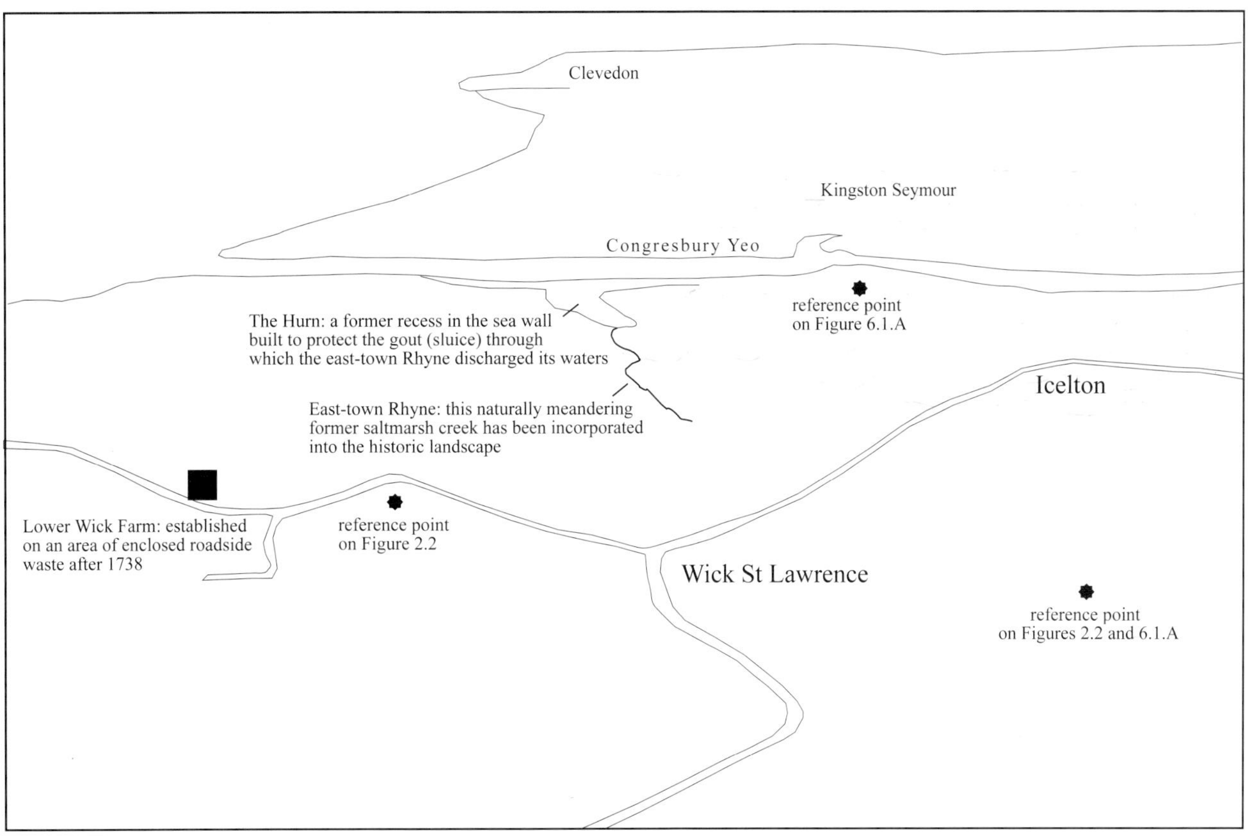

Figure 1.3 Aerial view of the tightly nucleated hamlets at Wick St Lawrence and Icelton, looking north across the estuary of the Congresbury Yeo towards Clevedon. Note how these compact settlements are in sharp contrast to the loosely arranged hamlets in Banwell Marsh (see Fig 1.4)

ual farmstead in north-west Somerset shown on the Ordnance Survey First Edition Six Inch maps. Their distribution was clearly uneven, with some areas unoccupied, and others showing a mixture of wholly dispersed through to wholly nucleated patterns. This variable distribution of farmsteads is interpreted in Figure 1.2.B with each settlement classified as either an isolated farmstead, a hamlet, or a village. There has been much debate over what constitutes a village or a hamlet and there is no simple definition that will work in all areas and for all periods (Taylor 1983, 15). In this study a village is regarded as a substantial nucleated settlement (and the dominant settlement within that parish), with the provision of central services (eg a chapel, church, school), and a strongly communal system of management in the surrounding landscape. Hamlets were smaller nucleated settlements that may also have been at the centre of a communally managed landscape, but on a much smaller scale and with several such foci within a parish. This analysis of north-west Somerset reveals some sharp contrasts, with village-based landscapes on the dry lands to the north and south of the Levels, and strongly dispersed settlements to the east. On the Levels themselves settlement is predominantly dispersed but with significant nucleation in places such as Puxton, Hewish, and Wick St Lawrence (Figs 1.3–1.4). This study will start to address the issue of why there is such varied landscape character within such a small area.

Working on a clean slate

In designing this research project, an attempt has been made to focus in on a limited number of the potential factors that could have led to local and regional variation in historic landscape character. The North Somerset Levels are an area of reclaimed coastal marshland, and so 'antecedent landscapes' will have had almost no impact on the form taken by the medieval countryside as they lie buried under a thick layer of alluvium that was deposited during an episode of late Roman–early medieval flooding. Apart from a number of naturally meandering former tidal creeks that were reused as field boundaries (eg Fig 1.3), the medieval landscape was created on a 'clean slate'. Because of its origins as reclaimed marshland, this landscape was also physically very uniform, comprising an almost flat homogeneous area of silty clays: if there were significant differences in the patterns of fields, roads, and settlements following the area's reclamation, then these can only have been due to contemporary cultural factors.

The north-west Somerset basin (Fig 1.5)

The North Somerset Levels

The North Somerset Levels are some 100km^2 of wetland in the north-west of the historic county of Somerset (latterly they formed part of the post-1974 county of Avon, and now lie in the unitary authority of North Somerset). The Levels comprise a *c* 20m-deep sequence of intercalated peat and silty clay alluvium deposited during the post-glacial rise in sea level (Chapter 3). Today most areas are covered by mottled grey/brown calcareous estuarine silty clay of the Upper Wentlooge Formation that was laid down when the Levels consisted of a huge tract of intertidal mudflats and salt marshes, giving rise to soils of the Wentlooge Series (Findlay 1965, 111–14). The surface of the Levels towards the coast is *c* 5.8–6.1m OD, though most areas are *c* 5.2–5.5m OD, falling to *c* 4.9m OD in the lower-lying backfens towards the fen-edge in the far east of the Levels. The present Mean High Water Spring Tide (MHWST) in the adjacent Severn Estuary is *c* 6.1m OD, with the Highest Astronomical Tides at *c* 7.5m OD. Coastal districts are higher than those inland because these areas are flooded most frequently, and so see the greatest sediment deposition as the estuary's waters flood across the marsh. In the north-east corner of the Levels, on Kenn and Tickenham Moors, soils of the Godney and Sedgemoor Series are derived from the underlying freshwater fen peat (Findlay 1965, 124–7), while much of the southern and eastern fen-edges are fringed by freshwater alluvium/colluvium washed off the adjacent drylands, giving rise to heavy clay soils of the poorly drained Compton, Fladbury, and Max Series (Findlay 1965, 118–22).

A series of bedrock islands – Wains Hill, Middlehope, and Worlebury – rise above the coast, while within the Levels there are a number of minor bedrock islands including The Oar (west of Congresbury), Nye and Rookery (in Sandford), and Wick Mill Hill (in Wick St Lawrence). The coastal frontage between Wains Hill and Middlehope is currently protected by artificial sea walls, while between Middlehope and Worlebury, and Worlebury and Uphill, there are belts of natural sand dunes. The date when this sand started to form is unclear, though to the south of Brean Down a similar belt of dunes was in place by the Bronze Age (Fig 1.1; Bell 1990). Immediately to the south of Worlebury, excavations at the Melrose Car Park and Weston-super-Mare Technical College revealed 2nd- to 4th-century AD occupation stratified within sand (SMR 00126), while earthmoving behind the Royal Terrace to the north revealed a Romano-British occupation horizon and two burials stratified high up within the same dunes as they lap over the bedrock of Worlebury Hill (SMR 45793; Rippon 1997a, 35). There is no direct dating evidence for the dunes between Middlehope and Worlebury, though there is no reason to assume that they did not similarly exist by the Roman period.

The dunes between Worlebury and Uphill are breached in two places. The first is a substantial palaeochannel immediately to the south of Worlebury, along which a small stream still flowed in the 19th century (Jackson 1877, 49, 69; Findlay

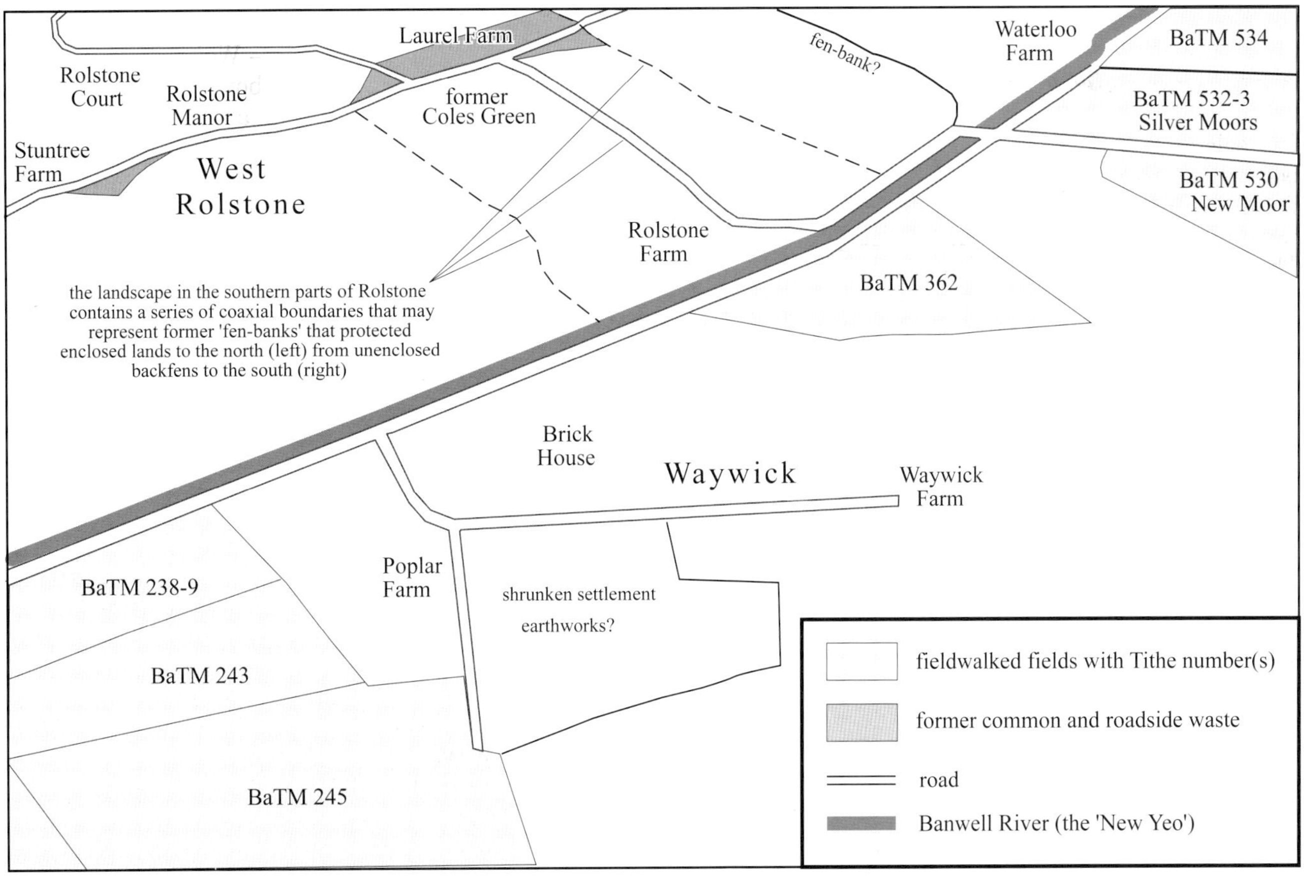

Figure 1.4 Aerial view of the loosely nucleated hamlet at Waywick in Banwell Marsh. Fieldwalking in adjacent fields suggests that the area was occupied from around the 12th century, while New Moor and Silver Moors were enclosed by the early 18th century

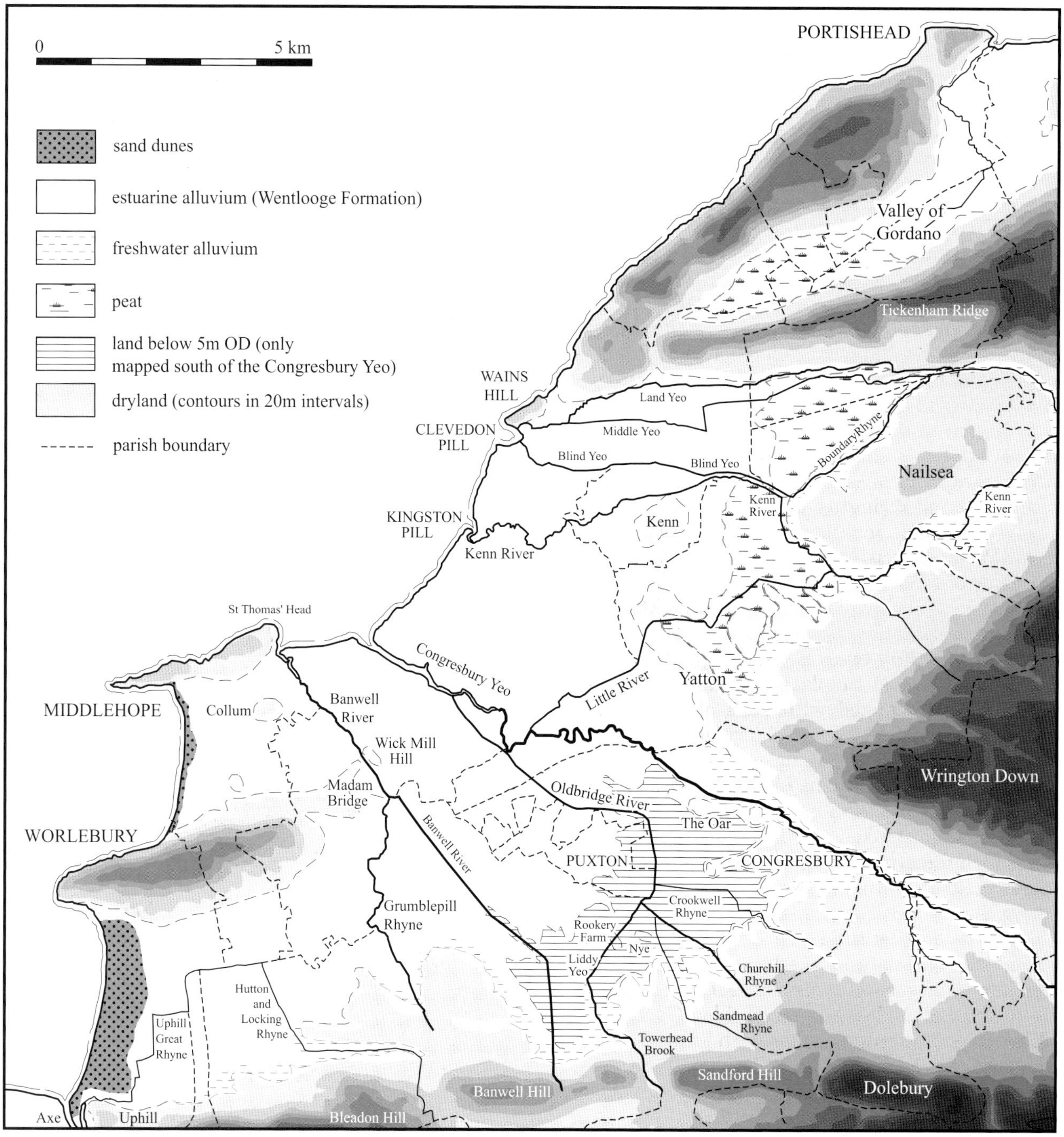

Figure 1.5 The topography, soils, and drainage of north-west Somerset

1965, sheet 279). In 1885 'the remains of an ancient galley', comprising part of the prow and keel piece almost 12 feet long, were found on the northern edge of this former tidal creek beneath Grove Terrace (Poole 1885). The second breach in the dunes, to the south at Uphill, remains open today and is the means by which the Uphill Great Rhyne discharges into the River Axe. The antiquity of this channel is unknown though it appears to have been cut through bedrock. As a series of drilled holes suggest the use of dynamite, this outfall must be of post-medieval date in its present form (Vince Russett pers comm).

Whatever their antiquity, neither of these tidal inlets appears to have led to significant inundation of the area behind the dunes between Middlehope, Worlebury and Uphill during the past two millennia, as the height of the present ground surface on the adjacent marshes (*c* 5.2–5.5m OD) is lower than the area further east around West Wick and St Georges (roughly the line of the M5 motorway: *c* 5.5–5.8m OD) (Fig 3.1). These patterns of relief, combined with the network of palaeochannels reflecting the former pattern of salt marsh creeks, suggest that the major source of tidal flooding – and hence greater sediment deposition – was via the estuaries of the Banwell River and the Congresbury Yeo to the north, with the areas behind the sand dunes forming a lower-lying backfen, equivalent to that found to the far east of the Levels (see above).

The hills and foothills surrounding the Levels

Apart from the Severn Estuary to the west, the North Somerset Levels are surrounded by a series of high Carboniferous Limestone hills, the steep slopes of which are today mostly wooded. To the south lie Bleadon, Banwell, Sandford, and Dolebury Hills that together form the western continuation of Mendip and extend as far as the Severn Estuary at Uphill. The watersheds of these hills lie just 0.5–1.5km south of the fen-edge giving a very small catchment for the spring-fed streams that flow northwards onto the Levels (see below). The hills are capped by shallow, well-drained stony red/brown loamy soils of the Crwbin Series (formerly the Lulsgate and Wrington Series), and are flanked by lower-lying and more gently undulating foothills of softer Permo-Triassic rocks (notably Keuper Marl and the Lower Lias), which give rise to fertile, mainly slowly permeable, clayey loams of the Brockhurst 2, Evesham 1, Whimple 1, and Worcester Series.

To the east of the Levels lies the high steep-sided Carboniferous Limestone plateau of Wrington Down that is similarly capped with soils of the Crwbin Series. Between this and Dolebury lies the broad, lowland plain of the Congresbury Yeo river that has a substantial catchment of $66km^2$, while to the north lie the valleys of the Land Yeo and Kenn River. Wrington Down is flanked by broad, gently undulating foothills including the Yatton ridge with fertile slowly permeable clayey loams of the Honet and Whimple 1 Series. Nailsea is separated from these foothills by the small valley of the Kenn River, and has well-drained loamy soils of the Neath Series derived from the underlying Carboniferous Coal Measures. To the north of the Levels lies the steep-sided Carboniferous Limestone Tickenham ridge. With just 0.5–1.0km between the fen-edge and the watershed, the run-off on the northern side of the Levels is relatively insignificant, and the band of foothills, once again with fertile soils of the Whimple 1 Series, is just a few hundred metres wide.

The drainage system on the Levels

With such a restricted catchment just two major rivers drain into the North Somerset Levels: the Land Yeo (the local term for a river is Yeo) to the north-east, and the Congresbury Yeo to the south-east. The waters of the Land Yeo disperse into a series of minor rivers (the Land Yeo, Middle Yeo, Blind Yeo, and Kenn River), the first three of which discharge their waters into the Severn Estuary at Clevedon Pill (pill is the local term for a small estuary), and the latter at Kingston Pill. Although before reclamation the Congresbury Yeo would have drained most of the southern part of the North Somerset Levels, today it is heavily embanked and this area is drained by a series of artificial watercourses (rhynes) that also carry the waters of several minor streams flowing off the adjacent uplands (Crookwell Rhyne, Churchill Rhyne, Sandmead Rhyne, Towerhead Brook, the Banwell River, Grumblepill Rhyne, and the Hutton/Locking Rhyne). The historical development of this drainage system is explored in Chapter 6.

A 'marginal' environment?

Marginality and landscape potential

In providing a physically almost uniform environment, free from the remains of any earlier cultural landscapes, reclaimed coastal wetlands such as the North Somerset Levels offer unparalleled potential for examining the socio-economic reasons why regional and local variation emerged in the countryside of medieval Britain. In the past such wetland areas would have been regarded as marginal, though the traditional idea of marginality has attracted much criticism (eg Postan 1972; M Bailey 1989; Dyer 1989; Young and Simmonds 1995; Rippon 1997a, 263–7), and the extent to which environmental change has shaped cultural landscapes has also been questioned (eg Tipping 2002). Indeed, rather than regarding some areas as core and others as marginal, it is more appropriate to think of landscape *potential* in terms of a series of interconnected natural and cultural factors:

- physical potential (ie relief, geology/soils, and drainage etc)
- environmental potential (ie weather (including vulnerability to storminess), climate, and relative sea level etc)
- economic/demographic potential (ie population pressure, rents and labour costs, food prices etc)
- locational potential (ie proximity to centres of consumption, such as towns and military establishments, and the communications network including roads, rivers, and the coast)
- socio-political and tenurial potential (ie patterns of lordship and landholding, and the relationship to centres of power etc)
- technological potential (ie drainage, and agricultural regimes etc)
- non-agricultural potential (ie minerals such as salt, stone, and metals).

It is important to remember that most if not all of these variables can change over time. In the case of coastal wetlands, for example, erosion, alterations in the course of a river, or the creation/breaching of a belt of sand dunes will all affect the potential of these areas for human settlement. They are also particularly vulnerable to rising sea level and deteriorating climate, although these can often be countered by technological developments (eg drainage and the raising of sea defences). The emergence of new centres of consumption, alongside improvements in the transport system, can make agricultural and mineral production in what were formerly less favoured areas more profitable, and while some socio-tenurial structures such as weak manorial authority and an active land market made it easier for farmers to adapt to new economic circumstances, tighter institutional control and/or a strongly communally managed landscape encouraged conservatism. Political decisions can also affect the landscape, for example invasion, conquest and colonisation, and the resulting changes in patterns of land tenure, such as the creation and fragmentation of lordships.

Coastal wetlands illustrate many of the complex issues surrounding marginality and landscape potential, and there are broadly three approaches that human communities can take towards utilising such marshlands (Rippon 2000a, 52–3):

- *exploitation* of the rich natural resources, such as fishing, wildfowling, producing salt, grazing livestock, and even growing a limited range of crops on the marshes
- *modifying* the landscape to make it more suitable for agriculture, most notably through digging drainage ditches and constructing low embankments (summer dikes) to keep the occasional high summer tide off small areas of arable
- *transforming* the landscape through reclamation which involves constructing a sea wall along the coast that was capable of keeping the tide at bay all year round, and then controlling the water-table through the construction of a drainage and flood defence system, making permanent settlement and large-scale arable cultivation possible.

In their natural, intertidal, state coastal marshes are undoubtedly marginal from the perspective of settled arable-based agriculture, and even when reclaimed they remain vulnerable to flooding at times of increased rainfall and storminess. They also require capital and recurrent investment in the construction and maintenance of the drainage and flood defence systems and so life in a reclaimed wetland can be regarded as high risk and high cost. But reclamation is also a high-return strategy towards landscape utilisation: in terms of agricultural productivity areas of reclaimed wetland were usually more highly valued than adjacent dryland areas, and during the late medieval period, for example, many reclaimed wetlands experienced less settlement desertion than their adjacent dryland areas due to their productive soils and proximity to markets and ports (Rippon 2000a, 2–7; 2001b; forthcoming a). All these risks, costs, and benefits will, however, also vary over time: the costs of sustaining a reclaimed landscape increased at times of lower population (leading to higher wages), while the risks of living on coastal marshlands increase at times of rising relative sea level, increased precipitation, or increased storminess. The return on reclamation would also fluctuate with changing economic conditions, for example when falling population led to declining food prices and lower rent income, or the growth of urban markets led to increased demands for foodstuffs. Any individual landscape can only be understood in the context of these wider issues, and as such a case study like that of the North Somerset Levels can be used as a means to gain a better understanding of these cultural processes.

'A rich, well-cultivated district': early accounts of the North Somerset Levels

Early accounts of the North Somerset Levels confirm that, whilst presenting a number of challenges, notably with regards to managing water, this reclaimed wetland landscape was far from being viewed as marginal. The earliest, probably fanciful, description is contained within the 12th-century biography of St Congar, who was one of three early 6th-century missionaries sent by Dubricius, the first Bishop of Llandaff (in south Wales), to work in Somerset. This 'hotch-pot of hagiographical and folklore elements mainly drawn from the Lives of other Welsh saints' (Farmer 1987, 98) purports to describe early reclamation, but its value here is really the very positive 12th-century perception of the agricultural productivity of this post-reclamation landscape: 'The following was the first miracle performed through the Divine Mercy by the most holy Congar. Places covered with water and reeds, which surrounded his dwelling, and at that time being no use to man, were converted into fields most suitable for cultivation, and into flowering meadows. The people acknowledged Congar's miracle by saying 'We see clearly fields and meadows where the reeds of the marsh used to grow" (Cran 1983, 2).

In the mid-16th century John Leland wrote of the area in less than complimentary terms: 'Two or three miles from Wick is Banwell, where the Bishop of Bath has a good estate . . . The position of Banwell, with the fennes close by, is not very salubrious, and Wick is worse (*Leland*, 430).[1] Leland was, however, an outsider, and a survey of Congresbury and Wick [St Lawrence] in 1567 gives us a more informed view of how this area was perceived by local communities, as this manor embraced both marshland and the adjacent dryland areas. The survey divided the manor into seven districts, the soil quality of which was graded into 'best', the 'second', and 'the worst'. The fact that 'the best [land] is in the districts of Laurence Wyke and the Marshe' suggests that local communities, which could compare the agricultural potential of both the wetlands and the adjacent dryland areas, clearly valued the wetlands most highly (Cran 1983, 48)! In the late 18th century Collinson (1791, 598, 611) described the lands around Puxton and Wick as 'mostly converted to the uses of grazing and dairy, and are very rich', and in 1836 Phelps described the 'North Marsh [of Somerset]' as being 'a rich, well-cultivated district, chiefly in pasture'. In 1825 Bennett described the lands in the parish of Puxton as 'uncommonly rich and fertile, and are mostly applied to the business of the dairy and grazing for which latter purpose they are nearly if not quite equal to any lands in Somersetshire' (SRO DD/SAS G/1740 1/1/7). In 1885, a survey of Merton College lands described the soils as 'rich alluvial loam and though varying in quality is all of good character' (BodL MC 1204–35). Once reclaimed, this was far from marginal agricultural land.

'A certain wonderfull overflowing of waters'

Whilst these reclaimed wetlands were agriculturally highly fertile, giving a high return on the considerable investment that reclamation entails, they remained vulnerable to flooding. A series of documented floods are known to have affected Somerset (Rippon 1997a, 243), as in 1703 when the sea broke through the sea walls at Woodspring flooding an area up to six miles inland (Defoe 1742, 24; Coles 1912, 24). The flood of 20 January 1607 was, however, particularly devastating and we are fortunate in having a series of contemporary accounts including a pamphlet entitled *A true report of certaine wonderfull overflowings of waters, now lately in Somerset-shire, Norfolke, and other places of England destroying many thousands of men, women and children, overthrowing and bearing downe whole townes and villages, and drowning infinite numbers of sheep and other cattle* (Fig 1.7; reprinted in Baker 1884; and see Fig 1.6; Anon 1762; Green 1872; Morgan 1882; Knight 1902; Bryant and Haslett 2002; Haslett and Bryant 2005). A number of churches around the Estuary also have plaques marking the height to which the water reached, which at Goldcliff and Peterstone, on the Welsh side of the Estuary, was 7.14m OD (*c* 1.5m from the present ground surface; Boon 1980, fig 16; Williams 1970, 88). Another plaque at Kingston Seymour does not itself mark the height to which the flood reached but similarly records that the water in the church was 5 feet high (ie *c* 7.3m OD) and lay on the ground about ten days (Fig 1.6).[2] The height of the early 17th-century sea wall along this coast is not known as it has since been demolished, though in the 19th century it was *c* 8 feet (2.4m) high. At Kingston Pill this replaced an earlier, but undated, embankment that was *c* 6 feet high (1.8m), the top of which was *c* 7.9m OD (heights given on the First Edition Ordnance Survey Six Inch map).

The height to which these waters reached must, however, have been an exaggeration as other contemporary accounts describe how a large building in nearby Kenn was used as a shelter during the floods (Green 1872, 53). The small island at Kenn lies at 6.4m OD (just 0.6m above the surrounding areas) and so would have been entirely inundated if the waters at Kingston Seymour had been five feet high (7.3m OD) and lain for ten days. What is more

Figure 1.6 Wooden plaque in the porch of Kingston Seymour church commemorating the great flood of 20 January '1606' (1607 in our modern calendar)

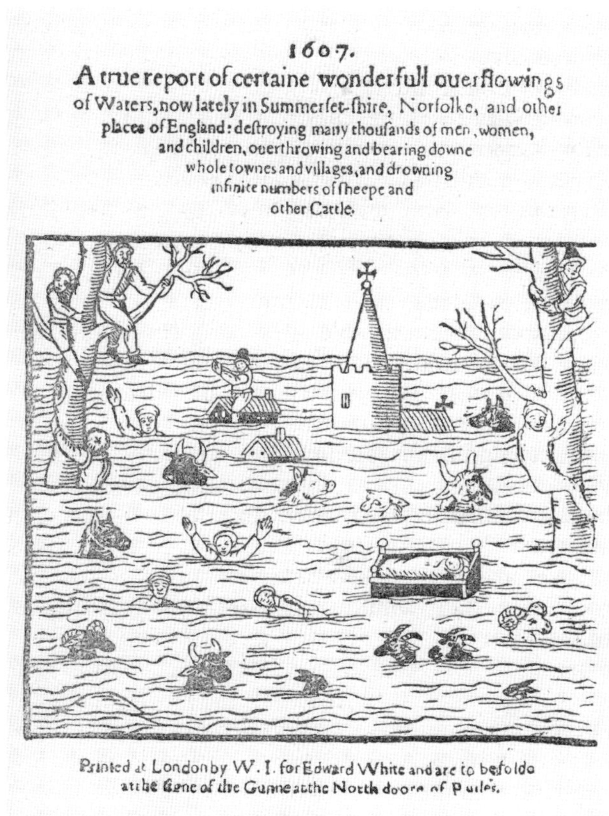

Figure 1.7 Engraving showing the 1607 flood from a contemporary account entitled 'A true report of certaine wonderfull overflowings of waters, now lately in Somerset-shire ...' (reproduced in Baker 1884). Note that the height to which the waters reached is greatly exaggerated, being far higher than recorded on plaques such as that shown in Fig 1.6

likely to have happened is that as the waters broke through the sea wall at Kingston Seymour they were indeed 5 feet high (1.5m, giving a height of 7.3m OD), though as the water dissipated across the

Figure 1.8: Aerial view of the oval-shaped Church Field that forms the earliest focus for settlement in Puxton. Looking north across Congresbury Marsh, Hewish, and Kingston Seymour towards Clevedon on the coast

landscape its depth would soon have reduced. There has been some recent speculation that this flood may have been caused by a tsunami, as opposed to the traditional view that it was due to a storm surge (such as that which devastated coastal areas around the North Sea in 1953). This is discussed further in Chapter 11.

The North Somerset Levels Project

The North Somerset Levels Project (NSLP) began in 1993 with the aim of trying to understand how the historic landscape of today, with its significant local and regional variations in character, came into being, and how this reflects the different and changing ways that human communities have chosen to utilise the same wetland environment. Work focused on the southern part of the Levels that by the 12th century was known as Wring Marsh (*Bruton* No. 134; 1304: *CPR* Edw I 1304–07, 279), after the Old English name (Wring) for the Congresbury Yeo river (and which is still preserved in the place-name Wrington to the east of Congresbury). In the 16th century the area was known simply as 'the marsh' (BRO BMC/4/37) and by the 19th century the Levels as a whole were known as the North Marsh of Somerset (Phelps 1836, 49–50). Those parts of Banwell and Congresbury parishes that extended onto the wetland were also known as 'the Marsh' (Locke 1806, 125). Although largely overlooked in Williams' (1970) seminal study *The Draining of the Somerset Levels*, this region formed part of the author's earlier study of *Landscape Evolution and Wetland Reclamation around the Severn Estuary* (Rippon 1993; published as 1997a), which compared the patterns of landscape utilisation on a series of coastal wetlands. Two key issues that emerged from this overview were our poor understanding of the nature of Romano-British wetland exploitation, and the reasons for such marked local variation in the character of the medieval landscape, and these formed the focus of this study.

The first phase of the NSLP (1993–97) focused on the Roman period. At a limited number of locations, air photographs had revealed the earthworks of extensive relict landscapes, and a 5-year programme of survey and excavation at Kenn Moor and Banwell Moor established a later 3rd-century AD date for both these ditched enclosure systems. A wide range of palaeoenvironmental indicators suggested a wholly freshwater (ie reclaimed) environment at that time, as did molluscan evidence from smaller-scale work at Puxton (a late Romano-British ditch sealed beneath a medieval bank at Church Field). The site at Banwell Moor also revealed a salt production site dating to the end of the Iron Age, suggesting that reclamation must have occurred sometime between the early 1st and later 3rd centuries AD. This element of the NSLP was published in *Britannia* (Rippon 2000b).

Stratigraphic and palaeoenvironmental evidence at Banwell Moor showed that these reclaimed landscapes were abandoned some time in the late Romano-British or early medieval periods when the North Somerset Levels were flooded and once again became an intertidal environment. Their subsequent recolonisation, which led to the creation of the present historic landscape, was the focus of the second phase of the NSLP (1996–2004). Analysis of the historic landscape suggested that the earliest surviving features are a series of small, roughly oval-shaped enclosures that seemed to pre-date the surrounding pattern of fields and roads, and which are found throughout the higher coastal wetlands all around the Severn Estuary (Rippon 1994a; 1996a; 1997a; 2002). Church Field at Puxton was typical of these infield enclosures (Fig 1.8), and in addition had several areas of abandoned settlement earthworks around the village, presumably representing a phase of later settlement expansion and contraction. Along with the investigation of an early Romano-British relict landscape on Puxton Dolemoor, the work within the medieval/modern settlement at Puxton gave the potential for comparing the medieval economy and environment on the North Somerset Levels with that of the Roman period.

The structure of this volume

Recent publications have seen landscape-based research projects presented in a range of different ways. Some have adopted a strongly chronological structure, with the various strands of evidence woven together in order to provide a history of that landscape period by period (eg Barker 1995; McOmish *et al* 2002; Riley and Wilson-North 2001). Others have described their results as a series of parish essays that gives a strong sense of spatial coherence (parishes being the primary unit of the medieval community), though a substantial general discussion is required in order to pull together the broad chronological and thematic developments (eg Wade Martins 1980a; Silvester 1988; Croft and Mynard 1993). Other landscape studies have adopted a structure that is neither chronologically nor spatially determined, but is instead based on different categories of evidence with separate discussions of documentary, field survey, excavation, artefactual, and palaeoenvironmental material (eg Cox and Hearne 1991; Davison 1990; West and McLaughlin 1998). Other landscape-based research projects have adopted a more thematic approach, addressing topics such as territorial structures, settlement patterns, and agrarian economy (eg Everitt 1986; Fleming 1998; Muir 2001; Corcos 2002a), while in some cases data and discussion are published in separate volumes (eg Fowler 2000; Fowler and Blackwell 1998; Astill and Davies 1997; Davies and Astill 1994).

This volume has tried to draw on many of the successful aspects of these earlier studies, with separate sections for the Roman and historic periods, as they are clearly separated by a significant change in the character of the landscape (a phase of late/post-Roman flooding). Within each section there is then a thematic as opposed to a source-based structure. Rather than a separate section on specialist reports, that contains much of the vital evidence from which overall conclusions are drawn but that most readers would probably skip over, as far as possible discussion of the artefactual and palaeoenvironmental evidence has been integrated with the overall narrative. Although this has led to some of the palaeoenvironmental reports being split between the Roman and medieval chapters, it hopefully has the advantage of integrating this important data with the other archaeological evidence. Finally, it should be stressed that this is not an attempt to write a definitive history of this landscape, and discussion is focused on the specific themes of the way in which human communities changed from simply exploiting the rich natural resources of this wetland, through modifying their environment to improve its agricultural productivity, to ultimately transforming the landscape through reclamation. In summary, therefore, the structure of this report is as follows:

In the remainder of **Part One** (***Chapter 2***) the sources and methods used in this project are discussed. Though one area, Puxton, saw the most intensive research through excavation and palaeoenvironmental sampling, it is placed in context through a nested series of study areas ranging from the southern part of the North Somerset Levels, that saw extensive archaeological survey, documentary research, standing building recording, and historic landscape analysis, through to a wider examination of certain issues across north-west Somerset and indeed the Severn Estuary region as a whole, providing the wider socio-economic context within which local lords and communities decided to manage their environment.

Part Two examines the Roman period when human communities first modified and then transformed the wetland landscape. ***Chapter 3*** examines the upper part of the alluvial sequence that makes up the North Somerset Levels (the Upper Wentlooge Formation) whose alluvial deposits are interleaved with cultural horizons corresponding to the prehistoric, Romano-British, and medieval landscapes. ***Chapter 4*** describes the archaeological and palaeoenvironmental examination of buried and relict (earthwork) landscapes of late Iron Age to Romano-British date at Puxton. In ***Chapter 5*** these are placed in context by further discussion of the previously published later Romano-British sites at Banwell Moor and Kenn Moor, along with a series of recent development-led excavations to the west of the study area in West Wick and St Georges, and elsewhere around the Severn Estuary.

Part Three of this volume relates to the second episode of wetland modification and transformation that led to the creation of today's historic landscape. It is structured through a series of thematic chapters that integrate a wide range of different source material. ***Chapter 6*** provides a characterisation of the historic landscape that integrates the morphological analysis of cartographic sources with a wide range of other evidence, including earthworks (identified through aerial photography and field survey) and material from fieldwalking (that together represent elements of the landscape that have gone out of use), documentary material, and field- and place-name evidence. In starting with a discussion of the historic landscape in its mature form, as depicted on the 19th-century cartographic sources which show the landscape following the final stages of enclosure but before the degradations of 20th-century farming and urban expansion, a fundamentally retrogressive approach has been adopted based on the premise that we should start with what we know and work back towards the unknown.

Subsequent chapters explore in greater detail the creation of this historic landscape, which as a cultural artefact can only be understood in the context of the human society that created it. ***Chapter 7***, therefore, examines the tenurial framework within which the landscape evolved. Part of the study area, in common with around a third of medieval England, was held by the church (the manors of Banwell and Congresbury being held by the bishops of Bath and Wells), while other areas, most notably Puxton and Rolstone, were held by a sequence of lesser aristocratic families. ***Chapter 8*** then considers the peasants and farmers who actually cultivated the land and managed the livestock, as reflected in documentary sources, their vernacular architecture, and the church within which they worshipped. ***Chapter 9*** reports on survey and excavation within one of those communities – the village of Puxton – including the artefacts that its occupants have left behind. In ***Chapter 10*** the palaeoenvironmental evidence is presented for both the local environment and the agricultural economy.

In **Part Four** these various strands of evidence are woven together. In ***Chapter 11*** the archaeological and documentary evidence for environmental and economic change over the first two millennia AD are discussed, with the particular intention of providing the non-specialist reader with a single summary of the detailed palaeoenvironmental reports presented in Chapters 3, 4, and 9. ***Chapter 12*** then brings together the evidence for when, how, and why the historic landscape was created, and in studying the creation of a medieval landscape in a relatively homogeneous physical environment that was devoid of the remains of earlier cultural landscapes, the specific role of lordship and community will be explored.

Archive

The archive and artefacts from the North Somerset Levels Project (including the excavations at Banwell Moor, Kenn Moor and Puxton) have been deposited at North Somerset Museum, Burlington Street, Weston-super-Mare, Somerset, BS23 1PR, under the accession number WESTM: 2006.47.

Notes

1 Chandler (1993, 430) suggests that Wick is Aldwick near Butcombe, but as Leland states that 'About a mile from Wick is the village of Kenn . . . and three miles from Wick in the Bristol direction is Wraxall' it can only be Wick St Lawrence.

2 This plaque can now be seen in the porch, although it used to hang in the vestry (*Bristol Times and Mirror*, 19 November 1910).

2 Researching the origins and development of an historic landscape

Historic landscape as the focus for research

All too often 'landscape' is used simply to provide the background or context for an essentially site-based programme of research. In the NSLP individual sites were indeed investigated through survey, excavation, palaeoenvironmental analysis, documentary archives, and standing building recording, but these individual strands of research were simply a means to the far broader end of understanding how the historic landscape as a whole came into being. The landscape as a whole was the focus of this research project, with the dominant theme being the changing ways that different human communities have chosen to utilise the same wetland environment

The NSLP was not an attempt at total landscape archaeology or history: resources were limited, and many questions had to go unanswered. Prehistoric landscapes, for example, are deeply buried under later alluvium and so could not be studied systematically, though on several occasions deep sections across Romano-British features revealed the underlying Iron Age ground surfaces. The starting point for studying the historic landscape was an analysis of the 19th-century maps – a common approach in landscape archaeology and history – but in this project the aim was to explore the antiquity of the different patterns of fields and settlements depicted on those maps (and that largely still survive today). Fieldwalking and the collection of pottery from the gardens of extant farmhouses allowed the development of the settlement pattern to be understood, while fieldwalking and documentary research provided a chronology for the development of field systems. A series of Romano-British and medieval landscapes were investigated through deliberately small-scale excavations. The aim of this project was not to reveal building plans and the like, but to understand the landscape as a whole and so a series of trenches were carefully targeted on features that would provide dating and palaeoenvironmental material. Such was the success of this sampling exercise that, along with the excellent preservation afforded by the wetland conditions, larger-scale work would simply have triggered the law of diminishing returns. This sampling strategy was rewarded with comparative palaeoenvironmental assemblages from two late Iron Age–early Romano-British salterns, a 1st- to 2nd-century ditched enclosure complex dug on the surface of a salt marsh, several later Romano-British enclosure complexes that lay within a reclaimed environment, early medieval flood deposits, an early medieval summer dike constructed on the surface of that salt marsh, and a 12th- to 13th-century settlement that exploited what was once again a reclaimed landscape.

The evolution of the research programme

A traditional way of studying landscape is to identify a study area (usually a parish, group of parishes, or county) across which research is spread relatively evenly. In this project, however, rather than a single study area, with hard boundaries within which all work was constrained, a different approach was developed through the creation of a series of nested study areas that were the subject of differing intensities of research (Fig 2.1).

This approach was born out of an earlier study in which the author compared patterns of wetland exploitation and reclamation all around the Severn Estuary during the Roman and medieval periods, and which noted marked local and regional variation in landscape character during those times (Rippon 1993; published as 1997a). This work was based mainly on a synthesis of existing archaeological and documentary research alongside a simple analysis of the historic landscape, and it became clear that there were many questions that could only be answered through a programme of fieldwork and primary documentary research. There were a series of crucial, and linked, questions: when and why did human communities decide to reclaim the coastal marshes that fringe the Estuary (and, in particular, were the extensive unstratified finds of Romano-British material indicative of reclamation); when was today's historic landscape created and why were its patterns of fields, roads, and settlements so varied across what is a physically uniform area. In the summer of 1993 the author therefore set out on a tour of the Severn Estuary wetlands with the aim of locating a suitable study area by visiting a series of potential sites identified through Site and Monuments Records, maps, and air photographs. It soon became apparent that the North Somerset Levels offered the greatest potential for archaeological research, with the earthworks of three well-preserved relict landscapes of probable Romano-British date (on Banwell Moor, Kenn Moor and Puxton Dolemoor), a series of oval-shaped infield enclosures (that were typical of those found throughout the Severn wetlands and which appeared to represent the earliest stages of marshland colonisation), and the earthworks of several shrunken medieval settlements (including Puxton).

The southern part of the North Somerset Levels was also of particular interest as for most of the medieval period the area was held by the bishops

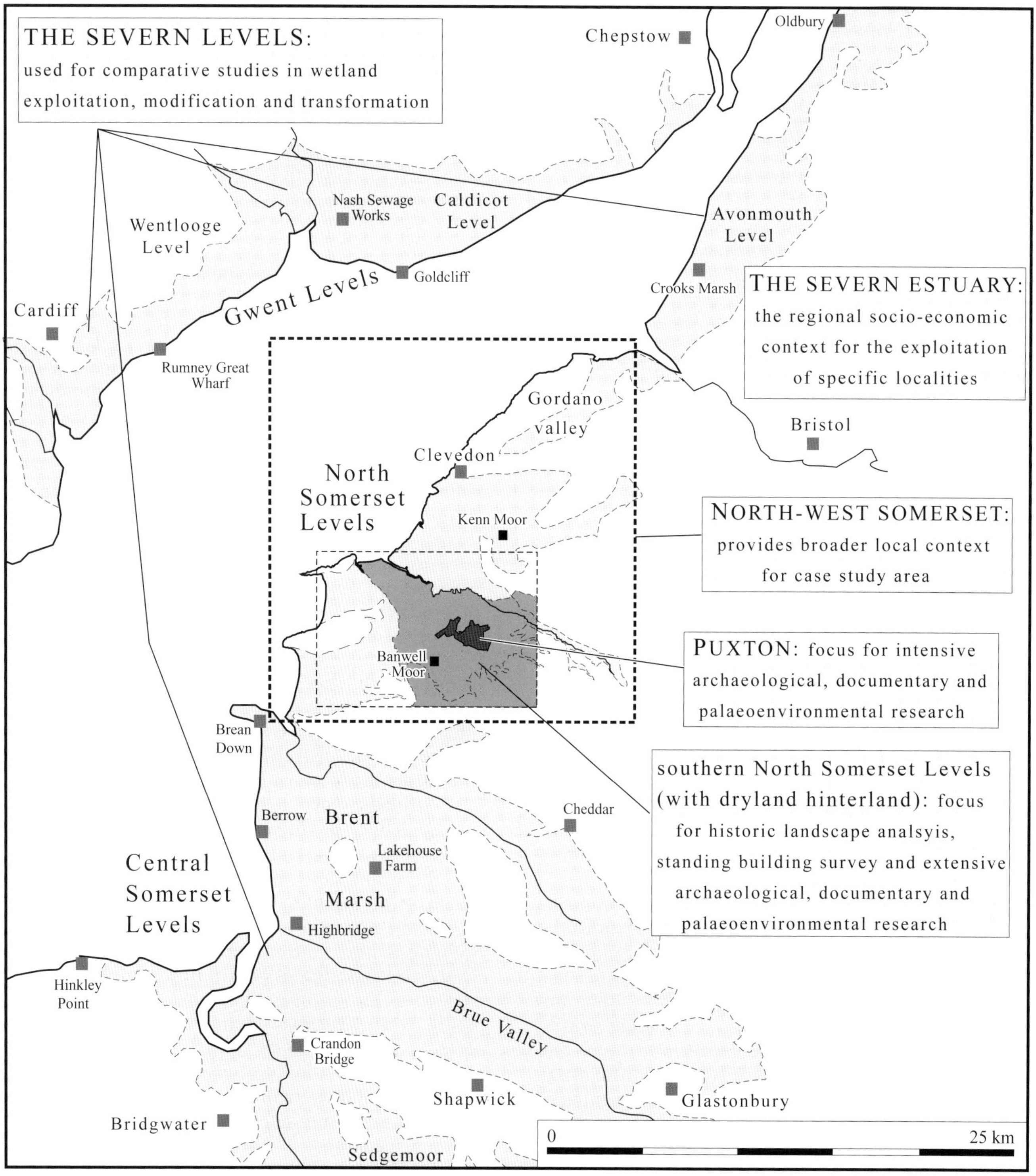

Figure 2.1 The series of nested study areas that provided data, and context, for the landscapes studied in the North Somerset Levels Project

of Bath and Wells, providing a potential comparison with the great monastic houses, notably Glastonbury Abbey, that have hitherto dominated agrarian and landscape research in Somerset (eg Postan 1952/53, 1956/57, 1975; Lennard 1955/56, 1975; Keil 1964; Stacey 1972; Holt 1987; Carley 1988; Abrams and Carley 1991; Ecclestone 1996; Harrison 1997; Thompson 1997; Corcos 2002a). When the NSLP began Mick Aston and his colleagues had also begun a detailed study of one of Glastonbury's Somerset manors at Shapwick (Aston and Gerrard 1999), and so the bishops' estates on north Somerset had the potential for comparing the estate management practices of these two institutions.

And so it was that the North Somerset Levels were selected for this programme of research, with work starting on two of the potentially Romano-British relict landscapes at Kenn Moor (1993–95) and Banwell Moor (1996–97) (published separately in Rippon 2000b). In 1996 the first season of excavations at the shrunken medieval village of Puxton also took place, and at this point in the discussion it is tempting to describe how Puxton offered an exceptional opportunity for exploring a landscape with a rare mixture of excellent earthwork preservation, but with significant areas available for fieldwalking, and what for a small non-monastic manor was an unusually rich archive. Such a statement would not, however, be altogether honest. In 1996 whilst the owners of two areas of shrunken settlement earthworks (in Church Field, and Home Ground north of Mays Lane) were amenable to archaeological investigations, a large area known as the Dolemoor, which included an extensive relict landscape thought to be of Romano-British date, along with several other potential deserted medieval farmsteads, was in the hands of a landowner who refused access as he was hoping to develop a hotel complex. The excellent preservation of earthworks around Puxton also meant that in 1996 the opportunities for fieldwalking were virtually non-existent, and while the archives held in the Somerset Records Office (SRO) included a wealth of post-medieval documents, there was little medieval material.

Any research project needs some luck, and Puxton was soon blessed as in September 1997 the probable early settlement core at Church Field was ploughed, providing a fortuitous opportunity for fieldwalking. Indeed, a pattern of periodic ploughing and then returning fields to pasture was seen across the study area in the following years, allowing the amount of fieldwalked land to grow slowly, but steadily. The prospects for fieldwork at Puxton improved further when the proposed hotel development on the Dolemoor was refused planning permission, and the land put up for sale. It was purchased by the Avon Wildlife Trust which encouraged a programme of survey and excavation which revealed that the relict landscape there dated to the earlier Roman period (mid-1st–2nd century), providing a fascinating contrast with the two later Romano-British (3rd- to 4th-century) examples previously investigated on Banwell Moor and Kenn Moor. There were also important developments with regards to the documentary research as it became clear that the manors of Puxton and nearby Rolstone had passed through the hands of several families and institutions whose archives had become scattered throughout records offices in Cornwall, Devon, Somerset, North Somerset, Wiltshire, Bristol, Gloucestershire, Cardiff, Birmingham, Oxford, and London (Lambeth Palace Library and the Public Records Office). Gill Bedingfield and Martin Ecclestone, who worked through many of these archives, were able to uncover far more material than it was assumed existed at the start of the project, including some important late medieval sources.

The NSLP also benefited from links established with other research programmes, notably the Shapwick Project directed by Mick Aston and Chris Gerrard. Two techniques used in the NSLP – shovel test pitting in and around an extant settlement, and heavy metal soil chemistry as a means of archaeological prospection in pasture – were both inspired by having seen them at work in Shapwick, and the same is true of the programme of standing building recording which benefited from another unforeseen event. A survey of Puxton church was first carried out in 1998, when the roof space was obscured by a ceiling. In 2002, however, several of the roof trusses gave way during a Sunday service (the congregation of four carried on regardless!), and in 2003 the church was declared redundant and taken into the care of the Churches Conservation Trust. During the subsequent repairs it was possible to gain access to the roof space, revealing important evidence for a potentially early date for the structure (see Chapter 8).

The cumulative effect of these developing circumstances at Puxton – including land sales, changes of land use, the discovery of unexpected archives in far flung places, and a dodgy church roof – was that far more was achieved than was originally expected. Fortunately, the NSLP was established without a rigid project design and so a flexible and pragmatic approach could be adopted, taking advantage of the new opportunities. But all good things must come to an end and the time was reached when it was right to finish the fieldwork, to stop visiting the records offices, and put pen to paper. Even as this text is being edited for the last time new fields have been ploughed up in Puxton and Wick St Lawrence, and several boxes of uncatalogued documents have been located in the Somerset Records Office, but no research programme can go on for ever. Hopefully these fields will be walked in time, and this archive examined, but now it is time to present the story so far.

The nested series of study areas (Fig 2.1)

There is an enormous range of sources available for studying the Romano-British, medieval, and post-medieval landscape, including archaeology, palaeoenvironmental assemblages, cartographic and documentary material, field- and place-names, and the physical fabric of the historic landscape itself, including the standing buildings. With the origins and development of this landscape as the focus for research, a strategy had to be designed that would balance the need for work that must be carried out on an extensive scale, such as fieldwalking, and the intensive site-based investigations needed to retrieve certain palaeoenvironmental assemblages. The result was not a single case-study area, but a series of nested study areas that were subjected to varying intensities of research:

1. Main study area comprises the marshland and fen-edge communities within the parishes of Banwell (including the hamlets of Rolstone,

Waywick, West Wick, and St Georges), Congresbury (including the communities at Puxton, the Marsh, and Wick St Lawrence), and Yatton (including the hamlets of East and West Hewish) (Fig 1.2.D). This area was subject to detailed historic landscape analysis, along with archaeological and standing building survey, and documentary research. Recent urban expansion to the east of Weston-super-Mare has also led to a number of development-led archaeological investigations close to the M5 motorway whose unpublished results have also been used.

2. Within this main study area, Puxton was selected for particularly detailed archaeological, palaeoenvironmental, and documentary research due to the presence of a Romano-British relict landscape, a classic example of an oval-shaped infield enclosure, other shrunken settlement earthworks, a well-preserved wider historic landscape, and what turned out to be relatively rich documentary sources. This area was subjected to detailed survey, excavation, palaeoenvironmental sampling, standing building recording, and documentary research, integrated through a detailed historic landscape analysis.
3. The broader study area comprises the North Somerset Levels as a whole and the adjacent dryland areas (the north-west Somerset basin). The inclusion of two very different physical environments within this broad study area reflects how in part many wetland areas were exploited from dryland/fen-edge places. This study area was used for selected research themes such as the context of the Romano-British wetland utilisation and the structure of early medieval estates.
4. The wider context. As this study unfolds, it will be seen that the development of the landscape within each of these nested study areas can only be understood in the context of a far wider region. The reclamation of these wetlands in the 3rd century AD, for example, forms part of the general trend towards prosperity, investment, and agrarian innovation seen in the wider Cotswold-Wessex region of Roman Britain. The emergence of a medieval landscape characterised by both small villages with communally managed open fields, and isolated farmsteads with enclosed fields farmed in severalty, reflects how the North Somerset Levels lie on the very western edge of that part of England that saw the creation of midland-style village landscapes.

The sources and techniques

The NSLP investigated landscapes that were preserved in three ways: the *buried* landscapes of later prehistory, the earthwork *relict* (ie abandoned) landscapes of Romano-British date, and the *historic* (ie still functioning) landscape of the medieval and post-medieval periods. The buried landscapes were only observed unintentionally in deep sections exposed when aspects of the relict or historic landscape were being investigated, and these sections had to be carefully cleaned and left to weather before the buried landsurfaces and associated features became clear. The relict and historic landscapes were investigated through a wide range of archaeological techniques alongside a detailed analysis of the historic landscape that goes well beyond simple morphological classification through the integration of documentary sources, field- and place-name evidence, and the vernacular architecture. This field survey and documentary research was designed to test the hypotheses derived from historic landscape analysis; where appropriate archives survived, and extensive fieldwalking was possible, this provided very successful.

Mapping the historic landscape

A central aspect of this project was its focus on the origins and development of the present countryside, and in this respect the historic landscape was both a source of information in itself and a means of integrating a wide range of other archaeological and documentary evidence. The earliest cartographic source to cover the entire study area systematically is the First Edition Ordnance Survey Six Inch to the Mile sheets surveyed in 1882–84. The earliest complete cartographic coverage for individual parishes are the *c* 1840 tithe maps for Banwell, Congresbury, Puxton, Wick St Lawrence, Yatton (including Hewish), and Kewstoke (including several detached parcels in Congresbury and Puxton). The accompanying tithe award schedules give details of land ownership and occupation, field-names, acreages, and land use. Large parts of the study area are also covered by 18th-century estate maps, notably the manors and estates belonging to the Chamber of Bristol in 1738–39 (which included large parts of Congresbury and Wick St Lawrence: Fig 2.2), the *c* 1770[1] map of the manors of Puxton and Rolstone, and the 1792 map of Sandford (Fig 6.15.B). The accompanying schedules for the Congresbury, Wick, Rolstone, and Sandford maps give details of field-names and landowners, though only a fragment of that for Puxton survives. The area between Puxton, Congresbury and Banwell is also covered by the Congresbury Drainage Act map of 1826.

Historic landscape analysis: adding time-depth and understanding to the historic landscape

These various cartographic sources allow the historic landscape to be comprehensively mapped in *c* 1840 (the tithe surveys), while for large areas a composite map can be drawn up based on the various 18th-century cartographic sources. The resulting maps

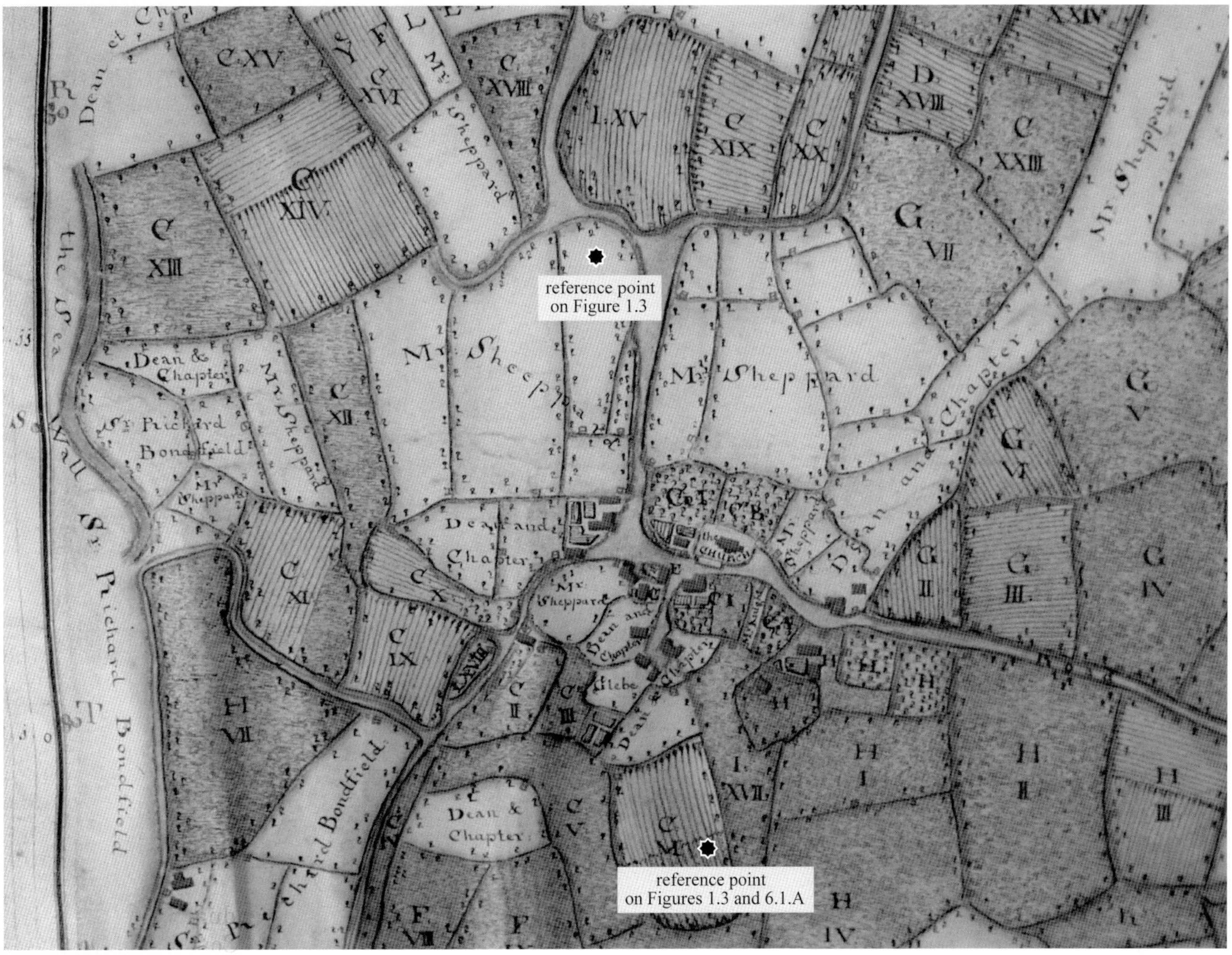

Figure 2.2 Extract of the de Wilstar map of Wick St Lawrence, 1738 (BRO 04480, ©Bristol Records Office). North is at the top. Tenements labelled C, G, H etc were held by Queen Elizabeth's Hospital, while those labelled Sir Sheppard and Sir Pritchard Bondfield had been sold off in the late 16th century

provide a remarkable resource for landscape research. The 1990s saw the development of techniques known as Historic Landscape Characterisation (sponsored in England and Wales by English Heritage and Cadw respectively), and Historic Landscape Assessment (sponsored in Scotland by Historic Scotland). In essence, these techniques attribute areas of the historic landscape to one of a series of predetermined types based largely on morphology and land use criteria (eg 'ancient' [ie medieval] enclosure: see Herring 1998; Fairclough and Rippon 2002; Rippon 2004a). They are designed to inform planners and countryside managers of the time-depth present within the landscape, and this work is starting to make an important contribution to planning and management decisions. As these historic landscape characterisations are forward-looking exercises, designed to inform decision making about the future of the countryside, the starting point is to characterise the landscape of today. Analysis of the historic landscape can, however, go much further in aiding our understanding of the origins and development of the countryside, particularly when it is applied on a smaller scale, in far greater detail, and is used to integrate a wide range of non-morphological data (see Rippon 2004a for a discussion of future- and past-oriented approaches to characterisation).

The approach preferred here is, therefore, to take as its starting point the landscape in its 19th-century form – after the long process of enclosure was complete but before the ravages of modern urban and industrial sprawl and agricultural improvement – and to disaggregate it into its separate components. This allows a more detailed examination of the field boundary patterns, the network of roads and commons, and the settlement pattern, while it is also important to map non-physical facets of the landscape such as ecclesiastical and manorial jurisdictions, patterns of landownership and tenure, and the nature of field- and place-names (see Chapter 6). Breaking down the historic landscape down into its component parts reveals marked spatial variation in the character of settlement, fields, roads, landholding, and field-names. The historic landscape must, however, ultimately be studied as a whole as these individual components did not exist in isolation,

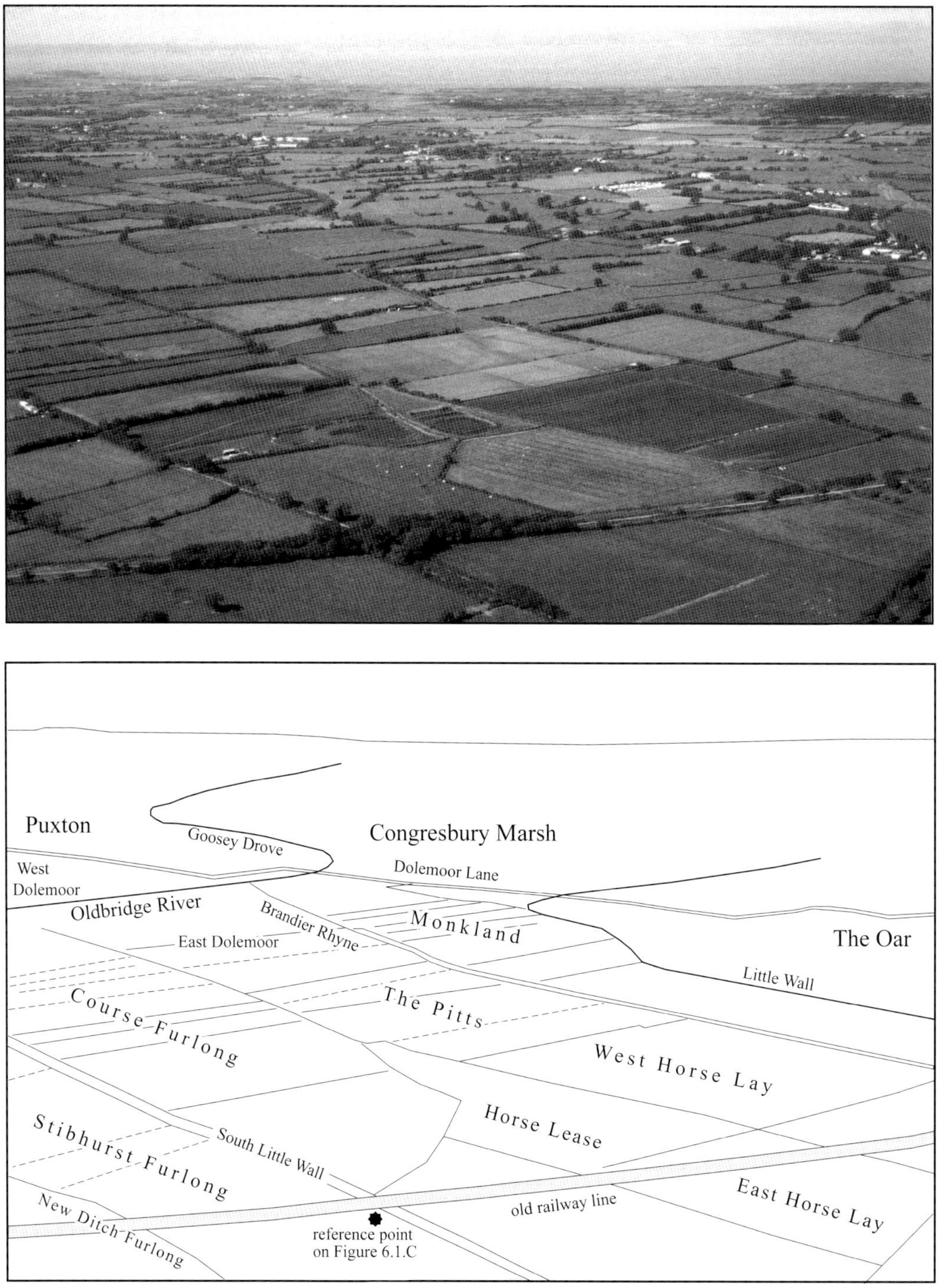

Figure 2.3 Aerial view of the former common fields west of Congresbury village. The carefully planned, coaxial, furlong boundaries still form the skeleton of this landscape, and many of the strips within this former common meadow are still preserved as field boundaries

but rather articulated with each other as part of a single working countryside. When variations in all the different components are taken together, what emerges is a series of unique character areas, each with its own set of character-defining features. Puxton and Rolstone, for example, are characterised by a settlement pattern of loosely nucleated hamlets and isolated farmsteads, associated with fragmented landholdings spread across complex and irregularly arranged field systems whose morphology and field-names suggest were derived from the enclosure of small common fields. The landscape in Wick St Lawrence and around St Georges, West Wick, and Waywick was similar though the settlement pattern was far more nucleated. In Congresbury Marsh, by contrast, the landscape was characterised by the almost total predominance of isolated farmsteads, associated with compact landholdings, and spread out alongside broad droveways.

There is, however, more to historic landscape

analysis than simply mapping morphology, and various techniques can be used to add time-depth and an understanding of the processes which created the countryside. Crucial to understanding the processes of landscape change is dating, both relative and absolute, and two basic principles can be used: stratigraphy and typology/analogy. All historic landscapes contain stratigraphic relationships that in the first instance can be identified through looking at a sequential set of maps of the same area (Williamson 1987 remains one of the clearest demonstrations of this retrogressive approach). Many 19th-century railways, for example, post-date the earliest maps of the areas through which they pass, allowing the impact of superimposing such a linear feature on an earlier landscape to be examined. The most distinctive signature is triangular-shaped fields created when a railway slices diagonally through an earlier field (eg Fig 2.3), and once this principle is recognised it can be seen, for example, that the Banwell and Oldbridge Rivers on the North Somerset Levels (Figs 6.1, 6.6 and 6.8) also post-date the historic landscape across which they run.

In these examples a linear feature is later than the historic landscape through which it passes, though in other cases the reverse is true, and relatively early features can be identified around which the rest of the historic landscape was created. One example is the enclosure of common field by agreement, where, in contrast to Parliamentary enclosure, the network of roads and furlong boundaries was retained in the post-enclosure landscape to form the major axial boundaries around which the new pattern of fields was created. A fine example on the North Somerset Levels is the Dolemoor between Congresbury and Puxton, where the map of 1739 shows around three-quarters of the former common field having been enclosed, with long blocks of closes laid out between the old furlong boundaries, and retaining names such as Course Furlong, Stibhurst Furlong, and New Ditch Furlong (Fig 2.3; note how the interpretation of this landscape as a former common field is based not just on the morphology, but also the 'Dole-' and '-Furlong' field-names).

These ancient enclosures have slightly curving or sinuous boundaries, whereas those postdating the map of 1739 are notably straighter (as are those of the final Parliamentary enclosures). As a set of observations such as these are built up, one can start to suggest at least relative dates for other aspects of the landscape by analogy with these absolutely dated features. The enclosure of roadside waste, for example, similarly produced a very distinctive historic landscape signature. The old droveways had sinuous/irregular boundaries up to 200 feet (60m) apart, and are depicted on various 18th-century estate maps. They were usually enclosed by laying out a straight, parallel-sided, road down the centre of the droveway, and dividing the areas of former waste either side into long, narrow fields with one side being sinuous (the boundary of the old droveway) and the other dead straight (following the new road). The retrogressive analysis of the various tithe, enclosure and estate maps clearly shows how such distinctive fields were created through the enclosure of droveways and roadside waste, and based on this understanding other examples can then be recognised elsewhere (Fig 2.5).

Morphology-based hypotheses, such as those described above, can be tested through documentary research. An example is shown in Figure 2.4. Banwell Moor was enclosed in 1797, though an analysis of the historic landscape suggests that this was the last remaining area of what had been a far larger common. Documentary evidence shows that the landscape around Rolstone was settled by the 12th century, and the landscape here is characterised by dispersed settlement and mostly irregularly shaped fields, sometimes laid out between long, sinuous, coaxial boundaries that may represent furlongs or former fen-banks built to control flooding (see Chapter 6). Between Rolstone and Banwell Moor as it survived in 1797 lies an area of rectilinear and polygonal fields with the names Castle Moor and Puddy Moor. These lack the regularity of Banwell Moor, but their individual boundaries are straight, suggesting that they are closer in date to the enclosure of Banwell Moor in the late 18th century, than the occupation around Rolstone in the 12th–13th centuries. This hypothesis is supported through documentary research as Puddy Moor was undergoing enclosure by 1672 (Fig 2.4). This sequence of enclosure is confirmed by the results of fieldwalking. Fields in Rolstone produced a light manure scatter of 12th-century and later pottery, whereas fields in Puddy Moor produced one possible medieval sherd but a relatively dense manure scatter of 17th- to 18th-century material. That part of Banwell Moor enclosed in 1797 which was fieldwalked (Twenty Acres) produced very occasional 17th- to 18th-century sherds (probably mixed in with later manure), but mostly pottery dated to the late 18th–19th centuries.

An analysis of the historic landscape can also be used to give a spatial context and meaning to otherwise dry historical documents, such as the late medieval account and court rolls for Puxton that refer to a series of landscape features such as watercourses, fields (both held in common and as closes), roads, and settlements (Fig 2.5):

The COURT ROLL of John Sayntlo knight held on the eve of SS. Philip and James in the said year [30 April 1492] (BodL RAWL. B 317):

- They present [order] Richard Craas to make a *ward* [bank] at Blackstones called Blackstones walle; on pain of 20d.
- At this court the Lord's officers approve the exchange made by Nicholas Hayne (one acre of pasture in le West Dolmore and one heystede on the west side of the King's road called le Northouswey) with William Sesse (one acre of pasture in le Longcrofte); each of them will pay the same rent as before.

Linking documentary sources to the historic landscape

New and Silver Moors

In 1705 there is reference to a close of 16 acres called North Silver Moor (which equates with the acreages of fields 532 and 533, both called Silver Moor, on the Tithe map) and South Silver Moors (field 526 on the Tithe map). To the west of Silver Moors lay New Moors which in 1731 was a single close of 29 acres (which can be identified in the Tithe Survey as four four fields of the same name whose total acreage is 27a 2r 22p) (WCL 10189). Clearly, the western part of Banwell Moor had been enclosed by that date, albeit in a rudimentary fashion, and the large closes so created were only later sub-divided into the fields of today.

West Rolstone

this relatively sinuous boundary is parallel to those to the north and south, suggesting that it may have been a furlong boundary within a common meadow, or a former fen-bank

these boundaries are very straight, especially compared to the sinuous boundaries to the north and south, suggesting they are later: they may have been created following the enclosure of a common meadow

the southern boundary of this block of fields is noticeably sinuous and probably represents a 'fen-bank' dividing the drained agricultural land to the north from the open moors to the south

the pattern of 'gripes' (spade-dug gullies cut into the surface of fields) is very different in this area, which is bounded to the south by a sinuous lane that separates these relatively irregularly shaped fields, with sinuous or curving boundaries, from the straight-sided and clearly later fields further south

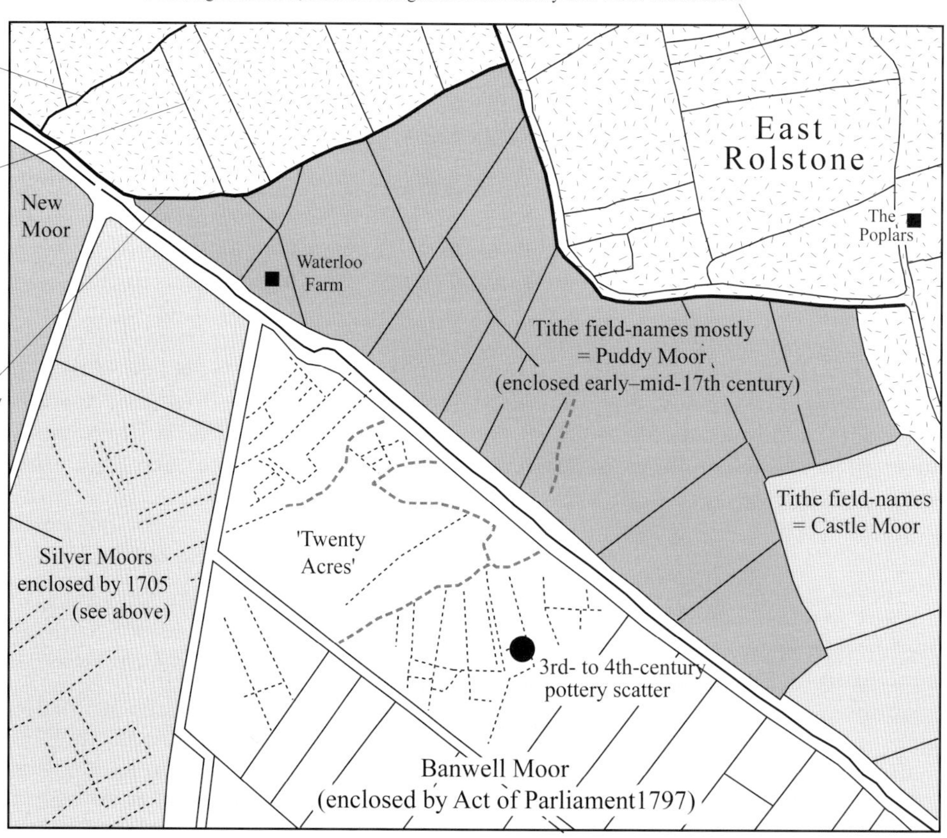

later Romano-British relict landscape

palaeochannel (former saltmarsh creek)

0 200 m

Figure 2.4 Aerial view and interpretation of the north-west corner of Banwell Moor (including Twenty Acres), with Puddy Moor to the north and Silver Moors to the west. The integration of documentary sources and fieldwalking with historic landscape analysis allows the sequence of enclosure in this area to be worked out (aerial photograph: © National Monuments Record RAF/3G/TUD/UK/21 fr 5096, January 1946). For survey and excavation of the late Romano-British relict landscape see Rippon 2000b

Figure 2.5 Aerial view and interpretation of Puxton and the Dolemoor with documented medieval features identified through later sources such as field- and place-names. Note how areas of enclosed former roadside waste can be identified in the field boundary pattern (aerial photograph: © National Monuments Record RAF/58/1354 fr 0053, February 1954)

- They present [order] Wm Coke, John Jeve jnr and John Carpenter well and sufficiently to make a *fossata* [ditch] from Chaundelersmede to the land of Thomas Browne before 24th June next, on pain of 20d each.
- They present [order] Wm Coke and John Carpenter to scour the *fossata* from the Rector's land to Knyvescrofte before 24th June next, on pain of 20d each.
- Also Wm Coke for a *fossata* between Shorteacre and the land called Freemans, on pain of 20d.

The ACCOUNT ROLL John Jeve the bailiff there from Michaelmas the 16th year of King Henry VII to the same feast in the 17th year [1500–01] (BodL RAWL. B 317):

Income from demesne lands:

- 46s 8d from demesne land called Twyndyke.

Expenditure:

- 12d paid to the bishop as customary for the meadow called Brodmed.
- 7d for repairing five ropes of the New Yoo.
- 5d for the new door at West Dolmore called le Clyfs.
- 20s for the rent of a close called Twyndyke this year.
- 2d for his breakfast on the court day.

Tenants, tenements, and houses

An important part of the historic landscape is the settlement pattern, which is made up of farmsteads (associated with a working agricultural landholding), cottages (that were often the homes of landless labourers), and other buildings such as the rectory or parsonage, church houses (alehouses), poor houses, and schools. Archaeologists and historical geographers have long studied the spatial disposition of settlement across a landscape, notably whether it is nucleated in a single location or spread across a parish in small hamlets or as isolated farmsteads (see Chapter 6). The emphasis in this study, however, was not just on settlements as dots on maps, but on the entire landholdings, or tenements, that they were associated with. In particular, an attempt was made to integrate two aspects of the medieval and post-medieval landscape that all too often are studied in isolation: the vernacular buildings, and the patterns of landownership and leasing.

Standing buildings form a distinctive part of any historic landscape and this is true of the North Somerset Levels. This is not a landscape of grand country houses, and indeed, not a single manor house can be identified within the study area. There are, however, a large number of distinctive farmhouses characterised by their long south-facing frontages and grey cement rendering. Over 30 farmhouses and cottages were recorded as part of this project in order to establish when they were first built and the major phases of development that were subsequently undertaken. Tracing the history of these houses, however, proved to be more complicated than expected as before the 19th century very few had proper place-names. What is actually recorded in pre-19th-century records is the tenement of which they were part, and these tenement-names refer to individual tenants who had held them sometime in the past. What is now called Grange Farm, south of Mays Green, for example, was purchased in 1593 by Edward Muttlebury, and although from at least 1687 it was held by the Cooke family and their successors, as late as 1881 the tenement was still known as Muttleburys (Cran 1983, 72; BRO 08835(1) and 18845(10); SRO DD/SOG 341–2; and private deeds).

The use of surname-based tenement names is found throughout the study area and many landholdings periodically changed their names as they passed from one tenant to another, occasionally retaining earlier affinities (eg in 1755 John Bailey paid 18s rent for a tenement called 'Tuckers late Wasons': SRO DD/WY box 70). Tracing tenements that kept changing their names back through a discontinuous documentary record was not easy, but a range of other sources enabled the vast majority of 19th-century tenements to be traced back to at least the early 17th century (and in many cases the 16th century). The starting point was the tithe map/award that gave the landowners and occupiers for all the farmsteads (and indeed all parcels of land). The major landowners can be identified in the 1832 Register of Electors that list the premises of each elector. Some of these premises are proper place-names (usually the first occasion when these are recorded), but most are surname-based tenement names. The next source consulted was the Land Tax returns that list the owners and occupiers of land in the parish, and the tax they paid. The latter is crucial, as the tenement name is not always listed but while the owners/occupiers changed over time, the tax paid usually remained constant. The Land Tax records go back to 1760, which provides a link with the next set of records: a series of 17th- to 18th-century lease books for the manors of Puxton and Rolstone along with a series of rentals for *c* 1630,[2] 1642, 1651, and 1755, and the map of *c* 1770. Pre-17th-century documentation is more patchy, though a number of late 15th- and 16th-century accounts and court rolls allow some tenements to be traced back even further. For example:

South Farm, Puxton: On **tithe map** (No 95) as a farmhouse when it was owned and occupied by John Howell. In 1832, John Howell paid £1 11s 8d **Land Tax** for Whites. In 1782 William White paid the same tax, as did Jane Brookman in 1766. The **lease book** of *c* 1778 records leases to Jane Brookman (widow) in 1756 and Robert White in 1775. Tenement U on **map of *c* 1770**, held by widow Brookman (for a tenement called Warnell's) with a house and 27a 0r 0p (29 customary acres).* John Brookman paid £1 7s 0d rent for Wormells in the **rental of 1755**, which Joseph and John Cooke also paid for Wornells in 1642. In the **rental of *c* 1630** Agnes Irish paid £1 8s 0d for Wornells; an annotation states that Cooke acquired it in 1642. The **court roll for 1560/62** records that Joan, late wife of John Wornell, and now wife of John Hurdytts, was ordered to repair the windows of her house (WRO 2667/13/452).

* The *c* 1770 survey of Puxton conveniently gives the size of tenements in both customary and stautory acreages, and while the former were occasionally smaller than the latter they were generally slightly larger, with 1 customary acre averaging 1.1 statutory acres.

Testing historic landscape analysis through archaeological fieldwork

In the ways described above, historic landscape analysis can produce a set of hypotheses relating to the antiquity of our countryside and the processes that may have been responsible for its creation. These hypotheses, however, must then be tested through a programme of archaeological fieldwork.

Topographical survey and coring

Although the Levels appear essentially flat, a crucial question was why the potentially early oval-shaped enclosures such as Church Field were located where they are. Previous work on several similar sites in nearby Kingston Seymour had established that they were not related to bedrock outcrops (Gilbert 1996, 56), and a programme of coring and topographical survey (over an area *c* 1.0 by 1.5km centred on Church Field) similarly established that Church Field was created on estuarine alluvium. Subsequent to this survey LIDAR data (Light Detection and Ranging, an airborne mapping technique which uses a laser to measure the distance between the aircraft and the ground) became available for the area immediately around Puxton, showing that the northern edge of the infield enclosure in fact lies on the very slightly raised banks of a palaeochannel (Fig 9.2).

Fieldwalking

During the course of the NSLP's initial work at Banwell Moor (1996–97), only around a dozen fields within the study area were ploughed and so it was assumed that fieldwalking would play a relatively minor part in the Project. Over the following years, however, a pattern emerged of fields being ploughed up and cultivated for a few years before being put back down to pasture, and this rotation cumulatively allowed a significant area to be walked. Two techniques were used. As the aim of the fieldwalking survey was to locate and investigate both deserted settlement and manure scatters of the Roman and medieval periods, the majority of fields were walked using lines 20m apart, surveyed from a baseline laid out beside the longest straight side of the field, and with collection units (stints) 20m long (the same approach was adopted on the Romano-British relict landscape at Kenn Moor: Rippon 2000b). Ground conditions were generally good, the fields having been ploughed, rolled, and weathered, and 180ha in 48 modern fields (that were 80 fields at the time of the tithe surveys) were walked in this way, ranging from parts of the historic landscape that represent the earliest areas to be enclosed and settled (eg around Puxton), through areas that represent slightly later colonisation (eg around Rolstone and Waywick), to post-medieval enclosures (eg Banwell Moor enclosed in 1797, and the adjacent New Moor, Puddy Moor, and Silver Moors that were probably enclosed in the 17th–18th centuries: see below).

A different fieldwalking strategy was adopted in Wick St Lawrence. During the fine spring of 2004 there was very little rainfall between seeding and the crop emerging, and although several former settlement sites were readily visible, mainly through scatters of stone rubble, a manure scatter of pottery was not apparent due to the poor visibility. It was decided, therefore, simply to locate any deserted settlements by walking along lines 20m apart, and no attempt was made to recover any manure scatters. This approach was also adopted in a large field west of Puxton Church Field that was ploughed for the first time in 2005 and had insufficient time for it to weather before the crop emerged (tithe numbers 121–7; 7ha).

Aerial photography and earthwork survey

A series of high-quality aerial photographs taken by the RAF shortly after the Second World War reveal an almost wholly pastoral landscape within which most fields contained earthworks (eg Figs 2.4, 2.5, 6.1, 6.6, and 6.8). Most were spade-dug gullies (known as gripes) that drained the surface of the fields and so formed a functioning part of the historic landscape, though in places the earthworks relate to parts of the historic landscape that have fallen out of use (including a number of field boundaries, the platforms of several deserted farmsteads and cottages, and certain stretches of road). Air photographs also revealed what were once extensive relict landscapes on a different orientation to the historic landscape (at Banwell Moor, Kenn Moor, and Puxton Dolemoor), and where significant areas survived as earthworks these were also subject to detailed field surveys (for the RCHME surveys at Kenn Moor see Rippon 1994b, figs 12–14; 2000b, fig 8).

Geophysics

It is well known that magnetometry does not work well in alluvial geologies (Gaffney and Gater 2003,

79), and this was confirmed at Kenn Moor when it failed to locate a known site comprising ditches, a building platform, and a spread of stone rubble. Resistivity was, in contrast, used with some success at Banwell Moor and Kenn Moor in fields that had been ploughed flat, locating a series of substantial ditches (Rippon 2000b), though in Church Field at Puxton it failed to locate any significant features.[3] As elsewhere earthwork preservation was so good, no further geophysical survey was undertaken.

Soil chemistry

In largely pastoral areas such as the North Somerset Levels, the worse case scenario for the landscape archaeologist is for fields to have been ploughed in the past (so destroying any earthworks), but then reverted to pasture (preventing the opportunity for fieldwalking). Locating sites in such circumstances can be extremely difficult, made worse in the case of estuarine alluvium because geophysical survey is notoriously ineffective (see above). During the course of the NSLP, the author paid a visit to the Shapwick Project, where multi-element soil chemistry was successfully tested by Mike Martin and Andrew Jackson. They expressed an interest in working at Puxton in order to test the technique in an area of uniform geology and soils, resulting in surveys of phosphate and heavy metals on the known medieval settlement site in Church Field, and as a control, in Puxton tithe map fields 110–11 to the south (Rippon *et al* 2001). Following its success, Andrew Jackson carried out a further survey in and around a curiously shaped field, with the potentially settlement-indicative field-name of Hardingworth (see Costen 1992b for the significance of these '-worthy' names), while further surveys were carried out by students at the University of Exeter in several locations where earthworks suggested the presence of deserted settlements to the east of Church Field (Butts and Oxlease) and to the north of Mays Lane (Home Ground).

Shovel test pitting

Documentary research, fieldwalking, earthworks (surviving and/or on aerial photographs), and soil chemistry surveys revealed a number of platforms that were possible deserted settlement sites, and those in the vicinity of Puxton itself were subject to a programme of shovel test pitting. Test pits 1m square were excavated through the topsoil in a line that extended from the platforms onto the surrounding areas, so that on-site and off-site pottery concentrations could be compared. A total of 54

Table 2.1 Summary of phasing and broad environmental/landscape conditions at the excavated sites

phase	date	natural environment	cultural landscape
10	modern	freshwater (reclaimed)	• topsoil
9	18th–19th century	freshwater (reclaimed)	• latest infilling of ditches/gripes at Church Field and Home Ground
8	17th century	freshwater (reclaimed)	• reoccupation at Home Ground
7	14th to 16th century	freshwater (reclaimed)	• contraction of Puxton village and abandonment of tenements at Church Field and Home Ground
6	late 11th to 13th century	freshwater (reclaimed)	• continued occupation in Church Field and expansion of settlement to Home Ground
5	?*c* late 10th/early 11th century	decrease in inundation?	• 'summer/ring dike' at Church Field • earliest features within Church Field (on a different orientation to the 12th- to 13th-century ditched enclosure
4	early medieval	intertidal saltmarsh	• alluvium above upper dark horizon
3	late Romano-British	freshwater (reclaimed)	• upper dark horizon (buried soil) at Home Ground and Hardingworth • upper fill of ditched enclosure system at Dolemoor • drainage ditch/gullies beneath later bank in Church Field
2b	early Romano-British	decrease in inundation?	• creation and lower fill of ditched enclosure system on Dolemoor
2a	late Iron Age	intertidal saltmarsh	• salt production at Dolemoor • alluvium below upper dark horizon at Home Ground
1	middle Iron Age	decrease in inundation	• lower dark horizon at Home Ground
0	Pre-middle Iron Age	intertidal saltmarsh	• alluvium below lower dark horizon at Home Ground

Table 2.2 Summary of preservation of palaeoenvironmental indicators (all sites published here unless otherwise stated)

site	feature/context	samples					
		soil micro.	diatoms	foraminifera	pollen	plant macros	Mollusca
upper part of Upper Wentlooge sequence							
Banwell Moor (Rippon 2000b)		*	*	*	*	*	*
Home Ground		*		*	*	*	*
Hardingworth	context 417					*	
late Iron Age							
Banwell Moor (Rippon 2000b)	saltern F.281					*	*
Dolemoor	saltern 361						*
early and late Romano-British							
Dolemoor	ditch F.365		*	*	*	*	
	ditch F.311						*
	pit F.301					*	
late Romano-British							
Banwell Moor (Rippon 2000b)		*	*	*	*	*	*
Kenn Moor (Rippon 2000b)			*	*		*	*
Church Field	gully F.156						*
late 11th to 13th century							
Church Field	surface beneath bank (503)	*			*	*	
	enclosure ditch F.103		*	*	*	*	*
	ditch F.128		*	*	*	*	*
	ditch F.140 (recut of F.128)					*	*
	ditch F.115					*	
	ditch F.135					*	*
	ditch F.510					*	
	ditch F.526					*	
Home Ground	gully F.243					*	
	pit F.265					*	*
	ditch F.267		*	*		*	*
	ditch F.308					*	*
?medieval or post-medieval							
Dolemoor	ditch F365 (upper cut)		*		*	*	
Moor Dairy						*	*
17th/18th century							
Church Field	ditch F.140 (recut of F.128)					*	*
Home Ground	ditch F.209					*	*

shovel test pits were dug on seven sites, all of which located medieval occupation. In addition, pottery was collected from a number of gardens both within Puxton and during the wider standing buildings survey, and the opportunity was also taken to report on the results of a comprehensive garden survey by local resident Linda Jenkins in the parish of Wick St Lawrence.

Excavation strategy

The excavation strategy had two clear aims: to date key elements of the relict and historic landscapes, and to obtain comparative palaeoenvironmental and palaeoeconomic samples from landscapes of different periods. This was achieved through a total of twelve trenches strategically located across four sites (see Table 2.1 for a summary of the phasing):

- Dolemoor: four trenches (7, 8, 9, and 10) excavated in 1999 across different elements of a relict landscape that by analogy with other excavated examples (at Banwell Moor and Kenn Moor) was thought to be late Romano-British, but which turned out to date from the 1st–2nd centuries AD (Fig 4.2)
- Hardingworth: one trench (6) excavated in 1999 across a suspected settlement site identified by soil chemistry survey within a field with a settlement-indicative field-name (Fig 4.1). The soil chemistry anomaly turned out to be a dump of post-medieval debris in the topsoil, though the trench revealed a long exposure of a buried soil within the upper part of the natural Wentlooge alluvium where it had slumped into a palaeochannel.
- Church Field: five trenches within the infield enclosure and deserted medieval settlement south of the church, sectioning the enclosure ditch and bank (Trenches 3 and 11, excavated in 1996 and 1999 respectively), along with internal boundary ditches and a raised platform that was confirmed as an occupation site (Trenches 1 and 2, and 12, excavated in 1996 and 1999 respectively) (Fig 9.4)
- Home Ground: two trenches (4 and 5) excavated in 1998 in a second area of shrunken medieval settlement to the north of the village (Fig 9.7)

Palaeoenvironmental sampling and reconstruction

Unlike the better known Somerset wetlands in the Brue Valley and Sedgemoor, there are no deep peat sequences in the southern part of the North Somerset Levels, while those on Kenn Moor have lost their upper, Romano-British and later, stratigraphy.[4] During the course of the NSLP, however, the estuarine alluvium that makes up the upper part of the Upper Wentlooge Formation was extensively sampled and, while palaeoenvironmental preservation was variable, a continuous sequence covering the Iron Age and Roman periods was obtained from Banwell Moor and Puxton Home Ground. A range of ditches and other features dating from the late Iron Age through to the early post-medieval periods were also sampled for beetles, diatoms, foraminifera, Mollusca, pollen, and plant macrofossils, and preservation in these contexts was on the whole far better (Table 2.2). This was the first occasion when this range of analyses had been applied to Roman and medieval sites on the Somerset Levels.

The palaeoenvironmental work on the late Roman sites at Banwell Moor and Kenn Moor is published elsewhere (Rippon 2000b), while specialist reports on the work at Puxton appear in this volume in Chapters 3 (the natural alluvial sequence), 4 (the Roman period) and 10 (medieval period). Chapter 11 provides an overall synthesis and discussion including a series of schematic reconstructions of what the vegetation across a typical ditch would have looked like. As part of the post-excavation process the project director and two of the palaeoenvironmental specialists, Julie Jones (plant macrofossils) and Heather Tinsley (pollen), also went out into the field to seek modern analogies for these Roman and medieval ditches and to try to understand some of the management practices that would have created the palaeoenvironmental assemblages.

Notes

1 This map and accompanying survey is undated, but a comparison of the occupiers of several tenements listed in later lease books indicates a date between 1766 and 1771.

2 The list of tenants is similar to that of 1642, but entry for 'Agnes Irish (Wornells)' that has been annotated 'Cooke 1642' proves that it is earlier (the 1642 rental confirms that Wornell's was held by John and Joseph Cooke). Of the tenants listed in the rental, John Burge is described as 'lately John Burges' in the 1636 glebe terrier; the Congresbury Church Registers record that 'Margaret Knight, widow of Puxton' was buried on 10 October 1640, while Thomas Avery of Puxton was buried on 21 June 1634; one John Irish of Puxton was buried on 31 March 1627 and the fact that John Irish Junior is listed in the rental suggests that it dates to sometime between 1627 and 1634.

3 *Resistivity Survey Report: Church Field, Puxton, North Somerset*, by Kerry Ely, Richard McConnell and Alex Turner, November 1996 (copy in archive in the North Somerset Museum, Weston-super-Mare).

4 The results of coring and pollen analysis are described in Rippon 1995b. A sample of peat from 0.26m below the top of this sequence gave a radiocarbon date of 2410 ± 60 BP (Beta-099381).

Part 2: Late prehistoric and Romano-British landscape

In the late Iron Age the North Somerset Levels were a vast area of salt marshes and mudflats that offered a range of natural resources such as rich grazing and the opportunity to produce salt. In the early Roman period human communities intensified their use of these marshes, modifying the environment through digging localised ditched enclosure systems. The Levels remained, however, an intertidal environment until around the 3rd century when extensive areas were embanked, transforming them into a freshwater reclaimed landscape. Comparing the North Somerset Levels to other areas around the Severn Estuary, there was significant local variation in how other wetland areas were used which reflects wider issues such as the impact of local centres of consumption (such as the Roman military establishment in south-east Wales), and the agrarian wealth, investment and innovation seen in the *civitas* of the Dobunni and the Durotriges.

Chapter 3 describes the upper part of the alluvial sequence that makes up the North Somerset Levels (the Upper Wentlooge Formation), within which prehistoric and Romano-British landscapes lie buried. Chapter 4 describes the excavations and other fieldwork on one of those landscapes, at Puxton Dolemoor, including the palaeoenvironmental sequence from an excavated ditch (F.365) that shows the transition from intertidal to freshwater (reclaimed) conditions, marking the act of reclamation. The context of this transformation of the landscape is discussed in Chapter 5 which provides an example of how any one landscape can only be understood in its wider context, and how general topics such as the changing ways that the Roman-British landscape was exploited can be informed by detailed local studies.

3 The wetland wilderness: the late prehistoric and Romano-British environment

On the eve of the Roman Conquest the North Somerset Levels were a vast expanse of untamed wilderness, with intertidal mudflats and salt marshes towards the coast, occasionally inundated backfens in the lower-lying inland areas, and a freshwater peat bog in its north-east corner (Fig 1.5: Kenn and Tickenham Moors). This mosaic of natural environments was used for grazing livestock and producing salt by boiling sea water, yet by around AD 300 the area was protected from tidal inundation and was extensively settled and farmed, with a palatial villa at the heart of this transformed landscape. Chapters 3–5 examine the changing ways in which human communities utilised this wetland environment over the Roman period, initially through its modification in order to improve the quality of grazing, and then through its transformation (ie reclamation) to make arable cultivation possible.

Research into this landscape began in the 1880s when a Roman villa was excavated at Wemberham on the north bank of the Congresbury Yeo, but apart from the collection of a few unstratified assemblages of material by local amateur archaeologists from the 1950s onwards there was little further work and by the early 1990s we still had almost no idea of what this wetland landscape was like during the Roman period (see Rippon 1993). In a number of places, however, the extensive earthworks of abandoned settlements and their associated field systems occurred in close proximity to unstratified findspots of Romano-British material. Between 1993 and 1997 two of these landscapes – on Banwell Moor and Kenn Moor – were the subject of survey, excavation, and palaeoenvironmental sampling (Rippon 2000b). In addition to a late Iron Age saltern, this revealed that both landscapes were later Romano-British in origin (mid-3rd century), and that they lay within a landscape that was entirely free from tidal inundation: the flora and fauna living in the ditched enclosure systems were entirely freshwater,

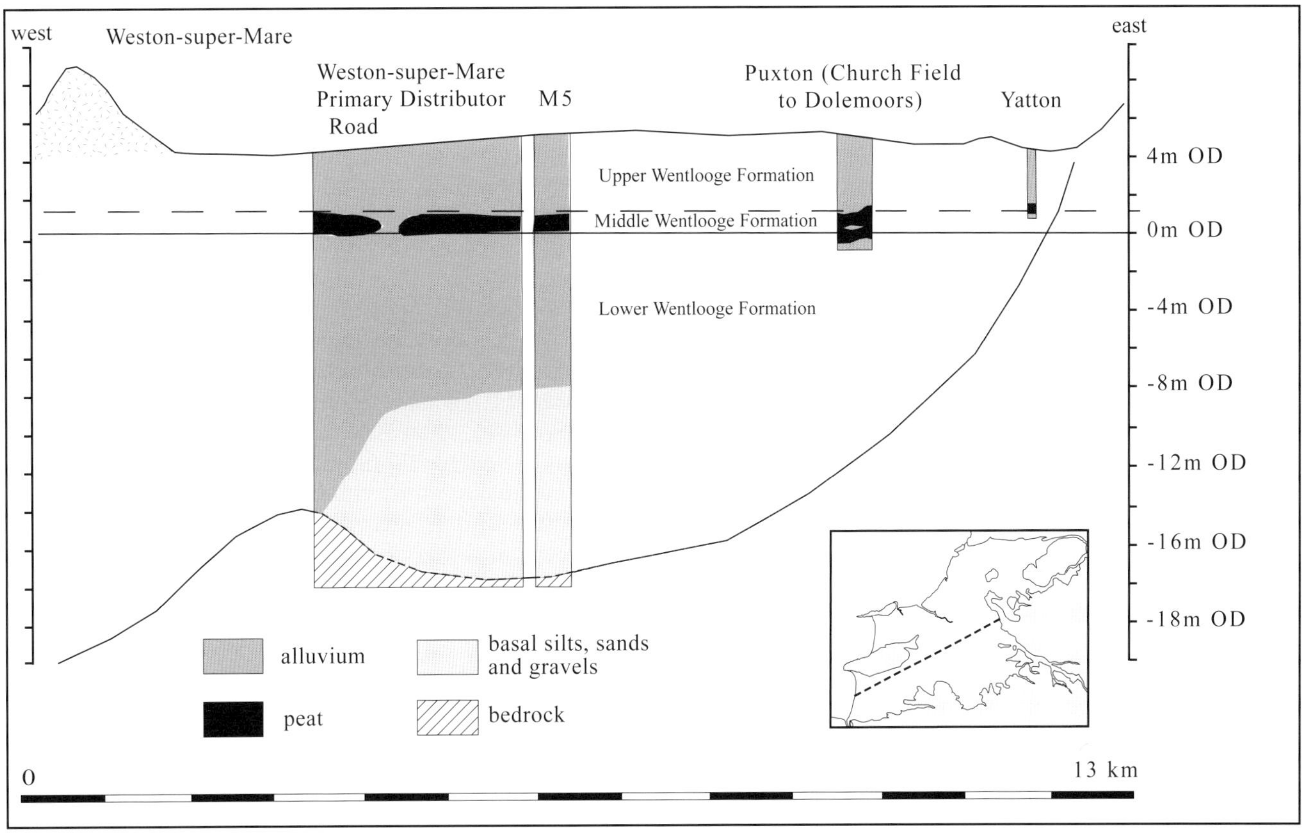

Figure 3.1 Cross-section through the alluvial and peat sequence that makes up the North Somerset Levels based on coring at Puxton, unpublished borehole logs along the line of the M5 motorway and Weston-super-Mare Primary Distributor Road (in the Highways Department of the former Avon County Council), and Murray and Hawkins 1976

and very similar to the ecology of the present day drainage system (see Chapter 11).

The subsequent programme of fieldwork at Puxton, whilst focused on the origins and development of the historic landscape, afforded the opportunity to investigate the Romano-British landscape in a third location. Unstratified later Romano-British pottery was found at various locations through fieldwalking and shovel test pitting, and the excavation of a ditch, sealed beneath a medieval bank in Church Field, produced a freshwater palaeoenvironmental assemblage. A surprise, however, came when a third relict landscape, in an area known as the Dolemoor, was investigated and was found to date to the earlier Roman period and to have occupied a very high intertidal salt marsh. In terms of the history of this landscape it filled the gap between the late Iron Age saltern excavated on Banwell Moor, and the late Romano-British reclaimed landscapes uncovered both there and at Kenn Moor. Taken all together, these sites demonstrate the changing nature of wetland exploitation, modification, and transformation in far greater detail than anywhere else in Roman Britain.

The Upper Wentlooge Formation

Archaeologists working on dryland sites are used to digging down to the natural and then stopping. In a wetland environment, however, the concept of the natural is less simple. The North Somerset Levels comprise a *c* 20m thick sequence of deposits that mirrors that found throughout the wetlands that adjoin the Severn Estuary: a diachronous basal peat, overlain by a thick layer of gravels, sands, silts, and clays (the Lower Wentlooge Formation), sealed by a near synchronous layer of mid-5th to early 2nd millennium BC peat (the Middle Wentlooge Formation), which in turn is buried beneath another layer of blue/grey silty clay (the Upper Wentlooge Formation: Hawkins 1971; Welin *et al* 1972; Murray and Hawkins 1976; Gilbertson and Hawkins 1978; 1983 (cf Coles 1984); Kidson and Heyworth 1978; Butler 1987). The historic landscape is cut into the surface of this sequence, and so the Upper Wentlooge Formation can be thought of as the natural, even though it was still being laid down at the same time as the earliest medieval settlers started to colonise what was then a high intertidal salt marsh. For earlier periods, however, the concept of natural is less straightforward as evidence for human activity is stratified within what was a continuously accumulating sequence of peat and alluvium. Opportunities to study the Wentlooge Formation are few, though elsewhere around the Severn Estuary large-scale development has led to a number of deep excavations, while the intertidal zone provides a remarkable cross-section through the whole post-glacial sequence (eg Aldhouse-Green *et al* 1992; Nayling and Caseldine 1997; Bell *et al* 2000; Nayling and McGrail 2004). Evidence for human activity has been found stratified throughout these deposits, and while much attention has been devoted to the remarkably well-preserved prehistoric timber structures contained within the Middle Wentlooge Formation, recent work, including that on the North Somerset Levels, is revealing that ephemeral traces of a series of buried landscapes are preserved within the Upper Wentlooge silty clays (Rippon 1995a; Locock 2000; Rippon 2000b; Gardiner *et al* 2002; Carter *et al* 2004; Masser *et al* 2005; Yates *et al* forthcoming).

Analysis of the upper part of the Upper Wentlooge Formation at Puxton

Coring at various locations in Puxton[1] revealed this typical Wentlooge Formation sequence, with the surface of a 1.8m thick layer of *Cladium* and *Phragmites* peat (the Middle Wentlooge Formation) lying at *c* 1m OD, sealed by *c* 4.0 to 4.5m of blue/grey silty clay of the Upper Wentlooge Formation (Fig 3.1). The uppermost part of the Upper Wentlooge Formation, including two buried land surfaces, was exposed in a series of long sections in Church Field and Hardingworth, and was explored in detail at Home Ground (the work at Banwell Moor has been published elsewhere: Rippon 2000b).

Home Ground

The lower horizon (layer 251/314/326) comprised a grey organically rich silty clay, 0.03 to 0.04m thick, occurring between +3.7 and +3.9m OD (Fig 9.9). It yielded an AMS (accelerator mass spectrometry) radiocarbon date of 2585 ± 50 BP (828–544 cal. BC; AA-32358), and foraminifera suggest that it was laid down in a high salt marsh environment (see Kreiser below). This lower buried ground surface was associated with a shallow U-shaped linear depression about 4m wide (F.320) which could have been a ditch, though its indistinct edges are more in keeping with a natural creek/palaeochannel.

This lower, Iron Age, buried ground surface was sealed beneath *c* 0.5m of alluvium, the foraminifera and Mollusca from which suggests greater marine influence and a return to mudflat conditions (see Kreiser, and Davies, below). This alluvium was sealed beneath another buried land surface, in the form of a more mottled and darker blue/black staining of the silty clay, undulating between +4.2 and +4.5m OD, and which at Home Ground (context 218/281) yielded radiocarbon dates of 1910 ± 45 BP (15 cal. BC–cal. AD 230) and 2775 ± 45 BP (1012–826 cal. BC; GU-9610). The latter date is clearly too old as this upper dark horizon also produced a sherd of Romano-British pottery (see Timby, below). Soil micromorphology shows that this upper horizon was a buried soil, bioturbated by earthworks, and subject to prolonged periods of drying, as was the case at Banwell Moor (see Heathcote, below).

Table 3.1 Radiocarbon dates from the North Somerset Levels Project

	context	sample	uncalibrated date	laboratory number	calibrated date (two sigma)
Home Ground, Puxton					
upper buried ground surface	281	organic-rich sediment	1910 ± 45	AA-32359	cal. BC 15–AD 230
upper buried ground surface (second sample for confirmation)	281	organic-rich sediment	2775 ± 45	AA-45870; GU-9610	cal. BC 1012–826
lower buried ground surface	326	organic-rich sediment	2585 ± 50	AA-32358	cal. BC 828–544
Dolemoor, ditch F.365, Puxton					
upper cut, basal fill	375	organic-rich sediment, 33–34cm	1340 ± 40	AA-45869; GU-9600	cal. AD 642–773
lower cut, lower organic-rich horizon	383	organic-rich sediment, 68.5–69.5cm	3280 ± 45	AA-45868; GU-9599	cal. BC 1684–1440
Moor Dairy					
trackway ditch	408	selected macrofossils	1575 ± 45	AA-50090; GU-10114	cal. AD 400–600

Palaeoenvironmental material was poorly preserved though the limited plant macrofossil assemblage supports the interpretation of a freshwater, and therefore reclaimed, landscape (see Jones, below). This upper dark horizon lies very close to the present ground surface and elsewhere around Puxton has been largely destroyed by later ploughing, and it only survives where it is sealed beneath later earthworks (eg Church Field in Trench 12 and Home Ground in Trench 4). Where preserved, the upper dark horizon was sealed beneath sterile alluvium within which palaeoenvironmental material was not preserved, but analogy with the nearby sequence on Banwell Moor shows that this represents a return to intertidal conditions (Rippon 2000b). It was the reclamation of these early medieval marshes that led to the creation of today's historic landscape (see Part III).

Hardingworth (Fig 9.3.B)

Trench 6 was positioned over a discrete soil chemistry anomaly within a field whose name (ending in the potentially settlement-indicative '-worthy') and shape (having several curvilinear boundaries) suggested that it might have been formerly occupied. Apart from two recent gripes and a spread of post-medieval domestic refuse in the topsoil, presumably from a manure heap that gave rise to the soil chemistry anomaly, there was no evidence of human activity. The trench did, however, provide another cross-section through the upper part of the Upper Wentlooge Formation, revealing the same sequence as Home Ground with an intermittent dark horizon (context 402) stratified between sterile alluvium *c* 0.4m below the present ground surface. The horizon became clearer (context 417) as it dipped to 0.8m below the present surface, sealing what appeared to be a *c* 4.5m wide palaeochannel. The greater degree of waterlogging at this lower depth gave rise to better plant macrofossil preservation than at Home Ground and duckweed, water crowfoot, water plantain, pondweed, rush, bulrush, gipsywort, brooklime, grasses, and hemp agrimony all suggest freshwater conditions in what by that time had become a shallow depression (see Jones, below).

Radiocarbon dates

Six samples from the NSLP were submitted by the Scottish Universities Research and Reactor Centre to the University of Arizona AMS Facility for AMS radiocarbon dating. All the samples were extracted in the Environmental Archaeology Laboratory at Bristol University from monoliths taken in the field. Calibrated age ranges are determined from the University of Washington, Quaternary Isotope Laboratory, Radiocarbon Dating Program, Rev. 4.0 (1998). The results are given in Table 3.1.

A number of these dates are problematic. The date for the lower dark horizon at Home Ground seems reasonable, as is the first date obtained from the upper dark horizon (that is compatible with a securely stratified Romano-British sherd recovered from the same context). This date is, however, slightly older than expected as the reclamation of the North Somerset Levels now appears to date to around the 3rd century AD (Chapter 4). The second sample from the upper dark horizon at Home Ground was therefore sent for dating in order to check the first, but turned out to be 1,040 years older and can be dismissed due to the Romano-British sherd. There was a very low organic content (<1%) in the sediment submitted which may account for the error. In ditch F.365 on the Dolemoor the date for the lower cut can also be dismissed: although no pottery was recovered from that context, sherds from other elements of the ditched enclosure system give a secure early Romano-British date, making the radiocarbon date *c* 1,600 to 1,700 calendar years too old. Once again there was very low organic content (<5%) in the sediment submitted. The dates from the later cut in F.365 and the enclosure at Moor Dairy are also rather unexpected as it was assumed that these features were either part of the Romano-British relict landscapes on Dolemoor and Banwell Moor respectively, or a later reoccupation of the area for which a date in the 11th–13th centuries was expected following traditional models for the expansion of settlement into marginal (in this case very low-lying) environments. Although there was a good amount of organic matter present in the samples submitted and humic acid was extracted, both dates remain curious, and by analogy with those described above, are probably too old.

The most likely explanation for so many of these dates being too old is the presence of hard (carbonate-rich) water in the drainage ditches due to freshwater run-off from the adjacent Carboniferous Limestone hills (where plants derive their carbon dioxide for photosynthesis from the water column rather than the atmosphere, and there is a source of carbonate in the catchment, then they will absorb this old carbon). For the bulk samples taken from organic-rich sediment another possible explanation for the early dates could be the incorporation of in-washed organic material eroded from some pre-existing deposits. There are certainly significantly more fern spores in the pollen assemblage from the lower cut of F.365 compared to the later contexts examined, and as a fern-rich ground flora would be unusual on reclaimed salt marsh it seems most likely that these spores originated in a different plant community. They could have come from woodland on the adjacent dryland areas, if water from this area reached the ditch (as fern spores are released close to the ground they do not usually travel far as a result of air currents), while it is possible that the spores in this lower band are not contemporaneous with the rest of the pollen assemblage but originated in some older, organic material. At a number of sites on the Somerset Levels peat is known to have been used as fuel (eg Banwell Moor: Rippon 2000b; East Huntspill: Leech *et al* 1983), and it is possible that if this was the case at Puxton, some of this material came to be incorporated into the ditch fill.

The set of dates from Puxton and Moor Dairy are not the only ones from the Severn Estuary Levels that appear to be too old. At Hill Farm, Goldcliff, just across the Estuary on the Caldicot Level in south-east Wales, a set of four dates were obtained from a buried ditched enclosure system, associated with a bank and buried soil similar to that at Banwell Moor and Puxton (Locock and Walker 1998). The two initial dates from the same buried soil were 2270±50 (402–192 cal. BC; Beta–120093) and 2110±120094 (339 cal. BC–cal. AD13; Beta–120094), while two further dates obtained from the surface of the buried soil and the gleyed clay below were slightly older (2600 ± 50 BP (770–400 cal. BC; Beta–126108) and 2440 ± 50 BP (596–362 cal. BC; Beta–125089) respectively). There is clearly a problem with the last two dates, and a general discrepancy between the first and second set, and while all four broadly point to an Iron Age date the same ditched enclosure system was associated with early 2nd- to early 4th-century Romano-British pottery (Bell 2000, 87–8; Bell *et al* 2000, 29–30; Marvell 2004, 98): the radiocarbon dates are clearly around 500 years too old. Archaeological evaluations along the line of the Cardiff to Newport Interceptor Sewer revealed two buried horizons that produced similarly unreliable radiocarbon dates: the lower peaty clay was dated to 1400–1050 cal. BC (Wk–9823), whereas the upper gleyed layer yielded a date of 3350–2910 cal. BC (Wk–9822) (Marvell 2004, 97). On the Avonmouth Levels a Romano-British buried ground surface, dated through artefacts, yielded a radiocarbon date of 2850± 40 (1190–900 cal. BC; Beta 134902: Yates *et al* forthcoming).

Soil micromorphology *by J L Heathcote*

The upper part of the Upper Wentlooge Formation at Home Ground was examined through soil micromorphology using two overlapping 0.5m monolith tins. In the laboratory each monolith was sub-sampled using 10cm long Kubiena tins. These sub-samples were dehydrated using acetone vapour baths and then consolidated using Crystic resin. Thin sections were manufactured at the Department of Environmental Science, University of Stirling, and unfortunately problems occurred with resin impregnation of the lower sample that meant that the bottom two thin sections (corresponding to the lower dark horizon) could not be produced. The thin sections for the upper part of the sequence were analysed at a range of magnifications from ×5.8 to ×400 using transmitted, polarising light microscopes. Formal micromorphological descriptions followed the terminology defined by Bullock *et al* (1985). In addition, the degree of organic decomposition was recorded according to the guidelines of FitzPatrick (1993).

Overall, the basic composition of the sequence is very similar throughout, with subtle variations in the colour of the fine mineral fraction being the main characteristic that allows the contexts to be differentiated in thin section (Table 3.2 CD). All contexts have a very low organic matter content, and that present is highly fragmented, strongly decomposed, and randomly distributed throughout the contexts: the only differentiating factor is the colour of the cell residues. Pedofeatures are present in all contexts and are dominated by gleying features (indicative of alternating oxidising and reducing conditions) found as mottles of iron and manganese. Features of bioturbation are also common. These mainly comprise channels that are partially filled with loose soil material that has a characteristic internal structure indicating it has been reworked by earthworms (earthworm passage features). Additional evidence of earthworm activity comprises the calcareous granules, up to 1mm diameter, that are occasionally identified. The final type of pedofeature that commonly occurs in this sequence comprises fragments of a fabric that is composed of variably oriented, laminated clay and silty clay. These fragments have clearly been reworked from their original site of formation, as the laminations lie at varying angles to horizontal, and the fragments are surrounded by unbedded material.

Context 242: the uppermost context of the sampled sequence shows a weak, horizontally bedded structure, observed as pale brown pure silt units up to 1mm thick alternating with silty clay units. Well-developed manganese and iron mottles are common and slaking features are occasionally present, both suggestive of episodes of wetting and drying. Earthworm passage features contain material having a higher organic content than the surrounding soil fabric.

Context 281 (the upper dark horizon): although the boundary between this unit and the overlying 242 was diffuse, context 281 was clearly differentiated from 242 by its lack of bedding structure and higher porosity. Earthworm passage features and granules are common. Occasionally, the earthworm passage features are filled with a dark brown, organic soil fabric that has no comparison elsewhere in the thin sections. This suggests the fabric represents remnants of a context that has been removed by erosion.

Context 282: this unit is differentiated from the overlying layer 281 by the paler colour of the fine mineral component and a decrease in the frequency and size of manganese mottles (iron mottles remain large and common). Rare thin silty clay coatings are present on pore walls and slaking features are occasionally present. Earthworm granules are rare but passage features, comprising fabric comparable to the surrounding soil material, are common. Discrete aggregates of laminated clay and silty clay fabric are found embedded within the soil matrix.

Context 283: the principal diagnostic characteristic of the fabric in this unit is that the mineral fraction contains a shell component. The shells are both fragmented and whole, the latter comprising small gastropods (<5mm). Rare, thin, strongly oriented clay coatings are present on pore walls and slaked features are common. Gleying features are also present, as both iron and manganese mottles and, occasionally, as zones of strongly gleyed fabric adjacent to pore walls. Fragments of variably oriented, laminated clay and silty clay fabric are found embedded within the soil matrix, the frequency of these increasing with depth. The bottom thin section of the sequence contains a large, highly disrupted fragment of bedded fabric comprising 1–5mm thick units of well-sorted fine sand, inter-bedded with 0.5–1mm thick units of silty clay. The bedding lies vertically oriented indicating it has been reworked, and the material lacks shell fragments.

Discussion

Thin section analysis has confirmed the preliminary field interpretation that context 281 (the upper dark horizon) represents a buried soil. The material has been bioturbated by earthworms, as evidenced by the calcareous granules and common passage features. The remnants of a dark brown organic soil fabric that is preserved in some of the channels, but which lacks a comparison anywhere else in the sampled sequence, suggests that it experienced some erosion, possibly losing the upper few centimetres of its 'A' horizon (topsoil). The soil profile is represented by contexts 281 and 282, with soil development characteristics (predominantly bioturbation) extending down into context 283, indicating a significant period of stability and, at least episodically, well-drained conditions. During this time, humification of organic material, biological reworking and limited, short-distance movement of silty clay occurred. In addition, repeated cycles of wetting and drying created both slaked and gleyed features, the latter a consequence of changes in oxidising and reducing conditions. The nature of the Home Ground sequence and its associated buried soil is comparable to the upper buried soil identified at Banwell Moor (Heathcote 2000) with one notable exception. Although both soils are developed in fine-grained alluvial deposits, at Banwell the material is calcareous whilst at Puxton it is non-calcareous, and therefore the soil horizons lack any evidence for decalcification. In both cases the uppermost part of the soil (the 'A' horizon) has been lost through erosion.

Pollen *by Heather M Tinsley*

General methodology

Pollen analysis was carried out on samples taken from the Romano-British ditch F.365 on Dolemoor (Chapter 4), the buried ground surface beneath the bank running around Church Field, the medieval enclosure ditch F.103 and boundary ditch F.128 in Church Field (Chapter 10), and the upper part of the Upper Wentlooge Formation at Home Ground (see below). Samples were prepared in the Environmental Archaeology Laboratory at Bristol University using standard techniques (Moore *et al* 1991). Initial

Table 3.3 Stratigraphy and pollen samples from the upper part of the Upper Wentlooge Formation alluvial sequence at Home Ground. Depths are from the top of the upper monolith tin, which was 0.79m below the present ground surface (5.25m OD)

depth	context	sample depth	stratigraphy
0–16.5cm (4.46–4.295m OD)	242	15–16cm	pale brown clay
16.5–17.0cm (4.295–4.29m OD)	242/281		blue clay, merging boundary
17–20cm (4.29–4.26m OD)	281	17.0–17.5cm 18.0–18.5cm 19–20cm	blue clay with black patches and streaks (upper dark horizon)
20–30cm (4.26–4.16m OD)	282		blue/grey clay, occasional black flecks, merging boundary
30–60cm (4.16–3.86m OD)	283		grey/brown clay mottled with orange, merging boundary
60–64cm (3.86–3.82m OD)	283/314		blue/grey/brown clay with diffuse black streaks, merging boundary
64–69cm (3.82–3.77m OD)	314	67–68cm	grey mottled clay with some black streaks (lower dark horizon)
69–84cm (3.77–3.62m OD)	252		grey mottled clay with some small snail shells

digestion in dilute potassium hydroxide was followed by sieving, then treatment with cold hydrofluoric acid for a week. Samples were washed with hot 10% hydrochloric acid and acetolysed, stained with safranin and mounted in glycerol. Two tablets of *Lycopodium* spores were added to each sample at the start of the preparation to allow pollen concentration to be assessed (Stockmarr 1971). Samples were counted at a magnification of ×400, with ×1000 magnification used for critical determinations. In the assessments the aim was to count at least 100 pollen grains from each sample level in order to assess the potential of the material for full pollen analysis, but in many cases this total was difficult to reach due to poor preservation and low pollen concentration. For these samples, the count was stopped when at least 50 of the added *Lycopodium* spores had been recovered. In addition to pollen, non-pollen palynomorphs such as fern, moss, and algal spores were counted. The relative concentration of microscopic charcoal was estimated by counting the number of charcoal particles >40μm long on two traverses of each slide. The relative abundance of metallic sulphide particles was also noted. In the full analysis of the samples from ditch F.365 at Dolemoor the pollen sum aimed for was >500 total land pollen (TLP), though in three cases low pollen concentrations meant this was not reached. The TLP counted for each sample level is shown on the pollen diagram.

Plant nomenclature follows Stace (1991), which was also used as a source for ecological information. Pollen types generally follow Bennett (1994). In this report pollen of *Corylus*-type includes pollen of *Corylus avellana* (hazel) and of *Myrica gale* (bog myrtle). The distinction between pollen of *Corylus* and *Myrica* is not easy to make, but Andrew (1984) noted that *Myrica* pollen could be identified by the sloping 'shoulders' leading to each pore; on this basis all *Corylus*-type grains in this material are believed to be *Corylus*. Pollen of cereal-type was distinguished from that of other grasses on the basis of size, with all grains >40μm in diameter considered to be in this group. Some (few) wild grasses also have grains of this size, including coastal species such as *Spartina anglica* (common cord grass), *Ammophila arenaria* (marram grass) and *Leymus arenarius* (lyme grass), and also *Glyceria* (sweet grass) that grows in mud by ponds, rivers, and ditches. Details of all pollen types are given at the end of the pollen archive report (Tinsley 2003).

The results of the assessments are shown in Tables 3.4, 10.1, 10.3, and 10.5 (all on CD) that list the number of grains of each pollen taxon counted. The taxa have been grouped into the woody types (trees and shrubs) and the herb taxa. The tables give an indication of the habitat preferences of the herbaceous taxa: cultivated fields, disturbed ground, heathland, salt marsh and other coastal habitats, freshwater ditch etc. These habitat preferences should be treated as a guide only as some taxa have members that grow in a variety of habitats. In particular there are problems at coastal sites where taxa, which in inland situations might be regarded as indicators of anthropogenically influenced habitats, grow on substrates disturbed by natural processes, or influenced by salt water. The Chenopodiaceae (goosefoot family) fall into this group, and this pollen taxon includes plants that grow on salt marshes and strandlines, and also on disturbed, grazed or cultivated ground. The same is also true of *Solidago virgaurea*-type (daisy, sea aster and related Asteraceae).

The results from the Upper Wentlooge Formation at Mays Lane

The upper part of the natural alluvial sequence at Home Ground, including two dark horizons stratified within the Upper Wentlooge Formation, was sampled using two overlapping 50cm monolith tins (Fig 9.9; Table 3.3). These were opened in the Environmental Archaeology Laboratory at Bristol University where they were described in detail prior to sampling for pollen. The results of this assessment were disappointing (Table 3.4 CD) as pollen concentrations were poor to very poor, and the preservation of the pollen was also poor to very poor. Only 10 grains were recorded from the lower buried surface (context 314). In the lower two samples from context 281 (upper buried surface) more pollen was recovered, but a large proportion of this was of Lactuceae (dandelion and related Asteraceae) (21 and 58 grains), a taxon which is particularly resistant to decay. This suggests that differential concentration of the more robust pollen taxa has occurred as a result of the breakdown of less resistant grains. These same two samples contained some spores of the algae *Mougeotia* and *Spirogyra* which grow in fresh (or slightly brackish) water, and also some spores of van Geel Type 128, a small spiny spore of unknown origin but typically found in freshwater sediments (van Hoeve and Hendrikse 1998). The pollen spectra from context 242, above the upper dark horizon, is very similar to that in the upper sample from the upper dark horizon (context 281), with a few grains of tree pollen (*Pinus*, *Quercus*, *Alnus*, and *Corylus*-type), and with the herbaceous pollen dominated by Poaceae with just occasional grains of taxa indicative of disturbed ground such as *Plantago lanceolata*. A few grains of Chenopodiaceae pollen occur in each sample, and in contexts 281 and 314 there are grains of *Plantago coronopus,* which is typically found growing on shingle at the strandline. Together these taxa may suggest some marine influence, but this is hardly convincing data. Overall it is not safe to make any ecological reconstructions from this assessment.

Foraminifera *by Annette Kreiser*

General methodology

Foraminifera analysis was carried out on samples taken from the Romano-British ditch F.365 on Dolemoor (Chapter 4), the medieval enclosure ditch F.103 and boundary ditch F.128 in Church Field, and the medieval boundary ditch F.267 at Home Ground (Chapter 10). The upper part of the Upper Wentlooge Formation was also investigated at Home Ground (see below). The aim was to reconstruct past water quality associated with these different phases of landscape development. The analysis follows earlier foraminifera analyses carried out on samples taken from the upper part of the Upper Wentlooge Formation and later Romano-British ditched enclosure systems at Banwell Moor and Kenn Moor (Haslett *et al* 2000).

10cm^3 of wet sediment from each sample was wet sieved through 500μm, 125μm, and 63μm mesh sieves. Any foraminifera retained on the 125μm sieve were picked out and identified at ×30–40 magnification under transmitted or incident light using a Brunel BMZ zoom stereo microscope. The 63μm fraction was also examined for the presence of juveniles but it is generally not possible confidently to identify juvenile tests to species level. For the purposes of this assessment, dominant taxa were identified to species level where possible, but in the Home Ground alluvial sequence varieties of *Ammonia beccarii* were not identified and agglutinated tests (where the hard shell-like part which surrounds the soft body of the living organism consists of a mass of mineral particles) typical of certain high marsh species were grouped together as agglutinated marsh species. Identification follows Murray (1973; 1979), and interpretation of their ecology follows Murray (1991) and Haslett *et al* (1997).

Home Ground alluvial sequence

This sequence of samples straddled the upper and lower buried ground surfaces and generally had excellent preservation (Table 3.5 CD). Samples 182 and 183 from context 252 (below the lower buried ground surface 251) were dominated by *Elphidium williamsoni*, *Haynesina germanica, Ammonia beccarii*, and small numbers of agglutinated tests of high marsh species. The 63μm fractions of these samples contained juveniles of the same species, while sample 183 contained the small individuals of *Brizalina*. These species live in a range of intertidal and marine environments including high marshes.

Sample 181 from context 324 (the possible palaeochannel F.320 associated with the lower buried ground surface 251) which contained a diverse assemblage of more than 100 individuals similar in character to context 252 below, including *Elphidium* species, taxa within *Ammonia beccarii*, *Haynesina germanica,* plus a small number of agglutinated tests of high marsh species. The 63μm fraction contained small individuals of the same species.

Throughout context 321 (sealing the possible palaeochannel, samples 177, 178, 179 and 180) foraminifera were comparatively abundant, exceeding 200 individuals in all samples. The assemblages of all these samples were dominated by *Elphidium williamsoni*, *Haynesina germanica* with some *Nonion depressulus*, a species commonly found in estuary mouth and nearshore sediments, suggesting a greater marine influence.

Three samples were taken from context 219 (overlying 321 and sealed by the upper dark horizon) which suggest decreasing marine influence. In sample 176 the total number of forams exceeded 100 and the assemblage was dominated by *Haynesina germanica* and *Elphidium williamsoni*, with the latter the more dominant of the two principal taxa. Sample 175 was also dominated by *Haynesina germanica* and *Elphidium william-*

soni and the 63μm fraction contained a number of small individuals of the *Brizalina* genus. Sample 174 contained around 100 individuals in total. The assemblage was dominated by the euryhaline species *Haynesina germanica* with *Elphidium williamsoni* also present, suggesting an intertidal mudflat environment. The 63μm fraction contained juveniles of these species.

Sample 173 from context 218 (the upper dark horizon) contained just three foraminifera tests: a high marsh agglutinated species and two individuals of *Haynesina germanica*. Though the sample size is very small a decrease in marine influence can be suggested though the environment cannot be inferred beyond the conclusion that some sediment was received from a brackish source.

Diatoms *by Nigel Cameron*

Diatom analysis was carried out on samples taken from the Romano-British ditch F.365 on Dolemoor (Chapter 4), the medieval enclosure ditch F.103 and boundary ditch F.128 in Church Field, and the medieval boundary ditch F.267 at Home Ground (Chapter 10). The upper part of the Upper Wentlooge Formation was also investigated at Home Ground though none of the samples contained diatoms. The absence of diatoms from these contexts may be the result of poor conditions for preservation of the diatom frustule, for example caused by a highly alkaline environment. Alternatively, diatoms may not have accumulated at the site, although this is unlikely in a water-lain context.

Plant macrofossil remains *by Julie Jones*

General methodology

Bulk samples for the analysis of plant macrofossils were taken from a variety of contexts including the alluvial sequences at Home Ground and Hardingworth, the early Romano-British landscape on the Dolemoor, and the shrunken settlement earthworks in Church Field and Home Ground. The samples were processed in the School of Geographical Sciences at the University of Bristol in a sieving tank with floats retained on a 250μm sieve and residues on a 500μm mesh. Where there was waterlogged preservation the floats were kept wet, otherwise they were air dried, with all residues dried before examination. The floats were fully sorted under low-powered magnification with all plant macrofossil remains extracted for identification with the aid of the author's reference collection. Nomenclature and habitat information for the weeds is based on Stace (1991), with grain and chaff determinations made with reference to Jacomet (1987). In Tables 3.6, 4.6, 10.6, and 10.8 (all on CD) the plant macrofossils have also been placed into habitat categories to complement the discussions, particularly in relation to the local environment of the sites, alongside the mode of preservation for each species.

Home Ground (context 218)

The only plant macrofossils preserved within the blue/grey silty clay (context 219/321) beneath the upper dark horizon at Home Ground were seeds of rushes (*Juncus*). The only plant macrofossils preserved within the upper dark horizon itself (context 218/281) were a few rush and duckweed seeds. Charred preservation included a single wheat tough rachis internode and grass caryopsis.

Hardingworth (context 417) (Table 3.6 CD)

One sample from the upper dark horizon in the upper part of the Wentlooge Formation was investigated from this site. The wet freshwater nature of the local environment is shown by the presence of duckweed, water crowfoot, water plantain and pondweed. There is also rush, bulrush, some gipsywort, brooklime, grasses, with frequent fragments of hemp agrimony (*Eupatorium cannabinum*).

Mollusca *by Paul Davies* (see Table 10.14 CD)

Mollusca were only preserved in context 321 (the alluvium beneath the upper dark horizon and sealing the possible palaeochannel). High numbers of *Hydrobia ventrosa* and *Hydrobia ulvae* clearly indicate that the alluvium is of estuarine or salt marsh origin.

Summary: changing environments in the 1st millennium AD

The analysis of the upper part of the Upper Wentlooge Formation both here at Puxton and at the previously reported Banwell Moor (Rippon 2000b) has provided a record of the changing environment on the North Somerset Levels since the late 1st millennium BC. Towards the end of the Iron Age there was a vast complex of intertidal salt marshes and mudflats, drained through a network of tidal creeks, and crossed by a series of rivers and streams flowing off the adjacent uplands. As described in Chapter 4, this environment was exploited for its rich natural resources such as producing salt by heating sea water and then modified through the creation of ditched enclosure systems. Intertidal conditions still prevailed, however, until the later Roman period when there was a significant change in environment marked by the upper dark horizon at Puxton Home Ground (and Banwell Moor). This horizon was produced through soil development in a freshwater environment indicating that the Levels were now free from tidal inundation, conditions which must have been brought about through reclamation. In the late-post-Roman period there was renewed tidal flooding following an episode of erosion that removed the upper 'A' horizon of the soil that had formed following reclamation, and over time the Romano-British landscape was sealed under alluvium deposited under salt marsh and mudflat conditions.

Note

1 At Mays Lane (ST 4049 6361), Church Field (ST 4066 6323) and from Butts to the Dolemoor (ST 4090 6323 to ST 4159 6311).

4 Landscape modification and transformation in the late Iron Age and Roman periods

The Romano-British landscape at Puxton was investigated through a series of sections cut across elements of the relict landscape on the Dolemoor, along with fieldwalking, shovel test pits, and excavations in and around the medieval settlement (Figs 4.1 and 4.2). The earliest feature was related to salt production in the late Iron Age–early Roman period, which is described below alongside a report on the briquetage. The excavations of several elements within the early Romano-British enclosure complex on Dolemoor, whose siltation continued into the later Roman period, are then described, followed by a brief description of several later Romano-British features uncovered in Church Field. The material culture assemblages are then described, followed by reports on the palaeoenvironmental evidence that shows a change from intertidal conditions in the late Iron Age–early Roman period, to a freshwater reclaimed landscape in the later Roman period.

The late Iron Age–early Romano-British saltern at Dolemoor

Feature F.397

The earliest evidence for human activity at Puxton lies within the alluvium that seals the lower, Iron Age, buried ground surface. Trench 8 on the Dolemoor was designed to section three of the north–south oriented ditches in the relict landscape, one of which (F.309) was found to cut through a shallow linear feature (F.397) that may have been a ditch or a natural creek, and that was filled with

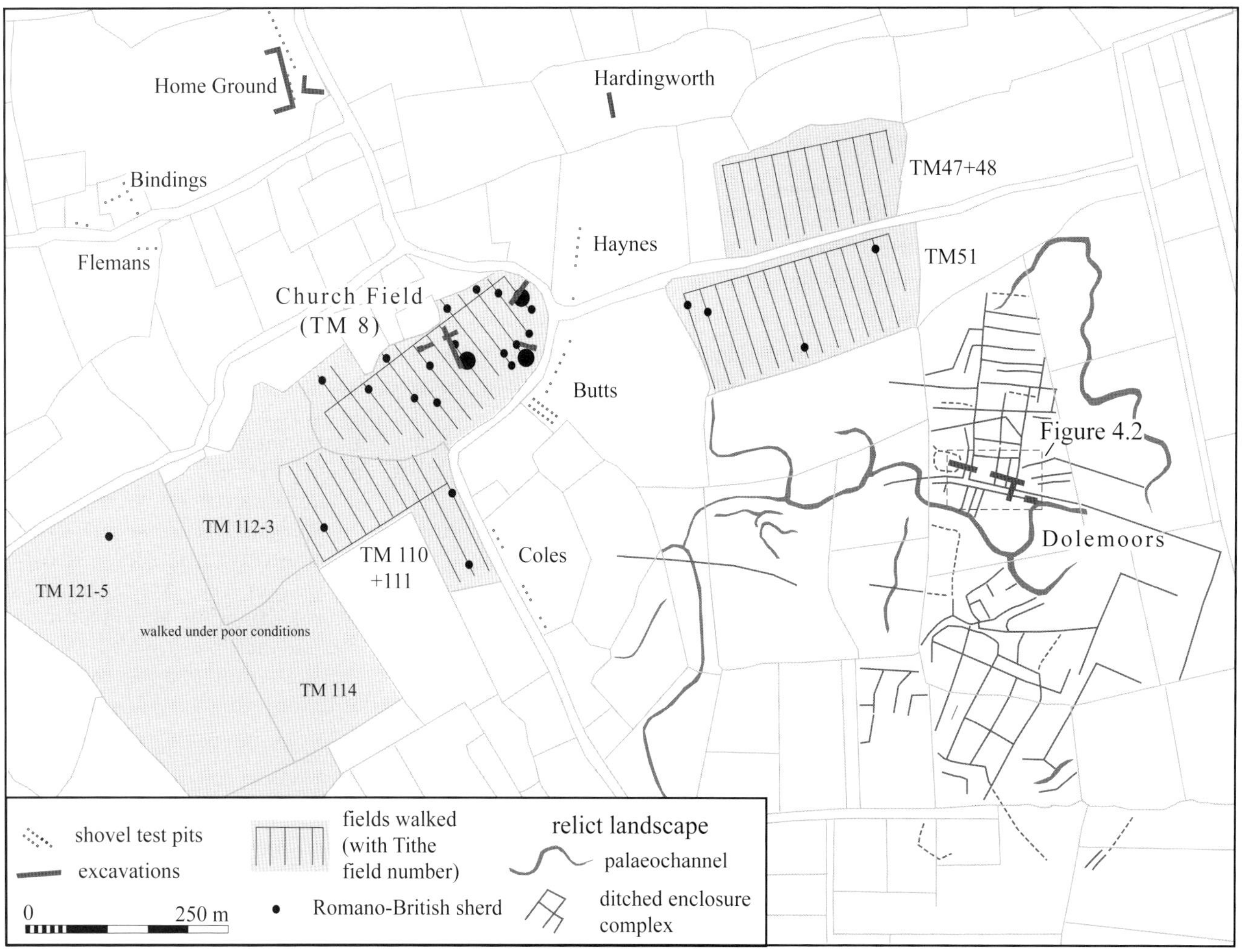

Figure 4.1 Romano-British archaeology at Puxton: the earthwork relict landscape on the Dolemoor (transcribed from air photographs in the National Monuments Record), and the location of fieldwalking, shovel test pits, and excavations (for location see Fig 5.1)

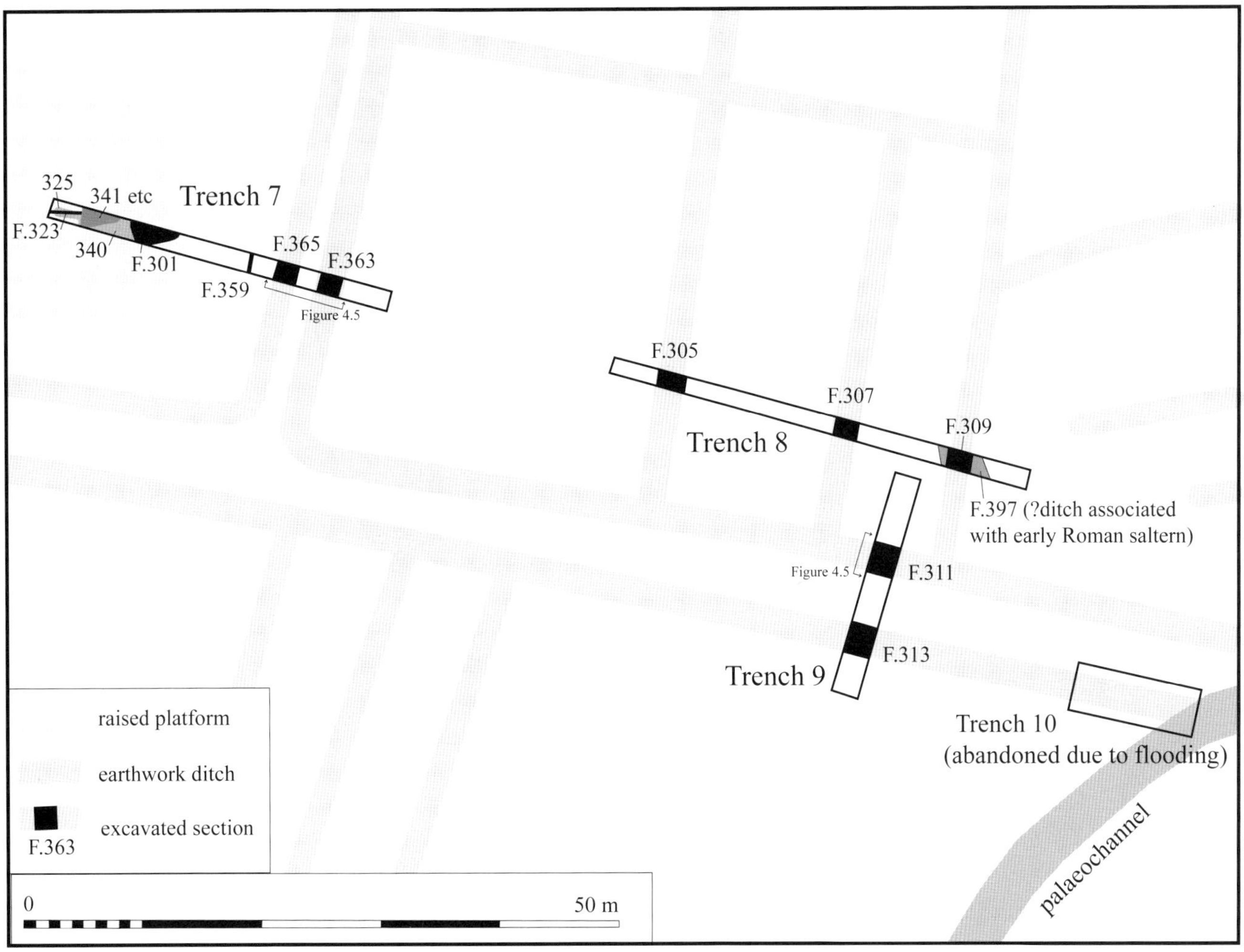

Figure 4.2 Trenches 7–10 in the Dolemoor. North is at the top of this and following plans

burnt debris (contexts 319 and 342) including large amounts of charcoal, stone, and burnt clay including saltern debris (Fig 4.2). The contemporary land surface from which this feature was cut has been lost to later ploughing. A small amount of late Iron Age pottery and a single sherd of 1st-century AD Roman grey ware suggests a mid-1st-century date. Overall, the fill of this feature was very similar to that of a contemporary saltern at Banwell Moor, and can be interpreted as the debris from salt production, presumably on the banks of the palaeochannel immediately to the south.

Briquetage and saltern debris

Although only a single feature was excavated, it produced an important assemblage of briquetage that was very similar to, though better preserved than, that at Banwell Moor. A total of 9,212g was examined.

Fabric

A soft, poorly fired, light–mid-orange/brown (5 YR 7/3 to 5 YR 6/4), slightly silty clay, with very few inclusions (just the occasional piece of grog and chopped plant material). Where fragments had a smoothed surface this tended to be harder and a lighter pinkish/orange/grey colour (10 R 6/4 to 5 YR 8/1), with occasional fragments showing signs of even higher temperatures giving a darker pinkish/red colour (7.5 R 4/6). There was no evidence of temperatures sufficient to cause vitrification. Many of the surfaces were covered in 'salt scale', a thin, white to buff-coloured skin on the exterior surface of saltern debris that results from the movement of soluble salts to the surface during drying and remaining there when the water evaporates (Lane and Morris 2001, 41).

Forms

1. Pedestals: A number of fragments had a curved surface and are clearly from pedestals (Fig 4.3). Though no complete example was recovered, the surviving fragments show that the majority (*c* 65%) were sub-square in section, with curving sides and heavily rounded corners, splaying out to a flat surface at one end. A smaller number (*c* 15%) of fragments appear to be from pedestals

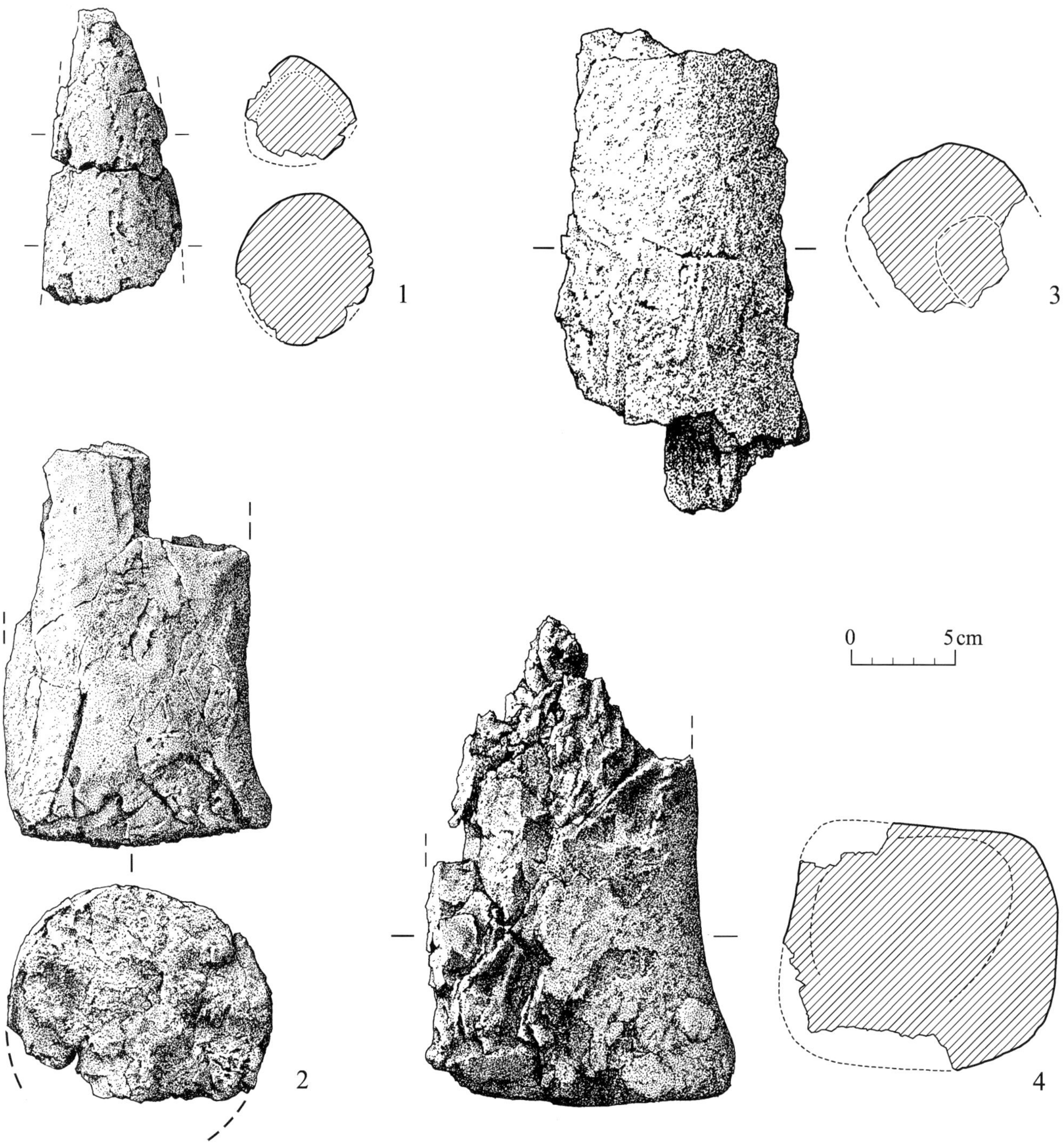

Figure 4.3 Briquetage/saltern debris (drawing by Mike Rouillard)

that were more angular in section, though still with rounded corners. The shafts of these pedestals are typically *c* 100–120mm across increasing to *c* 140–150mm at the splayed end; the maximum surviving length was 220mm. A small number of fragments (*c* 10%) were more circular in section tapering to a point at one end. These were only ever very poorly preserved as they appear to have experienced less heat, and may represent the top ends of the sub-angular pedestal fragments described above. These pedestals were probably designed to rest on their splayed ends, with their tapering ends supporting tanks or troughs of sea water. The relatively limited degree to which they are heat-affected suggests that they were used within an oven structure rather than an open fire.

2. Fragments with flat and right-angled surfaces: these fragments only ever had one smoothed surface, which was hardened to some degree by the effects of heat. The undersides are rough/broken and show little sign of heating. Not all the surfaces were covered with 'salt scale', and the surviving fragments were up to 40–50mm thick (from heat-affected surface to almost

unfired core). These fragments are too thick to be the remains of evaporating troughs (well-preserved troughs from some Fenland sites are just 10–15mm thick: Lane and Morris 2001, figs 126–32). This, along with the lack of the 'salt scale' on some surfaces, suggests they are the remains of oven structures.

Discussion

This late Iron Age–early Roman assemblage of saltern debris from Puxton is very similar to that from the contemporary site at Banwell Moor (Rippon 2000b). The pedestals at Puxton are, however, better preserved and a re-examination of the smaller fragments from Banwell suggests that they are of similar dimensions. One subtle difference is that the Banwell fabric contains slightly more organic tempering, though this is far less than is seen in the Brue Valley in the main Somerset Levels (see below). Little of the Banwell or Puxton material shows signs of having experienced prolonged heating to high temperatures (again contrasting with the Brue Valley material). The Banwell and Puxton material is comparable to another collection from nearby St Georges (Cox and Lankstead, 2004; and see Chapter 5 below). The assemblages are broadly similar with a fine silty clay fabric and little tempering. The most diagnostic forms are pedestals of the same broad shape as those at Banwell and Puxton but on an even larger scale (*c* 150–200mm across and *c* 0.5m long). Surfaces that are pink, lavender and even dark purple/red suggest exposure to higher temperatures than at Banwell and Puxton. Together with the larger size of the pedestals (presumably to support more substantial pans/troughs) this suggests larger-scale production.

This late Iron Age–early Romano-British saltern debris from the North Somerset Levels can be compared with that from the Brue Valley in the main Somerset Levels. Despite some 167 sites being known, there has been very little research into the Somerset salt industry (Leech 1977; 1981b; 1982a; Leech *et al* 1983; Rippon 1993, 436–43; 1997a, 68–74; Grove and Brunning 1998), although small assemblages of briquetage have been published (Bulleid 1914; Leech 1981b; Leech *et al* 1983). Using unstratified surface collections observed by the author from a number of sites in addition, it is possible to show that the character of this material from the Brue Valley is very different to that from the North Somerset Levels:

1. Rectangular and square bars/pedestals: typically rectangular in cross-section, *c* 25 × 40mm to *c* 35 × 60mm in section, sometimes tapering (reducing in breadth) at one end. Occasionally almost square (*c* 30 to 35mm) in cross-section. Edges are angular, and both flat and rounded ends are evident. Original length unknown (no complete examples have been recorded), but at least 200mm.
2. Cylindrical pedestals: circular in cross-section, *c* 30–40mm in diameter. Original length unknown (no complete examples have been recorded), but at least 0.4m.
3. Slabs/tiles ranging in thickness but appearing to have two distinct types, *c* 15–25mm thick and *c* 40–50mm thick. Edges both rounded and cut square. Nothing comparable from North Somerset.
4. Wedges: lumps of fired clay with a triangular cross-section, around 140mm long. Nothing comparable from North Somerset.
5. Evaporating vessels: walls *c* 14–18mm thick with knife-/wire-cut or plain rounded rims. Nothing comparable from North Somerset.

The Brue Valley salt industry started in the late Iron Age and continued through to the 4th century (Leech 1977; 1981b; Seagar Smith 2003) and there is no obvious significant variation in these forms over time or space. All the material is heavily tempered with chopped vegetable matter, and has clearly been exposed to sustained and/or repeated high temperatures giving rise to a hard, pinkish/grey colour throughout (this is particularly so with the pedestals).

The assemblages from the North Somerset Levels differ from this Brue Valley material in four significant ways: the fabric contains almost no organic temper, it does not appear to have been exposed to such sustained high temperatures, there is no evidence for evaporating vessels, and the pedestals are between three and four times larger (*c* 100–120mm diameter at Puxton and Banwell and *c* 150–200mm at St Georges, compared to *c* 30–40mm in the Brue Valley). This difference is all the more remarkable as the Brue Valley tradition of slender pedestals was long lived, stretching back to the middle Bronze Age examples from Brean Down (Bell 1990, 165–9), and geographically widespread, being found throughout the major coastal salt production centres in southern and eastern England (Hampshire/Sussex: Bradley 1975; 1992; Romney Marsh: Philip and Willson 1984; Kent: Barber 1998; Farrar 1975; Miles 1975; 2004; Essex: de Brisay 1978, 43–5; Fawn *et al* 1990, 11–12; Barford 1995, 175). The closest parallel in terms of size for the North Somerset pedestals comes from the late Roman (mid- to late 3rd- to 4th-century) saltern at Middleton in the Norfolk Fens, where supports with both square and circular cross-sections were typically *c* 100–120mm across the base, tapering to *c* 60–80mm at the top, and *c* 220mm high (the example with a base diameter of 160mm shown in Lane and Morris 2001, fig 69, may have been relined).

These pedestals are all interpreted as being designed to stand on a hearth or oven floor and support some form of vessel containing sea water (Lane and Morris 2001, figs 22 and 85). On the North Somerset sites there is no evidence for the nature of these evaporating vessels. Both in the Brue Valley and around the coast of prehistoric and Roman Britain, organic-tempered briquetage vessels predominate, though these were noticeably absent from the late Romano-British site at Middleton in Norfolk which has led to an assumption that lead pans were used (Lane and Morris 2001, 187, 190, 244, 352). Dribbles and offcuts of lead are commonly found on medieval salterns where documentary sources show that lead pans were used (Rudkin and Owen 1960, 76–84; Lloyd 1967; McAvoy 1994; Healey 1999; Lane and Morris 2001, 445), yet no lead was recovered from Banwell, Puxton, and St Georges (and despite the use of metal detectors at the latter). Whilst the possibility that lead pans were used cannot be ruled out, not least because of the proximity to Mendip, it is possible that wooden vessels, or even hollowed out tree trunks, were used. One complete pedestal from St Georges does have a concave cut into its apex suggesting that it held a round-bottomed vessel.

In conclusion, evidence for late Iron Age–early Romano-British salt production has been found on a number of sites on the North Somerset Levels. The saltern debris, and by implication the technology of production, is of a rather different character to that elsewhere in southern Britain, with the unusually substantial pedestals presumably supporting very large evaporating vessels, possibly made of wood.

The early Romano-British enclosure complex on Puxton Dolemoor

To the east of Puxton, in an area known as the Dolemoor, there are the earthworks of an extensive relict landscape, now much denuded by ploughing but revealed in the excellent RAF photography of the late 1940s (Figs 2.5 and 4.1). The central feature was one arm of an extensive creek system, to the north and south of which were ditched enclosure complexes. The northern complex appeared to have a roughly north–south oriented ladder-like arrangement, with trackways on its western and southern sides. To the west of the junction of these two trackways lay a slightly raised platform. To the south of the palaeochannel the southern enclosure complex had a less regular layout, though a broadly north-east to south-west orientation is evident (Fig 4.1). The northern enclosure complex was investigated through four trenches (7–10: Figs 4.2 and 4.4) spread across its major axial elements including the trackways (ditches F.363 and F.365 in Trench 7, and F.311 and F.313 in Trench 9), and a sample of the other ditches (F.305, F.307, F.309 in Trench 8). The platform was also examined in Trench 7.

The trackways and other ditches

All of the excavated ditches contained a remarkably similar sequence with two clear phases (eg Fig 4.5). The earliest was a relatively narrow and steep-

Figure 4.4 Puxton Dolemoor: view looking east along Trenches 7 (foreground) and 8 (background), with Trenches 9 and 10 top right. Looking towards the valley of the Congresbury Yeo on the skyline, with Dolebury Warren to the south (right) and Wrington Down to the north (left) (see Fig 1.5)

sided ditch, *c* 1.2m deep, *c* 1.2m wide at the top, and narrowing to *c* 0.6m at the base, and filled with light blue/grey silty clay containing several organic-rich bands. A small number of later 1st- to early 2nd-century Romano-British sherds were recovered from the first phases of these ditches (see Timby, below), establishing that a radiocarbon date from F.365 of 3280 ± 45 BP (1684–1440 cal. BC; AA-45868/GU-9599) cannot be correct (Chapter 3). Each of these early Romano-British ditches was recut with a broader (*c* 2.5–3.0m wide) but far shallower (*c* 0.6–0.8m) cut, each containing an organic-rich basal fill which graduated to mid-blue/grey silty clay towards the top. Thankfully, these shallow recuts left most of the Romano-British stratigraphy intact. The only artefactual dating from this second phase of ditches was more sherds of early Romano-British pottery, though a sample from F.365 produced a radiocarbon date of 1340 ± 40 BP (cal. AD 642–773; AA-45869/

GU-9600). Although contamination with recent carbon cannot be ruled out, it is likely that this date, like the other from F.365 (see above), is in fact too old and this recutting of all the ditches dates to the medieval/post-medieval period.

Ditch F.365, forming the western boundary of the ladder-like enclosure complex, revealed a typical sequence of fills and was subject to extensive palaeoenvironmental sampling (Fig 4.5). The lowest fill (384) comprised a light blue/grey silty clay with iron staining along root channels. The upper surviving fill comprised very similar layers of light blue/grey silty clay (382 and 376) separated by lenses of dark grey/black silty clay with some visible organic material (383, 381, and 380). This ditch F.365, along with ditch F.363 just 2m to the east, was recut by a wide, shallow feature F.303 whose lower fill comprised an organic-rich dark blue/black silty clay (367 and 375) which graduated into a mid- to dark blue/grey silty clay with some pale brown mottles that filled the rest of the profile (364/366 and 362). Palaeoenvironmental evidence (see Tinsley, Cameron and Dobinson, Kreiser, Jones, and Davies below) shows that when initially cut F.365 occupied a high intertidal environment (context 384), though by the time that it had substantially silted up the environment was largely freshwater (context 383). Evidence from Banwell Moor, Kenn Moor, and Puxton Church Field show that the North Somerset Levels were reclaimed around the mid-3rd century and the final silting up of the Dolemoor ditches may date to this period. Microscopic charcoal is present in the lower fill (384) of F.365 but is hardly represented at all in the upper fills (382 and 376), suggesting that during the active life of the ditch there was domestic occupation in the vicinity (probably on the raised platform to the west: see below), but that this occupation ceased as the ditch became substantially silted up.

The possible occupation platform

The slightly raised platform at the western end of Trench 7 revealed a number of features and an extensive spread of occupation debris (Figs 4.2 and 4.4). The earliest deposit appears to have been a layer of possibly redeposited natural alluvium (327 and 336), sealed by a spread of pale grey silty clay (layers 325, 326, 330 and 340). This was cut by a narrow, U-shaped gully (F.323), 0.34m wide and 0.16m deep, which lay to the west of a heterogeneous spread of mid-grey/brown silty clays containing fragments of burnt clay (337, 338 and 339), very dark grey/brown clay loam with abundant charcoal (329), and a spread of burnt clay (341). None of this burnt material included the distinctive saltern debris seen in F.397, and it may simply have been daub from a timber building or the dumped base of a hearth. To the east of this spread of occupation material was a large pit (or possibly the butt end of a ditch) F.301, which appears to have been backfilled from the west with tips of organic-rich material (320, 321, 322) and a dump of sterile silty clay (390). Finds included a small assemblage of 1st- to 2nd-century Romano-British pottery, frequent lumps of burnt clay (daub), charcoal, occasional charred cereal grains, and small amounts of stone. Unfortunately no animal bone was recovered.

The complexity of the archaeology on the platform and the amount of occupation debris including pottery in F.301 suggest that this was a focus of occupation and was presumably the settlement from which the contemporary ditched enclosure system was exploited. The scarcity of pottery from the ditches to the east indicates that very little domestic refuse was spread over the fields. This supports the palaeoenvironmental evidence in suggesting an essentially pastoral use of an area of partially enclosed and drained high salt marsh.

The later Romano-British landscape at Puxton

Evidence for later Romano-British settlement at Puxton was fragmentary (Fig 4.1). A relatively light scatter of pottery was recovered from fieldwalking in Church Field, with the greatest density of material to the east. One fragment of box-flue tile (Fig 4.6, No. 11) hints at a building of some status in the vicinity. Nearly 80 residual Romano-British sherds were also recovered from the excavations in Church Field (12 sherds from Trenches 1, 2, and 12, and 66 from Trenches 3 and 11), also reflecting the eastern bias. Metal detecting in Church Field has produced a small assemblage of twelve late 3rd- to mid-4th-century coins (see Trevarthen, below). A number of later Romano-British features were also excavated in Trench 3, sealed beneath the medieval bank around the eastern side of Church Field (see Rippon 2000a, 96–7). A small ditch, F.160 (0.60–0.85m wide, 0.55m deep), was oriented south-west–north-east, with a small parallel gully F.158 (0.25m wide, 0.16m deep) 1.2m to the west. This was cut by another gully F.156 (0.45m wide, 0.18m deep) running at right angles to F.160. The profiles of these gullies, with steep sides and a flat bottom, like other examples at Banwell Moor and Kenn Moor, are similar to medieval and later gripes: spade-dug gullies cut into the surface of a field to aid its drainage. F.156 produced a wholly freshwater snail assemblage (see Davies, below).

As part of the investigation of the medieval settlement of Puxton, shovel test pits and trenches were dug at five other locations and these revealed varying amounts of Romano-British pottery: Butts immediately east of Church Field (18 test pits, 17 sherds), Coles *c* 200m to the south (8 test pits, 16 sherds), Bindings *c* 400m to the north-west (9 test pits, 1 sherd), Flemans (3 test pits, no sherds), Home Ground (Trenches 4–5, 12 test pits, 24 sherds), Haynes immediately north-east of Church Field (6 test pits, no sherds), and Hardingworth *c* 400m to the north-east (Trench 6, no sherds). Along with the distribution of material from fieldwalking, this

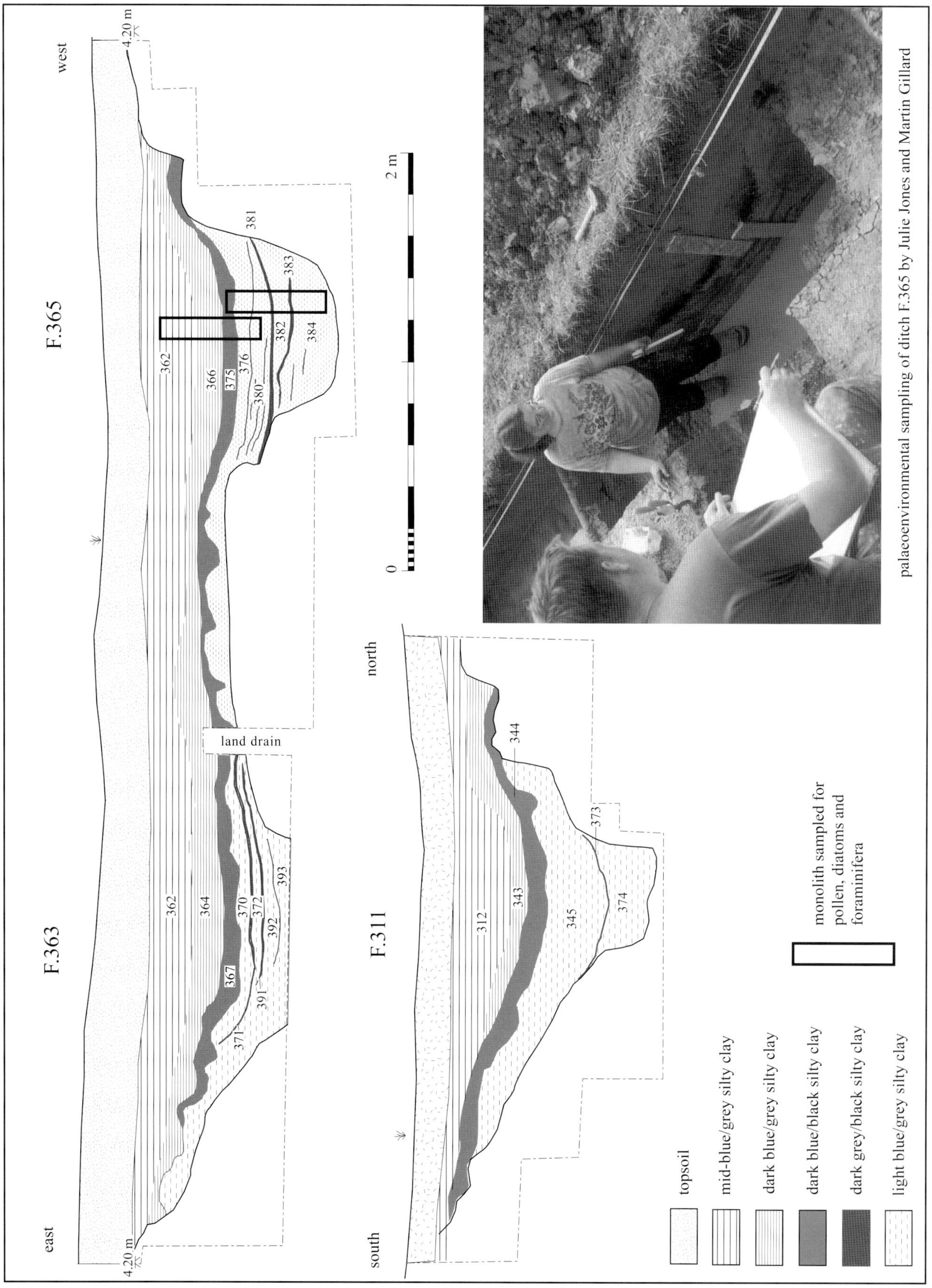

Figure 4.5 Sections of F.363, F.365 (and photo), and F.311 (for locations see Fig 4.2)

Table 4.1 ?Late Iron Age and Romano-British pottery from excavations at Puxton

	fabric code	description	number	%	Wt (g)	%
Prehistoric	Preh	?Prehistoric	4	4.3	5	0.4
LIA–Roman	L1	soapy limestone/vesic	17	18.3	144	12.7
	L2	Palaeozoic limestone	13	14.0	87	7.7
	L3	calcite-temper	3	3.2	19	1.7
	L4	pale, vesicular	7	7.5	39	3.4
	L6	Jurassic shell/limestone	9	9.7	141	12.4
	G2	grog-tempered	4	4.3	105	9.3
Roman	R9	grey very sandy	1	1.1	10	0.9
	R12	grey with limestone/cp	2	2.2	54	4.8
	R14	fine grey micaceous	8	8.6	289	25.5
	R20	fine black micaceous	4	4.3	15	1.3
	R21	black sandy ware	6	6.5	64	5.6
	R00	misc grey sandy	1	1.1	3	0.3
	SVW OX	Severn Valley ware	4	4.3	9	0.8
	SAV GT	Savernake type	8	8.6	113	10.0
	DOR BB1	Dorset BB1	2	2.2	36	3.2
TOTAL			93	100.0	1133	100.0

suggests that the later Romano-British settlement lay somewhere to the south-east of Church Field.

Overall, therefore, it would appear that around the 3rd century AD the landscape at Puxton was transformed, from a high intertidal salt marsh, to a freshwater reclaimed landscape, drained in places through a hierarchy of ditches and gullies, with other areas, such as the abandoned Dolemoor, presumably left as open pasture. The amount of later Romano-British pottery recovered from Puxton was limited, but, like the assemblages from Banwell Moor and Kenn Moor, it was dominated by locally produced coarsewares, though the fragment of box-flue tile hints at a building of some status in the area.

The ?late Iron Age and Romano-British pottery *by Jane Timby*

Introduction

The excavations at Puxton Dolemoor produced a modest assemblage of 93 sherds of ?late Iron Age to Romano-British pottery weighing 1,133g (Table 4.1). The material was in quite poor condition, especially the sherds with a limestone temper that had badly leached. Pottery was recovered from fifteen recorded contexts, most of which can be dated to the earlier Roman period, though context 337 (on the platform) produced just four small pot crumbs that may be of prehistoric date. The assemblage was sorted into fabric types broadly following the fabric series previously developed for this and other sites investigated on the North Somerset Levels (Timby 2000, 174). Where new fabrics occur these have been added to the sequence (L6, L7, G2 and R21). The sorted sherds were quantified by number and weight for each context. Significant assemblages of material were also recovered from various contexts around the medieval settlement of Puxton and the fieldwalking of Twenty Acres in Banwell Moor, and this material was also examined.

Description of fabrics and associated forms

Native wares

L1: Limestone-tempered
Fabric: Moderately soft brown ware with a grey core. The paste contains a moderate scatter of irregular-shaped voids up to 2mm across. Smooth soapy fabric. Forms: handmade simple, everted rim jars and beaded rim jars.

L2: Palaeozoic limestone-tempered
Fabric: Black with brown or black core. The matrix contains a moderate scatter of white limestone mixed with calcite up to 1.5–2mm in size. Occasional iron pellets. Similar to Rouillard 1989, Meare fabric 2b. Forms: handmade beaded rim jars.

L3: Calcite-tempered
Fabric: Reddish/brown to black exterior with a black core and interior. The paste contains a moderate frequency of ill-sorted calcite up to 1mm in size. Similar to Rouillard 1989, Meare fabric 2c; Peacock (1969) Group 3. Forms: handmade vessels.

L4: Limestone-tempered
Fabric: A white leached fabric with numerous surface voids. The cream fabric is mottled with pinkish or red patches. The paste contains grains of iron and irregular-shaped voids from leached calcareous material. Forms: handmade jars.

L6: Jurassic limestone and shell-tempered
Fabric: Mainly light brown or grey ware containing a sparse to moderate frequency of limestone up to 2mm in size accompanied by fine fossil shell, bryozoa and other fossiliferous matter. At ×20 the paste also contains sparse glassy grains of quartz. Forms: wheelmade necked rolled rim jars (Fig. 4.6, No. 5).

G2: Sandy with a grog-temper
Fabric: A moderately hard ware with a brown exterior grey core and grey/black interior. The ware has a sandy texture. The paste contains a sparse scatter of fine, rounded quartz sand and sub-angular multi-coloured fragments of grog. Form: handmade beaded rim jar.

Roman wares

R9
Fabric: A grey sandy ware with a pale to dark grey fabric. The paste contains a moderate to high frequency of fine, rounded quartz sand giving a distinctive sandy feel. Forms: wheelmade jars.

R12
Fabric: A hard, grey sandy ware with a moderate frequency of fine quartz sand, fine limestone and dark grey clay pellets. Form: wheelmade everted rim jar.

R14
Fabric: A fine to medium sandy ware distinguished by the presence of distinctive flecks of muscovite mica. Quartz sand varies from sparse to moderate. Forms: wheelmade jar.

R20
Fabric: Fine black, micaceous ware with a sandy texture. Brown core. Forms: wheelmade everted rim jar.

R21
Fabric: Black medium sandy ware with a brown, black or grey core. Similar to Gloucester type fabric 201 (Ireland 1983, 99). Forms: wheelmade necked bowls and jars.

R00
Fabric: miscellaneous grey sandy (one body sherd)

Traded wares

SAV GT: Savernake ware (Tomber and Dore 1998, 191). Forms: storage and other large necked, or beaded rim jars.

SVW OX: Severn Valley ware (ibid, 148). Forms: tankard.

DOR BB1: Dorset black-burnished ware (ibid, 127). Forms: flat-rimmed dish and jar sherds.

Catalogue of illustrated sherds (Fig 4.6)

1. Handmade bowl with a rolled, flattened rim. Light brown exterior with a dark orange/brown core. Fabric L2. Pit 301 (321).
2. Handmade jar or bowl. Pale orange/brown vesicular fabric. Fabric L4. Pit F.301 (321).
3. Wheelmade necked bowl with a carinated shoulder. Black sandy ware, fabric R21. Pit F.301 (321).
4. Handmade beaded rim jar. Black with an external burnish. Fabric L2. Pit F.301 (322).
5. Wheelmade wide-mouthed, necked jar. Grey in colour. Fabric L6. Pit F.301 (390).
6. Handmade rolled rim jar. Grey sandy with grog. Fabric G2. Pit F.301 (302).
7. Handmade jar. Orange/brown with a darker core and interior. Fabric R12. Saltern context 342.
8. Handmade rolled rim storage jar. Savernake ware (SAV GT). Disturbed top of natural, context 368.
9. Wheelmade thickened rim necked jar. Fabric R12. Ditch F.313 (388).
10. Wheelmade necked jar with traces of burnished line decoration in imitation of a BB1 type. Heavily sooted with internal and external encrustations. Fabric R21. Ditch F.363 (389).

Discussion

The early Roman enclosure complex on Puxton Dolemoor

The assemblage from Puxton Dolemoor comprised a mixture of handmade and wheelmade wares. The handmade wares for the most part are locally made native types typical of the later Iron Age but which continued to be made and used well into the early Roman period. In the early Roman period recognisable types include a small amount of Severn Valley ware, Savernake, or Savernake-type, ware and Dorset black-burnished ware. Of the 93 sherds recovered, 62 sherds, 577g, came from a single pit, pit F.301. The remaining 30 sherds were distributed across thirteen contexts so the individual groups were very small. This combined with a generally low presence of chronologically diagnostic wares or forms limits the degree of reliability that can be placed on the dating.

In the ditch or creek F.397 associated with saltern debris, layer 319 produced exclusive native calcareous-tempered wares, fabrics L1, L3 and L4, one sherd of which had been vitrified. The sherds were quite friable and vesicular and can be broadly dated to the later Iron Age–early Roman period by analogy with material recovered from Kenn Moor

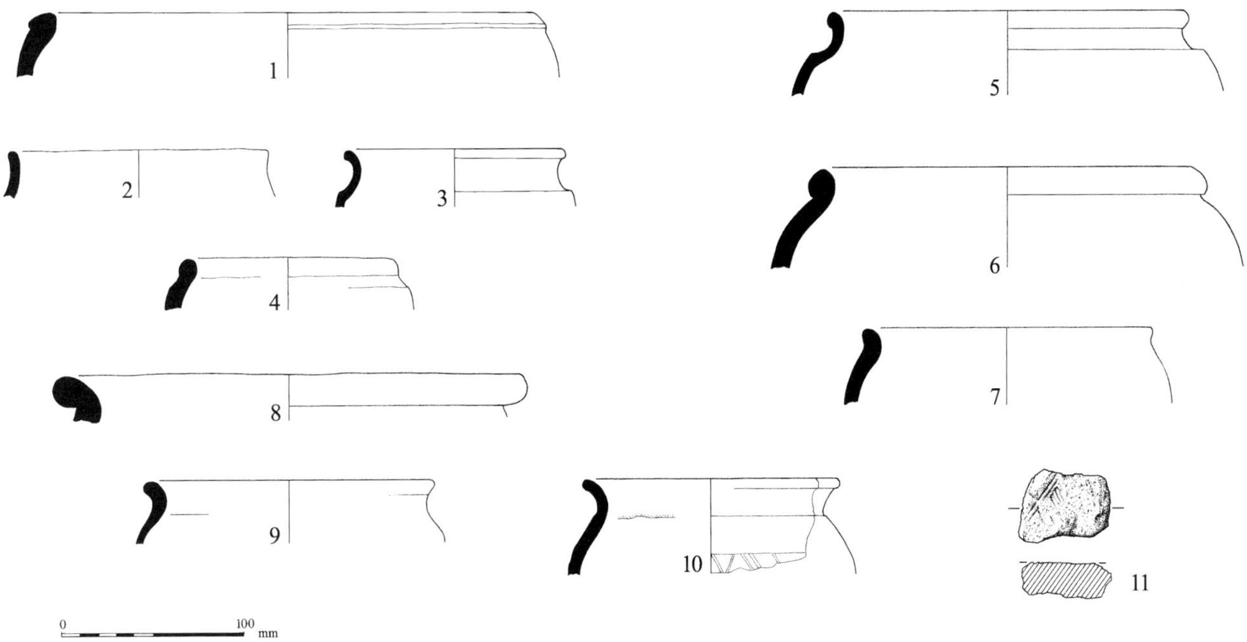

Figure 4.6 Romano-British pottery from Dolemoor (nos 1–10, drawing by Jane Timby), and fragment of comb-decorated box-flue tile from fieldwalking in Church Field (drawing by Mike Rouillard)

and Banwell Moor (Timby 2000, 181). Layer 342 yielded a single beaded rim jar sherd (Fig 4.6, No. 7) in fabric R12, which probably dates from the 1st century AD.

Several contexts from the platform in Trench 7 yielded pottery. Layer 337 produced just a few crumbs that may be later Iron Age–early Roman period or earlier. Layers 340 and 369 may be slightly later in that amongst the five sherds from 340 is a flat rim Dorset black-burnished ware bowl and fine grey ware sherd, and from 369, a fine black sandy micaceous ware jar rim, all suggestive of a 2nd-century date. The largest assemblage came from pit F.301: layer 322 produced exclusively native limestone-tempered wares, 21 sherds in both handmade and wheelmade forms including beaded rim and rolled rim jars (fabrics L1, L2, L3, and L6) (Fig 4.6, No. 4); layer 321 similarly produced largely limestone-tempered sherds accompanied by a beaded rim jar in a grog-tempered fabric, nine reduced wares (fabrics R20 and R21) and four sherds of Savernake-type ware (Fig 4.6, Nos 1–3); layer 320 produced just two sherds, one Savernake ware and one micaceous sandy ware; while layer 390 yielded a single limestone-tempered jar rim (Fig 4.6, No. 5). A further large jar in a sandy grog-tempered ware came from the uppermost fill layer 302 (Fig 4.6, No. 6). The assemblage suggests a date of infill in the later 1st or early 2nd century.

Ditch F.363 (layers 370 and 389) produced one and two sherds respectively in Roman fabrics R20 and R21. The latter two sherds are burnt with soot deposits and from a jar probably imitating a BB1 form (Fig 4.6, No. 10). Layer 367 (the basal fill of the upper cut) produced five sherds from a grey micaceous jar base which had had five holes drilled through after firing. Ditch F.313 (layer 388) produced just two sherds, one wheelmade sandy jar (Fig 4.6, No. 9) and one sherd of DOR BB1. Little further can be said about the dating of these ditches other than that they appear to date to the Roman period proper. A single large sherd of Savernake-type ware jar (Fig 4.6, No. 8) was recovered from the disturbed top of the natural (layer 368) at the northern end of Trench 9, and is indicative of a post-Roman Conquest date.

The assemblage is broadly comparable in date and composition to the early groups previously examined from Kenn Moor and Banwell Moor (Timby 2000). The native wares point to sources from at least two different geological outcrops, a palaeozoic limestone source such as the Mendip Hills and a Jurassic source such as that found in the Cotswold region but extending down through Somerset. The sources need not necessarily be distant geographically. Most of the Roman wares proper appear to be of broadly local origin with few traded regional wares and no imported fine wares.

Later Roman occupation around Puxton Church Field

Twenty-four Romano-British sherds weighing 206g were recovered from fieldwalking in Church Field. The sherds all comprise Roman grey sandy wares from the North Somerset industries, with the only distinctive featured sherd being a plain-rimmed dish. The character of the material suggests it belongs to the later Roman period.

Forty-two sherds weighing 420g were recovered from Trench 3 in Church Field, mostly from the topsoil but also in the medieval ditch F.103. This residual/unstratified assemblage included a single sherd of Central Gaulish samian, eight sherds of DOR BB1, a single sherd of Norton Fitzwarren-type ware, one oxidised sherd, and local grey sandy wares. Featured sherds include a DOR BB1 plain rimmed dish and jars, and local grey ware jars again indicating activity in the later Roman (later 2nd- to 4th-century) period. The fills of gully F.158 (context 159) and ditch F.160 (161) each contained two sherds, including a later 2nd- to 4th-century DOR BB1 jar. Trench 11, across the bank that encircled Church Field, yielded 24 sherds (235g) of which 21 were from the make up of the bank itself (contexts 502–3); local sandy grey wares predominate but there were also four sherds of DOR BB1 and one oxidised sherd. The remaining three sherds, all local sandy grey ware, came from the topsoil. The far more extensive excavations towards the church (Trenches 1, 2 and 12) yielded just twelve residual sherds (105g), mostly local sandy grey wares with one sherd of DOR BB1.

Twenty-five Romano-British sherds were recovered from the excavations at Home Ground. A sherd of local grey ware copying a DOR BB1 form came from buried soil 218, while the remaining material was all residual in medieval features and the topsoil including one burnt sherd of Oxfordshire colour-coated mortarium, five sherds of DOR BB1, and two sherds of Central Gaulish samian. The range of material suggests a date of activity in the later 3rd–4th centuries.

The shovel test pits at Butts produced 32 sherds of pottery weighing 225g. Nearly half of these sherds (fifteen in total) are probably medieval in date, including at least one jar with an applied thumb-pressed strip. The similarity of this fabric to some of the Roman wares means that designation of very small sherds may be incorrect. The remaining seventeen sherds, all local grey sandy wares, are probably Roman in date but the absence of any chronologically diagnostic material makes closer dating inappropriate. The shovel test pits at Coles produced sixteen Romano-British local greyware sherds weighing 105g. Featured sherds include a plain rimmed dish, and four everted rim jar sherds. The test pits at Bindings produced one Roman grey ware. No. Romano-British pottery was recovered from Bindings South.

Banwell Moor: Twenty Acres

When the late Romano-British enclosure complex on Banwell Moor was excavated, the field (Twenty Acres) was under pasture (Rippon 2000b). In 2004 this field was ploughed and fieldwalked. The enclosure complex that had previously been subject to limited excavation yielded just a handful of undiagnostic local greyware sherds, but in the eastern part of Twenty Acres there was a dense scatter of Romano-British pottery from the area of another enclosure complex that shows up as earthworks on early air photographs (Fig 2.4). Ninety sherds were collected with only four main wares present: North Somerset greywares (SGREY), Dorset black-burnished ware (DOR BB1), South-west white slipped ware (SOW WS), and a fine oxidised ware (OXIDF).

North Somerset greywares dominate the group, accounting for 87% by count. Within this group are several variants with slightly differing shades of grey or degree of sandiness but generally likely to belong to the same generic industry. Broadly speaking little is known about the Somerset greyware kilns and associated products other than that production spans the 2nd–4th centuries. Many of the later products imitate black-burnished ware forms. Some of the sherds present here broadly conform to material known from the Congresbury kilns but it is likely that there are several small kilns producing closely similar wares. Of the featured sherds in the group there is one flat-rimmed dish with a very slight groove (Fig 4.7, No. 1) that probably, typologically, dates to the 3rd century. Other forms include a jar decorated with a burnished wavy line, a bodysherd with a handle springing probably from a tankard, four everted rim jars (Fig 4.7 Nos 3 and 5), one flat rim jar (Fig 4.7, No. 6), and one plain-rimmed dish. One bodysherd is decorated with an obliquely set burnished line lattice. All these types probably belong to the later Roman period (3rd- to 4th-century). The second commonest ware is Dorset black-burnished ware, all eight pieces of which are also typical of the later Roman period. Featured sherds include a plain-rimmed dish (Fig 4.7, No. 2), a conical flanged bowl (Fig 4.7, No. 4), which cannot date before the later 3rd century, and a jar. The only other sherds in the Roman assemblage are single pieces of South-west white slipped ware, which generally dates to the later 2nd–3rd century, and a fine, oxidised bodysherd from a closed form.

On balance the assemblage seems to indicate activity dating to the 3rd through to the 4th century, making it contemporary with the excavated enclosure complex in the west of Twenty Acres, as well as Puxton Church Field and Kenn Moor. The assemblage is probably too small and too homogeneous to allow any refined dating given our general lack of knowledge of the greyware industries in this region. Most of the wares appear to be of local origin, the main traded wares being the Dorset black-burnished ware. The presence of the flanged bowl could indicate continuity into the 4th century but could also be seen as a late 3rd-century product. There are no other distinct chronological markers to demonstrate definite 2nd-century or definite 4th-century activity.

Catalogue of illustrated sherds from Twenty Acres

1. Flat rim dish. Light grey, hard sandy ware. Somerset greyware.

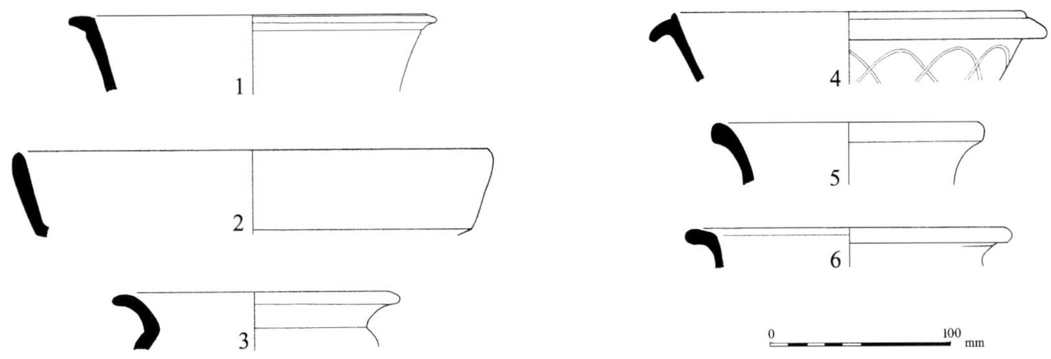

Figure 4.7 Romano-British pottery from Twenty Acres in the north-west corner of Banwell Moor (for location see Fig 2.4) (drawing by Jane Timby)

2. Plain rimmed dish. Dorset black-burnished ware.
3. Everted rim jar. Grey sandy ware imitating Dorset black-burnished ware. Somerset greyware.
4. Flanged rim conical bowl. Dorset black-burnished ware.
5. Everted rim narrow-mouthed jar. Dark grey, sandy ware. Somerset grey ware.
6. Everted rim jar with an internally bevelled surface. Light grey, sandy ware. Somerset greyware.

Roman coins and brooch
by Ciorstaidh Trevarthen

The twelve coins recovered from metal detecting by a local amateur in Church Field comprise five radiates of the late 3rd century, five bronzes of the House of Constantine and the usurpers (first half of 4th century), and two of the house of Valentinian (third quarter of the 4th century) (Table 4.2). A fragment of a probably 2nd-century bow brooch with triangular recesses for enamel was also recovered.

Palaeoenvironmental evidence for the changing environment in ditch F.365

Pollen *by Heather M Tinsley*

Excavations at Dolemoor revealed a series of ditches with two cuts, the upper, more recent one being broader and shallower than the lower Romano-British one. Ditch F.365 in Trench 7 exhibited this typical pattern and was sampled in the field using two overlapping 50cm monolith tins (Fig 4.5 and Table 4.3). The tins were described in detail prior to sampling for pollen, foraminifera, diatoms, and radiocarbon dating. Some additional samples for pollen analysis were added later.

The pollen preservation in these samples was variable; mainly it was moderately good, but in sample 54–55cm it was good and only poor to moderately good in sample 66–67cm. The concentration of pollen was fairly good in the top four samples but declined below 66cm. The results of the pollen analysis are shown in a pollen diagram (Fig 4.8) prepared using

Table 4.2 The Roman coins from metal detecting in Puxton Church Field

coin	obverse	reverse type	date range	denomination
4	Copy of bust of Postumous/Victorinus?	?standard	259–286?	?Contemporary copy (radiate)
6	Claudius II Gothicus	Provid Aug	268–270	Radiate
2	Claudius II Gothicus	Aequitas Aug	268–270	Silvered radiate
3	Tetricus I?	illegible	270–273	Radiate
5	Tetricus I	Virtvs Aug	270–273	Radiate
8	Constantine I	Soli Invicto Comiti	307–318	Nummus
9	House of Constantine	Victoriae Laetae Princ Perp	318–324	Silvered nummus
12	House of Constantine	Gloria Exercitus	330–335	Nummus
10	House of Constantine	Constantinopolis	330–335	Nummus
7	Magnentius/Decentius	Victoriae DD NN Aug et Cae	350–353	Nummus (possible copy)
1	Valens?	Securitas Reipublicae	364–378	Nummus
11	House of Valentinian	Securitas Reipublicae	364–378	Nummus

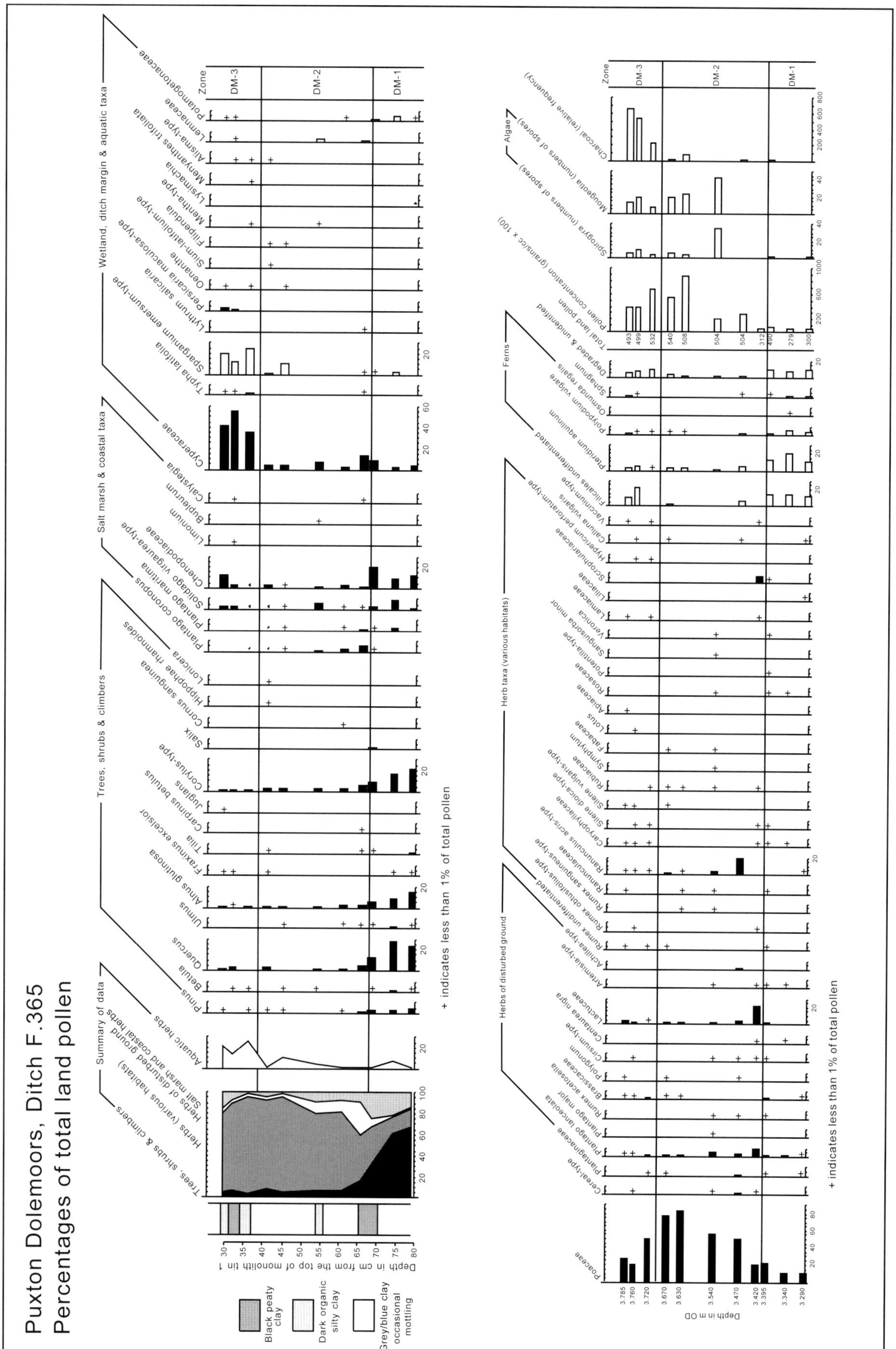

Figure 4.8 Pollen diagram for F.365 (drawing by Heather Tinsley)

Table 4.3 Stratigraphy, pollen, diatom, and foraminifera samples: Dolemoor ditch F.365. Depths are from the top of the upper monolith tin, 0.29m below the present ground surface (4.37m OD)

depth	context	sample depth: diatoms and forams	sample depth: pollen	stratigraphy
0–22cm (4.08–3.86m OD)	362			mid-blue/grey silty clay with some pale brown mottling, merging boundary
22–29cm (3.86–3.79m OD)	366			mid-blue/grey silty clay with some pale brown mottles and some streaks of black organic matter
29–31cm (3.79–3.77m OD)	375	29.5–30.0cm	29.5–30.0cm	dark grey/brown silty clay (organic-rich lower fill of upper ditch cut)
31–34cm (3.77–3.74m OD)	375	32–33cm	32–33cm	black peaty clay (organic-rich lower fill of upper ditch cut)
34–37cm (3.74–3.71m OD)	375	36–37cm	36–37cm	dark grey/brown silty clay (organic-rich basal fill of upper ditch cut)
37–54cm (3.71–3.54m OD)	376		41–42cm 45–46cm	light blue/grey silty clay with some orange/brown mottles and black streaking
54–56cm (3.54–3.52m OD)	381	54–55cm	54–55cm	dark grey/black silty clay with some visible organic material (upper organic-rich band within lower ditch cut)
56–65.5cm (3.52–3.425m OD)	382		61–62cm	light blue/grey silty clay with orange mottles and some black streaks, merging boundary
65.5–70.5cm (3.425–3.375m OD)	383	66–67cm 68.5–69.5cm	66–67cm 68.5–69.5cm	blue/grey silty clay with irregular lenses of black peaty clay (lower organic-rich lens within lower ditch cut)
70.5– 83cm (3.375–3.25m OD)	384		74–75cm 79–80cm	light blue/grey silty clay with iron staining along root channels (basal fill of lower ditch cut)

Tilia and *Tilia*.graph software (Grimm 1990). Pollen data are expressed as percentages of total land pollen (TLP). All taxa included in the pollen sum are shown on the diagram as solid bars. Obligate aquatic taxa are expressed as percentages of total land pollen plus aquatics (TPA). Fern spores and moss spores are expressed as percentages of total pollen plus spores (TPS). Algal spores are shown as numbers of spores counted, not percentages. All taxa excluded from the pollen sum are shown on the diagram as hollow bars. The pollen taxa are organised into ecological groups to aid interpretation: trees, shrubs and climbers, salt marsh and coastal taxa, wetland, ditch margin and aquatic taxa, herbs of disturbed ground, etc. These groups are not exclusive; some pollen taxa include plants inhabiting a variety of ecological niches. The diagram has been zoned on the basis of changes in the dominant taxa into three local pollen assemblage zones, DM-1–3, specific to this site. These zones are not pollen assemblage zones *sensu stricta*, and are merely used for the convenience of describing the data. The main characteristics of the individual zones are described below.

DM-1 (context 384 and lower part of context 383: lower fill of lower cut)

This zone is characterised by relatively high values for pollen of trees, shrubs, and climbers, which form 60% TLP at the start of the zone, falling to 32% TLP by the end. The principal woody taxa are *Quercus* (oak) and *Corylus*-type (hazel), with some *Alnus* (alder). *Pinus* (pine) forms 3–5% TLP with *Betula* (birch), *Tilia* (lime) and *Ulmus* (elm) present throughout at low frequency. Of the herbaceous pollen taxa, the most characteristic is Chenopodiaceae (goosefoot family) at 10–20% TLP, along with Solidago *virgaurea*-type (sea aster and related Asteraceae) at 1–8% TLP and occasional grains of *Plantago maritima* (sea plantain). These taxa suggest marine influence at the site. Pollen of Potamogetonaceae (pondweed), usually indicative of fresh water, is present throughout the zone at low frequency. Poaceae (grasses, including *Phragmites*, common reed) form 11–23% TLP, rising towards the end of the zone, and Cyperaceae (sedges) are present at 3–9% TLP. The flowering herb taxa include taxa typical of disturbed ground such as *Plantago lanceolata* (ribwort plantain) (<3% TLP) and *Artemisia*-type (mugwort, but also the halophyte sea wormwood) (<1% TLP). The zone is also characterised by relatively high frequencies of fern spores, including *Pteridium aquilinum* (bracken) <20% TPF, *Polypodium vulgare* (polypody fern) <5% TPF, and Filicales (undifferentiated) <15% TPF. The relative concentration of microscopic charcoal >40μm is low in this zone. Pollen concentration is also very low; preservation is only moderately good and the percentage of degraded and unidentified grains recorded is relatively high.

DM-2 (upper part of context 383, contexts 382, 381, 376: upper fill of lower cut)

Pollen of trees, shrubs, and climbers falls markedly at the start of the zone to 16% TLP and then falls again to around 7% TLP, which is maintained throughout. The principal woody taxa remain *Quercus*, *Corylus*-type and *Alnus;* all other tree taxa are reduced to just occasional grains. The taxa indicative of salt marsh and coastal locations are also markedly reduced, though the group maintains a presence at low frequency throughout the zone; pollen of Chenopodiaceae falls to <4% TLP and there are small peaks of <2% TLP of *Solidago virgaurea*-type and of *Plantago coronopus* (buck's horn plantain). There are occasional pollen grains of taxa from the wetland and aquatic group including *Filipendula* (meadow sweet) and *Lemna* (duckweed); pollen of *Sparganium emersum*-type (bur-reeds, lesser bulrush) starts to increase towards the end of the zone. The zone is characterised by a marked increase in pollen of Poaceae (grasses, including common reed) which rises to more than 80% TLP by the end of the zone. Taxa indicative of disturbed ground increase at the start of the zone, most noticeably *Plantago lanceolata* and Lactuceae (dandelion and related Asteraceae); pollen of Brassicaceae (cabbage family) occurs throughout at low frequency and *Cirsium*-type (thistles), *Plantago major* (greater plantain) and *Rumex acetosella* (sheep's sorrel) are also present. The diversity of flowering herbs is higher than in DM-1, and a wide range of taxa typical of a variety of habitats are represented by occasional grains. A peak in *Ranunculus acris*-type (buttercup and related Ranunculaceae) (19% TLP) is found mid-zone. All fern spores are reduced in frequency compared with DM-1. In the upper part of the zone, above 55cm, spores of the algae *Spirogyra* and *Mougeotia* start to occur. The relative concentration of microscopic charcoal >40μm remains low throughout. Pollen concentration rises markedly at the top of the zone, suggesting slower sediment accumulation. Pollen preservation is generally better than in DM-1 and this is reflected in fewer degraded and unidentified grains. Black metallic sulphide particles were observed frequently, indicative of deposition in aquatic environments of low redox potential, both freshwater and marine (Wiltshire *et al* 1994).

DM-3 (context 375: base of upper cut)

Pollen of trees, shrubs, and climbers continues to be represented at the very low levels typical of the end of DM-2. A single pollen grain of *Juglans* (walnut) was found in the uppermost sample: walnut is a non-native tree introduced to Britain during the Roman period (Rackham 1990). The start of the zone is characterised by a marked increase in pollen of Cyperaceae (sedges), *Sparganium emersum*-type and *Typha latifolia* (bulrush), which are all plants found in wet ditches. Pollen of Poaceae undergoes a corresponding decline, though still forms more than 30% TLP. Other taxa associated with freshwater ditches occur occasionally, for example *Oenanthe* (water-dropworts), *Persicaria maculosa*-type (knotweeds, including *P. lapathifolia* and *P. hydropiper* which both grow in damp places), *Alisma*-type (water plantain) and Potamogetonaceae. Taxa associated with disturbed ground decline compared with DM-2, though *P. lanceolata*, Brassicaceae and Lactuceae continue to be represented at low frequency. Occasional pollen grains of a range of taxa possibly associated with meadowland are found, including Caryophyllaceae (pink family), *Silene dioica*-type (red campion), and Apiaceae (carrot family). In the upper part of the zone there is a clear increase in pollen taxa associated with salt marsh and coastal habitats, as Chenopodiaceae rise to 12% TLP, *Solidago virgaurea*-type also increases, and there are occasional grains of *Limonium* (sea lavenders). Fern spores (undifferentiated) also increase somewhat towards the end of the zone. Spores of *Mougeotia* and *Spirogyra* continue to occur, though at reduced frequency compared with DM-2. Pollen concentration remains high, but preservation is rather variable and numbers of degraded and unidentified spores rise to around 10% TLP + unidentifiable. There is a marked increase in the relative concentration of microscopic charcoal fragments in this zone.

Interpretation

The pollen diagram from ditch F.365 at Dolemoor gives some clear indications of the changing nature of the local landscape throughout the period of ditch infilling although the complication of the later recutting means that there is a hiatus in the sediment sequence, between contexts 376 and 375, giving rise to a gap in the record of unknown length.

At the time when the basal sediments (contexts 384 and 383) were accumulating in the early Romano-British ditch there is evidence of marine influence at the site. This is demonstrated in zone DM-1 by the characteristically high frequencies of Chenopodiaceae pollen (10–20% TLP). This family includes a wide range of plants, some of which are halophytic such as *Suaeda* (sea-blite), *Salicornia* (glasswort) and *Atriplex* (oraches), while others are weeds of disturbed ground such as *Chenopodium album* (fat-hen). However, values for Chenopodiaceae pollen in excess of 5% TLP are usually only found in pollen assemblages from salt marsh communities, rather than plant communities modified by human activity. Within the Chenopodiaceae, different genera occupy specific niches on salt marshes; sea-blite and glasswort are characteristic of the lower zones, whereas oraches and beets (*Beta* spp.) are more typical of higher parts of the marsh. Clearly, it would be valuable for palaeoecological reconstruction if these pollen taxa could be distinguished, but it is not possible in routine analysis. Other pollen taxa likely to have originated from salt marsh plants occur in this assemblage, in particular *Solidago virgaurea*-type (which includes sea aster as well as a range of other related Asteraceae). This pollen taxon is frequently associated with high Chenopodiaceae frequencies in salt marsh deposits at Walpole, beside the Parrett Estuary in the main Somerset Levels (Tinsley 2003). The source of the salt marsh pollen in DM-1 was probably the upper salt marsh communities growing on the tidal flats closest to the ditched enclosure system, with pollen from these communities having blown into the ditch, or been washed in with tidal incursions. In view of the evidence from the diatoms and foraminifera at the site (see Cameron below; see Kreiser below), the latter is most likely.

The high frequencies of tree pollen, which are a very characteristic feature of DM-1, also lend support to the view that tidal water had access to the ditch when it was first silting up. The tree pollen taxa concerned are principally oak, hazel and alder, but there are also regular occurrences of low frequencies of pine pollen. The source area for this woodland pollen cannot have been the immediate landscape of salt flats, but woodland must have existed in the wider region on higher ground around the margins of the Severn Estuary, and it is likely that this was washed into the ditch with the tide and thus forms an allochthonous (transported from elsewhere) element in the pollen assemblage. Such in-washed pollen is always a possibility at estuarine sites and in particular the presence of pine in the DM-1 assemblage is indicative of far-travelled pollen: pine is very unlikely to have grown in the woods of this part of Somerset in the mid- to late Holocene but its pollen is very buoyant and it has previously been recorded in sediments at a number of sites around the Severn Estuary (Scaife 1987; 1993; 1995; Walker *et al* 1998; Tinsley 2003). High frequencies of washed-in fern spores are another feature characteristic of some Severn Estuary sediments, for example those at Barlands Farm on the Caldicot Levels (Walker *et al* 1998), and these are also found in DM-1. Taken together, all these features of the basal pollen assemblage in F.365 very clearly suggest that the initial environment of the ditch was influenced by estuarine water. However, occasional pollen grains of pondweed (*Potamogeton*) establish the presence of some freshwater in parts of the ditch system, even in this early stage of drainage and enclosure. The local vegetation immediately around the ditch at this time appears to have been a somewhat weedy grassland with a range of herbs including ribwort plantain and mugwort.

The initial silting of the ditch involved the deposition of a largely inorganic clay, but this was followed by the accumulation of organic detritus (context 383). The pollen assemblage in the base of this organic lens indicates continuity of environment with that of the lower clays. However, the pollen assemblage from the upper part of context 383 demonstrates a change in local conditions and in the pollen diagram this is marked by the boundary between zones DM-1 and DM-2. Chenopodiaceae pollen falls at the start of DM-2; tree pollen and all fern spores also decline and together these features suggest a reduction in tidal influence in the ditch although halophytic pollen taxa are still represented (though at considerably reduced frequencies). Small peaks of pollen of the strandline plants buck's horn plantain (*Plantago coronopus*) and sea plantain (*P. maritima*), which occur at the opening of DM-2, may well have resulted from pollen blown in to the ditch from the coast.

The freshwater plants duckweed (*Lemna*) and bulrush (*Typha latifolia*) appear in the pollen record at the start of DM-2, suggesting colonisation of the ditch itself. The nature of the ditch sedimentation changes during this zone, from an organic-rich lens (context 383) to a largely inorganic silty clay (context 382), but the pollen evidence does not indicate any return to tidal inundation. The diatom evidence similarly indicates a marked decline in salinity at the start of DM-2, though diatom taxa typical of slightly brackish water still made up a significant part of the assemblage (see Cameron below). It appears that context 382 was deposited under the influence of fresh or brackish water, at a time when the pollen evidence suggests an increasingly grass-dominated community around the site and the waterlogged plant macrofossils indicate the presence of abundant *Phragmites* (common reed) (see Jones, below). It is therefore likely that the ditch at this stage was lined with reeds, including some bulrush, and the pollen evidence also suggests some associated tall herbs such as meadow sweet (*Filipendula*). The ditch became drier at some point, when the organic debris of context 381 accumulated, but this change in sedimentary type is not reflected in the pollen record and the plant communities around the ditch do not appear to have changed. The increasing pollen concentration in the sediments from context 381 and above suggests that the rate of sediment accumulation slowed at this point. Following the drier phase, alluvial deposition was re-established to produce context 376. Towards the end of DM-2 bur reeds and/or lesser bulrush (*Sparganium emersum*-type) started to spread in the ditch and spores of *Spirogyra* and *Mougeotia* indicate the development of algal mats. The plant macrofossil evidence revealed abundant seeds of water crowfoot (*Ranunculus* sub-genus *Batrachium*) in context 382, a sub-aquatic plant which is a common ditch coloniser (see Jones, below); the peak of 20% TLP in pollen of *Ranunculus acris*-type (a taxon including water crowfoot), which also occurs in context 382 in the middle of DM-2, could be from this source.

At this stage the wider environment beyond the

ditch was an open one, with very few trees. The reclaimed land was probably used for grazing, which is suggested by an increase in the frequency of pollen taxa indicative of disturbed ground which occurs at the start of DM-2, particularly of types associated with pasture such as thistles, sheep's sorrel, dandelion, and ribwort plantain. The disturbance herbs decline somewhat towards the end of the zone. The presence of occasional grains of cereal-type pollen in DM-2 (and also in DM-3) is unlikely to be significant in terms of crop growing in the immediate fields, given the general poorly drained environment. The grains may well be from *Glyceria* (sweet grass) which could have grown in the ditch, or they may have blown into the site from coastal communities of marram or lyme grass. It is also possible that cereal pollen, released from sites of crop processing which may have existed in the wider area, could have blown in to the ditch.

Subsequently the ditch was recut and organic sedimentation was re-established (context 375). The hiatus is reflected in the marked changes that occur in the pollen diagram between DM-2 and DM-3. At the time of deposition of the organic debris of context 375 the pollen evidence suggests that sedges (Cyperaceae) and bur reeds or lesser bulrush (*Sparganium emersum*-type) now dominated the ditch, along with bulrush, instead of common reed. The expansion of sedges does not appear to be reflected in the plant macrofossil remains, but *Typha* species (bulrush and lesser bulrush) were recorded abundantly in the organic fill of the upper cut (see Jones, below). The pollen diagram also indicates the presence of water-dropwort (*Oenanthe*) and knotweed (*Persicaria maculosa*-type) in the bank side vegetation at this stage, with water plantain (*Alisma*-type), bogbean (*Menyanthes*), pondweed (*Potamogeton*), and green algae colonising the water itself.

The herbs of disturbed ground are reduced compared with DM-2; it may be that use of the surrounding grasslands was less intensive. There is also, however, the possibility that the land was being used differently after the second cutting of the ditch and some herbaceous pollen taxa occurring in DM-3, which are not present in DM-2, are suggestive of meadowland, including red campion (*Silene dioica*) and carrot family (Apiaceae, for example herbs such as cow parsley). The increase in relative concentration of microscopic charcoal, which occurs at the start of DM-3, suggests that human use of the wider area had increased compared with DM-2. Such microscopic charcoal particles may travel some distance in the wind and are usually interpreted as originating from domestic fires, though it is also possible that they resulted from the burning of vegetation.

In the upper part of DM-3 there is a clearly marked increase in pollen of salt marsh taxa, in particular Chenopodiaceae and *Solidago virgaurea*-type, and there are also occasional grains of sea lavender. As a group, the halophytes do not reach the levels of DM-1, but nevertheless the increase is enough to suggest that there was some resurgence in tidal influence at this stage, bringing pollen of salt marsh taxa into what was essentially a freshwater environment. Diatom preservation in this organic fill was too poor to give percentage counts but the assessment showed the presence of marine, marine–brackish, brackish and freshwater/aerophilous types (see Cameron, below), which is entirely consistent with the pollen evidence.

Summary

The pollen data from ditch F.365 at Dolemoor suggest that the early Romano-British ditch was originally dug in a salt marsh environment influenced by tidal water. Over time marine influences declined and the ditch became a largely freshwater environment. This may correspond to the reclamation of the North Somerset Levels that is now known to have occurred around the mid-3rd century. The surrounding landscape was lacking in woodland and was largely poor-quality grassland probably used for grazing. There is then a hiatus in the pollen record that reflects the recutting of the ditch. Freshwater conditions still existed at the time of the recut and in the period of initial sedimentation that then took place, and a meadow environment is suggested. There is then evidence to indicate that tidal influences returned to affect the ditch and presumably its associated field system.

The pollen evidence from F.365 can be compared with a similar ditch sequence that has been described from a late Romano-British ditch at Banwell Moor (ditch F.6) 3km south-west of Dolemoor (Rippon 2000b). At Banwell Moor ditch F.6 appears to have been cut as a drain in a freshwater environment and the earlier ditch environment at Dolemoor must have been a much more challenging undertaking. However, the ditch plant communities that eventually established at Dolemoor, once tidal inundation ceased, appear to be very similar to those associated with the Banwell ditch.

Diatoms *by Nigel Cameron and Simon Dobinson*

Diatom preparation followed standard techniques (Battarbee 1986): the oxidation of organic sediment, removal of carbonate and some clay, concentration of diatom valves, and washing with distilled water. Two coverslips, each of a differing concentration of the cleaned solution, were prepared from each sample and fixed in a mountant of suitable refractive index for diatoms (Naphrax). Slides were first scanned under phase contrast illumination at magnifications of 400 and 1000. In order to evaluate the type of diatom assemblage present in the samples, where diatom preservation is adequate, diatom counts have been made and are presented in the diatom diagrams. Total counts of between approximately 300 and 400 valves were made where possible, and where insufficient numbers were present an evaluation was carried out from extensive scanning of coverslips. Several diatom floras and taxonomic publications were consulted to assist with diatom identification, including Hendey (1964), Hustedt (1930–66), Krammer and Lange-Bertalot (1986–91). Diatom species' salinity preferences were classified using the halobian groups of Hustedt (1953; 1957, 199) and are summarised below:

1. Polyhalobian: >30g l^{-1}
2. Mesohalobian: 0.2–30g l^{-1}
3. Oligohalobian–halophilous: optimum in slightly brackish water
4. Oligohalobian–indifferent: optimum in freshwater but tolerant of slightly brackish water
5. Oligohalobian–halophobous: restricted to freshwater and intolerant of brackish and marine water
6. Unknown: taxa of unknown salinity preference.

Figure 4.9 (CD) and Table 4.4 (CD) show diatom taxa classified into halobian groups. The principal source used for diatom ecological data was Denys (1992).

Six samples from the Romano-British ditch F.365 were prepared for diatom analysis, taken at the same levels as sub-samples for foraminifera and pollen analysis (see Table 4.3): the basal fill 375 in the upper cut where preservation was poor (29.5–30.0cm, 32–3cm, and 36–7cm), and the upper organic band (54–5cm) and lower organic band in lower cut (66–7cm, 68.5–69.5cm) where preservation was good. Diatoms are well preserved in the three samples from the organic lenses in the lower cut and it is therefore possible to make percentage diatom counts for these samples (see Fig 4.9 (CD)).

The basal sample (68.5–69.5cm) is dominated by a mixture of marine (polyhalobous) diatoms comprising almost 50% of the assemblage, with brackish water (mesohalobous) species accounting for over 35% of the assemblage and marine–brackish (polyhalobous to mesohalobous taxa) representing almost 10% of the diatom assemblage. A number of diatom species represent each of these salinity groups. The most common polyhalobous taxon is the planktonic (floating in the water) diatom *Paralia sulcata* (almost 35% of the total diatom count). Other marine taxa include *Rhaphoneis* spp., *Podosira stelligera* and *Cymatosira belgica*. Amongst the marine–brackish species *Pseudopodosira westii* (a semi-planktonic species) is most common and *Nitzschia navicularis* (almost 20% of the total diatom assemblage) is the dominant mesohalobous diatom. As well as *Nitzschia navicularis* a number of other diatoms from the basal sample are non-planktonic, for example *Caloneis westii, Diploneis interrupta, Navicula digitoradiata, Navicula peregrina,* and *Nitzschia punctata*. The environment represented by this basal diatom assemblage is clearly fully tidal, with estuarine conditions predominating. Freshwater and even halophilous (brackish–freshwater) diatoms are absent.

The diatom sample from 66–7cm depth (context 383, lower organic-rich lens in the early Romano-British ditch cut) shows a clear change from the basal sample analysed for diatoms. The component of marine species is reduced to less than 15%, marine–brackish species to just over 5%, and brackish (mesohalobous) species account for less than 20% of the total. Halophilous (brackish–freshwater) diatoms are dominant, comprising over 35% of the diatom assemblage and freshwater (oligohalobous indifferent) diatoms are over 20% of the total. The dominant halophilous species is the non-planktonic diatom *Navicula cincta*. The mesohalobous, benthic species *Diploneis interrupta* is relatively abundant, comprising over 10% of the assemblage, and other saline diatoms include the marine–brackish benthic diatom *Navicula forcipata*. The freshwater taxa include species likely to be from semi-terrestrial habitats such as *Hantzschia amphioxys* and *Pinnularia microstauron*. The diatom assemblage from 66–7cm therefore represents a reduction in salinity compared with the basal sample and, whilst tidal influence is still evident, marine planktonic diatoms such as *Paralia sulcata* and *Cymatosira belgica* are a relatively small component of the diatom assemblage.

The diatom sample from 54–5cm depth (context 381, upper organic-rich lens in the Romano-British ditch cut) shows that salinity decreases further with a trace of less than 1% of the total assemblage being of marine or marine–brackish origin. Freshwater (oligohalobous indifferent) diatoms account for over 45% of the diatom assemblage. However, brackish water and halophilous diatoms make up a significant part of the assemblage (approximately: mesohalobous diatoms 20%; mesohalobous to halophilous 10%; halophilous 5%; halophilous to indifferent 15%). *Synedra tabulata* (10%) and *Synedra pulchella* (7%) are brackish water, epontic (growing attached to submerged surfaces, but not the mud surface) species. They are typically found growing as epiphytes (plant growing, but not parasitic, on another) on the submerged stems and leaves of aquatic macrophytes (higher plants). In contrast, the brackish water species *Cyclotella meneghiniana* present in this sample (5%) is a planktonic species. The halophilous species *Navicula cincta* is present at almost 5% abundance. All of these brackish water diatoms are usually found at their highest abundances in slightly brackish water at the low end of the mesohalobous, or the halophilous, salinity range and none is associated with full estuarine conditions. Amongst the most abundant, halophilous to indifferent and oligohalobous to indifferent, halobian diatom groups at 54–5cm all of the species are non-planktonic. Further a large proportion of these species are likely to have been epiphytes (see above), including the *Epithemia* spp., *Gomphonema* spp., *Cocconeis placentula* (including var. *euglypta*), and *Rhoicosphaenia curvata*. Other species such as *Surirella ovata* would have lived on the surface of submerged mud. The aquatic environment was therefore one of slightly brackish water with abundant aquatic macrophytes that was either at the very highest end of the tidal range or infrequently affected by tides from the Severn Estuary. The environment was stable enough for the development of a diverse diatom flora including a halophilous planktonic species *Cyclotella meneghiniana*. The increased diatom diversity, development of a planktonic diatom flora and inferred growth of macrophytes may reflect a decrease in the rate of current flow in the channel and the maintenance of a fairly constant water level.

The concentration of diatom valves and species diversity in the basal fill of the upper cut of ditch F.365 (samples 29.5–30.0, 32–3, and 36–7cm, context 375) is very low and the quality of diatom preservation is poor, with the majority of diatoms represented only by fragments; it is not, therefore, possible to make percentage diatom counts for the samples. However, a diatom assessment produced from skeleton counts is presented in Table 4.4 (CD) and this shows that a mixture of marine, marine–brackish and brackish water diatoms (*Podosira stelligera, Pseudopodosira westii, Nitzschia navicularis*) is present in all three samples. These species are derived either directly or indirectly from the Severn Estuary. In addition, the freshwater/aerophilous diatom *Pinnularia major* is relatively common along with chrysophyte stomatocysts, particularly in the uppermost two samples from this part of the sequence. The presence of the aerophilous diatom and relatively high numbers of chrysophyte resting cysts suggests that the ditch was subject to drying out or that soil algae were introduced into the channel as a result of erosion. The diatom and chrysophyte remains are heavily silicified, so it is also likely that the fossil assemblage represents the effects of preferential preservation. Silica dissolution would be anticipated in an aquatic habitat that dried out.

Overall, the diatoms in the lower cut represent a sequence of salinity changes that are consistent with the idea of enclosure and drainage in the Roman period. The basal sample is from a full tidal habitat with no freshwater component to the flora. In the middle and uppermost samples from the lower organic-rich horizon there is a reduction and then almost complete absence of marine diatoms. At the same time there is an increase in the abundance of brackish water species, followed by an expansion of freshwater species. An increase in the stability of the water body results in the development of an epiphytic diatom flora, halophilous plankton, and an increase in species diversity. Together these changes indicate a reduction of direct tidal influence and in mean salinity levels. The fragmentary diatom and chrysophyte remains in the basal fill of the upper cut represent both a semi-terrestrial freshwater habitat and full tidal conditions. These components are not inconsistent if, for example, a ditch is envisaged that periodically dried out or had diatom input from the (freshwater) catchment. The marine–estuarine component of the flora represents either the direct (tidal) input of diatoms along the ditch from the Estuary or diatoms from redeposited estuarine sediment.

Foraminifera *by Annette Kreiser*

Six samples from ditch F.365 on Dolemoor were prepared for foraminifera analysis, taken at the same levels as sub-samples taken for diatom and pollen analysis (Table 4.3 above). Foraminifera were absent from most of the samples analysed apart from 33.0–33.5cm (375, the organic-rich basal fill of the upper cut), which contained just one test, probably eroded from the Upper Wentlooge alluvium, and 68.0–68.5cm (383, lower of two organic-rich lenses within the lower cut) that contained twelve tests of high–mid-marsh species, which are more likely to be autochthonous (Table 4.5 CD). This assemblage comprises organic, agglutinated forms from vegetated high or middle marsh habitats. With only twelve individuals found any conclusion must be tentative, but the foraminifera appear to support the plant macrofossils (see Jones, below) and diatom data (see Cameron, above) in suggesting a vegetated intertidal environment in the earliest phase of the ditch, though this decreased over time as it silted up. No. foraminifera were present in the 63μm fractions.

Plant macrofossil remains *by Julie Jones*

Bulk sampling of several features within the early Roman ditched enclosure complex on Puxton Dolemoor yielded a series of plant macrofossil assemblages (Tables 4.6 and 4.7 both CD).

Pit F.301 (context 322)

The fill of pit F.301 (at the western end of Trench 7) contained a limited assemblage of predominantly charred cereals including barley (*Hordeum*), wheat (*Triticum*), rye (*Secale cereale*), and oat (*Avena*) grains. The presence of two *Triticum spelta* (spelt wheat) glumes, as well as poorly preserved hulled wheat glumes and spikelet forks indicate the presence of spelt, the wheat most commonly recovered from Romano-British sites. A single pedicel of *Avena fatua / ludoviciana* (wild oat) suggest some at least of the oats present are of the wild variety, likely to have occurred as crop weeds with other grasses (Poaceae) and brome (*Bromus*) present in the sample, plus weeds of disturbed ground chickweed (*Stellaria media*), bartsia/eyebright (*Odontites / Euphrasia*), and wild radish (*Raphanus raphanistrum* ssp *raphanistrum*), often found in association with charred cereal remains. Charred nutlets of sedges (*Carex*), common club-rush (*Schoenoplectus lacustris*) and great fen-sedge (*Cladium mariscus*) would have originated from a freshwater environment, although the presence of grey club-rush (*Schoenoplectus tabernaemontani*), which also occurs in brackish water marshes, may suggest a location prone to occasional brackish water incursions. Waterlogged preservation was restricted to a few disturbed ground species including fat-hen (*Chenopodium album*) and bramble (*Rubus* sect *Glandulosus*).

Ditch F.365 lower cut, middle fill (contexts 382 and 381)

Context 382, a blue/grey silty clay lying between two dark organic-rich horizons (381 and 383), was typical of the predominant fill of ditch F.365. A 20-litre bulk sample produced a 700ml organic float with well-preserved waterlogged plant remains. In contrast a 5-litre bulk sample from the narrow organic lens (381) overlying context 382 and below 376 (see below) produced a 2.2 litre float, although only a 300ml sub-sample was examined in detail. Despite the differing organic content of these two deposits the assemblages from both samples are very similar and illustrate the local environment of the ditch. There are abundant stem/root fragments of common reed (*Phragmites australis*) as well as aquatic species, notably water crowfoot (*Ranunculus* subg. *Batrachium*), pondweed (*Potamogeton*), and horned pondweed (*Zanichellia palustris*). Common reed is a tall stout perennial up to 3.5m or more which can form extensive beds in either freshwater or brackish margins on damp clayey slopes (Fitter *et al* 1987). Although largely freshwater plants, some species of both water crowfoot and pondweed, as well as horned pondweed, can also tolerate brackish water conditions and traces of two other species, sea arrowgrass (*Triglochin maritimum*), a perennial of short turf in saline marshes, and annual sea-blite (*Suaeda maritima*), typical of muddy salt marshes, may suggest that there were at least temporary incursions of brackish water inundation, perhaps associated with the nearby palaeochannel. Other species in the sample, however, are more suggestive of freshwater conditions. These include the aquatic spiked water-milfoil (*Myriophyllum spicatum*), as well as marsh/bank side species such as common club-rush (*Schoenoplectus lacustris*), great fen-sedge, and spike-rush (*Eleocharis palustris/uniglumis*) with true fox-sedge (*Carex vulpina*), a plant of damp places often occurring in standing water in ditches, usually on heavy clay soils (Jermy *et al* 1982).

Away from the ditch side the environment appears to be one of rough grassland, with damp areas suggested by taxa such as silverweed (*Potentilla anserina*) and hairy buttercup (*Ranunculus sardous*), but with a greater range of species of drier grassland (selfheal, *Prunella vulgaris*; and black medick, *Medicago lupulina*) with areas of disturbed ground supporting weeds such as orache (*Atriplex*), docks (*Rumex*), and thistles (*Cirsium/Carduus*). A few charred remains in 382 included a single barley grain and spelt wheat glume base, suggestive of human activity nearby.

Ditch F.365 lower cut, upper fill (context 376)

The upper fill of the lower cut of F.365 comprised a blue/grey silty clay identical to 382 (see above). Occasional fragments of common reed and water crowfoot continued to dominate the sample. Duckweed (*Lemna*), whose free-floating fronds blanket the water's surface, and rigid hornwort (*Ceratophyllum demersum*) both suggest still water conditions. Rigid hornwort, a submerged aquatic of stagnant or slow-moving fresh water, also occasionally occurs in brackish dykes and is a rapid coloniser frequently choking areas of water. Similarly duckweed, very abundant in this sample, whilst mostly a freshwater aquatic, has some species that can tolerate brackish conditions.

Despite the tolerance of these species to brackish water conditions, other species present point to a predominantly freshwater environment. Water plantain (*Alisma plantago-aquatica*) is a medium to tall perennial of aquatic freshwater habitats of still to moderate flow in shallow margins up to 0.75m deep and mare's-tail (*Hippuris vulgaris*) is an aquatic perennial with erect shoots appearing above the water's surface often in still waters in sheltered shallow margins. Many of the bank side and marsh species are also freshwater taxa. Some of the taller species that may have lined the ditch sides include common club-rush (although again in association with grey club-rush which can also occur in brackish water), bulrush (*Typha*) and tubular water-dropwort (*Oenanthe fistulosa*), a medium to tall perennial of shallow water and marshy habitats. Lower growing herbs include water mint (*Mentha aquatica*), gipsywort (*Lycopus europaeus*), and celery-leaved buttercup (*Ranunculus sceleratus*). A freshwater environment is also indicated by the presence of occasional leech cocoons and caddis fly larvae, as well as frequent statoblasts (overwintering bodies of bryozoans, which hatch in spring) of *Lophopus crystallinus. Lophopus* are freshwater creatures belonging to the Bryozoa which are often found adhering to submerged objects such as rotting wood, stems of water plants and amongst fronds of duckweed (Clegg 1965). Other species present in the sample are similar to those found in earlier fills and include taxa of grassy areas (hairy buttercup and silverweed) and disturbed ground (thistles and orache, red/oak-leaved goosefoot (*Chenopodium rubrum/glaucum*)).

Ditch F.365 upper cut, basal fill (context 375)

A much smaller assemblage was recovered from the dark grey/brown silty clay that comprised the basal fill of the upper cut, although the sample is again dominated by freshwater aquatic species, particularly water crowfoot, duckweed and pondweed, suggesting still to slow water conditions in the ditch with the water's surface covered with vegetation. Bogbean (*Menyanthes trifoliata*), which can grow either as an aquatic in shallow water or semi-aquatic in fens and bogs, together with bulrush, rushes, sedges, and water mint, would have formed the bank side vegetation and also suggest freshwater conditions. There appears to be little change in the wider environment away from the ditch with occasional thistle, orache, and elder (*Sambucus nigra*).

Ditch F.365 upper cut/middle fill (context 366)

Only six species were recovered from the mid-blue/grey silty clay that comprised the middle fill of the upper cut, presumably due to poorer conditions of preservation. Little change can be seen, the ditch remaining water-filled with water crowfoot, duckweed, and bulrush.

Discussion

Assuming F.365 is typical, during the early Roman period the enclosure ditches on Dolemoor were well vegetated with predominantly freshwater species such as duckweed and water crowfoot forming a cover on the water's surface, with horned pondweed as a slender submerged aquatic and spiked water-milfoil suggestive of slow-moving or still water conditions. The ditch sides would also have been well vegetated with common reed, common clubrush, spike-rush and other sedges perhaps forming a fairly closed community varying in height from 1–3m. Whilst most of the taxa recovered suggest a freshwater ditch environment, some species recorded, notably common reed, horned pondweed and some species of duckweed and water crowfoot, can also tolerate brackish water conditions. The presence of two definite salt marsh plants, annual sea-blite and sea arrowgrass, although only present as a trace in 382 and 381, suggest either that salt marsh was somewhere not too far distant from the enclosure or that incursions of brackish water were bringing this material into the ditch system. The vegetation community away from the ditch sides appears to be one of mixed grassland supporting taxa of both damper areas and drier ground. Though preservation was poorer in the samples from the upper ditch cut, a similar freshwater environment is suggested by the species present.

The only evidence relating to the economy of the site came from the lower cut (context 382) of ditch F.365 and the fill of pit F.301. The pit fill contained a small charred assemblage with charcoal and cereal remains suggesting domestic activity at this time. The assemblage is fairly limited although it does show that crops of spelt wheat (confirmed by spelt glumes), barley, and rye were being utilised at the site. Oat grains were also present but identification of some wild oat pedicels suggests these occurred as crop weeds with the other arable weeds recovered. It is difficult to be sure if crop production would have been local from such small assemblages but the presence of grain as well as chaff, weed seeds and small silicified wheat awns suggests that this material may have come from the disposal of debris from hearths or ovens or spillage from crop cleaning, presumably in close vicinity to these features.

The presence of charred nutlets of club-rushes and sedges is interesting. Great fen-sedge (*Cladium mariscus*) is a tall stout sedge up to 2.5m tall, which often occurs in dense stands in fens and swamps. A variety of wetland plants including great fen-sedge and common club-rush (*Schoenopletus lacustris*) have been used in the past as thatching material or as fuel or kindling (Letts 2000) so it may have been deliberately collected for such purposes. Spelt wheat and common reed stems, both known to have been locally available, were also used as thatching materials.

Mollusca *by Paul Davies*

Dolemoor: the late Iron Age–earlier Romano-British saltern deposit 361

The saltern deposit 361 produced a low diversity assemblage with a dominant brackish water component (*Hydrobia ventrosa*); the very small freshwater assemblage is dominated by *Anisus leucostoma* which lives in ponds, ditches, and marshes that are prone to drying out and so would not be out of place on a raised mound within a salt marsh where localised areas of poor quality freshwater might accumulate. The terrestrial species (*Pupilla* and *Vallonia*) suggest adjacent open-country. This small assemblage is from a comparable estuarine environment to that at the nearby late Iron Age saltern at Banwell Moor (Rippon 2000b, 165).

Dolemoor: the earlier Romano-British ditched enclosure complex

The extensively sampled ditch F.365 failed to reveal any snails, although the upper dark horizon (373) within the lower cut of ditch F.311 which has the same broad sequence of fills as F.365 produced a low diversity freshwater aquatic assemblage, dominated by Limnaeidae with *Anisus* and *Gyraulus crista*. Together with the low numbers of Succineidae this would seem indicative of a sluggish, but perhaps reasonably vegetated, freshwater environment (the individual *Hydrobia ventrosa* comprises just 0.8% of the assemblage of 123 Mollusca). This freshwater assemblage provides an instructive contrast with the earlier saltern: clearly a significant change had occurred within the landscape that altered the environment from intertidal to freshwater. The low-diversity assemblage is dominated by *Anisus leucostoma, Gyraulus crista,* and *Lymnaea peregra,* and can be paralleled by elements within the late Romano-British reclaimed landscapes at Banwell Moor (eg ditch F.2, context 35) and Kenn Moor (eg ditch F.13, context 48; silted-up palaeochannel F.61, context 59) which appear to relate to the period very soon after reclamation had occurred (Rippon 2000b). Context 373 was relatively high up in F.311, suggesting that by the time that this ditch had substantially silted up it formed part of a landscape free from tidal waters and so was probably reclaimed. The wholly freshwater assemblage from the late Romano-British gully F.156 in Church Field (see below) may be contemporary.

Church Field: the late Romano-British gully F.156

The small gully F.156 (context 157) produced a small assemblage comprising 59 Succineidae and one *Cepaea hortensis / nemoralis*. The former are terrestrial marsh species that prefer damp, freshwater places alongside aquatic plants.

Reflections and discussion

One of the reasons why archaeological research is so exciting is that it occasionally throws up surprises. On previous sites that the NSLP investigated there was evidence for two very different approaches to wetland utilisation: the simple exploitation of natural resources (eg through salt production and the grazing of livestock) in the Iron Age–early Roman period and the transformation of the landscape through reclamation in the 3rd–4th centuries. When work began at Puxton the focus was very much the early medieval oval-shaped infield enclosure and later medieval shrunken settlement. An extensive relict landscape on the Dolemoor was *assumed* to be later Romano-British, as was the case at Banwell Moor and Kenn Moor. When the project began permission to carry out fieldwork on the Dolemoor was refused but following the area's acquisition by the Avon Wildlife Trust, a season of survey and excavation was carried out in order to confirm its date. What was revealed was far more interesting than yet another later Roman field system located in a reclaimed landscape free from tidal inundation. Following more evidence for late Iron Age–early Roman salt production, a ditched enclosure system was dug during the 1st–2nd centuries AD into the surface of what remained an intertidal marsh, with occupation on a slightly raised platform nearby. This was subsequently abandoned and as the ditches began to silt up there was a marked change in environment from brackish and intertidal to freshwater and reclaimed, reflected in the flora and fauna living within and beside these ditches, and by the formation of a soil (now only preserved where later earthworks have protected it from ploughing). The focus of settlement in this later Roman period now appears to have shifted west, probably somewhere to the south-east of Church Field. The uppermost stratigraphy within these Romano-British ditches at Puxton has been lost, but elsewhere (eg Puxton Home Ground and Banwell Moor) the alluvial sequence then shows a reversion to intertidal conditions. There was some erosion of the formerly reclaimed land surface that was then buried under more estuarine clays deposited on salt marshes and mudflats. The evidence from Puxton confirms a later 4th-century date for the abandonment of this landscape.

So this is the story from this particular site, but what of the questions it raises: what was happening elsewhere on the North Somerset Levels, and indeed the other marshlands fringing the Severn Estuary, and why did human communities change from simply exploiting the rich natural resources to first modifying and then transforming the landscape? As Chapter 5 will show, the answers can be found partly by examining the evidence from north-west Somerset as a whole and partly by looking even further afield, reflecting how the study of any one landscape can only be understood when it is placed in its wider context and how the study of individual landscapes can inform issues of far wider significance.

Note

1 Shaking Drove, Woolavington (ST 372 433 and ST 371 431), and Woolavington Bridge (ST 348 437).

5 The Romano-British landscape reconstructed and in context

The North Somerset Levels in the early Roman period: a landscape modified

North-west Somerset is an area rich in Romano-British archaeology (Fig 5.1), though making sense of this evidence is difficult as much of it comes from antiquarian or otherwise poorly reported finds. Few sites have produced well-dated assemblages and many recorded findspots are simply described as 'Romano-British'. What is emerging, however, is that conditions on the North Somerset Levels during the early and later Roman periods were very different.

The palaeoenvironmental material recovered from Banwell Moor, Kenn Moor, and Puxton Dolemoor suggests that in the late Iron Age and early Roman periods most of the Levels were intertidal salt marshes with more frequently flooded mudflats towards the coast, an infrequently flooded backfen around its southern and eastern margins, and a freshwater peat bog in its north-east corner (Kenn and Tickenham Moors: Fig 5.2).[1] The exact position of the Romano-British shoreline is unclear though analogy with the opposite side of the Estuary suggests that it may have lain around 0.8km further out into the Estuary (Allen and Rippon 1997a, 356; Allen 2002a), and indeed a scatter of later Romano-British pottery from the intertidal zone south-west of Kingston Pill lies 0.5km from the present sea wall (SMR 40550; Fig 5.1). Sand dunes are known to have existed at Weston-super-Mare (see Chapter 1) though analogy with Berrow in the main Somerset Levels, where the dunes have now surrounded the medieval church, suggests they are likely to have drifted inland during the late medieval period (Rippon 2000c, fig 3). These dunes would have impeded the natural drainage of what were relatively low-lying areas immediately to the east, whereas the rest of the Levels were traversed by a series of tidal rivers and streams flowing off the adjacent uplands and which presumably flowed to the coast along broadly similar lines to those in the early medieval period and which came to be fossilised in the historic landscape.

The surface of this intertidal marsh would have been drained by a network of creeks such as that preserved as an earthwork on Puxton Dolemoor (Fig 4.1), and recorded in section at Hardingworth and Home Ground (Fig 6.10). Aerial photography and the Environment Agency's LIDAR survey have revealed a complex network of palaeochannels in the low-lying backfens, below the 5m contour, that suggest that the Grumblepill Rhyne, Bourton Rhyne, the predecessor of the now canalised Banwell River, and possibly the Towerhead Brook, drained north-west to an estuary by St Thomas' Head, while the Sandmead, Churchill, and Crookwell Rhynes drained into a low-lying basin west of Congresbury village from which the water probably flowed into the Congresbury Yeo (Fig 5.2).

At Puxton Dolemoor the drainage of this landscape was improved through the construction of a ditched enclosure system from which the palaeoenvironmental evidence and lack of pottery from manure scatters points to a largely pastoral economy. Fragmentary traces of what may be a comparably early field system were also recorded at Kenn Moor on a different alignment to the later Romano-British enclosure complex, and though none of these early features produced any direct dating evidence a small number of residual later 1st- to early 2nd-century sherds was recovered from later contexts (earthworks in Field 6 and 7; F.13 in Trench C; F.159 in Trench J: Rippon 2000b, 82, 90, 95–6).

More evidence for the condition of the North Somerset Levels during the earlier Roman period has come from a series of recent evaluations, excavations, and watching briefs at West Wick and St Georges *c* 2.5km west of Puxton (Fig 5.3). Conditions in the field were difficult, and the opportunities for proper excavation and the careful cleaning of deep sections very limited, but what appears to be emerging is a very similar sequence to that at Banwell and Puxton, with two buried ground surfaces dating to the later Iron Age–early Roman and later Roman periods (Clarke 1998; Ducker 2002a; 2002b; Young 2002). At the Scott Elm Drive site (immediately east of Westacre Farm) a shallow pit, or the butt end of a ditch, containing Iron Age pottery, charcoal, heat-affected clay, and heavily burnt bone (Young 2002, 10) sounds very similar to F.281 in Trench 2 at Banwell Moor and F.397 at Puxton Dolemoor which were associated with the debris from salt production. At the West Wick bypass to the south of Westacre Farm no buried ground surface was observed but a linear gully and two shallow oval-shaped cut features were sealed by 0.3–0.9m of alluvium that was itself sealed by a dark grey silty clay at *c* 4.4–4.9m OD which is elsewhere dated to the later Roman period (see below; Ducker 2002a, 10–11). An initial assessment of the plant macrofossil assemblage showed it to be dominated by rush, with some freshwater species such as water crowfoot and water mint, alongside the salt marsh species sea club-rush (Hunter 2002, 5). The latter forms often dense stands in ill-drained brackish sites on coastal salt marshes and along creeks and is more typical of the upper marsh which is only affected by occasional inundation. The rushes and watercrowfoot could be either fresh or brackish but water mint is freshwater: such mixed communities occur at the level of the upper marsh where

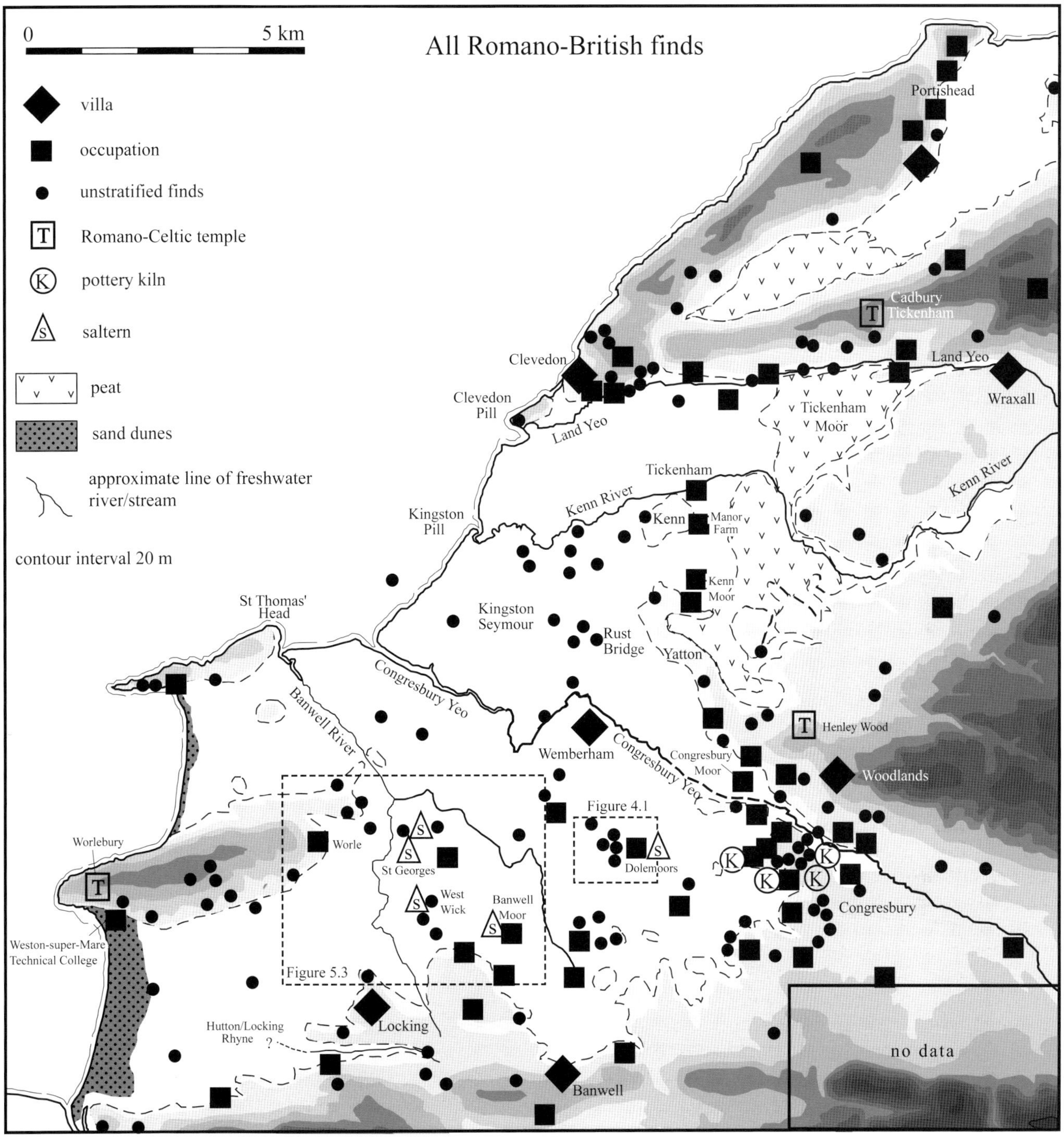

Figure 5.1 The Romano-British archaeology of north-west Somerset (based on the North Somerset SMR). For location see Figure 2.1

soils have low salinity levels and are perhaps only affected by Highest Astronomical Tides, but where there is some freshwater input too (Julie Jones pers comm). Lumps of peat from one of the oval-shaped features must have been cut elsewhere but may have been brought to the site as fuel (as was also seen at Banwell Moor in the late Iron Age: Rippon 2000b).

To the north of West Wick, at St Georges, there is extensive evidence for salt production of very similar character to Banwell Moor and Puxton (I must thank Simon Cox and Ed McSloy for allowing access to this unpublished material). At Rose Cottages, a spread of burnt clay in Trench 1 may relate to a saltern, though its absence in the remaining five trenches suggests that any activity was localised (Cullen and Cox 2004). The clearest evidence for late Iron Age–early Romano-British salt production comes from a series of evaluations, excavations, and watching briefs to the north (SMR 46412; Cox and Lankstead 2004). A series of late Iron Age and early Romano-British (1st-century BC–1st-century AD) ditches/gullies were recorded intermittently across a development site of *c* 35ha, associated with

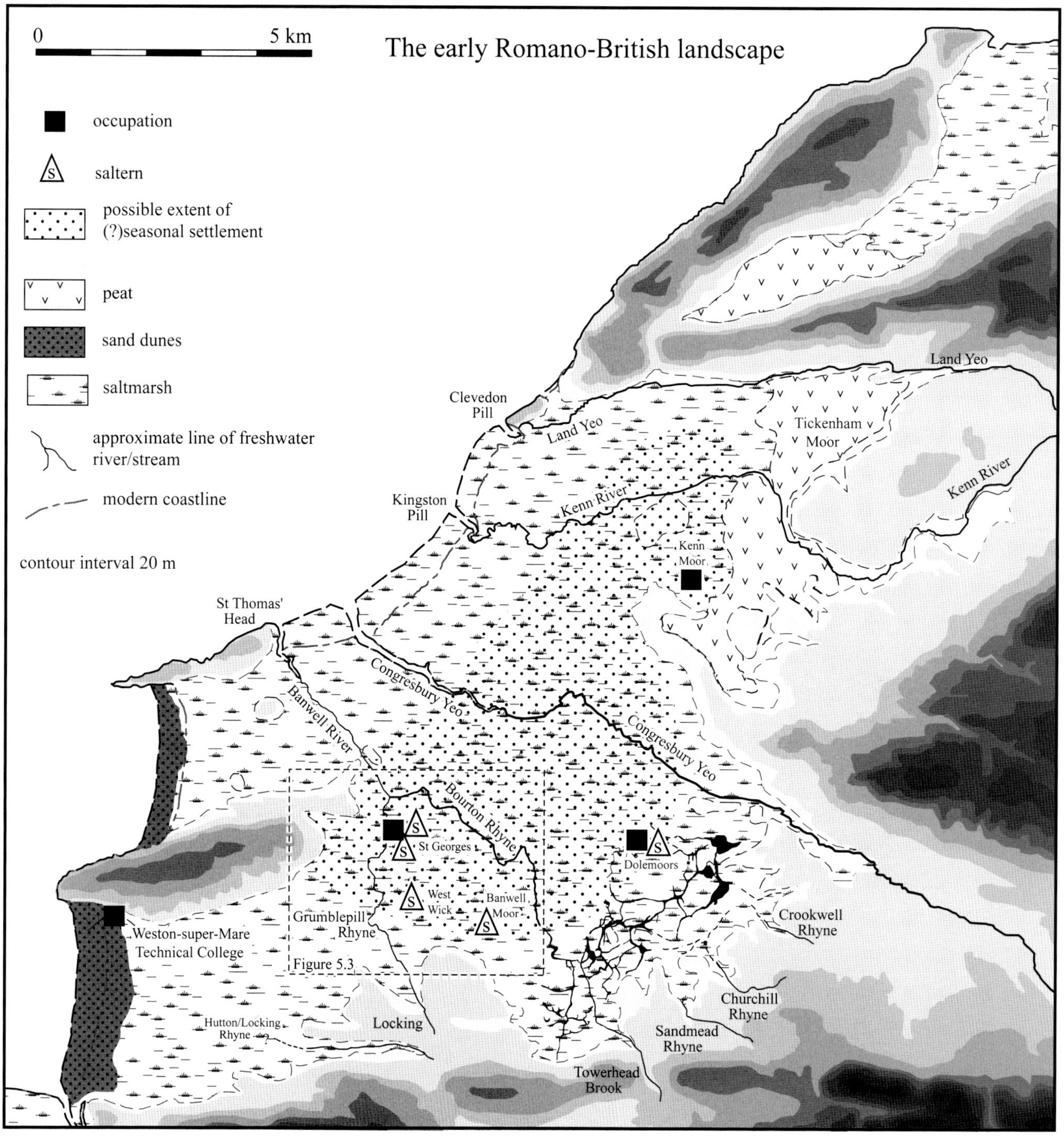

Figure 5.2 A possible reconstruction of the early Romano-British landscape of north-west Somerset showing known sites and the probable extent of settlement avoiding the most frequently flooded coastal zone, and poorly drained areas behind the sand dunes. Earthworks of an extensive relict creek system in the low-lying backfens in the south-east corner of the Levels probably dates to this period, but across the rest of the Levels is buried under later alluvium

a number of larger features that were probably tidal creeks. These features produced large amounts of saltern debris, notably large fragments of oven structures and substantial pedestals comparable in design, though larger, to those from Banwell Moor and Puxton. Pedestals with both circular and square cross-sections are present, with the shafts typically 130–60mm across, sometimes splaying at one end to 180mm. The surviving fragments are up to 400mm high, though one possible complete example was just 200mm high and with a concave depression that probably supported a rounded-bottomed evaporating vessel. As at Banwell Moor and Puxton there was no evidence for ceramic evaporating vessels, and metal detecting produced no evidence for the repairing of lead pans. Salt production ceased by the end of the 2nd century and there are hints that, as at Puxton Dolemoor, it may have been replaced by a field

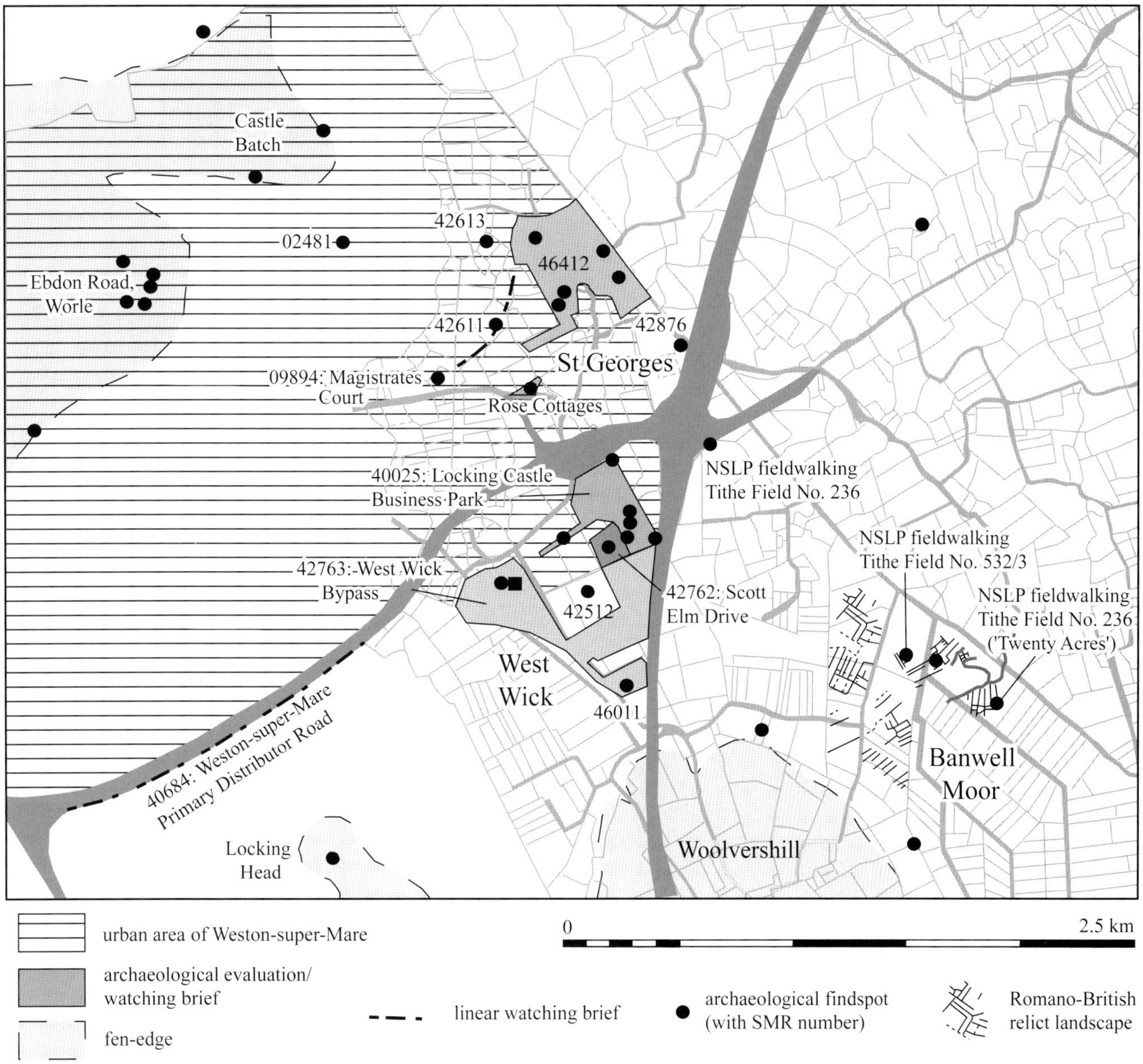

Figure 5.3 Recent PPG16-related work around West Wick and St Georges, and results of survey work carried out as part of the North Somerset Levels Project on Banwell Moor (based on the North Somerset SMR, and unpublished reports by the Avon Archaeological Unit and Cotswold Archaeology referred to in the text). For location see Figure 5.1

system as several ditches produced assemblages of 2nd-century pottery indicative of settlement in the vicinity. Ditch 307 at the Scott Elm Drive site also produced 33 sherds from a single vessel imitating south-east Dorset black-burnished ware, probably dating to the second half of the 2nd century.

These various known sites with early Romano-British occupation all occur some distance from the coast (Fig 5.2). This in part reflects the location of recent development-led archaeological investigations, and the fact that several of these inland locations were not sealed under later alluvium. Analogy with coastal wetlands both elsewhere around the Severn Estuary and beyond suggests that while the margins of the intertidal marsh and the largely freshwater backfens was a favoured location for settlement and salt production, the higher coastal marshes would also have been occupied (eg Silvester 1988; Hayes and Lane 1992; Lane 1993; Hall 1996).

Early Romano-British marshland landscapes elsewhere around the Severn Estuary

Although the survival as earthworks of an early Romano-British ditched enclosure system on Puxton Dolemoor may be unique around the Severn Estuary, recent developer-funded work has revealed a number of very similar landscapes buried under later alluvium. Much of the evidence is in unpublished reports, but cumulatively it suggests that during the early Roman period the Severn Estuary was fringed by unreclaimed intertidal marshes that were extensively modified through the digging of ditched field systems.

On the Avonmouth Level, north-west of Bristol (Fig 2.1), a series of 1st- to 2nd-century sites, including several ditched enclosure systems, have now been recorded and although palaeoenvironmental evidence is sparse sheep appear to dominate the small animal bone assemblages (Lawler *et al* 1992; McGill 2001b, 34, 49–55, 91–144; Young 1992). Sheep can be successfully grazed on salt marshes where they do not suffer from foot rot and liver fluke. At Northwick, parts of a late Iron Age–early Romano-British field system were excavated producing a strongly intertidal snail assemblage in its lower fill, with a mixed brackish and freshwater assemblage in the upper fills (a change in environment over time that possibly mirrors that seen at Puxton Dolemoor). Layers of sterile alluvium interleaved with domestic refuse suggest periodic inundation of the site. Very few plant remains were recovered, and no cereals were present (Barnes 1993; Gardiner *et al* 2002, 10–19). At Farm Lane, a 2nd-century ditch similarly produced brackish foraminifera and snail assemblages (Burchill *et al* 2001, 207; Masser *et al* 2005). On the Gwent Levels, a number of early Romano-British sites have been recorded suggesting fairly extensive settlement (Rippon 1996a, 32–5; 1997a, 101–3; Meddens 2001). Two sites, at Goldcliff (Locock and Walker 1998; Bell *et al* 2000, 9) and Nash Sewage Works (Meddens and Beasley 2001), have seen extensive excavation and palaeoenvironmental analysis revealing ditched enclosure systems used mainly for pasture in what was a very high intertidal salt marsh.

South of Mendip, in the central part of the Somerset Levels, the early Romano-British landscape was dominated by salt production (Leech 1981b). Just a single late Iron Age saltern has been recorded, at Badgworth, though a single late Iron Age sherd has been recovered from a site in Highbridge (Seagar Smith 2003). In the early Roman period production spread across the coastal marshes, with a further expansion of the industry towards the inland margins of the salt marshes in the 3rd–4th centuries (Leech 1977; 1981b Rippon 1995a; 1997a; Grove and Brunning 1998; Hollinrake and Hollinrake 2003; Seagar Smith 2003). Most of the pottery assemblages are dominated by utilitarian coarseware jars with a restricted range of fabrics, and are suggestive of temporary, perhaps seasonal, industrial activity though a number of sites may have seen domestic occupation.

Overall, it appears that the intertidal marshes on both sides of the Severn Estuary were extensively settled in the 1st–2nd centuries AD, with occupation starting in the late Iron Age and increasing in intensity during the earlier Roman period. Salt production was restricted to the Brue Valley and Brent Marsh in Somerset, though elsewhere largely pastoral settlements exploited and improved the rich marshland grazing. Palaeoeconomic evidence is scarce, though sheep appear to have dominated the livestock husbandry on the English side of the Estuary, and cattle on Caldicot Level (a difference which may be due to Roman military dietary preferences, as this area may have been exploited by the nearby military garrison at Caerleon). There is little evidence for the cultivation of cereals on these unreclaimed marshes.

The North Somerset Levels during the later Roman period: a landscape transformed

There has been some discussion over the character of the Severn Estuary Levels in the later Roman period, and this was a specific focus of the NSLP, with the results published in an earlier report (Rippon 2000b). In a recent paper Andrew Marvell (2004, 101) states that 'There is no empirical evidence for the construction of sea defences on the Severn Levels', though this is then contradicted by his own statement that 'some areas, such as that between the Rivers Axe and Siger, were reclaimed'. The reasons why Marvell sometimes seems determined to refute the very clear evidence for reclamation is unclear, but the publication of his paper makes it necessary to reiterate the key evidence that has either not been understood, or has been selectively ignored (notably the most comprehensive recent review of the evidence in Rippon 2000a). On the North Somerset Levels the crucial evidence was published in the journal *Britannia* (Rippon 2000b), and in denying that reclamation had taken place Marvell makes no attempt to address the evidence presented in this paper, notably, how a palatial Roman villa such as Wemberham, complete with its mosaic pavements and underfloor heating, could have been built on an intertidal salt marsh. He similarly ignores the wide range of palaeoenvironmental indicators (beetles, diatoms, Mollusca, plant macrofossils, and pollen) at Banwell Moor, Kenn Moor, and Puxton, which all point to a wholly freshwater environment during the mid-3rd–mid-4th centuries, and the buried soil at Banwell Moor that cannot have formed in a landscape that was subject to tidal inundation.

The more recent work at Puxton Dolemoor confirms that there was a very marked change in environment around the 3rd century AD, reflected in the shift from intertidal to wholly freshwater conditions in ditch F.365. This change in environment on the North Somerset Levels is all the more significant as on the opposite side of the Estuary intertidal conditions continued to prevail in the ditched enclosure system at Nash Sewage Works on the Caldicot Level (Meddens and Beasley 2001). The continued intertidal conditions here, just across the Estuary from the North Somerset Levels, rules out the possibility that the changes in environment seen at Banwell Moor, Kenn Moor, and Puxton were the result of a natural fall in

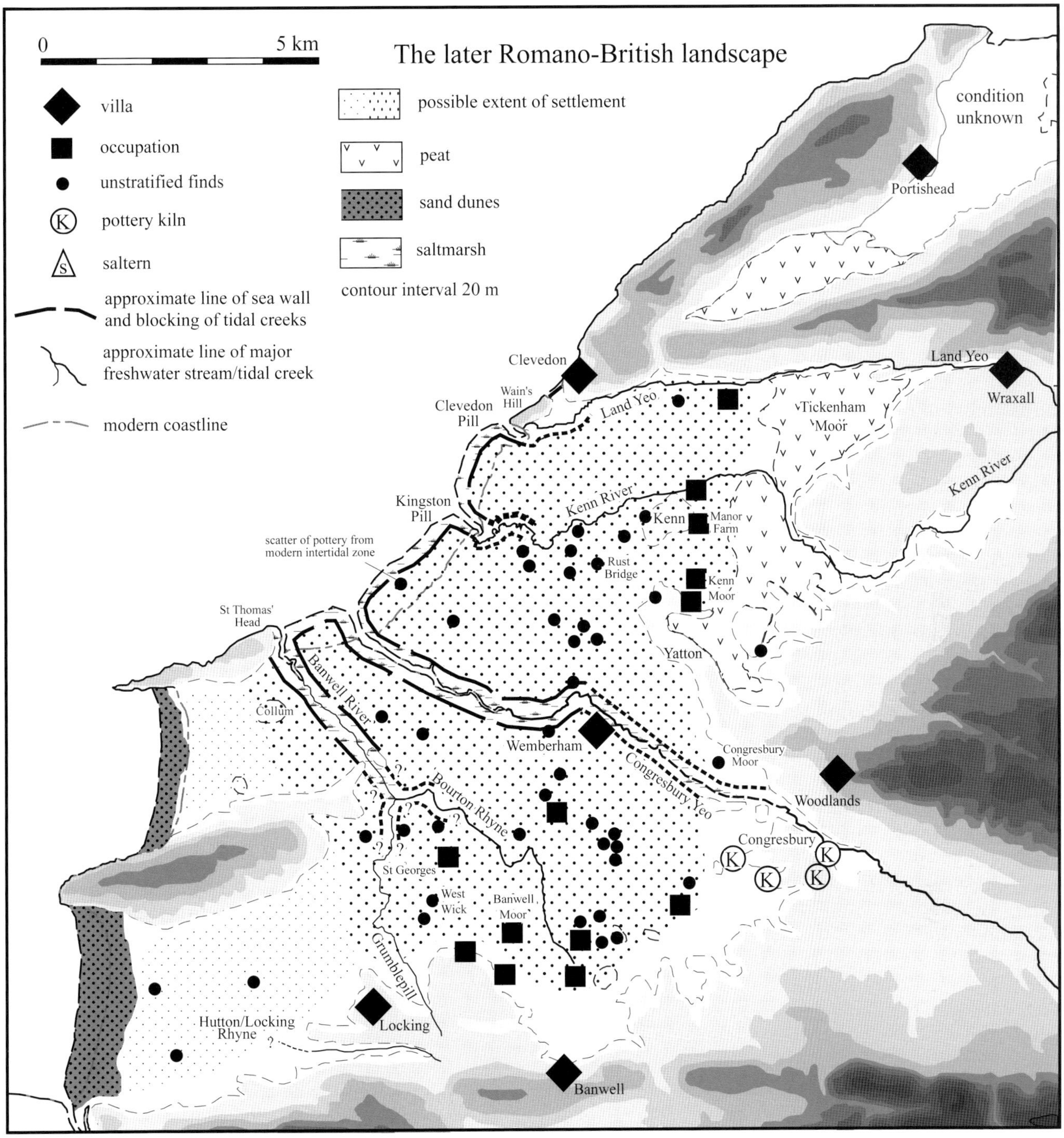

Figure 5.4 A possible reconstruction of the later Romano-British landscape of north-west Somerset. The exact location of the sea walls is unknown

relative sea levels. Admittedly no sea walls dating to the Roman period have been found on the North Somerset Levels and it is highly unlikely that they will, having been either buried under later alluvium (that towards to the coast is *c* 0.7m deep), or lost to later erosion (which on the Welsh side of the Estuary amounts to *c* 0.8km lost since the Roman period), but this dramatic change in environment including soil development, and the construction of at least one palatial villa, can only have occurred through these marshes having been protected from tidal inundation.

The date of reclamation

The small assemblage of material from the pre-reclamation enclosure complex at Puxton Dolemoor dates to the later 1st to 2nd centuries AD (see Timby, Chapter 4), while the pottery and coins from Banwell Moor, Kenn Moor (Rippon 2000b), and Puxton Church Field (see Timby, and Trevarthen, Chapter 4) suggest a date in the second half of the 3rd century for the creation of the ditched enclosure complexes there. The fieldwalking assemblage from another enclosure complex on Banwell Moor Twenty

Acres is similarly 3rd- to 4th-century in date (see Timby, Chapter 4). Taken alongside the construction of the villa at Wemberham in the later 3rd century, it appears that the North Somerset Levels were embanked around the mid-3rd century.

The buried land surface

Across most of the Levels the Romano-British landscape is buried under later alluvium, and at Puxton and Banwell Moor it is marked by a buried soil that micromorphology and palaeoenvironmental analysis has shown formed under flood-free and freshwater (ie reclaimed) conditions (see Chapter 4; and Rippon 2000b). This same horizon appears across most of the Levels. Just to the west of Kenn Moor, at Rust Bridge, the description of a ditched enclosure system and associated buried soil *c* 0.5m below the present ground surface, and a similar buried land surface at Broome Manor Nursery in Tickenham, bear a marked resemblance to that at Banwell Moor, though the few Romano-British sherds that were recovered are not diagnostic as being early or late (Hume 1993; Smith 1993).

The development-led evaluations and watching briefs at West Wick and St Georges have also revealed an extensive buried ground surface possibly dating to the later Roman period. Fairly consistently across these sites, a dark horizon has been recorded *c* 0.7–1.0m below the present ground surface (*c* 4.4–4.9m OD; Clarke 1998; Ducker 2002a, 2002b; Young 2002). In trenches to the east of Westacre Farm this 0.05–0.10m thick horizon comprised a dark grey, organic-rich silty clay, which in places was associated with flecks of charcoal and fragments of animal bone, burnt clay, and Romano-British pottery including mid-3rd- to 4th-century sherds (Clarke 1998, 6–9; Young 2002, 12). In trenches on the West Wick Bypass site this buried land surface is associated with features including a V-shaped gully (0.7m deep) and a series of parallel ditches (1.6 to 3.0m wide) spaced *c* 10–20m apart that are associated with a dark horizon (Ducker 2002a, 10). Assessment of the plant macrofossils from one of the ditches (F.307) revealed a freshwater assemblage and occasional grains of charred barley and wheat, while the lower fill of gully F.114 produced a similarly freshwater assemblage, with sea club-rush in its upper fill suggesting some brackish influence after it had largely silted up (Hunter 2002, 5–7), a sequence also seen at Banwell Moor. Further to the west, a large number of U-shaped ditches, *c* 1–3m wide and *c* 0.8–1.2m deep, were recorded on Locking Moor during the construction of the Weston-super-Mare Primary Distributor Road. No buried land surface was recognised though the ditches once again appear to have been cut from 0.3 to 0.5m below the present ground surface (*c* 4.6–4.7m OD). The only artefact was a single sherd of Romano-British grey ware from ditch 8100 (Smith and Young 1995).

These ditches and gullies at Westacre Farm and on Locking Moor are mostly aligned NW–SE. This is similar to the general orientation of the historic landscape, which raises the question of whether the buried features could also be medieval in date. Closer examination of where buried ditches lie close to elements of the historic landscape, however, reveals that their orientations are in fact subtly different. There is also little context for the 0.3–1.0m of overlying alluvium deposited in the medieval/post-medieval period, and a later Roman date for the whole system appears most likely. The similarity in alignment between the buried and historic landscapes is probably due to both systems of ditches having been laid out perpendicular to the fen-edge, and if these buried ditches do indeed represent one drainage system extending for some 2.5km to the west of West Wick, then this is far more extensive than the relict landscapes at Banwell Moor and Kenn Moor.

A similar buried ground surface was also observed to the north of West Wick at the Magistrates' Courts site west of St Georges (Burchill 2000), and further work to the north has also revealed a buried soil at between 4.2 and 5.0m OD (Jordan 2002; Cox and Lankstead 2004). An assemblage of 3rd- to 4th-century pottery and a fragment of possible imbrex tile from a large shallow depression at Grapevine Farm, along with some residual 2nd- to 4th-century pottery from Grove Farm, point to a late Roman settlement in the area (Lankstead 2003; CAT 2002a). A large assemblage of 3rd- to 4th-century pottery has also been recovered from *c* 300m to the south-west of Grove Farm, reportedly associated with a large amount of building stone (North Somerset Museum Acc. No. WESTM: 2002.90; SMR 42876). The composition of the assemblage was very similar to those from Banwell Moor and Kenn Moor, being dominated by coarsewares, notably BB1 and Congresbury ware with just 1% fineware.

Unfortunately relatively little palaeoenvironmental work has been carried out on the features associated with this buried soil, though eight of the undated ditches on Locking Moor were sampled, and both the plant macrofossil and snail assemblages point to a wholly freshwater environment (Jones 1995). Aquatics such as duckweed (*Lemna* sp), pondweed (*Potamogeton* sp), water-milfoil (*Myriophyllum* sp), hornwort (*Ceratophyllum* sp), and water crowfoot (*Ranunculus* subg *Batrachium*) would have formed a carpet on the surface of the water, while water plantain (*Alisma* sp), greater spearwort (*Ranunculus lingua*), reedmace (*Typha* sp), spike-rush (*Eleocharis palustris*/*uniglumis*), sedges (*Carex*), and rushes (*Juncus*) grew at the water's edge. The Mollusca include Lymnaeidae (pond snails) and Planorbidae (ram's horn snails), both of which prefer slow or standing weedy water.

The sea defences

Analogy with the Welsh side of the Severn Estuary suggests that the Romano-British coastline has

Figure 5.5 The bridge over Grange Pill in the high salt marshes of Woolaston, Gloucestershire, which may have had its origins as a dam and sluice analogous to those used in the Roman period on reclaimed marshlands such as the North Somerset Levels

been lost to later erosion, and the intertidal scatter of 3rd- to 4th-century pottery in Kingston Bay (see above) suggests that it probably lay at least 0.8km beyond today's sea wall. While parts of the coast were protected by natural sand dunes, stretching from St Thomas' Head on Middlehope to Wains Hill at Clevedon, parts must have been protected by embankments. An estimate can be made of the scale of these sea walls. The present MHWST at Kingston Seymour is *c* 6.1m OD, with the Highest Astronomical Tide *c* 7.5m OD. Heyworth and Kidson's (1982) sea level curve for the Severn Estuary/Bristol Channel region stops short of the Roman period, though extrapolation suggests that relative sea level at the start of the 1st millennium AD was around 3m below that of today. This figure is, however, too high as it is based on radiocarbon dated peat sequences and fails to take into account the fact that they will have been compressed by overlying sediments (Haslett *et al* 1998). Allen (1991) has calculated that there has been *c* 1.3m of salt marsh accretion in the Inner Severn Estuary since the Roman period (Allen 1997a, 20), and if the scale of sea level rise at Kingston Seymour was of the same order then MHWST in the Roman period was *c* 4.8m OD (the present MHWST of 6.1m minus 1.3m), and Highest Astronomical Tide of *c* 6.2m OD (7.5m minus 1.3m).

So would these Romano-British high tides have flooded the Levels? The height to which the intertidal salt marshes had accreted on the eve of reclamation will have varied, with the higher ground near the coast falling away to lower-lying areas to the south and east (as these areas were flooded less often and by waters carrying less sediment). In Kingston Seymour the buried Romano-British ground surface has been recorded at 5.4m OD by Broadstone Rhyne 0.9km from the present coast (Usher 1967), and 5.3m OD at Rust Bridge and Phipps Bridge 3km from the present coastline (Lilly and Usher 1972, Nos 9 and 10). This suggests that the coastal salt marshes of the North Somerset Levels had probably accreted to a height whereby they were flooded only at the very highest tides, and so any embankments along the coast could have been of a relatively modest scale compared to the massive flood defences of today. However, tidal waters would still have flowed up the creeks and rivers and at Banwell Moor, West Wick, and Puxton, some 5km from the coast, the buried Romano-British ground surface was at *c* 4.8–5.0, *c* 4.6–4.7, and *c* 4.2–4.5m OD respectively, well below the contemporary MHWST.

So how were these tidal creeks dealt with in the later Roman period? One way of preventing tidal

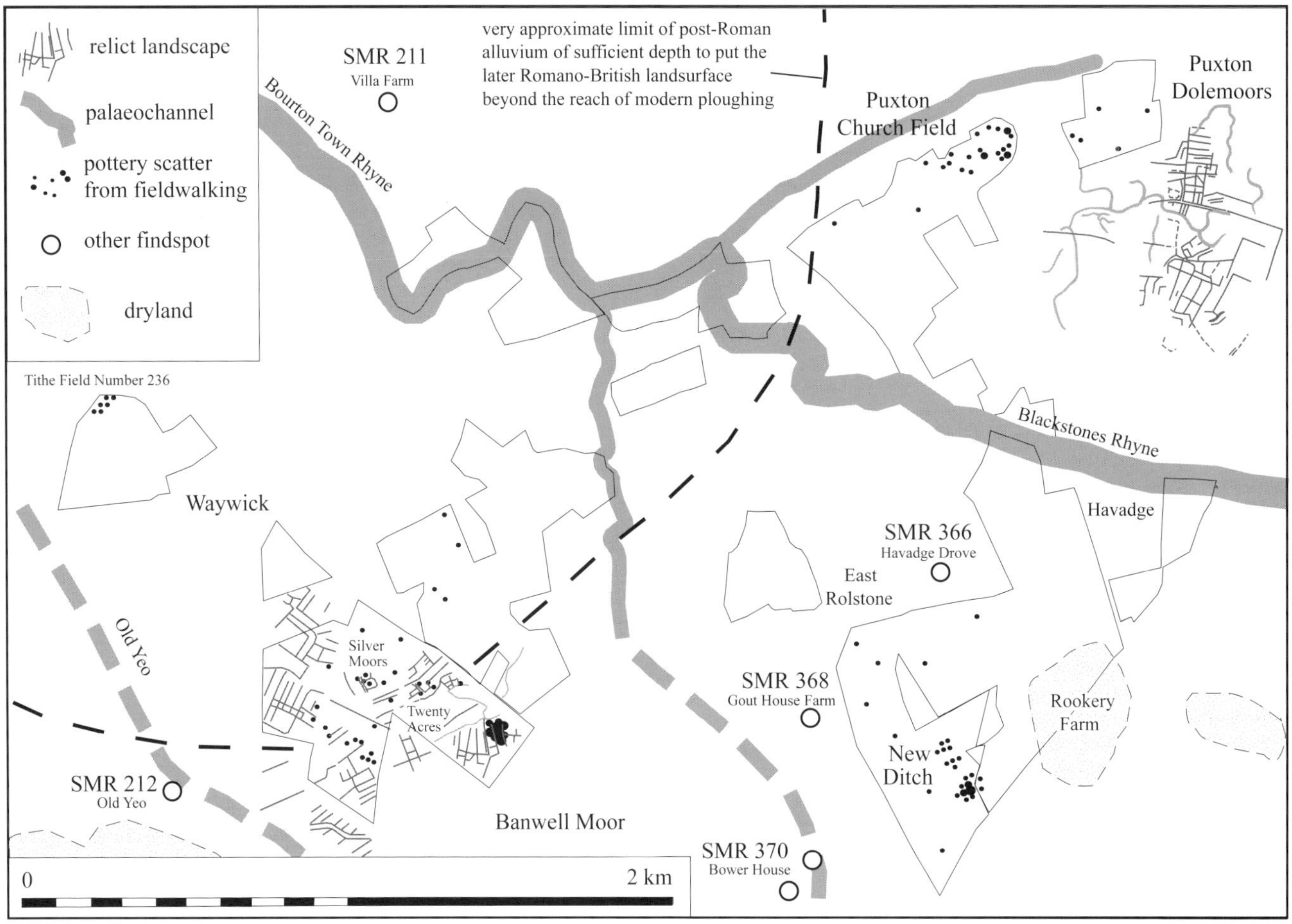

Figure 5.6 Romano-British material from the fieldwalking survey around Puxton, Rolstone, Banwell Moor and Waywick. Note that the scarcity of material from the northern and western areas may be due to the greater depth of post-Roman alluvium. The results from Puxton and Havadge, where the Roman landscape is within reach of modern ploughing, suggests that areas of around half a kilometre around each settlement was manured, with areas of pasture in between

flooding was for the sea walls to turn inland and run alongside the major tidal rivers, as was the case with the Congresbury Yeo until the post-medieval period (Fig 6.7). What is less clear is what happened to the minor streams that crossed the Levels: they too could have been embanked, or they may have been blocked by dams with the freshwater water discharge flowing through a sluice structure. This technology is known to have existed on the Continent during the Roman period, with water carried beneath timber-revetted earthen dams through hollowed out tree trunks with carefully crafted flap-valves at their mouths (Rippon 2000a). A possible post-medieval analogy survives at Grange Pill, Woolaston, on the western bank of the Severn Estuary in Gloucestershire (Figs 1.1 and 5.5). At first sight this structure appears to be simply a bridge across this creek, but it lies in what remains a very high intertidal salt marsh that still floods during high spring tides. The freshwater stream now flows through a narrow arched tunnel under the structure, though a simple sluice/valve here would prevent sea water from flowing up the channel.

Settlement, field systems, and land use

This act of reclamation resulted in a substantial area of land becoming free from tidal inundation and later Romano-British settlement on the North Somerset Levels appears to have been widespread, with most of the dated unstratified assemblages collected by local amateur archaeologists containing 3rd- to 4th-century material (Fig 5.1; WESTM: 1989.245–343, 459; Usher 1967; Timby 2000, 181). The extent to which even the lower-lying areas of the Levels were occupied in the Roman period is also seen on Congresbury Moor where a scatter of pottery, bone, coins, vessel glass, and charcoal was associated with a spread of stone rubble (Broomhead 1999, 8). The predominance of Congresbury ware and black-burnished ware (Category 2) suggests a late Roman date (3rd–4th century).

Only where the Romano-British landscape lay beyond the later flooding, and has survived as earthworks, do we know what it looked like (Fig 5.6). At both Banwell Moor and Kenn Moor the later Romano-British landscape consisted of loose clusters of farmsteads (what in the medieval period might be termed a hamlet), comprising slightly raised platforms and small paddocks/enclosures, set amongst larger fields through which passed narrow trackways (eg Rippon 2000b, figs 3–4, 8). The density of settlement is difficult to determine due to the limited extent of fieldwalking in those areas that are not sealed by later alluvium, though an analysis of the relict landscape on Banwell Moor identified six possible settlement-related enclosure complexes within an area *c*750 by 750m (0.56km2), of which upon excavation one (Silver Moors) lacked large amounts of domestic occupation, but a second (enclosure V) was confirmed as a settlement (Rippon 2000b, fig 3); fieldwalking has now produced sufficient material from site VI to suggest that it too was occupied. In nearby East Rolstone three sites are known through earlier finds (at Bower House, Gout House Farm, and Havadge Drove), while a fourth was located through fieldwalking at New Ditch, giving four sites within 1km^2. At West Wick and St Georges there are similarly at least four sites per square kilometre. This density of settlement cannot, however, be simply extrapolated across the whole of the Levels, as fieldwalking in East Rolstone also revealed areas that were devoid of settlement (eg Havadge): as there also appears to have been almost no manuring of these areas, they were presumably permanent pasture. The combination of earthwork and fieldwalking evidence at Kenn Moor similarly suggests a discrete zonation of land use, with an area up to *c* 350m around the settlements being divided into large fields and manured, with unmanured areas beyond. Palaeoenvironmental evidence from both Banwell Moor and Kenn Moor suggests that land use included arable cultivation, hay meadows, and rough pasture (Rippon 2000b, 104–5). At Banwell Moor, cattle and sheep were present in equal numbers in a small assemblage, while at Kenn Moor cattle were clearly dominant. The growing of hay also points to a significant pastoral dimension to the economy. The arable crops were predominantly wheat (largely spelt, but also emmer and bread wheat), alongside two- and six-row hulled barley, oats, and horse/celtic beans.

Communications

The relict landscape at Banwell Moor contains short stretches of trackways through the enclosure complexes, though there is no evidence for major Roman roads or tracks crossing the intervening areas. In fact, very few substantial Roman roads have been identified in north-west Somerset (Fig 5.7), though there is clear evidence for the use of rivers. In 1974 timbers of a boat were recovered from a depth of 18ft (5.5m) from close to the Banwell River, immediately to the east of Collum Farm, one of which was radiocarbon dated to 350±90 AD (Clarke 1979; no laboratory number was published).

The products of the Congresbury ware pottery industry may also have been transported by water (ie via the Congresbury Yeo: Fig 5.4). A number of mid-3rd- to 4th-century kiln sites producing coarse cooking and storage vessels and some poor quality tableware have been recorded around Congresbury village and although only a short published note has appeared on the excavations (Usher and Lilly 1964), fabric series have been published for the assemblages from Henley Wood (Watts and Leach 1996, 98–9) and Kenn Moor (Timby 2000). North of Mendip, Congresbury ware was abundant at Henley Wood (62% of the pottery assemblage: Watts and Leach 1996), and was used at Brean Down (ApSimon 1965), Butcombe (Fowler 1968), Chew Valley (15%, Rahtz and Greenfield 1977), Gatcombe (32%, Branigan 1977), Havyatt (Neale 1970), Pagan's Hill (Rahtz and Watts 1989), and Star (Barton 1964). There has been no proper study of the wider dispersal of Congresbury ware, though it certainly reached south of Mendip, forming 95% of the assemblage at Lympsham (Broomhead 1991) and 26% at Rooksbridge in East Brent (Russett 1989). It was also present in smaller amounts at Cheddar (Rahtz 1979), York Farm in Edingworth (Rippon 1995a), Cannington (Rahtz *et al* 2000, 293), and Crandon Bridge (Timby, forthcoming). The significance of riverine and coastal transport in the trading of Congresbury ware is also seen at Hinkley Point on the coast of west Somerset where it comprised 45% of the assemblage (Cox and Broomhead 1993). It does not appear to have reached (or have been recognised in assemblages from) the small towns and adjacent settlements at Bath (Cunliffe 1979), Ilchester (Leach 1982; Leech 1981a; 1982b), Shepton Mallet (Leach 2001a), and Sea Mills (Bennett 1985) to the north and east of Congresbury.

Later Romano-British wetlands elsewhere around the Severn Estuary

It appears that there was widespread reclamation on the eastern side of the Severn Estuary during the later Roman period. The marshes north of the now silted-up river Siger in central Somerset must have been embanked, allowing the formation of a probable buried soil and the construction of a villa at Lakehouse Farm, alongside other substantial mid-3rd- to mid-4th-century stone buildings at Rooksbridge and Burton Row Rhyne (Fig 5.7; Russett 1989; Broomhead 1991; Rippon 1995a; 1997a). On the Avonmouth Levels also there is now growing evidence for reclamation in the later Roman period. The earlier Romano-British sites all appear to have been abandoned by the late 2nd–early 3rd centuries apart from possibly Farm Lane where several mid-3rd- to mid-4th-century ditches are on the same orientation as a series of 1st- to 2nd-century boundaries (McGill 2001a, 87–114). The diatoms, foraminifera, plant macrofossils, ostracods, and snails suggest an essentially freshwater environment that was subject to occasional tidal inundation.

Cereals were present, with wheat dominating and some barley and oats, associated with typical arable and freshwater grassland weeds (Burchill *et al* 2001, 199, 201, 207; Masser *et al* 2005). The presence of crop-processing waste suggests there was local cultivation, and as wheat will not grow on a salt marsh this supports the other palaeoenvironmental indicators in suggesting an embanked landscape largely free from tidal inundation. A further mid-3rd- to mid-4th-century field system has been recorded at Crooks Marsh where various ditches have yielded wholly freshwater plant macrofossil and snail assemblages, though diatoms, foraminifera, and ostracods suggest occasional influxes of tidal waters; the ditches lay within a largely grassland environment with some arable cultivation suggested by the presence of crop-processing waste (Everton and Everton 1980; Juggins 1982; Allen and Fulford 1986, note 83; Burchill *et al* 2001, 202, 207, 210; Gardiner *et al* 2002, 26; McGill 2001b, 186–210; Masser *et al* 2005). As at Kenn Moor, the animal bone assemblage is dominated by cattle, while cereal pollen, crop-processing debris, and associated weeds indicative of heavy clay soils suggest local cultivation. The fen-edge of the Avonmouth Levels was once again a focus for settlement, including the villa at Kingsweston built in the late 3rd century (Boon 1950).

Further up the Estuary, on the eastern side, surface scatters and intertidal exposures of Romano-British pottery suggest that smaller areas of marshland were also extensively settled. As the Roman ground surface appears be within reach of the plough, these areas may have been protected from flooding since the later Roman period (Allen 1997b; Allen and Fulford 1987; 1990a; 1990b; 1992). Whilst some of the sites have yielded some late Iron Age–early Romano-British pottery, the bulk of the assemblages are later Romano-British (mid-3rd- to mid-4th-century). Just one site, immediately south of the nuclear power station at Oldbury, has seen more intensive fieldwork (Allen and Fulford 1992; Allen and Rippon 1997b; Hume 1992). The occupation here was long-lived, with the earlier (1st- to 2nd-century) settlement restricted to the banks of a palaeochannel, and the 3rd–4th centuries seeing a three-fold increase in the area of occupation. Little palaeoenvironmental analysis has been carried out to determine whether or when reclamation had occurred, though a plant macrofossil assemblage contained some cereals and chaff, with wheat dominating alongside some barley, oats, and vetches; the associated weeds indicate cultivation of damp soils. If this cultivation was in the vicinity of the site then this must have been a reclaimed landscape as wheat will not tolerate saline conditions. Fragments of comb-decorated box-flue tile, tegula roof tile, a bath stone ornamental roof fitting, and a stone shaft (probably a column from a colonnade) suggest that the later 3rd- to 4th-century settlement included a building of considerable status.

On the Welsh side of the Estuary these settlement-indicative scatters of material are absent from the upper/middle Estuary, though the Gwent Levels, adjacent to the outer Estuary, clearly saw extensive settlement. It has been suggested that the Wentlooge Level was reclaimed in the Roman period (Allen and Fulford 1986; Fulford *et al* 1994; Rippon 1996a, 25–32), although this is disputed by Marvell (2004) on the basis that there is no archaeological, literary, or epigraphic evidence for a Roman sea wall between Cardiff and Caldicot. The absence of a sea wall should not, in fact, be surprising as the Romano-British coastline has been lost to later erosion, and it is difficult to know what literary evidence we should expect from Roman Britain for such a structure. There is little or no epigraphic evidence for the vast majority of the rural landscape in Britain. In Fenland, for example, a series of well-dated canals were dug during the Roman period – major feats of engineering on a comparable scale to the construction of a sea wall – yet no epigraphic evidence survives (Crowson *et al* 2000). Marvell also disputes the evidence from the excavated settlement at Rumney Great Wharf where a Romano-British settlement and ditched enclosure system was associated with a freshwater environment comprising 'damp rich pasture which although showing maritime influences, was not full salt marsh', the maritime influences being seeds of *Juncus gerardi* which 'could have been derived from more distant salt-marshes, either windblown or brought in as fodder, or [having] persisted following the reclamation of the land' (Robinson 1994, 203–4). Marvell also suggests that pottery from the ditches was residual even though the published report clearly comments on 'the excellent condition of the sherds which included the preservation of carbonised material beneath the rim of the BB1 jars, as well as the presence of external sooting of these vessels'. The average sherd weight of 14.2g and very large sherd size (including one complete vessel!) is also hardly indicative of a residual assemblage (Fulford *et al* 1994, 190, table 3, fig. 8), which Marvell would have appreciated if he had actually examined the material in the National Museum of Wales. This is not the place for a blow-by-blow critique of what is a consistently flawed paper, that overlooks or misinterprets published data and other material in the public domain, but suffice to say that until new evidence is forthcoming a Roman date is still most plausible for the Wentlooge field system. Marvell's erroneous inferences are too many to correct here, but it should be observed that Rippon (1996a or any other reference) has never claimed that the regularly planned landscape around Peterstone 'provides an example of what the whole of the Gwent Levels would have looked like in Roman times' (Marvell 2004, 94). Indeed, in *The Transformation of Coastal Wetlands* (Rippon 2000a, 56), a source that Marvell rather curiously appears to have overlooked, it is suggested that 'a number of banks and ditches recently recorded at Goldcliff do *not* appear to form a coherent rectilinear plan as is the case on Wentlooge, suggesting a less systematic and more localised approach to drainage' [italics added].

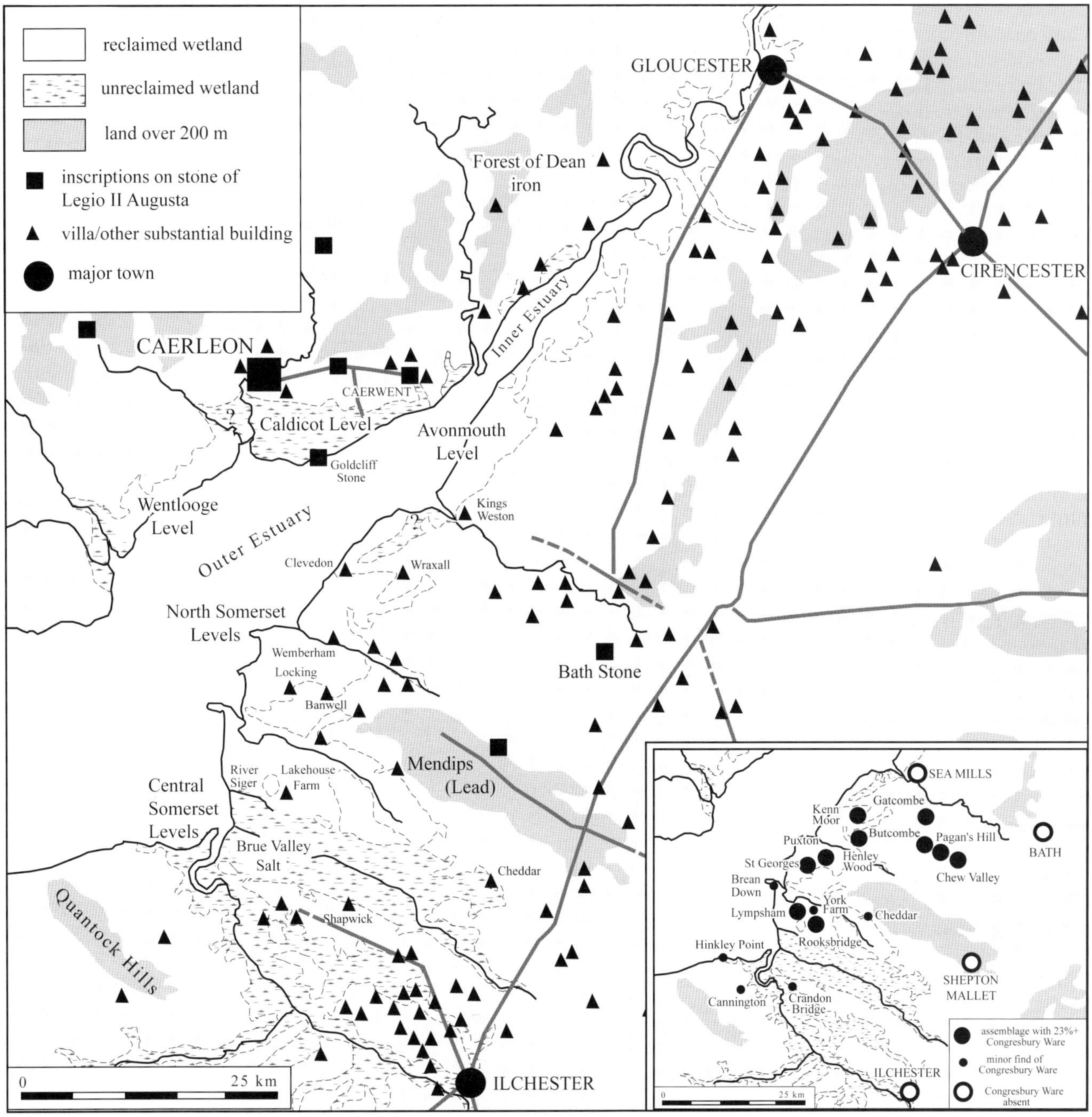

Figure 5.7 The context of later Romano-British reclamation (with distribution of Congresbury ware inset). The distribution of villas and other substantial buildings based on information in the Historic Environment Records of Gloucestershire, South Gloucestershire, Bristol, Bath and north-east Somerset, north Somerset, Somerset, and Wiltshire (collected by Chris Webster as part of the English Heritage-sponsored South-West Archaeological Research Framework)

This evidence from the Caldicot Level reveals that the early Romano-British approach of modifying a wetland environment seen at Puxton Dolemoor, whereby the drainage of a high intertidal marsh is improved through the digging of an enclosure system, continued into the later Roman period. On the English side of the Estuary, in contrast, the majority of wetlands do appear to have seen even more intensive activity and ultimately their transformation into a freshwater environment with the exception of one area, the Brue Valley to the south of the now silted up river Siger in the central Somerset Levels, that was left in its natural, intertidal state and was used for salt production (Leech 1981b; Rippon 1997a, 65–72; Grove and Brunning 1998). Overall, therefore, the mid-3rd century saw most of the marshlands on the eastern side of the Severn Estuary being transformed through reclamation. Where palaeoenvironmental evidence is forthcoming this clearly shows that these settlements and field systems existed in a freshwater environment that can only have existed if there was protection from tidal inundation. The scale of these defences, however, would have been much smaller than those of today as sea levels were far lower in the Roman period, and fairly modest embankments alongside the coast and major rivers, and dam/sluice structures across the minor creeks, would have protected this landscape from the majority of tidal flooding. These reclaimed wetlands supported quite a high density of settlements that were clearly engaged in both arable cultivation and animal husbandry, with cattle dominating. Only the Brue Valley in Somerset, along with the Caldicot Level on the Welsh side of the Estuary, appear to have been left as intertidal marshes, and exploited for their rich natural resources.

A landscape in context: who reclaimed the North Somerset Levels?

The desire to increase agricultural productivity presumably explains *why* these marshes were reclaimed, and we know *when* this occurred (around the mid-3rd century); the remaining question is *who* was responsible. This important issue was addressed in just one paragraph when the sites at Banwell Moor and Kenn Moor were published (Rippon 2000b, 194–5, a classic example of dodging an admittedly difficult issue), and so a fuller discussion is now attempted. Two obvious contexts for reclamation present themselves:

- that it was the work of the army, perhaps based just across the Severn Estuary at Caerleon, or in the context of a putative imperial estate possibly based near Bath.
- that it was the work of either a single entrepreneur who built the villa at Wemberham, or that it was a collaborative venture by various local villa owners.

A military context?

The role of the Roman army in exploiting landscape resources in the south-west of Britain has been the subject of a number of recent research projects. An extensive area of intertidal marshland (the Caldicot and Wentlooge Levels) lay within the hinterland of the legionary fortress at Caerleon (Fig 5.7), much of which presumably lay within the *prata legionis* (the area of land falling under the direct control of a legionary fortress: Mason 1988). The boundary of this territory is unknown, though to the east it must have lain somewhere between Caerleon and the *civitas* capital of Caerwent, 11km to the east. One logical boundary is the natural predecessor of the now canalised Monks Ditch Stream, the most substantial natural watercourse between Caerleon and Caerwent. Monks Ditch flows into Goldcliff Pill adjacent to which the Goldcliff Stone was discovered in 1878 (Morgan 1882; Rippon 1997a, fig 29). This probably 3rd-century inscribed stone records the completion of 33½ paces of work on some unspecified linear structure by the century of Statorius Maximus of the first cohort (presumably of the *Legio II Augusta*) (Collingwood and Wright 1965, No. 395). Its shape suggests that it was designed to stand upright in the manner of a milestone, but there has been much discussion over its interpretation (Knight 1962; Boon 1967, 125–6; 1972, 17; 1980, 24–36; Locke 1970–71; Allen 2002b). Allen (2002b) has argued convincingly that the stone was related to the construction of a low bank and an associated ditched enclosure system. Along with the character of the reclamation of the nearby Wentlooge Level this provides clear evidence for Roman military involvement in the utilisation of these wetlands: an example of local variation in landscape character resulting from its proximity to a centre of consumption. Further support for military involvement comes from the character of the animal bone assemblages at Rumney Wharf on Wentlooge, with an unusually high proportion of horses, and Nash Sewage Works on Caldicot, with indications of specialist cattle raising.

The Roman army may also have been involved in exploiting the South-West's rich mineral resources in the 1st century AD. Their direct role in extracting Mendip lead is well known (Beagrie 1989; Fulford 1996, 11–19), and evidence for cupellation (the separation of silver from base metals such as copper) from the late occupation of the legionary fortress (*c* AD 69–75) at Exeter suggests that the military authorities may similarly have been involved in exploiting the region's other minerals (Bayley 2001). Further down the south-west peninsula, the fort at Nanstallon, occupied between *c* AD 55 and *c* AD 80, is in a region rich in metal ores just to the west of Bodmin Moor, and the discovery of silver-rich slag on a crucible fragment, and iron working debris, hints at the army's involvement in their production (Fox and Ravenhill 1972). A series of forts in northern Devon and west Somerset may testify to an interest in both Exmoor and the Blackdown Hills where recent work has shown that iron was both mined and smelted. Trial excavations of a quarry pit adjacent to a furnace and slag heap at Upottery on the Blackdown Hills, for example, produced a pottery assemblage of military character dating to the later 1st century AD (Frances Griffith pers comm; Griffith and Weddell 1996, 33–4).

This clear evidence for Roman military interest in resource exploitation is, however, all 1st century AD, though from the later Roman period there may also have been official involvement in the exploitation of Bath Stone, at Combe Down near Bath, in the form of a 3rd-century lead seal stamped P(*rovinciae*) BR(*itanniae*) S(*uperioris*), and an inscription dedicated to Caracalla (198–217) recording the restoration of a *principia* by a procurator's assistant

(Fig 5.7; Collingwood and Wright 1965, No. 174; Bird 1987, 57; Rivet 1966, 113). While this points to the involvement of the Roman authorities in resource exploitation within the broader West Country region, there is, however, no evidence for their having any role in the colonisation of the North Somerset Levels, in terms of the morphology/character of the settlements and field systems, the material culture recovered, or the economy, and in fact it is the number of villas in this area, usually regarded as an indication of private property, that is most remarkable.

A villa estate context?

The North Somerset Levels probably lay within the southern part of the Dobunni polity which formed the basis of the Roman *civitas* based at *Corinium Dobunnorum* (Cirencester), and was divided from the northern sub-division of the Durotriges, based at Ilchester, by the vast expanse of wetlands that comprised the southern and central divisions of the Somerset Levels (the Brue and Parrett Valleys: Fig 5.7) (Peacock 1969; Van Arsdell 1994; Cunliffe 2003; Darvill 2003). These *civitas* formed a wealthy and culturally vibrant region in the Roman period, with a relatively high density of villas and Romano-Celtic temples, three schools of mosaicists (two in Cirencester and one in Dorchester), and a number of possible sulpture workshops, all reflecting substantial levels of investment in the later Roman period (Jones and Mattingly 1990, 220–4; Henig 1993; 1995). The relatively high numbers of lead curse tablets at temples such as Uley and Bath, and stone inscriptions with dedications to Roman and Romano-Celtic deities, suggest a particularly widespread use and understanding of Latin (Fulford 2003). There are also signs that this was an area of agricultural innovation reflected, for example, in the adoption of iron plough shares and coulters, and large numbers of late Roman T-shaped corn drying ovens (Morris 1979; Rees 1979, 153, 174; Jones 1981; Millett 1990, 187; Fowler 2002, 184). It is within this context of a prosperous and highly Romanised region that we must examine the North Somerset Levels.

A series of villas has been identified close to the fen-edge while a substantial villa at Wemberham lay at its centre. In publishing the excavations of Banwell Moor and Kenn Moor the author was somewhat cautious in discussing the possible role of the owners of these villa estates in reclaiming the North Somerset Levels, observing that the low status of the settlements, and potentially specialised pastoral economy at Banwell, raises the question of whether these communities were pioneering free farmers who colonised the newly reclaimed marshland, or were tenants of villa-based estates whose owners may well have been responsible for the initial act of reclamation (Rippon 1997a, 194; 2000b). So were the North Somerset Levels reclaimed as part of a collaborative venture on the part of the several villa estates whose territories extended onto the wetlands, or was it the owner of the villa at Wemberham who was solely responsible?

An initial observation is that a comparison of the villas in north-west Somerset shows that they were far from all being of the same status (Figs 5.4 and 5.8).

Locking: Only a brief note on the limited excavations of the villa at RAF Locking in the late 1950s has ever been published (Linnington and Rogers *c* 1961). The site lies just to the south of Locking Head Farm, close to the fen-edge on the northern side of the Locking peninsula. The earliest occupation is represented by a late Iron Age roundhouse, possibly within a ditched enclosure. A 2nd-century timber building was replaced in the mid-3rd century by a timber barn constructed on a rammed stone floor that sealed three infant burials. Around AD 300 this was replaced by several stone buildings arranged around at least two sides of an open area, and containing a small bath house comprising a hot room with hot bath, and a warm room, both with painted wall plaster, but no mosaics. In the mid-4th century the bath block was dismantled and levelled, with the robbed material being used to refloor the adjoining rooms. This does not have the appearance of a palatial villa, but rather a relatively wealthy farmstead whose owners were able to invest in a small bath house.

Banwell: A second, also not fully published, Roman villa was discovered in 1967 on the fen-edge at Banwell (Rendell 1986/87; Rye 1986/97). Traces of several 3rd- to 4th-century buildings were located around an open area, though only the well-appointed bath house was fully excavated, which comprised a hot room with hot bath, a warm room with apsidal annex, both with mosaic pavements, an adjacent cold room also with a mosaic, and a fourth room that was simply paved. Geophysical survey (Gait 2001) suggests the presence of further buildings to the south and west of this yard, with the entire complex measuring around 100m north to south and 50m east to west (for which a close parallel may be the villa at Pitney: Leach 2001b, 89).

Congresbury: In 1867 a possible villa was discovered at Woodlands in Congresbury, on a hillside just under 1km from the fen-edge. Scarth (1887) refers to the discovery of 'Roman remains consisting of much pottery and bronze implements and the foundations of a dwelling'. Bramble (1891) gives further details of the finds including a bronze spoon, a brooch, ten sherds of samian pottery, and a 3rd-century coin. In 1903 members of the Somerset Archaeological and Natural History Society visited the site, and reports published in the *Weston Mercury* (30 May 1903, 2) and *Weston Gazette* (30 May 1903, 7) describe the party visiting the remains of the villa. Haverfield (1906, 307) gave credence to a villa at Woodlands based on a letter from William Long that described how in 1867 Mr White of Woodlands 'uncovered two rooms of the villa and took away everything he found. I did not see them, but heard it was an unusually [illegible]

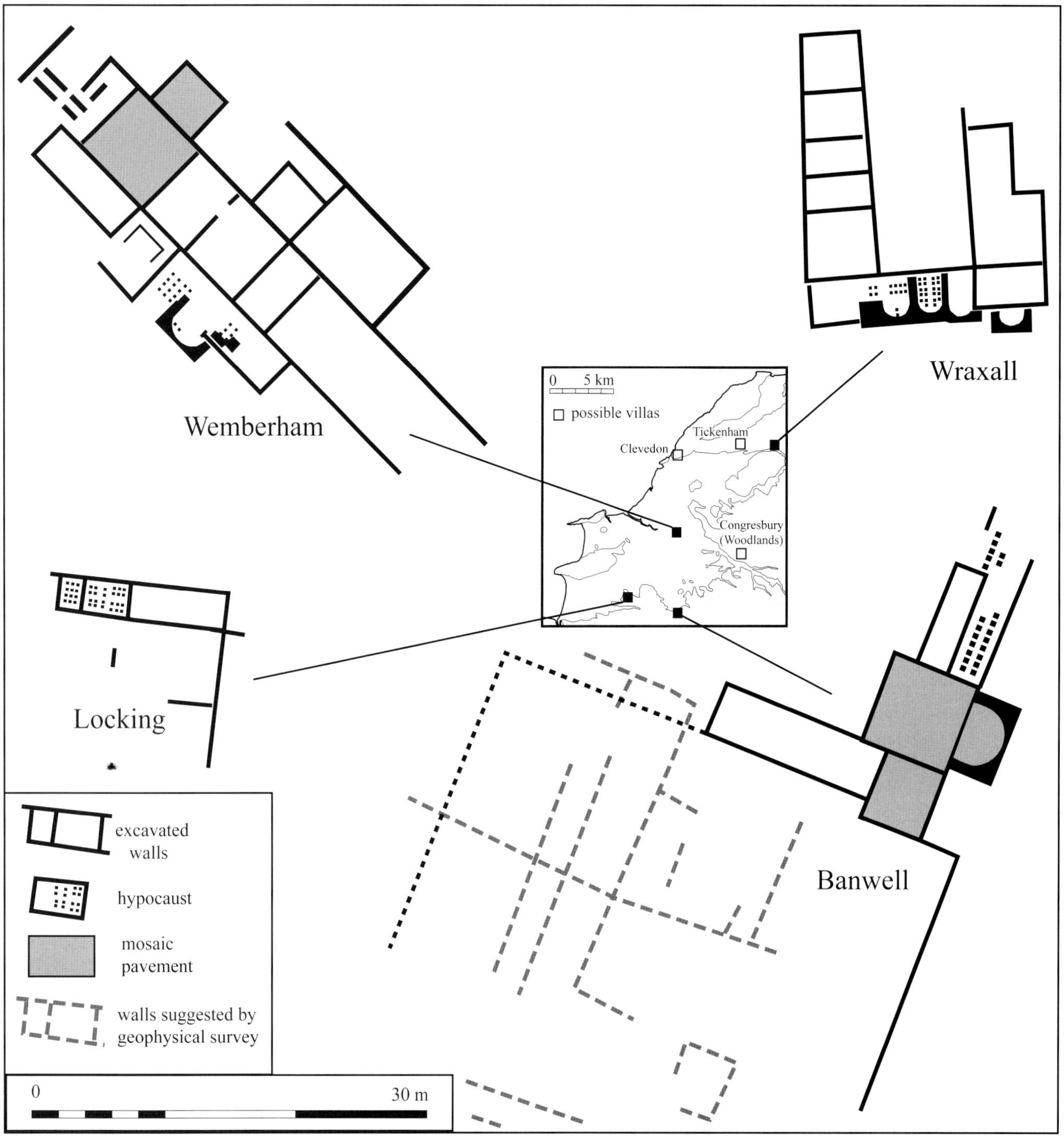

Figure 5.8 Comparative plans of excavated Romano-British villas in north-west Somerset (after Reade 1885 and Scarth 1885 (Wemberham); Sykes and Brown 1960/61 (Wraxall); Linnington and Rogers c 1961 (Locking); Rendell 1986/87 and Gait 2001 (Banwell))

find. This oblong [referring to a sketch plan] represents the spot he cleared, while the circle on the left represents what I believe to be a hypocaust, with at the point A what I believe to be a flue running under other rooms'. The location of this possible villa is a little curious, lying on the slopes of the limestone hills rising above the valley of the Congresbury Yeo, and there has been no recent investigation of the site. A second possible villa in Congresbury lies on the lower-lying foothills at Clarence Court, where there are antiquarian references to Roman remains including a mosaic pavement (SMR 394). Both these possible villas lie *c* 1km to the north of an extensive fen-edge settlement beneath the modern village of Congresbury where mostly unstratified finds of occupation debris and pottery kilns are spread over *c* 30ha (Rippon 1997a, 25).

Wraxall: A small compact building covering just 20 by 30m, with three ranges of rooms around a small internal courtyard, including a fine bath suite, occupied from the mid-3rd to the mid-4th century (though 1st- to 2nd-century pottery suggests earlier occupation on the site). At least one room appears to have had a mosaic pavement, though only a single line of tesserae survived (Sykes and Brown 1960/1).

Tickenham: The evidence for a villa or substantial settlement at Tickenham is circumstantial. Referring to the discovery of a coin hoard in 1821, the antiquary Seyer (1821; cited in Branigan 1977, 167–8) says that 'many old foundations of buildings at different times have been discovered on this spot'. This site comprises an earthwork platform on the side of Tickenham Hill, a position not dissimilar to the probable villa at Congresbury Woodlands.

Clevedon: A scatter of Romano-British material, comparable in extent to that in Congresbury, has been recorded over an area of *c* 20ha close to the fen-edge in Clevedon. The evidence for a villa is simply the discovery of Roman tesserae, pottery, coins, and three or four burials with their heads to the north-east, from Hangstone Hill (*Clevedon Mercury*, 5 February 1883; Anon 1922, lxxxix; SMR 469).

Wemberham: Finally, there is a substantial villa at the very centre of the North Somerset Levels, at Wemberham, currently in the parish of Yatton. Though also only partly excavated, this villa was clearly on a different scale to at least Locking and Wraxall. In 1828 a stone coffin containing an inhumation was discovered 'in the meadow called Great Wemberham' (Rutter 1829; Scarth 1885, 1), and in 1884 stone walls were uncovered during drain laying, and the resulting excavations revealed part of what was clearly a substantial house (Reade 1885; Scarth 1885; Haverfield 1906, 306–7). Of fourteen excavated rooms five had mosaics, including two in the bath block. Hypocausts were found in both the baths and elsewhere, and even this incomplete wing is at least 46m long and 15m wide. The coin sequence ran from Gallienus (253–68) to 'Constantius' (giving a date range of 305 to 361).

These villas that are spread around the North Somerset Levels form part of a marked concentration of such sites on the northern flanks of Mendip and in the Yeo valley of north-west Somerset (Fig 5.7). The construction of villas in the 3rd century is seen throughout much of Somerset and has led to suggestions that before this date the region formed part of an imperial estate based at Combe Down near Bath, which was succeeded by large villa-based estates many of which were held by Gallic immigrants (eg Branigan 1976, 125–7; 1977, 47). Closer examination of the evidence, however, reveals that many villas have pre-3rd-century occupation (including Locking and Wraxall), and that what appears to be happening around the later 3rd century is the investment of resources into making existing farmsteads increasingly opulent (Leech 1982a; Leech and Leach 1982, 66). The villas at Locking, Wraxall, and perhaps Woodlands appear to have been of modest scale, while Banwell and Wemberham were more substantial, but what was their relationship to the reclamation and settlement of the North Somerset Levels? There are at least three possibilities:

1. That it was the work of a single entrepreneur who assumed control of a large area of waste land, building an embankment along the coast/major tidal river(s), constructing the villa at Wemberham, and leasing areas of the newly embanked land to tenants who lived in a series of low-status settlements such as Banwell Moor and Kenn Moor. This assumes that reclamation was a relatively major undertaking.
2. That it was a collaborative venture by a number of landowners whose estates were based at fen-edge villas and whose territories extended from the uplands, across the foothills onto the wetlands, perhaps with tenant farms in the more distant locations. One of those estate owners may have moved his villa onto the newly embanked land at Wemberham. This also assumes that reclamation was a relatively major undertaking.
3. That individual estates owners gradually improved the drainage and flood defence on their own individual areas of marshland. This assumes that reclamation was a relatively small-scale undertaking.

The first of these now seems unlikely. An important addition to our understanding since the author's speculations in 1997 (see above) is that the North Somerset Levels were settled during the earlier Roman period. Following the work at Kenn Moor, Puxton, West Wick, and St Georges, we now know that this was not an unoccupied waste land waiting to be seized by an entrepreneurial reclaimer, but an area with valued natural resources, notably salt production, and already used for at least semi-improved grazing. Another development since writing in 1997 is that it now seems that the villa at Wemberham could have been on the southern banks of the Congresbury Yeo, the same side as the other substantial villa at Banwell. The latter's location right on the fen-edge makes it very unlikely that its estate did not extend onto the marshes, and so both villa owners were presumably engaged in reclamation. Fragments of comb-decorated box-flue tile from Puxton, and imbrex tile from Grapevine Cottage, St Georges, also suggest a degree of stratification within the settlement pattern. Overall, it would appear that several villa-estates were involved in the reclamation and colonisation of the North Somerset Levels.

When writing in 1997, the author also may have over estimated the effort required to protect the North Somerset Levels from tidal flooding. The landscape is today protected by a substantial and continuous sea wall all along the coast, with recessed gouts through which the major rivers discharge their waters (eg The Hurn: Fig 1.3; and see Allen and Rippon 1995). Until the 20th century, however, the Congresbury Yeo was tidal, being embanked on both its northern and southern sides all the way from the coast to the fen-edge; in practice there were separate reclamations to the north and south of the river. If other major tidal watercourses, such as the predecessor of the Banwell River, were also embanked, then there may in fact have been a larger number of individual reclamations between these rivers. Therefore rather than a single monolithic sea wall to protect all of the North Somerset Levels, that would have required the considerable resources of either a single wealthy villa estate or the active co-operation of several estates, we can perhaps envisage the more piecemeal improvement, with individual areas of marsh being embanked by individual villa estates.

Wiping the slate clean: late Roman and early medieval flooding

During the course of the Roman period, the North Somerset Levels were first exploited, then modified, and ultimately transformed by human communities which sought to increase agricultural production, reflecting the wider pattern of agricultural innovation, expansion and prosperity seen in the later Romano-British *civitas* of the Dobunni and the Durotriges. The work at Puxton has confirmed that in the 3rd century this landscape was transformed from one in which brackish, intertidal conditions prevailed, to a wholly freshwater environment. This can only have been brought about by preventing tidal flooding, though with lower relative sea level this would not have been such a major undertaking as was previously thought and low embankment along the coast and major river, and a system of dams and sluices across the minor tidal creeks, may have been sufficient. There is no evidence for military or official involvement on the North Somerset Levels, and instead this appears to have been an example of agricultural innovation and investment on the part of local villa estate owners.

Sometime after the mid-4th century nature reclaimed the North Somerset Levels. In most areas the later Roman-British landscape is sealed by a layer of sterile alluvium laid down under intertidal conditions which at Banwell Moor is reflected in the foraminifera (dominated by *Ammonia beccarii*, *Elphidium williamsoni*, and *Haynesina germinca*), and snail assemblages (comprising the brackish/estuarine species *Hydrobia ventrosa* and *Hydrobia ulvae:* Rippon 2000b). This indicates a dramatic change from a freshwater, reclaimed, environment to initially open mudflats, followed by the formation of salt marshes. It would appear that Banwell Moor lay close to the inland limit of tidal flooding, as pollen and plant macrofossil assemblages also contain some freshwater species, but there was still sufficient inundation to deposit *c* 0.4m of alluvium (though the period over which this was deposited is unclear). Puxton, further inland, would presumably have been flooded at only the very highest tides, and far less post-Roman alluvium was deposited with the result that in most places the Romano-British ground surface has been lost to ploughing, only surviving where it has subsided into the top of a palaeochannel (in Hardingworth) or has been buried under medieval house platforms (in Church Field and Home Ground).

The obvious cause of this marine transgression is a change in the natural environment such as a short-term increase in storminess that breached the flood defences or a longer-term rise in relative sea level. Evidence for the latter can be found in the sequences of dated buried ground surfaces at Banwell Moor, Puxton Home Ground, West Wick, and St Georges which reflect the increasing height to which mature salt marshes had accreted. At Banwell Moor, for example, the late Iron Age land-surface lay at *c* 4.3m OD, rising to *c* 4.8m OD in the 3rd century AD (a rise of 0.16m per century), and *c* 5.1m OD around the 10th century (a rise of 0.04m per century). Traditional ideas of post-glacial sea level suggest that it showed a steady rise, but more recent work in places such as the Thames Estuary has indicated a series of fluctuations with periods of both rising and falling sea level (Rippon 2000a, fig 12). Unfortunately, there is no independent evidence from the Severn Estuary as to whether there was a steady or fluctuating rise in sea level there, though in either case the changes would have been relatively gradual (and at a pace that local communities could have coped with simply by improving flood defences). For a densely settled and agriculturally productive landscape such as the North Somerset Levels, into which there had been much investment in the form of flood defence, enclosure, and settlements (including at least one villa), there must have been other factors that led to their abandonment.

It is possible that the initial flooding of the Levels was a relatively rapid process. Soil micromorphology at both Banwell Moor and Puxton Home Ground indicates that the upper A horizon of the buried late Roman soil had been lost, presumably to erosion, and this might suggest a sudden flooding of the Levels. Its causes are unclear: a natural event is possible, such as an increase in storminess, though cultural factors, such as a failure to maintain the flood defences could also have contributed. The date of the initial inundation would appear to be in the later 4th century based on pottery and coins from Kenn Moor, Banwell Moor, Puxton Church Field, and the Wemberham villa. This confirms the impression gained from sites elsewhere around the Estuary that these coastal marshes were abandoned before the end of the Roman period, and perhaps starting in the third quarter of the 4th century (Rippon 1997a, 124–7; Masser *et al* 2005). This was a period of wider change, reflected in the villa at Locking, where the bath block was demolished, and the villa at Wraxall that was abandoned. The landscape was not, however, deserted – at Locking, for example, material robbed from the bath block was used to refloor adjacent rooms, and the nearby temple of

Henley Wood was still in use (Watts and Leach 1996) – but the impression is that highly Romanised sites such as these were on the wane. This is also seen at nearby sites such as Gatcombe, which was abandoned around the 370s, and although the site was partially reoccupied, possibly *c* 380–90, this was on a far smaller scale than before (Branigan 1977). Towns such as Shepton Mallet were also undergoing changes in the late 4th century, with stone buildings going out of use while timber structures continued to be occupied into the early 5th century (Leach 2001a, 95). This pattern of apparent decline is seen throughout the region (Leach 2001b), and could represent a social phenomenon such as a declining fashion for the trappings of Roman life, or growing economic problems as the market-based economy started to collapse. In such circumstances the motivation to farm agriculturally difficult environments would have reduced, and if the North Somerset Levels were indeed suffering from increased flooding due to the gradually rising relative sea level then the incentive to maintain flood defences would have gone. One other thread of evidence from the NSLP suggests that the abandonment of the reclaimed marshlands may have been primarily due to these wider socio-economic processes. The pollen from sediments directly overlying the buried late Roman soil at Banwell Moor show an increase in dryland tree pollen at the same time as there was increased maritime influence locally (Rippon 2000b, 159). Just as agricultural land was being lost on the Levels, there appears to have been a decline in the intensity with which the adjacent drylands were exploited.

That the abandonment of once reclaimed coastal marshes appears to be part of the far wider decline in the countryside of late Roman Britain illustrates how an individual landscape can only be understood in its wider context, and how an individual landscape-based case study can inform wider research into our past. It also marks the end of one period when some human communities increased the intensity with which they utilised a physically marginal environment of enormous agricultural potential, by going through the cycle of landscape exploitation, modification, and transformation. Elsewhere, other communities preferred to continue in the traditional exploitation of the rich natural resources of these wetlands, but by the early medieval period this local and regional variation in how the landscape was managed appears to have disappeared, as reclaimed and unreclaimed marshes alike were buried under salt marshes. By the 11th century, however, the North Somerset Levels were once again reclaimed, following their initial colonisation around a century earlier, and it is to the origins and development of the historic landscape that was created by this second phase of reclamation that we must now turn.

Note

1 This peat has been mapped in Rippon 1994b, fig 11, and 1995b, fig. 15. The results of an auger transect and pollen core are described in Rippon 1995b, 35–8. Two radiocarbon dates were subsequently obtained from the pollen core:
0.26m below the present ground surface:
2410 ± 60 BP (756–394 cal. BC; Beta-099381)
0.59m below the present ground surface:
2690 ± 60 BP (979–780 cal. BC; Beta-099382).

Part 3: The making of the historic landscape

In the early medieval period most of the North Somerset Levels once again became salt marshes and mudflats: in terms of the preceding cultural landscape the slate was wiped clean and a physically almost homogeneous environment returned. Around the 10th century human communities once again started to colonise these marshes, and the long process of drainage and enclosure that followed led to the creation of today's historic landscape that forms the focus of Part III of this study. Once again we will see how successive human communities changed from simply exploiting their environment, through its modification, to its ultimate transformation by reclamation. Of particular significance will be the origin and development of local variation in the character of the historic landscape that was created following reclamation, with an examination of the potential significance of environmental factors, antecedent landscapes, and cultural issues such as patterns of landholding. In this historic period, a wide range of sources and techniques are called upon to unravel the story of how this historic landscape was created, and to explain why its character is so varied.

In Chapter 6 the character of the historic landscape is examined in depth, and documentary and archaeological evidence is used to trace its origins back to the medieval period. Chapter 7 examines the tenurial framework within which this historic landscape was created, notably the development of estates and manors. Chapter 8 describes the peasant and yeoman tenements that made up these manors, including a study of the surviving pre-19th-century buildings. Chapter 9 describes the results of excavations in one of the medieval settlements, Puxton, including the artefactual material recovered, while Chapter 10 reports on the palaeoenvironmental material.

6 Created on a cleaned slate: a characterisation of the historic landscape

Working from a clean state

During the early medieval period the North Somerset Levels were reclaimed by nature: the later Roman freshwater landscape, that had been embanked and partly enclosed, reverted to intertidal salt marshes and mudflats. The following centuries are a 'dark age', with little archaeological or documentary evidence. Even the Domesday survey is not as helpful as one might have hoped as large areas south of the Congresbury Yeo fell within estates that straddled both the wetlands and the adjacent drylands (eg Banwell, Congresbury, and Yatton), and while it is suspected that several unnamed subtenancies within these manors represent places on the Levels (including Puxton and Wick St Lawrence: see Chapter 7) we cannot be sure. To the north of the Yeo, however, there were two wholly marshland manors, both in Kingston Seymour, and it is these two entries that demonstrate that reclamation was well underway as with 41 villagers, smallholders, and slaves, along with 21 ploughs, there must have been a substantial area of agricultural land that was free from tidal inundation. Sometime in the later 1st millennium AD the North Somerset Levels started to be reclaimed for a second time.

This recolonisation occurred at a particularly interesting period when villages and open fields were being created in England's central province (Chapter 1), and on the Levels too there emerged marked variations in landscape character. In Wick St Lawrence, for example, most settlement was concentrated into a few small hamlets that were linked by narrow lanes (Fig 6.1A; and see Fig 1.3), while in areas of Banwell and Congresbury Marsh the settlement pattern was more dispersed, with isolated farmsteads and loosely arranged hamlets strung out along a network of broad droveways and small commons (Fig 6.1.B; and see Fig 1.4). The landscape immediately west of Congresbury village is different again, with a series of long, roughly parallel (coaxial) boundaries reflecting the furlongs in an area of former common field adjacent to a substantial village (Fig 6.1.C; and see Fig 2.3). The reasons why the medieval countryside developed such different character areas have led to much debate between archaeologists, historians, and historical geographers. Part of the problem is that in dryland areas historic landscape character could have been influenced by a range of factors, including variations in the physical topography and soils, or the structure of the earlier cultural landscapes. In coastal wetlands, in contrast, this cannot have been the case as they were a cleaned slate, physically almost uniform, and largely uncluttered by the debris from antecedent cultural landscapes that were mostly buried. It was upon this almost blank canvas that human communities created entirely new settlement patterns and field systems in the medieval period.

Using the historic landscape as a focus for research

Although one aim of this research project is to tell the story of an historic landscape, starting with its origins and ending up in the early 19th century, the actual research process often went in reverse: just as an excavation peels away the layers on an archaeological site before revealing the earlier deposits, so it is with historic landscape analysis. The rest of this chapter will therefore explore the character of this 19th-century landscape using a wide range of evidence to then trace its origins back into the medieval period.

The historic landscape can be thought of as comprising various physical **elements** (eg field boundaries, buildings, roadside ditches), that together form discrete spatial **parcels** (eg a field, settlement, road), that when mapped over a large area combine to form a series of **components** (eg field systems, settlement patterns, road networks: see Rippon 2004a for a fuller account of this approach to historic landscape analysis). Within this particular wetland landscape a number of key components can be identified which will be discussed in turn – the natural environment, tenurial structures, unenclosed land (coastal salt marshes and the backfen commons), and the enclosed landscape (including artificial drainage and flood defence, settlements, field systems, and communications) – before considering how they combine with each other to create different historic landscape character areas.

A central premise of this study is that the historic landscape itself is an invaluable record of the history of the countryside, but although large areas are covered by a series of 18th-century estate maps, the earliest occasion for which we can map the whole study area is through the tithe surveys of *c* 1840. In recent years there has been considerable emphasis on using 19th-century cartographic sources as a base from which to hypothesise about the medieval countryside (eg Roberts 1987; Roberts and Wrathmell 2000; 2002), but is this really a valid approach? In England's central province the 19th-century landscape bears relatively little resemblance to its medieval predecessor due to the transformation brought about by Parliamentary enclosure, but elsewhere there are signs that many of the key elements of the historic landscape's physical fabric

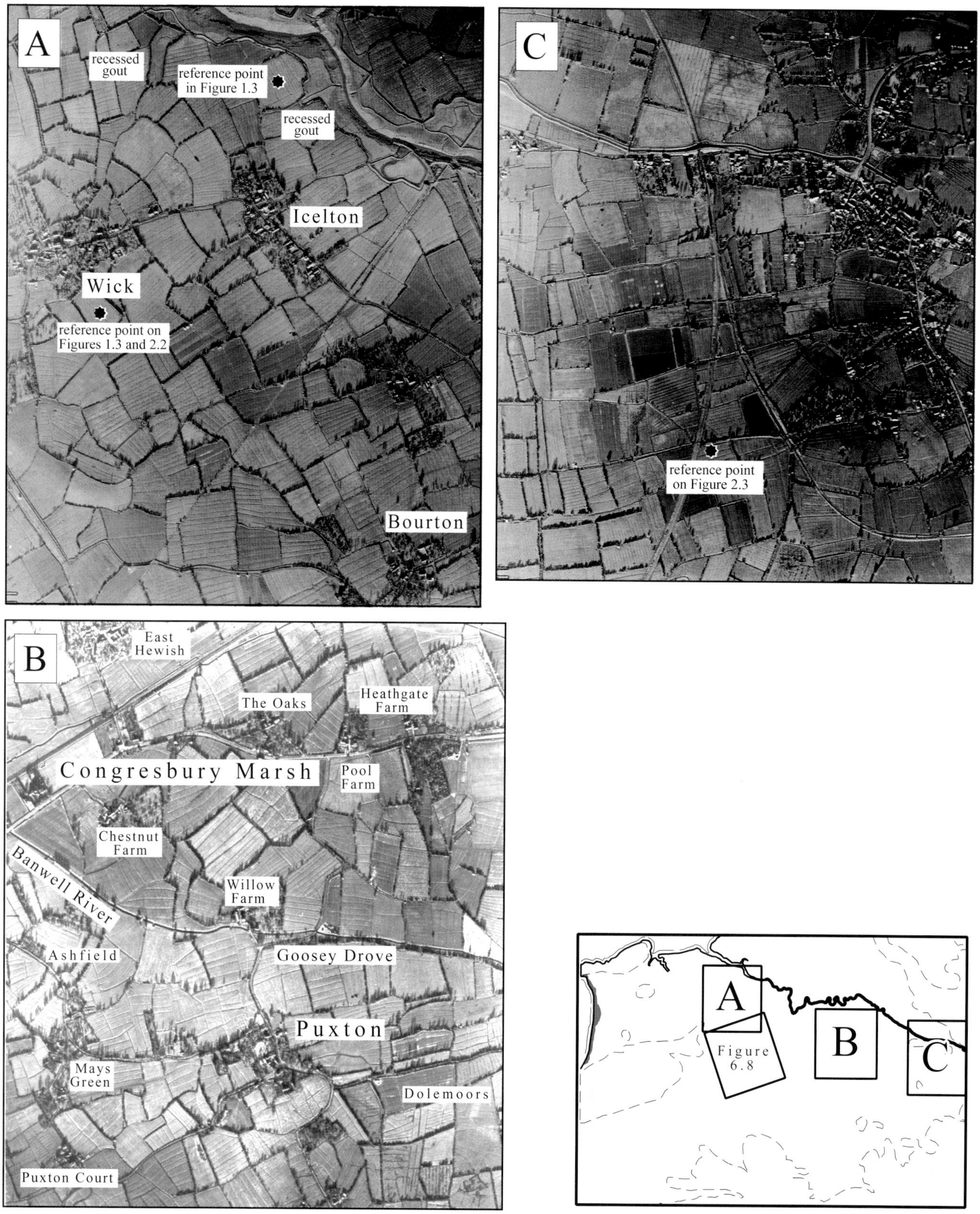

Figure 6.1 Contrasting historic landscapes of (A) Wick (a series of small tightly nucleated hamlets), (B) Puxton (a mixture of hamlets and isolated farmsteads) and Congresbury (isolated farmsteads on Congresbury Marsh, and (C) a substantial nucleated village on the fen-edge to the east of a substantial common meadow; see Fig 2.3) (aerial photographs © National Monuments Record RAF/CPE/UK/1869, December 1946, photo A: fr 4148, B: fr 3155; C: fr 4265)

have been remarkably stable, and do date from the medieval period. Many pre-Conquest land charters, for example, include a description of the estate boundaries which can usually be identified today (and in the case of Banwell appear to be coterminous with the 19th-century parish). The place-names in Domesday are mostly familiar, and many of the field-names recorded in other documentary sources from the 13th century onwards appear in the tithe surveys of *c* 1840. Just as these documents record a medieval landscape that is readily familiar to anyone studying the countryside of today, so is the archaeological record: some late medieval houses are still occupied and lie adjacent to roads that must themselves therefore be medieval in date. Abandoned settlements and field boundaries, as revealed through fieldwalking or earthwork survey, similarly fit into the historic landscape rather than form an underlying relict landscape on a different orientation and of a different character.

Whilst some elements of the historic landscape are, therefore, clearly medieval, the countryside of today is of course a palimpsest created over many centuries, and in some cases we can show that its character in the 19th century was significantly different to that in the medieval period. Puxton, for example, appears in the tithe survey as a small hamlet with several outlying cottages and farmsteads, though aerial photography from the 1940s reveals that the intervening spaces are filled with the earthworks of abandoned houses that shovel test pitting, excavation, and 15th- to 16th-century documents reveal are deserted tenements (see Chapter 9). Taken altogether, this reveals that Puxton is a severely shrunken village and while 19th-century maps on their own may have given little indication of this, there is plenty of other evidence for the landscape detective to use (notably earthworks, documentary material, and field-names). The rest of this chapter, therefore, presents an interdisciplinary analysis of the palimpsest that is the historic landscape within the southern part of the North Somerset Levels and the adjacent dryland areas. It disaggregates the landscape into its different component parts, each of which are characterised as they are mapped in the 19th century, before exploring their antiquity through the integration of archaeological and documentary sources. The various strands of evidence are then combined in order to identify a series of landscapes of distinctly different character, as well as forming the basis of a series of maps discussed in Chapter 12 that plot the evolution of this landscape over the course of the historic period.

The natural environment

Relief and soils (Fig 1.5)

A key character-defining feature of the North Somerset Levels, as with any wetland area, is their apparent flatness. Although the Levels certainly do appear featureless compared to the surrounding hills, there are subtle variations in relief with areas towards the coast being slightly higher than those inland. The present ground surface in coastal areas is *c* 5.8 to 6.1m OD, with most of the Levels at *c* 5.2 and 5.5m OD, falling to *c* 4.9m OD in the lower-lying backfens. This difference in elevation is due to these coastal marshes being the first areas to be flooded by the tide, and so experiencing the greatest sediment deposition. Apart from areas of peat in the north-east corner of the Levels, and very localised areas of freshwater alluvium around the southern and eastern fen-edge, all of the soils are uniformly estuarine silty clays.

Development of the river system (Figs 1.5 and 6.2)

The evolution of the drainage system can be reconstructed through an analysis of the historic landscape, earthworks, documentary sources, and field- and place-names (Fig 6.2). The largest river is the Congresbury Yeo though as it currently crosses the Levels it is embanked and so makes no contribution to the drainage of the area through which it passes. The Levels themselves are drained through a series of rhynes that today mostly form part of two systems: the Oldbridge River system that discharges its waters into the Congresbury Yeo at Sampson's Clyce in Wick St Lawrence (clyce = sluice gate), and the Banwell River system that flows directly into the Severn Estuary south of St Thomas' Head. The Oldbridge River system drains the south-eastern parts of the Levels, including the Brandier, Carditch, Crookwell, Churchill, Sandmead, and Towerhead Brook Rhynes, while the Banwell River system drains the central-southern parts of the Levels and includes the Old Yeo, Grumblepill and Bourton Town Rhynes.

The Congresbury Yeo

For the most part the Congresbury Yeo retains a naturally meandering course, though as it crosses the lower-lying backfen of Congresbury Moor, between Binhay Rhyne and The Oar, its course has clearly been straightened. Further west at Wemberham there may have been a more significant change in the river's course. Following the Norman Conquest, Domesday records that Wemberham was transferred from Congresbury to Yatton, and this area can be identified as the extension of Yatton parish south of the Yeo, now known as Hewish (Fig 1.2.D). What is now called Wemberham, however, lies to the north of the present course of the Yeo, raising the possibility that Hewish and Wemberham were once a continuous block of land to the south of a possible older course of the Yeo preserved by a meandering field boundary to the north of Wemberham, running from the end of Wemberham Lane to Wemberham

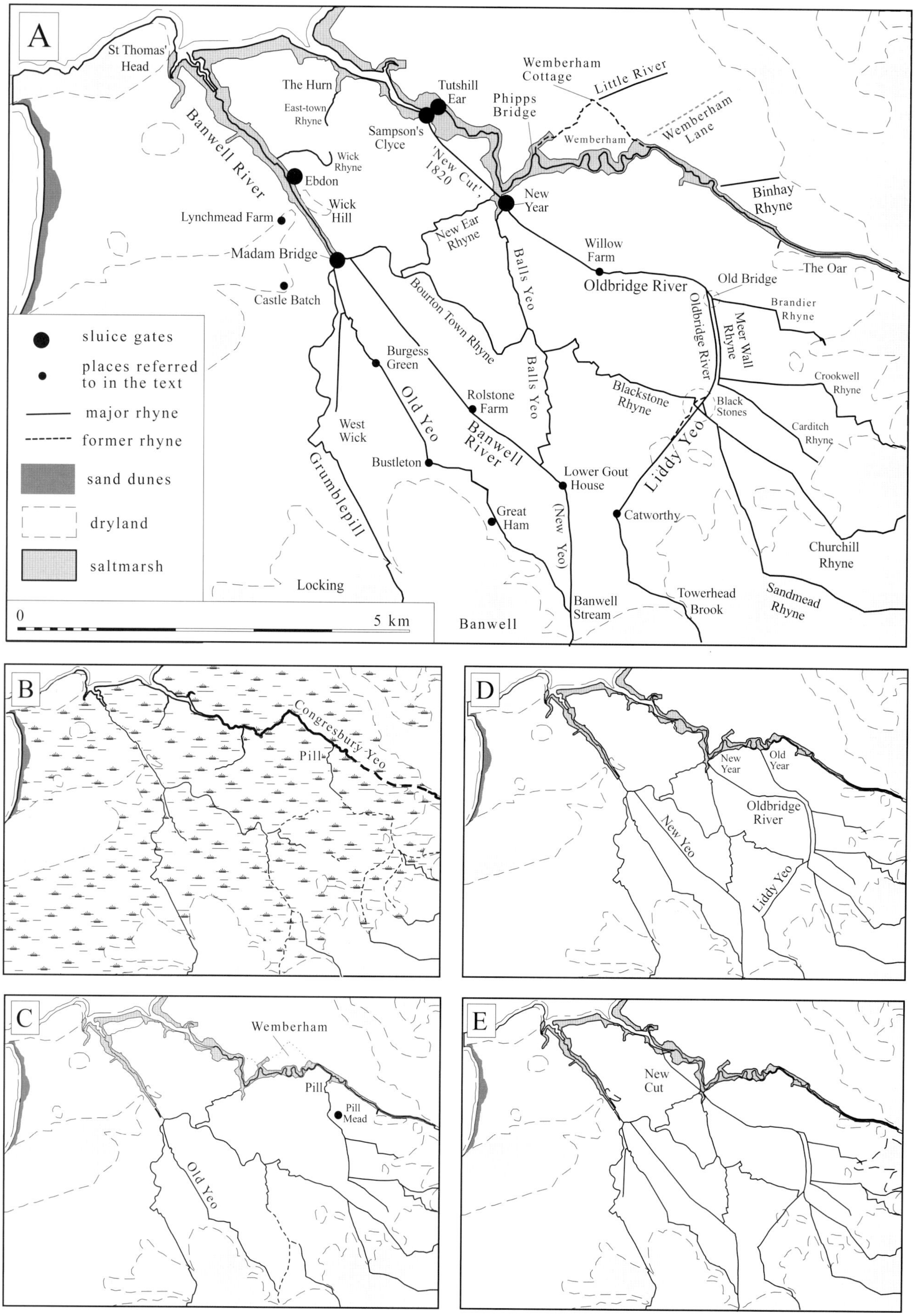
A
St Thomas' Head
The Hurn
East-town Rhyne
Tutshill Ear
Sampson's Clyce
Wemberham Cottage
Phipps Bridge
Little River
Wemberham
Wemberham Lane
Banwell River
Wick Rhyne
Ebdon
'New Cut', 1820
New Year
Binhay Rhyne
Wick Hill
Lynchmead Farm
New Ear Rhyne
Willow Farm
Madam Bridge
The Oar
Balls Yeo
Oldbridge River
Old Bridge
Castle Batch
Bourton Town Rhyne
Brandier Rhyne
Meer Wall Rhyne
Oldbridge River
sluice gates
places referred to in the text
major rhyne
former rhyne
sand dunes
dryland
saltmarsh
Burgess Green
Balls Yeo
Crookwell Rhyne
Rolstone Farm
Blackstone Rhyne
Black Stones
Old Yeo
West Wick
Carditch Rhyne
Banwell River
Bustleton
Lower Gout House
Liddy Yeo
Grumblepill
Great Ham
(New Yeo)
Catworthy
Churchill Rhyne
Locking
Towerhead Brook
Sandmead Rhyne
0
5 km
Banwell
Banwell Stream
B
Congresbury Yeo
Pill
D
New Year
Old Year
Oldbridge River
New Yeo
Liddy Yeo
C
Wemberham
Pill
Pill Mead
Old Yeo
E
New Cut

Cottage, and hence down to Phipps Bridge (Fig 6.2.A and see p 135).

The extent to which the Yeo was used for navigation is unclear, although until the construction of the sluice at Tutshill Ear in the 20th century, the Congresbury Yeo was tidal as far as the village and in 1736 Graffin Prankard shipped 232cwt of iron from Bristol to Congresbury (SRO DD/DN 439 f.177). In 1794 the tannery in Congresbury was described as having a navigable river running alongside (*Sherborne and Yeovil Mercury*, 24 February 1794).

Before its embankment a series of tidal creeks would have drained into the Congresbury Yeo, and several of these are now fossilised in the historic landscape as rhynes, such as East-town Rhyne and New Ear Rhyne in Wick. Other former creeks may be reflected by the line taken by meandering field boundaries, 'pill' field-names, and recesses in the line of early sea walls such as that to the east of Pillhay Farm where the line of a former creek divides the land associated with Heathgate Farm to the west from the former demesne pasture of Pill Field to the east (Figs 6.5.D and 6.12). The minor streams that enter the south-eastern side of the Levels (Crookwell, Churchill, Carditch, and Sandmead Rhynes) probably originally flowed into the Congresbury Yeo via this tidal creek at Pill (Fig 6.2).

The Banwell River, the Old and New Yeo, and the Balls Yeo

The central-southern parts of the Levels are drained through a series of rhynes known as Grumblepill Rhyne, the Old Yeo, the Banwell River, and the Bourton Town Rhyne (the *Ealdan Wrinn,* Old Wring river, in the 1068 bounds of Banwell), that converged at Madam Bridge (Madamesbrugg in 1352: SRO DD/SAS/C/795), before flowing down the Banwell River to its estuary below St Thomas' Head. This last stretch, between Madam Bridge and the coast, may be the 'watercourse between Ebdon [at the head of the Banwell River] and land of Mr Bustle' that the Winterstoke and Banwell hundred court rolls for 1351–52 state was the responsibility of the Prior of Woodspring, Lord of Norton, and Walter le Irish (SRO DD/SAS C/795). The Old Yeo and Banwell River rise from a spring that gave Banwell its name (AD 904 *Bananwyll,* 'spring or stream of *Bana*': Mills 1991, 22), though the name Banwell River is a recent one. In 1730, for example, Strachey describes how the Banwell stream divided into two branches: what is still called the Old Yeo flowing north-west along the southern and western sides of Banwell Moor, and the New Yeo (now known as the Banwell River) flowing directly north before turning west at Lower Gout House (*Strachey I*, f.B; *Strachey II*, 81).

The Old Yeo is an embanked watercourse that skirts around the southern side of Banwell Moor. Between Banwell village and the south-west corner of Banwell Moor at Great Ham it has a slightly sinuous course, though this may simply reflect the way that it skirts the fen-edge. Between Great Ham near Bustleton and Burges Green at St Georges it is certainly a wholly artificial creation that cuts across what must have been open moorland to the west of Waywick. The Banwell court roll for 1598 refers to stooks (stockades) between 'Bustilandgate and Burgeways Bowe' that also probably lay along the Old Yeo (Burges Bow being where the Old Yeo passes under the St Georges to Worle road: Coward 1980, 153). It would appear, therefore, that while older than the New Yeo (the modern Banwell River), the Old Yeo was itself an artificial creation.

The New Yeo (the Banwell River) in its current form is a wholly artificial one that when initially created ran directly north from the fen-edge at Banwell village across unenclosed moorland to Lower Gout House, then turning north-west through what was still open common until it reached the edge of the enclosed lands at Rolstone Farm in Waywick, whereupon it changed direction slightly before following a straight course past St Georges to the Bourton Town Rhyne, cutting through the earlier patterns of fields and roads (see Figs 1.4, 6.2, and 6.8). The embankments either side of this channel prevent it from draining the land through which it passes, and while this major feat of engineering may have been designed simply to carry the water of the Banwell Stream to the coast, it is tempting to suggest that it was at least in part designed to act as a canal, linking the Bishop of Wells's manor at Banwell with the Estuary (in the same way that the Abbots of Glastonbury constructed a network of canals in the main Somerset Levels: Rippon 2004c; 2005; forthcoming b).

The naturally meandering predecessor of the Banwell River still survives as a substantial palaeochannel that flows north from the fen-edge across The Hams and Cormoor (that is shown on a sketch map of 1815 as Easter Mead Rhyne: Fig 6.13.A), meandering past the modern Lower Gout House and then probably linking up with the naturally

Figure 6.2 (opposite) The drainage system in the southern part of the North Somerset Levels
A: the rhynes as recorded on the First Edition Ordnance Survey Six Inch maps of the 1880s
B: the conjectural natural drainage system in the early medieval period
C–E: development of the artificial system of rhynes showing how the outfall of the Sandmead and Churchill Rhynes (and later the Oldbridge River) was progressively shifted down the Congresbury Yeo from Pill, to what must have been the Old Ear at East Hewish, then to the New Ear at West Hewish (by 1521), and ultimately Sampson's Clyce (in 1820)

Figure 6.3 The Oldbridge River and Goosey Drove (to the left) at Old Bridge (from ST 4160 6365 looking west towards Willow Farm; for location see Fig 6.2)

meandering stream now called Balls Yeo Rhyne which joins the Bourton Town Rhyne (Fig 6.2.B). In 1351 the Banwell court rolls specify that all tenants were responsible for scouring the *Banewellesyeo* [Banwell River] and *Baillyesyeo* [Balls Yeo], and the fact that the two are described as separate watercourses by this date suggests that the *Banewellesyeo* is the artificial Banwell River. In 1352 it is specified that the tenants of Banwell were responsible for the *Banewellesyeo*, while the tenants of Puttingthorpe [St Georges] were responsible for the *Ballesyeo* which must refer to that stretch of the Balls Yeo between Lower Gout House and the Bourton Town Rhyne (SRO DD/SAS C/795). North of Bourton Town Rhyne the Balls Yeo currently continues along a clearly artificial course through Puxton and West Hewish to the recessed gout at New Year on the Congresbury Yeo. It is not known when this artificial stretch of Balls Yeo Rhyne was dug, though it pre-dates the surrounding historic landscape and so must be relatively early.

The Oldbridge River system

A series of streams enter the south-eastern part of the Levels: the Towerhead Brook (described as the *Ture broc* in the 1068 description of Banwell's bounds), Sandmead Rhyne, Churchill Rhyne, Carditch Rhyne, Crookwell Rhyne, and Brandier Rhyne. The Towerhead Brook was later canalised as the Liddy Yeo, which itself becomes the Oldbridge River (formerly known as the Holebridge Yeo) (Figs 6.2 and 6.3). Before reclamation it is unclear whether the Towerhead Brook flowed into the Balls Yeo/Bourton Town Rhyne, or into the system of palaeochannels around Rookery island that probably flowed north into the Congresbury Yeo possibly at the former tidal creek at Pill (see above). This drainage system appears to have been disrupted when a wall (the *Morewal*, that the Congresbury hundred court ordered all tenants to repair in 1351: SRO DD/SAS C/795) was constructed through the middle of the Dolemoor in order to divide Congresbury from Puxton. This necessitated the construction of the Meerwall Rhyne to the east to carry the waters of the Carditch and Crookwell Rhynes to Pill, which had probably occurred by 1325 when there is reference to East and West Dolemoor that lie either side of Meerwall (Knight 1902, 229). At an unknown date a second major artificial rhyne was constructed to the west of the Moor Wall to carry the waters of the Towerhead Brook/Liddy Yeo and Crookwell Rhyne northwards, though in 1383 there is reference to this 'Holeyo' and 'Holebrugge' [now known as the Old Bridge, where the Meer Wall Rhyne and Oldbridge River join] (LPL 1182). At some stage the outfall of the Meer Wall Rhyne/Oldbridge River appears to

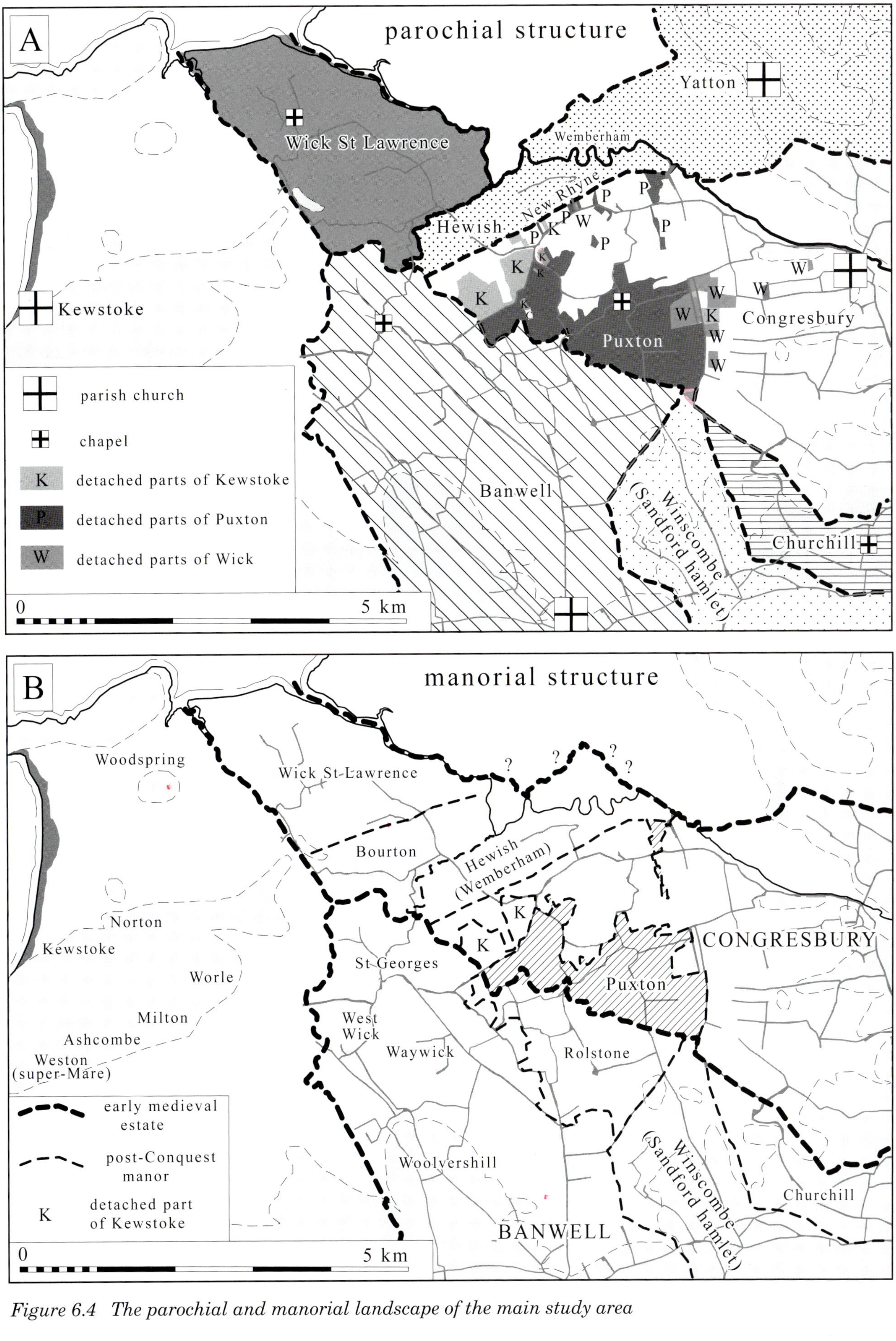

Figure 6.4 The parochial and manorial landscape of the main study area

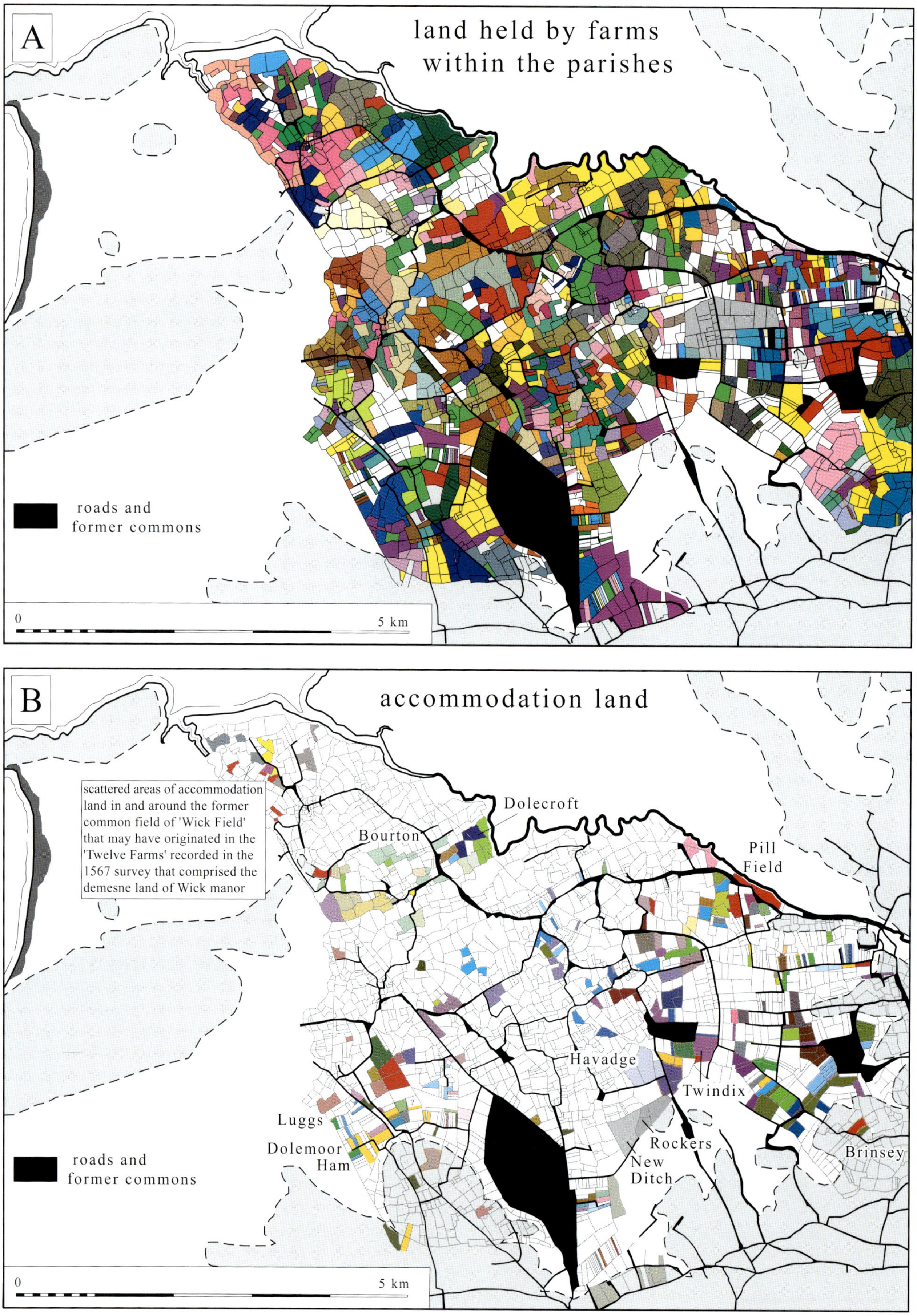

Figure 6.5 Characterisation of 19th-century landholding (occupancy) in the main study area
A *All land held by farms located within the parishes of Banwell, Congresbury, Puxton, Wick St Lawrence, and Yatton (Hewish).* ***B*** *Accommodation land (ie land held by distant farms)*

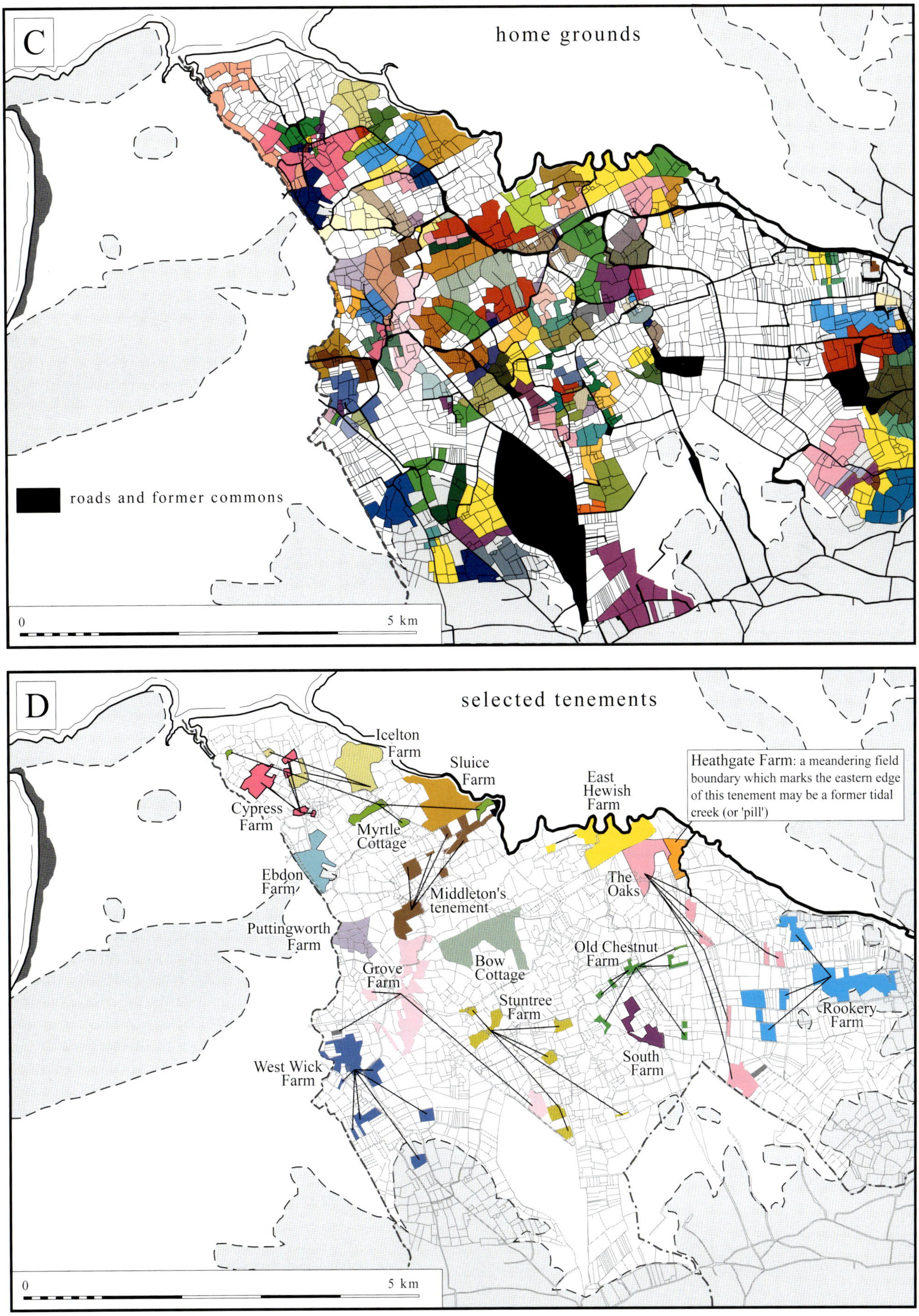

Figure 6.5 Characterisation of 19th-century landholding (occupancy) in the main study area
***C** Home grounds (ie closes located immediately adjacent to the tenement's farmhouse).* ***D** Selected estates illustrating the diversity of ways that the land belonging to individual tenements was distributed*

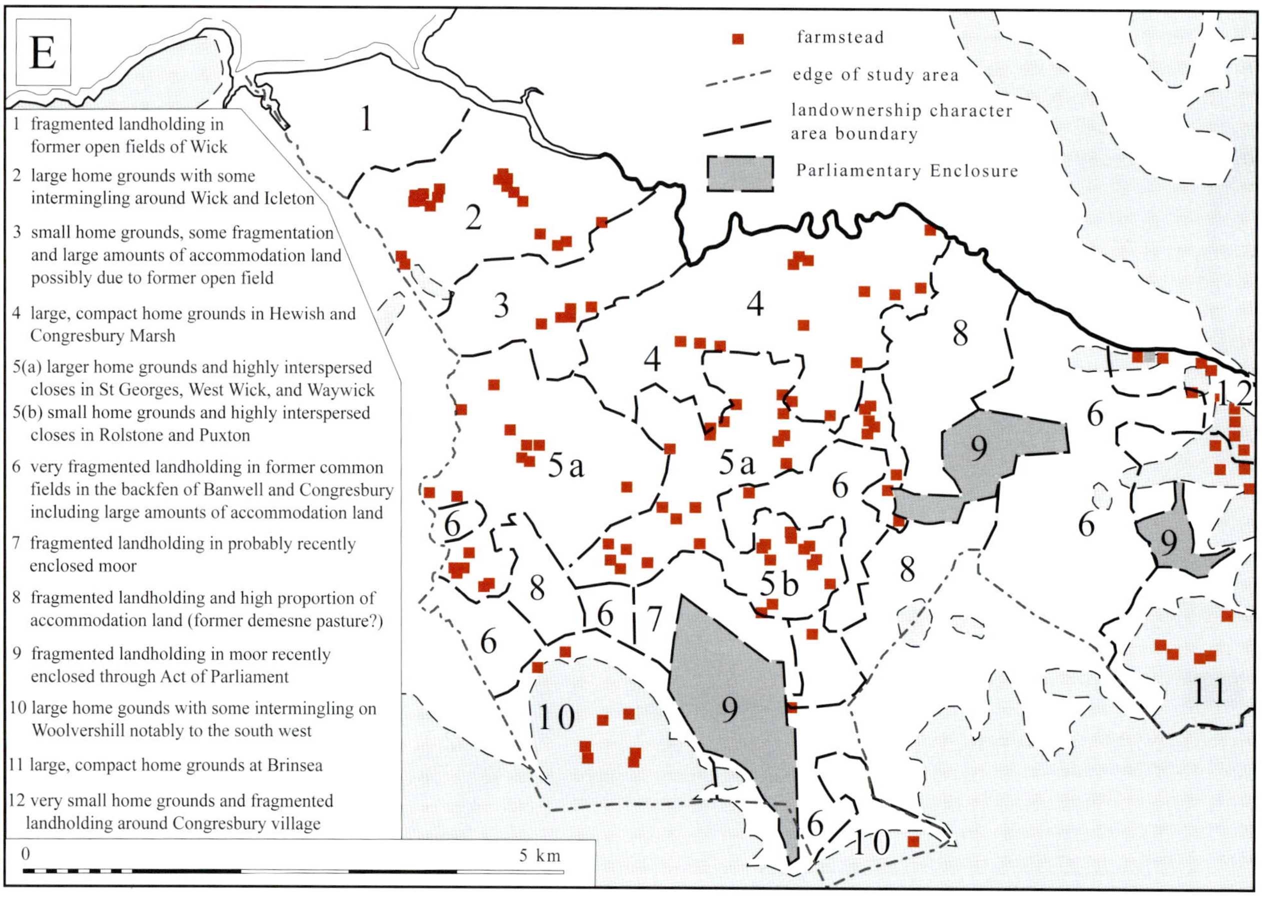

Figure 6.5 Characterisation of 19th-century landholding (occupancy) in the main study area
***E** Characterisation of the patterns of landholding*

have been diverted downstream from the Pill via an artificial rhyne that is still preserved as a field boundary running between Pill Mead and what was presumably a sluice just east of East Hewish. The river and its outfall was then diverted downstream again as a new stretch of rhyne was created from the Old Bridge, along the pre-existing Goosey Drove, and then cutting across the historic landscape between Willow Farm and West Hewish (Fig 6.6) to the New Ear where there was a substantial recessed gout off the Congresbury Yeo into which the New Ear and Balls Yeo Rhynes also discharged their waters. The New Ear existed by 1521 (*Yatton Churchwardens*, 139), and was presumably new in relation to the outfall at East Hewish (shown as Old Ear in Fig 6.2.D). In 1820 the outfall was moved further downstream to Sampson's Clyce (SRO Q/RDe 139).

The Grumblepill Rhyne

The Grumblepill Rhyne marks the western boundary of Banwell. It rises at the *Fulle Welle* recorded in the 1068 bounds of Banwell, which can be identified as Fullens/Full Lands in the tithe survey (Coward 1980). Having flowed onto the Levels, it has been canalised as far as West Wick, though thereafter it retains its naturally meandering course as far as Madam Bridge where it joins the Bourton Town Rhyne. In 1352 it is recorded that the Prior of Worspring [Woodspring], the Lord of Norton [in Kewstoke], and Bishop [of Bath and Wells, lord of the manor of Banwell] were responsible for the maintenance of Grumblepill Rhyne (SRO DD/SAS C/795). By the early 15th century part of it was bounded on its western side by an earthen wall, one section of which was known as the Wowwall 'made and commissioned to bar the flooding of the fields between the *dominia* [manor] of Banwell on the one side [east] and the *dominia* of Worle, Hutton, Ashcombe, Weston, Milton, Uphill, Oldmixon, and Locking [to the west]' (Coward 1980; 1981). The responsibility for its construction and maintenance lay with the Prior of Worspring and his tenants of Locking and Worle, the lord of Norton and his tenants, and the vicar of Locking. The name is probably in part derived from the Old English *woeg/wo* (meaning bent) and may indicate that it lay next to the meandering stretch of Grumblepill between West Wick and Madam Bridge.

The social and tenurial landscape

The manorial and parochial structure

Before considering the physical fabric of the historic landscape, we should first establish the social/

tenurial framework within which these patterns of roads, fields and settlements were created. The starting point has to be the tithe maps of *c* 1840 which show the study area divided between eight parishes: Yatton, Congresbury, Churchill, Winscombe, and Banwell (all of which extended from the drylands onto the Levels), the wholly marshland parishes of Puxton and Wick St Lawrence, and several detached parts of Kewstoke (Fig 6.4.A). The morphology of the parish boundaries strongly suggests that Puxton was carved out of Congresbury though it became a chapelry of Banwell, probably when the chapel there was granted to Bruton Priory (that also held the church at Banwell) in the late 12th century (see Chapter 7). Churchill was also a chapelry of Banwell, while Wick was a chapelry of Congresbury that in 1326 was granted a licence for burial (*Drokensford, 251*; Collinson 1791, 612; Manchee 1831, 3).

The manorial history of this area is discussed in detail in Chapter 7 but, in summary, during the early medieval period the study area was divided between two large estates based at Banwell and Congresbury, which by the 11th century had started to fragment into a series of smaller manors (Fig 6.4.B). The greater Congresbury estate broke down into the manors of Congresbury with Wick (from which Bourton was detached at a later stage), Puxton, and Hewish (that was transferred to Yatton), while the manors of Churchill, East and West Rolstone, and Sandford (that was transferred to Winscombe) were carved out of Banwell.

Within these large parochial and manorial territories there were smaller divisions of the landscape. Within Congresbury there were separate tithings of Congresbury, Puxton, and Wick from at least the 14th century (LPL ED 1176 f.22), while the survey of 1567 divided the Congresbury tithing into six areas: Middletown, Venus Street, Above the Yeo, Land [also north of the Yeo], Brinsea, and The Marsh. By the 16th century Banwell was broken down into the tithings of Upland, Woolvershill, and Churchill (PRO SC2/198/1b). A separate tithing covering 'le Marsh' (which included St Georges, West Wick, Waywick, East Rolstone, and West Rolstone) is recorded by the late 16th/early 17th century in both the parish registers and manor lease book (WCL 10189).

A characterisation of 19th-century landholding

During the medieval period these manors were divided between the lord's own land (the demesne), and the land held by tenants. From the late medieval period the demesne was first leased out and then sold off, as was the case with many of the tenements in Congresbury and Wick. In Puxton and Rolstone, by contrast, most tenements were still part of a single estate until well into the 20th century. The first occasion for which we have a complete record of land ownership and the occupation of individual tenements is in the tithe surveys of *c* 1840 (Fig 6.5).

The patterns of tenements can be characterised in three ways.

1. Whether or not land was held by farms located within the parish (Fig 6.5.A) or outside (Fig 6.5.B). The latter, known as accommodation land, was often used for fattening livestock on the rich summer pastures, and is concentrated in a few locations notably Bourton in the southern part of Wick St Lawrence, and the backfens of Banwell and Congresbury. Field-names (eg Dolemoor Ham and Luggs in Banwell, and Wick Field in Wick St Lawrence) and field boundary morphology (ie long, narrow strip-like fields) suggest that many of these areas were either former common fields, or areas of former manorial demesne that were leased out and then sold off (eg Pill Field in Congresbury Marsh; Havadge, and New Ditch in Banwell; and Twindix in Puxton).
2. The structure of landholding within individual areas. In a number of places there are compact blocks of fields all in the same ownership immediately adjacent to a farmhouse (their home ground), suggesting a set of closes held in severalty (Fig 6.5.C). Elsewhere the pattern of landholding was far more fragmented; this is greatest in areas of former common fields.
3. The disposition of fields associated with individual farmsteads (Figs 6.5.D). In Wick St Lawrence farmsteads are typically associated with a large home ground, and detached parcels in former open fields to the north (eg Wick Field, parts of which were held by Cypress and Icelton Farms on Figs 6.5.B and D). Several farms in the central part of Wick had wholly compact landholdings (eg Ebdon and Sluice Farms) but in Bourton, to the south, farmsteads were typically associated with a small home ground and detached parcels in the probable former common fields to the east (eg Dolecroft; Fig 6.5.B: Middleton's tenement). St Georges, West Wick, and Waywick are characterised by farmsteads with home grounds that show a degree of interspersion with each other, suggesting that they represent the subdivision of once larger tenements, along with detached parcels in various former common meadows and moors (eg Fig 6.5.D: Grove Farm and West Wick Farm). In Rolstone and eastern Puxton farmsteads typically had very few fields immediately adjacent to the farmhouse with the majority scattered across surrounding areas (Fig 6.5.D: Old Chestnut and Stuntree Farms; Fig 6.6: Rushworths), though in western Puxton and around Puxton Moor the holdings were a little more compact (Fig 6.5.D: South Farm). In Congresbury Marsh the farmsteads had large compact home grounds, with a few detached fields in the former common fields east of Dolemoor (Fig 6.5.D: Heathgate and Rookery Farms; Fig 6.6: Chestnut Farm). These

Table 6.1 Merton College lands in the surveys of 1601, 1756 and 1840 (tithe)

1601	area 1601	1756	area 1756	Tithe Number
1. One ground called Great Rushwoods, half pasture, half tillage, having a partition in the midst	8a 0r 0p	Rushey in Dolemore Lane	10a 0r 0p	TM 49 [abuts Dolemoor Lane]
2. One other ground called Little Rushwoods, pasture	4a 0r 0p	Five acres opposite	5a 0r 0p	TM 50 [on the opposite side of Dolemoor Lane to TM 49]
3. One piece of pasture ground abbutting upon Flemming Gout*, half acre	0a 2r 0p	Cod Acre	1a 0r 0p	TM 143* 'Smock Acre'
4. One halfe acre of pasture lying in a ground called Whatlys parrock	0a 2r 0p	Puxton Paddock	½a	TM 202
5. Arable called Little Ashfield	2a 0r 0p	Ashfield	2½a [with TM 200+202]	TM 205
6. Arable lying in Great Ashfield	1a 0r 0p	Ashfield	2½a [with TM 205]	TM 200+202 'Ashield'
7. One acre and halfe of meadow in a close called Prince, being disjointed	1a 2r 0p	in common with lands of James Arundell	1½a	TM 193 'Prints'
8. A little orchard	0a 2r 0p	orchard	1½a	?
9. One 4th part of an acre of arable adjoining to the orchard	0a 1r 0p			TM 219
10. A little cut full of elms containing the 6th part of an acre	0a 0r 27p	Withy Bed	¼a	?
11. One half acre meadow lying in a ground called Leydens Hurst	0a 2r 0p	The Yeo	½a	TM 204 'Yeo Ground'
meadow	2a 0r 0p			
pasture	9a 0r 0p			
arable	7a 1r 0p			
orchard	0a 2r 0p			
a [?]platt of elms	0a 0r 27p			
in all	18a 3r 27p		22a 3r 0p	
common for two great cattle or thereabouts in a great moor called Puckstons Moor: for which common, work in two rivers, Bawles ewe [Balls Yeo] and Hole ewe [Oldbridge River], one and twenty feet a piece, is to be performed, and fifty feet thereabout, about the said moor				TM 88a in the enclosed Puxton Moor

* this parcel can be identified as No. 143 ('Smock Acre') in the Tithe Survey, which lay next to No. 142 (Flemans: Fig 6.6, bottom right).

remarkable different patterns of landholding are summarised in Figure 6.5.E.

The antiquity of the 19th-century tenements

This characterisation of the 19th-century landscape is quite straightforward, but how old are the patterns that have been identified? Surveys of Puxton and Rolstone (*c* 1770, 1755, 1642, and *c* 1630), of Congresbury and Wick (1738–39), and of Hewish (1700) show that while individual tenements may have lost or gained odd fields, many were unchanged, as were the fundamental differences in the spatial disposition of fields shown in Figure 6.5.E. The study of individual tenements shows that these patterns can, in some cases at least, even be traced back to the late medieval period. For example, one area that had a particularly fragmented pattern of landownership in the tithe survey and on the map of *c* 1770 was around Ashfield and Prints in western Puxton, both of which had surviving areas of open fields. Not only does this support the link between highly fragmented patterns of landownership and former open fields, but the exceptionally good documentation for one freehold tenement shows how little it had changed over the course of the post-medieval period (Fig 6.6 and Table 6.1). In 1468 the copyhold tenancy of 'Russhworths' (named after the family who held the tenement in the 14th century) was granted to Merton College, Oxford, by the executors of the will of Thomas Beckington, Bishop of Bath and Wells (BodL MC 1204–35). The tenement represented the amalgamation of two earlier holdings: 'half a furlong of land, in length and breadth, as it lies in the East Field between the common road to Congresbury on its south side and the furlong of Thomas Crossman called Elleneacris on its west side' (29 Sept. 1404: BodL MC 1205), and '18 acres of arable land and three acres of pasture' (1 July 1428: BodL MC 1207). The '18 acres' of 1428 were surveyed in 1601 and 1756 and can be identified through field-names on the tithe map as the scattered fields of Samuel Bisdee's tenement (leased to Henry Sparkes and Samuel Hurley) lying in and around Ashfield and Prints (along with three post-enclosure fields in the former Puxton Moor leased in lieu of the tenement's former common rights). There is complete continuity in the scattered fields that made up this tenement. The 'half furlong of land in East Field' can also be traced through to the 19th century as TM 49 at the eastern end of Dolemoor Lane (Fig 2.5).

This example illustrates that there is more to historic landscape analysis than simply mapping the morphology of its physical components such as settlement and field boundary patterns. This examination of the patterns of landholding has revealed marked local differences in the 19th century, and for those tenements with good documentation the patterns do appear to have been remarkably stable. The broad variations in the character of landholding – such as the smaller fragmented tenements in Puxton contrasting with the large compact holdings in Congresbury Marsh – can certainly be traced back at least as far as the 15th–16th centuries, although the extent to which they can be back-projected beyond the post-Black Death consolidation of landholding is unclear (see 'Documentary evidence for the management of land' p 110 below).

The unenclosed landscape

A fundamental division within any historic landscape is between those areas that are covered within an enclosed fieldscape, and open or unenclosed areas. This distinction is most evident in upland areas, but is also of fundamental importance in some lowland landscapes including the wetlands of the North Somerset Levels. Before reclamation, the whole wetland landscape was unenclosed, and even after the construction of the sea wall areas of intertidal salt marsh remained along the coastal frontage and the embanked tidal rivers (Fig 6.7). Even the area behind the sea wall was not necessarily all enclosed as for many centuries, and while the higher coastal areas were settled and farmed, the lower-lying backfens were left as unenclosed common pastures. Earthen fen-banks often marked the division between the enclosed areas and backfens (see below; Fig 6.7).

The last surviving areas of common land, the Moors in Banwell, Brinsea, Congresbury, and Puxton, were enclosed by Act of Parliament in the late 18th–early 19th centuries (Fig 6.16). Before then they were permanent pasture, and the right to graze animals there was attached to certain tenements, as was the case with Merton College's holding at Ashfield (see Table 6.1). These backfen commons were once far larger, and an interdisciplinary analysis of the landscape can establish their former extents. Large areas around Banwell Moor, for example, appear to have been enclosed in the centuries preceding the Act of Parliament. Documentary and fieldwalking (manure scatter) evidence suggests that Puddy Moor to the north of the Banwell River was enclosed in the early to mid-17th century. By the late 17th century a 29-acre close called New Moor was carved out of the western side of Banwell Moor, followed by the *c* 30-acre close called Silver Moors that was itself later sub-divided (Fig 2.4).

The enclosed landscape

Artificial drainage and flood defence

One of the key features characterising the North Somerset Levels today is that they have been entirely handcrafted by human communities which transformed an intertidal salt marsh into a freshwater agricultural landscape. The success of this landscape relies upon a complex system of water management that stops the sea from entering the Levels at the coast whilst dealing with freshwater run-off from the adjacent uplands and precipitation that falls on the Levels themselves.

Summer ring dikes: the infield enclosures (Figs 6.6–6.8)

A common feature of the historic landscape in the reclaimed marshes of not just the North Somerset Levels but all of the Severn Estuary wetlands are oval-shaped enclosures preserved within the field boundary pattern. These infield enclosures share a number of common characteristics (Rippon 1994a; 1996a; 1997a; 2002; 2004b; Gilbert 1996; Allen 2004):

- they mostly occur individually but occasionally in pairs
- they are restricted to the higher, coastal areas that were the first to be settled, enclosed, and drained (they are not found in the lower-lying backfens that were enclosed later)
- their shape is generally oval, and this unconstrained shape suggests that they were created in a landscape that was largely devoid of other features

Figure 6.6 Aerial view and interpretation of Ashfield and Chestnut Farm in Puxton and Congresbury, illustrating examples of landscape stratigraphy, the way in which documentary sources can be given a spatial dimension through their integration with the physical fabric of the historic landscape, and the contrasting structure of tenements – Merton College's scattered holding in Ashfield (based on the survey of 1601) contrasts with the extensive home ground of Chestnut Farm (aerial photograph © National Monuments Record RAF/3G/TUD/UK15/21 PART I, January 1946, fr 5037)

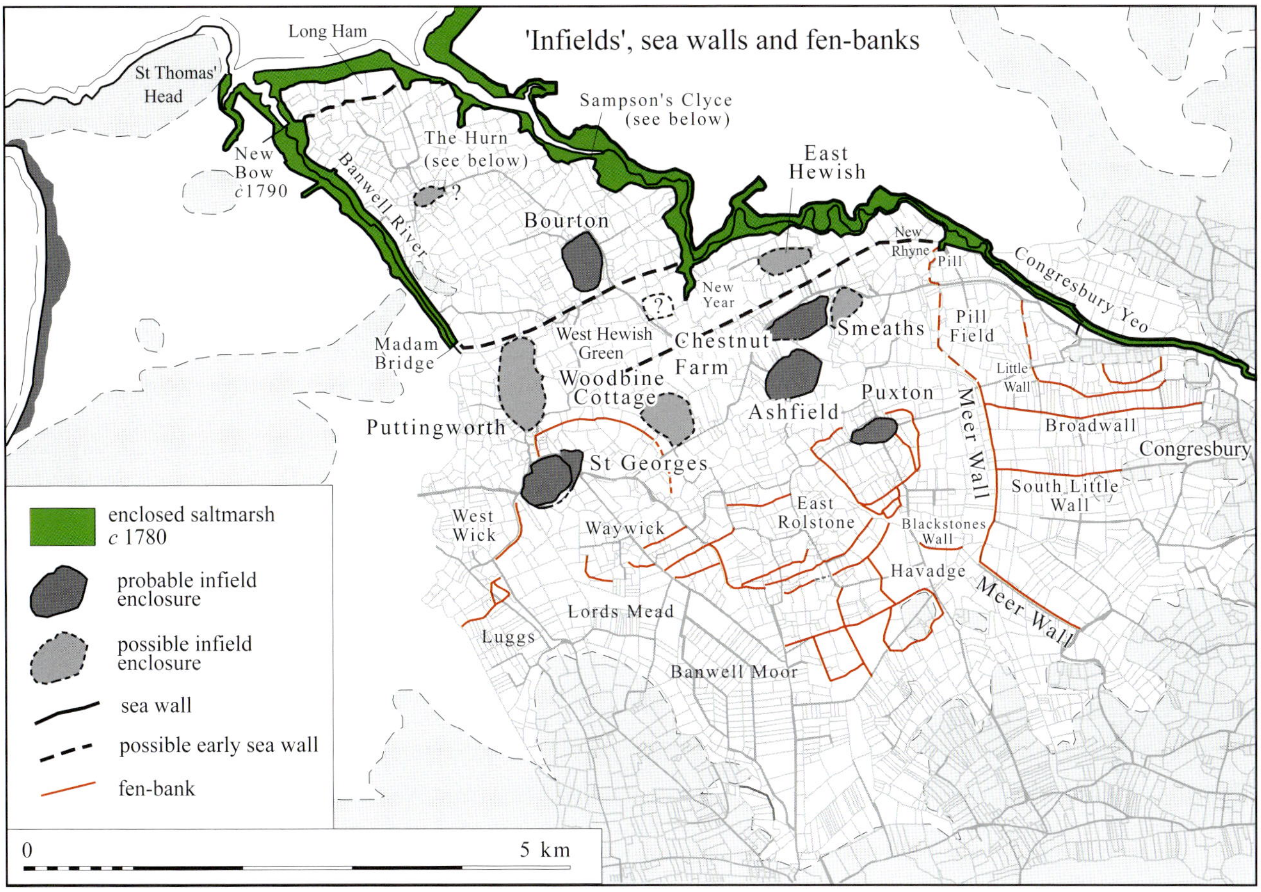

Figure 6.7 Landscape elements related to flood defence (infields, sea walls, and fen-banks) in the main study area, and aerial view of the estuary of the Congresbury Yeo looking south-east down the New Cut of the Oldbridge River at Sampson's Clyce towards Banwell and Dolebury Hills (on the skyline, centre). The spade-dug gullies (gripes) cut into the surface of the fields in the foreground were to aid drainage

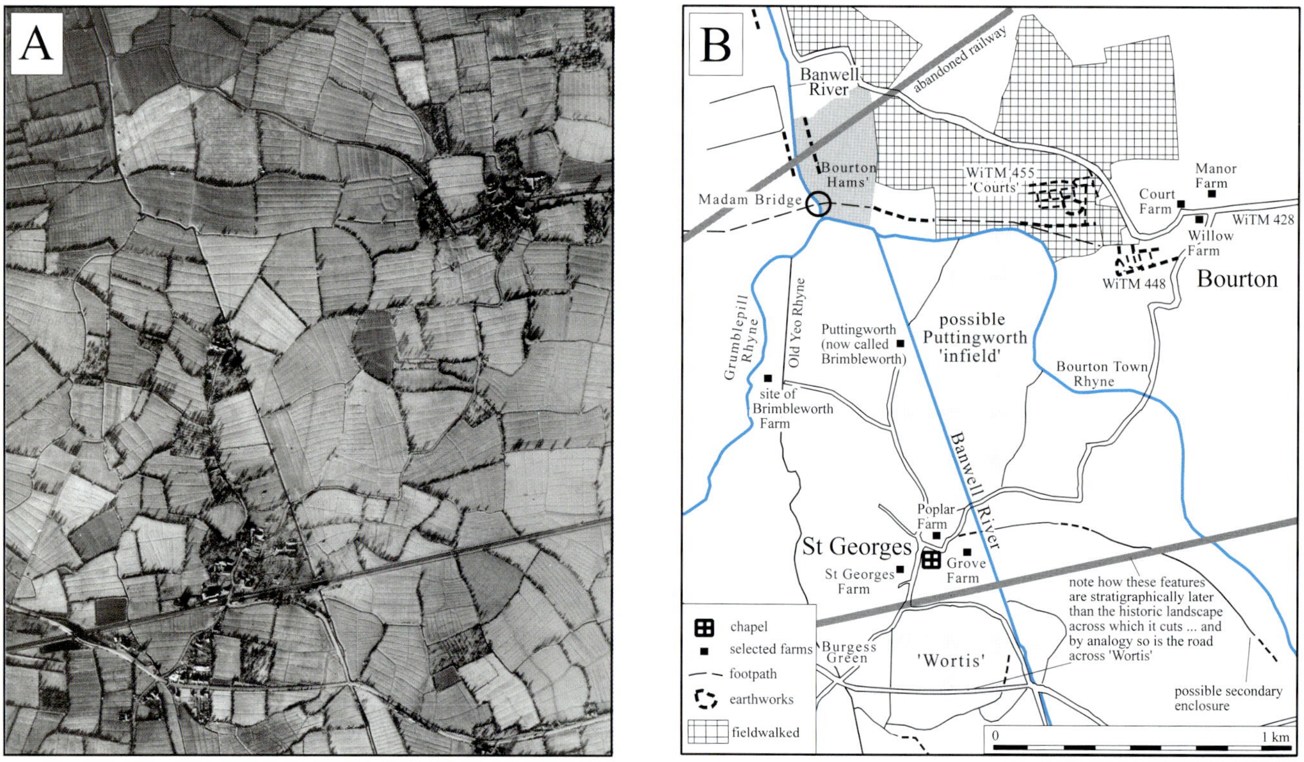

Figure 6.8 Aerial view and interpretation of St Georges and Bourton. Note how earthworks, mostly gripes, were preserved in almost every field, including the deserted settlement of 'Courts' west of Bourton which has been fieldwalked. There are several clear examples of landscape stratigraphy where linear features (two railways and the road across 'Wortis') were constructed after the earliest maps of the area were drawn. The Banwell River shows the same type of stratigraphic relationship to the historic landscape and by analogy is also later than the fields through which it passes (aerial photograph © National Monuments Record RAF/540/640, December 1951, fr 4008)

- roads and droveways run towards the enclosures, but then pass around them
- their size is typically *c* 5–20ha (12–50 acres; average 13ha, 32 acres)
- extant settlements are almost always located on the edge of or just outside the enclosed area suggesting that they represent areas of agricultural land, not an enclosed settlement
- a number are associated with churches or chapels, suggesting some pre-eminence in the settlement pattern, again possibly indicating their relatively early origins
- at least some had a bank running around the enclosure's perimeter
- some have 'worthy' field-names that may indicate an early enclosure
- in some cases they are associated with larger, concentric enclosures.

The clearest examples within the study area are at Puxton and St Georges, though another nine possible examples have been identified (Table 6.2 and Fig 6.7). There is a wide range of ways that such oval configurations of roads and field boundaries can arise. They could potentially be small bedrock islands, as occur elsewhere in wetlands, including river floodplains (eg Taylor 2002, fig 6), although coring at several infield enclosures, including Puxton, has shown that this is not the case in these coastal marshes (Gilbert 1996; and see Chapter 9 below). Other examples of oval-shaped enclosures in the English landscape originated as greens and commons (Oosthuizen 2002; Taylor 2002), though there is nothing to indicate this was the case here; in fact where there are areas of common they tend to occur beyond the edge of the infield enclosure (eg Puxton: Fig 9.4). Another potential analogy, that they are early Christian enclosures similar to the *llans* of Cornwall and Wales (eg Silvester 1997), can also be dismissed as there are far too many: there are ten possible examples south of the Congresbury Yeo and a further six to the north.

Closer parallels for the infield enclosures of the Severn Estuary marshes are assarts in areas of common, moorland, and woodland (eg Warner 1987; 1996, fig 7.6; Rippon 1997a, fig 49; 2004a, fig 13.1; Roberts and Wrathmell 2002, figs 4.12, 4.5 and 6.3). When creating an enclosure in an unenclosed area of waste the most economical shape is an oval as this gives the shortest length of perimeter per area enclosed (for the same reason medieval deer parks often adopted this shape as the pale (fence) around the perimeter was expensive to both build and maintain). The same applies in the context of

Table 6.2 The infield enclosures in the main study area (in decreasing order of certainty): see Fig 6.7 for location

site	circuit	settlement in 19th century	chapel
Puxton	complete (Figs 1.8, 2.5 and 9.2)	hamlet to north	yes
St Georges	complete (Fig 6.8)	hamlet to north	yes
Ashfield	nearly complete (Fig 6.6)	hamlet to south	no
Bourton	nearly complete (Fig 6.11)	Hippisleys and Hodders Farm on NW edge	no
Puttingworth	nearly complete (Fig 6.8)	Puttingworth Farm on western edge	no
Chestnut Farm	nearly complete (Fig 6.6)	single farm at centre	no
Smeaths	complete (Fig 6.6)	The Oaks on northern edge	no
East Hewish	conjectural: around three quarters of circuit can be reconstructed from earthworks and extant field boundaries	hamlet to east	no
Woodbine Cottage	conjectural: around three quarters of circuit can be reconstructed from earthworks and extant field boundaries	single farm to south; part of detached part of Kewstoke parish	no
Wick village	a number of curvilinear boundaries around the hamlet at Wick are suggestive of an 'infield' enclosure obscured by later settlement (Fig 1.3)	occupied by village	yes
West Hewish Green	sub-rectangular arrangement of field boundaries, seemingly cut by Greenstreet Common	no	no

marshland colonisation, where the enclosing ditch will have been dug into heavy clay. In some cases the curvilinear enclosure may also incorporate a naturally meandering tidal creek.

These infield enclosures on the North Somerset Levels would appear, therefore, to be the earliest intakes on an area of otherwise relatively featureless marsh though it is not apparent from historic landscape analysis alone whether they pre- or post-date the construction of a sea wall along the coast. This leads to two possible interpretations: firstly, that they were themselves sea walls built on the surface of a high intertidal salt marsh and were designed to prevent summer flooding of a small cultivated area, or secondly, that they were the first areas to be enclosed following the construction of a more substantial sea wall along the coast. These hypotheses were tested through fieldwork at Puxton, discussed further in Chapter 9, and the former proved to be the case.

The sea walls (Fig 6.7)

Today, the North Somerset Levels are protected from tidal inundation by a continuous sea wall that runs along the coast from Middlehope to Clevedon, with the Congresbury Yeo discharging its waters through a sluice at Tuthill Ear north of Bourton. Until the 20th century, however, the Congresbury Yeo was tidal all the way back to the fen-edge at Congresbury village, and so in effect the areas to the north and south were separate reclamations (Fig 6.7). Before the construction of the sluice at Tutshill Ear the sea wall ran from Congresbury along the southern side of the Yeo, then along the open coast in Wick St Lawrence before turning south along the eastern side of the Banwell River. The Banwell River currently enters the Severn Estuary in a recessed sluice at New Bow though this was only constructed around *c* 1790 (Allen 1997a). Earthworks and field boundaries show that before then the sea walls ran as far south as Madam Bridge which may have been the site of an earlier sluice gate (which also provided a convenient bridging point for the river, perhaps comparable to the surviving structure at Grange Pill, Woolaston, Gloucestershire: Fig 5.5).

There are also hints, in the form of earthworks aligned with extant field boundaries and footpaths depicted on early maps, that the sea wall which ran down the eastern side of the Banwell River may originally have turned north-east from Madam Bridge running through Bourton and then along the northern side of the New Ear Rhyne, joining up with the sea wall on the south side of the Congresbury Yeo just to the west of the New Ear (Figs 6.7 and 6.8). If this was the case, then the earliest sea wall may simply have encircled Wick St Lawrence, with the western side of the Banwell River having been embanked separately by constructing a sea wall from St Thomas' Head to Lynchmead Farm (Fig 12.2.B).

In order to reclaim the land between Wick St Lawrence and the fen-edge at Congresbury an embankment would have had to be constructed to the south of the Congresbury Yeo. The current structure hugs the riverbank very closely, and has clearly been constructed in a piecemeal fashion as areas of salt marsh within the river's meanders were progressively enclosed. The original embankment is likely to have been a simpler structure with a relatively straight course, and set back from the river itself to avoid the risk of erosion. The line of this original sea wall may be preserved by an alignment of field boundaries and roads running west from the Oar up to Pillhay Bridge, and then along New Rhyne to the south of West Hewish (Figs 6.7 and 12.2.C). Only later was Hewish itself protected by a sea wall on the southern bank of the Yeo between Pillhay and the New Ear.

The exact line of the original sea wall along the open coast is not known. On the Welsh side of the Severn Estuary the present sea wall clearly cuts across the grain of the historic landscape, having been moved back to this position by coastal erosion in the late medieval period (Rippon 1996a, 97–9; Allen 2004). The original line of the medieval sea wall is not known but analogy with the opposite side of the Estuary suggests that it may have been over 800m further out into the Estuary (Allen and Rippon 1997a; Allen 2002a). On the North Somerset Levels the oldest extant sea wall in Kingston Seymour similarly cuts across the grain of the historic landscape and so must have been set back to that position, though in Wick St Lawrence the situation is less clear. The earliest definite sea wall is that shown on the map of 1738 which runs to the north of Long Ham, though an alignment of field boundaries to the south may represent the line of an earlier sea wall that does not obviously post-date the adjacent field boundaries and so may be the original structure.

Drainage and inland flood defence

Once these sea walls were built there remained the problem of freshwater flooding which was dealt with in two ways: a hierarchy of drainage channels cut into the surface of the fields to deal with precipitation, and a series of embankments (fen-banks) to protect settled areas from flooding from the lower-lying back fens. The hierarchy of drainage channels started with a network of spade-dug gullies or gripes (a term that can be traced back to at least 1636: BRO DC/E/25/2), that were cut into the surface of fields in order to collect precipitation (Figs 6.7 and 6.8). From there water flowed into the network of field boundary ditches which in turn flowed into the major drainage watercourses known as rhynes within which water levels could be managed through the construction of small sluices known as gowtes or gouts (gates). These rhynes discharged their waters into the major rivers and estuaries via sluice gates (years, ears, or clyces). Very few examples of traditional gouts remain (and none on the North Somerset Levels), though at Hill, in Gloucestershire, two early structures survive. The earliest gout, probably early 17th-century in date, now serves simply as a bridge across Hill Pill as the sea wall has now been moved forward, while its possibly 18th-century successor is now a ruin out on the salt marsh. The modern sea wall/sluice lies between the two. These structures reveal how an early gout was built with two substantial stone walls to the front and back of an earthen dam, through which a narrow arched tunnel allowed the freshwater rhyne to discharge its waters. A sluice gate/valve on the seaward side would have been forced shut by the rising tide, so preventing sea water from flowing through the tunnel (Rippon 2000a, figs 29–33).

The second source of flooding was freshwater run-off from the backfens which was dealt with through the construction of earthen fen-banks, known as walls, and an adjacent ditch, such as the bank and ditch [*ripa et fossata*] between 'Twyndycke' and the 'Common' in Puxton that John Cooke was ordered to repair in 1568 (Fig 2.5; SRO DD/WY/W/CR 46/1). The importance of these structures is shown by an incident in 1560 when John Herdiche 'broke certain walls called banks so the stream over ran walls called Blackstones [also in Puxton] to the serious loss of all the tenants' (Figs 2.5 and 6.9; WRO 2667/13/452). In Puxton the term ward appears to relate to both an embankment and a ditch: in 1492, for example, Richard Craas was ordered to make a ward at Blackstones called 'Blackstoneswalle' (BodL RAWL B317), while in 1495 tenants were ordered to make and scour [clean out] the ward called Blackstonesward (BodL RAWL B317). Once the backfens were enclosed fen-banks became redundant and so most have been destroyed, though wall names are sometimes preserved in place- and field-names. Others survive simply as long, sinuous alignments of field boundaries that divide areas of medieval enclosure from what were the open common pastures of areas such as Banwell Moor and Havadge (Figs 2.4 and 6.7).

The maintenance of the drainage and flood defence system

In a wetland landscape such as this ditches need regular cleaning to prevent them becoming choked with vegetation and silt. Today, the major rivers are cleaned out every year (a process traditionally known as keeching: Beisly 1996, 49), and ditches every four to six years (Storer 1985, 14; and see Chapter 11). During the medieval period maintaining the drainage and flood defence system was the responsibility of the hundred court, the manorial courts, the lord of the manor, and the customary tenants. The lord of the manor appears to have had responsibility for surveying the condition of the embankments and watercourses, and two of the Bishop of Wells's manorial officials at Banwell were 'wardens of the River Yeo' (PRO SC11/951; Hembry 1967, 20). In 1449/50, for example, the accounts of the Bishop of Wells included expenses at Banwell to view (survey) the 'Lytheyoo' [Liddy Yeo?] (*Wells II*, 78). The responsibility for carrying out any necessary maintenance was part of the customary tenure and services owed

Figure 6.9 Blackstones Rhyne, which marks the southern boundary of Puxton parish (looking east from ST 4095 6235). References in the Puxton court rolls suggest that in the 15th century there was a fen-bank adjacent to the ditch (BodL RAWL B317). Palaeoenvironmental evidence suggests that this relatively open ditch, without the scrubby hawthorn hedges that fringe many field boundaries on the Levels today, is probably very much what the landscape looked like in the later Roman and medieval periods

to the lord of the manor. In 1497, for example, John Payne held 100 acres of land in Banwell off Woodspring Priory by service of finding two men for a day to scour a weir beside Banwell called Kinges River (*CIPM* Hen VII Vol I, No1150). The major rivers (or yeos) and fen-banks were divided into 20-foot stretches known as ropes, each of which was the responsibility of a specific tenement, as was the case with Merton College's land in Puxton (Table 6.1; and BRO BMC/4/376; SRO D/RA 1/2/124; SRO D/P/Kenn 4/1/2). In 1654, for example, the Congresbury court roll records that John Ewens surrendered a customary tenement and 28 acres in Wick, the services including scouring two ropes 'in the common river called the main Yeo' [the Congresbury Yeo] (BRO BMC/4/376). The sea walls appear to have been measured out in 'lugs' and 'spadeworks' marked out by 'mere-stones' (SRO DD/X/BUE 1–2; SRO DD/BR/U 5). In 1432, for example, a lease for 20 acres at 'Cradworth', 'Oddieworth', and 'le Busshehyron' in Clevedon specifies such work on both the sea wall and 'Moor Wall' (ie a fen-bank) (SRO DD/X/RY c.1968). Even dryland tenements, presumably with lands and/or common rights on the Marsh, had attached duties to maintain the drainage system. In 1654, for example, John Jones and Thomas Lascom were admitted to a tenement in Brinsea with the responsibility of making and sufficiently scouring four ropes in the common river called the Main Yeo (BRO BMC/4/376). Tenants were also paid for maintaining drainage gripes, ditches, rhynes, and rivers. In 1653, for example, jurors in the Congresbury manorial court instructed John Rouswell to throw and ground the ditch that lay against Manor Hill from the poole down as far as Gode Croft, by payment of two shillings a rope (BRO BMC/4/376), while in 1655 Thomas Selwood was paid £1 7s 0d for keeching [cleaning out] the Balls Yeo, Rockers Yeo, and Liddy Yeo (WRO 2667/23/37).

Water levels within the different watercourses were maintained through a series of sluice gates – known as gouts – and the construction of these was a costly affair that required the employment of skilled labourers. In 1686, for example, the accounts of Puxton manor included payments for work at Havadge and Rolstone Gouts amounting to £1 3s 0d for stone and mortar, 18s 0d for two sacks of lime, 6s 0d for a new door, and £2 2s 9d for Samuel White the mason (to put this figure in context, the total cost of keeching the various rhynes in Puxton and Rolstone

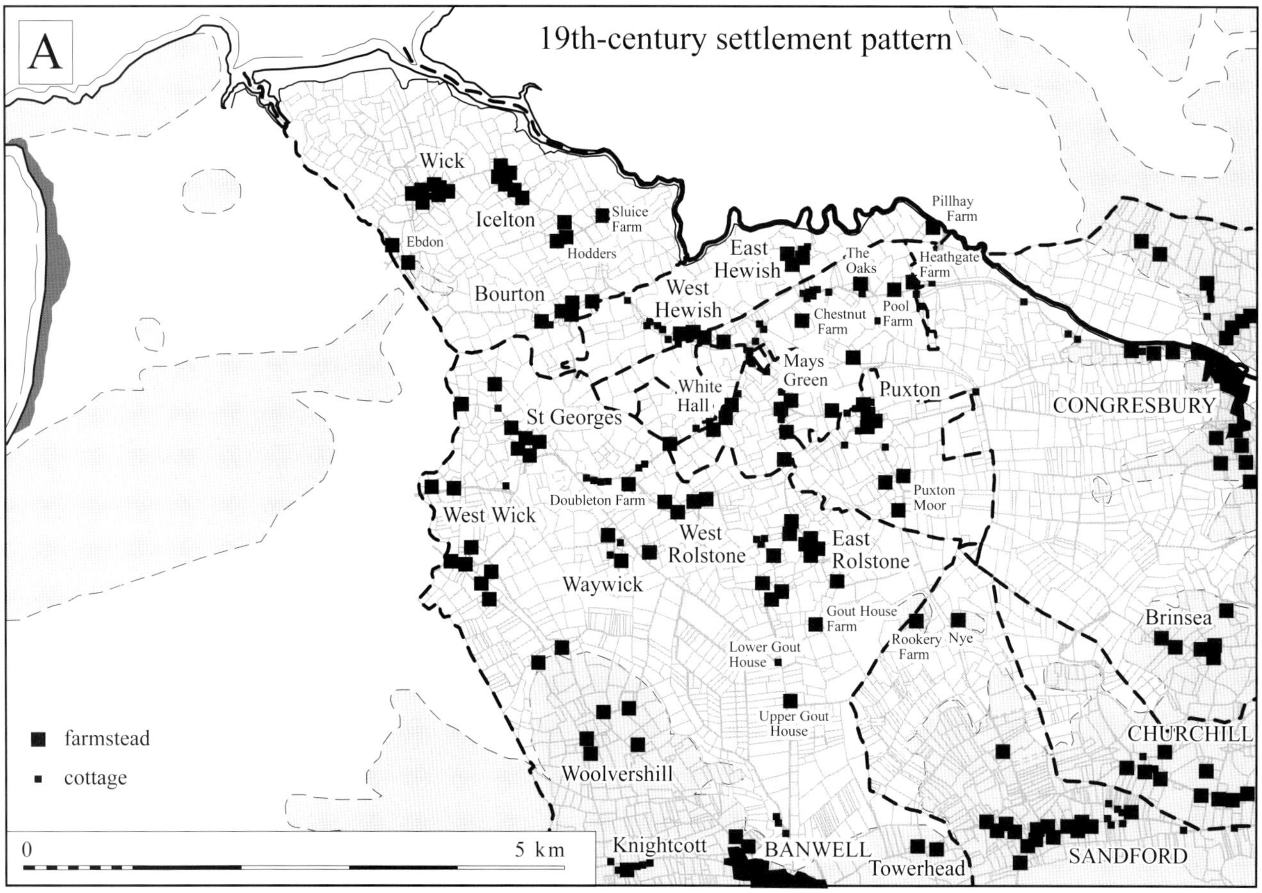
A
19th-century settlement pattern
Wick
Icelton
Sluice Farm
Ebdon
Hodders
Bourton
East Hewish
West Hewish
The Oaks
Pillhay Farm
Heathgate Farm
Chestnut Farm
Pool Farm
Mays Green
White Hall
Puxton
St Georges
CONGRESBURY
Doubleton Farm
Puxton Moor
West Wick
West Rolstone
East Rolstone
Waywick
Gout House Farm
Brinsea
Lower Gout House
Rookery Farm
Nye
Upper Gout House
CHURCHILL
farmstead
cottage
Woolvershill
0
5 km
Knightcott
BANWELL
Towerhead
SANDFORD

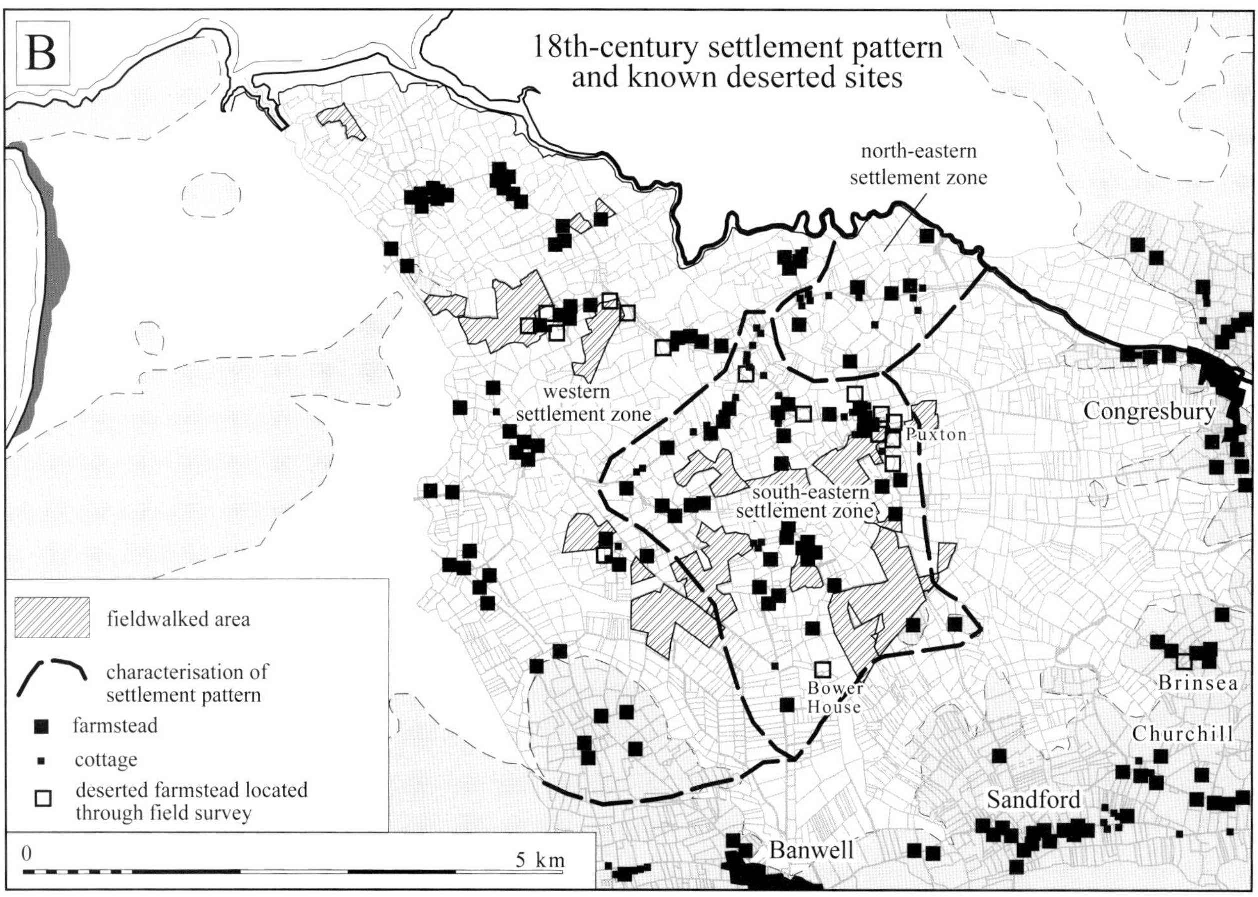
B
18th-century settlement pattern and known deserted sites
north-eastern settlement zone
western settlement zone
Puxton
Congresbury
south-eastern settlement zone
fieldwalked area
characterisation of settlement pattern
farmstead
cottage
deserted farmstead located through field survey
Bower House
Brinsea
Churchill
Sandford
0
5 km
Banwell

that year came to just £1 12s 6d) (WRO 2667/23/37). The integration of historic landscape analysis with documentary sources such as these reminds us how the countryside of today was created through the work of many generations of past farming communities.

The settlement pattern

The 19th-century settlement pattern (Fig 6.10)

As described in Chapter 1, despite the physical uniformity of the case-study area, the 19th-century settlement pattern shows significant diversity, ranging from the compact hamlets in Wick St Lawrence to the dispersed farmsteads of Congresbury Marsh. Figure 1.2 presents a basic characterisation of the settlement pattern within each parish in north-west Somerset, and Figure 6.10 shows a more detailed analysis for the study area. In terms of the distribution of settlement within the study area in the 19th century, a broad division can be drawn between four areas (Fig 6.10.B):

- Congresbury Marsh (the north-eastern settlement zone): predominantly isolated farmsteads, with small clusters of cottages on areas of enclosed roadside waste
- Puxton and Rolstone (the south-eastern settlement zone): predominantly loose conglomerations of both farmsteads and cottages
- Wick St Lawrence, Hewish, and the western part of Banwell Marsh (Waywick, West Wick, and St Georges) (the western settlement zone): predominantly nucleated, hamlet-based settlement pattern, with occasional isolated farmsteads. The hamlets in Wick St Lawrence are notably more compact that those in Banwell Marsh.
- the major fen-edge villages of Banwell, Sandford, and Congresbury, with the looser conglomerations of Churchill and Brinsea.

Most nucleated settlements within the study area appear to have grown in a gradual and piecemeal fashion with little sign of any planning (eg Waywick: Fig 1.4; St Georges: Fig 6.8). The exception is West Hewish whose morphology is suggestive of a small rectangular block measuring 110 × 340m, possibly divided into three compounds, corresponding to West Hewish Farm (now called Manor Farm), a now deserted site to the east, and the deserted site of Plentys to the west (Fig 6.12). Although the farms in Icelton have the appearance of forming a planned row, this arrangement probably reflects the underlying set of coaxial field boundaries in this part of the parish.

Place-names and documentary evidence

The place-name **Wick** (St Lawrence) could have several origins. Although Draper (2002; and see Gelling 1978, 63–74) has recently reaffirmed the association of 'wick' place-names in Wiltshire with Romano-British sites, the 3rd- to 4th-century pottery found in this example is likely to have been brought to the surface through ditch digging as by analogy with Kingston Seymour, that lies an equal distance from the coast, the Romano-British ground surface is likely be around 0.7m below the present (Usher 1967; Lilly and Usher 1972). There is no evidence for a coastal trading centre, or salt production, and in this marshland landscape the name probably reflects the origins of this settlement as a specialised dairy farm (Cameron 1996, 27), out on the marshes of the greater Congresbury estate. The dedication of Wick to St Lawrence is in keeping with the area's colonisation in the late pre-Conquest or immediately post-Conquest period, it often being found in areas of reclamation and colonisation away from the primary settlement areas (Arnold-Forster 1899a, 508–15; Everitt 1986, 225–57).

The names of **West Wick** and **Waywick** also probably reflect their origins as specialised dairying settlements within the marsh of the greater Banwell estate. West Wick, first recorded in 1660 (SRO DD/HB1), literally means the western wick, while Waywick, first recorded in 1475 as 'Wheywyck' and 'Wey wyke' (SRO T/PH/VCH 5i), may mean 'wick by the road' derived from the Old English (OE) *weg* = road).

The original name for **Icelton** appears to have been **East Town**, which is still the name of one of the farms, and of the rhyne flowing from Wick village to the Congresbury Yeo. There are references to Easton Town in the Churchwardens' records of 1831, 1836, and 1841, and in 1728 they refer to the 'hauling of William Andrewe's goods to Weeke from Easentown'. The earliest reference is in 1242–43 when it was recorded that 'it is agreed that William Lussier, guardian of the land and heirs of Philip

Figure 6.10 (opposite) ***A*** *The 19th-century settlement pattern within the main study area (based on the tithe surveys of c 1840).* ***B*** *A comparison with the 18th-century settlement pattern for those areas with estate maps (see Figure 6.15) which reflects very little change between then and the tithe surveys other than the emergence of several clusters of roadside cottages. Extensive areas have also been fieldwalked and, apart from some shrinkage of Bourton, East Rolstone and Puxton, the fundamental character of the different settlement patterns does not appear to have been significantly different in the past. Sources: maps of Congresbury 1739 (BRO 33041/BMC/4/PL1/1–4), Puxton and Rolstone c 1770 (SRO DD/X/WI 66), and Wick St Lawrence 1738 (BRO 04480)*

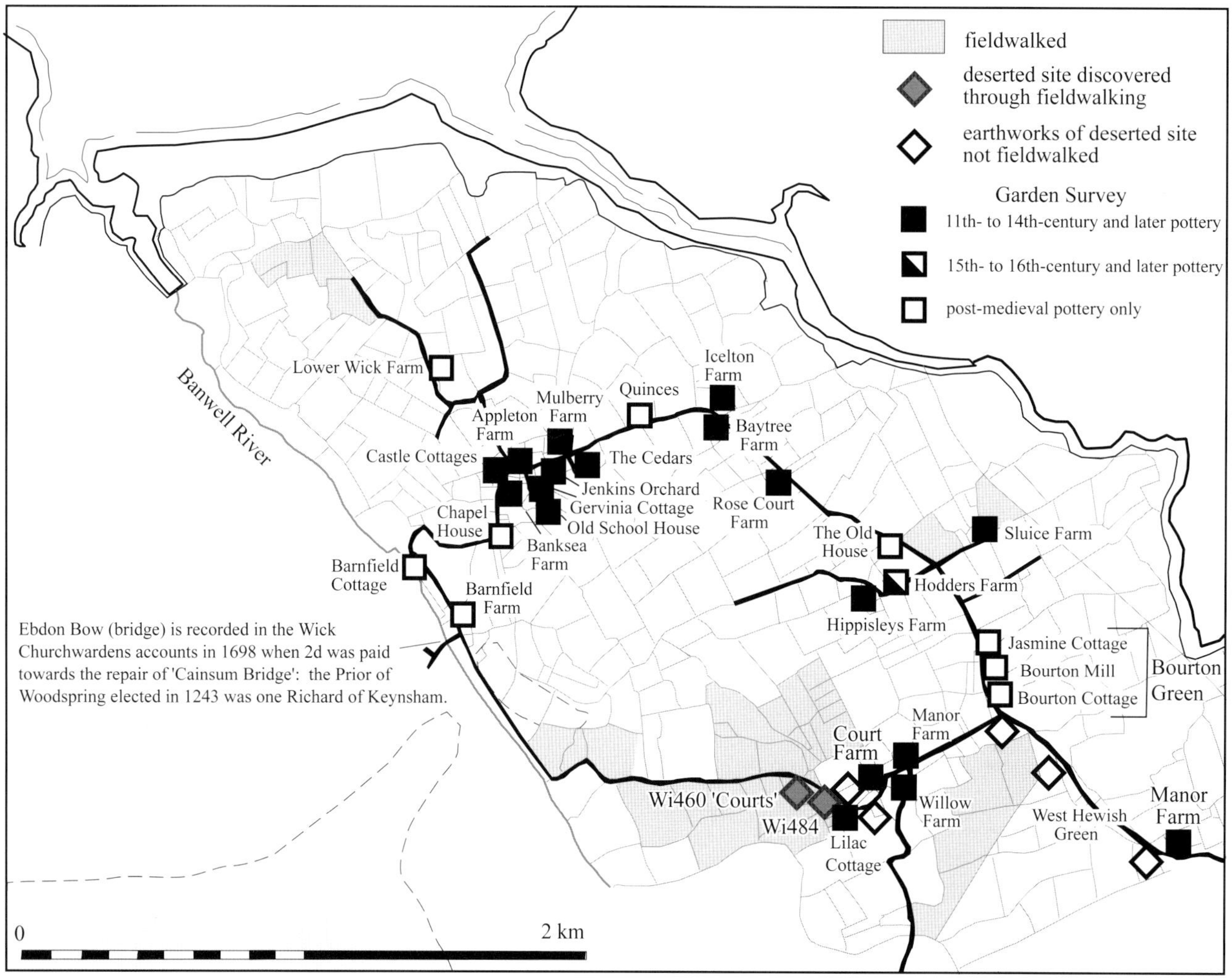

Figure 6.11 The results of garden survey and fieldwalking in Wick St Lawrence. The vast majority of those properties from which only post-medieval pottery was collected are known to be recent in origin (post-dating the map of 1738 in the case of Quinces, or being on enclosed roadside waste in the case of Bourton Green)

la Wyke . . . should grant to Philippa [la Wyke] the manor of Wyke . . . except a certain hamlet which is called Aeston' (*Pleas*, No. 505). The place-name **Bourton** (first recorded as Burton in 1274: *CIPM* II, No. 17) is interesting as it is usually thought to be derived from the OE *burh-tūn*, meaning 'fortified farmstead, or farmstead near a fortification' (Mills 1991, 44), or 'fortified enclosure or village' (Watts 2004, 73). This could refer to the possible infield enclosure. Such minor habitative *-tūn* names, combined with a geographical location (as in Easton) or a personal/family name (eg **Puxton**: see Chapter 7), are rare in documents predating the 8th century and are compatible with a period of colonisation in the centuries either side of the Norman Conquest (Cox 1976; Gelling 1978, 126; Costen 1992a, 121; Cameron 1996, 143). The origins of the names **Rolstone**, first recorded in the late 12th century as Rolveston (*Bruton* No. 133[2]), and **Doubleton** Farm, which is named on the map of *c* 1770 and is one of the very few farmsteads in the study area to have a proper place-name in the 18th century, are unknown. **Ebdon** (first documented as 'Ebdon ys bowe' [bridge] in 1475 (SRO T/ph/vch5i) may be the OE personal name Aebba and *tūn* (Michael Costen pers comm), or may contain the *dūn* element reflecting the nearby small bedrock island (Gelling and Cole 2000, 164–7).

The settlement of **St Georges** has an interesting history, and until recently it was known as **Puttingthorpe** and before that **Putteworth**. Around the late 12th/early 13th century Walter, rector of Publow, near Pensford in North Somerset, granted Bruton Priory all his land in Putteworth (*Bruton* 136). The 'worth' place-name element may be derived from the OE *wyrth* = enclosed farmstead, perhaps again referring to the infield enclosure. In 1324 a grant by John, Bishop of Bath and Wells, to John son of Robert de Strode, was confirmed as comprising 'the whole tenement with land, feedings, meadows and pastures, late held in villenage by Alice Offre, in Puttingthrop in the manor of Banwell, to hold for their lives at a yearly rent of 26s 8d' (*Liber Albus I*, 209). In 1331 Bishop Ralph of Shrewsbury granted a tenement and lands in Puttyn-

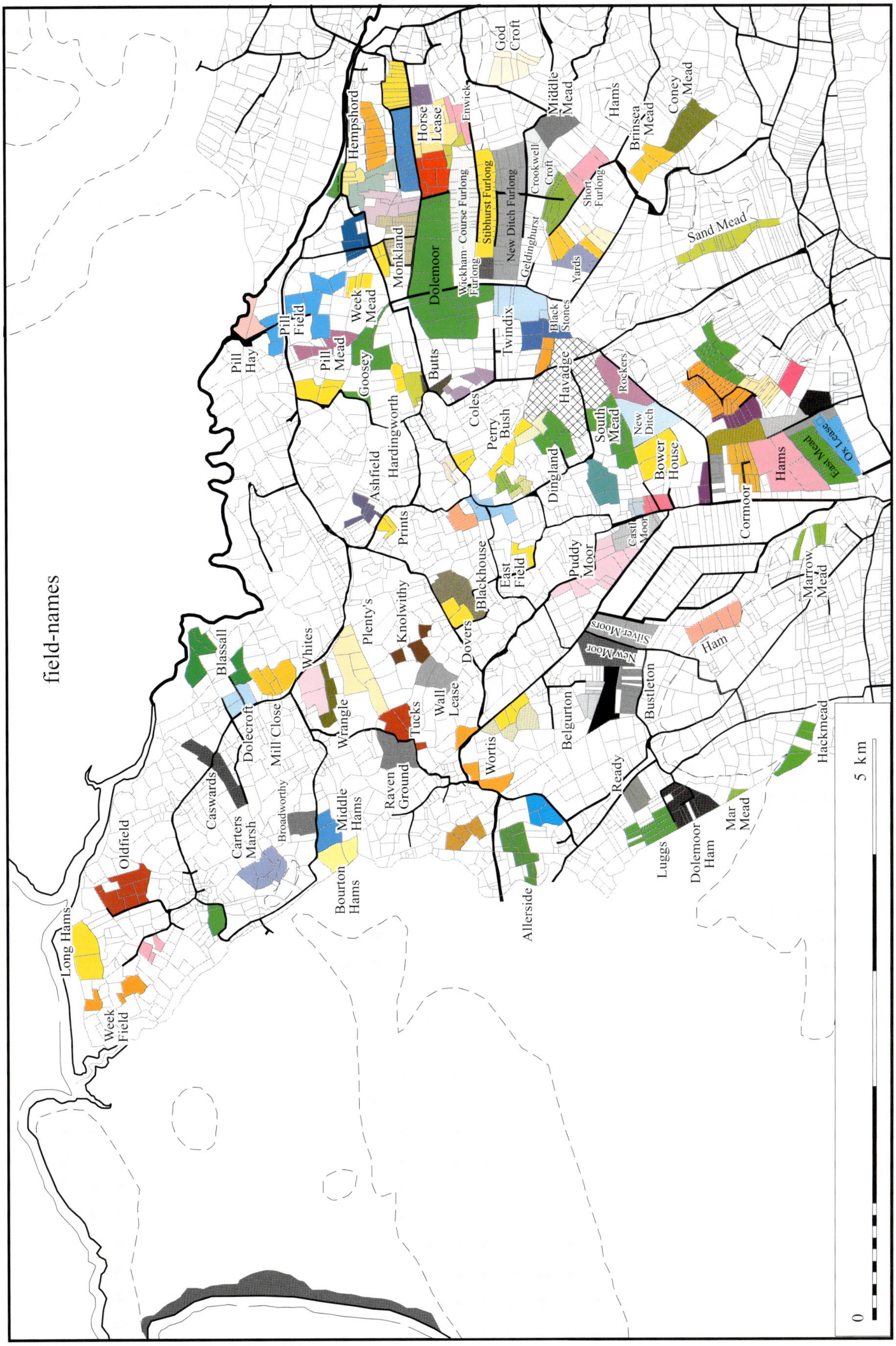

Figure 6.12 Selected field-names from the tithe surveys and earlier estate maps in the main study area. Fields with the same name have the same shading

gthrop in the manor of Banwell, that John de Acres and John son of Robert de Strode lately held, to Richard of Clivedon (*Shrewsbury*, No. 288; *Bath Chartulary*, No. 735). The 'throp' place-name element is derived from the OE *throp*, meaning a settlement or farmstead; it is very rare in the South-West but common in the east midlands where it appears as 'thorp'. It may suggest a pre-Conquest date (Michael Costen pers comm). In 1336 John de Chaumflour and Richard de Clyvedon were granted a licence to have divine services in the Chapel of **St George** of Pottyngthrop, in the parish of Banwell (*Shrewsbury*, No. 1050), and in 1521 the Banwell churchwardens' accounts refer to a chapel at St Georges (Knight 1902, 456). St George is a distinctively late church dedication, the saint becoming particularly popular from the 13th century (Arnold-Forster 1899b, 464–74; Everitt 1986, 256). The Survey of Chantries in 1548 includes the chapel of Saint George with one rood of ground, which in 1564 was granted to Thomas Reve, William Revette, and William Hechus (*Chantries*, 73–4; *Chantry Grants*, No. 72). This chapel appears to have been destroyed in the early 18th century, though its site is remembered in the tithe map field-name Chapel Hay (BaTM 35), from where skeletons are alleged to have been found (Knight 1902, 457; Fig 6.8). Bruton Priory's rectory manor also appears to have had one of its two tithe barns at Puttingthorp, the other being at Balls Barn in Rolstone (LPL: COMM.XIIa/1, f. 290; PRO SC6/HenVIII/3137m.45; PRO E134/1654/Mich 16). The place-name Puttingthorpe is found throughout the 17th century (PRO REQ2/168/4; WCL 10189, 23, 56, 99), at which time the name St Georges also appears for the first time (SRO DD/WY 75).

In the tithe survey fields within the infield enclosure at St Georges were known as Wortis, which may be derived from the OE *Word* that means enclosure. No 'worth' place-names are found in Anglo-Saxon records before the mid-8th century (Cox 1976). The possible infield enclosure to the north of Woodbine Cottage (in the detached part of Kewstoke) includes two fields called Knolwithy in the tithe survey, though it is unclear whether this is derived from 'worthy'. To the north of St Georges lies a farm that is today called **Brimbleworth**, but on the First Edition Six Inch map was called Puttingworth Farm; Brimbleworth was a recently deserted farm at the end of Brimbleworth Lane next to Grumblepill Rhyne. One or other of these may be the messuage and half yardland of old auster in Puttingworth comprising 40 acres (of which 20 acres arable) recorded in 1661 (WCL 10189, 17).

A noticeable characteristic of the local farm names is the very large number that related to trees, and this tradition appears to date back to the early 19th century. The Oaks, in Congresbury Marsh, for example, can be traced back through the Land Tax records as Oak Farm until 1803, but before that date was simply listed by its owner and occupier. The Poplars is first recorded in deed of 1804 (in private hands). In the 19th century other tree place-names in the study area were elm and willow (three examples each), myrtle, laurel, poplar, and chestnut (each with two examples), and single examples of bay, box, cedar, cypress, mulberry, oak, and rose. The meaning of Stuntree is unknown.

Settlement-indicative field-names

Elsewhere in Somerset and beyond it has been suggested that medieval and later field-names sometimes preserve the name of earlier settlements that were swept away when nucleated villages and open fields were created (eg Costen 1992b; Hey 2004, 37). Evidence for such settlement-indicative field-names from the study area is very limited. A cluster of fields named **Enwick** (CoTM 554, 578–9, 718) at the very end of the Silver Street promontory in Congresbury may preserve the name of another small dairying settlement later subsumed by the coaxial field system (Fig 6.12). **Wickham Furlong** in the same common field system may include the 'wick' place-name element, but is probably related to the adjacent fields that were detached parts of Wick St Lawrence parish (WiTM 488–90). There is nothing in the pattern of field boundaries, earthworks, or fieldwalking at **Broadworthy** in Wick St Lawrence (WiTM 368) to suggest a former settlement or enclosure. Two fields in at the junction of the Towerhead Brook and Liddy Yeo in Banwell are called **Catworthy** (BaTM 892 and 912), though the adjacent field in Sandford (No. 106 in the Winscombe tithe survey) is called Catwithy, giving an alternative derivation for the name (ie a withy or willow bed). Two fields in Puxton are called **Rushwoods** in the 1601 survey of Merton College's lands (Table 6.1; PxTM 49 and 50). Rushwood is derived from the name of the tenement focused on the Ashfield infield enclosure, and that in deeds of 1401 and 1468–69 is variously recorded as 'Rushyworthy', 'Russhworthis', and 'Russheworth', and in the 1547–48 court rolls as 'Russhworthies' and 'Rushford'. The name can be traced back to one John Rushworth who held the tenement before his death in 1378. It is not impossible that this is an example of a surname derived from a place-name, as was quite common in the 14th century (Aston 1983), suggesting that the Ashfield infield enclosure was called Rushworthy. Finally, two fields called **Hardingworth** in Puxton (Nos 43–4) have a rather curvilinear northern boundary, although a soil chemistry survey revealed only one small localised concentration of phosphate and heavy metals (in addition to the backfilled field boundary between field numbers 43 and 44) which upon excavation proved to be a dump of post-medieval material in the topsoil (Fig 9.3.B). The Hardingworth field-name appears in the survey of *c* 1770 but in the 1552 court roll is spelt 'Hardingforth'.

Archaeological evidence for the antiquity of the settlement patterns

With the exception of some tenements within Puxton recorded in late 15th-century court rolls, the medieval documentary sources relate to whole settlements (eg East Town, Puttingworth, Rolstone etc) rather than the individual farmsteads within them. Archaeological evidence, in contrast, can help establish the antiquity of both. A previous archaeological survey of Congresbury revealed a large number of findspots of medieval and post-medieval pottery in the gardens of surviving settlements,[1] or adjacent plots[2] in the dryland areas, and the same pattern can now be seen across the reclaimed marshland of Puxton, Rolstone, Congresbury Marsh, St Georges, and Wick St Lawrence.

The results from the collection of pottery from the gardens of extant houses as part of the NSLP (pottery identified by Alejandra Gutiérrez), a previous survey by a local resident Linda Jenkins (the pottery being identified at Weston-super-Mare Museum), and work by Cotswold Archaeology in St Georges is presented in Table 6.3 (CD). Many assemblages are small, but significantly all those farmhouses depicted on the tithe maps that had material collected from them produced 12th- to 13th-century and later material. Whether these sites were occupied any earlier than this cannot be determined as the possibly earlier pottery fabrics AA1 and AA2, that elsewhere in Somerset have been dated to the late 10th–11th centuries, were only found in association with later 11th- to 12th-century fabrics in the excavations at Puxton; before that date Somerset appears to have been aceramic. Most of the properties that failed to produce medieval material are known to be relatively recent such as Lower Wick Farm and the cottages on the former Bourton Green, both of which are on areas of former roadside waste (Fig 6.11). The one exception may be Ebdon, on the opposite side of the Banwell River in Worle, which probably does have medieval origins as Ebdon Bow Farm, and has produced fifteen sherds of medieval pottery including Ham Green ware (information from Linda Jenkins).

Extrapolation from these surveyed areas suggests that most 19th-century farmsteads were in place by at least the 12th–13th centuries, but does this represent the maximum extent of medieval settlement? The excellent survival of earthworks in the late 1940s (when the RAF photographed the area from the air) reveals just one wholly deserted settlement (the isolated farmstead at Bower House to the south of East Rolstone: see below), though hamlets such as Bourton (Fig 6.8), West Hewish, East Rolstone, Puxton (Fig 9.3.A), and Waywick (Fig 1.4) show signs of shrinkage. In Puxton this shrinkage was confirmed through fieldwalking and shovel test pitting, and appears to have been most pronounced during the late medieval period (see Chapter 9) though in some cases it was as late as the 19th century (eg BaTM 770 in East Rolstone and WiTM 454 in Bourton which were still occupied at the time of the tithe survey). Extensive areas were also fieldwalked in the lower-lying backfens and although these areas had been settled in the Roman period, no deserted medieval settlements were discovered. Just one deserted farmstead is known from earlier work in these backfens: a scatter of 12th- to 14th-century pottery, stone, and daub that Clarke (1976) recovered from a field called Bower House which is documented in 1379 as 'Bower', and in 1632 as the 'roofless tenement of Bower House'. In 1637–38 a 36-acre 'roofless tenement commonly known as Bower House' was held of the manor of Rolstone by Lord Paulett (SRO DD/SS 42). This is one of the lowest-lying locations to have been occupied in the medieval period and its desertion in the 14th century probably represents a classic example of settlement expansion into, and contraction from, the margins.

Overall, therefore, fieldwalking, shovel test pitting, and garden surveys, coupled with earlier finds, lead to three fundamental conclusions. Firstly, a large proportion of 19th-century farmsteads, many of which can be traced back through documentary sources to the 16th–17th centuries, were in fact occupied from at least the 12th–13th centuries. Secondly, while some individual tenements within the villages and hamlets have been deserted – that is there has been some settlement shrinkage – the overall distribution of medieval settlement was no greater than it was in the 19th century. There was no significant expansion of medieval settlement into areas that by the 18th and 19th centuries were devoid of occupation (notably the lower-lying backfens). Thirdly, the significant local variation in the character of the settlement patterns as mapped in the 18th–19th centuries can similarly be traced back to at least the 12th–13th centuries. There is no evidence that the fields in Wick, for example, were ever full of isolated farmsteads, or that Rolstone once had substantial nucleated villages. Overall, the distinctly different settlement character areas mapped in Figure 6.10. B are certainly of medieval origin.

Field systems

Field-names

In the tithe surveys the majority of fields have their names listed. In a number of places, adjacent fields share the same name and alongside other documentary evidence and the field boundary patterns, these field-names can be interpreted in a number of ways (Fig 6.12):

- former arable open fields (eg Ashfield and East Field in Puxton; Week Field in Wick St Lawrence).
- former common meadows such as Mead, Luggs (lug = small measure of land: Skeggs 1992, 111), and Dolemoor/Dolecroft (dole = common land divided into shares: Field 1972, 65). These common meadows were usually divided between tenements in several settlements: Dolemoor Ham, for example, was divided between tenements in St Georges, Waywick, Woolvershill, and Banwell

village; Luggs and Ready Mead were split between West Wick, Woolvershill, and Banwell village.

- former open fields of indeterminate type where blocks of long, narrow fields share names that are not in themselves indicative of former common arable or meadow, such as Belgurton and Bustleton in Waywick, and Allerside in West Wick (aller = alder).
- former common pasture (eg Castle Moor, Cormoor, New Moor, Puddy Moor, and Silver Moors all in Banwell).
- topographical names that describe the nature of the area (eg Ready in West Wick, West Yeo in St Georges).
- personal names relating to a previous tenant (eg Coles and Haynes in Puxton).
- the sub-division of large areas of backfen that documentary sources show were former demesne pastures (eg Havadge in Banwell, Twindix in Puxton, and Pill Field in Congresbury.

Documentary evidence for the management of the agricultural land

From the 16th century, when we start to have good documentary sources for Congresbury, Puxton, and Wick, large parts of the study area were held in severalty, in enclosed fields or closes. In 1636 the Puxton glebe, for example, consisted of five 'severall grounds' called Priests Leaze (15 acres) bounded by parcels called 'Southfield', 'Hardingforth', and 'Longland'; a piece of ground called 'Westmeade' bounded to east and south by parcels of ground called 'Freemans'; and 1 acre of ground bounded to the south by Puxton Moor and to the north by 'Longmeade' (BRO DC/E/25/2). A comparison with tithe map field-names allows most of these places to be located (Fig 2.5)

The 1636 glebe survey also refers to one and a half acres in the 'Middle Twindick', which can be identified as a large, now sub-divided, area south of West Dolemoor. A further parcel of Twindix was accommodation land in 1655 when 1 acre and 2 roods of pasture was let by Simon Marriott of London to George Clarke, though the larger part (23 acres) was demesne land maintained at the manor's expense (WRO 2667/18/25; 2667/23). In 1472/3, for example, 3s 6d was paid for bread, ale, and other food bought for 21 men who came on boonwork [seasonal labour service owed by tenants] to dig ditches there (SRO DD/WY box 84). By the end of the medieval period Twindix appears to have been rented out, and the 1500–01 manorial account roll records 46s 8d received for 'the demesne land called Twyndyke' (SRO DD/WY W/CR 46/1). There were other extensive demesne pastures, mostly towards the margins of the lower-lying backfens, such as Havadge in Banwell, and 'Pillfeelde' to the east of Heathgate Farm in Congresbury which in 1457 amounted to 187 acres in 34 closes which were let as pasture (SRO DD/CC).

Returning to Puxton, two other common fields are shown on the map of *c* 1770. Ashfield, in the western part of the parish, is first recorded in 1491 when the manorial court ordered the inspection of 1 acre of land called 'Princisacre in Asshefeld' (BodL RAWL B317; Fig 6.6). Several parcels were still arable in 1601 (Table 6.1 above). The other small common field shown on the map of *c* 1770 was 'Chout Feelde', a detached part of Puxton lying in Congresbury Marsh within which Merton College also held a parcel (Fig 6.6). It is possible that larger common fields once lay to the south and east of Puxton village, where the pattern of landholding was highly fragmented in *c* 1770, and the field boundary morphology (blocks of relatively long, narrow fields laid out between parallel, sinuous boundaries) is very similar to the known former common fields (Fig 2.5). The area to the east of Puxton was known as East Field in 1404 (BodL MC 1205), and the tithe survey records several 'Butts' field-names that generally refer to irregularly shaped end-pieces of the former common field (Field 1972, 34). Though not documented as such, the putative open field south-west of Puxton may have been known as West Field.

The largest area of common meadow, known as the Dolemoor, lay between Congresbury and Puxton and was only enclosed in 1811. The Dolemoor is first documented in 1325 when Alicia Ofre gave Woodspring Priory half an acre of meadow in 'Estredolmore' and half an acre in 'Westredolmore' (Knight 1902, 229). The management of the Dolemoor is particularly well documented in the Congresbury manorial surveys of 1567, 1647, 1655, and 1737, the Accounts of the Overseers of the Dolemoor of 1685–1766, and several contemporary accounts written in the 18th and 19th centuries including that of local historian George Bennett (SRO DD/SAS G/1740 1/1/7; Collinson 1791; and see Williams 1853; Knight 1902, 228–33; Jervis and Jones 1935; Gardner 1985; Rendell 1985/86Brian 1999). The Dolemoor was unenclosed between Lammas (1 August) and Candlemas (2 February) when the ground was open for common grazing for all those who held rights, though in 1568 and 1570 it was agreed at the manorial court that no one should put more than one ox per acre in 'Dolemede' (SRO DD/WY W/CR 46/1). For the rest of the year the livestock was excluded in order to produce hay. Plots were not in permanent ownership, but were allocated each year in order to ensure a fair distribution of the hay crop. The Dolemoor was divided into large blocks, known as furlongs, each permanently marked by wooden posts. Each year, the furlongs were divided into strips, with names such as 'Dungpick', 'Pole-axe', and 'Four Pits', each of 1 acre measured out using a chain 18 yards long (the distance between Puxton church's west door and the front of the rood screen). Twenty-four apples had already been marked with symbols representing the different tenements which held rights in the meadow, and these were placed in a bag. As each strip was measured out, an apple was drawn from the bag and the turf cut with that

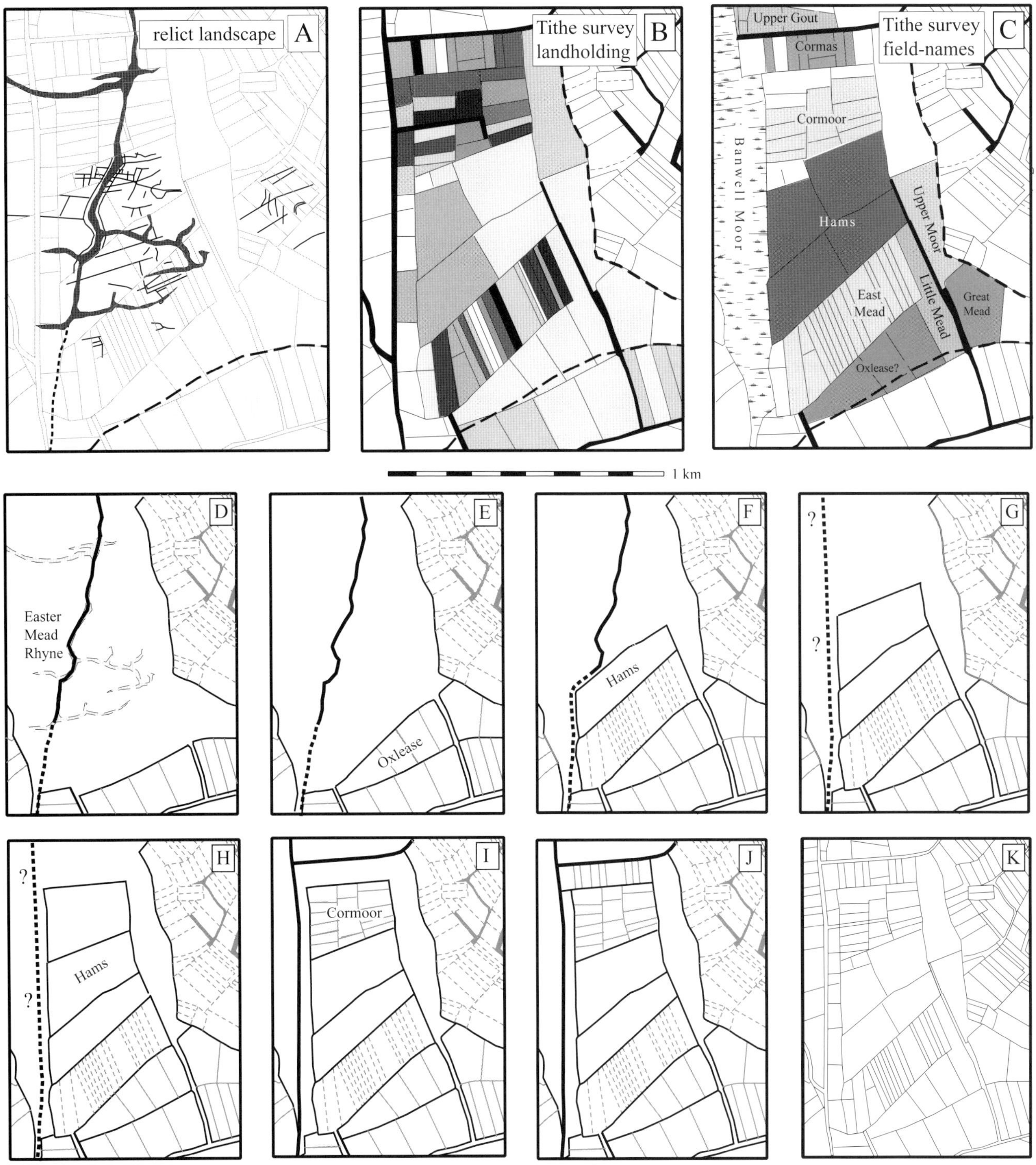

Figure 6.13 The evolution of the landscape around the Banwell Hams. ***A–C*** *show the sources used in this analysis (the earthworks of an extensive relict landscape, and the 19th-century pattern of field boundaries, landholding and field-names), while* ***D–K*** *suggest the possible sequence in which this historic landscape was created through the progressive enclosure of this low-lying backfen in order to create common meadow (East Mead), closes held in severalty (Hams), and former common pasture (Cormoor)*

symbol. The strip was then allocated to the owner of the tenement represented by that symbol until the following Lammas. A separate part of the Dolemoor, the 'Out Drift' or 'Out Let', was auctioned each year to raised funds to cover expenses.

The Dolemoor appears to have been the last remnant of a vast common field that once stretched as far as the fen-edge in Congresbury and Brinsea. The area was divided by a series of broadly east–west oriented droveways, rhynes, and in some cases embankments (walls), that defined a series of furlongs (Figs 2.2 and 6.12).[3] In 1567 these furlongs contained a mixture of closes held in severalty and a series of 48 named common fields each with between two and 25 tenants (Cran 1983, 50–2). This arrangement appears to be of considerable antiquity, as one of those common fields, 'Horsecroft', is mentioned in 1215 when 1 acre and 3 perches were granted to the Bishop of Wells (*Liber Albus I*, 241). In 1351 a long list of land exchanges in this area may represent a reorganisation of tenements following the Black Death. Hugh Egebrok, for example, consolidated a series of parcels in 'Guldenehurst' when he acquired two acres from Henry Burgh in exchange for the same in 'Le Fairforlong'; two acres from William Whitecok for the same in 'Quatterham'; and two acres from Nicholas Selok for the same in 'Croukhele' (SRO DD/SAS BA1).

A further set of common meadows (East Mead) can be identified close to the fen-edge to the east of Banwell Moor (Fig 6.13). The first area to be enclosed, adjacent to the fen-edge, was Oxlease and Great Mead which lay either side of a funnel-shaped droveway that led to what was an open moor that was subsequently enclosed in several stages as East Mead, the Hams (itself representing two stages of enclosure), Cormoor, and Cormas. These areas had very different field boundary morphologies and patterns of landownership: East Mead was divided into a series of long, narrow strip-like fields that in the tithe survey were either accommodation land or were held by tenements in Banwell village, suggesting that this was formerly common meadow, while Hams comprised four large closes held in severalty. The date of these reclamations are not known though the 'ham' and 'mead' field-names are suggestive of a medieval date. A pasture close called Ham is recorded in 1541 (PRO REQ2/17/22). The next area to be enclosed was Cormoor whose ownership was highly fragmented, with over half the area being accommodation land and the rest belonging to farms in Banwell village, as was the case in the final area to be enclosed, between Cormoor and the Liddy Yeo (Cormas). Both were probably former common pasture enclosed by agreement by 1513, when a 5-acre close in 'Cornmowres' was part of a tenement in the village (GRO D547a/M6).

Patterns of manuring: the fieldwalking evidence for arable cultivation and the date of enclosure

The integration of documentary evidence with the physical structures of the historic landscape allows certain distinctive field systems to be identified whose origins can be attributed to certain past land uses. Such hypotheses can be further tested through archaeological fieldwork. A total of 48 modern fields were fieldwalked in Puxton, Rolstone, and Waywick, amounting to 180ha. In terms of the historic landscape the fields walked straddled areas of medieval and post-medieval settlement (with their associated field systems), and the lower-lying backfens that included common meadows (South Mead), demesne pastures (Havadge), and areas enclosed from Banwell Moor (Puddy Moor, New Moor, Silver Moors and Banwell Moor itself) (Fig 6.14.A and Table 6.4).

Not surprisingly all the sherds of the earliest fabric (AA1, late 10th–11th century) were found in Puxton, East and West Rolstone, and Waywick, though interestingly several sherds were recovered from areas some distance from known settlement foci suggesting that sizeable areas were already within manured fields (BaTM 687 in West Rolstone, BaTM 194–6 in East Rolstone, and the two possible sherds from PxTM 51 within Puxton's East Field). Far more material was recovered dating to the 12th–14th centuries, with 1.5 to 3.0 sherds per hectare in fields around Rolstone and Waywick, and double this density in Puxton. In the lower-lying backfens, the few sherds from Rockers were found on the small bedrock island by Rookery Farm, and a small scatter of pottery, stone, and burnt clay (daub) in Blackstones may represent a dwelling of some kind in the north-east corner of the demesne pasture of Havadge. Somewhat unexpectedly there were also very small amounts of medieval material from Silver Moors, Banwell Moor, New Ditch, and possibly Puddy Moor. While some of these sherds could have been mixed in with post-medieval farmyard manure, other evidence from Banwell Moor suggests that there was actually some agricultural improvement in the 12th–13th century (see Chapter 12).

Limited amounts of late medieval pottery were recovered from the fieldwalking, the majority coming from Puxton and Waywick, and very little from Rolstone. This suggests an overall decline in the manuring of the fields, but also local differences with Puxton, for example, consistently having greater amounts of manuring (see below). The absence of material from the lower-lying backfen pastures and commons suggests that these areas were no longer being agriculturally improved. Far greater amounts of material were recovered from the 17th–18th centuries. As before, the most intensive manuring was in Puxton, East and West Rolstone, and Waywick, though it would appear that the enclosure of Puddy Moor dates to this period as it yielded 3.8 sherds per acre (which is more than in Rolstone and Waywick). Very small amounts of material were recovered from the other backfen areas, and this could have been mixed in with later manure. Generally, there was surprisingly little post-medieval and modern pottery on the fields, though this reflects the predominantly pastoral patterns of land use in recent centuries. At the time of the tithe survey, for example, just 8% (49 acres) of Puxton was cultivated.

It is only in the post-medieval period that we have documentary evidence for agricultural land use on the North Somerset Levels, and in addition to showing the general shift towards pasture it also reflects the greater significance of arable in Puxton (Table 6.5). The 1567 survey of Congresbury Marsh shows that 16–19% of the land was arable (a precise figure cannot be calculated as 19% of the area was described as 'land, meadow and pasture'; in Wick the

Table 6.4 Densities of pottery from fieldwalking survey

district	area (ha)	sherds of fabric AA1	C12th–14th sherds/ha	C15th–16th sherds/ha	C17th –18th sherds/ha	C19th–20th sherds/ha
Puxton Church Field	4.02	8	27.36	1.24	18.66	14.93
rest of Puxton	7.68	?2	6.31	1.14	14.28	5.47
East Rolstone	23.14	1 or ?2	2.75	0.19	2.73	2.56
West Rolstone	29.63	1 or ?3	1.48		3.24	4.29
Waywick	14.00	3	1.48	1.40	2.01	2.16
South Mead	12.88			0.05	0.61	1.41
Puddy Moor	10.21		0.15?		3.87	4.06
New Moor	6.50				0.43	0.43
Silver Moors	11.73		0.35		0.67	1.36
Rockers	9.71		0.19		0.43	1.46
Blackstones	3.03		0.99		0.66	0.99
Havadge	19.16				0.23	1.73
New Ditch	12.49		0.07		0.07	0.70
Banwell Moor	8.65		0.12		0.69	1.97

Table 6.5 Post-medieval land use from documentary sources

		acres	pasture	meadow	arable
1567	Congresbury Marsh	437*	57%	23%	16–19%
1601	Merton College lands, Puxton	18.5	49%	10%	41%
c 1770	Puxton	142	28%	48%	24%
c 1770	East Rolstone	167	28%	68%	4%
c 1770	West Rolstone	220.5	50%	45%	5%
1840	Puxton	603			8%

* the full acreage was 544.25 but 107.25 acres was described as 'land, meadow and pasture'

vast majority of the land is described as such and so it is impossible to assess the relative significance of the different land uses). In 1601, 41% of Merton College's tenement in Puxton was arable, and while this may not have been typical, it is noticeable that in *c* 1770 a higher proportion of Puxton was arable compared to Rolstone. Of those parishes wholly on the North Somerset Levels, the 1801 crop returns only survive for Kingston Seymour, which was by then a largely pastoral district. The cultivated land was predominantly sowed with wheat, with lesser amounts of potatoes, barley, peas, and beans (Williams 1969). Of those parishes wholly on the North Somerset Levels, the tithe files of *c* 1840, which also provide information on crop yields, unfortunately only survive for Wick. Although once again predominantly pastoral, the wheat yield of 24–32 bushels per acre was amongst the highest in Somerset, testifying to the potential productivity of the soils (Kain 1986).

A characterisation of the field systems

Reference has already been made to the way that field boundary patterns can be a guide to past land management and, unlike the documentary sources whose survival is patchy, and fieldwalking that can only be carried out in areas that are cultivated today, field morphology can be examined for the whole study area. The earliest date at which the whole landscape can be mapped is by piecing together the tithe maps of *c* 1840 (Fig 6.15.A), while for large areas there are earlier estate and enclosure maps (Fig 6.15.B). Figure 6.15.C characterises these field boundary patterns based on their predominant morphology, with areas being classified as regular, coaxial, intermediate, and irregular, while the integration of documentary, archaeological, and field-name evidence allows some of these different patterns to be interpreted in terms of their origins and past management (Fig 6.15.D).

The irregular-type field boundary patterns appear to have come into existence through a long process of piecemeal enclosure. Large areas may always have been closes held in severalty, though a number of small common fields can be identified (eg Oldfield, Wick Field, and Dolecroft in Wick St Lawrence; Perry Bush in East Rolstone; Ashfield, Chount Field, and East Field in Puxton). The naturally meandering lines of former salt marsh creeks are

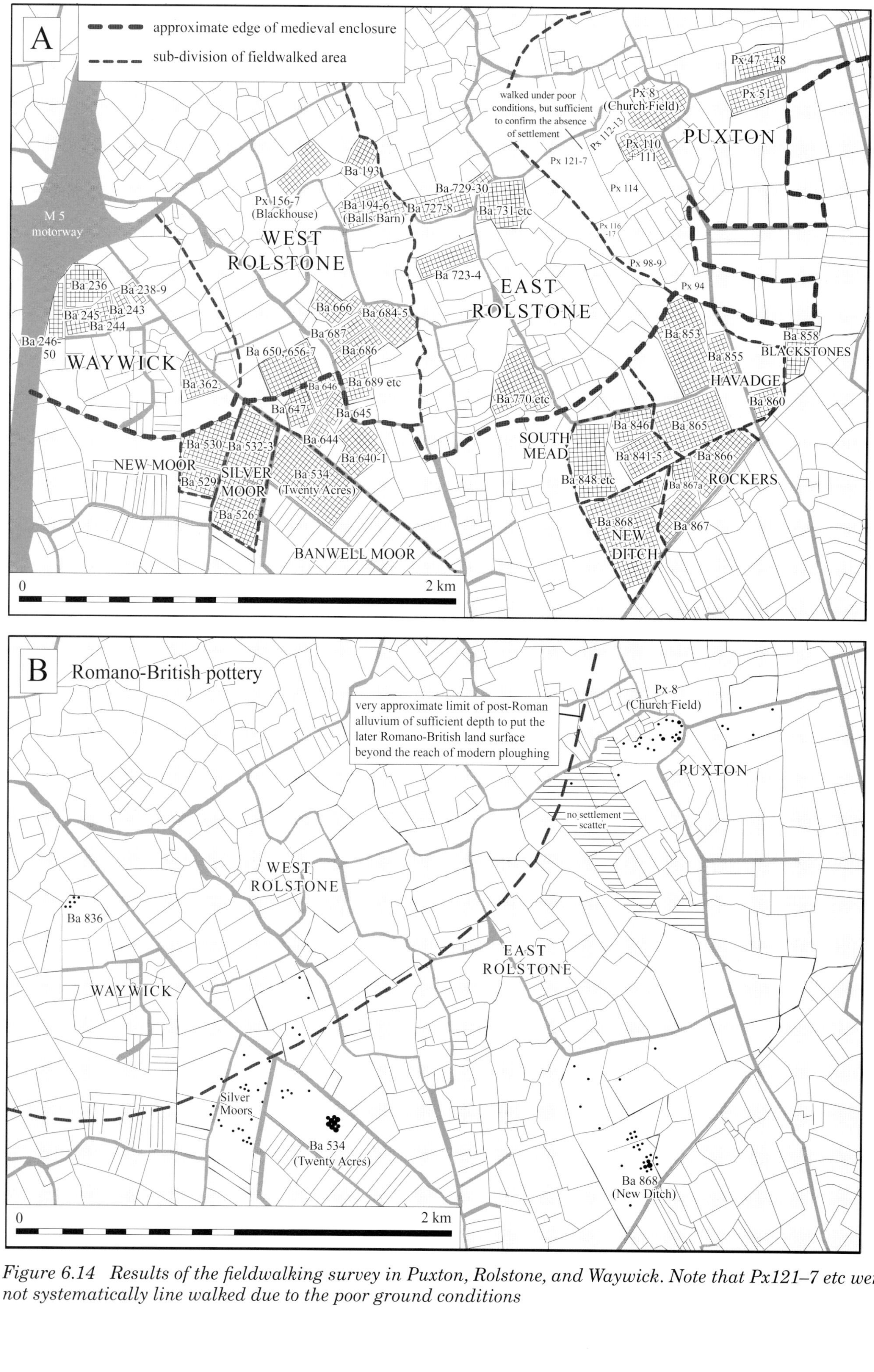

Figure 6.14 Results of the fieldwalking survey in Puxton, Rolstone, and Waywick. Note that Px121–7 etc were not systematically line walked due to the poor ground conditions

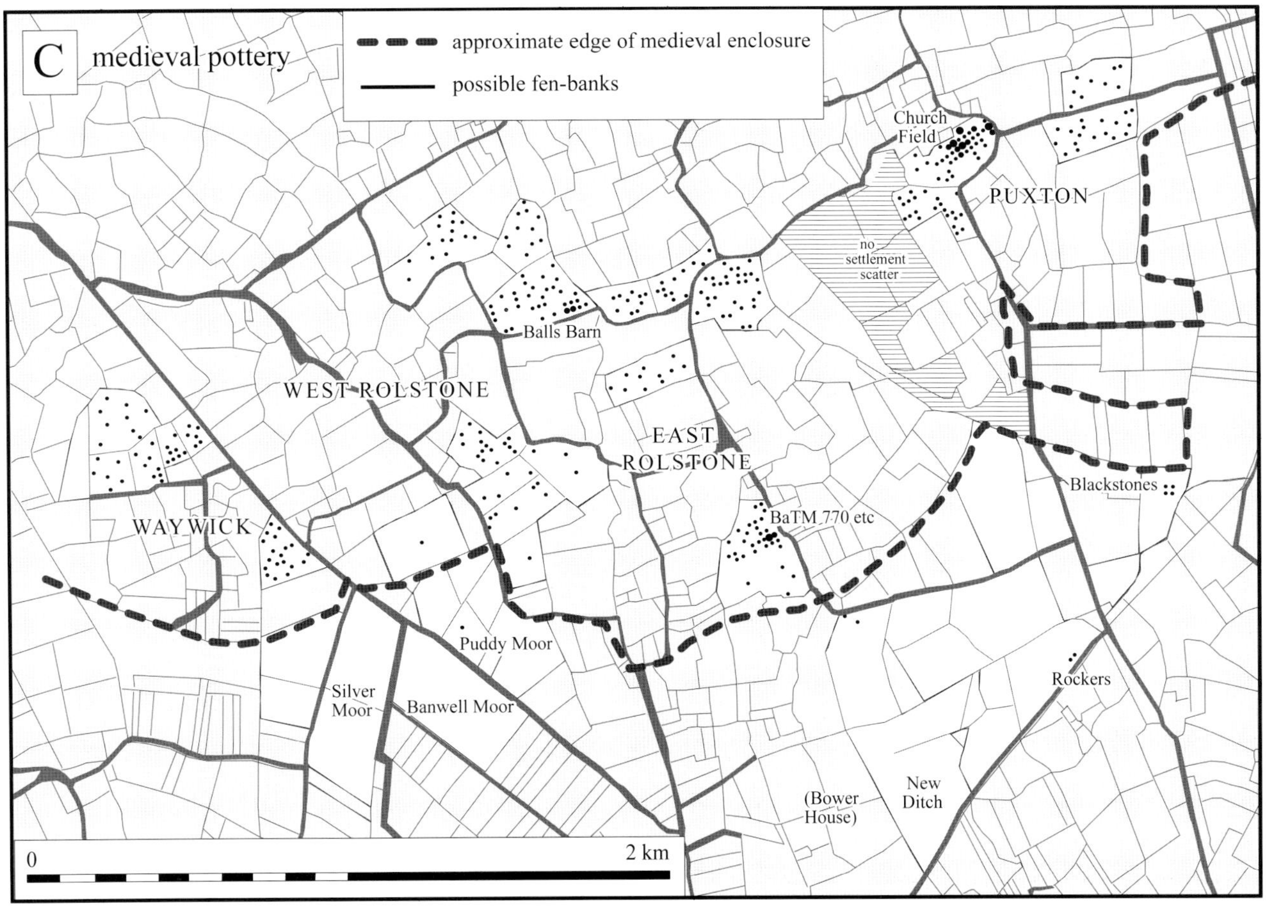
C medieval pottery
approximate edge of medieval enclosure
possible fen-banks
Church Field
PUXTON
no settlement scatter
Balls Barn
WEST ROLSTONE
EAST ROLSTONE
Blackstones
WAYWICK
BaTM 770 etc
Puddy Moor
Silver Moor
Banwell Moor
Rockers
New Ditch
(Bower House)
0
2 km

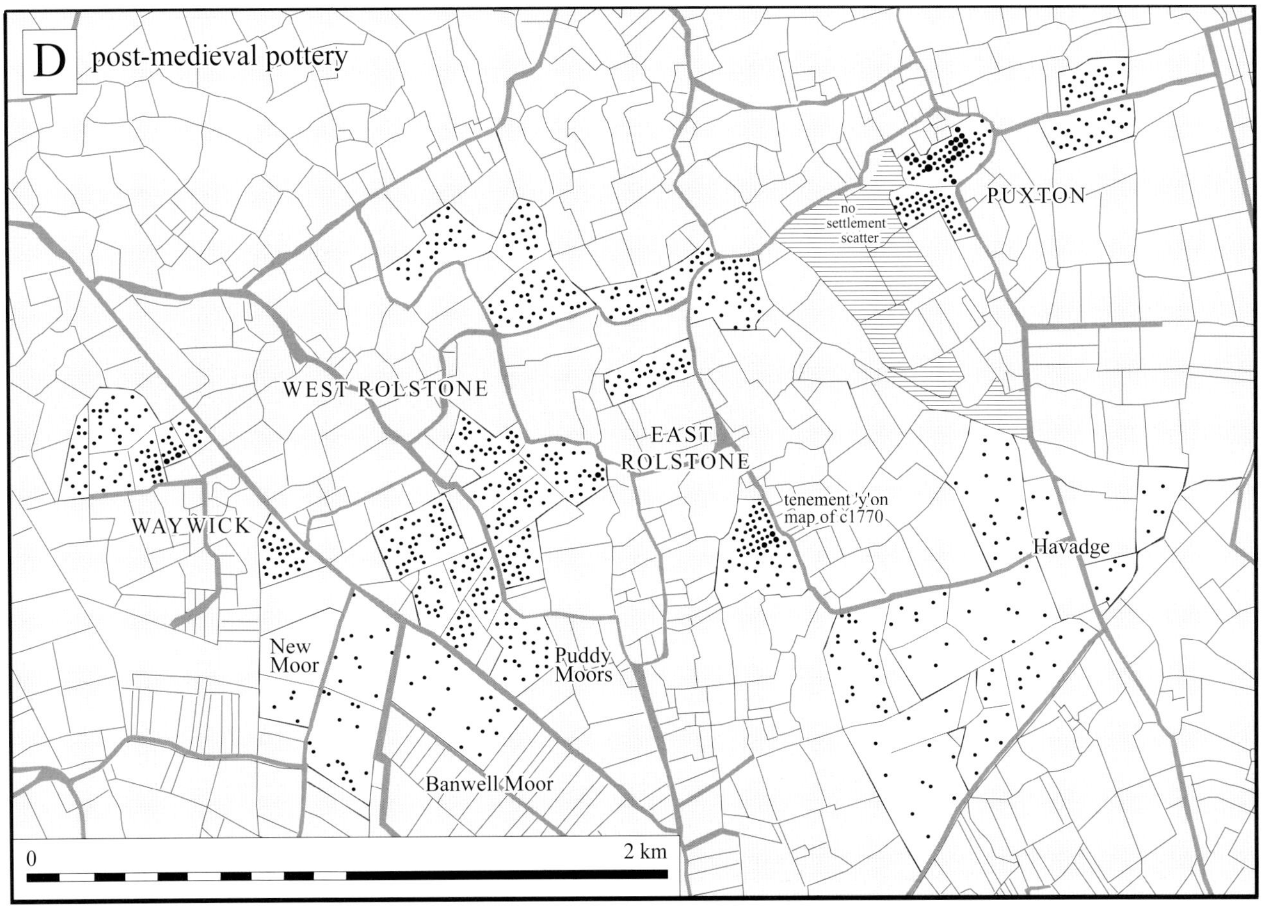
D post-medieval pottery
PUXTON
no settlement scatter
WEST ROLSTONE
EAST ROLSTONE
tenement 'y'on map of c1770
WAYWICK
Havadge
New Moor
Puddy Moors
Banwell Moor
0
2 km

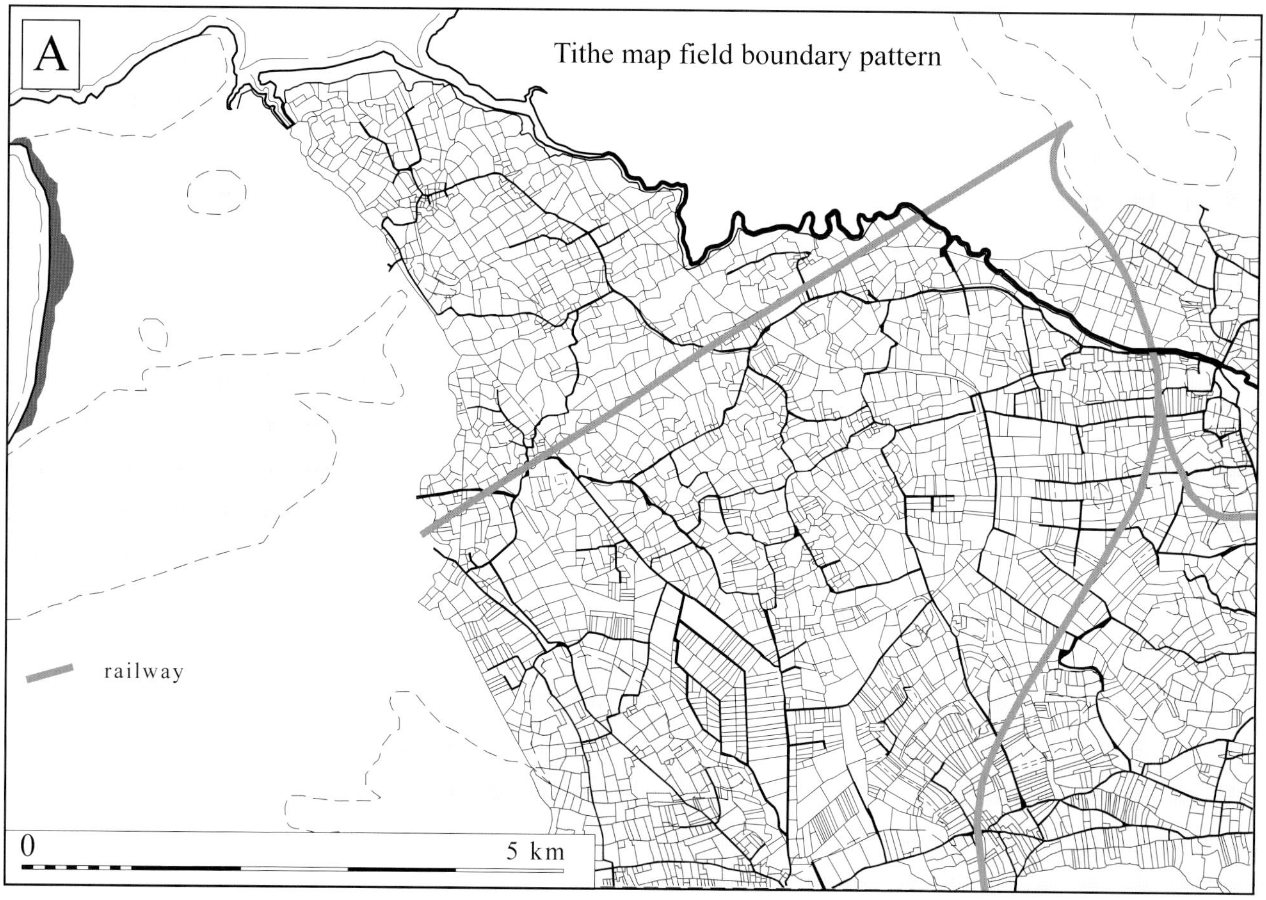

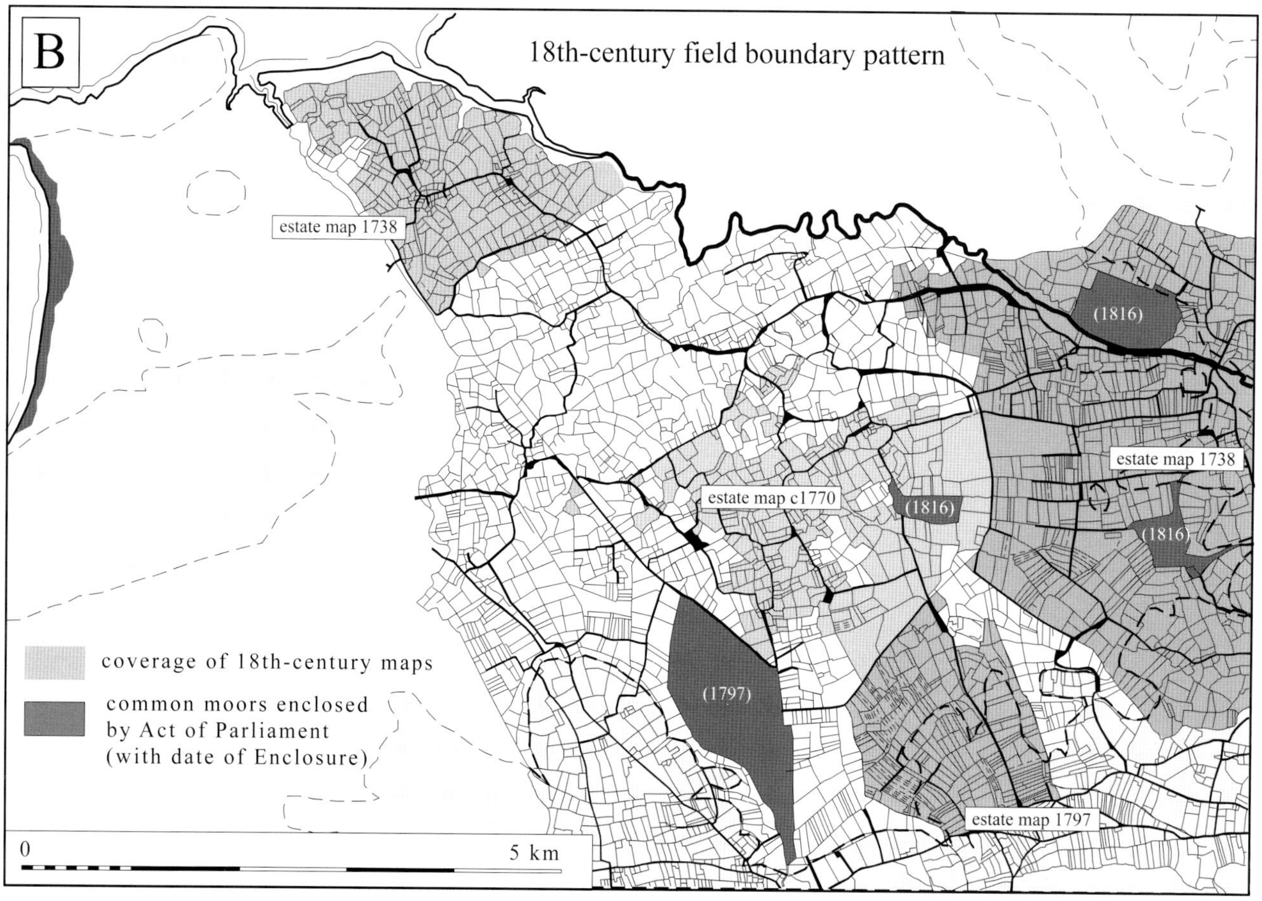

Figure 6.15 A characterisation of the field boundary patterns across the main study area. ***A*** *Tithe map field boundary patterns.* ***B*** *18th-century field boundary patterns*

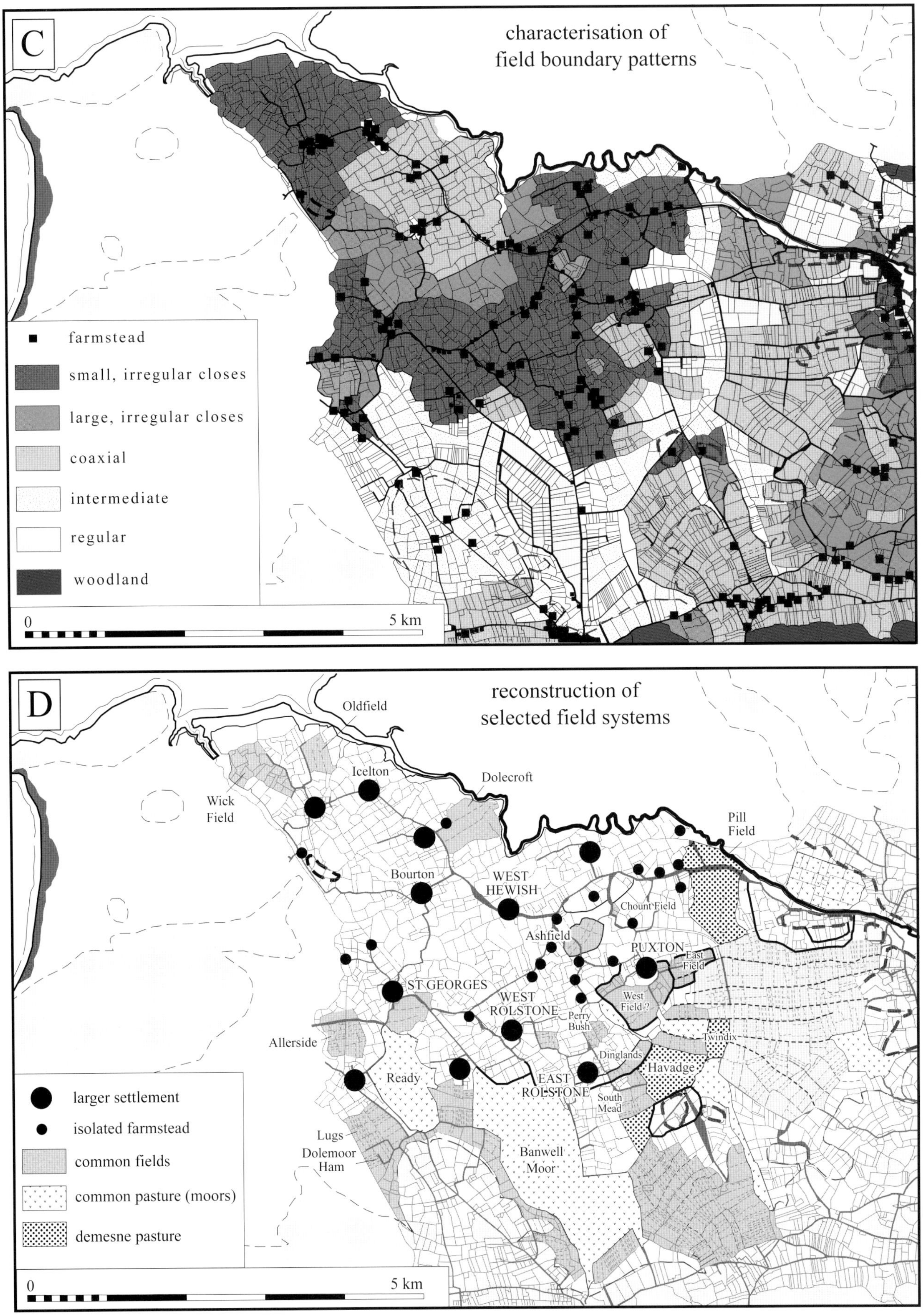

Figure 6.15 A characterisation of the field boundary patterns across the main study area. ***C*** *A characterisation of the field boundary patterns based simply on their morphology.* ***D*** *An interpretation of the field systems based on their morphology, field-names and documentary sources*

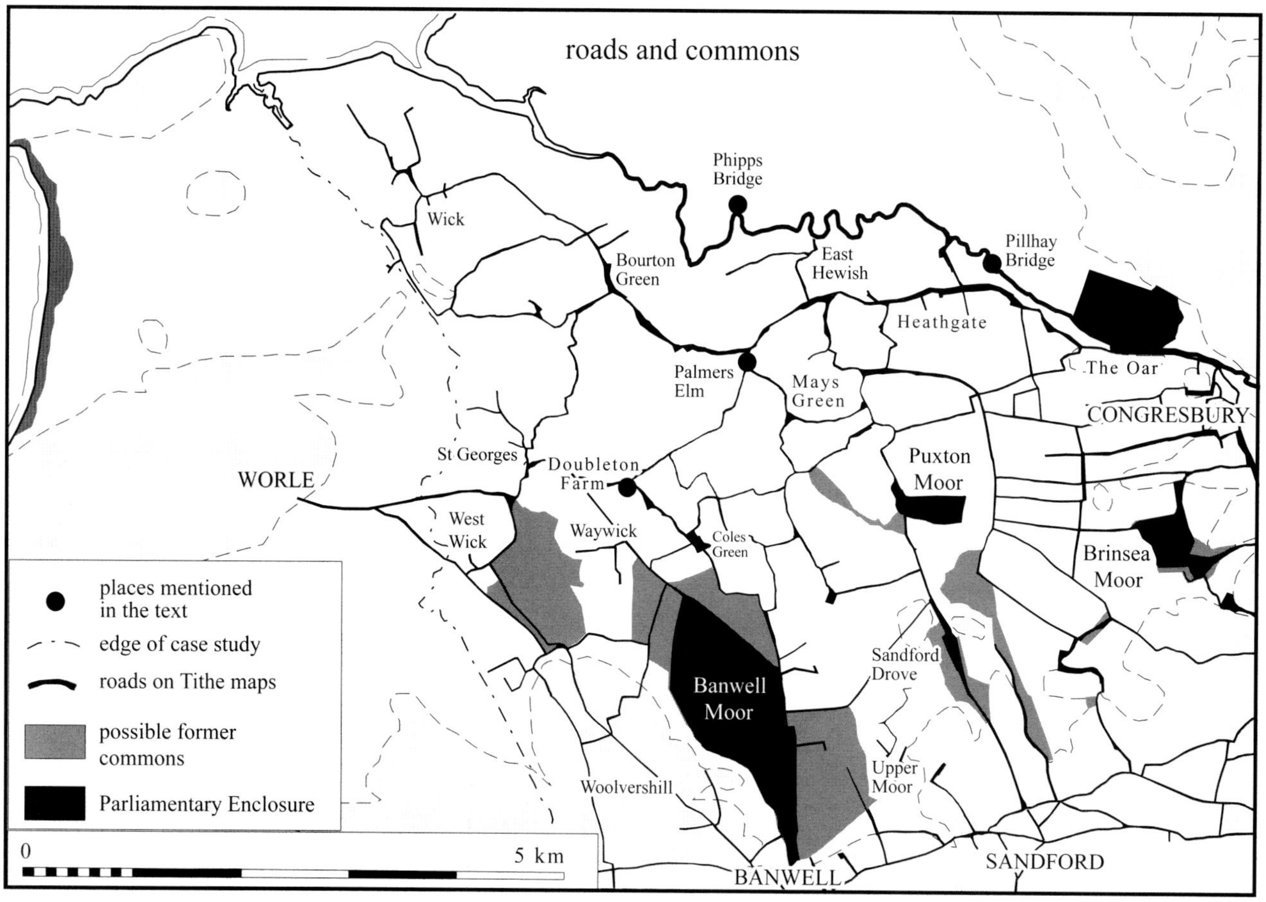

Figure 6.16 Roads and commons in the main study area

often preserved within the field boundary pattern. Around Icelton, Bourton, and West Hewish, there is a broad north-east/south-west orientation to the field boundaries though without the obvious furlong boundaries seen in the former common fields west of Congresbury. There are also a number of areas within Rolstone where the field boundary pattern is structured around a series of roughly parallel boundaries. Although in a number of cases these marked the boundary of former common meadows (eg Dinglands), in origin they may have been a sequence of fen-banks. The area between Bourton and St Georges, along Bourton Town Rhyne, is characterised by relatively large, irregularly shaped closes, several of which share the same field-name (eg Bourton Hams, Raven Ground, Tucks, Wall Close), and when the boundaries between these fields are removed, the impression of an area with large, presumably pastoral, closes is even clearer.

A number of areas, mostly in the lower-lying backfens, have rectilinear field boundary patterns, including the carefully planned rectangular fields that are the result of Parliamentary enclosure of former common pasture (Banwell, Brinsea, and Puxton Moors). A number of other, often adjacent, backfen areas also have areas of straight-sided fields but lack the overall planned coherence of the Parliamentary enclosures. 'Moor' field-names and fragmented patterns of landholding suggest that they were areas of common moor enclosed by agreement.

The roads and commons (Fig 6.16)

Today we think of roads as linking settlements and forming a skeleton around which the historic landscape developed. In the past, however, roads were not just the means whereby people moved around the landscape; they were also the way of driving livestock from settlements to pastures without them straying into the arable and meadow. In the medieval landscape some of the most important reserves of pasture were in the backfen moors, and the droveways that led to them were in fact a simply a continuation of this common, the final pieces of which were enclosed by Act of Parliament. Rather than being the primary skeleton around which the historic landscape was created, droveways may simply have evolved as long narrow strips of common land that were left after the adjacent areas had been enclosed (eg Upper Moor in Banwell: Fig 6.13.C). Areas of irregular landscape around Puxton, Hewish, and Rolstone are characterised by an abundance of such roadside waste and small, often triangular-shaped greens where these

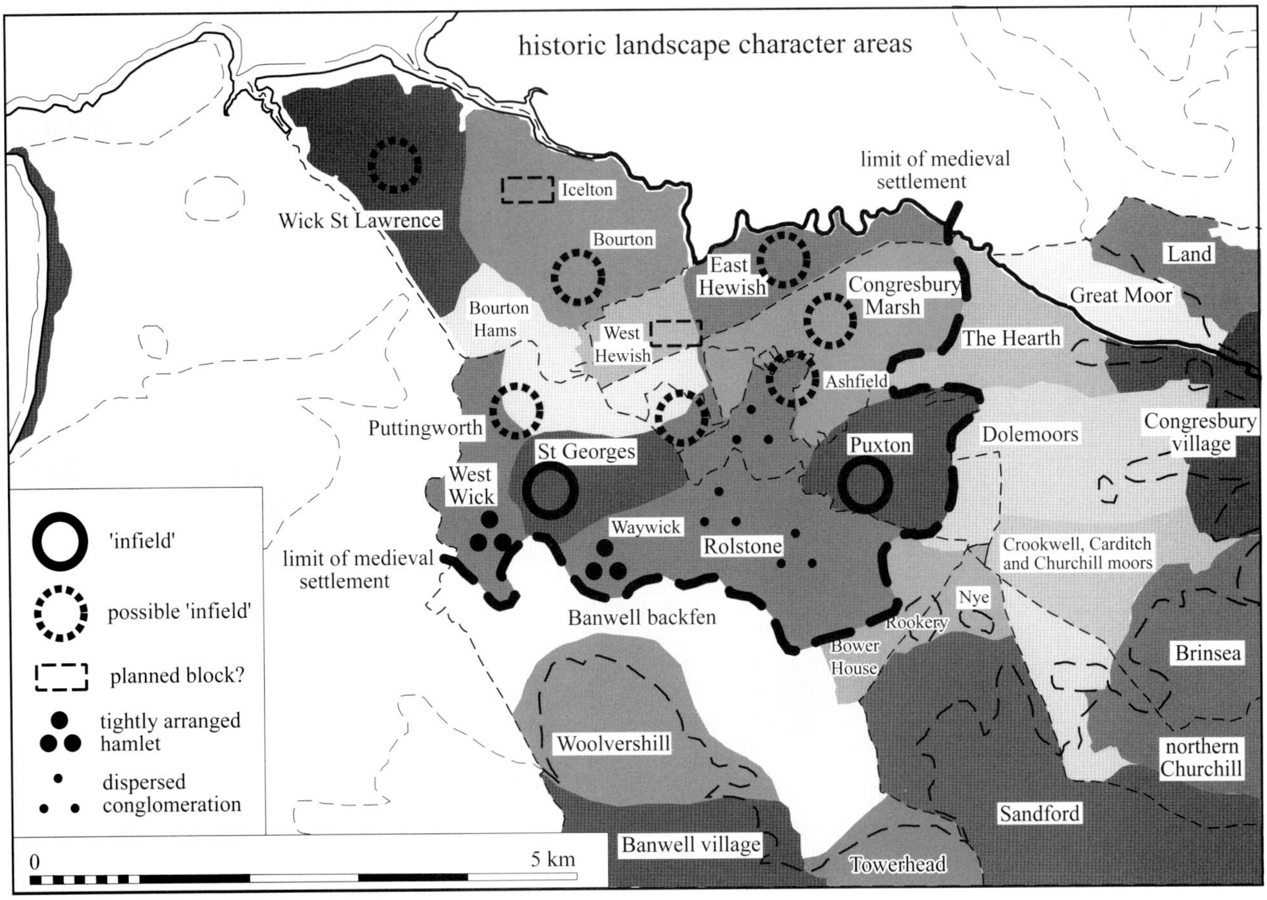

Figure 6.17 The major historic landscape character areas within the main study area. The darker tints represent the earlier areas to be enclosed

droveways met (eg The Wash and Mays Green in Puxton: Fig 2.5).

A characterisation of the historic landscape

The discussion so far has been about individual components of this historic landscape: the natural environment, patterns of landholding, the drainage and flood defence systems, settlements, field systems, roads, and commons. While disaggregating the historic landscape into these components is a useful way of understanding them individually, in practice it is the way in which they articulate with each other that gives different areas their individual local characters. A total of eleven wholly wetland character areas can be identified along with seven that are focused on the adjacent dryland but which extend into the backfens (Table 6.6 and Fig 6.17). Some character areas have fairly clear boundaries, sometimes along a specific field boundary, while in other cases the edges are far from clear and what is mapped is simply an attempt at drawing a best fit line to divide two character areas that in practice merge together.

In the wetland areas a clear division has emerged between the coastal and central areas (Wick, Hewish, St Georges, Rolstone, Puxton, and Congresbury Marsh) that have a settled landscape that appears to have developed in a largely piecemeal fashion, and the lower-lying backfen areas that have landscapes with a more planned character but lacking in settlements. This simple two-fold division, however, hides a series of subtle, but significant, differences in historic landscape character that suggest the broad sequence of colonisation and enclosure.

Three areas – Wick St Lawrence, St Georges, and Puxton – have broadly similar landscapes characterised by field systems of irregular morphology, in part derived from the courses of naturally meandering former salt marsh creeks, with closes probably held in severalty intermingling with small common fields. Landholding was fragmented; the roads were meandering with abundant areas of roadside waste and small greens; and each of these three areas had a clear primary settlement focus around a chapel, which at least in the case of Puxton and St Georges lay within or adjacent to an infield enclosure. Each of these character areas saw the development of presumably secondary settlement foci, such as Ebdon in Wick, Puttingworth and Brimbleworth Farms in St Georges, and Ashfield and Puxton Moor in Puxton. East Hewish is not dissimilar in character to these areas, with a tentative infield enclosure, though there is no evidence for a chapel or former common fields. The landholdings are also relatively compact.

Table 6.6 Historic landscape character areas

character area	the natural environment	tenurial structures	unenclosed land	artificial drainage and flood defence	settlements	field systems	roads
DRYLAND							
Banwell village	on northern flanks of Banwell Hill, extending down to fen-edge, including Hack Mead and Marrow Mead	(not mapped)	none	only extends very slightly onto the wetland	substantial nucleated village of Banwell and small hamlet at Knightcott	coaxial field systems, suggestive of former open field, with large numbers of long narrow fields and a small number of unenclosed strips shown on the Tithe map	long, slightly sinuous, roads without roadside waste
Woolvershill	low gently undulating dryland area and adjacent wetland fringes on almost four sides	small, mostly compact holdings with some detached parcels	none	only extends very slightly onto the wetland	dispersed	intermediate, with little evidence for an underlying structure; currently large closes, possibly laid out between coaxial boundaries, but no evidence for former strip fields	long, slightly sinuous, roads without roadside waste
Towerhead	on northern flanks of Banwell Hill, extending down to fen-edge, including Ox Lease and Great Mead	land split between two substantial landholdings, whose holdings are in places interspersed	none	only extends very slightly onto the wetland	two adjacent farmsteads at Towerhead	series of large closes laid out between the edge of Banwell Wood, the through road, and the fen-edge	long, slightly sinuous, roads without roadside waste
Sandford	on northern flanks of Banwell Hill, extending across low foothills down to fen-edge, including a substantial area of backfen to north (including Sidcot Mead), and east (Sandmead)	extremely fragmented	none	bounded by Nye Drove/Liddy Yeo to north	with the exception of one isolated farm (Droveway Farm), all settlement located in a single loosely nucleated settlement	coaxial field system laid out between a series of long boundaries, that encompass both dryland and wetland; large numbers of long narrow fields and unenclosed strips with furlongs depicted on map of 1792	one droveway extends from village towards Nye

(table continued)

Table 6.6 (*cont.*) Historic landscape character areas

character area	the natural environment	tenurial structures	unenclosed land	artificial drainage and flood defence	settlements	field systems	roads
Brinsea and northern Churchill	low foothills in Wring Valley extending down to fen-edge including Coney Mead	fairly compact tenements though some with detached parcels	extends down to Brinsea Moor	not applicable	loosely nucleated settlements in both Brinsea and Churchill	large, mostly irregular fields, with occasional blocks with a coaxial layout, but showing no overall coherence or evidence for unenclosed strips on the map of 1739	long, slightly sinuous, roads without roadside waste
Congresbury village	low foothills in Wring Valley including God Croft	fairly compact tenements though some with detached parcels to south of village, though highly fragmented landholdings to the west (the Oar)	extends down to Brinsea Moor	not applicable	large compact nucleated village	small, mostly irregular fields, paddocks and orchards, with occasional blocks with a coaxial layout, but showing no overall coherence; occasional unen-closed strips on the map of 1739 but restricted to meadow	long, slightly sinuous, roads without roadside waste
Land	on the flanks and foothills of Candbury Con-gresbury Hill		none	not applicable	beyond the extension of Congresbury village north of the Yeo, set-tlement is dispersed	predominantly coaxial layout with long narrow fields laid out between broadly east–west boundaries; long narrow fields and unenclosed strips on map of 1739	sinuous droveways without areas of roadside waste
WETLAND							
Wick St Lawrence	highest areas of marsh beside the coast	mostly fragmented, especially in Wick Field to the north of the village	intertidal salt-marshes beyond sea wall	bounded by sea walls along open coast and beside Banwell River and Congresbury Yeo	large nucleated settlement possibly associated with an 'infield' enclosure	largely small, irregular field systems, with some coaxial blocks suggesting a greater degree of planning of some areas; some unenclosed strips on map of 1736	sinuous droveways formerly with limited areas of roadside waste
Icelton and Bourton	highest areas of marsh beside the Congresbury Yeo	some compact blocks of fields associated with the farmsteads, though other areas have predomi-nantly fragmented pattern with much accommodation land	Bourton Green	bounded by sea walls along the Congresbury Yeo, and possible sea wall along New Ear Rhyne to the south	small to medium-sized compact hamlets (one possibly associ-ated with an 'infield' enclosure)	several sets of coaxial block fields, all broadly NE–SW but showing little sign of an under-lying cohesion	sinuous droveways formerly with areas of roadside waste

(table continued)

Table 6.6 (*cont.*) Historic landscape character areas

character area	the natural environment	tenurial structures	unenclosed land	artificial drainage and flood defence	settlements	field systems	roads
Bourton Hams, Raven Ground	beside Banwell River, Bourton Rhyne and New Ear Rhyne	mostly compact blocks of closes	none	either side of the Bourton Town Rhyne	none	area of larger irregular fields between Wick St Lawrence/ Bourton and St Georges, Rolstone, and Puxton	sinuous droveways without areas of roadside waste
East Hewish	area of high marsh beside the Congresbury Yeo	compact blocks of closes	none	bounded by sea wall alongside the Congresbury Yeo and the New Rhyne to the south	compact hamlet possibly associated with 'infield' enclosure	area of small, irregular closes	sinuous droveways without areas of roadside waste
West Hewish		compact blocks of closes	West Hewish Green	between the natural creek of New Ear Rhyne to the north and New Rhyne to the south	single compact, possibly planned, hamlet	several sets of coaxial block fields, all broadly NE–SW	sinuous droveway that broadens to form a wide funnel-shaped common
St Georges, and Puxton	intermediate area between the higher coastal marshes and low-lying backfens	fragmented	small greens and areas of roadside common	series of possible fen-banks to south	compact hamlets associated with 'infield' enclosures	dominated by small, irregular field systems, and some small coaxial blocks suggestive of former open fields	sinuous droveways formerly with areas of roadside waste
Congresbury Marsh	area of high marsh beside the Congresbury Yeo	compact blocks of closes	none		isolated farmsteads	area of small, irregular closes	sinuous droveways with large areas of roadside waste
West Wick, Waywick and Rolstone	intermediate area between the higher coastal marshes and low-lying backfens	fragmented	Coles Green	series of possible fen-banks to south	small, loosely nucleated hamlets	area of small, irregular closes	sinuous droveways with small areas of roadside waste
Banwell backfen	lowest-lying backfen immediately north of the fen-edge		Banwell Moor enclosed 1797	bounded by several possible fen-banks to north	occasional dispersed farmstead	intermediate, with substantial areas divided into long narrow fields	long and straight without roadside waste

(table continued)

Table 6.6 (*cont.*) Historic landscape character areas

character area	the natural environment	tenurial structures	unenclosed land	artificial drainage and flood defence	settlements	field systems	roads
Nye, Rookery Farm and Bower House	on northern edge of backfen in Banwell and Sandford	large compact landholdings associated with the farmsteads; remaining area mostly accommodation land	field-names (eg Havadge) suggest large areas were once unenclosed pasture	to south of Rolstone's fen-banks	three isolated farmsteads, two (Nye and Rookery) on small bedrock islands	predominantly very large, polygonal closes, with clusters of smaller fields adjacent to the farmsteads	long and straight without roadside waste
Crookwell, Carditch and Churchill Moor	low-lying backfens in south west Congresbury (west of Brinsea) and Churchill	highly fragmented pattern of landholding with a relatively large amount of accommodation land	Crookwell Common Mead	found either side of the Meer Wall where it marks the Congresbury/Churchill parish boundary	none	short coaxial systems mostly divided into open or enclosed strips on the 1739 map	long, slightly sinuous, roads without roadside waste
Dolemoor	low-lying backfens in Congresbury (west of village) and Puxton	highly fragmented pattern of landholding with a relatively large amount of accommodation land	East and West Dolemoor common meadows, and Puxton Moor enclosed in 1816	coaxial boundaries cut by the Meer Wall; several of the coaxial boundaries have 'wall' names	none	long coaxial system, mostly divided into open or enclosed strips on the 1739 map, with larger closes in far west (east of West Dolemoor in Puxton)	long, slightly sinuous, roads without roadside waste
The Hearth	area of Congresbury's backfen immediately south of the Congrebury Yeo	highly fragmented pattern of landownership with a relatively large amount of accommodation land	very broad areas of roadside waste beside droveway	east of Pillhay (the original outfall of the Oldbridge River)	none	predominantly irregular field system that in the east includes small blocks of open and enclosed strip fields	sinuous droveways formerly with areas of roadside waste
Great Moor	low-lying backfen north of the Congresbury Yeo	[not studied]	Great Moor itself enclosed in 1816	southern boundary marked by the northern sea wall along the Congresbury Yeo	none	Great Moor itself was subject to Parliamentary Enclosure and has a regular-block layout of fields; areas to the east and west were enclosed earlier and have large irregular closes	long and straight without roadside waste

Three other character areas – Icelton and Bourton, West Hewish, and West Wick, Waywick and Rolstone – would appear to represent secondary colonisation. In Bourton there is a possible infield enclosure, though in West Hewish there appears to be a small row-plan settlement to the north of New Ear Lane that marked the boundary between Hewish and Congresbury. West Wick and Waywick are two relatively compact hamlets, while in Rolstone there are two loose conglomerations of farmsteads (East and West Rolstone). The patterns of roads and fields in each of these areas have greater coherence than in Wick, East Hewish, St Georges, and Puxton, with a series of roughly parallel coaxial boundaries which appear to have been established in a fairly open landscape. In Bourton the boundaries run parallel to the putative sea wall just to the north of New Ear Lane, while those in West Hewish are parallel to New Rhyne (which marked the division between Hewish and Congresbury). In Rolstone a parallel set of boundaries to the south would appear to represent successive fen-banks enclosing areas of the backfen. Most land was held in closes, though with a number of common meadows.

The landscape in Congresbury Marsh also has an irregular morphology, and while there are possible infield enclosures at Chestnut Farm and Smeaths these never formed the basis of nucleated settlements. The pattern of isolated farmsteads was associated with relatively compact landholdings, with large home grounds, and while there was no evidence for open fields these tenements did hold parcels in the common meadows between Puxton and Congresbury.

The low-lying backfens to the south and east were certainly enclosed later than these settled landscapes, and both the roads and the field systems here have a more planned appearance. In Puxton and Congresbury most of the backfens appear to have been divided up by a single set of coaxial boundaries (later cut by the Meer Wall, Oldbridge River and the Puxton–Congresbury parish boundary). Relatively small areas were left as common moors. The oldest enclosures in the Banwell backfens would appear to have been a series of small meadows around the fen-edge (eg Luggs, Dolemoor Ham, Bustleton, Ham, Marrow Mead, and East Mead). Large areas of the backfen in Banwell was, however, left as unenclosed common pastures until the 17th–18th centuries when Puddy Moor appears to have been enclosed, followed by New Moor, Silver Moors and finally Banwell Moor in 1797. Other parts of the backfen, notably to the north of the Liddy Yeo, were divided up into a series of exceptionally large closes that appear to have been either associated with isolated farmsteads (Bower House, Rockers/Rookery Farm) or were simply areas of pasture (New Ditch, Havadge).

Summary

The historic landscape analysis presented in this chapter has gone beyond simply classifying the morphology of settlement and field systems, by using the physical fabric of the countryside not just as a source of information in itself but as a means of integrating a range of other evidence including field- and place-names, archaeological survey, and documentary archives. This chapter has also gone beyond simply classifying landscapes as being of one particular type, but has also explored their origins and development. Having disaggregated the historic landscape into a series of discrete components – the natural drainage system, the pattern of landholding, the drainage and flood defence systems, the settlement patterns, and field systems – the way that they articulate with each other can be used to understand the processes that led to the creation of a series of broad character areas. A number of places emerge as probably being the primary settlement foci, centred on an infield enclosure (Wick, St Georges, East Hewish, and Puxton), from which there were areas of secondary colonisation resulting in both nucleated (Icelton, West Hewish, West Wick, Waywick, and Rolstone) and dispersed settlement patterns (eg Congresbury Marsh, and the area around Bower House in East Rolstone). Some areas, notably Puxton and Wick, saw a high degree of communal management of the landscape with open fields, common meadows, and a common moor. Tenements in the other hamlets usually had access to a share of at least one common meadow and one of the backfen commons, though there were striking differences in how compact these settlements were, and in Congresbury Marsh there is a pattern of wholly isolated farmsteads. Each of these landscapes are, therefore, significantly different both morphologically and socially (reflected in the extent to which people chose to live together and manage their resources communally), despite having evolved within a physically almost homogeneous environment free from the influences of antecedent cultural landscapes. Clearly, this local variation in historic landscape character must be due to socio-economic factors, and these will be explored in the next chapter.

Notes

1 The North Somerset SMR also records medieval material from the gardens of extant farms on the dryland in Congresbury at (all pottery unless otherwise stated): Brinsea Batch Farm (SMR 7230); Brinsea Manor Farm (SMR 7229); Brinsea Road Farm, (SMR 7218); Cherry Tree Farm, Brinsea (SMR 7234); Congresbury village (SMR 388; 396; 7269; 7281; 7283); Honey Hall, Brinsea (pottery and coin of Edward III: SMR 7205; 7207); Honey Hall Farm, Brinsea (includes pre-Conquest material: SMR 7208; 7209); Honey Hall Lodge, Brinsea (SMR 7206); Ivy House Farm, Brinsea (SMR 7211); Willow Farm, Congresbury (SMR 7882).

2 SMR records of shrunken settlements: south of

Brinsea Farm (includes pre-Conquest material: SMR 7215–16); Brinsea Green Farm (SMR 7228); Mays Green (SMR 7932; Clarke 1978); Honey Hall, Brinsea (SMR 7210).

3 There has been some speculation over the name 'Wickham Furlong', which forms the westernmost block of 'Courses Furlong' and lies adjacent to the early Romano-British settlement on Dolemoor. 'Wickham' names generally are thought to have a strong correlation with Romano-British settlements (Costen 1992a, 58), but in this case it appears to mean the 'ham' (ie meadow) of Wick (St Lawrence): it was a detached parcel of Wick parish, reflecting the common rights that the tenants of Wick held there, such as William Tucker who in 1655 held land 'in Wickham Furlong upon the Yeo Bank' (BRO 04237).

7 Of kings, bishops and knights: the social and tenurial context of landscape change

The historic landscape was a cultural construction by many generations of human communities who farmed the land. In the case of the North Somerset Levels this occurred in the context of wetland reclamation, itself undertaken within the context of a series of estates. As described in Chapter 6, there is marked local variation in the character of the historic landscapes that were created, and in such a physically uniform environment, where antecedent cultural landscapes cannot have been significant (as they were largely buried under later alluvium), it is to the patterns of lordship and community that we must look for an explanation.

Pre-Conquest territorial divisions and estates

During the Roman period, it is likely that north-west Somerset was at least partly divided between a series of large villa-based estates (Chapter 5). Some have argued that such estates may have survived into the medieval period and the proximity of some hillforts, villas, and medieval church/manor complexes in north-west Somerset is certainly intriguing (eg Banwell, Congresbury, and Portbury: Rippon 1997a, 136–7). The early medieval period is, however, one with few sources and it is only in the 11th century that the Domesday survey reveals the structure of landowning with a landscape that was divided between a multiplicity of manors that were often part of larger, but discontinuous, lordships held by the Crown, ecclesiastical institutions, and the aristocracy. So where had these manors come from?

A variety of evidence suggests that across southern Britain the early medieval landscape was once divided up into large territorial units that may have originated as folk territories, sometimes referred to as *regiones*, equating to around ten to twenty later parishes (K Bailey 1989; Bassett 1989, 17; Bassett 1997; Brooks 1989, 71; Blair 1991, 12; Fleming 1994; Fleming 1998, 18–32; Hooke 1998, fig 3). Similar-sized territories, that Jones (1979; 1985) has called 'multiple estates', are recorded in 13th-century Welsh lawbooks that describe a system of landscape exploitation in which a hierarchical network of primary and subsidiary settlements lay within a territory that characteristically embraced a range of environments (eg straddling both uplands and lowlands). This multiple estate model of landscape exploitation has been widely applied to early medieval Britain, though Bassett (1989, 20) rejects the term as 'unhistorical' as there is no evidence that forms of agrarian organisation based on ownership existed during the centuries in which the early English kingdoms developed (and see Gregson 1985; Jones 1985). What is clear is that irrespective of whether the multiple estate structure as described in the 13th-century lawbooks ever existed in that precise form during earlier periods, or indeed outside Wales, many of its underlying principles towards exploiting a landscape are apparent. Such territories can be regarded as federative, with a hierarchy of settlement, dependent on a single centre, spread across areas that embraced a diverse range of environments, leading to some specialist and even seasonal settlements that owed food, rent and services to the centre (eg Blair 1991, 24–5; Faith 1994; Lewis *et al* 1997, 23; Hooke 1998, 122–3; Dyer 2002, 25–30). Eventually the idea of individual ownership of land emerged and these territories became great estates that around the 9th century started to fragment, and while the king, church, and great magnates often retained sizeable areas, usually on the best land, thegns were increasingly granted landed endowments of typically one to six hides (Dyer 2002, 30). These ultimately led to the multiplicity of manors that existed in 1066 as recorded in the Domesday survey. Following the Norman Conquest there was a major redistribution of land, with most estates of the English thegns being seized and granted to the King's followers, and some of the estates that Earl Harold had seized from the Church being restored (eg Banwell: see below).

Following the principles of retrogressive research – starting with the well-documented post-medieval period and working back towards the poorly recorded pre-Conquest period – a range of evidence can be used to reconstruct a series of early federative estates in north-west Somerset by locating both their centres and their teritorial extents:

- royal centres, known through both documentary and archaeological evidence (eg Cheddar: Rahtz 1979)
- ecclesiastical relationships (Fig 7.1.A): early minster parochia are likely to reflect the pattern of early estates and this is sometimes reflected in later ecclesiastical relationships such as one place being a chapelry of, or owing other dues to, another church (the discussion below uses Youngs 1979 unless otherwise stated)
- hundredal arrangements
- territorial relationships (Fig 7.1.B): detached parochial parcels (which may be derived from the fragmentation of what was once a single jurisdiction, or an area of intercommoning), and where a parish boundary zig-zags through, and so post-dates, the historic landscape (of which a clearly

Table 7.1 Possible components of an early estate based at Portbury

parishes	ecclesiastical relationship	detached parcels	1086	1066	charters	place-names
Portbury		Clapton Wick, Ham Green, Happerton, and Failand Farm	5, 33: Bishop of Coutances	Godwin, 8 hides	S.1707 (899 x 925): land granted by K. Edward S.1781 (979 x 1016): land granted by K. Aethelred	shares 'port' prefix with Portishead
Portishead			5, 25: Bishop of Coutances	Aelfric the Young, 8 hides		shares 'port' prefix with Portbury
Clapton-in-Gordano		Clapton Wick part of Portbury	5, 27: Bishop of Coutances	Algar, 5.5 hides		shares '-ton' suffix with other Gordano parishes
Easton-in-Gordano			5, 24: Bishop of Coutances	Alric, 12 hides		'East-ton' of Portbury?
Walton-in-Gordano			29, 1: Ralph of Mortimer	Gunni the Dane, 3.5 hides		shares '-ton' suffix with other Gordano parishes
Weston-in-Gordano			5, 22: Bishop of Coutances 5, 26: Bishop of Coutances	Brictnoth 7 hides Algar, 3 hides 1 virgate		'West-ton' of Portbury?
Abbots Leigh		Ham Green part of Portbury	16, 9: Thurston	father of Thurston, 1 hide		
Wraxall	mother church of Nailsea	Happerton, and Failand Farm part of Portbury	5, 40: Bishop of Coutances	Aelfric, 20 hides		
Nailsea	chapel of Wraxall		[un-named 4.5 hides in Wraxall?]	[absent: included under Wraxall?]		
Flax Bourton	chapel of Wraxall		[absent: included under Wraxall?]	[absent: included under Wraxall?]		
Backwell			5, 30: Bishop of Coutances	Thorkell, 10 hides		
Tickenham			26, 8: William of Eu 41, 2: Arnulf of Hesdinc	Saewulf + Theodulf as two manors, 8.5 hides Edric, 1 hides 3 virgates		
Clevedon			44, 1: Matthew of Mortagne	Hildebert, 5.5 hides		

documented example is when Cleeve was carved out of Yatton in 1841: Youngs 1979, 422)

- place-names indicating early estate centres (topographical features such as river + ton: eg Wring-ton); hierarchical relationships and the relative locations of primary and subsidiary settlements, such as Norton (North-ton) and Sutton (South-ton); and a common origin such as East and West Harptree (Fig 7.1.B)
- large Domesday manors of 20 hides or more that include unnamed sub-tenancies, or manors that other evidence suggests included places that are not themselves named (Fig 7.1.C)
- pre-Conquest charters giving hidage, and occasionally estate boundaries (eg Banwell: Fig 7.1.D).

Greater Portbury (Table 7.1)

An early federative estate was clearly based at Portbury reflected in part by a series of linked place-names (Portbury and Portishead; Clapton-in-Gordano,

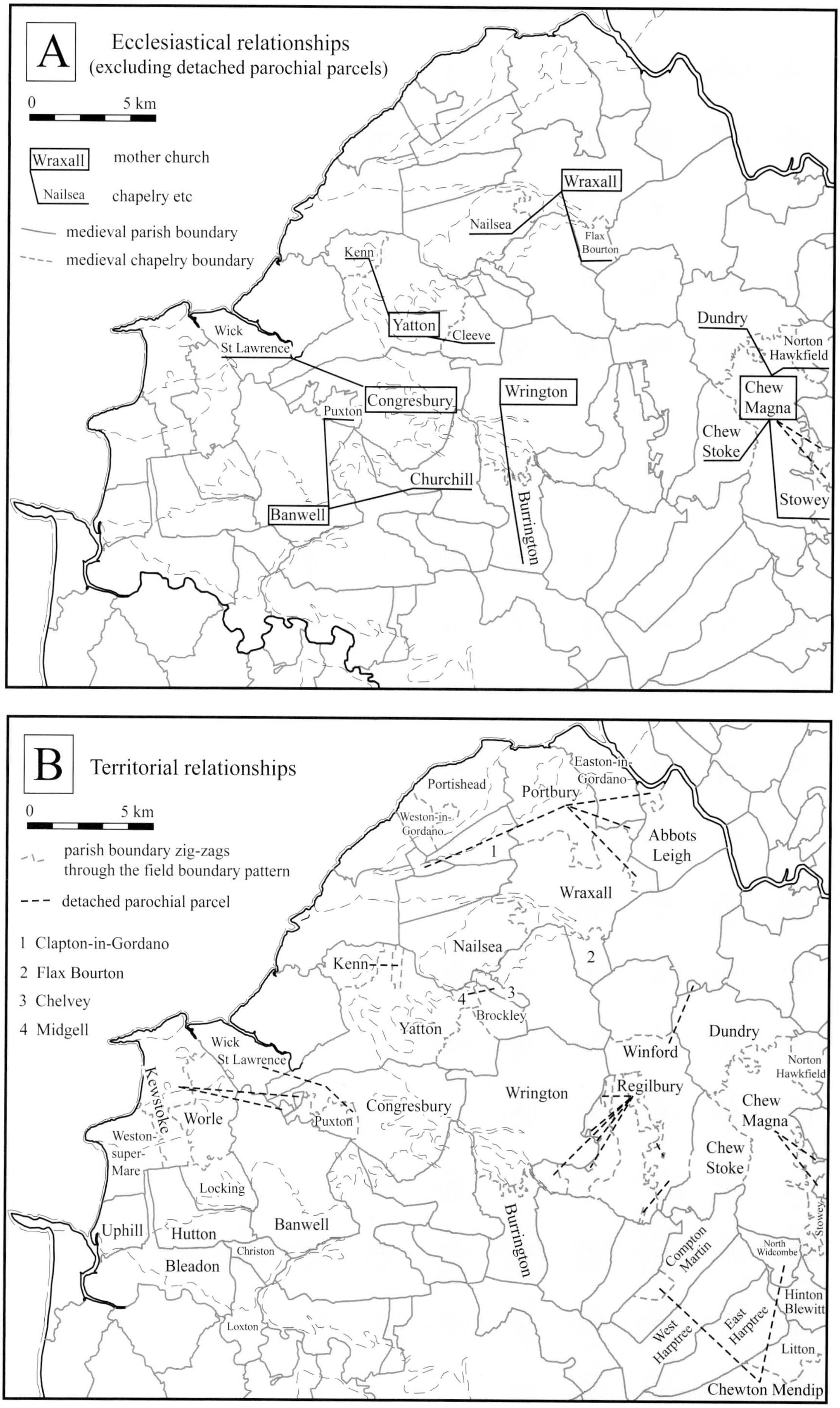

Figure 7.1 The evidence used to reconstruct the early estates in north-west Somerset

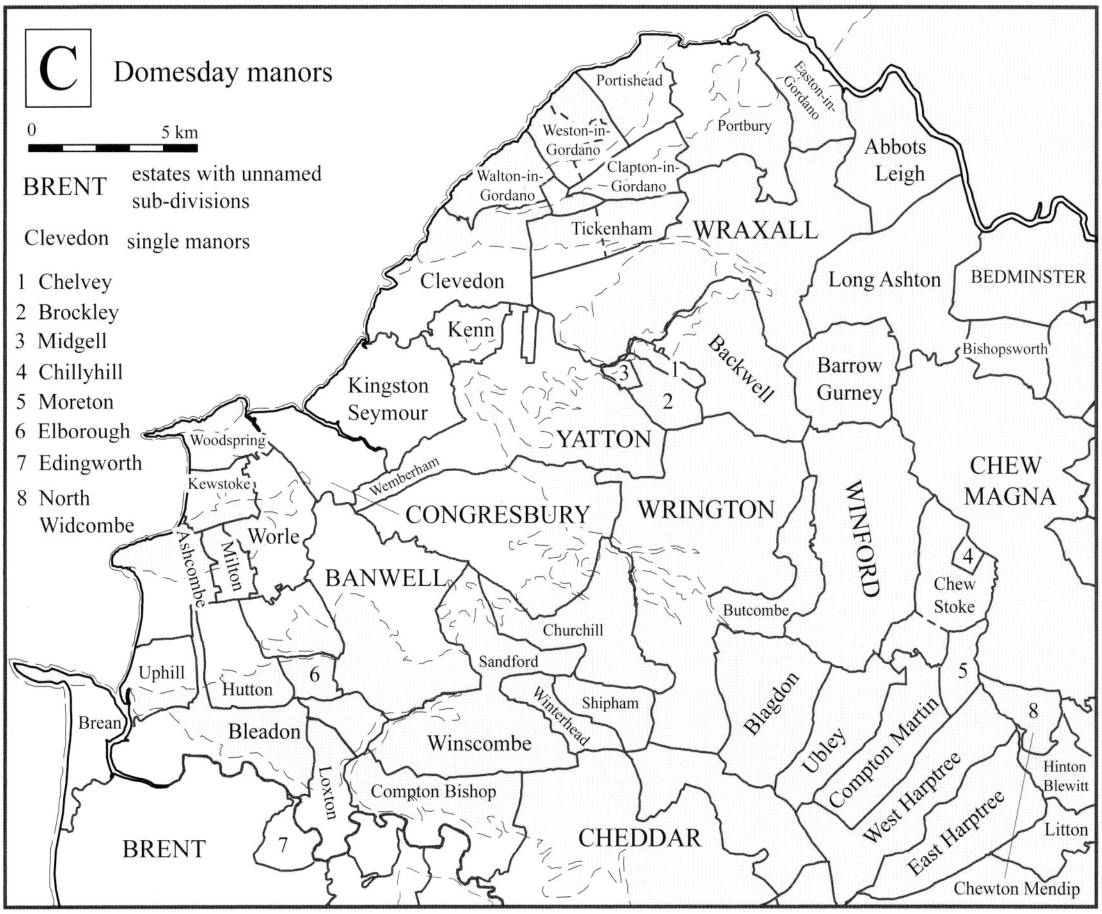
C
Domesday manors
0
5 km
BRENT
estates with unnamed sub-divisions
Clevedon
single manors
1 Chelvey
2 Brockley
3 Midgell
4 Chillyhill
5 Moreton
6 Elborough
7 Edingworth
8 North Widcombe
Portishead
Easton-in-Gordano
Portbury
Weston-in-Gordano
Abbots Leigh
Walton-in-Gordano
Clapton-in-Gordano
Tickenham
WRAXALL
Clevedon
Long Ashton
BEDMINSTER
Kenn
Backwell
Barrow Gurney
Bishopsworth
Kingston Seymour
YATTON
Woodspring
Wemberham
CHEW MAGNA
Kewstoke
CONGRESBURY
WRINGTON
WINFORD
Worle
Ashcombe
Milton
BANWELL
Chew Stoke
Butcombe
Churchill
Sandford
Uphill
Hutton
Shipham
Blagdon
Winterhead
Brean
Bleadon
Winscombe
Ubley
Compton Martin
West Harptree
Hinton Blewitt
Loxton
Compton Bishop
East Harptree
Litton
BRENT
CHEDDAR
Chewton Mendip

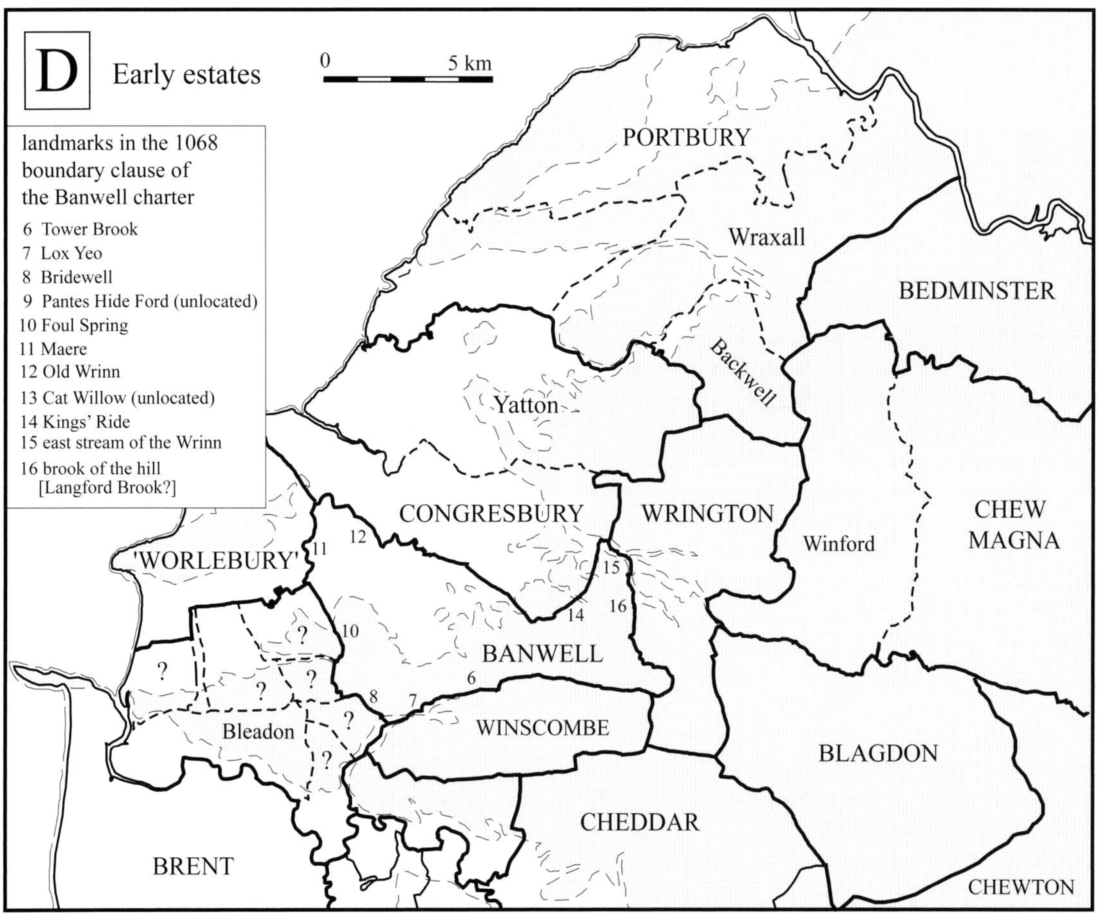
D
Early estates
0
5 km
landmarks in the 1068 boundary clause of the Banwell charter
6 Tower Brook
7 Lox Yeo
8 Bridewell
9 Pantes Hide Ford (unlocated)
10 Foul Spring
11 Maere
12 Old Wrinn
13 Cat Willow (unlocated)
14 Kings' Ride
15 east stream of the Wrinn
16 brook of the hill [Langford Brook?]
PORTBURY
Wraxall
BEDMINSTER
Backwell
Yatton
CONGRESBURY
WRINGTON
Winford
CHEW MAGNA
'WORLEBURY'
BANWELL
Bleadon
WINSCOMBE
BLAGDON
CHEDDAR
BRENT
CHEWTON

Easton-in-Gordano, Walton-in-Gordano, and Weston-in-Gordano), with Easton to the east of Portbury and Weston to the west. Portbury parish also had detached parcels at Clapton Wick (in Clapton parish), and Ham Green (in Abbots Leigh). The south-eastern boundary of Abbots Leigh is the 5km-long Beggar Bush Lane that is clearly of great antiquity and pre-dates the surrounding historic landscape. This continues as the southern boundary of Wraxall and Flax Bourton, and also marks the boundary of Portbury hundred. The boundary between Portbury and Wraxall, in contrast, zig-zags through the historic landscape, and there are two further detached parcels of Portbury in Wraxall (Failand Farm and Happerton). Wraxall was the mother church of Nailsea and Flax Bourton, neither of which appears in Domesday. Clevedon and Tickenham may also have originally been part of this greater Portbury estate as they also lay to the north of the Kenn River that formed the southern boundary of Nailsea, and were part of Portbury hundred. It would appear, therefore, that the bounds of this early estate were coterminous with Portbury hundred which was then divided between Portbury with the Gordano parishes in the north, and Nailsea with its dependencies in the south. In total this reconstructed estate amounted to 64 hides and a virgate (as assessed at Domesday). In addition, the 10 hides at Backwell (*DB Som* 5,30) may have been part of this estate as, like Flax Bourton and Wraxall, it faces into the Kenn Valley with its unenclosed commons up on Wrington Down to the south-east, and topographically it makes no sense for it to have belonged to Wrington or the greater Congresbury estate (Fig 7.1.D).

Greater Chew Valley (Table 7.2)

The zig-zagging parish boundaries between Chew Magna and its adjacent parishes (Dundry, Norton Hawkfield, and Stowey) clearly suggest that these once comprised a single territory, while the boundary between Chew Magna and Chew Stoke cuts across a series of parallel furlong boundaries running between the two villages. Dundry was a chapelry of Chew Magna, and Chew Stoke, Norton Hawkfield, and Stowey all paid tithes and mortuary fees to Chew Magna; Chew Stoke also paid half the offerings of newly weds to Chew Magna, and the vicar of Chew was responsible for maintaining the church at Stowey (Corcos 2002a, 54). The Vestry Book of 1752 records that parts of the Chew Magna churchyard wall belonged to, and were repaired by, the parishioners of Chew Stoke, Stowey, Dundry and Norton (Aston 1985, 49). The common place-name element in Norton Hawkfield and Norton Malreward suggests these were once the 'North-ton' of this postulated greater Chew Valley estate, to the north of Chew Magna. Sutton (Sutton Court, Bishop Sutton and Knighton Sutton) are the south-ton.

The southern boundary of Chew Magna parish (with North Widcombe) follows the long sweeping curve of what appears to be an ancient boundary on the watershed of Burledge Hill,[1] but to the west the boundary is more complex, as the parish of Compton Martin extends north into Chew Stoke to include the hamlet of Moreton (Fig 7.1.C). In 1086 Moreton, along with Compton Martin, was held by Serlo de Burcy but in 1066 it was held by three thanes as three manors for 5 hides (*DB Som*, 37,11; Rahtz and Greenfield 1977, 91). It is possible that these three manors originated as peripheral parts of the greater Chew Valley estate that, having fallen into the same hands as Compton Martin, were combined into one parish. In total this reconstructed estate amounted to 43 hides and 2 virgates (as assessed at Domesday).

To the east of Chew Magna, the boundary with the royal manor of Stanton Drew (and its two chapelries of Pensford and Publow, altogether assessed as 10 hides) cuts across a series of furlong boundaries that run between the two villages, and the boundary between Norton Malreward and Stanton similarly zig-zags through the historic landscape. Stanton Drew may have been part of the greater Chew Valley estate that was retained by the king after he had granted Chew Magna to the Bishop of Wells (Sawyer 1968, No. 1042) and so administratively became part of the royal manor at Keynsham. With Stanton Drew, the greater Chew Valley estate amounted to 53 hides and 2 virgates.

To the west of Chew Stoke, the parishes of Winford, Nempnett Thrubwell, Butcombe, and Barrow Gurney, along with the extra-parochial Regilbury (Kain and Oliver 2002, 183), were clearly once part of a single estate as their boundaries zig-zag through the historic landscape. There are also numerous detached parcels of Regilbury throughout these other parishes. Only Winford (11 hides), Barrow Gurney (10 hides), and Butcombe (3 hides) are in Domesday (though Regilbury may be the 1 hide added to Winford after the Conquest). The boundary between Winford and Chew Stoke cuts cut across a series of probable furlong boundaries and the inclusion of these five parishes in the greater Chew Valley estate gives a final total of 77 hides and 2 virgates.

Wrington

The 20-hide estate at Wrington was described in a charter of 904, its bounds being coterminous with the later parishes of Wrington and Burrington (the latter was a chapelry of Wrington during the medieval period). The place-name is river + ton type indicative of an early estate centre (Costen 1992a, 87; and see Corcos 2002b for a discussion of Burrington).

Greater Chewton and Greater Blagdon

Corcos (2002a) has suggested that the royal manor at Chewton may have also been the centre of what

Table 7.2 Possible components of an early estate based at Chew Magna

parishes	ecclesiastical relationship	parish boundaries	1086	1066	charters	place-names
Chew Magna		detached parcel Folly Farm east of Stowey	6, 13: Bishop of Wells	Bishop of Wells, 30 hides	S.1042 (1065): spurious confirmation held by Bishop of Wells	The 'South-ton' of Chew Magna could be Sutton in Stowey
Chew Stoke	tithes paid to Chew Magna	boundary with Chew Magna cuts through furlong boundaries	37, 3: Serlo de Burcy 37, 4 (Chillyhill): Serlo de Burcy 37, 4: Serlo de Burcy 47, 16: Aldwin	Everwacer, 0.5 hide Everwacer, 3 virgates Aelfric, 0.5 hide Aldwin, 1 hide 3 virgates		
Dundry	chapel of Chew Magna	interweaved with Chew Magna and Norton Hawkfield	[absent: included under Chew Magna?]	[absent: included under Chew Magna?]	S.1042 (1065): spurious confirmation held by Bishop of Wells	
Norton Hawkfield	tithes paid to Chew Magna	interweaved with Dundry	[absent: included under Chew Magna?]	[absent: included under Chew Magna?]		'North-ton' of Chew Magna?
Norton Malreward		interweaved with Publow	5, 16: Bishop of Coutances	Alfwold, 5 hides		'North-ton' of Chew Magna?
Stowey	tithes paid to Chew Magna	interweaved with Chew Magna	[absent: though Aelfric of Stowey held 7 virgates of Chew Magna]	[absent: included under Chew Magna?]		
Moreton		interwoven with Chew Stoke	37, 11: Serlo of Burcy	three thanes as three manors, 5 hides		'Marsh-ton' of Chew Magna?
Stanton Drew			1, 28 (as part of the King's manor of Keynsham)	the King, 10 hides		
Penford	chapelry of Stanton Drew		[absent: included under Stanton Drew?]			
Publow	chapelry of Stanton Drew	interweaved with Stanton Drew and Norton Malreward	[absent: included under Stanton Drew?]			
Winford		Detached parcel in Nempnett Thrubwell, and to north of Dundry	5, 41: Bishop of Coutances	Alfwold, 10 hides Aelfric, 1h [Regilbury?]		
Regilbury		detached parcels in Winford and Butcombe	[see Winford 1066]	[see Winford]		
Nempnett Thrubwell		Includes detached parcel of Winford				
Butcombe		includes detached parecls of Regilbury	5, 41: Bishop of Coutances	Alfward, 3 hides		
Barrow Gurney		boundary with Winford zig-zags through the historic landscape	5, 32: Bishop of Coutances	Edric, 10 hides		

was once a far larger estate, encompassing most of the hundred of the same name. The place-name is river + ton type indicative of an early estate centre (Costen 1992a, 87). The boundary of Chewton Mendip parish itself is interweaved with Litton and Emborough, while Ston Easton (note the directional name), Emborough, Farrington Gurney, and Paulton (all to the east of Fig 7.1) were chapelries of Chewton Mendip, of which North Widcombe (to the north-east of Hinton Blewitt) was a detached tithing. Some issues concerning the eastern boundary are unclear but a territory of around 60 hides appears likely.

These eastern parishes of Chewton hundred are all physically interwoven and most have an ecclesiastical relationship with Chewton Mendip, in contrast to the parishes in the western part of the hundred (East Harptree, West Harptree, Compton Martin, Ubley, along with Blagdon in Winterstoke hundred) that form a set of strip parishes running from the Mendip Hills down into the Chew and Yeo Valleys (Fig 7.1.C). With the exception of the possible Roman road (Stratford Lane) that formed the parish boundary between Compton Martin and West Harptree, the boundaries between these parishes appear to post-date the historic landscape, and in Domesday every manor within this block of parishes was assessed as 5 hides or multiples thereof giving a total of 40 hides. Ubley was certainly royal land, being held by King Edgar in 959 x 75 (Sawyer 1968, No. 1771), while Compton Martin may be the Mertone held by Cynewulf in 757 x 86 (Sawyer 1968, No. 1690; Finberg 1964, 635).

Greater Banwell

The early history of Banwell and Congresbury

According to the *Life of Alfred*, written in 893, Alfred the Great granted the *monasteriis* at *Cungresbyri* [Congresbury] and *Banuwille* [Banwell] to the Welsh priest Asser in 885–86 (*Asser* f.81, 22; Smyth 1995, 226, 355, 450). The word *monasteriis* has usually been translated as monasteries (eg Stevenson 1904, 353; Smyth 1995, 355) but is probably more correctly thought of as minster (Blair 2005, 324–5). Asser went on to become Bishop of Sherborne sometime between 892 and 900, and upon his death in 908–09 the See was divided in three (Sherborne in Dorset, Crediton in Devon, and Wells in Somerset), when logically Banwell and Congresbury would have passed to the new bishopric of Wells (*Asser*, f.81, 22; Keynes and Lapidge 1983, 50–2, 264, n.192; Smyth 1995, 226, 355, 450; Whitelock 1967, 13). Wells subsequently lost the two estates as they returned to the Crown, possibly because they had been given to Asser as his personal property rather than to the former See of Sherborne itself.

Unfortunately we do not have any genuine early charters for Wells, the earliest being a confirmation (Finberg 1964, No. 542; Sawyer 1968, No. 1042) purportedly by King Edward in 1065 but which must be post-Conquest as it includes Mark (an appurtenance of Wedmore) that was only granted to Wells in 1066 x 75 (Finberg 1964, No. 545). A charter of 904 *claims* that Banwell had passed to Winchester Cathedral's manor at Taunton as in that year Winchester granted King Edward 20 hides at Banwell, 10 hides at Compton Bishop, and a number of other estates, in consideration of the remission of certain rights which the king possessed over Taunton (Sawyer 1968, No. 373; Hugo 1859; Knight 1902, 412). Finberg (1964, No. 424) regards this charter as interpolated and possibly containing some element of truth, but Sawyer (1968, No. 373) and Stevenson (1904, 192 n.5) argue that it is simply a forgery not least because Asser did not die until *c* 909 (Banwell could, perhaps, have reverted to the Crown after Alfred's death in 899 though there is no record of its subsequent granting to Winchester). In a charter of 968 x 78 that Stevenson (1904, 202 n.2) regards as doubtful, but which Finberg (1964) argues is authentic, King Edgar renewed the liberties of Taunton as granted by King Edward and it is mentioned that the land at Banwell and Compton Bishop had since been given to the monastery at Cheddar in exchange for Carhampton (Sawyer 1968, No. 806).

In the 11th century we return to firmer ground when sometime between 1016 and 1033 King Canute granted Banwell and Congresbury to a royal priest called Dudoc who in 1033 became Bishop of Wells (Finberg 1964, No. 528). In 1060 Dudoc left the estates in his will to the See, though they were seized by Earl Harold upon the bishop's death in the same year (*Wells I*, 431; Hunter 1840, 15). A spurious charter of 1065 claiming to be a confirmation by King Edward of Wells's estates included Banwell and Congresbury (*Wells I*, 428–9; Finberg 1964, No. 542), but in fact upon Harold's death in 1066 the estates passed to King William. In 1068, Giso, Bishop of Wells, petitioned the king and a charter of 1068 confirms the restoration of 30 hides at Banwell including Compton Bishop. The king retained Congresbury but granted Yatton to the bishop instead, along with one hide of land in Congresbury called Wemberham (modern Hewish; *DB Som*, 1,21; 6,14; *Liber Albus II*, 431).

The 1068 charter bounds of Banwell (Fig 7.1.D)

The 1068 charter includes the following description of its bounds (Grundy 1932, 167):

> *Aerest aet Hylsbrookes Ea Willme east on thone Cumb eall abutan Losa Leh. Swa west on thone Cumb. And swa west of tham Cumbe to Bibricge. Of Bibricge into ture Broc. Of ture Broc into loxcs. Of Loxs into bridewell to Pantes hyd ford to Fule Welle ut on thone Maere. Of tham Maere on Ealdan Wrinn into Catt widig. Up forth be Cyng Roda. Aestt in thone Wrinnaest Straeme. Forth that hit cymth in thone Hyls Broc. Up that hit cymth aest inne tha Eaa Willme.*

Following Grundy (1932, 167), the translation reads:

> . . . First at the large spring of the Brook of the Hill east to the Combe (and) all round *Losa* clearing. So west to the Combe. And so west from the Combe to the place by the bridge. From the place by the bridge to Tower Brook. From Tower Brook to the Lox Yeo River. From the Lox Yeo to Bridewell. To Pantes Hide Ford to Foul Spring out to the *Maere*. From the *Maere* to the Old Wrinn. Into Cat Willow. Up on by King's Ride east to the East Stream of the Wrinn. On till it comes to the Brook of the Hill. Up till in comes again to the large Spring.

Ture Broc must be Towerhead Brook that forms the eastern boundary of Banwell, which indicates that the bounds up until then relate to an area to the east in what is now Sandford and Churchill (a chapelry of Banwell), neither of which are named in Domesday (Fig 7.1.C–D). The next section corresponds to the southern, western, and northern boundary of Banwell parish as it is first mapped in 1815: the *Loxcs* is the Lox Yeo, while *Bridewell* Lane forms Banwell's south-western boundary, with Christon. *Pantes Hyd* ford is *Panteshede* in Domesday (*DB Som* 21,80).[2] It cannot now be identified but must lie somewhere near Manor Farm at Hillend, as the next landmark, *Fulle Welle* (Foulwell), is the source of the Grumblepill Rhyne. The *Maere* could mean boundary (Dickinson 1877, 61) or bank (Grundy 1932, 169) and is presumably the Grumblepill Rhyne. Dickinson, Grundy, and Taylor (1905, 51) all assume the *Ealdan Wrinn* ('Old Wrinn', ie a former course of the River Wring now called the Congresbury Yeo) is the Oldbridge River, with the implication that Banwell included Puxton, but a range of other evidence clearly points to Puxton having been carved out of Congresbury (see below) suggesting that the *Ealdan Wrinn* was the Bourton Town and Blackstones Rhynes which formed the Banwell/Puxton parish boundary. Grundy identifies the last stretch of the bounds as being the present eastern boundary of Banwell that runs past a field that in the tithe survey was called 'Catwithy' at the junction of the Liddy Yeo and Towerhead Brook, but this cannot be the same place since the King's Ride is probably King Road between Churchill and Congresbury and the 'east stream of the River Wrinn' is the Congresbury Yeo that now flows past Wrington, forming the northern boundary of Churchill.

The charter bounds clearly show that Banwell in the 11th century contained the later parishes/manors of Banwell and Churchill, along with Sandford that was later part of Winscombe (Fig 7.1.C, D). The 15 hides of Winscombe, including Winterhead that was removed from it by the time of Domesday, may originally have been part of the greater Banwell estate as it was also royal property, being granted by King Edgar to Aelfswith in 959 x 75 from whom it appears to have passed to Glastonbury Abbey (*John of Glastonbury*, 43; Finberg 1964, No. 502; Sawyer 1968, No. 1762; Abrams 1996, 248–9). Logically, Shipham was also part of this early territory.

Banwell in Domesday

The Domesday account of Banwell is relatively detailed as, in common with the rest of south-west England, the Exchequer volume is supplemented by the *Liber Exoniensis*, a 'survivor of the mass of original documents produced in connection with that inquest' (Welldon Finn 1964, 1). In the following transcription (from Thorn and Thorn 1980) the additional information in the *Liber Exoniensis* is in italics.

> BANWELL. Earl Harold held it before 1066; it paid tax for 30 hides. Land for 40 ploughs, of which 6 hides are in lordship; 3 ploughs there; 52 slaves; 24 villagers and 12 smallholders with 18 ploughs *and 7 hides.*
> A mill that pays 7s 6d; meadow, 60 acres; pasture 200 acres; woodland 1 league long and 1 furlong long; *1 cob; 25 cattle; 30 pigs; 200 sheep.*
> Value £10, *for the Bishop's use.*
> Of this manor's lands **Serlo *of Burcy*** holds 3 hides from the Bishop, *land for 8 ploughs, in lordship 1 plough and 2 slaves, 5 villagers have 3 ploughs, 3 smallholders, value 60s, when acquired* £6; **Ralph *Crooked Hands*** 5½ hides, *in lordship 3 ploughs, 6 villagers have 5 ploughs, 2 smallholders, value 100s*; **Roghard 5½ hides**, *in lordship 2 hides, 2 ploughs and 3 slaves, the villages have 3½ hides and 4 ploughs, 9 villagers, 10 smallholders, 1 cob, 20 cattle, 30 pigs, 100 sheep, 6 unbroken mares, value 100s, £4 when he acquired it;* **Fastrad 1 hide**, *in lordship 1 plough, 1 villager, value 20s*; **Bofa 1 hide**, *in lordship 1 plough, 1 villager has 1 plough, value 10s*; **Alfwy *son of Banna(?)*** 1 hide, *in lordship 1 plough, 1 villager has half a plough, value 10s.* In Lordship 9 ploughs; 5 slaves; 25 villagers and 15 smallholders who have 13½ ploughs. 2 mills of Roghard's which pay 10s; Ordwulf, 1 mill which pays 40d.
> Value of the whole manor £15, for the Bishop's use; for the men's use, £15 likewise.

Thorn and Thorn (1980, 354) suggest that Ralph Crooked Hands' 5½ hides was Churchill with Stock, lying adjacent to his 1 hide manor in Winscombe (which is probably Sandford) as in the early 14th century Roger Fitzpayn held both Sandford (of Glastonbury Abbey: *Monington*, 32), and Churchill with Stock (*Feudal Aids VI*, 307). Banwell's other subholdings, of Serlo, Roghard, Fastrad, Bofa, and Alfwy, cannot be identified but might include Compton Bishop and the hamlets/tithings of Knightcott, Rolstone, St Georges, Woolvershill, and Yarborough which all lie beyond the main village and open fields in Banwell. Winscombe may also have been part of an early greater Banwell, taking the boundary of the territory up to the watershed of Mendip as was the case with Wrington (Burrington) and the greater Blagdon block of manors.

Greater Congresbury (Fig 6.4 and Table 7.3)

The early history

Congresbury is named after the late 5th- to early 6th-century Welsh missionary St Cyngar (Congar), and the '-bury' name, derived from the Old English *burh/byrig*, probably refers to a monastic site (as in Glastonbury, Amesbury, Malmesbury, and Tewkesbury), rather than a hillfort (such as its use in Cadbury: Rahtz *et al* 1992, 5; Oakes and Costen 2003, 285–6). Two late 14th-century lists of the early endowments of the church at Sherborne refer to a lost charter of King Ine, dated 688 x 726, that granted seven hides at *Predian* [Priddy] and 20 hides at *Conbusburie/Cungresbury* [Congresbury] to the church at Sherborne (Finberg 1964, No. 372; O'Donovan 1988, xxxvii). Congresbury is next recorded in 885–86 when Alfred granted it, along with Banwell, to Asser from whom it passed to the See of Wells (see above). Following its seizure by Earl Harold, King William retained most of Congresbury but granted the adjacent Yatton to the Bishop instead, along with one hide of land at Wemberham that was removed from Congresbury (*Liber Albus II*, 431; Sawyer 1968, No. 1042).

The location of the early British monastery is unknown, though it may have lain within the hillfort at Cadbury (reoccupied in the 5th–6th centuries: Rahtz *et al* 1992), or the nearby Romano-Celtic temple at Henley Wood where there was an extensive Christian cemetery (Watts and Leach 1996). The monastery may then have moved to a large rhomboidal enclosure on the edge of the Levels (within which the medieval parish church was constructed), of approximately 11.25 acres (4½ ha) in extent. Romano-British and possibly early medieval pottery have been recovered from this enclosure, along with a sherd that has been interpreted as 'Saxon' (Fowler *et al* 1970, fig 9, no. 26; Rahtz *et al* 1992, 6, microfiche 1). This enclosure is very reminiscent of those in Dorset that Hall (2000; 2003; and see Aston 2003) has argued were created following the Saxon Conquest, as although initially the British church was supported by the new Saxon kings, by the late 7th century it was seen as 'unorthodox' and in need of reformation. This 'Romanisation' led to a number of other sites being abandoned and refounded within new rectilinear enclosures, a process particularly associated with Aldhelm, Abbot of Malmesbury and Bishop of the See at Sherborne created in 705. If King Ine did indeed grant Congresbury to Sherborne in the early 8th century, then it is very tempting to see a British monastery as having been moved to a new rectilinear enclosure in the early 8th century. A collection of late 10th- to mid-11th-century carved stone found in a barn in Brinsea also probably came from close to the present parish church (a 13th-century structure: Pevsner 1958, 176), and may represent a shrine to the cult of St Congar that had developed under the See of Wells (Oakes and Costen 2003).

Congresbury in Domesday

The 20 hide estate of Congresbury was larger than the 19th-century parish and some progress can be made in reconstructing its extent, starting with its Domesday entry (from Thorn and Thorn 1980, with the additional information from the *Liber Exoniensis* in italics):

> CONGRESBURY. Earl Harold held it before 1066; it paid tax for 20 hides. Land for 50 ploughs, of which 5 hides are in lordship; 6 ploughs there; 12 slaves; 34 villagers and 34 smallholders with 34 ploughs *and 9½ hides.*
> 2 mills that pay 17s 6d; meadow, 250 acres; pasture 2 leagues long and ½ a league wide; woodland 2½ leagues long and ½ a league wide; *2 cobs; 20 cattle; 40 pigs; 200 sheep; 40 goats.*
> It pays £28 15s white silver; *when William the Sheriff acquired it, as much.*
> Of this manor three thanes, Alfward, Ordric and Ordwulf, hold 3 hides and 3 virgates of land*; *Alfward, Ordric and Ordwulf hold three hides of thaneland*; they could not be separated from the lord of the manor. In lordship 3 ploughs; 4 slaves; 6 villagers and 17 smallholders with 3½ ploughs. *Alfward 1h, in lordship 3v, 1 plough, the villagers have 1v,* ½ *a plough, 1 villager and 5 smallholders; Ordric 1h 1v, in lordship 3v and 1 plough, the villagers have 2v and 2 ploughs, 4 villagers and 8 smallholders; Ordwulf 3v, in lordship 2½v and 1 plough, the villagers have ½v and 1 plough, 1 villager and 4 smallholders.* Meadow 20 acres; woodland 30 acres. Value of the whole 60s.
> Bishop Maurice holds this manor's church with ½ a hide. Value 20s.
> From this manor's land have been taken away 2 hides which lay there before 1066. Bishop Giso holds 1, value £4; *when he acquired it, as much.*
> Serlo of Burcy and Gilbert son of Thorold hold the other hide; value 40s; *they each hold* ½ *a hide and the values are 20s each*; *when they acquired it, as much.*
>
> * 3 hides and 3 virgates is incorrect: the details given in *Exon.* add up to 3 hides, which also combine with the other hides to give 20 (Thorn and Thorn 1980, 296).

The three hides held by Alfward, Ordric and Ordwulf cannot be identified directly, but one may be Puxton that was clearly carved out of Congresbury (see below). The others may have been Iwood and Brinsea that also lay at the edges of the estate. Of the two hides removed from Congresbury after the Conquest, one, held by Giso, Bishop of Wells, is probably Hewish as the Domesday entry for Yatton includes reference to 'A pasture called *Waimora* [Wemberham?] . . . which before 1066 belonged to Congresbury' (Fig 7.1.C; *DB Som* 6,14). The *Exon.* Domesday elaborates: 'Of this manor's [Yatton] land Hildebert [holds] four hides. Of the four hides . . . a woman, Aethelrun, had one hide jointly in 1066. With this hide, which Aethelrun held, lies a pasture called Wemberham' (Thorn and Thorn 1980, 317). Therefore, this hide, with the pasture at Wemberham, was transferred from the king's manor of Congresbury to the bishop's manor of Yatton between 1066 and 1086. The hide in question is logically Hewish, which, although lying south of the river, was part of the medieval parish of Yatton (Costen 1992b). The place-name Hewish is derived from *hid* (a hide of land), through a common root in *higan* (a family), and means 'the land for the support of a family' (Costen 1992b, 65). The boundaries of Hewish, as shown on the tithe map, also suggest that it was carved out of Congresbury. Its northern and western boundaries follow a naturally meandering stream (the New Ear Rhyne), whereas its southern boundary is the very straight and clearly artificial New Rhyne. The northern boundary of Hewish is the current course of the Congresbury Yeo, though in the 19th century, when the landscape was first mapped, a large meadow called Wemberham lay on the northern side of the river, even though it paid Land Tax in the Hewish division of Yatton to the south, and it is possible that the original course of the river was around the north and west of this meadow (see Chapter 6).

The other hide removed from Congresbury after the Conquest was held as two half hides by Serlo of Burcy and Gilbert son of Thorold (*DB Som* 1,21 *Exon.*). Gilbert held 1½ hides in Kewstoke (*DB Som* 42,1), and presumably the half was his share of the hide removed from Congresbury and was probably the detached part of Kewstoke parish sandwiched between Puxton, Congresbury, and Hewish (Fig 6.4).

Serlo of Burcy held Woodspring for a short time after the Conquest (*DB Som* 27,3) as 6 hides and 1 virgate, to which were added 3 hides 'in Serlo's time'. The *Liber Exoniensis* explains that these three hides comprised half a hide that Cola held before 1066 as a manor (perhaps Bourton?), and 2½ hides that Alfward had held before the Conquest as a manor (which is logically Wick St Lawrence, adjacent to Woodspring, which does not otherwise appear in Domesday).

North of the Congresbury Yeo: the Greater Yatton estate

It seems clear, therefore, that the 20-hide royal estate of Congresbury encompassed the later parishes of Congresbury, Puxton, and Wick St Lawrence, along with Hewish and the detached parts of Kewstoke in Puxton. Logically the northern edge of this estate should be the Congresbury Yeo, but the parish/manor of Congresbury itself actually extends to the north where it shares a boundary with another royal estate centred at Yatton. This area of Congresbury, known as Land, included the reoccupied hillfort on Cadbury Hill (the parish boundary running along the northern rampart of the hillfort) but not the nearby, contemporary, and surely associated cemetery at Henley Wood. The division of these two sites, and the extension of Congresbury north of the Yeo, suggests that there was once a single estate that was initially divided into Congresbury and Yatton, perhaps by 688 x 726 if the charter is genuine.

A range of evidence suggests that Yatton originally included the parishes of Brockley, Cleeve, Kenn, and Kingston Seymour. Cleeve and Kenn were medieval chapelries of Yatton. The place-name Kingston suggests it was once royal property (Bourne 1988; Gelling 1978, 184), as does the Domesday entry: one of its two manors was assessed as 1 hide, land for 17 ploughs, and valued at £6 in 1066 and 1086 (*DB Som* 5,63), the other as 4½ hides, land for 7 ploughs, and valued at 60s in 1066 and 1086 (*DB Som* 5,64). The fact that 'before 1066 this manor did not pay tax except for 1 hide', and the huge difference between the 1 hide and 17 ploughlands in the first manor, suggests tax exemption on former royal demesne (Costen 1992a, 123; and see Corcos 2002a, 126–9). It might be expected that as a recently colonised and pasture-rich area, the marshland manors of Kingston Seymour would have had a relatively high proportion of smallholders compared to the national average of 40% of the recorded population (Dyer 2002, 97); in fact, at 29% in Kingston, this was lower than the average of 40% in Banwell, Congresbury, and Yatton. In the regional context, however, this was a very relatively high proportion, as in the neighbouring wholly dryland estates of Winscombe and Wrington just 19% of the recorded population were smallholders. The proportion of arable land that was cultivated by the peasants was, however, virtually the same (78% in Kingston, 83% in Banwell, Congresbury, and Yatton, and 78% in Winscombe and Wrington).

Yatton (with Cleeve and Kenn), Kingston Seymour, and Brockley also formed a detached part of Chewton hundred (itself a royal manor with a recorded tax exemption in 1086: *DB Som* 1,29), and Corcos (2002a, 129) suggests that this resulted from the Bishop of Wells carving this block of land out of its Yatton estate and granting it to the royal manor at Chewton, to compensate the Crown for its loss of good pasture when the king's manor of Chew Magna was granted to the See in or after 909. The final part of this complex story is that Chelvey, with its detached parcel at Midgell, appears to have been carved out of Brockley. As Chelvey was not in the detached part of Chewton hundred it was presumably removed before 909.

Discussion: Cadbury Hill, Yatton, and the greater Congresbury estate

It seems clear, therefore, that Yatton, with Kenn, Cleeve, Brockley, and Kingston Seymour, once

Table 7.3 Possible components of an early estate based at Congresbury

parishes/ vills	ecclesiastical relationship	parish boundaries	1086	1066	charters	place-names
Congresbury		intermixed with Puxton and Wick St Lawrence	1, 21: the King	Earl Harold, 20 hides	Finberg 1964, No. 372 (688/726); *Asser* f.81, 22; S.1042 (1068)	
Puxton		intermixed with Puxton and Wick St Lawrence	[absent: part of Congresbury?]	[absent: part of Congresbury?]		
Wick St Lawrence	chapelry of Banwell	intermixed with Puxton and Wick St Lawrence	[absent: part of Congresbury?]	[absent: part of Congresbury?]		
Wemberham (Hewish)	part of Yatton		6, 14: Bishop of Wells	Kings manor of Congresbury, 1 hide		
Yatton			6, 14: Bishop of Wells	Bishop of Wells, 20 hides		
Kenn	chapelry of Yatton	carved out of Yatton	5, 29: Bishop of Coutances	No reference to 1066		
Kingston Seymour			5, 63: Bishop of Coutances	Aldred, 1 hide		King's-ton
Kingston Seymour			5, 64: Bishop of Coutances	Four thanes, 4.5 hides		King's-ton
Brockley			45, 16: Aldred	Aldred, 4 hides		
Midgell	detached part of Chelvey	carved out of Brockley	5, 68: Bishop of Coutances	Aelmer, 1 hide		
Chelvey			44, 2: Matthew of Mortagne	Thorkell the Dane, 1 hide		

comprised a single territory, which itself appears to have been part of the greater Congresbury estate that included Puxton, Hewish, and Wick St Lawrence. A hidage in Kingston Seymour is impossible to calculate, though its land for 24 ploughs may represent around 16 hides,[3] giving a total for this greater Congresbury estate of around 62 hides.

A Worlebury estate? (Table 7.4)

Although there are no charters for places west of Banwell, there is a good case for reconstructing another substantial estate based on the coastal bedrock island of Worlebury Hill which shows interesting parallels with Congresbury in having a substantial Romano-British settlement on the slope below an Iron Age hillfort that has produced large amounts of Romano-British material, including 200 coins, along with a Saxon spearhead and a 6th-century pennanular brooch (Burrow 1981, 281; Evans 1980; Rippon 1997a 106–7). In 1066 Worle was held by Asgar as 6½ hides (*DB Som* 24,1). Weston-super-Mare does not appear in Domesday, but Ashcombe (in the 19th century a small hamlet in the east of the parish) was held by Brictric in 1066 as 3½ hides (*DB Som* 5,13).[4] Kewstoke is a large parish whose church is on the northern side of Worlebury. Its boundaries with Worle to the east and Weston-super-Mare on the west zig-zag through the historic landscape in a way that clearly suggests that they are relatively late. The parish of Kewstoke extends over Worlebury to include the hamlet of Milton and the wetlands to the south, and as far north as the coastal bedrock island of Middlehope. In 1066 it was held by Edric as just 1½ hides (*DB Som* 42,1), and much of the parish appears to have been assessed as Woodspring, held by Everwacer as 6 hides and 1 virgate (*DB Som* 27,3). There were also two manors of 1 and 1½ hides at Milton in Kewstoke (*DB Som* 24, 2; 46,19: Thorn and Thorn 1980, 24). It would appear, therefore, that Kewstoke, Worle, and Weston-super-Mare were once a single estate possibly focused on Worle, which gave its name to Worlebury Hill, and with a 'West-ton' (Weston), 'Middle-ton' (Milton) and 'North-ton' (Norton) suggesting, not surprisingly, that Worle was the estate centre. Excavations in Worle in 1969–71 revealed a large ditched enclosure associated with large amounts of domestic refuse including pre-Conquest pottery (Chris Richards pers comm). The total hidage was 20 hides and 1 virgate.

Table 7.4 Possible components of an early estate based at Worlebury

parishes/vills	ecclesiastical relationship	parish boundaries	1086	1066	charters	place-names
Worle		interwoven with Kewstoke	24, 1: Walter of Douai	Asgar, 6.5 hides		
Kewstoke		interwoven with Worle and Weston-super-Mare	42, 1: Gilbert son of Thorold	Edric, 1.5 hides		Middle-ton and North-ton (see below)
Milton (in Kewstoke)		–	24, 2: Walter of Douai 46, 19: Ansketel Parker	Alwaker, 1.5 hides Osward, 1 hide		
Woodspring (in Kewstoke)		–	27, 3: William of Falaise	Everwacer, 6hides 1 virgate		
Ashcombe (in Weston-super-Mare)		interwoven with Kewstoke	5, 13: Bishop of Coutances	Brictric 3.5 hides		West-ton

Discussion

In the early medieval period it would appear that north-west Somerset was divided between a series of large estates including Portbury (64 hides), Chew Magna (77 hides), Chewton (*c* 60 hides), Blagdon (40 hides), Wrington (20 hides), Banwell (20 hides), Congresbury (*c* 62½ hides), and Worlebury (20 hides). Each of these estates was based at a central place located in a river valley or close to the fen-edge, with subsidiary and sometimes specialised settlements spread across the different environments, and their boundaries extending onto the surrounding uplands where they probably ran unmarked through areas of rough grazing. To the west of Banwell, however, there is no evidence that the parishes of Bleadon, Uphill, Hutton, Locking, Christon and Loxton were ever part of a single estate and it may be that this area always consisted of a series of smaller holdings.

Some of these large federative estates appear to have fragmented in several stages, initially into large territories such as Wraxall (20 hides) and Yatton (20 hides), and if King Ine's (688–726) grant of 20 hides at Congresbury is genuine then this process appears to have been underway by the 8th century. Many of these estates were in turn sub-divided into smaller manors that by 1066 had been acquired by great magnates and lesser thanes alike in order to create large but often discontinuous lordships. The Norman Conquest saw a major transformation of secular landownership with the wholesale confiscation of the estates of the Saxon aristocracy followed by the redistribution of this land amongst the new Anglo-Norman elite, such as the Bishop of Coutances who was a major recipient of manors in the coastal districts of north-west Somerset,[5] and Serlo de Burcy who built up a small lordship around the Chew Valley.[6] Other changes in landholding following the Conquest included restoring to the Church a number of estates that had been seized by Earl Harold (eg Banwell and Congresbury were returned to Wells in 1068 and 1217–19 respectively), and in time the endowment of new monasteries (eg Woodspring Priory; Willis Watson 1908). The rest of this chapter will focus on the history of just those estates that extended into the study area, notably Banwell and the manor of Rolstone that was carved out of it, Congresbury, and Puxton.

Post-Conquest Banwell

In 1316 the *Nomina Villarum* records that Banwell contained three fees held by the Bishop of Bath and Wells [Banwell Manor], the Prior of Bruton [the Rectory Manor], and John FitzPayne [Rolstone] (*Feudal Aids VI*, 325–6).

Banwell Manor

Throughout the medieval period, the manor of Banwell was held by the Bishops of Bath and Wells, and was one of their favoured residences (second only in importance to Wells: Hembry 1967, 18; Thompson 1998, 170–1). Under Edward VI the manor was seized by the Duke of Somerset and then returned to the Crown. In 1553 it was granted to Sir William St Loe but within a year was restored to the bishop by Queen Mary and it remained an episcopal manor until the late 18th century (Collinson 1791, 567). The extent of its lands is evident from a lease book of 1695–1743 that covered extensive areas of the dryland part of the parish, along with Waywick ('Wheywick'), West Wick, and St Georges ('Puttingthorpe') (WCL 10189; Powell 1999).

Rectory Manor and Balls Barn

The church at Banwell was granted to Bruton Priory by Robert, Bishop of Bath and Wells, sometime between 1136 and 1166, and in a series of subsequent grants the priory built up an estate comprising the advowson and the rectory manor with its lands and share of the tithes. Following the Dissolution this estate was granted to the newly established cathedral in Bristol which retained the tithes but sold the manor to a Mr Lacy, whose descendant, Edmund Lacy, died in 1613 leaving it to his daughter Elizabeth (*Wills*, 76). Surveys of 1712, *c* 1745–50, and 1766 indicate that most of this manor's property lay in and around Banwell village, interspersed with those of the bishop's manor (DRO 2065m add 28/m1; Bromwich 1984).

The only tenement in the Banwell Rectory Manor located on the Marsh was the tithe barn for Puxton known as Balls Barn (LPL COMM.XIIa/15; PRO E134/1654/Mich 16). As this '17 acres of land called Balls Barn, Butchers Lease, and Brewton' is described alongside the first tenement listed in the 1712 survey, Bromwich (1984, 33–4) suggests that it equates with the original grant to Bruton in the late 12th century, by Thomas la Warre, lord of Rolveston, of land in augmentation of the 'barton' of their grange of Rolveston (*Bruton* No. 133[2]). In 1538–39 the Ministers Accounts for the Rectory of Banwell refer to a capital messuage and barn called 'Ballsbarne' formerly held by the Abbey and Convent of Bruton (PRO SC6/HenVIII/3137m.45), and in 1595 there was a dispute over the lease, dated 1562, by Dean and Chapter of Bristol Cathedral, of the Chapel of Puxton, and other appurtenances of the Rectory of Banwell, including 'a moiety of the tything corn belonging to the barn called Balles Barn' (PRO REQ2/226/13). Balls Barn lay in a field adjacent to the parish boundary with Puxton to the north of Balls Barn Lane (Figs 6.14.C and 7.3: BaTM 194 'Balls Barn'), and survives as a slightly raised sub-rectangular platform. When fieldwalked it yielded a scatter of stone and medieval pottery.

Rolstone

By the 17th century the single manor of East and West Rolstone occupied most of the land in the north-east corner of Banwell, and in *c* 1770 East Rolstone covered 327½ acres and West Rolstone 516 acres (Fig 7.3; SRO DD/WY 70). During the medieval period these two manors were held separately by the la Warre/de Coker and FitzPayne families respectively, being united in common ownership in the early 17th century.[7]

The FitzPayne manor of West Rolstone

The first of the Rolstone manors may have been included in Ralph Tortmanus's 5½ hides in Banwell (*DB Som* 6,9) that he held alongside 1 hide in Winscombe (*DB Som* 8,2: Sandford?), Pilton (*DB Som 8*,20), and 6½ hides at Alhampton in Ditcheat (*DB Som* 8,30). Morland (1963–64, 97) and Thorn and Thorn (1980, 354) suggest that Ralph Tortmanus's 5½ hides in Banwell was Churchill with Stock, which along with Pilton, Sandford, and Alhampton passed to the FitzPayne family by 1180 (Hodges 1996, 24). In 1307, however, it is specified that Roger FitzPayne was tenant in chief of Churchill with Stock, and Rolstone (*Feudal Aids VI*, 307), and the latter could, therefore, either have been included in the 5½ hides that Ralph Tortmanus held in Domesday, or added to the estate at a later date.

During the early 14th century the FitzPaynes were actively acquiring land in the Banwell area, for example in 1309 when Gregory de la Mare granted to Roger FitzPayne and his wife Margery a messuage, two carucates of land, 49 acres meadow, 62 acres wood, and £3 16s rent in Churchill-juxta-Banwell and Rolvestone (*Fines II*, No. 14). In 1316 the *Nomina Villarum* records that John FitzPayne held a fee in Banwell (*Feudal Aids VI*, 325–6), and in 1343 he held knights fees in Churchill, Rolstone, and Stock (LPL 1176), which passed to Roger FitzPayne by 1345–46 (*Feudal Aids VI*, 351), and to John FitzPayne by 1428 (*Feudal Aids VI*, 368). In the mid-15th century Churchill (along with Puxton: see below) passed to the Austell and then the St Loe families, though no further reference is made to Rolstone. That part of the fee may have been retained by the FitzPaynes who now lived in Hutton as in 1497 the *Inquisition Post Mortem* of John Payne includes 100 acres in Banwell, and 200 acres in Rolstone, Wolvershill, and Puxton which were held of Woodspring Priory (*CIPM Hen VII* I, No. 1150). The inclusion of land on Woolvershill suggests that this was the manor of West Rolstone, which included land there in the *c*1770 survey, as does a dispute in 1551 between Thomas Payne and Richard Morgan (a servant of Sir John St Loe, Lord of Puxton) over a 6-acre field called 'Cocks Close' within the parish of Banwell and their manor of 'Paynesbarne' which included land in Rolstone, Puxton, and Hewish (Coward nd). Two fields are called 'Cocks' in the Banwell tithe survey (Nos 232 and 234), both of which were part of the manor of West Rolstone in *c* 1770. A survey of the late 17th century similarly refers to 'Rolstone alias Paynesbarne' (SRO DD/PT box 46).

The la Warre/de Coker manor: East Rolstone

The FitzPaynes were not the only family to hold a fee in Rolstone. In the late 12th century Thomas la Warre, described as 'lord of Rolveston', granted Bruton Priory a piece of land called 'Suxacres' in augmentation of the 'barton' of their grange in Rolveston (*Bruton* No. 133[2]); this charter is undated but the witnesses include Roger FitzPayne. This can be identified as the Puxton tithe barn at Balls Barn in East Rolstone (see above). In 1317–18 'the manor of Rolstone' was held by John la Warre (*Fines II*, Nos 8 and 54), while in 1330–31 it is recorded that one-third of the manor, formerly held by Christina, wife of Thomas la Warre, was now in the possession of John son of Thomas le Baiocis, who granted it to Hugh son of Robert Draycote (*Fines II*, No. 4), while in 1341–42 Hugh de Draycote and Elizabeth his wife granted their one-third part of the manor of Rolstone to John de Bonham and Thomas de Pykes (*Fines II*, No. 10). The fee then passed to the de Coker family as in 1345–46 William de Coker and Elizabeth his wife held two parts of the manor of Rolstone (*Fines II*, No. 62). In 1357 there is reference to William de Coker of Rolstone (*Fines III*, 35), and in 1375–76 Simon Draycote died, granting his estates to the church, including land in Rolstone worth half a mark a year held of William Coker (*CIPM XIV*, No. 115). Draycote's other property lay in Uphill, Christon, Oldmixon, Wrington, South Brent, Burnham, and Brean, suggesting that, like Puxton, Rolstone formed part of the scattered estates typical of the lesser aristocracy in Somerset.

The combined manor(s) of East and West Rolstone

It is unclear who held the de Coker manor of Rolstone between the mid-14th and mid-16th centuries though a distinctive element of the manor of East Rolstone in the 17th century was a messuage in Axbridge, and this can be traced back to at least 1491–92 when John FitzJames the younger held a messuage, 12 acres of land, and 2 acres of meadow in Banwell, 'Wodebarough', and Axbridge, of the manor of 'Rolstone' by service of a knights fee; the lord of the manor of 'Rolstone' is unfortunately not given (*CIPM Hen VII* I, No. 716).

Sometime before 1571–72 Sir Ralph Jenyns acquired 'Rolstone' [East Rolstone?], which he held alongside the manors of Puxton, Churchill, and Edingworth (SRO DD/WY W/CR 46/1), while in 1584 Christopher Payne sold all his lands in Hutton, Banwell, [West] Rolstone, Hewish, Congresbury, and Puxton to Christopher Kenne (*Deeds*, No. 212). In 1609 Sir John Jennings died, holding the manors of Churchill, Puxton, Edingworth, and Rolstone, with divers lands and tenements recently purchased from Thomas Leigh in Rolstone, Banwell and Kewstoke, which probably represents the unification of the two manors (*Wards*, No. 185). His estates passed to his son Sir John and Lady Jennys and then to their son Richard, who sold the manors to Sir Wadham Wyndham in 1649 (SRO DD/WY 75).

The East Rolstone manor house appears to have been at Land Farm, described in the *c* 1770 survey as 'Court Place', and which an indenture of 1627 described as a 'capital messuage called Court Place' (SRO DD/WY 75). An indenture of 1649 describes the 'messuage called Court, 31 acres, and pasture called Havadge [a demesne pasture in the backfens]' (SRO DD/WY 75). The manor house of West Rolstone has not been located but may have been either Rolstone Court Farm or the nearby Rolstone Manor Farm. Alternatively, it may have been that as the Paynes were resident in Hutton there was no manor house in West Rolstone.

The map of *c* 1770 shows Lord Paulett as holding various tenements, with their characteristically scattered parcels, outside the manors of East and West Rolstone, which in the 17th century were leased from the manor of Rolstone alias Paynesbarn and included the roofless tenement at Bower House (SRO DD/SS 42). This may have been the demesne that had been farmed out, or freehold land (as Paulett also held a freehold tenement in Puxton).

Post-Conquest Congresbury

Following William's retention of Congresbury in 1066, King John restored the manor to Wells in 1217–19 and in 1229 it was disafforested and granted the licence for a weekly market and annual fair (*Liber Albus I*, 76–7; *Liber Albus II*, 494). In 1316 there were five fees in Congresbury: the Bishops of Bath and Wells (the main manor), John FitzPayne (Puxton?: see below), John le Ireys (Wick?), John de Ledewell, and the Prior of Woodspring (who held several tenements: see below).

During the 13th century the manor of Congresbury appears to have been directly managed by the bishop, though this was reversed from the early 14th century when it was leased to the earls of Kent for £54 a year, and labour services were commuted to cash rents (*CIPM VII*, No. 300; *X* No. 46; *CIM(C) VII*, No. 111; PRO SC6 1131/3). In 1391, the bishop's buildings within the manor were demolished on account of their being 'utterly ruinous and altogether useless' (*Cosyn*, 87). In 1548 the manor of Congresbury with Wick St Lawrence, and the advowson of the vicarage of Congresbury and the chapelry of Wick, was seized from the bishop by Edward Seymour, Duke of Somerset and Lord Protector to the young King Edward VI (Cran 1983, 40). After a few years the manor was granted to Sir George Owen, from whom it passed to his widow Mary who then married Sir William Allen, who made a detailed survey in 1567. Meanwhile, in 1562 Richard Owen, eldest son of Sir George and Mary, sold the manor to William Carr for £3,500, on condition that he did not take possession until the death of Mary Owen, now Allen. William Carr died in 1574–75 having never taken possession of Congresbury as Dame Mary was still alive, and he left the estate to his son John who finally acquired it in 1578 on her death (Manchee 1831, 3; Bowen 1971, 7; Cran 1983, 40, 44; Avery 1990, 1). In his will of 1586 John Carr made provision for the foundation of a 'hospital or place for bringing up poor children' which was created through Act of Parliament in 1590 as Queen Elizabeth's Hospital in Bristol. The estate included the manor of Congresbury, lands and tenements in Wick, and the ground called Harthe [on Congresbury Marsh] (Manchee 1831, 3). In 1836 local government reform in Bristol led to the creation of the Bristol Municipal Charities that acted as the managing agents for individual endowed charities, including Queen Elizabeth's Hospital (Costello and Burley 1997, 16–17).

In total the manor of Congresbury with Wick St Lawrence amounted to *c* 5,000 acres of which *c* 3,500 acres were tenanted by copyhold and 1,500 acres were demesne, including 300 acres of woodland (Cran 1983, 42). By 1567 the demesne was leased out, and between 1592 and 1596 1,445 acres were sold off, including ten of the fourteen Marsh tenements. Many of the beneficiaries were outsiders but some were the tenants themselves. Another series of sales in 1600–01 amounted to a further 1,112 acres including The Oaks, and by 1739 of the Marsh tenements only Palmers Elm Farm and Pool Farm were still within the manor.

Post-Conquest Wick St Lawrence

Throughout the post-Conquest period Wick was part of the Bishop of Wells's manor of Congresbury, apart from four tenements held by the Dean and Chapter. These were surveyed in 1812 as 95 acres (the modern Mulberry Farm, Cypress Farm, Gervinia Cottage, and a dwelling on the opposite side of School Lane: SRO DD/CC 10877), and could be the one virgate of land at Wick granted by Bishop Jocelin to the church at Congresbury in 1216 that were occupied by John Aylward, Adam Algar, William Oswal, and Geoffrey Toky (*Wells I*, 241). Along with Congresbury, Wick was surrendered to the Crown in 1548, and then passed to George Owen and later William Carr (see Congresbury above). In 1586 Wick, along with Congresbury, was granted to Queen Elizabeth's Hospital. The 1567 survey of Wick records that the estate included 25 customary tenants (copyholders), a freehold of some 40 acres called 'Beard's Land' which had been purchased by William Carr before he acquired the rest of the manor, and 'twelve farms' of the former demesne that were held by Richard Roberts and leased out to nine sub-tenants (Cran 1983, 46, 59). The use of the word 'farm' in this sense probably refers to parcels of the demesne that were 'farmed' (ie leased) out (Dyer 2002, 346). The Twelve Farms consisted of 340 acres in 1544–45, leased by the bishop to one Cuthbert Walker, and this lease was bought out by William Carr, who in 1562 purchased the rest of the manor (Cran 1983, 40, 46, 70). The Twelve Farms can probably be identified on the map of 1738 and the tithe survey as the scattered areas of accommodation land held in the former common field to the north of Wick.

Between 1593 and 1596 a number of tenancies were sold off including Sluice Farm, purchased by Francis Knight of Bristol, Baytree Farm, purchased by John Irish of Yatton, and Banksea Farm, acquired by John Sheppard (Cran 1983, 72). By 1738, therefore, the land in Wick can be divided into one of four groups: tenements still held of Queen Elizabeth's Hospital, the four tenements owned by the Dean and Chapter of Wells, several private holdings that lay outside these two estates scattered around Wick village and Icelton,[8] and a series of small blocks of accommodation land that was the former demesne.

The area around Bourton in the southern part of the parish, called 'Vanoms Land' in 1738, was sub-divided into a series of separate tenements held by James Somerville Somerville at the time of the tithe survey. This area may always have been outside the main manor, as Collinson (1791, 612) states that there was a manor of Bourton which 'anciently belonged to the family of Percival of Weston-in-Gordano. In 1658 Sir John Percival sold the estate to Mr William Vanham from whom descended Mr John Vanham who left it to his niece Mrs Yate of Arlingham, who left it to her nephew Rev Mr Somerville, the present possessor'. In the late 13th century George de Cantilupo held 'Burton' (a quarter fee held by Adam le Irys) along with Kewstoke and Locking, all owing suit at the court of 'Wrleston' [Worle?] (*CIPM II, Edw I*, No. 17). A number of leases of land within the manor of 'Bourton alias Bourtonhams' survive from the mid-17th century (SRO DD/BR/py 134; DD/BC/63), and a series of surveys, rentals, leases and presentments at court baron survive from the late 17th century to the mid-18th century, although it has not been possible to identify any of the tenements with those listed in the tithe survey. The now deserted site that was fieldwalked to the west of Bourton was probably the site of its manor house (Fig 6.8). This field was called 'Courts' on the tithe survey, and the fairly dense scatter of pottery and stone contained several indicators of a relatively high-status site, including fragments of green-glazed ridge tile and roof slate, and several fragments of worked Dundry stone.

Post-Conquest Puxton

Like Rolstone, Puxton was a small secular manor with a complex history that can now be written for the first time (based on the transcription and translation of documents by Martin Ecclestone). It is described in some detail as an example of the complex development of the estates of the minor aristocracy, which stands in such sharp contrast to the continuity in the management of better-documented (and so more researched) major royal and ecclesiastical estates. In the absence of an English Place-Names Society volume for Somerset, the development of the place-name Puxton, and that of Rolstone with which it has in the past been confused, is outlined in Table 7.5. The earliest form is Pukereleston (1212: *Fees*, 82); rather than being a combination of Puxton and Rolstone it means 'Pukerel's estate' (the Old French family name Pukerel and Old English *tūn*: Mills 1991, 265; Watts 2004, 486). The Pukerel family held the manor from at least 1166 to 1212 (*Red Book*, 221; *Fees*, 82).

Table 7.5 The evolution of the place-names Puxton and Rolstone

date	Puxton	Rolstone	source
1174/91	Wringmareis (chapel of) [Puxton?]		*Bruton* No. 134
late C12th		Rolveston	*Bruton* No. 133[2]
1212	Pukereleston		*Fees*, 82
?1215	Pokereleston (chapel of)		*Bruton* No.135
1308/09		Rolustone (land in)	*Fines II*, 11
1312/13	Pokerelston (land in)		*Fines II*, 31
1317/18		Rolveston (lands in)	*Fines II*, 75
1326/27		Rolueston	*Fines II*, 11
1330/31		Rolveston (lands in)	*Fines II*, 154–5
1333	Pokerston (chapel)		*Shrewsbury*, No. 599
1341/42		Rolveston (manor)	*Fines II*, 215
1345/46		Rolveston (manor)	*Fines II*, 229–30, 235–7
1371	Pokerelston		*CIM*(C) vol. III, No. 822
1379		Rolveston (land in)	*CIPM XIV*, No. 115
1380/81		Rolleston (lands in)	*Fines III*, 107
1383/84	Pokereleston (manor)		*Fines III*, 124
1385	Pokerleston (manor of)		Batten 1901, 69
1410	Pokerolleston	Rolleston (land in)	*CPR* 11 Hen.IV, 191
1412	Pokeston		*Feudal Aids VI*, 509
1423/24		Rolleston	*Fines IV*, 61
1441/42	Pokerelleston (manor)		*Fines IV*, 196
1449/50	Poxton (chaplain of)		*Bekynton*, No. 487
1463	Puckeston (chaplain of)		*Bekynton*, No. 1522
1468	Paxston (chaplain of)		*Stillington*, No. 118
1468	Puckerelliston		MC 1234
1487	Pukeston		*CIPM* Hen.VII, vol. I, No. 87
1497	Pokerilston/Pokerelston	Rollyston/Rolleston	*CIPM* Hen VII, vol. I, No. 1150
1499	Pukrelston (manor of)		*CIPM* Hen.VII, vol. II, No.189
1502		Pokeston and Rouleston	*CIPM* Hen.VII vol. III, No.1105
1534	Puxston		Weaver 1905, 28
1539	Puxton		*Knyght*, No. 584
1544	Poxston		*Wells Wills*, p.80
1624	Puxton		*Quarter Sessions*

The detaching of Puxton from Congresbury

Until 1772 Puxton was a chapel of ease of Banwell (SRO DD/SAS G/1740 1/1/7, p.10; *Bekynton* Nos 487, 1522; *Knyght* No. 584; *Shrewsbury* No. 599; *Stillington*, No. 118), and from the 16th century the manor of Puxton was in the same hands as Rolstone (in the adjacent part of Banwell). Along with the apparent similarity of the place-names (see above) this led to the conclusion that Puxton was carved out of Banwell (Collinson 1791, 599; Locke 1806, 125; Taylor 1905, 51; Grundy 1932, 167). However, several threads of evidence suggest that the manor, tithing, and subsequently parish of Puxton was in fact carved out of Congresbury:

- the Puxton glebe partly lay within Congresbury parish (as recorded in a Terrier of 1636: BRO DC/E/25/.2).
- in (?)1215 the parson of Congresbury confessed he had no rights in the chapel of Pokereleston and sought a pardon from the Prior of Bruton (*Bruton* No. 135) who held the chapel along with the church at Banwell. There must have been some reason why the parson of Congresbury claimed Puxton, and Bruton's possession of Puxton chapel dates

back no further than the later 12th century when Henry Tortmanus granted his chapel of *Wringmareis* to the priory (*Bruton* Nos 134–5).

- the coterminous southern boundary of Puxton manor (as mapped in *c* 1770) and parish (as mapped in 1840) is a simple one, following a naturally meandering stream (Blackstone Rhyne). To the east, north, and west, in contrast, the manor and parish are not coterminous, and the boundaries of each zig-zag through what were clearly earlier field boundaries, including Ashfield and the series of coaxial furlong boundaries that extend west from the Congresbury fen-edge. A series of detached parcels of Puxton are spread throughout Congresbury Marsh.
- the earliest collection of medieval deeds (from 1378 to 1459), relating to the lands acquired by Merton College, clearly refer to Puxton as lying in the manor and hundred of Congresbury, but the parish of Banwell (BodL MC 1204–11, 1214, 1217–18, 1220–21, 1230–34).
- the 'free tithing'[9] of Puxton was part of Congresbury hundred. The court roll for November 1351 includes earliest reference to the *libera decenna* (free tithing) (SRO BA1 DD/SAS C/795). The roll for May 1379 lists the same tithings but this time specifies that the '*Libera Decenna* for which William Ruyssworth, William Greve, and John Stretend paid a common fine of 6s 8d' (LPL ED 351 f.1). William Ruyssworth held land in Puxton later owned by Merton College. The Puxton manorial account rolls for 1472–73, 1474–75, and 1477–78 all include a payment of 4d to the 'tithingman of the freemen's tithing' for the common fine (along with a common fine of 3d to the hundred of Frowardeshill (Winterstoke). The court rolls for Congresbury hundred in May 1560–70 list the 'libera decenn de Puxton' ['free tithing' of Puxton] followed by Kenn, Cleeve, Claverham, Yatton, and 'Wike' [Court de Wyke in Yatton?] (BRO 04235). In the 1622 Lay Subsidy, and 1664–65 Hearth Tax returns, Puxton was still part of the tithing of 'Congresbury, Weeke [St Lawrence], and Puxton' (SRO DD/SASc/275 BK81; Dwelly 1916; and see *Quarter Sessions* 1650 and 1651: Bates 1907, 158, 170). Congresbury court rolls for 1653 record that Edmund Cooke was appointed constable for Wick and Puxton (BRO BMC/4/37b).

The post-Conquest manor of Puxton

The 11th–12th centuries: the Pukerels and Tortmanuses

In Domesday, Puxton may have been one of the three unnamed hides within Congresbury held by Alfward, Ordric, and Ordwulf, implying that Puxton was yet to become fully detached from the greater Congresbury estate (*DB Som* 1,21). In 1166 Robert Pukerel held one knights fee of the Bishop of Bath (*Red Book*, 221), which must be the same fee that in 1212 was named as Pukereleston and held by Lady Constance (wife of Robert Pockerell) (*Fees*, 82). It will become significant later that Lady Constance, widow of Robert Pokerell, is the only lord of the manor recorded as being 'of Puxton' (*Fees*, 82), the other owners living elsewhere, notably in Churchill (eg John Austell, MP for Wells in 1432: PRO IPM C140/8).

In 1174 x 91 Henry Tortmanus granted his chapel of *Wringmareis* (which is almost certainly Puxton: *Bruton* No. 135) to the church at Bruton (*Bruton* No.134). Henry was presumably descended from Ralph Tortmanus [or 'Crooked Hands'] who in 1086 held 5½ hides of the Bishop of Wells's manor of Banwell (see above). How Tortmanus acquired Puxton chapel is unclear as the Pukerels held the manor from at least 1166 to at least 1212, though there was clearly a link between the two families as in 1158–59 and 1166 Robert Puckerel also held one knights fee of the Abbot of Glastonbury that was once held by Galfrid Tortesmains (*Red Book*, 18, 223). In 1189 the same fee, now specified as 'Alenton' [Alhampton in Ditcheat] with its appendages Pilton and Sandford, was held by Henry Tortesmains, and later by Roger Fitzpayn (*Monington*, xxxviii, 112).

The 14th to early 15th century: the FitzPaynes

Puxton does not appear in the *Nomina Villarum* of 1316 though it may have been John FitzPayne's fee in Congresbury (see above). In the 14th century the FitzPaynes were actively acquiring property in the Banwell and Congresbury area (*Feudal Aids VI*, 326; *Fines II*, No. 14, 31) and in 1312 William Malerbe granted to John FitzPayne of 'Rodewell' and his wife Joan a messuage, 4 bovates of land and 12 acres of meadow in Kywestoke and Pokereleston (*Fines II*, No. 31). This message in Puxton and Kewstoke is logically in the west of the parish of Puxton where there are detached parts of Kewstoke. In 1385 the manor of Puxton was granted to Sir John FitzPayne, his wife Eleanor, and their son Thomas by Philip Maybank and John Glastonbury, though how they acquired it is unclear (*Fines III*, 124; and see Batten 1901, 69). Sir John FitzPayne also held a number of other manors including Alhampton and Churchill in Somerset, and Cheriton Fitzpayne, East Stoodley, West Stoodley, Hederland, Mere, Combe and Cove in Devon. These manors appear to have been split between Sir John's sons, with Thomas receiving Alhampton, Churchill, and Puxton, and Elias receiving the Devon estates. In 1430 John FitzPayne, son of Thomas, conveyed Puxton, along with Alhampton and Churchill, to trustees, though for what purpose is unclear (Batten 1901, 69).

The early 15th century to 1479: the Austells

John FitzPayne had no issue from his marriage to Alice, and so Alhampton, Churchill, and Puxton then passed to his uncle Elias's only child, Margaret wife of John Austell of Churchill (MP for Wells) (1405–62) (Batten 1901, 69). On the death of John Austell his manors at Puxton, Churchill, and half of Camerton passed to his daughter Agnes (wife of Sir Nicholas Sentlo), while Alhampton and the other half of Camerton passed to his other daughter Joan (wife of John Kelly, d.1465: PRO C140/17) (Batten 1901, 69). In 1447 Agnes (daughter of John and Margaret Austell) married Sir Nicholas de Sancto Laudo [St Loe] (1424–86) (PRO C139/131), and on the death of Agnes in 1479 Puxton, Churchill, and Camerton passed to her husband (PRO C140/70m.28).

The St Loes (1479–1564/65), Jennings (1564/65–1649), and Wyndhams (1649–20th century)

On the death of Sir Nicholas Seyntlo in 1486 the manors of Puxton, Churchill, and half of Camerton (along with Stoke Orchard, Knighton Sutton) passed to Sir John Seyntlo (*CIPM Hen.VII* 1, No. 87). The *Inquisition Post Mortem* of Sir John in 1499 records that the manors of Puxton and Churchill were left to his widow Isabel and two under-age daughters, Mary and Eleanor, and were held on Isabel's behalf by her new husband Edward Wadham (*CIPM Hen. VII*, II, No.189). The manors then passed to John Sentloo in 1535–36 (SRO DD/HI 122) and hence to his son William in 1558–59 (WRO 2667/13/452) who sold his manor of Puxton to Ralph Jennyns of Islington (London). In 1649 Richard Jennyns sold part the manor to Wadham Wyndham for £666, who paid Richard a further £33 in 1663 following the death of Lady Jennyns the previous year (SRO DD/WY box 75), which explains how, during the 1650s different indentures cite both John Jennings and Wadham Wyndham as lord of the manor (SRO DD/WY box 75). Puxton was still in the hands of the Wyndhams in 1672 (WRO 2667/23), though by 1755 it was inherited by James Everard Arundle of Ashcombe in Wiltshire by right of his wife Anne, only child of John Wyndham (of Salisbury) (WRO 2667/18/25). On the death of James, sometime after 1791 (Collinson 1791, 598) the manor passed to his wife Anne, on whose death the estate was returned to the Wyndham family. By 1801 Puxton and Rolstone were the property of William Wyndham [IV] of Dinton (Wiltshire) (Bennett 1804, 201; Knight 1902, 216; Rutter 1829, 38; Wyndham 1950), whose family held the estate until the 1960s.

The manorial property (Figs 7.2 and 7.3)

The manor of Puxton had all the usual features including customary and freehold tenants, a manorial court, systems of record keeping (account rolls, rentals and surveys), and demesne land. There is no evidence, however, for a manor house. Two buildings in Puxton stand out as being more substantial than the others. Puxton Court is a large 19th-century double-pile farmhouse, and although a fragment of an earlier building survives, its character cannot be determined (see Chapter 8). Despite its place-name, this is, however, a well-documented customary tenement and its location, far to the west of Puxton church, is not logical for the manor house. The other significant house is Puxton Moor Farm where the present, largely 20th-century farmhouse appears to incorporate the west wing and other fragments of a substantial earlier house (Fig 8.3, No. 20) which Knight (1902, 216) suggests was the manor house though seemingly only on the basis of its appearance as an old building with ornate stone and wood carvings. In *c* 1770 it lay outside the manor and in the tithe survey its lands amounted to just 12a 3r 5p, clearly insufficient to have supported such a substantial house. It was not one of the freehold tenements listed in the 16th century, suggesting that this land may have been part of the demesne that was sold off.

The demesne is otherwise difficult to identify. The account roll for 1500–01 includes 46s 8d rent from demesne land called Twyndyke but this is not associated with a house. The earliest rental of *c* 1630 includes 'John Inman for the demesne being 59 acres' but no rent is given. John Irish is recorded separately as holding 7 acres in South Twindix and 16 acres in Middle Twindix (in the tithe survey Twindix amounted to 31a 0r 27p), suggesting that the 59 acres of demesne and this part of Twindix were separate. In 1642 'the demesne' was leased to John Inman and here the rent is specified as £1 5s 0d. The lease was for 'one life upon half and two [lives] on the other half' indicating that it had been, or could be, held as two tenements (SRO DD/WY box 75). Part of the demesne could also be accounted for by the 21 customary acres of Tenement T which is shown on the map of *c* 1770 but cannot otherwise be identified in the rentals of *c* 1630 and 1642. Tenement T may have been carved out of Puxton Moor Farm as in the tithe survey they shared field 109, and taken together their lands formed a fairly coherent block. There is no evidence from fieldwalking or earthwork survey that Tenement T ever contained a farmhouse, though it must have held the right to graze livestock in Puxton Moor as it included a field there following enclosure. It is possible, therefore, that Puxton Moor Farm and Tenement T (amounting to *c* 33 acres) once formed a substantial part of the demesne land, and that while part (Tenement T) was retained as a roofless tenement, the other part was sold off to become Puxton Moor Farm. The house may have been built new in the 17th century. The rest of the demesne may have been in North Twindix.

If there ever was a manor house in Puxton a possible location is the abandoned site excavated in Church Field. This site produced tantalising hints of high status, such as the bones of a number of goshawks, several fragments of glazed roof tile (which along with fragments of slate suggest a stone roof), and a sherd of Stamford ware pottery (see Chapter 9). It is curious that the occupation of this site ceased in the

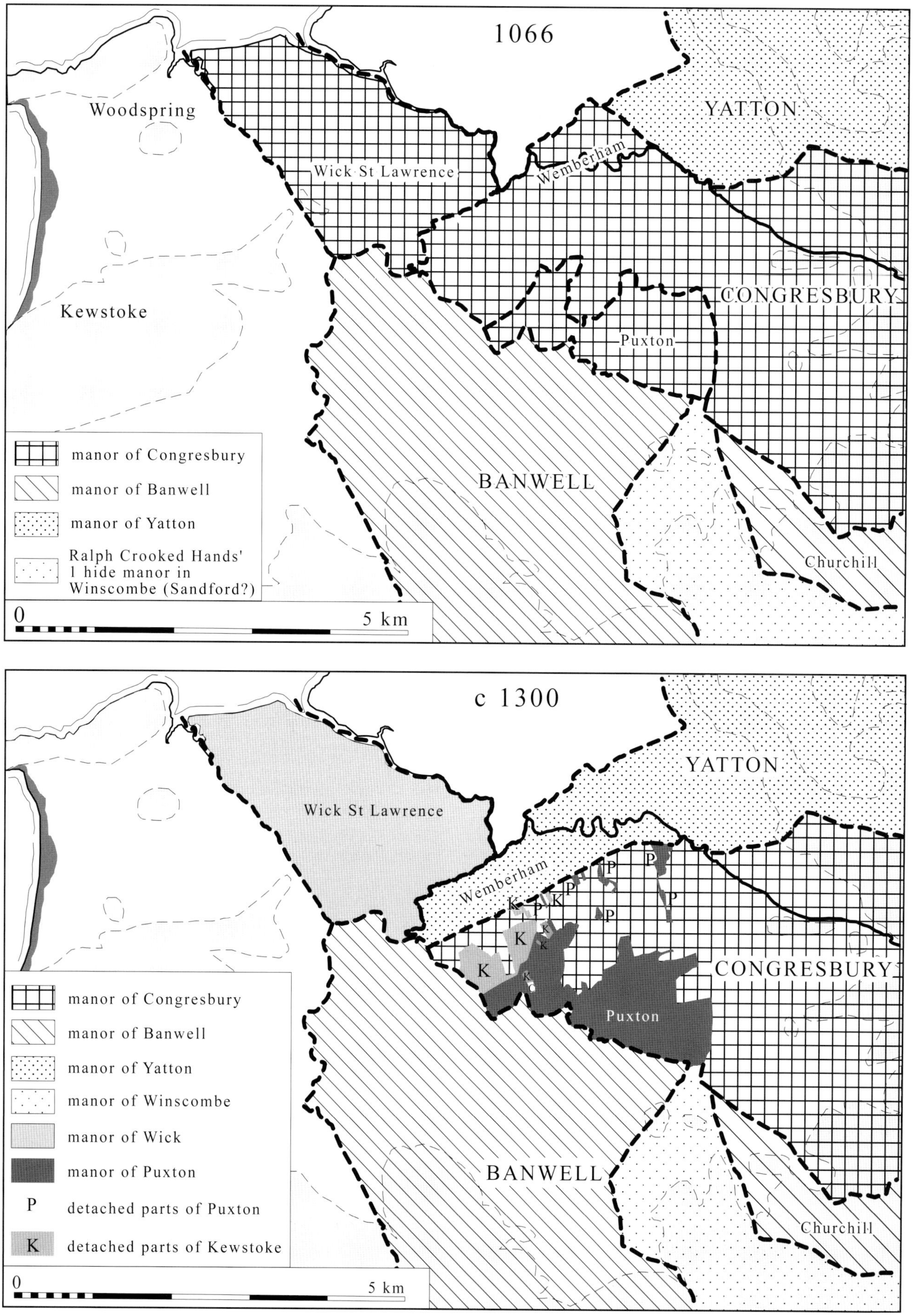

Figure 7.2 The Domesday manors and possible sub-tenancies within the main study area, and manorial structure c *1300*

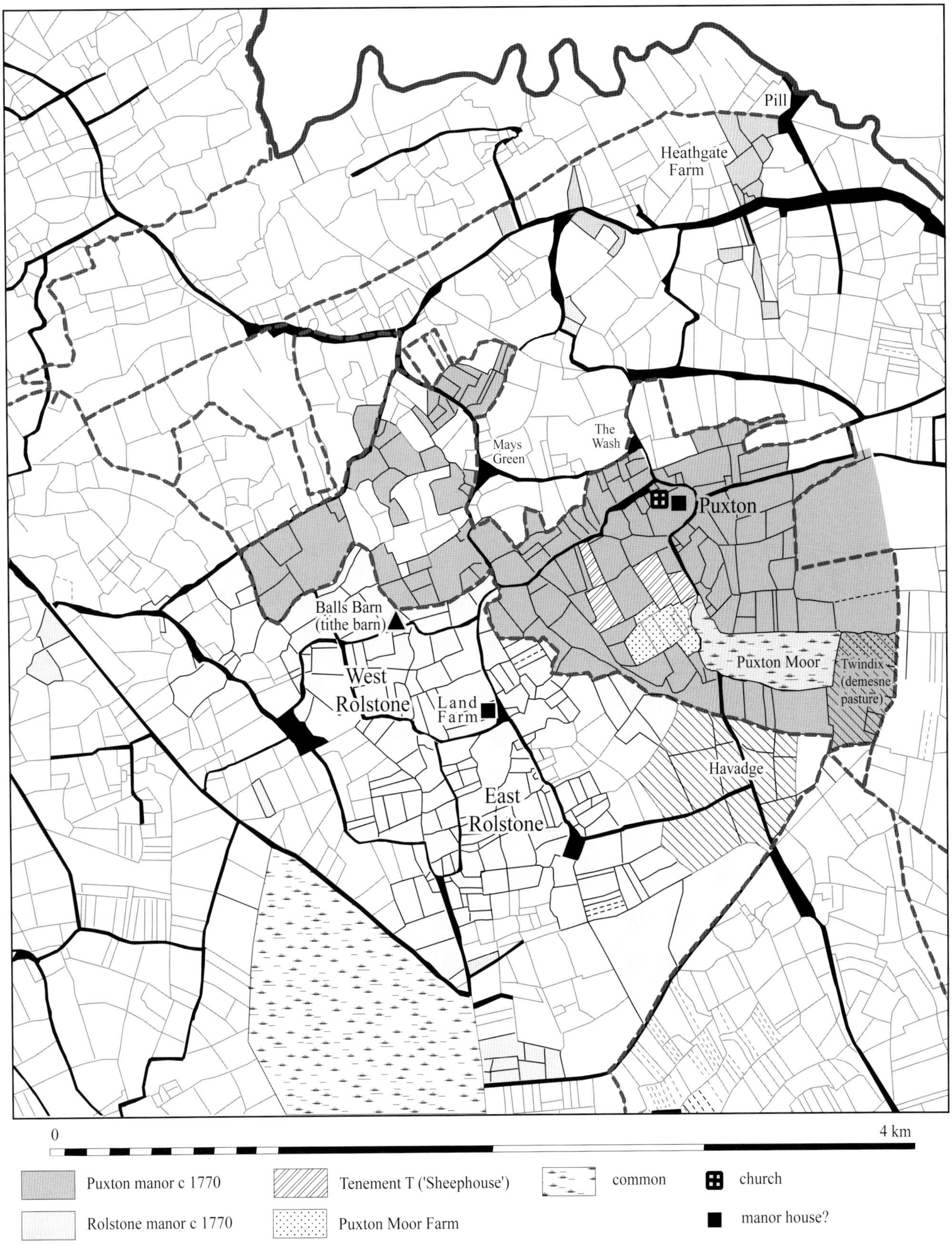

Figure 7.3 The extent of the manors of Puxton and East and West Rolstone in c *1770, and selected elements such as the demesne pastures and common moors*

early 13th century, and it is noticeable that Lady Constance (wife of Robert Pockerell) is the last lord of the manor who is said to have lived in Puxton (in 1212). By the 16th century even the Puxton manor court was held at Churchill (WRO 2667/13/452). This shift in the centre of power may have provided a context for the demolition of the manor house in the early 13th century.

Discussion: lordship, community, and the landscape

Chapter 6 identified a series of marked local differences in the character of the historic landscape that emerged in what was a physically almost uniform natural environment. With the old Romano-British landscape buried beneath up to a metre of later alluvium, this was also an area that lacked antecedent landscapes that elsewhere in England may have influenced how the medieval countryside evolved. So if variations in the natural environment or the preceding cultural landscape cannot explain why some areas saw the development of nucleated settlements and open fields, and others had a landscape characterised by isolated farmsteads and fields held in severalty, it must be due to socio-economic factors. A crucial issue that follows from this is the relationship between landlords and their communities in shaping historic landscape character.

In the early medieval period, a large part of the North Somerset Levels lay within two large estates centred on Banwell and Congresbury, which appear to have switched periodically between royal and episcopal hands. Both these federative estates encompassed a range of environments with areas of high limestone upland fringed by gently undulating foothills, and substantial tracts of marshland down on the Levels. The origins of these two estates will never be known though it is intriguing that their centres both lay in the shadow of substantial Iron Age hillforts with a major Roman settlement on the slopes below, and close to early medieval monasteries documented in the 9th century. Actual continuity of a high-status settlement and its associated estate is almost impossible to prove during this period, though this juxtaposition of Romano-British and early medieval high-status sites has been noted quite widely in Somerset and beyond (Finberg 1955; Fowler 1975; Aston 1986; Rippon 1997a, 132–8). Over time these two great estates fragmented, forming the manors that are recorded in Domesday. To the north of the River Yeo, Yatton, Kingston Seymour, and Kenn were removed from Congresbury, while to the south Puxton obtained autonomy. Churchill and Rolstone were detached from Banwell (though both remained within the ecclesiastical jurisdiction of the old mother church), while Sandford was transferred to Winscombe. By the time of the Norman Conquest, however, what remained of the episcopal manors of Banwell and Congresbury had embarked on a period of relative stability, in contrast to Puxton and Rolstone that formed parts of the ever-changing lordships of the lesser aristocracy.

By the 12th–13th centuries the study area was divided between a series of manors of which the two largest – Banwell and Congresbury – were both in the hands of the same landlord, the bishops of Bath and Wells. This is significant as the fact that the historic landscape in areas such as Congresbury Marsh (characterised by isolated farmsteads with large, compact home grounds consisting of closes held in severalty) is so different to areas such as St Georges, West Wick, and Waywick in Banwell Marsh (characterised by small compact hamlets, and a mixture of small common fields and closes held in severalty) is presumably due to the way that local communities decided to manage their environment, as opposed to the estate management policies of their common landlord. Apart from a brief spell in the mid-11th century when it was seized by Earl Harold, Hewish has also always been in the hands of the bishops of Wells, having been detached from their manor of Congresbury shortly after 1066, and transferred to their manor of Yatton. The landscape of Hewish is also of interest as it provides one of the few well-dated horizons in this historic landscape: the creation of New Rhyne that marked the boundary with Congresbury shortly after 1066. There is no evidence that this boundary cuts through the historic landscape, and apart from a possible infield enclosure at East Hewish, surrounded by a small area of irregular landscape, the rest appears to have been enclosed and drained sometime later, with the broadly north-east/south-west trend in the field boundaries running parallel to the New Rhyne boundary. The very similar landscape in the south-east of Wick, around Icelton and Bourton, may similarly reflect how these areas were enclosed after the area around the main village, and after the construction of the sea walls alongside the Congresbury Yeo and New Ear Rhyne from which this roughly coaxial landscape was laid out.

In Wick and Puxton the situation is slightly more complicated since during the crucial years leading up to 1066, when these marshlands appear to have been initially colonised, both appear to have become sub-tenancies of Congresbury. The same could have been true of Rolstone. Wick was soon returned to the bishop's manor of Congresbury, though Puxton and Rolstone became separate manors. In these cases the way in which the landscape subsequently evolved may have been influenced by both lord and/or community, though the basic fabric of the landscape was clearly in place long before Puxton was carved out of Congresbury as reflected by the way that the boundary between them zig-zags through a pre-existing pattern of fields, roads and settlements. Another dated horizon in this historic landscape is the creation of the ecclesiastical jurisdiction of Puxton when Henry Tortmanus granted his chapel at *Wringmareis* to Bruton Priory sometime between 1174 and 1191, whereby it became a chapelry of Banwell. What is interesting is the way in which the eastern and western parts of Puxton had already evolved in very different ways despite both forming part of Congresbury Marsh. The nucleated village in eastern Puxton, surrounded by its open fields, stands out as being very different from the surrounding areas, with the western part of the parish having a landscape that had far more in common with the rest of Congresbury Marsh.

Rolstone may also have been a sub-tenancy at the time of Domesday (held by a predecessor of

Table 7.6 Summary of the history of the estates and manors

date	Banwell	West Rolstone	East Rolstone	Congresbury	Wick	Puxton	Yatton
400							
500				St Congar			
600							
700				688 x 726: Ine to Sherborne?			
	?			?			
800				Crown			?
	886/87: Crown to Asser 909: Asser to Wells			886/87: Crown to Asser 909: Asser to Wells			
900							909: Wells to Crown?
	? 904: Winchester to the Crown			?			
	? 968 x 78: the church at Cheddar			?			
1000				Crown			
	1016 x 33: Crown to Dudoc 1060: Dudoc to Wells; seized by Harold	1016 x 33: Crown to Dudoc 1060: Dudoc to Wells; seized by Harold		1016 x 33: Crown to Dudoc 1060: Dudoc to Wells; seized by Harold			
1066	seized by Crown	Tortmanus?		seized by Crown	sub-tenancies of Congresbury?	sub-tenancies of Congresbury?	Crown
1086	Crown to Wells	?					Crown to Wells
1100						?	
			?			Puckerel	
			le Warre				
1200				1217 x 19: Crown to Wells	1217 x 19: Crown to Wells	?	
1300		?				?	
		FitzPayne				FitzPayne	

Tortmanus), but this landscape is very different in character. Firstly, it had a more fragmented history of landownership, and secondly, large areas may have been colonised slightly later than areas such as Wick, St Georges, or Puxton, as it is very slightly lower lying and historic landscape analysis suggests there is no infield enclosure. Indeed, the landscape has a degree of regularity that, by analogy with places such as Icelton and West Hewish, is indicative of areas of secondary colonisation. Taken together, these factors may account for the more dispersed settlement pattern.

Overall, therefore, we can make significant progress in explaining when historic landscape character varies at a local level. In this particular study area, the physical environment was relatively insignificant with uniform soils and just a very slight decrease in elevation away from the coast. There were also no antecedent landscapes to influence how the medieval countryside evolved. Puxton, Rolstone, and Hewish may have seen their development affected by the fact that they were sub-tenancies and then separate manors, but the remaining areas were all in the same hands, whether the bishops of Bath and Wells, the Crown, or briefly Earl Harold. That areas such as Wick, St Georges, and Congresbury Marsh developed in different ways suggests that it was decisions taken by the local colonists, rather than their landlord, that led to the differing degrees of communality in the landscape.

Notes

1 The parishes of both Chew Magna and Stowey are interwoven with Cameley to the south in a way that might suggest that the three were once a single estate. The south-western boundary of Cameley, however, also zig-zags through the historic landscape, appearing to cut across the furlong boundaries of a former open field that extends into Hinton Blewitt, which was part of an estate centred on Chewton (see below). Indeed, Cameley was in Chewton hundred, and in the 1334 Lay Subsidy it is listed as 'Hinton Blewitt and Cameley' (Glasscock 1975, 261). It would appear, therefore, that Cameley was part of an estate centred on Chewton. The original boundary with the 'greater Chew Valley' estate may have run along the lane between White Cross to Clutton that continues the long sweeping southern boundary of Chew Magna over Burledge Hill.

2 *Pantesida* in the late 12th century (*Bruton* No. 133[1], *Pontyessde* in 1327 (Dickinson 1889, 267), *Ponteshyde* in a rental of 1482 (BRO AC/M8/14; Coward 1971/72, 34), and *Ponteside* in 1497 (*CIPM* Hen VII, vol I No. 1150).

3 In the other manors that make up the 'greater Congresbury' estate there was an average of 1.7 ploughlands per hide; in the Worlebury manors this figure was 1.9, while in Banwell it was 1.3 and 'greater Portbury' 1.2.

4 Weston is documented by *c* 1230 (Mills 1991, 353) and it is not clear whether it was included under another Domesday entry, or whether it was in fact a post-Conquest creation, perhaps even a subsidiary, coastal, settlement of Ashcombe.

5 Receiving Hutton and Elborough, Winterhead (in Winscombe), Ashcombe (in Weston-super-Mare), Claverham (in Yatton), Kingston Seymour, Kenn, Backwell, Wraxall, Portishead, Weston-in-Gordano, Easton-in-Gordano, Clapton-in-Gordano, Portbury, and Long Ashton.

6 Receiving Blagdon, Chew Stoke, Chillyhill, Compton Martin and Moreton, along with Uphill by the coast.

7 Rutter (1829, 133) and Knight (1902, 456) follow Collinson (1791, 567) in arguing that Rolstone once formed the head of the 'barony of Worleston' which can be traced back to 1272, and which at one time was held by the Percival family and later Sir William Wyndham. It comprised half a knights fee in Kewstoke, the fourth part of a knights fee in 'Burton' (Bourton in Wick St Lawrence), half a virgate in Locking, half a knights fee in Tarnock, and Edingworth in Brent, all in Somerset, and Stonenhalle in Devon. The *Calendar of Inquisitions Post Mortem* vol II (p19) makes it clear that these formed the barony of Worle alias Worleston (which following the Dissolution was also held by Sir William Wyndham).

8 Barnfield Farm: held by Sir Pritchard Bondfield; Baytree Farm: Mr and Mrs Irish; Wick House: late John Read; Sluice Farm: Colonel Prowse; and a series of tenements without a house.

9 Tithings were the smallest unit of governance in medieval England, being responsible for the local administration of justice and tax collection. In origin, they were groups of ten customary tenants called frankpledges or tithings (*decenna*), one of whom was its head (chief pledge or tithingman). The tithing was responsible for producing in court any of its members accused of a misdeed. The county sheriff was originally responsible for ensuring that all men belonged to a tithing through an inspection known as a view of frankpledge, which took place through the hundred court, though by the 13th century this role had often been assumed by the manorial lord, and was overseen through the manorial court. The Views of Frankpledge were also courts of justice, and the 'Courts of the View' dealt with minor misdemeanours (Homans 1941, 309–27). Each tithing brought a sum of money to court to meet its expenses, originally 1d per head – the tithing-penny – though it later became a fixed amount, often called the common fine. The meaning of the term free tithing is unknown.

8 Peasants and yeomen: the tenements and houses of a marshland community

Introduction

So far this study has focused on the physical fabric of the historic landscape, and the patterns of landholding within which it was created and managed, but we must not forget the farming community itself: the people who lived in the houses, ploughed the fields, tended the livestock, maintained the flood defence systems, and are buried in the churchyards (eg Fig 8.1). This chapter, therefore, is about the marshland community who made this landscape. In the early medieval period the North Somerset Levels lay within a series of great estates, based at a number of major fen-edge centres such as Banwell and Congresbury, and it was probably from these dryland settlements that colonists first moved onto the Levels. By the time of the Domesday survey these great estates had started to fragment into a series of smaller manors (whose history is outlined in Chapter 7), a number of which were based entirely on the wetlands (including Puxton and Rolstone). The land within all these manors was divided between the lord's own demesne and a series of peasant tenements, some of which were held by his customary tenants in return for rents and the obligation to perform certain services (such as ploughing the lord's arable fields, mowing his meadows, and maintaining drainage and flood defence systems), while others were freehold tenements that were exempt from these obligations and paid just a nominal rent.

In Chapter 6 the landholdings of all the 19th-century tenements within the study area were characterised in terms of their size and spatial distribution, highlighting marked local variation. In Hewish, for example, each tenement was typically associated with a relatively large and compact 'home ground' (ie fields immediately adjacent to the farmstead), which was also the case in Congresbury Marsh although these holdings also had a few outlying parcels in what had been the common fields around Dolemoor. In Puxton, by contrast, tenements were far smaller and much more scattered, with the home ground often limited to just one or two fields. Although in Puxton a number of tenements can be traced back through the court rolls to the late 15th century, and the deeds for Merton College's Rushworth's tenement go back to 1378, we only have a clear picture of the structure of landholding from the mid-16th century onwards. The patterns that these records portray can only be regarded as reflecting the late medieval situation as the surveys and court rolls we have for this period show that a number of tenements were deserted and their lands absorbed by others, while areas of demesne were leased out and ultimately sold off providing another means by which wealthier tenants could enlarge their holdings. The emphasis in Chapter 6 was on studying different components of the historic landscape in order to identify its different character areas, and thereafter to try to understand the processes that led to its creation. In this chapter attention will focus on what we know of the community who lived in and farmed those tenements.

Congresbury and Wick in the later 16th century

For Congresbury and Wick the surveys of 1567 and 1593 provide a comprehensive list of tenements, the majority of which can be traced through later records[1] to the tithe survey (apart from Bourton in Wick which was a separate manor) (Table 8.1). In Congresbury Marsh thirteen tenants held the same number of tenements which, apart from Palmers Elm Farm and The Grange (which formed part of the small hamlet of West Hewish), formed a series of isolated farmsteads with compact landholdings of typically between three and eight closes amounting to 50–90% of the total land held in severalty, the rest being detached parcels in the former common fields around Dolemoor. On average 13% of each holding lay in the surviving common fields, which was largely in Dolemoor with smaller shares of Broad Field, East Mead, East Moor, West Moor, Gildenhurst, and Smallhurst. Interestingly the most substantial detached part of Puxton in this area – Heathgate Farm, owned by William Counsell in the 18th century (Figs 6.5D and 8.1) – forms a similarly compact landholding, quite unlike those in the main area of Puxton (see below). Most of these tenements were described as half yardlands (*c* 40 acres) along with one yardland (which appears to equate to earlier virgates, ie quarter hides), and two fardells (*c* 20 acres) of 'old auster' (see below), all of which comprised a messuage (house), curtilage (yard), garden and orchard, an amount of land, meadow and pasture held in severalty in separate closes, and an amount of arable and/or meadow in the common fields. The mean acreage was 42 acres.

In Wick 23 tenants held 25 tenements, of which three represent the amalgamation of two earlier properties. That one tenant held several tenements suggests that there was a level of sub-letting that is entirely undocumented. Several tenements in Wick were also referred to as cottages, 'tofts called an eighth acre', and in one case 'half a pill'. The landholdings associated with these tenements were more varied than in Congresbury, with typically one

Table 8.1 The tenements in Congresbury Marsh and Wick St Lawrence in the survey of 1567, placed in order of their acreages

tenant	customary measure	acres		1593–96, sold to	modern name
CONGRESBURY MARSH					
BROWNE, John	fardel	18	mess. etc	William Younge	Tile House
ORTON, Joan	fardel	20	mess. etc	Thomas Farr of Wick St Lawrence	Home Ground
TAYLOR, John	half yardland	32	mess. etc	Mr Kedwyn of Bristol	unlocated
Isabell Cade and son [?]	third yardland	34	mess. etc		unlocated
PAYNE, John	half yardland	39	mess. etc	Thomas Farr of Wick St Lawrence	Bindings
KNIGHT, John	half yardland	40	mess. etc	Francis Knight of Bristol	?Burnt House
HARDWILL, Edmond	half yardland	41	mess. etc	[retained]	Pool Farm
IRYSH, John	half yardland	42	mess. etc	John Irish of Congresbury	Grange Farm
BUMER, Ralph	half yardland	43	mess. etc	Edward Muttlebury of Congresbury	Grange Farm
WILLOT, Cuthbert	half yardland	48	mess. etc	[retained]	Palmers Elm Farm
WILLETT, Robart	half yardland	51	mess. etc	Francis Knight of Bristol	Willow Farm
KEENE, Thomas	half yardland	71	mess. etc	Mr Cole in 1600	The Oaks
CADE, Isabel and daughters	yardland	90	mess. etc	John Irish of Congresbury	Chestnut Farm
WICK ST LAWRENCE					
BODYE, Johann	toft	1	cottage		?
GEFFRYS, Edith	cottage	3	cottage		?
DAWKES, Christopher	toft	3	toft		?
TUCKER, Thomas	eighth acre	3	cottage		?
CUSSH, Richard	toft and cottage	4	toft and cottage		?
TYRELL, Julyan	eighth acre	4	toft		?
KYNGE, John	fardel	14+	closes		pt of Castle Cottages
NYE, Thomas	fardel	15	mess. etc		?
BODYE, Johann	fardel	16	mess. etc		?Hippisleys Farm
FARRE, Ansell	fardel and toft	17	mess. etc		?
ANDREWES, Thomas	fardel	19	mess. etc	[retained]	East Town Farm
TUCKY, John	fardel	19	mess. etc		?
FARRE, Thomas	fardel and toft	19	mess. etc		Hodders or Manor Farm
WILLYE, William	fardel + half a pill	20	mess. etc		Wick House
KYNGE, John	fardel	21	mess. etc		Castle Cottages
SARE, William	fardel	23	mess. etc		?TM 428
SMYTH, Henry	half yardland	30	mess. etc		?
BODY, James	half yardland	30	mess. etc	[retained]	Rose Court
BADMAN, Margaret	half yardland	32	mess. etc	John Irish	Baytree Farm
TUCKER, John	half yardland	33	mess. etc	[retained]	Ebdon Court
KYNGE, John	half yardland	33	mess. etc	[retained]	Little Orchard
BANWELL, George	half yardland	34	mess. etc		?
TUCKER, Thomas	half yardland	34	mess. etc	[retained]	Old House
ANDREWES, Richard	half yardland + toft	40	mess. etc	[retained]	Appleton Farm
HARDWELL, Thomas	half yardland	45	mess. etc		Westhouse
QUARR, John	yardland	72	mess. etc	Francis Knight	?Sluice Farm
WILLIAMS, Richard	yardland	85	mess. etc	[retained]	The Cedars
CRASE, Richard	yardland	88	mess. etc	[retained]	Icelton Farm

to four closes adjacent to the messuage amounting to 10–50% of the total land held in severalty. On average 17% of each holding lay in common fields, which was largely over in the Puxton/Congresbury Dolemoors (along with nearby Wickham Furlong, Small Hurst, Monkland, Gildenhurst, Hemshorde, and Small Yardes etc), while smaller amounts were in Wick itself (North Field, The Fleet, and Carter's Marsh). The mean acreage was 32 acres (excluding the six cottages and tofts).

The term old austers is a relatively common one in Somerset and for which we have an 18th-century explanation: when the manor of Banwell Bruton was acquired by the Buller family of Cornwall this term would not have been familiar to them and the survey of *c* 1745–50 helpfully explains that 'many of the above premises are said to be of Old Auster whereby the occupiers have a right of commonage for shutting cattle as they term it in Banwell Marsh [the common Moor] and on Banwell Hill [the upland common]' (Bromwich 1984). In fact, grazing rights were only part of customary attributes of an Old Auster tenement, for they also shared the burden of maintaining specified stretches of sea walls and drainage ditches (Nash 1974; Rippon 1997a, 216). Nash (1974, 158–61) suggests that this form of tenure began in the late 13th–early 14th century as a result of rising population placing increased pressure on grazing resources, though Sabin (1968) disputes this, arguing that it resulted from a general late medieval trend towards the commutation of labour services. In the 16th century all tenements with a house and agricultural land were referred to as old austers, though in Banwell and Puxton its use from the 15th century is so erratic as to suggest that it represents the remnants of a formerly more coherent system, being applied to some tenements that no longer had a house. Sharps, for example, was described in the court roll for 1491 as 'de antiquo astro' (literally meaning 'of the ancestral home or hearth') despite consisting of just four acres of land (this abandoned house can be located in the field south of Puxton Moor that was called Sharps in the tithe survey: Fig 9.3.A).

Puxton in the 16th to mid-17th century

For Puxton a number of tenements can be identified in the surviving 15th- to 16th-century court rolls, though the rentals of *c* 1630 and 1642 provide the first comprehensive list of tenements the majority of which can be traced through later records to the rental of 1755 and survey of *c* 1770, and hence the tithe map. There are no references to yardlands, though the freehold tenement that came to be Villa Farm was described in the 1569 court roll as 'a messuage, half virgate of land [*c* 40 acres], 10 acres of land called Freemans, and 5 acres 1 rood of other land'; the rent was 5 shillings, one pound of cumin, an iron *acus*,[2] and a red rose (SRO DD/WY W/CR 46/1). The other freeholds are a curious collection of landholdings in the west of the parish or amongst the detached parcels to the north on Congresbury Marsh. The Earl Paulett's Puxton freehold appears to have been Ball Barn field in Banwell (PxTM 194, 4a 3r 20p), the site of Bruton Priory's tithe barn for Puxton; Lord Paulett held other land in Rolstone. Merton College's freehold was Rushworths, granted to them in 1468; it amounted to 22 acres and included the now deserted house platform in PxTM 205 (Fig 6.6). Mark May's freehold was described in the 1567 court rolls as half an acre of meadow in Dolmore Meade, a 10-acre pasture close called 'Yedhays', 1 acre of arable in 'Coxe Channders', 1 acre of meadow in 'Ashfield', one acre of arable in 'Brenfylde', and 4 acres of land in Chonnehyll (17½ acres in total; SRO DD/WY W/CR 46/1),[3] which can probably be identified as a scattered tenement outside the manor held by George Hardwick in *c* 1770 and based at the now-deserted house site PxTM 191. William Counsell's freehold was a detached parcel of Puxton now occupied by the Full Quart public house (PxTM 214–15) amounting to 1a 3r 20p (Fig 8.1.A). Finally, there is Purbecks which cannot be located although a field of that name appears in the survey of *c* 1770 (PxTM 149) immediately north of Puxton Court Farm. This cannot itself have been the freehold, however, as in the same 1642 rental this field was part of George Whippey's customary tenement.

The manor of Puxton was clearly carved out of Congresbury and Wick, yet the tenements there were far smaller. The rental of *c* 1630 lists 27 tenants holding 34 tenements with a mean acreage of 15 acres, and this small size of the typical Puxton landholdings is reflected in the detailed history of the larger tenements recorded in the court rolls which reveal that they were the product of the amalgamation of several landholdings. In 1570, for example, John and Agnes Atwill held three tenements (two of which were ruinous) which comprised 40½ acres, to which Agnes added one further tenement in 1571. By 1642 these four tenements had passed to Thomas Inman who held 51 acres altogether (Table 8.2 CD). The first occasion at which we can reconstruct the spatial disposition of the landholdings associated with each tenement in Puxton is through the map of *c* 1770, though the stability in rents and acreages since the 16th century suggests that this pattern is at least late medieval in origin.

In eastern Puxton the pattern is remarkably different from Congresbury and Wick, with the fields held by farmsteads adjacent to the church scattered across the surrounding areas in exactly the way that one would expect in a nucleated village surrounded by open fields: on average just 22% of closes held in severalty were adjacent to the farmstead themselves. The three extant farmsteads around Puxton Moor (Goose Acre Farm, Puxton Moor Farm, and South Farm) had rather more compact landholdings though still with parcels in these putative open fields. A combination of these patterns of landholding, field-names, and field boundary mor-

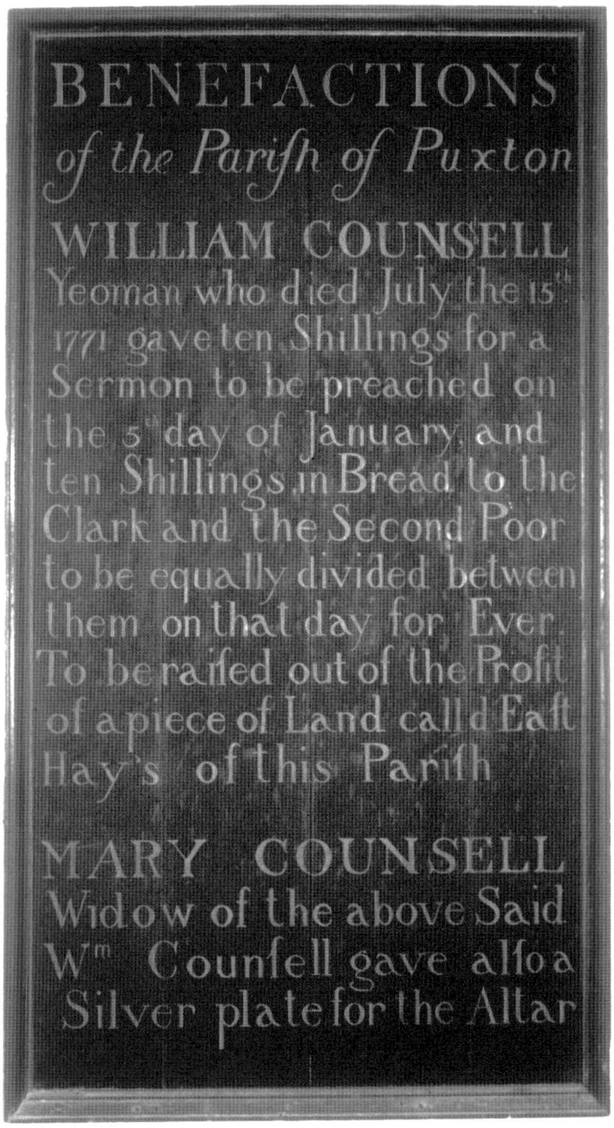

Figure 8.1 (A) Monument in Banwell church commemorating the benefactions of William and Mary Counsell of the parish of Puxton. That part of the survey of c *1770 which covers William Counsell's tenement has been lost, though later sources show that it was Heathgate Farm, the detached part of Puxton by Pill (see Figure 7.3). On the Puxton tithe map this tenement was held by James Reeves from William Wyndham. In the 1832 register of electors one James Broackes occupied Heathgate Farm, while in the same year he paid £1 14s 9d land tax for 'late Counsells' from William Wyndham. The same tax was paid by William Counsell in 1782, and in 1766 for 'Wilcoxs'. The lease book of* c *1778 records 'Tenement 5' leased to William Counsell in 1749, Mary Counsell in 1771, and Edward Blackford in 1787. This was, therefore, tenement 'c' on map of* c *1770 [ie Heathgate Farm] when it amounted to a house and 27a 2r 14p. In 1755 William Councell paid £1 3s 2d rent which John Inman paid in the 1651, 1642 and* c *1630 rentals for 24 acres*

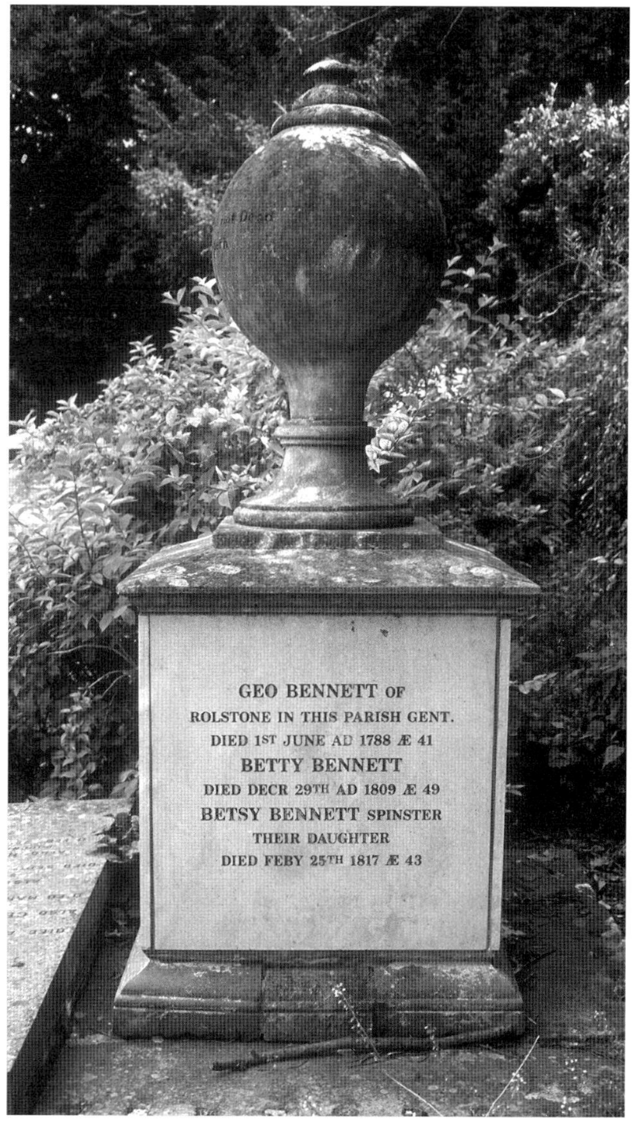

Figure 8.1 (B) The monument of George Bennett in Banwell churchyard. In the tithe survey George Bennett owned and occupied what is now called Land House in East Rolstone, though the 40a 2r 15p of land was leased to Thomas Urch. This tenement lay outside the manor in c *1770 (when it was owned by Joseph Shepherd). Bennett (1812, 57) argues that the name Land House reflects its origins as the only freehold dwelling in the manor of Rolstone, and a deed of 1569 shows that it was freehold from at least that date. Its landholding was typical of Rolstone, comprising a compact block of land around the farmhouse with detached parcels in the former common fields of Dingland, Perry Bush, and East Field. The present house is a late medieval or 17th-century three-celled cross-passage house, though around 60 sherds of medieval pottery, including green-glazed ware, and a 14th-century silver penny have been recovered from the garden (SMR 217; 2483; 4649; Isles 1978)*

phology suggests there were two open fields: the documented East Field either side of Dolemoor Lane, and a putative West Field lying between Church Field and the entrance to Puxton Moor, in addition to the common meadow on Dolemoor which was only enclosed in 1816. The survey that accompanied the map only survives for seven tenements, which shows that on average 5% of each landholding in both eastern and western Puxton lay in the Dolemoor. Whilst this figure is lower than in Congresbury or Wick it should be remembered that the sources are of different date (1567 for Congresbury and Wick, compared to *c* 1770 for Puxton).

The landholdings in western Puxton were somewhat different in character. While they also had shares in Dolemoor, and grazing rights in Puxton Moor, the farms were mostly compact home grounds (accounting for 90–100% of the closes held in severalty), apart from a number of tenements with *c* 40% of their fields scattered across the former open field at Ashfield. Along with the character of the large detached block of Puxton at Heathgate Farm, which is closer in character to the rest of Congresbury Marsh than Puxton (see above), it seems clear that the parish and manor of Puxton was a fairly artificial creation made after this area had been colonised and different communities had gone about structuring their landscapes in very different ways.

Rolstone in the mid-17th century

The manors of East and West Rolstone were carved out of Banwell and as such the structure of the tenements might potentially show significant differences from Congresbury, Wick, and possibly Puxton (Table 8.3 CD). The average tenement size in 1651 was 21 acres in East Rolstone and 25 acres in West Rolstone, and while there were a couple of *c* 40-acre tenements in each there is nothing like the recurrent halfyardland seen in Congresbury Marsh. In part this may reflect fragmentation of the tenements, though it is probably also due to the piecemeal way in which the manors were created.

The earliest occasion for which we can comment on the spatial disposition of landholding in Rolstone is the map of *c* 1770, and the accompanying survey which is complete. Across Rolstone 45% of the closes held in severalty lay adjacent to the farmstead though this figure masks significant variation in the degree of fragmentation, with some, such as Boxbush and Laurel Farms, having *c* 80% of their fields in a compact home ground, and around half of the tenements averaging just 21%. The majority of tenements also had parcels in the former common meadows at Dinglands and South Mead, while the highly fragmented pattern of landholding around Perry Bush (to the east of Land House) and East Field (to the east of Rolstone Court) are suggestive of other common fields. This scattered pattern of landholding is seen in both the customary and the copyhold tenements (such as Land House, the home of local historian George Bennett: Fig 8.1.B).

The emergence of the yeoman farmer

Throughout the manors within the study area, the late medieval and early post-medieval periods saw the emergence of tenants with more substantial landholdings, created through the leasing of the demesne and amalgamating tenements for which the lord of the manor could not find tenants. In Puxton, for example, the 16th-century court rolls record a series of such amalgamations such as in 1567 when Emota and Alice Webbe took up two tenements (one ruinous) amounting to 26 acres on the death of William Webbe (see Table 8.2 (CD)). By the 17th century the court rolls even record a list of tenants who wished to take over tenements that were 'in hand' (ie for which the lord had no tenant).

Another notable trend by the 16th century was the extent to which tenements in Congresbury Marsh, Puxton, Rolstone, and Wick were held by non-resident owners or lesees. Many lived in local, fen-edge villages such as Banwell, Congresbury, and Worle, while others lived in parishes on the surrounding limestone hills such as Blagdon, Christon, Shipham, Winscombe, and Wraxall. Some of these tenements down on the Levels could have been acquired through marriage/inheritance. Diana Crossman, for example, held lands in Puxton and that upon here death in 1634 passed to her husband the Revd Hugh Waterman of Bristol (SRO DD/GB 148). In other cases, these tenements appear to have been acquired as an investment. John King, for example, a merchant of Bristol, held what is now called Villa Farm and who in turn sold it to Samuel Hardwick, apothecary, also of Bristol; in 1799 his successor James Hardwick sold it to William Bisdee whose family was emerging as a major landowner in Puxton, Rolstone, and Wick (SRO DD/SOG 342, 903). Other landholdings may have been acquired specifically to provide rich summer grazing for fattening livestock as these estates included not just occupied tenements, but also areas of accommodation land. An *inquisition post mortem* in 1616 records Francis Knight of Bristol's holding of three tenements (with 18, 50 and 38 acres) along with 16 acres of meadow and pasture in two blocks, and 14 acres of former demesne land (BRO 4726.11). In the post-medieval period the Somerset Levels were well known for their rich pastures, used to fatten cattle particularly from Devon and Cornwall (Defoe 1742, 23), and there are occasional explicit references to grazier-butchers acquiring land there: in 1755 Richard Jolliffe of the city of Bristol, butcher, leased 7½ acres in Rolstone (WRO 2667/23/44) and in 1594 John Bythsea, a tanner of Axbridge, held 8 acres of land in Congresbury Dolemoor (SRO DD/FS 57/3/1–2).

This acquisition of estates by the gentry was characteristic of the Bristol region in the post-medieval

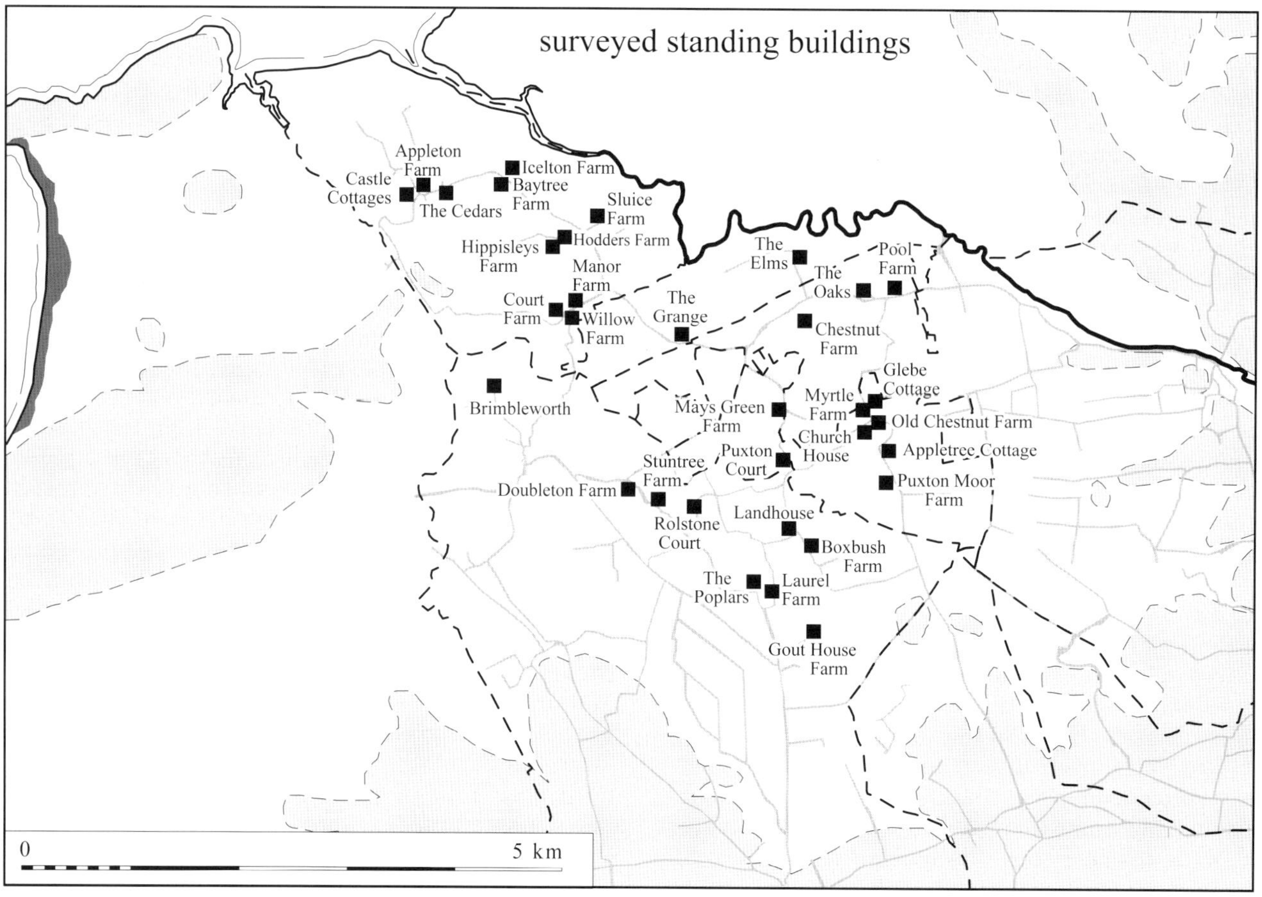

Figure 8.2 Location map for the standing buildings that were surveyed as part of the North Somerset Levels Project, and early surveys

period (Bettey 1983) and it is noticeable how many tenements on the North Somerset Levels were acquired by people living in the city, including three of the nine farms in Congresbury Marsh sold off in 1593–94 (see Table 8.1). Christopher Kedgwin, a grocer of Bristol, for example, held 40 acres in Congresbury Marsh in 1595 (BRO 00576(8)). The extent to which land was held by outsiders is impossible to quantify as most documents do not record where tenants actually lived, though the 1762 list of fee farm rents in Wick St Lawrence shows that seven were held by residents of Wick, four by residents of Bristol, one from Winscombe, and another from Whitchurch in Dorset (BRO BMC/4/12).

The vernacular buildings *by Colin Humphreys and Stephen Rippon*

Introduction

Different regional styles in standing buildings form an important part of the character of any historic landscape. Parish churches often still dominate our villages and hamlets, while farmhouses and their associated agricultural buildings were the centres from which the surrounding countryside was managed. In many places the oldest surviving building is the medieval parish church, though detailed survey projects and in particular the increasing use of dendrochronology is revealing the extent to which some farmhouses also date back to the late medieval period, making them contemporary with the earthworks and pottery scatters of shrunken and deserted settlements that archaeologists have traditionally studied. The standing building survey undertaken as part of the NSLP therefore had as its central aims to identify the main phases of building and rebuilding within individual structures and across the study area as a whole, and to examine how these relate to the wider socio-economic factors that shaped the wider historic landscape. Thirty-three vernacular buildings were surveyed as part of this project (along with the church at Puxton); additional information was available for five[4] based on previous surveys by E H D Williams and his colleagues. They had also recorded three further structures[5] to which access could not be gained during this project (Fig 8.2). The majority of these houses were, until recent decades, working farms (some still retaining this traditional function), along with one outbuilding (a former detached kitchen), several cottages, and the parsonage in Puxton. The dominance of working farms within this sample, as opposed to artisans' and labourers' cottages, is unusual when compared to the other published surveys of vernacular architecture in Somerset (eg Dallimore 2001; SSAVBRG 1982; 1984; 1986; 1988; 1993; 1994; SVBRG 1996; 2001; 2004). This reflects the different character of the historic landscapes, with a settlement pattern dominated by hamlets and isolated farms associated with relatively small landholdings on the North Somerset Levels, and nucleated villages containing large numbers of cottages and a few farms of larger size in the other study areas.

Methodology

The chosen study area for the standing building survey covered Puxton, Rolstone, Hewish, Congresbury Marsh, and Wick (Fig 8.2). All houses shown on the 18th-century estate maps or tithe survey (whichever was earlier) were visited and those which appeared to be 18th-century or earlier in origin, and for which permission was obtained, were surveyed. All buildings had a measured ground-floor plan, with first-floor plans and elevations/cross-sections drawn where appropriate.

A wide range of evidence was used in order to establish the relative sequence and absolute dating for the different phases of construction. In a number of cases stratigraphic relationships were visible, while in many cases there were changes in wall thickness. It is a well-observed phenomenon that the thickness of walls in domestic buildings has reduced over time as builders improved their techniques and materials. In Somerset generally the walls in 15th- to early 17th-century structures are typically 70–80cm (28–32 inches), reducing to 50–60cm (20–24 inches) in the 18th to 19th centuries (SVBRG 1996, 35). In southern Gloucestershire, Hall (1983, 32) suggests that it is rare for 16th-century and earlier houses to have walls less than 30 inches (76cm) thick, and that most 17th-century walls are less than 27 inches (69cm) thick; by the late 17th century most had walls that were 24 inches (61cm) thick or less. On the North Somerset Levels wall thicknesses within the different phases of individual buildings also reduce consistently over time, allowing a relative chronology to be established for individual buildings, though it is difficult to use this as an absolute dating technique. The well-dated 15th-century Brimbleworth Farm, for example, had walls just 61cm (24 inches) thick, while the other probable examples of three-room cross-passage houses with an open hall had walls 66cm (Castle Cottages) and 70cm (Glebe Cottage and Gout House) thick. Wall thicknesses in the other three-room cross-passage houses show a broader range, from 50 to 70cm, and these relatively narrow walls may reflect the lack of building stone on the Levels. The larger 17th-century houses also show wall thickness ranging from 51cm (20 inches) to 71cm (28 inches), with the thicker walls being found in the larger structures. The smaller 17th-century houses have wall thicknesses around 50cm (20 inches), which is also the case in datable 18th- to 19th-century structures and extensions to the earlier houses. Clearly, changing wall thicknesses in domestic buildings on the North Somerset Levels are partly related to social status (which is in turn a reflection of the lack of immediately local building material), as well as changing building design and technology over time.

In a small number of cases roof structures provided useful dating evidence, though sometimes there was no access to the roof space,[6] and sometimes the whole roof had been replaced in the 19th–20th centuries.[7] All the observed roofs were of elm, making a programme of dendrochronology impossible. In some buildings structural phases could be dated typologically through their roof structures, although only Brimbleworth Farm appears to have a surviving late medieval cruck (that at Glebe Cottage was removed in the 1980s). This scarcity of crucks is in keeping with the rest of Somerset north of Mendip and southern Gloucestershire (where there are just nine), and is in sharp contrast to central, eastern, and southern Somerset where they now number several hundred (R Hall 1970; 1973; Gilson 1976; Penoyre 1998, 81; Williams and Gilson 1981; L Hall 1983). In the remaining roofs there were broadly three types of roof structure:

- mortice and tenoned joints that were in use from at least the 16th century, and in the study area certainly continued in use into the 17th century such as at Puxton Moor Farm which is securely dated by other internal fixtures and fittings to the early to mid-17th century (Fig 8.3, No. 20). Also seen in secondary extensions to Chestnut Farm and Hodders Farm that probably date to the 16th/17th centuries.
- Lapped 'fish-tail' collars (eg Hodders Farm, Fig. 8.3, No. 5), which in southern Gloucestershire is generally found in the 18th century but in Somerset is found in buildings from the mid- to late 17th century (Hall 1983; Penoyre 2005, 50). At The Grange this style is firmly dated to the mid- to late 17th century by doors, hinges, and stair balusters of that date found throughout the house. Their use certainly overlaps with the mortice and tenoned tradition (as seen at Hodders Farm where the surviving roof of Phase 1 has fish-tail collars, but the later extension has the traditional mortice and tenoned joints).
- lapped and notched ('dove-tail') collars (eg Castle Cottages: Fig 8.3, No. 3) that in Devon are found in smoke-blackened roofs and so probably date from the 16th century, though their use extended into the 18th century. At Chestnut Farm their use in an extension to the main house can be firmly dated by the two-light ovolo-moulded windows with catches dating to the late 16th century or slightly later (Alcock and Hall 1994, 32). Also found at Myrtle Farm where a wide range of internal fixtures and fittings date from the early 17th century (SRO DD/V/AXR/24/4).

Other structural elements were also used as dating evidence including doorways, fireplaces, staircases, and beams. In the 16th and 17th centuries, for example, chamfering on beams was relatively deep (5–11cm), reducing to about 3cm in the 18th century (SVBRG 2004, 25). Stop ends were of limited use, with the common step and run-out style being used in the 16th–17th centuries (see Alcock and Hall 1994; Hall 1983). Finally, a number of the more recent extensions to buildings could be dated by whether they appeared on the tithe maps, or the maps of 1738–39 for parts of Congresbury and Wick; the map of *c* 1770 of Puxton and Rolstone shows buildings only in a very schematic fashion and was of no use in dating. The Hearth Tax returns (Holworthy 1916) were of little use as it was rarely possible to identify a single house belonging to the persons listed.

During the standing building survey gardens were also examined for any pottery and the results were added to a similar exercise carried out by Linda Jenkins in Wick St Lawrence (Fig 6.11 and Table 6.3 (CD)). The owners of each house surveyed were also asked about any documentary material they held and in several cases this revealed important collections of deeds. A documentary history of each tenement was drawn up, making particular use of the *c* 1640 rentals and *c* 1770 survey in Puxton and Rolstone, and the 1567 and 1736 surveys in Congresbury and Wick St Lawrence (eg Fig 8.1; and see Chapter 2 for South Farm in Puxton).

The development of the house plans

Late medieval to16th-century three-roomed cross-passage houses

The development of the vernacular architecture on the North Somerset Levels is, not surprisingly, very similar to the rest of Somerset, western Dorset, and southern Gloucestershire (Machin 1978; Hall 1983; Penoyre 2005). The medieval house in this region had as its main characteristic a hall that was open to the roof and heated by an open hearth, which, if the roof survives, has led to distinctive blackening of the roof timbers (and sometimes even thatch). The simplest surviving dwellings contained just this one room (see the possible examples at Hodders and Appleton Farm below: Fig 8.3 Nos 5–6), while more substantial houses had a separate inner room or private chamber separated from the hall by a screen. More substantial still, and the most frequent in the region, was for an arrangement of three rooms in a line with the high end comprising family living quarters (the hall and inner room), divided from the low end (a service room) by a screened cross-passage. In the more substantial houses there was usually a first-floor solar over the service and/or inner rooms (restricting smoke blackening of roof timbers to the hall), while in lower-status houses all three rooms were open to the roof (so that where roof timbers survive they are all smoke blackened). From the 15th century lofts were created above the inner chamber and sometimes the service room even in peasant houses, reflecting how architectural fashion drifted down the social scale (Gilson 1985; Hall 1983, 7–8; SVBRG 1996, 40; Walrond and Powell 1985; M Johnson 1990; 1997). These three-roomed cross-passage houses tended to have an asymmetrical façade with the hall and inner room on one side of the passage being longer than the service room on the other. A variant on this plan that is increasingly being recognised is a two-roomed cross-passage house with an open hall (without an inner room) and a service chamber on either side of a cross-passage, as at West End Farm in Barton, Winscombe, which has a dendrochronological date of 1278–79 (Penoyre and Penoyre 1999, fig. 1; and see Anon 1986a, 171, 179; Austin and Hall 1970; 1972; Dallimore 1995; SVBRG 2004, 18). As the rooms in these two-unit cross-passage houses tended to be of different size, they had an asymmetrical façade, and a possible example in the North Somerset Levels study area is Glebe Cottage in Puxton (Fig 8.3, No. 2).

From around the early to mid-16th century in both Somerset and Gloucestershire open hearths were replaced by chimney-stacks usually constructed in the gable wall of the service end, which served as a kitchen, and in the hall with their backs usually against the central passage (Somerset Vernacular Building Research Group plan type A1 and B1). These chimneys were sometimes inserted into what remained open halls, though from the mid-16th century these open halls were also increasingly divided into two rooms through the insertion of a first floor, as had already often occurred in many of the inner and service rooms. This innovation led to the need for a staircase to be inserted, which was often located either in the hall next to the stack, winding over the doorway from the passage, or in an external stair turret. This enclosing of halls was a gradual process, and some halls are known to have remained open into the 17th century, as poorer households could not necessarily afford the cost of bringing their homes up-to-date (Hall 1983, 9; Walrond and Powell 1985; Rodwell 1991; SVBRG 1996, 40). This design of a chimney built against the central passage was also found in newly constructed houses from the mid-16th century, which were all of two storeys, and it is unlikely that open halls were constructed after the mid-16th century (Hall 1983, 9). The two- or three-room cross-passage tradition of house construction extended into the 17th century in North Somerset as elsewhere (eg Shipham Manor House just to the east of Winscombe: Anon 1986a, 169), but the vast majority of examples are 16th-century or earlier (Anon 1986a; 1986b; 1988; 1989; 1990; 1991; 1992; 1993; SSAVBRG 1982; 1984; 1986; 1988; 1993; 1994; SVBRG 1996).

Within the study area **Brimbleworth Farm** (Fig 8.3, No. 1) is the only definite late medieval domestic building with a 15th-century jointed cruck roof above the inner room and lower end. The roof above the hall has been replaced and no smoke blackened timbers survive, though a building of this date must have had an open hall as demonstrated by the jetty of the solar above the inner room that extended 0.3m into the open hall. When a first floor was inserted into the hall and service room, their floors were at a higher level than the floor above the inner room (Williams 1977/78). This difference in height between the floors is also seen in one of the three-roomed cross-passage houses surveyed as part of the NSLP – **Gout House Farm** – suggesting that it too contained a hall that was originally open to the roof (Fig 8.3, No. 4). **Castle Cottages** also appear to have had an open hall as the removal of internal plasterwork showed that the central stack between rooms B and C was inserted into an earlier three-roomed cross-passage house that was presumably, therefore, mid-16th century or earlier (Fig 8.3, No. 3). **Hodders Farm** is a particularly interesting structure as the removal of external render reveals that what initially looked like a classic three-roomed cross-passage house was in fact constructed in a series of phases, with rooms A and B (the lower end and cross-passage) being constructed before C–D (the hall and inner room); the stack was a later addition to this extension suggesting that C was formerly an open hall (Fig 8.3, No. 5; Fig 8.4). The plan of **Appleton Farm**, with a substantial wall dividing the putative service room from the cross-passage, suggests that it too originated as a single-room structure which was later extended (Fig 8.3, No. 6). In three further three-roomed cross-passage houses – at **Boxbush Farm** (Fig 8.3, No. 7), **Landhouse** (Fig 8.3, No. 8), and **Rolstone Court** (Fig 8.3, No. 9) – it is impossible to say whether they originally had an open hall (and so are pre-mid-16th century), or were built with a complete first floor (and so are mid-16th to early 17th century). Five further houses would appear to contain substantial elements of three-roomed cross-passage houses: **Doubleton** (Fig 8.3, No. 11), where a splayed window shows that the original south range pre-dates the rear kitchen wing which contains a 16th-century fireplace; and **Hippisleys Farm** (Fig 8.3, No. 14), **Laurel Farm** (Fig 8.3, No. 15), **Sluice Farm** (Fig 8.3, No. 13), and **The Cedars** (Fig 8.3, No. 12) whose dimensions and plan layout suggest they contain the remnants of three-roomed cross-passage houses. The plan of **Chestnut Farm** was difficult to

Figure 8.3 (pp 158–70) Examples of the historic houses in the southern part of the North Somerset Levels. They are shown in broadly chronological / typological order as follows:

Late medieval houses with dated roof structures (Brimbleworth Farm and Glebe Cottage)
Other three-roomed cross-passage houses that are late medieval–16th century (Castle Cottages, Gout House Farm)
Three-roomed cross-passage houses that developed from a single-celled unit (Hodders Farm, Appleton Farm)
Other three-roomed cross-passage houses that are cannot be closely dated and may be late medieval–17th century (Boxbush Farm, Landhouse, Rolstone Court)
Houses that probably contain substantial remnants of a three-roomed cross-passage house (Chestnut Farm, Doubleton Farm, The Cedars, Sluice Farm, Hippisleys Farm, Laurel Farm)
Large 17th-century symmetrical central-passage houses with two rooms (Icelton Farm, Myrtle Farm, Pool Farm)
Substantial C-shaped houses (The Grange, Puxton Moor Farm)
Small 17th- to 18th-century symmetrical central-passage houses with two rooms (Church House, Mays Green Farm, Old Chestnut Farm, Baytree Farm)
Large 17th-century symmetrical central-passage houses with three rooms (Manor Farm, Willow Farm, Stuntree Farm)
Double-pile houses (The Poplars, Puxton Court Farm)
Cottage (Appletree Cottage)

Shading on the plans simply identifies the different phases of construction, with the earliest in black. Selected datable features (windows and roof structures) are shown in inset boxes

Key for building plans in Figure 8.3

- first phase
- first or second phase
- second phase
- third phase
- modern (20th century)

A, B etc domestic rooms
1, 2 etc agricultural rooms rooms
S staircase
F fireplace

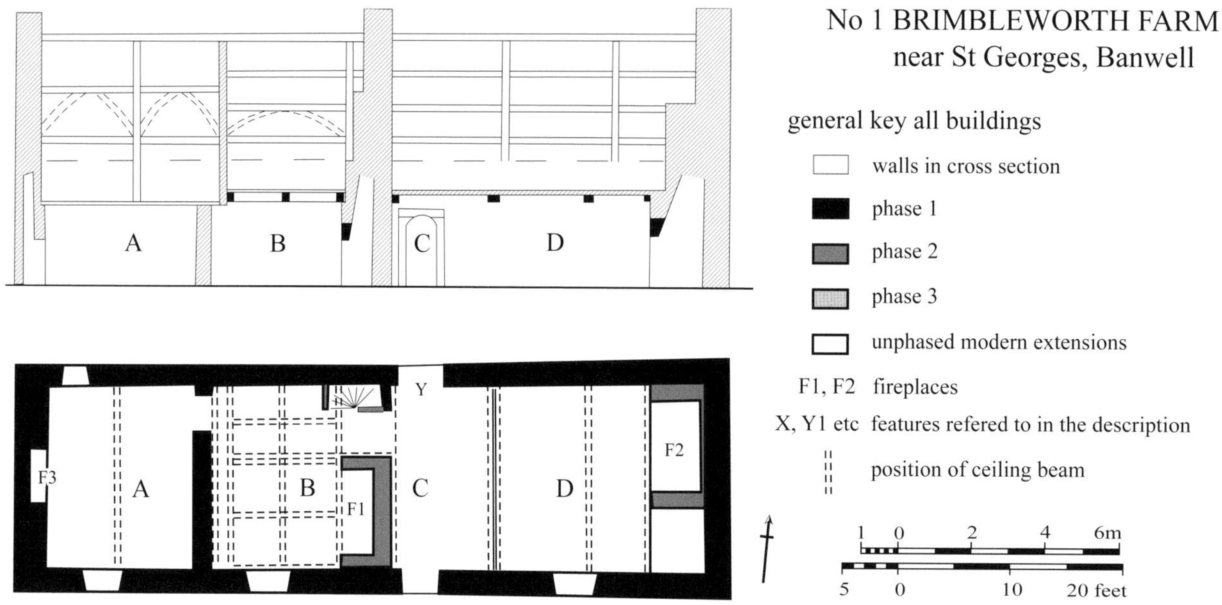

Late medieval three-roomed cross-passage house previously surveyed by Williams (SRO DD/V/AXR.3.3) comprising what was an open hall (B) with an inner room (A), cross passage (C), and service room (D). Rear door of the passage is in a three-centred wooden frame which is identical to that into the hall. At the upper end of the hall the framed ceiling is set against a lower plain plastered area 18 inch wide showing there was a jettied upper floor (the solar) to the inner room.The roof over the solar includes a mortice and tenoned jointed cruck, not blackened, with cambered mortice and tenoned collar, and purlins that have halved scarf joints in the principals. Stack added to hall backing onto the passage. A date stone in the western gable of 1737 may relate to the insertion of the fireplace in that end wall. The length of the lower end, including the cross passage, almost equals that of the hall and inner room combined, and the face-pegged jointed cruck in the lower end is a less sophisticated form of structure than the tenoned jointed cruck over the solar, leading Williams to suggest that this was a longhouse with rooms C and D originally used as a byre for liveststock.

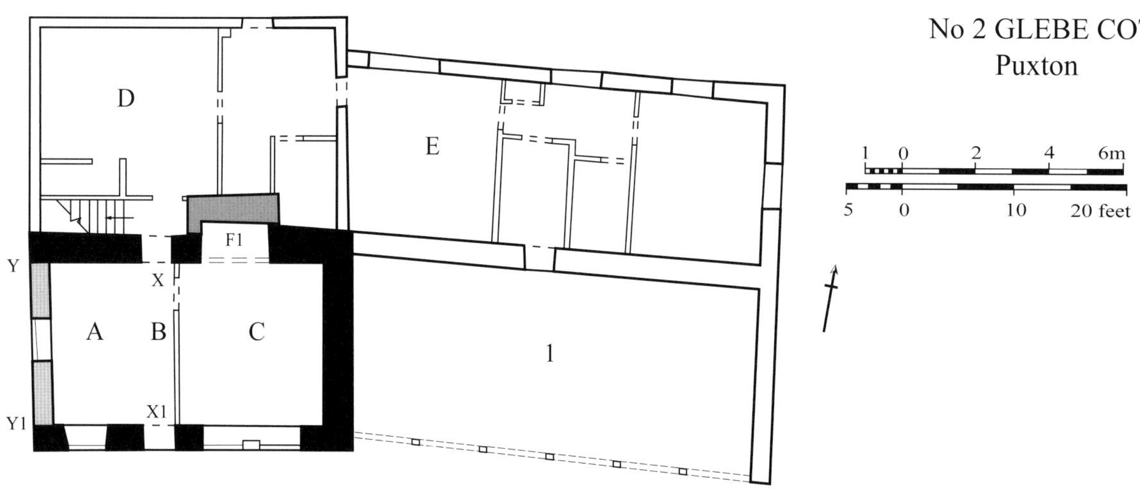

Phase 1: Late medieval? The surviving plan suggests a two-roomed house with central passage (B), though Williams (SRO DD/V/AXR/24) reports having seen a photograph taken a few years prior to 1988 (and before extensive rebuilding) that showed a heavy, arched, and windbraced truss over room C that he regarded as 'probably a cruck', suggesting that room C was in fact the open hall of a late medieval house, with A the inner room. He suggests that the modern extension (1) may be on the site of a cross passage and service room (giving a three-roomed cross-passage layout), though this may in fact have been a two-roomed house with a cross-passage between X and X1 giving the asymmetrical facade typical of late medieval houses.

Phase 2: Addition of external stack on the north side of the formerly open hall C. Chamfered and stopped lintel and moulded stone uprights are not very datable but could be 17th century.

Phase 3: Rebuilding of the west wall of room (A) which is narrower than the rest of the walls.

Phase 4: 20th century. Conversion of outbuilding (E) to domestic accommodation and the addition of extension (D).

Figure 8.3

No 3 CASTLE COTTAGES
Wick St Lawrence

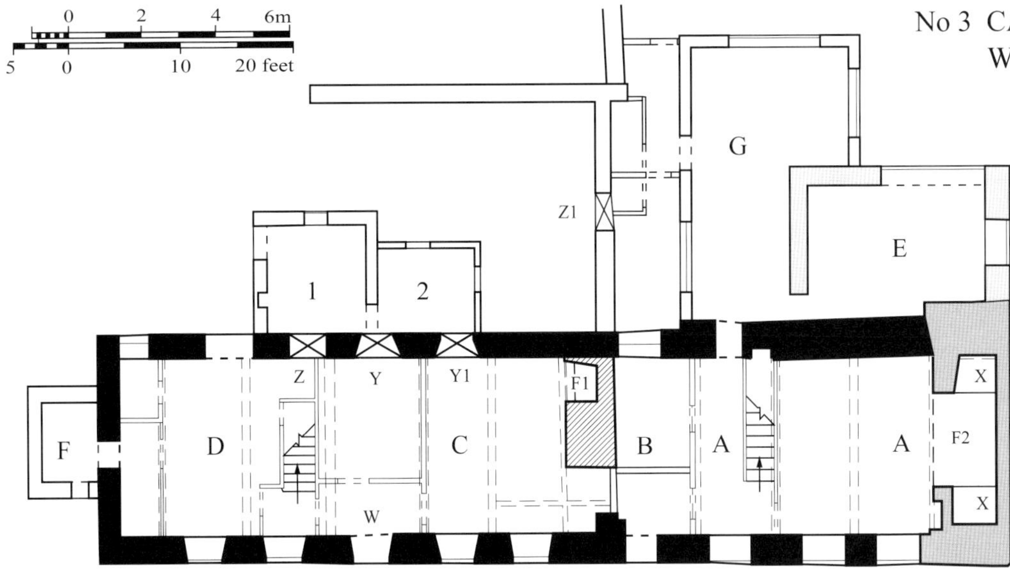

plan and phasing based on initial survey

The initial survey of Castle Cottages was carried out before the interior of the western half was stripped out, including removal of all the plaster and ceilings. The initial interpretation of the structure was as follows:

Phases 1/2: either a three-roomed cross-passage house with an inner room (D), hall (C) with a stack backing onto the passage (B) and a service end (A), or a 17th-century two-roomed central-passage house (like Nos 16–18) consisting of rooms C and D either side of a passage between doorway W and a putative doorway at Y (which was evidenced externally as a blocked window), or central entry three-roomed house with central unheated servivce room (like Nos 25–7), to which was added rooms A and B later in the 17th century (based on the roof structure and chamfered beams with stop ends).

Phase 3: Eastern gable end rebuilt to include a large stack with deep recesses (smoke bays or large ovens: X).

Phase 4: Addition of small wing (E) to the north of service room (A).

Phase 5: Addition of store (1) to the north that closes window Y, and later extension (2) that closes window Y1.

Phase 6: 20th century. Addition of room (F) to west and room (G) to the north.

A-frame truss with notched collar

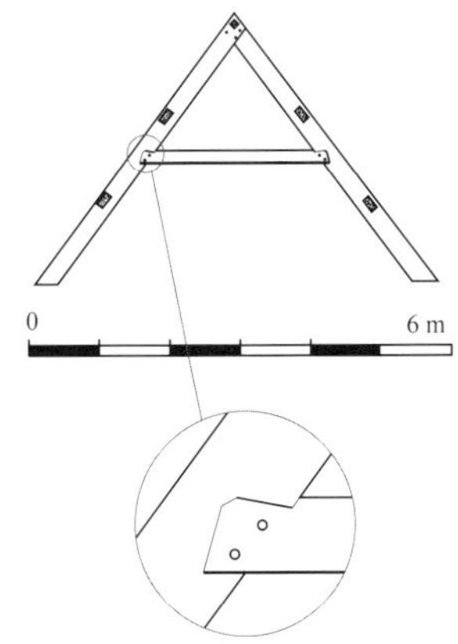

Following the stripping of the interior a number of key observations were made:

1. the front and rear walls of C and D are of different construction, with a mud bonding in the north wall, and a lime mortar used in the south wall.
2. the modern door W was originally a window.
3. window Y was never a door, ruling out the possibility that rooms C and D once formed a symmetrical two-roomed house.
4. the stack post-dates the construction of the north wall, suggesting that it was inserted into an open hall (C).
5. the western gable end has been rebuilt in the 19th century 1m to the west of its predecessor. The former gable end wall was next to the westernmost floor beam in room D (*-* on plan below), which has a flat back. A fireplace was added to the first floor at the same time.
6. chamfered beams with stop ends, and the roof structure with half lapped, pegged notched collars are identical throughout A–D.
7. the uneven thickness of the walls of room A is due to the application of thick external rendering.

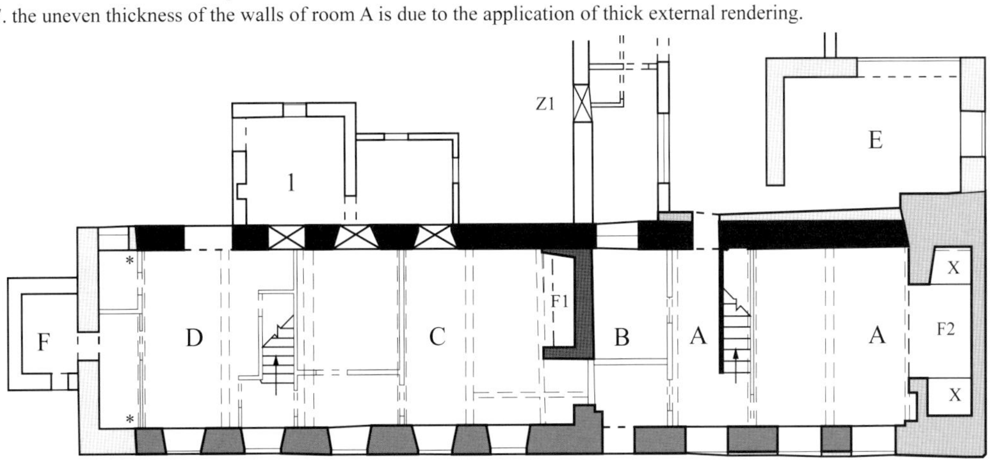

plan and phasing based on survey after the interior of C and D were stripped out

Based on these observations the following phasing can now be proposed:

Phase 1: late medieval. A three-roomed cross-passage house with an open hall (C) and inner room (D), cross-passage (B), and service room (A).
Phase 2a: ?16th century: stack inserted into the hall (C).
Phase 2b: 17th century. The front wall of the house is rebuilt, along with a new first floor and a new roof.
Phase 3: rebuilding of the eastern gable end.
Phase 4: 19th century. Rebuilding and extension of the western gable end, and addition of extension E.

No 4 GOUT HOUSE FARM
East Rolstone

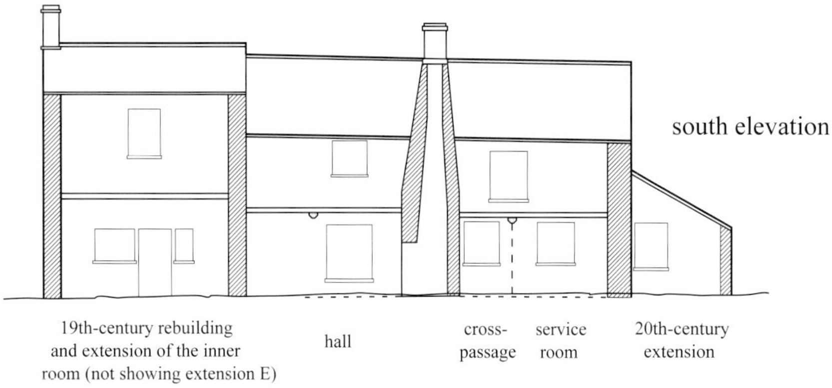

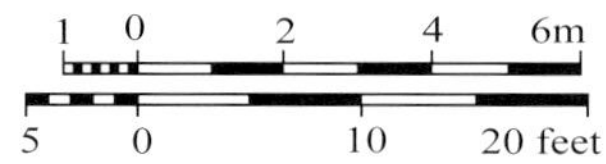

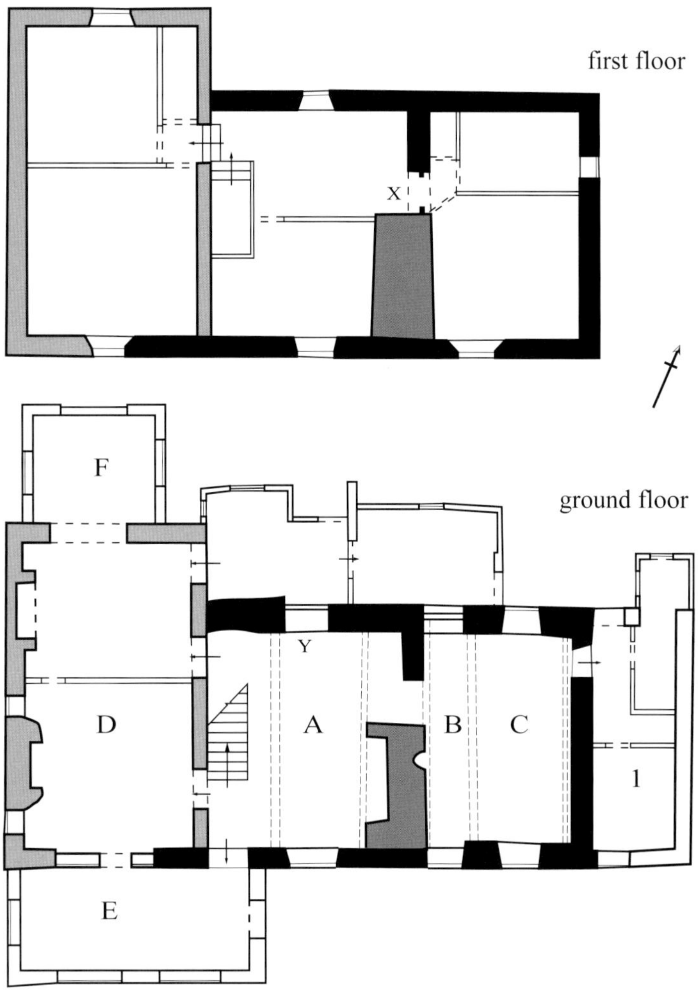

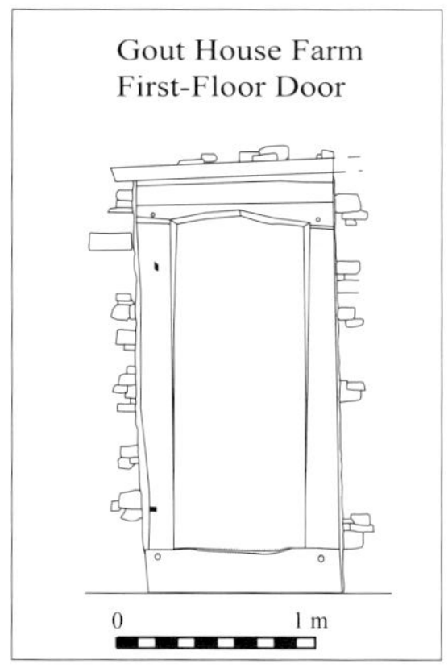

Phase 1: ?late medieval. A three-roomed cross-passage house consisting of (A) hall, (B) cross-passage, (C) service room, and in the position of the later room (D) an inner room. A slot in the beam between B and C marks the position of a wooden partition. The ground-floor doorway Y and adjacent thickening and curvature of the north wall in room A may represent the remains of an external stair turret giving access to the first floor before the construction of the present, modern, stairs.

Phase 2: insertion of ceiling into hall (note the higher elevation of the first floor compared to that over B and C) . The first floor doorway X is late 16th- or early 17th-century, as are the very deeply chamfered ground floor beam stop ends in room A.

Phase 3: 19th century. Demolition, rebuilding, and extending to the north, of inner room (D).

Phase 4: 20th century. Addition of animal house/store (1).

Phase 5: 20th century. Addition of room (E).

Phase 6: 20th century. Addition of room (F).

No 5 HODDERS FARM
Wick St Lawrence

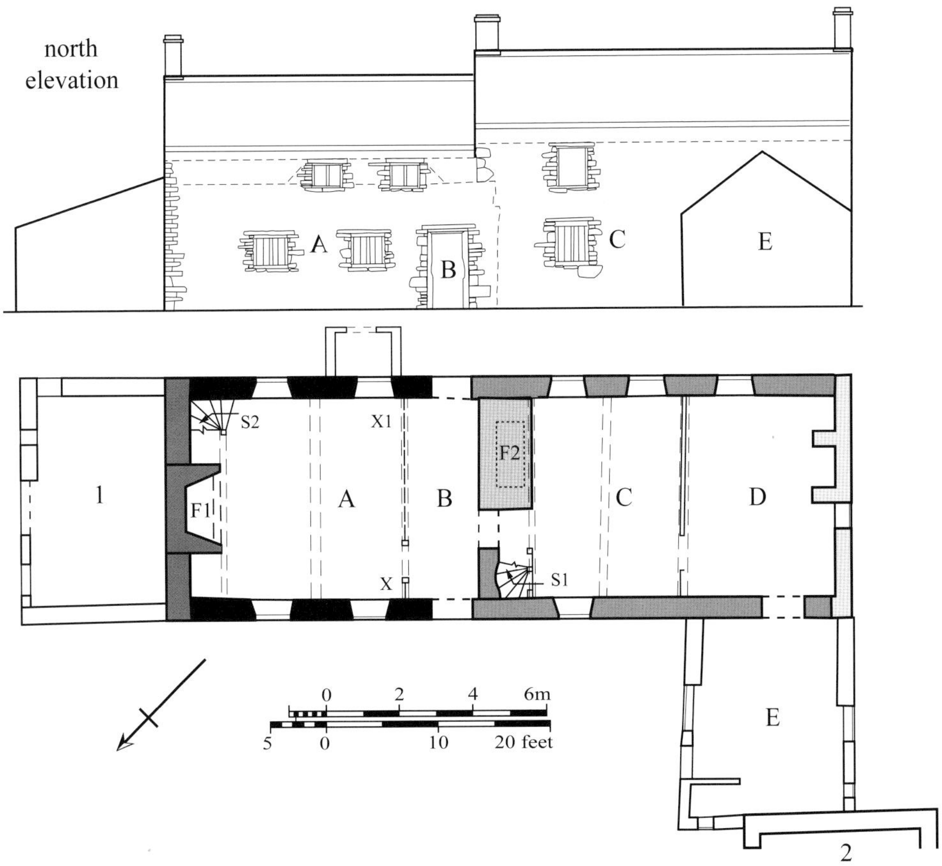

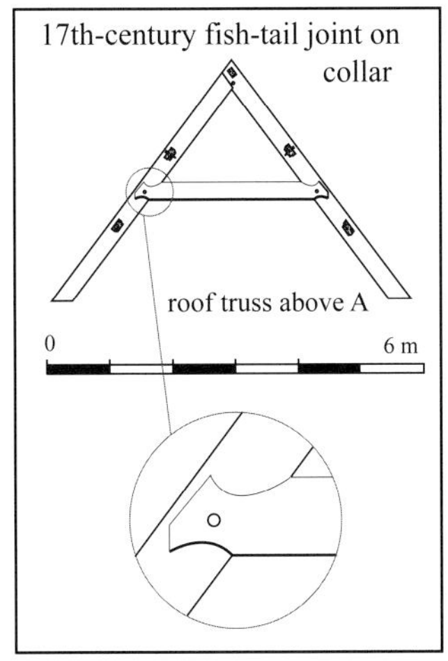

Phase 1: ?late medieval. Single storey, single-cell building comprising the later rooms A and B (the removal of external render reveals that the lower walls of A and B are of different construction to the first floor, that of the chimneystack in the eastern gable end, and of rooms C and D). The late medieval to 17th-century 'plank and plank' screen between the hall (A) and passage (B) may have been an original feature or added later.

Phase 2: east wall of A rebuilt with gable end stack (F1), and the other walls raised to allow the insertion of a first floor giving 1½ storeys with low dormer windows to a first floor accessed by stair (S1) adjacent to the stack. A series of quoins above the west side of the rear doorway match those in the east gable confirming that A/B was raised as a single cell. The roof comprises A-frame trusses with half-lapped, rounded fish-tail joint on straight collar.

Phase 3: late 16th–17th century. Creation of three-roomed cross-passage house through the addition of a two-storey extension to the west comprising a hall (C) and inner room (D) with stack against cross-passage (B) (the stack is possibly not tied to the south wall and so may have been inserted later). The first floor is accessed by a stair (S1) adjacent to the stack. Roof comprises a thatched 3-bay, A-frame with mortised and tenoned collars. The dormer windows of the earlier end (rooms A and B) are now incorporated into the wall to give a level wall plate height throughout building though the lower ridge height of the east end is retained. The same rubble construction is used to infill between the dormer windows in A/B as is found in the construction of C and D. The front and rear openings to the passage have 17th-century ovolo-moulded wooden frames and two-panel plank doors, suggesting that new doors were provided for this older part of the building when it was extended to the west.

Phase 4: 19th-century rebuild of west gable with new brick stack incorporated in the construction of the wall.

Phase 5: 20th-century conversion of rear lean-to into kitchen.

No 6 APPLETON FARM
Wick St Lawrence

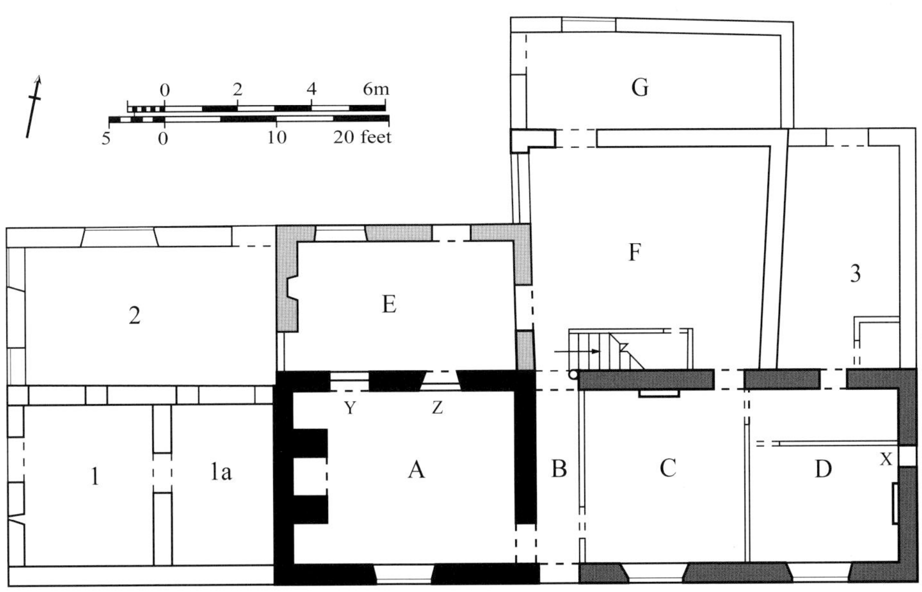

Phase 1: a single-roomed structure (A). Note that the wall between A and B is too substantial to have originated as a partition in a cross-passage house, and room A is too large to have originated as the service end of such a structure. At the first-floor level there is a reused wood mullioned window looking out from the east wall of A that was blocked when B–D were built.

Phase 2: the addition of a cross passage (B), hall (C), and inner room (D) to create a three-roomed cross-passage house.

Phase 3: after 1738. Addition of room E, the closed window (Z) showing that this extension post-dates room A.

Phase 4: Addition of domestic room F and outbuilding (3).

Phase 5: Addition of room (G); 19th-century reroofing of A; 20th-century reroofing of B–D

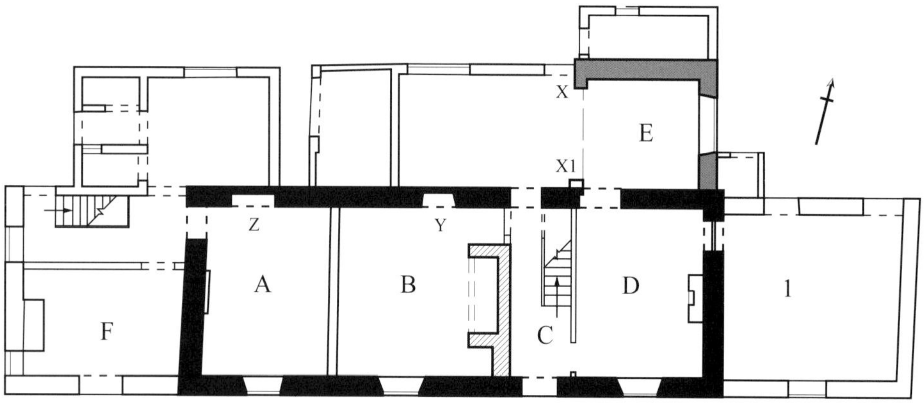

No 7 BOXBUSH FARM
East Rolstone

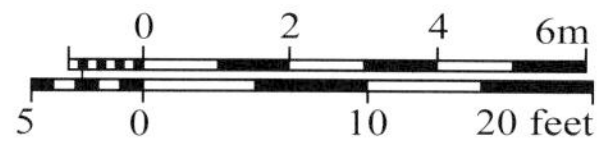

Phase 1: late medieval to 17th century. Three-roomed cross-passage house with (A) inner room, (B) hall, (C) cross-passage, and (D) service room. Chimney-stack backing to cross-passage.

Phase 2: A small extension (E) to the north, with access from the lower room (D). Such extensions are a common feature in the area and may have been used as dairies (eg Appleton Farm, Baytree Farm, Castle Cottages, Laurel Farm, Manor Farm, Rolstone Court, and Stuntree Farm).

Phase 3: Extensions to the building with a stable (1) to the east and possibly the same to the west (F) though this part of the building is now in domestic use and the original function is hard to establish. Modern roof structure over whole building.

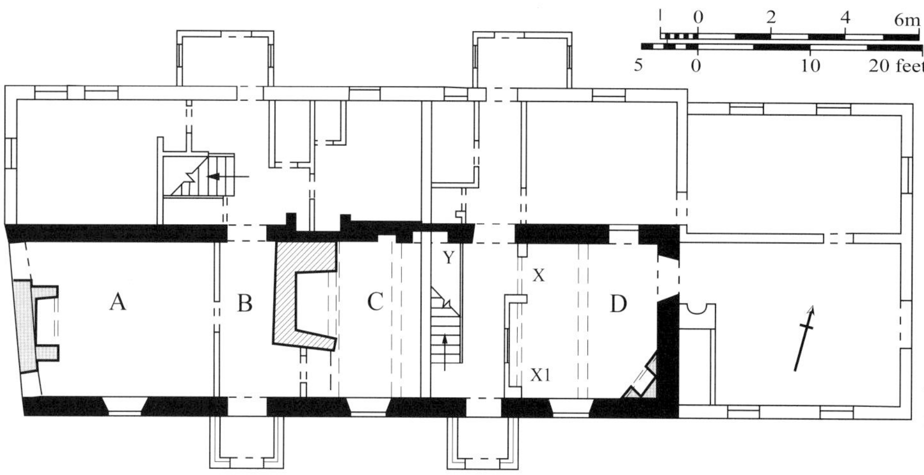

No 8 LAND HOUSE
East Rolstone

Phase 1: late medieval to 17th century. Three-roomed cross-passage house comprising (A) service room, (B) cross-passage, (C) hall, and (D) inner room. Chimney-stack backing to cross-passage. Blocked doorway (Y) and change of wall thickness in north wall of hall (C) may represent position of winder stair (as seen in Chestnut Farm, No 10) Slotted beam X–X1 in inner room (D) is probably the upper rail of a screen that separated the hall and the inner room.

Phase 2: West wall of service room (A) rebuilt with stack. The angle of this wall to the rest of the building suggests that it may be the rebuild of a collapsed wall (not untypical of the area) and care was not taken to square the rebuild to the rest of the building.

Phase 3: 20th century. Extensions to north and east and division of the house into two dwellings. New roof over whole structure.

No 9 ROLSTONE COURT
West Rolstone

Phase 1: late medieval to 17th century. Three-roomed cross-passage house comprising (A) inner room, (B) hall, (C) passage, and (D) service room. Stack with its back to the passage.

Phase 2: ?17th/18th century. Addition of unheated extension (E) to the north side of the building.

Phase 3a: ?19th century. Rebuilding and extending of the west end (D and F) of the main range (as seen at Gout House and Hippisleys).

Phase 3b: 19th century. Addition of long range of agricultural outbuildings (1 and 2), including stables, tack room etc.

Phase 4: 19th/20th century. Infill of area (G) between rooms (F and E) to the north of the building.

Phase 5: 20th century. Rebuilding of the south wall of rooms (B and A) and the east walls of rooms (A and E). New roof over whole structure.

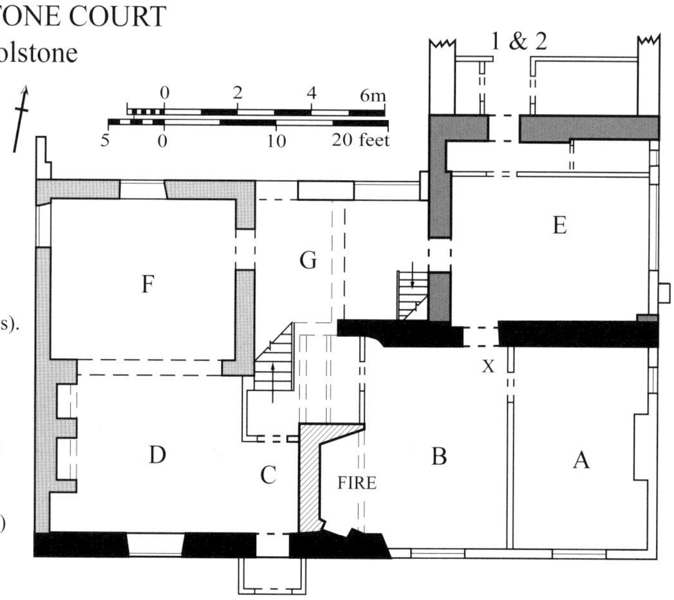

No 10 CHESTNUT FARM
Congresbury

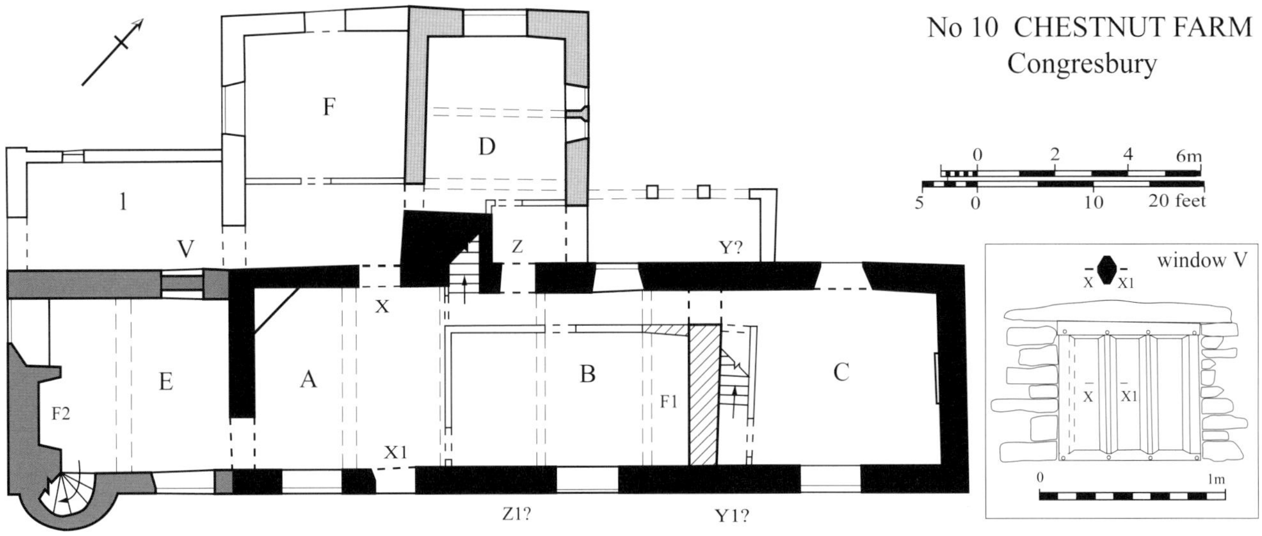

Phase 1: three possible interpretations for the original plan

1. Late medieval to 17th-century three-roomed cross-passage house with (A) an unheated inner room, (B) the hall with the stack backing the cross-passage which would have required doors between (Y and Y1), and (C) the unheated service room. Stair turret to the first floor projecting behind the rear of the hall (B).

2. Late medieval to 17th-century three-roomed cross-passage house with (A) the unheated service room, the cross-passage between (X and X1), (B) the hall with the stack backing (C) the inner room. Stair turret to the first floor projecting behind the rear of the hall (B).

3. 17th-century two-roomed house with a parlour (A) and kitchen (B) either side of a slightly offset central passage between Z and a putative blocked Z1. Door X has 17th-century hinges, but the width (6m) and wall thicknesses (0.71m) of the central block (A and B) are both greater than in other 17th-century central passage houses and so this plan interpretation is thought unlikely.

Phase 2: Extension (E) with stair turret to east of main range with remains of 17th-century hipped roof with dormer windows front and back. Blocked window V has chamfered (flat splay) mullions. Rooms A and B have a very similar roof with mortice and tenoned joints and so were probably reroofed at a similar time as E was built. Door X1 in room A has mid-17th-century strap hinges and latch.

Phase 3: Rear extension (D), with 17th-century half-lapped notched collars on the roof trusses, truncating the north stair turret in order to give access to the wing, and closing a first-floor window in north wall of the main range. Two-light ovolo-moulded windows on the ground and first floors with late 16th/early 17th-century latches.

Phase 4: 19th century. Renewing and raising of roof above A and B. Phase 5: Late 19th century. Filling in of angle between rooms A and D with room F.

No 11 DOUBLETON FARM
West Rolstone

Phase 1: The dimensions of the front wing are suggestive of a three-roomed cross-passage house with (A) service room, and (B and C) the hall and inner room. Rear doorway of cross-passage may be (X) in room (B). The splayed window (Y) demonstrates that the wing (D) post-dates this part of the building.

Phase 2: Addition of kitchen wing (D) to earlier front range. The beams are deeply chamfered with scroll stop ends, and the fireplace (F1) is 'at least early16th century' (SRO DD/V/AXR 3.7), though the roof structure is not chronologically diagnostic. The insertion of the stack (F2) in the western gable end of A may have been contemporary as the first-floor fireplace dates to c1560 to 1630; this is a high-status feature with two carved shields.

Phase 3: The wing (E) could have been added at this stage. The original function of this part of the building is not clear: it may have been built as domestic accommodation although the square-cut rather than splayed windows may suggest an agricultural function or dairy. Either way it created a building with a U-shaped plan that possibly mirrors that at The Grange (No 19). The thickness of the walls suggests that this part pre-dated the rebuild of the front range.

Phases 4: addition of animal house, probably pig sty (F); 5: mid- to late 18th-century rebuild of front range rooms (A, B and C) and construction of present staircase; roof structure with tusk tenons on the purlins and surface spiked collars; 6: infill of courtyard (G) between the two rear wings (D and E) with a 2-storey domestic block; 7: addition of room (H) to the north of the west wing.

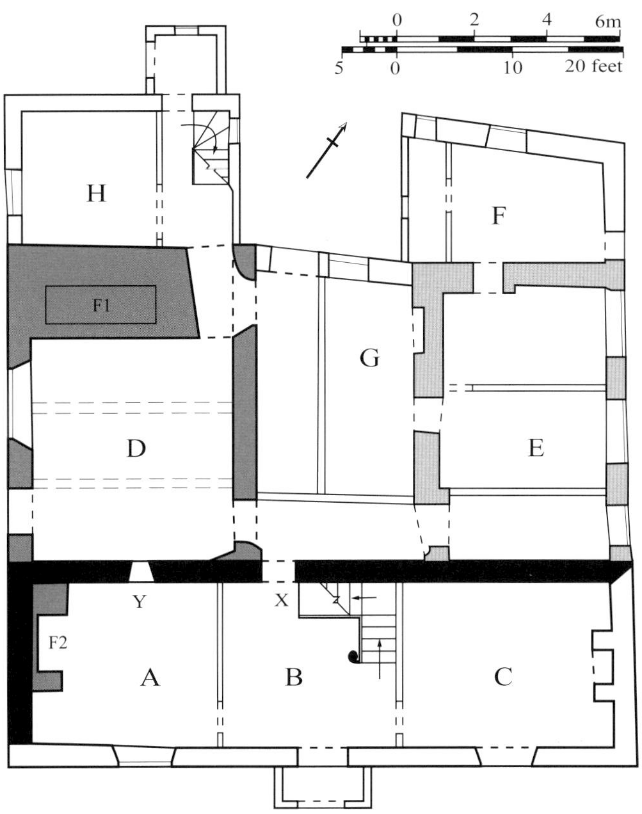

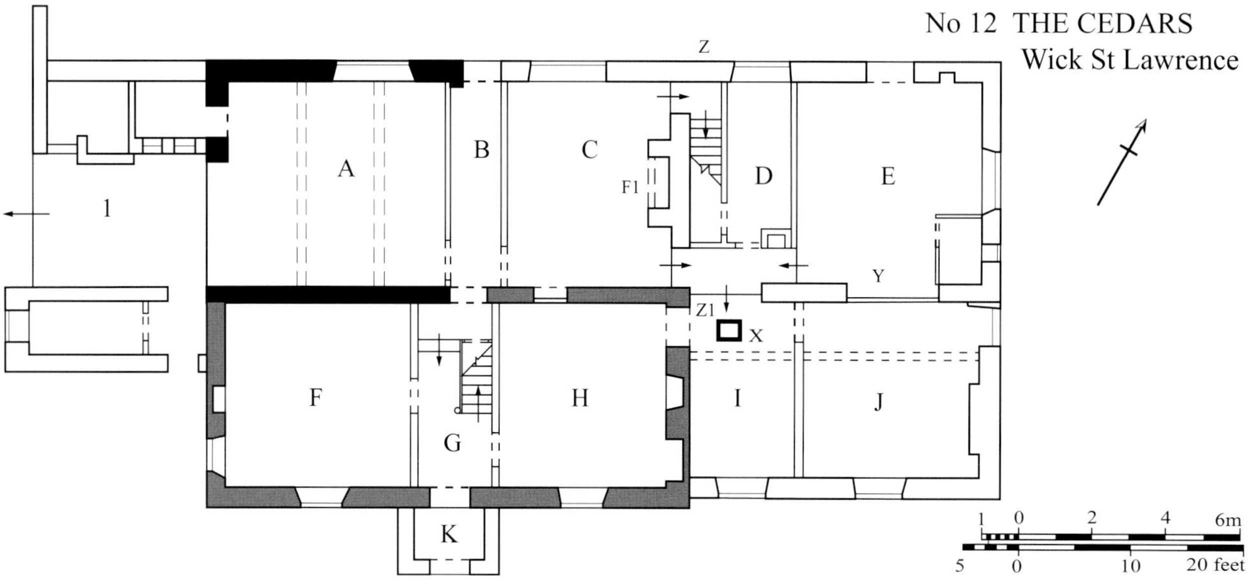

Phase 1: ?late medieval–17th century. Probably a three-room cross-passage house, the likely layout being (A) inner room, (B and C) hall, with a cross-passage between Z and Z1 (next to a well, X), and D and E (or part of) forming a service room (only A surviving, but B–E being rebuilt on an earlier footprint). The only surviving part is rooms A and B which are still 1½ storeys (typical of earlier buildings in the area), with moderately chamfered beams. An 18th-century painting suggests that there was a stack backing the passage in the same position as the 19th-century structure (F1) in the rebuilt room C .

Phase 2: late 18th century (post-1738). Addition to the south of two-storey extension consisting of two heated rooms (F and H) either side of a central hallway and staircase (G).

Phase 3: late 19th century. Replacement of the east end of north range and extension to south range by new build consisting of heated domestic rooms I and J, and agricultural rooms D and E (the latter probably a cheese room). Addition of porch (K).

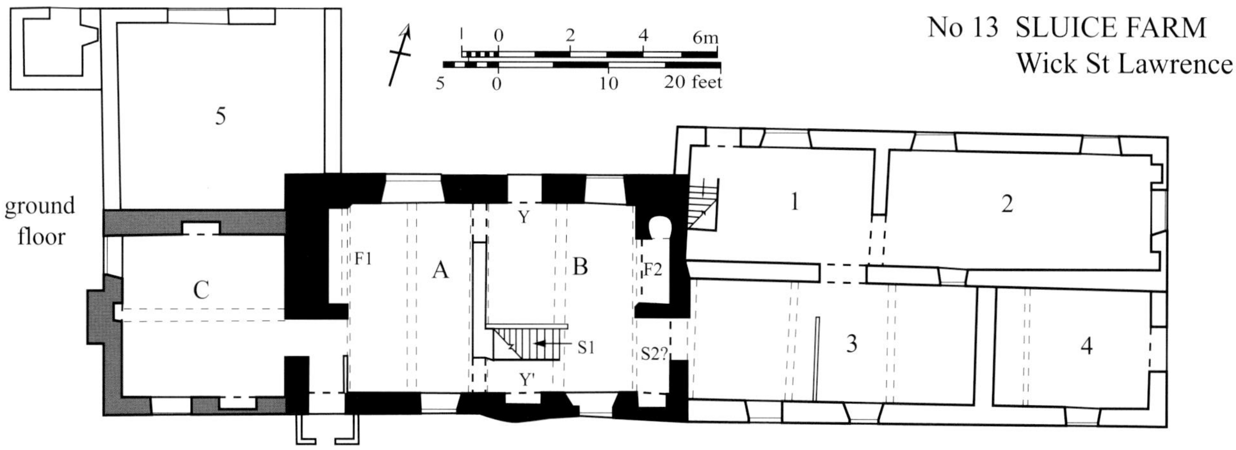

Phase 1: late medieval to 17th century. The earliest part of Sluice Farm is clearly rooms A and B, whose length (11.1m), width (6.3m), and thick north walls (0.72m) are comparable to late medieval–17th-century three-roomed cross-passage houses with B the hall and A the inner room, suggesting there was originally a cross passage behind the stack F2 (with moulded stone jambs) beyond which lay a service room. Alternative interpretation is a two-roomed gable-entry house which is also a 16th- to 17th-century form.

Phase 2: mid 17th century. Extensive renovation and creation of a central through passage between extant north door (Y) and possible blocked doorway (Y'). Insertion of fireplace (F1) in west gable end with deep chamfered lintel and moulded and chamfered shelf. F2 in the east gable end may also have been added at this date. Access to the first floor may have been via a winder stair next to the fireplace F2 whose former existence is suggested by a change in floor level in the first floor. The present roof is a 17th-century through purlin structure with half-lapped collar notched top and bottom.

Phase 3 mid- to late 18th century. Present staircase inserted along with most of the internal first-floor doors. Room C added at this time along with the door between A and C which matches those on the first floor (the beam supporting the first floor is chamfered and has stop ends).

Phase 4: 19th century. Addition of outbuildings 1–5 with 19th-century windows. 1 and 2 clearly pre-date 3 and 4 as there is a window in the south wall of 1.

No 14 HIPPISLEYS FARM
Wick St Lawrence

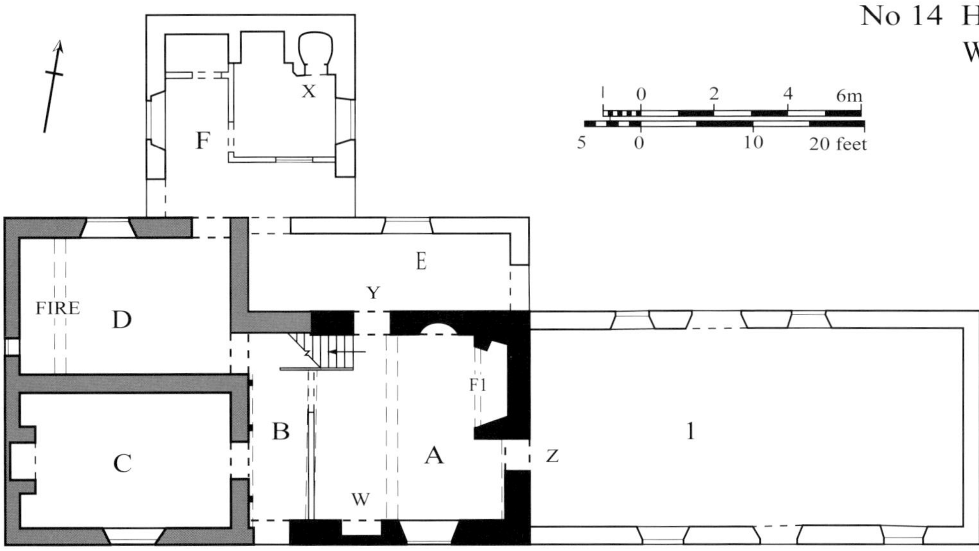

Phase 1: The central core (A and B), with a large stack, is either the remains of a two-roomed through-passage house, with a central passageway running from the present cupboard W through to Y, either side of a kitchen (A) and parlour (B), or the hall of a three-roomed cross-passage house of which A was the hall, with a cross-passage and service room under the later room 1 (the otherwise inexplicable doorway Z being typical of such a layout), and an inner room rebuilt as C. The width (6.1m) of the core block (A and B) is also typical of three-roomed cross-passage houses, and far wider than well-dated 17th-century houses. Stopped and chamfered beams in room A are not closely datable but probably 16th–17th century.

Phase 2: 19th century. Rebuilding of western end with a heated domestic room (C) and kitchen (D) with full width fire. The change of wall thickness (at the current staircase) clearly demonstrates the truncating of the earlier building.

Phase 3: 19th century. Building of cider house (1) to the east of the main chimneystack, and re-roofing of A and B. This may have involved the demolition of the serviceend (cross-passage and service room) of the original three-roomed cross-passage house.

Phase 4: Room E built into re-entrant angle between old house and new west wing.

Phase 5: Further extension (F) (containing large bread oven) to the north.

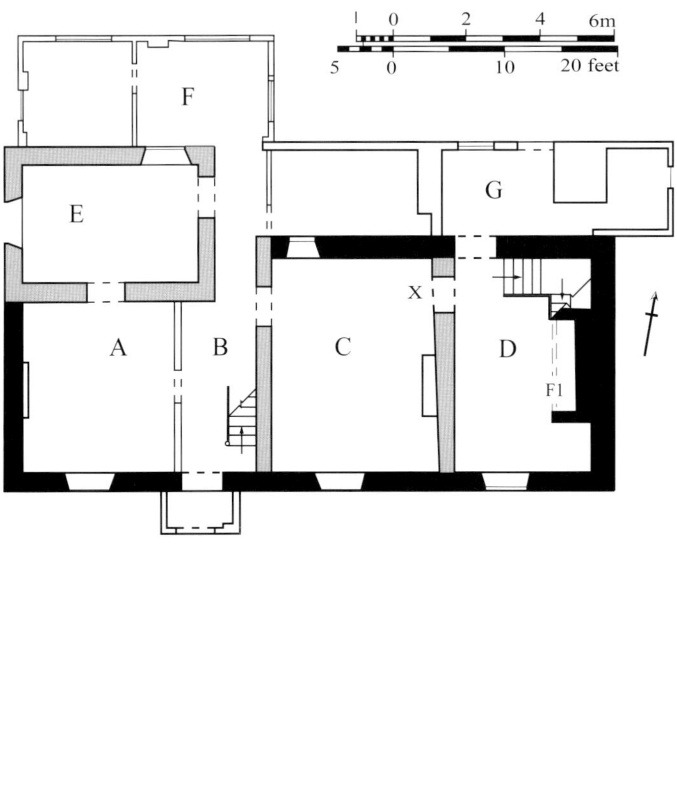

No 15 LAUREL FARM
East Rolstone

Phase 1: late medieval to 17th century? Probably a three-roomed cross-passage house consisting of (A) service room, (B) cross-passage, (C) hall, and (D) inner room.

Phase 2: The wall between the hall and the passage has been rebuilt, possibly at the same time as the house was extended through the addition of the unheated room E (perhaps used as a dairy). The wall between C and D is of uneven thickness and may also have been inserted at this time.

Phase 3: 20th century. Extensions to north and east, and division of the house into two dwellings.

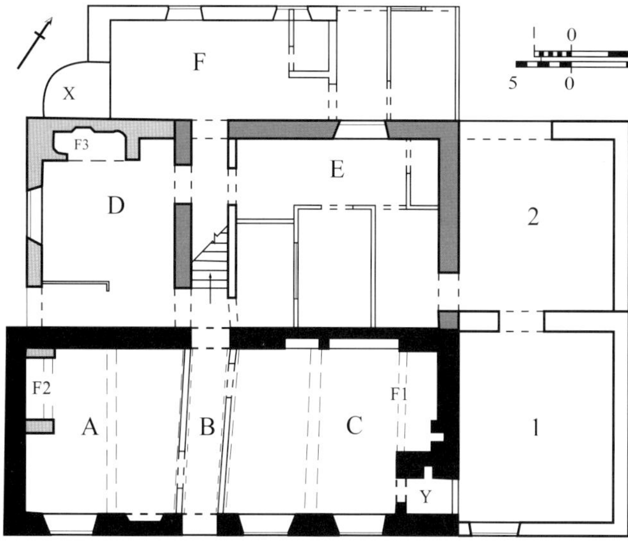

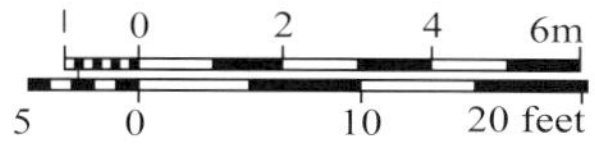

No 16 ICELTON FARM
Wick St Lawrence

Phase 1: early 17th century. Two-room house (rooms A and C) with central passage (B). Access to first floor by winder stair (Y) in room (C) adjacent to the stack. Principal room (C) heated from the start with a fine early 17th-century fireplace (F1) with moulded freestone jambs and large moulded shallow arch timber lintel. Stopped and moderately chamfered beams throughout this first phase.The fireplace in room (A) is probably a later insertion.

Phase 2: Pre-1738: addition of wing (E).

Phase 3: 18th/19th century. Infill of angle between the wing (E) and the main range probably as a kitchen (D), though the bread oven (X) is a later addition. New staircase fitted.

Phase 4: early 19th century. Two-storey extension (rooms 1 and 2), to the east of the main range, probably with agricultural function. Main range reroofed at same time. Refronting of main range.

Phase 5: Addition of a further single-storey room (F).

Phase 6: Conversion of room (1) and floor above to domestic use.

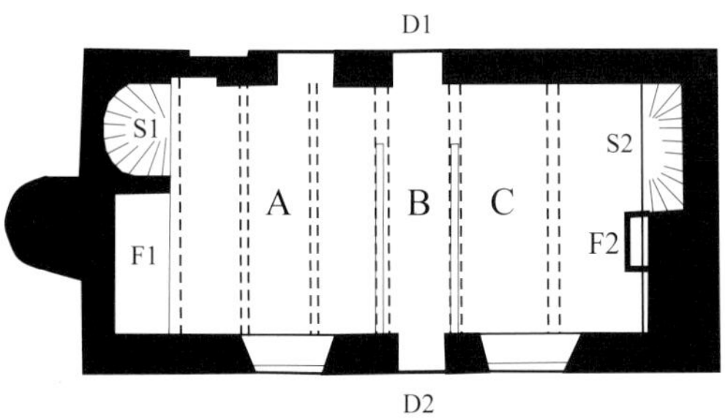

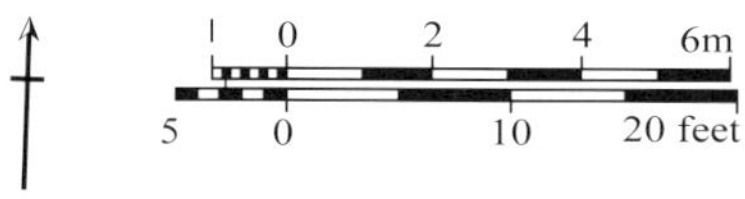

No 17 MYRTLE FARM
Puxton

Previously surveyed by P. Brimacombe (SRO DD/V/AXR/24/4): early 17th-century one and a half storey, two-roomed house with a central passage between doors D1 and D2.

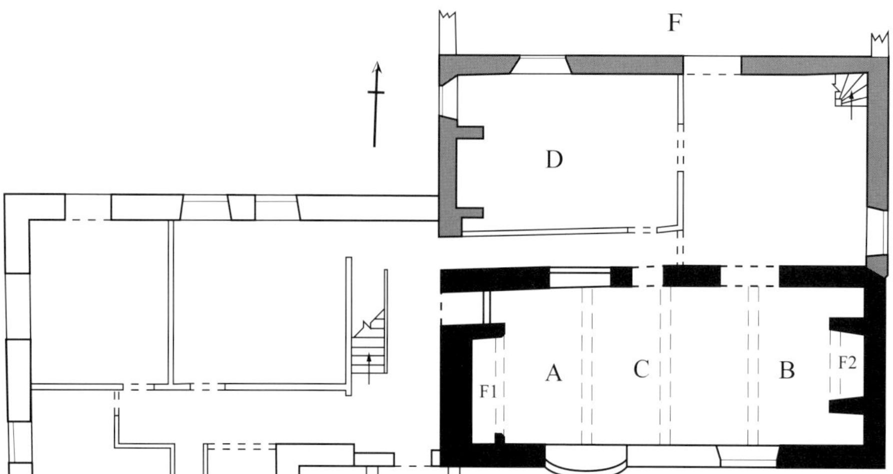

No 18 POOL FARM
Congresbury

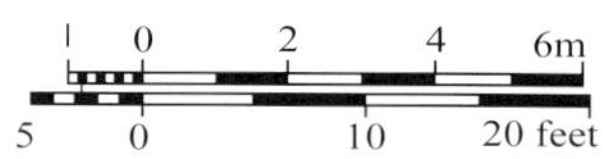

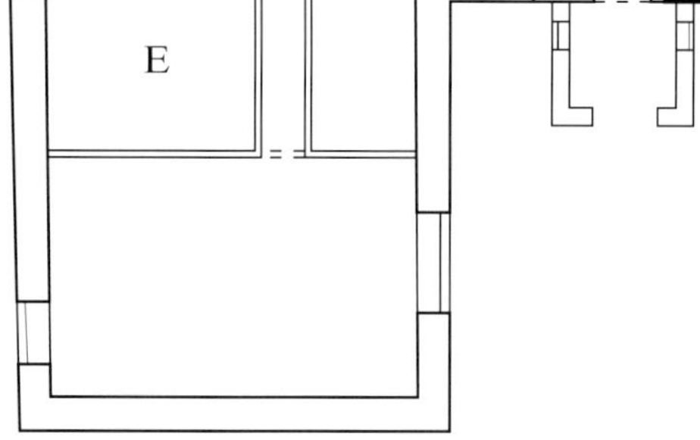

Phase 1: ?17th century. Probable two-room house with a central passage consisting of (A) kitchen, (B) parlour, and a front to back passage approximately in the position of (C). The beams on the ground floor of this part of the building are reused, although the origin of this timber is not known.

Phase 2: post-1739 to 19th century. Addition of two-storey extension (D) with chimney-stack, and reroofing of A–C, to create a house of double-pile plan.

Phase 3: Post-1840. Addition of south wing with connecting rooms to primary range (E).

Phase 4: 20th century. Addition of single-storey extension (F) (not recorded).

No 19 THE GRANGE
West Hewish hamlet, Congresbury parish

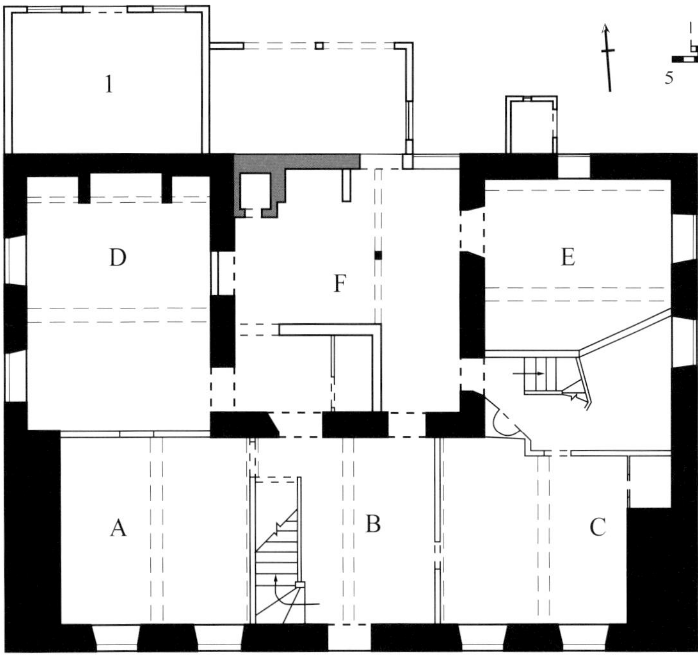

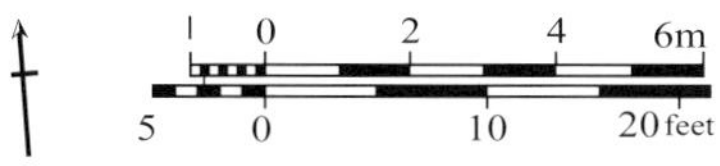

Phase 1: mid- to late 17th century. A substantial house with a long south-facing front range comprising a central unheated lobby (B) with staircase to the first floor, with heated rooms to west and east (A and C). The two wings at the rear are of the same date, demonstrated by the continuous string around entire building. The west wing contains a fireplace in the gable, which though much rebuilt may indicate that this was originally the kitchen, above which was a cheese storage room (suggested by the slatted louvre vent operated by an internal lever). It was approached from below by a narrow ladder stair against the gable which if removed could have provided space for a vertical hoist for the cheeses. Mid- to late 17th-century doors, hinges, stair balusters etc. Stopped and chamfered beams throughout. Roof structure mostly intact with dovetailed collars.

Phase 2: 19th century. Windows replaced in the south front; porch added; and infilling of space between rear wings as kitchen.

No 20 PUXTON MOOR FARM
Puxton

Phase 1: mid-17th century. Two rooms (A and B): may be the west wing of a substantial U-shaped house, or a detached late medieval chamber block that was remodelled in the 17th century (the latter can survive when the hall does not). Room A to the south is heated and has a framed/cross-beam ceiling, and mid-17th-century Cockshead-type door hinges on cupboard, and door through to room B has mid-17th-century divided scroll strap hinge. Room (B) has a lower ceiling with stopped and chamfered beams and a four-light oak mullion window in north wall. Roof structure intact over A with mortice and tenoned collars (B has a modern roof). Blocked oak mullion window in rear section of first-floor west wall. The east wall of the east wing (X–X1) is thicker than the rest and has splayed windows, and may represent a fragment from this early phase. Alternative interpretation of A and B is as a detached chamber block.

Phase 2: 20th century. Main range and east wing demolished in 1929, but the new house may have been built on the footprint of the old. Part of east wall of old building may be incorporated in new structure (X–X1).

Phase 3: 20th century. Addition of outbuildings (1, 2 and 3).

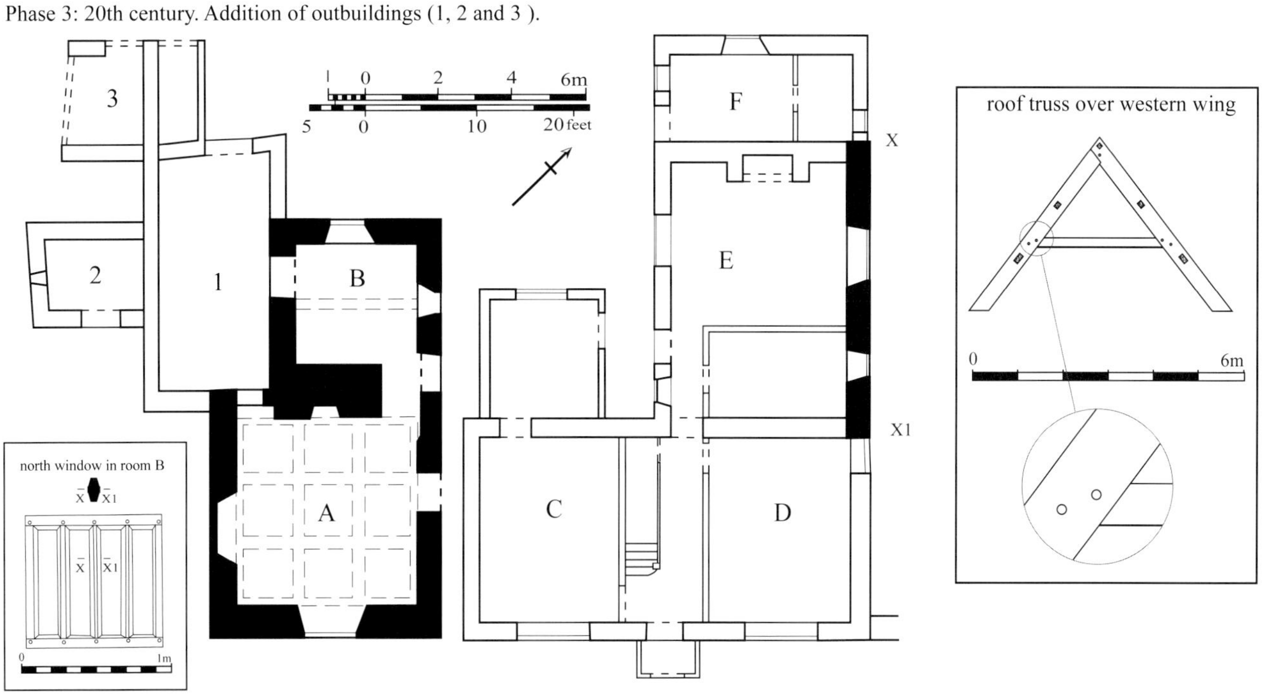

No 21 CHURCH HOUSE
Puxton

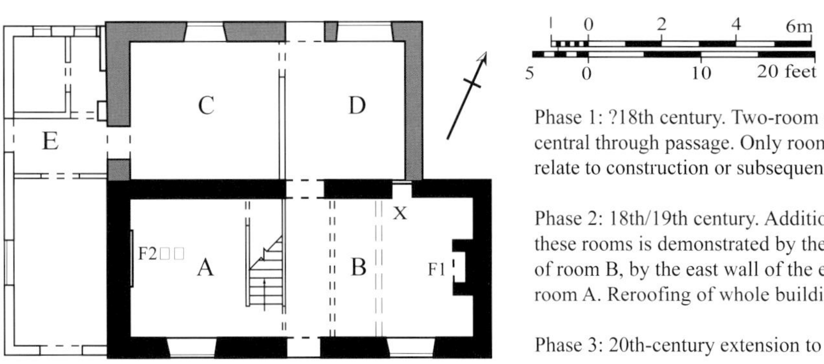

Phase 1: ?18th century. Two-room cottage consisting of rooms A and B and a central through passage. Only room B heated. Date stone of 1786 on east gable may relate to construction or subsequent repairs.

Phase 2: 18th/19th century. Addition of rooms C and D. The later addition of these rooms is demonstrated by the closing of the doorway (X), in the north wall of room B, by the east wall of the extension. Addition of chimney-stack to room A. Reroofing of whole building and raising of stacks in brick.

Phase 3: 20th-century extension to the west; reroofing of whole building.

No 22 MAYS GREEN FARM
Puxton

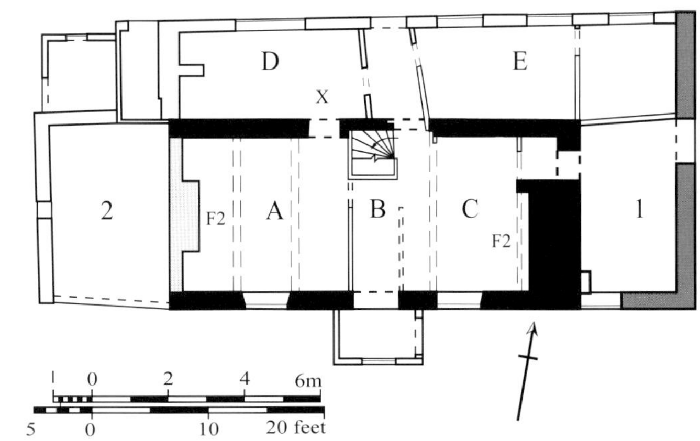

Phase 1: 17th/18th century.Two-roomed house with central passage (B), leading to kitchen (C), and parlour (A). Passage now blocked by staircase but this may be later alteration. Opening (X) in north wall of parlour (A) now acts as a door. Chamfered and stopped beams in both main rooms on ground floor not closely datable but probably 17th century.

Phase 2: Addition of cellar (store room) (1) to the east.

Phase 3: 20th century. Rebuilding of west gable with chimney-stack.

Phase 4: 20th century. Single-storey extension to the north incorporated under main roof. Removal of partition between passage (B) and room (C).

No 23 OLD CHESTNUT FARM
Puxton

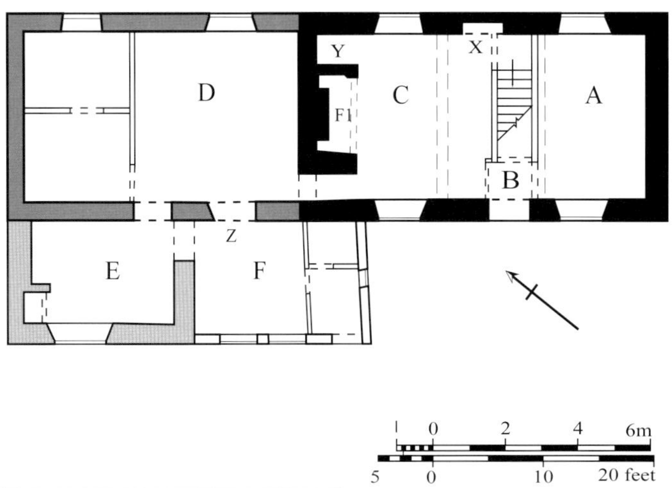

Phase 1: 17th/18th century. Two-roomed house with offset central passage, consisting of passage (B), giving access to unheated parlour (A) and kitchen with large fireplace (C). Blocked doorway (X) giving external access to passage. The current staircase is modern: the original one may have been a winder stair, positioned next to the chimneystack (Y). Stopped and chamfered beams in rooms (A and C), not closely datable but possibly 17th century.

Phase 2: 18th/19th century. Addition to the west of 2-storey extension (D) with brick stack in west wall. East wall of earlier phase rebuilt with chimney-stack.

Phase 3: Addition of small, single-storey extension (E) with chimney-stack.

Phase 4: 20th century. Extension (F) that overlaps the splayed window (Z).

No 24 BAYTREE FARM
Wick St Lawrence

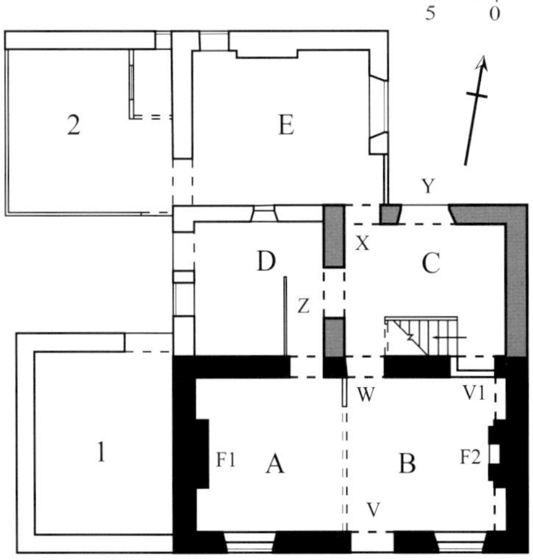

Phase 1: Pre-1738. Two-roomed cottage consisting of two heated room (A and B), with gable-end chimneystacks and a central through passage. External doorways in south (V) and north walls (V1).

Phase 2: Post-1738. Addition of extension (C) with window (Y) and external doorway (Z) (large frame and external door still in situ). Staircase inserted which blocks previous external doorway (V1). New doorway (W) forced in north wall of room (B).

Phase 3: Addition of dairy (D). This closes the external doorway (Z) and may be the point when the window (Y) is converted into a doorway. The outbuilding (1) could have been added at this stage.

Phase 4: Addition of kitchen (E) demonstrated by the closing of the small splayed window in the north wall of the diary (D). Addition of outbuilding (2). Whole structure reroofed in the 19th century.

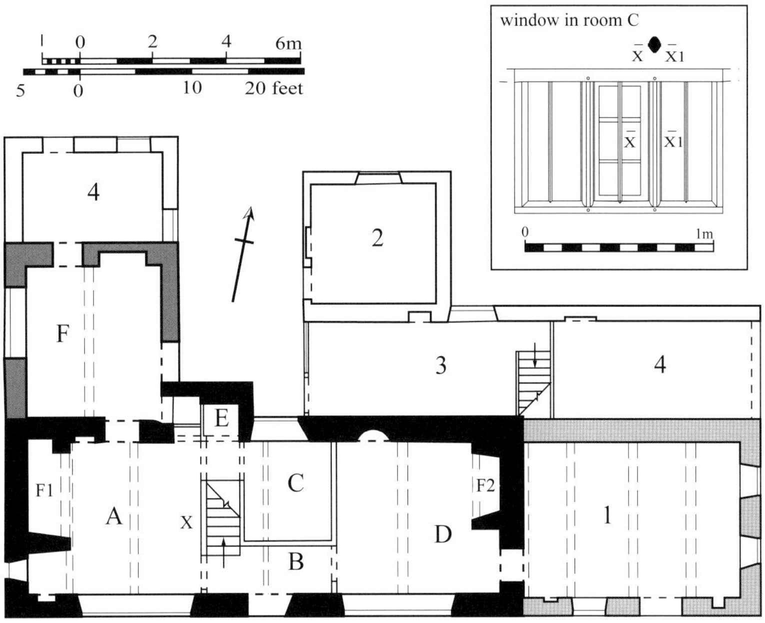

No 25 MANOR FARM
Bourton

Phase 1: 17th century. Three-roomed farmhouse with kitchen (A), hallway (B), service room (C) with three-light ovolo-moulded mullion window, parlour (D), and with first floor accessed by external winder stair turret (E) with a two-light ovolo-moulded mullion window with sunk chamfer and convex planes leaded with stays. The present staircase is a later addition. Moderately chamfered and stopped beams throughout.

Phase 2: ?17th/18th century, certainly pre-1840. Addition of wing (F) to the north of the kitchen (A).

Phase 3: Pre-1840. Addition of animal house (1) to the east of the main range.

Phase 4: Outbuildings (2, 3, 4) added to north side of building.

Phase 5: 20th century. Conversion of animal house (1) to domestic accommodation.

No 26 WILLOW FARM
Bourton

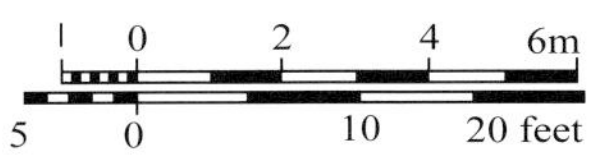

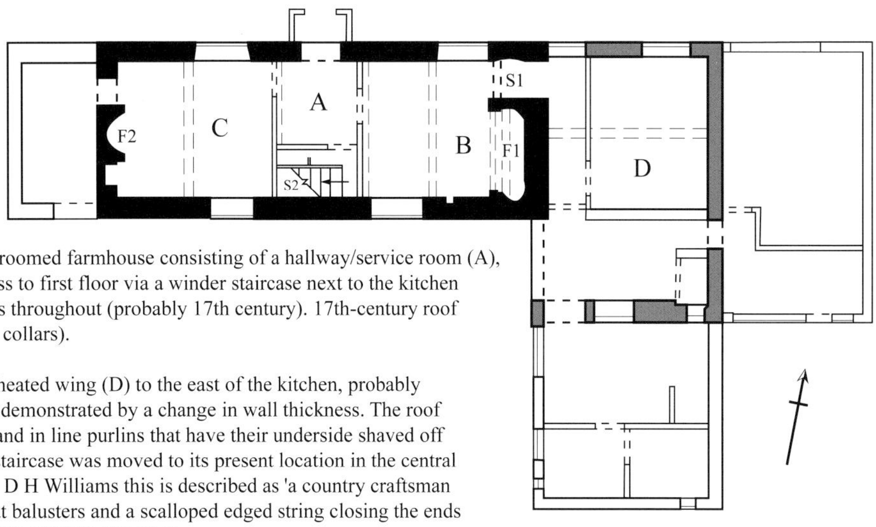

Phase 1: early 17th century. 1½-storey three-roomed farmhouse consisting of a hallway/service room (A), leading to (B) kitchen, and (C) parlour. Access to first floor via a winder staircase next to the kitchen fireplace (S1). Chamfered and stopped beams throughout (probably 17th century). 17th-century roof (with in line tenoned purlins and side-lapped collars).

Phase 2: late 17th century. Addition of an unheated wing (D) to the east of the kitchen, probably as a dairy. That this is a later addition can be demonstrated by a change in wall thickness. The roof has trusses with roughly side-lapped collars and in line purlins that have their underside shaved off close to the truss. In order to access this the staircase was moved to its present location in the central service room (S2). In a previous survey by E D H Williams this is described as 'a country craftsman copy of Jacobean style with small pierced flat balusters and a scalloped edged string closing the ends of the threads: probably late 17th century' (SRO DD/V/AXR.28.2).

Phase 3: Further outbuildings added at both the east and west ends.

No 27 STUNTREE FARM
West Rolstone

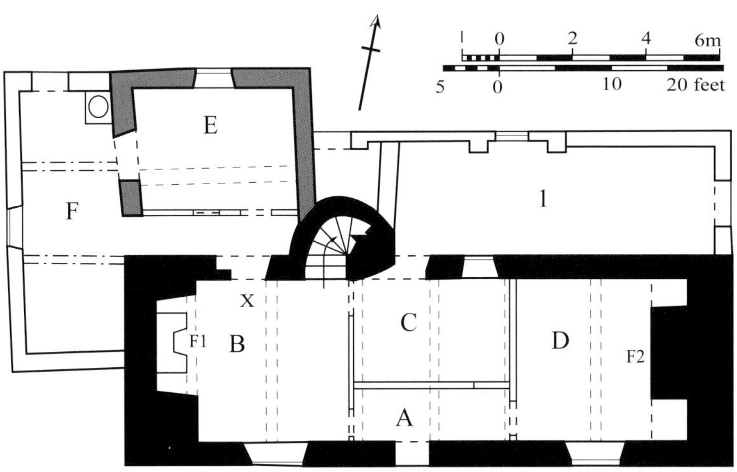

Phase 1: 17th century. 1½-storey three-roomed farmhouse consisting of a (A) hallway, (B) kitchen, (C) unheated service room, and (D) parlour. Access to first floor may have been via a stair turret on north wall of room (B). Stopped and moderately chamfered beams in all rooms (A–D) (probably 17th century).

Phase 2: Late 17th/18th century. Addition of unheated wing (E), probably as a dairy. That this is a later addition can be demonstrated by a change of wall thickness, the lack of alignment to what otherwise is an extremely square building, and the conversion of the window (X) in the north wall of room (B) into a doorway.

Phase 3: 19th century. Reroofing of whole building and raising of eaves to give 2 storeys. First floor rooms refurbished.

Phase 4:19th/20th century. Addition of single storey room (F). Dovetailed collar reused in the lean-to roof of this room.

Phase 5: 20th century. Addition of outbuilding (1).

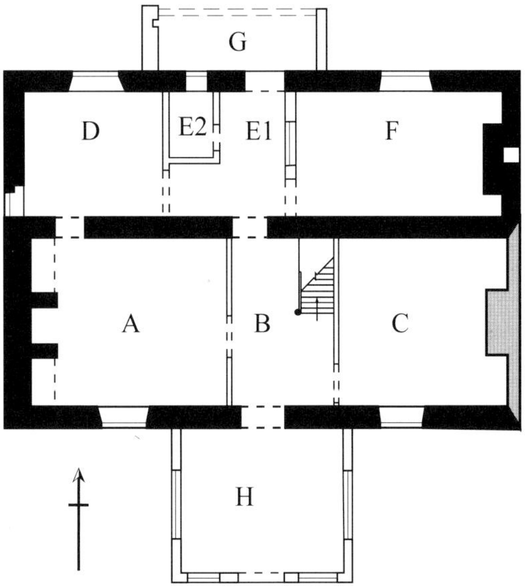

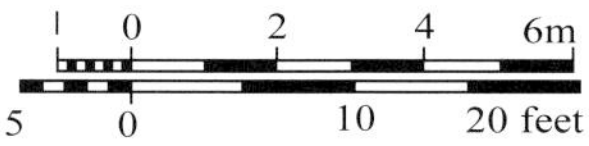

No 28 THE POPLARS East Rolstone

Phase 1: Late 18th-/early 19th century. Four-room symmetrical plan with an entrance lobby with late 18th/early 19th-century doors and staircase (B). Dining room (A), and parlour (C) to the south and service rooms (probable dairy (D), entrance lobby (E) and a kitchen (F)) to the north. Porch (G) to the north possibly of this date. East wall of parlour (C) is narrower than the rest and has probably been rebuilt at some stage

Phase 2: 20th century. Single-storey extension (H) attached to the south front of the house. Insertion of room (E2).

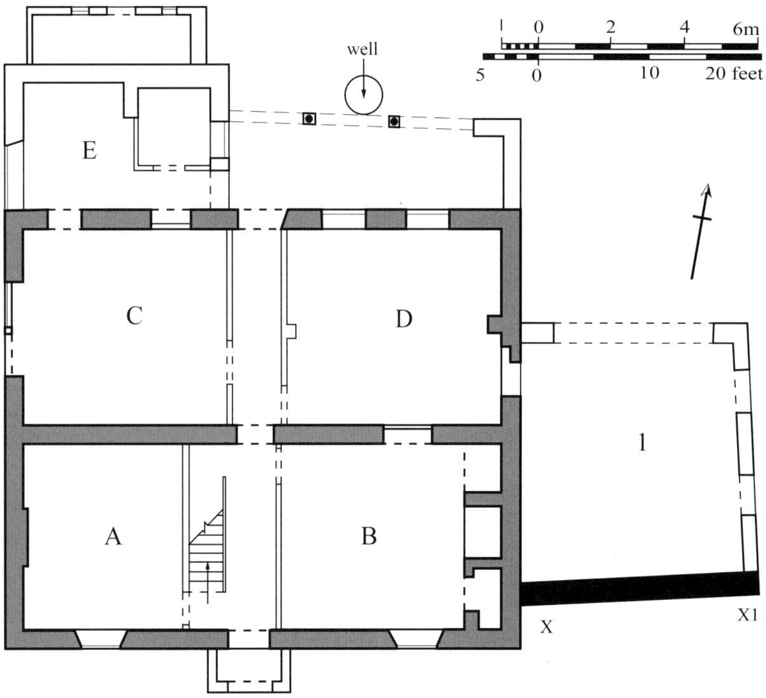

No 29 PUXTON COURT FARM Puxton

Phase 1: A fragment of an early building (X–X1), on slightly different alignment to current structure, may be preserved in the outbuilding (1) to the east of the present house.

Phase 2: 19th century. Double pile house of four rooms with central passage. 19th-century roof structure. Cast-iron manhole cover over the well in the yard to the north of the house, dated 1849.

Phase 3: Addition of outbuildings (E).

No 30 APPLETREE COTTAGE Puxton

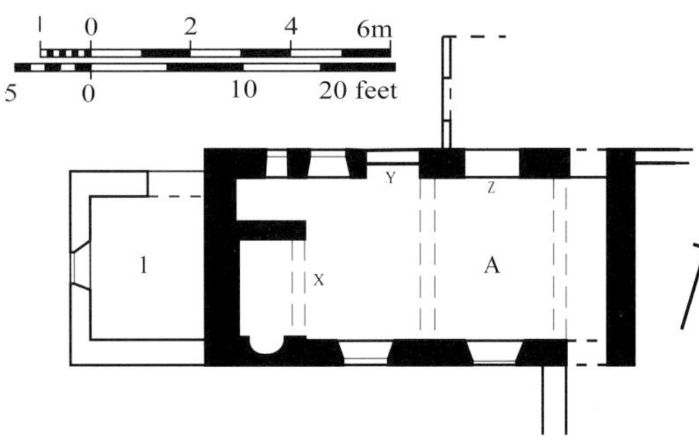

Phase 1: One or two roomed, one and a half storey cottage with doorway (Y) in north wall. Chamfered and stopped bressumer of inglenook; probably 17th century.

Phase 2: Addition of outhouse (1). Splayed window would suggest domestic use for such as a diary.

Phase 3: A substantial modern addition (not recorded).

Figure 8.4 Hodders Farm: this house is unusual in having had its grey external render removed (cf Fig 8.5), revealing a complex structural history starting with a single-celled house (centre left), whose walls were raised to accommodate a first floor, and then extended to create a three-roomed cross-passage house

interpret, with three possibilities for its origins (Fig 8.3, No. 10): a three-roomed cross-passage house is the most likely based on the wall thicknesses (71cm) and width of the main block (6.0m which is typical for three-roomed cross-passage houses, and significantly wider than 17th-century houses in the area which are mostly *c* 4.8–5.5m wide).

In all these examples the chimney-stacks were positioned within the house, usually against the cross-passage. In several examples, however, external chimney-stacks were built on the front of houses (Glebe Cottage in Puxton and Banksea Cottages in Wick). Both may reflect greater external influence in house design, Glebe Cottage being the parsonage and Banksea Cottages originating as a church house.

A detached kitchen block

In the late medieval period the more high-status medieval houses would have had a detached kitchen block, though from the 16th century the majority of houses had an integral kitchen utilising the fireplace in the service room (Hall 1983, 12). Detached kitchens are unlikely to have been constructed after this provision of a fireplace within a house and so are likely to date to the 16th century or earlier. One detached kitchen block was recorded as part of this survey at The Oaks. Here it took the form of a two-storey building measuring 7.4m by 5.5m, with walls 0.5m thick. It is entered by a doorway in the south end of the east wall with a heavy wooden frame with four-centred or curved early to late 16th-century arch, and strap hinges to a plank door. The ground floor consists of a single undivided room with windows in the east and west walls, and a substantial fireplace occupying the entire north wall. The single-roomed first floor, access to which was via a small open stair, was supported by a massive beam, suggesting that it was used for storage. There is a blocked loading door in the south wall.

Longhouses

Another type of three-unit cross-passage structure was the medieval longhouse, which consisted of two domestic rooms to one side of the cross-passage (the hall and inner room), and a byre for overwintering livestock on the other. The length of the hall and inner room was usually the same as or less than the byre end, which was also typically located downslope of the domestic rooms in order to aid drainage. A final indication of a longhouse is that

8.5 Stuntree Farm: a 17th-century house with a symmetrical front façade

the domestic end and the byre end were often rebuilt at different times, giving rise to a house whose ends are of different dates and quality of construction, and whose rooflines can be different (Hall 1983, 12–15). Longhouses are best known from Devon and Cornwall though examples are known in Gloucestershire (Hall 1983, 12–15) and possibly Somerset (Anon 1986a, 175), though no examples were recorded as part of this survey. Brimbleworth Farm (Fig 8.3, No. 1), however, may have been a longhouse as the lower end including the cross-passage represents 9m, out of a total length of 20m, and the face-pegged jointed cruck roof is less sophisticated than the tenoned jointed cruck over the solar. In Somerset and south Gloucestershire generally the service ends are typically about 6–7m long, forming around a third (or just over) of the total length, as in the vast majority of examples in the study area (see Table 8.4).

17th- to 18th-century symmetrical cross-passage houses

From the early 17th century the design of buildings changed significantly, with a growing desire for separate access to as many rooms as possible. This contributed to the fashion for a symmetrical design of two same-sized rooms with fireplaces in the gable ends (a hall/parlour and kitchen on the ground floor), on either side of a central passage, such as that excavated in nearby Sandford, in Winscombe, and dated to the mid-17th century (Gardiner 1996). If an extra room was needed, it tended to be built at the back, creating an L-shaped building maintaining the appearance of symmetry when viewed from the front. The stairs were sometimes accommodated in a D-shaped or rectangular stair turret on the back longitudinal wall, a feature not uncommon in northern Somerset and southern Gloucestershire in the late 16th to 17th centuries, with the D-shaped style perhaps being slightly earlier (Machin 1978; Hall 1983; SSAVBRG 1988; SVBRG 1996, 40; Dallimore 2001).

Several variants of the symmetrical house were recorded as part of the NSLP survey. The first, simpler plan comprised two equal-sized heated rooms on either side of a central passage which ran from front to back (Somerset Vernacular Building Research Group plan type B2). Some were fairly substantial houses, 11 to 14m long, such as Gervinia Cottage and Icelton Farm in Wick, Mays Green Farm in Puxton, and Pool Farm and The Oaks in Congresbury Marsh. At **The Oaks** access to the first floor was via an external stair turret to the west of the central passage, and a thickening of the wall and a splayed opening at this point in **Gervinia Cottage** may mark the position of an external stair turret there too. At **Icelton Farm** (Fig 8.3, No. 16) and **Myrtle Farm** (Fig 8.3, No. 17) there was a winder stair adjacent to the stack in the eastern room. At **Mays Green Farm** (Fig 8.3, No. 22) a staircase has been inserted into the central passage, though it may originally have had a similar winder next to the stack in room C (although the space might appear to be too small, a surviving winder stair occupies the same sized space at Icelton Farm). **Pool Farm** (Fig 8.3, No. 18) contained no chronologically diagnostic features, but Gervinia Cottage, Icelton Farm, Mays Green Farm, Myrtle Farm, and The Oaks all contain simple chamfered beams with stepped stop ends likely to be 17th-century in date. Icelton also has a fine early 17th-century fireplace with moulded freestone jambs and a large moulded shallow arch timber lintel.

This symmetrical house building tradition continued into the 18th century when **The Poplars** (Fig 8.3, No. 28) was built, and an almost identical extension was added to the front of The Cedars (Fig 8.3, No. 12, rooms F and H). Smaller variants of the simple two-room central-passage house are also represented by Church House and Old Chestnut Farm, both with just one room originally heated. **Church House** (Fig 8.3, No. 21) did not contain any datable features, though **Old Chestnut Farm** (Fig 8.3, No. 23) contained probably 17th-century stopped and chamfered beams in both the kitchen and the parlour, along with a 17th-century roof structure.

A second symmetrical house plan was for three rooms to occur in a line with an axial passage at the front of the house (Somerset Vernacular Building Research Group plan type A7). Heating was provided through gable end fireplaces in the two end rooms (a kitchen and parlour), while the central room was unheated (presumably having been used as a service room). At **Manor Farm** (Fig 8.3, No. 25) and **Stuntree Farm** (Fig 8.3, No. 27; Fig 8.5) access to the first floor was via an external stair turret on the north wall of the kitchen (to the west of the central service room), although at Stuntree this may be a later addition as the west side of the door in the north wall of the service room is slightly truncated by the stonework of the turret whose build is of a poorer quality than that in the rest of the building. At **Willow Farm** (Fig 8.3, No. 26) the stairway currently occupies the back part of the central passage, though originally they may have been located next to the fireplace in the kitchen (the same position as at Icelton Farm). The present stairs are described by Williams (SRO DD/V/AXR.28.2) as a 'country craftsman copy of Jacobean style with small pierced flat balusters and a scalloped-edged string closing the ends of the threads', probably late 17th-century in date, whereas the rest of the house is considered to be early 17th-century. Manor and Stuntree Farms are similarly 17th-century in date, the former having a three-light ovolo mullion window and a similar two-light window leaded with stays in the stair turret, and both having stopped and chamfered beams.

Farmhouses with a U-shaped plan

One of the largest farmhouses in Puxton is **Moor Farm** (Fig 8.3, No. 20). Much of the present structure was built in 1929 though part of its east wall is clearly older, as it contains two splayed windows (with modern frames) and is thicker than the rest of the structure. The west wing of this earlier house, however, survives intact and consists of two rooms of which that to the south (A) is heated and has a deeply chamfered framed/cross-beam ceiling suggesting it belonged to a house of some status. The northern room (B) was unheated and had a lower ceiling than in the main room, supported by stopped and chamfered beams. Other architectural features also point to an early to mid-17th-century date including the door hinges, a stopped ovolo surround to the doorway into the first-floor south room, and a four-light chamfered oak mullion window in room B. If the 20th-century rebuilding was indeed on the footprint of the earlier house then this was an impressive structure possibly with a U-shaped plan very similar to **The Grange** in West Hewish hamlet (though actually in Congresbury parish) (Fig 8.3, No. 19), the dimensions of which are virtually identical. This impressive farmhouse was all of one build, and may also have been imitated by **Doubleton Farm** whose rear extension would have created a U-shaped plan (Fig 8.3, No. 11).

The double-pile style

From the late 17th to the 18th century there was another major change in house design with the construction of 'double-pile' houses, with two rooms in the front (a parlour and dining room) either side of a central hallway, and two rooms at the back (a kitchen and service room) either side of the stairs, giving an almost square plan and with gable end fireplaces in most of the rooms. Initially the front and rear ranges were roofed separately with a valley gutter in between, though from the late 18th century the whole house was under a single roof. **The Poplars** is a fine example with a set of fine residential rooms in the front and smaller, probably service rooms at the rear (Fig 8.3, No. 28; almost identical to the early 18th-century Caswell Farm in Ryme Intrinsica, Dorset: Machin 1978, 104–5). **Puxton Court** is an example of a somewhat grander 19th-century double-pile house, probably built in the 1840s (Fig 8.3, No. 29).

Smaller houses

Very few pre-19th-century cottages have survived in the study area, though two buildings in their early form are appreciably smaller than the rest. One example is preserved within a complex of later additions at **Appletree Cottage** in Puxton (Fig 8.3, No. 30). Measuring just 8.5m by 4m this single-

Table 8.4 Comparative dimensions of dated houses within the study area

illustration number in Figure 8.3	building	dimensions			three-roomed cross-passage houses			wall thicknesses in primary build
		length	width	area	higher end	lower end	lower end as % of total length	
late medieval–early 16th-century three-room cross-passage houses with open halls								
1	Brimbleworth Farm	19.7m	6.4m	126.1m²	10.1m	9.6m	49%	0.61m
3	Castle Cottages*	?22.0m	6.1m	?134.0m²	?13m	?7.5m	?34%	0.66m
4	Gout House Farm**	?15.7m	6.7m	?105.2m²	?11.2m	4.5m	?29%	0.70m
5	Hodders Farm ***	18.4m	6.4m	117.8m²	10.0m	8.4m	46%	0.56m
* both gable ends rebuilt; ** inner room rebuilt; *** derived from single room structure								
late medieval–16th century two or three-room cross-passage house with open hall								
2	?Glebe Cottage	incomplete	5.9m	–	?9.6m			0.70m
late medieval–16th- (or possibly 17th-) century three-room cross-passage houses								
6	Appleton Farm *	17.5m	5.6m	98.0m²	10.4m	7.1m	41%	0.50m
7	Boxbush Farm	15.1m	5.7m	86.1m²	9.2m	5.9m	37%	0.50m
10	Chestnut Farm	19.8m	6.0m	78.0m²				0.71m
11	Doubleton	17.1m	5.4m	92.3m²	9.2m	7.9m	46%	0.52m
14	Hippisleys	incomplete	6.1m	–				0.60m
8	Land House	18.5m	5.3m	98.1m²	11.2m	7.3m	40%	0.55m
15	Laurel Farm	16.5m	6.7m	110.1m²	?10.6m	?5.9m	?36%	0.55m
9	Rolstone Court	17.0m	6.3m	107.1m²	9.8m	7.2m	42%	0.64m
13	Sluice Farm	incomplete	6.5m	–	?11.2m			0.70m
12	The Cedars	?21.6m	6.4m	138.2m²	13.2m	8.4?	39%	0.51m
* derived from single-room structure								
larger 17th-century two-room central-passage house (heating in both rooms)								
	Gervinia Cottage	13.8m	5.2m	71.8m²				0.66m
16	Icelton Farm	12.4m	5.3m	65.72m²				0.55m
17	Myrtle Farm	12.2m	5.6m	68.3m²				0.62m
18	Pool Farm	12.2m	5.2m	63.4m²				0.52m
	The Oaks	13.7m	5.2m	71.2m²				0.57m
U-shaped house, 17th-century								
20	Puxton Moor Farm	18.0m	6.5m					0.60m
19	The Grange	18.5m	6.2m					0.62m
smaller 17th-century two-room central-passage house (heating in both rooms or just one room)								
21	Church House	10.5m	4.6m	48.3m²				0.50m
22	Mays Green Farm	10.8m	4.9m	52.9m²				0.40m
23	Old Chestnut Farm	9.8m	5.4m	52.9m²				0.51m
three-room 17th-century axial-passage houses								
25	Manor Farm	13.8m	4.9m	67.6m²				0.56m
26	Willow Farm	12.1m	4.8m	58.1m²				0.51m
27	Stuntree Farm	16.3m	5.4m	88.0m²				0.60m
18th-century two-room central-passage house (heating in both rooms)								
28	The Poplars	13.4m	5.3m	71.0m²				0.51m
19th-century house								
29	Puxton Court Farm	14.0m	11.5m	161.0m²				0.48m
17th- to 18th-century cottages								
30	Appletree Cottage (C17?)	8.5m	4.1m	34.9m²				0.48m
24	Baytree Farm (C17–18)	8.4m	4.5m	37.8m²				0.49m

other buildings recorded

Banksea Cottages, Wick: Church House, converted into three Poor Houses by the 17th century, and now two cottages (SRO DD/V/AXR 28.1; Anon 198a6, 183).

Court Farm: 19th-century house using some farbric of earlier structure

Palmers Elm Farm (West Hewish), The Elms (East Hewish), and The Old School House (Wick): no fabric can be proved to be pre-19th century room, one and a half storey, gable-ended structure had a fireplace in its west wall with a probably 17th-century stopped bressumer. This cottage can be traced through documentary sources back to the rental of *c* 1630 as a customary tenement called North House comprising a house and two acres of land. In general, the cottages of landless labourers in Somerset were under 20m^2 (Dallimore 2001, 25), and the 34.9m^2 of Appletree Cottage suggests that it was more than simply the cottage of a landless labourer. The same is certainly true of **Baytree Farm** (Fig 8.3, No. 24) which at 37.8m^2 was the farmhouse for a tenement of 32 acres in 1567.

Building materials

In most of the structures recorded the walls are externally rendered, though where the fabric is visible all buildings are of stone rubble construction, as is common throughout Somerset and south Gloucestershire (Hall 1983, 29; Williams 1991, 124; Penoyre 2005). No cob construction was observed. Where whole elevations are visible there are clear changes over time in the stone sources being exploited; this is best illustrated at Hodders Farm, Bourton in Wick St Lawrence. In the earliest phase a mixture of Carboniferous and Lias limestone rubble with a little sandstone was used (late medieval–16th century?), while Lias dominated the second (early 17th-century) phase when the roof was raised. In later phases only Carboniferous limestone was used (Fig 8.3, No. 5). Brick was first used in some Somerset towns in the 17th century, but its use in the countryside, including on the Levels, was not common until the mid-18th century (Williams and Wilson 1982). Most internal walls are also stone built, though a number of timber screens survive. The stud and panel screen at Hodders Farm is of a type dated elsewhere in Somerset to the late medieval period to the 17th century (Williams 1991, 128).

All of the roof structures that could be viewed were made of elm. Elm is very common in 17th-century and later buildings across southern England (Ian Tyers pers comm), and why this should be the case is unknown. On the North Somerset Levels, however, there appears to be a local explanation as elms are by far the most common tree to be recorded in pre-19th-century records. In 1371, for example, Amice Nichols sold elms from a messuage in Puxton (*CIM(C)* III, No. 822). In the early 15th century Henry Bernard was ordered by the hundred court to make a ditch along his meadow between 'Elmham' and 'Becdonbridge' between Banwell and Worle (Coward 1980, note 10). In 1494 Richard Craas ordered to make a ward [bank/ditch] at Blackstoneselme (BodL RAWL B317), while in 1547 there was a dispute between William Webbe (the Lord's tenant) and the churchwardens of Congresbury parish church over four elms growing in the 'fossata' [ditch] of the close called Wallhay (BodL RAWL B317). A survey of Merton College lands in Puxton in 1601 included 'a little cut full of elms containing the 6th part of an acre' (BodL MC 17.12.00/B), and in 1739 Thomas Bunn of Frome paid fee farm rent for a little house below Palmers Elm on the south side of the way that leads to Worle called White Hall (BRO 04242, pp 76–7). The only other tree species documented is not surprisingly alder when Henry Louseft's grant to the church of Winscombe in 1236 included an alder grove called 'Durnehete' (*Liber Albus II*, 360–1), while the field-name Allerside in Banwell incorporates 'aller' which means alder (Jennings 1869, 4). There are no references to oak growing on the Levels until a lease of 1800 that refers to a field called Oak Ground (SRO DD/SOG 41).

Until the widespread use of ceramic pantiles and Welsh slate in the 19th century, thatch was by far the most common traditional roofing material in central and northern Somerset, apart from the north-east corner around Bath where, in common with south-east Somerset, stone tiles were used (Williams 1991, 133–4). Though none of the buildings in the study area are still thatched, a 19th-century print of The Cedars shows the 17th-century or earlier back range as thatched, and the late 18th-century front range with a slate roof. The renovation of Castle Cottages also revealed a thatched roof sealed beneath the present covering.

The 'great rebuilding' of the North Somerset Levels' farmhouses

The two main types of pre-19th-century vernacular buildings that dominate the landscape of the North Somerset Levels – the asymmetrical three-roomed cross-passage houses, with their central chimneys just to one side of the opposed front and rear doors, and the symmetrical two- and three-roomed houses with central or lateral passages and stacks in the gable ends – are found throughout Somerset and Gloucestershire. Chronologically, the former represent an evolution of the medieval tradition and are predominantly 16th-century and earlier, while the latter style dates from the 17th century. The improvement of medieval houses, through inserting chimney-stacks and floors into the formerly open hall, and the construction of new houses of both the asymmetrical cross-passage and symmetrical central-passage type, all reflect a period of considerable investment in rural housing. In Devon Hoskins (1953) described this as the 'great rebuilding' of between 1570 and 1640 when people below manorial status first began to construct houses that would stand for centuries rather than a few decades (and see Brunskill 1978, 27). It is now widely recognised, however, that large numbers of late medieval houses do survive. Beacham (1989, 74), for example, has shown that the rebuilding of Devon's farmhouses was a continuous process from the late 15th through to the early 18th century, and Hall (1983, 99), for example, has shown that in south Gloucestershire the emergence of the portfolio of vernacular buildings that survive today was a longer and more complex process than was previously believed. This suggests that the 15th century was the first period when houses were sufficiently well constructed to have survived to the present day, and that these were substantial enough to support modification in the 16th century when existing houses were brought up-to-date without the need for wholesale reconstruction.

This period of investment in rural housing is generally attributed to a range of socio-economic factors notably the emergence of more wealthy tenants who had expanded the size of their landholding through engrossing the land of other tenements for which the lord of the manor could not find another tenant. The emergence of this 'middling sort' – prosperous 'yeomen' farmers and the lesser gentry (Dyer 1997; Johnson 1997) – is certainly evidenced in and around the North Somerset Levels (see above). Another trend in the later medieval period was for lords to abandon the direct management of their demesne in the face of rising wages and falling prices, in favour of leasing it out for a fixed rent or 'farm' (the word farmer coming to mean an agricultural entrepreneur: Dyer 1997, 68). In Puxton, for example, the manorial account roll for 1500–01 records the receipt of 46s 8d for the demesne land called Twindix, while in Banwell the demesne was divided up. In 1592 the manorial accounts included £7 18s 10d for the farm of part of the demesne, and £26 6s 8d for the other part which was leased during a vacancy (PRO SC1/951).

In the case of the North Somerset Levels there are also a number of more local factors that may have played a part in the development of the rural housing. Ground conditions (notably the high but fluctuating water table), may have meant that buildings required more regular rebuilding, or at least extensive renovation that masks earlier fabric, compared to dryland areas. There is also no natural building stone on the Levels and it is noticeable that wall thicknesses are less than in many other areas of Somerset, making them even more vulnerable to subsidence, and several of the houses on the North Somerset Levels have had their gable ends rebuilt.[8] Local socio-economic factors may also have been significant in Congresbury and Wick St Lawrence where the new lord of the manor, Queen Elizabeth's Hospital in Bristol, sold off a number of tenements in the late 16th century (Sluice Farm and Baytree Farm in Wick, and Chestnut Farm and The Oaks in Congresbury), and this could have provided a context for the new owners investing in their buildings. This cannot, however, be the sole explanation since Pool Farm, whose house was also rebuilt in the 17th century, was retained by Queen Elizabeth's Hospital. Puxton and Rolstone also saw major rebuilding at that time (eg Church House, Mays Green Farm, Myrtle Farm, Old Chestnut Farm, and Stuntree Farm), although their customary tenements were still leased from the manor until the 20th century.

Another factor that must have been significant was the great flood of 20 January 1607 (see Chapter 1). Before the present survey late medieval houses appeared to be poorly represented on the Levels, with just one medieval roof structure identified (at Brimbleworth Farm in St Georges), though a second probable example was destroyed fairly recently but recorded in a photograph (Glebe Cottage in Puxton). Following this survey, however, there are now between eight and fourteen examples of three-roomed cross-passage houses of which at least four (Brimbleworth, Castle Cottages, Gout House Farm, and Hodders Farm) had an open hall and so almost certainly pre-date the 1607 flood. Outside the study area, in Kingston Seymour, a three-roomed cross-passage house at Gout Farm also dates to *c* 1500 (Williams 1987). The other certain (Appleton Farm, Landhouse Farm, and Rolstone Court), and possible (Chestnut Farm, Doubleton Farm, Hippisleys Farm, Laurel Farm, Sluice Farm and The Cedars) three-roomed cross-passage houses are impossible to date precisely and, while the majority of houses of this type in both Somerset and south Gloucestershire date to the 16th century or earlier, the style is known to have continued into the early 17th century. It is possible that following the flood some houses were rebuilt in this traditional style (on the footprints of the earlier structures) as the new fashion for houses with symmetrical façades and a central passage had not yet taken root. Leaseholding tenants were responsible for their own houses and agricultural communities tend to be conservative in their outlook (Dallimore 2001, 31).

Irrespective of whether these houses are in fact late medieval, the 17th century certainly saw a major programme of investment. Castle Cottages in Wick, for example, had the first floor inserted throughout the building and the roof replaced, at the same time as the south frontage was rebuilt. The front of the house was rebuilt and not the back which would have faced the flood waters, suggesting that this rebuilding was for socio-economic reasons (as presumably was the case in the 18th century when the front of Doubleton Farm was rebuilt). Indeed, the north walls of Castle Cottages and of Hodders Farm, Bourton in Wick St Lawrence, are bonded with little more than mud, and while these could have survived the rising waters and relatively slow currents of flood water created when sea walls are breached during periods of extreme storminess, it is questionable whether they would have survived a tsunami-type wave.

A comparison of the North Somerset Levels with the wider region

If the 1607 flood really had devastated the North Somerset Levels then we would expect to see far fewer 16th-century and earlier buildings surviving there compared to the adjacent dryland areas. Elsewhere around the North Somerset Levels some impression of the building stock can be gained from

Table 8.5 Summary of the initial date of construction for surveyed houses in the North Somerset Levels study-area and other surveys in the region

	sample size	C16 and earlier	C17	C18	source
Somerset					
Alford and Lovington	24	6 (25%)	14 (58%)	4 (17%)	SSAVBRG 1986, 14
Barton, Winscombe	9	2 (22%)	2 (22%)	5 (56%)	Sue Shaw pers comm
Batcombe	29	9 (31%)	12 (41%)	8 (28%)	SSAVARG 1988, 18
Butleigh	54	19 (35%)	22 (41%)	13 (24%)	SVBRG 2001, 15–16
Chiselborough	36	11 (31%)	9 (25%)	16 (44%)	SSAVBRG 1983, 40
Compton Dundon	43	16 (37%)	15 (35%)	12 (28%)	SVBRG 2004, 20–21
Haselbury Plucknell	39	10 (26%)	18 (46%)	11 (28%)	SSAVBRG 1994, 33
Long Load	27	10 (37%)	10 (37%)	7 (26%)	SSAVBRG 1982, 24–9
Shapwick	26	7 (27%)	9 (35%)	10 (38%)	SVBRG 1996, 44
West and Middle Chinnock	23	9 (39%)	10 (44%)	4 (17%)	SSAVBRG 1984, 30–47
Somerset average		99 (32%)	121 (39%)	90 (29%)	
Somerset average of C16 and C17		45%	55%		
Newton St Loe **		0	24 * (53%)	21 (47%)	
South Gloucestershire	67	87 (49%)	91 (51%)		Hall 1983, 11
North Somerset Levels	30	14 (47%)	15 (50%)	1 (3%)	

* of which 17 were constructed *c* 1690–1700
** Newton St Loe is excluded from the main Somerset average as it was clearly atypical in having a very high number of cottages, and an extensive programme of rebuilding from *c* 1690 through into the 18th century

the Listed Buildings schedule, and the surveys of individual buildings of interest by E H D Williams and P Brimacombe (SRO DD/V/AXR). A number of 16th-century three-room cross-passage houses are known,[9] with a roughly equal number of early to mid-17th-century structures.[10] These subjective surveys will, however, tend to favour what are regarded as more interesting early structures, and the only systematic survey to date which can be compared with that on the North Somerset Levels was carried out by Sue Shaw at Barton hamlet in the parish of Winscombe directly to the south of Banwell. In a survey of 1792 (SRO DD/CC 110735) there were fourteen houses, of which nine survive today, and all of which were surveyed. The oldest structure is at **West End Farm,** a two-roomed cross-passage house with walls comprising small pieces of stone rubble bonded with clay and no lime (DD/V/AXR/29/2), as was seen in the north walls of Castle Cottages and Hodders Farm. The roof includes two heavily smoke-blackened true crucks, one of which has yielded a dendrochronological date of AD 1278–79 (Penoyre and Penoyre 1999, fig 1). During the 16th century a fireplace and ceiling were inserted into the hall with the service room possibly converted into a kitchen that for a few decades was open to the roof before itself having a ceiling inserted perhaps in the late 16th–early 17th century. **Home Farm** currently also survives as a two-roomed cross-passage house, though the long hall may have been sub-divided in the past. A range of architectural features, and a jointed-cruck roof in a later extension, all suggest a 15th-century or earlier date. **Nut Tree Farm** is a three-roomed cross-passage house with the fireplace backing onto the passage and of the type seen both on the Levels and the surrounding dryland. The ceiling beams and windows all indicate a 17th-century date, though the 17th-century roof appears to be a replacement and the 76cm thick walls may also suggest a pre-17th-century date (DD/V/AXR/29/3). **Barton Farm** is a two- or three-roomed cross-passage house which is undated, though the wall thickness of 68cm points to a 16th- to 17th-century date; an extension bears a date stone of 1703 providing a *terminus ante quem* for the main house. The remaining five houses in Barton are all 18th-century or later in date.

In this very small sample in Barton, buildings of the late medieval tradition make up 22% of the total number of 18th-century and earlier buildings surveyed, compared to an average in Somerset of 32% in the parish studies published by the Somerset Vernacular Buildings Research Group (Table 8.5). In these Somerset studies as a whole it is noticeable that on average buildings that are 16th-century or earlier occur in roughly equal proportions to those which are 17th-century (albeit with marked differences in some parishes). In the North Somerset Levels Study area there are five clearly 16th-century or earlier structures (14%), four definite (14%) and six possible (17%) three-roomed cross-passage houses that could be 17th-century but are probably 16th-century or earlier, compared to thirteen clearly 17th-century houses (52%). Just one clearly 18th-century building was recorded. Overall, there appears to be little significant difference in the age structure of the pre-18th-century vernacular buildings on the North Somerset Levels compared to elsewhere in Somerset and in southern Gloucestershire, and the extent of 17th-century building compared to the extent of the survival of 16th-century and earlier structures is no greater. The great flood of 1607 did not sweep away the domestic houses of the North Somerset Levels.

Overall, it is clear that there was a major period of investment in the houses of the North Somerset Levels in the 16th and 17th centuries, with the insertion of chimney-stacks and ceilings into what had been open halls, and the construction of fashionable new houses in the symmetrical style. These are familiar trends within vernacular architecture and reflect the lesser gentry and tenant farmers emulating fashions towards greater comfort and privacy seen in preceding decades in higher-status households. The proportion of the surveyed buildings on the Levels which have a plan layout whose origins are late medieval – the three-roomed cross-passage house – is in keeping with the rest of Somerset and southern Gloucestershire. While some of these structures clearly saw considerable renovation in the 17th century which may have resulted from damage caused by the 1607 flood, social as opposed to environmental factors are likely to have been more important.

Social status/relationship between buildings and size/nature of landholding

Standing buildings are all too often interpreted simply on the basis of their architecture and not the nature of the landholding that sustained them, and Johnson (1997, 146) has suggested that 'such houses rarely have the necessary documentation to be sure about the social status of their late medieval builders and owners'. Hall (1983, 103) notes that 'It is common practice to define vernacular houses in terms of the social status of their original builders or occupants', which she defines as the nobility, lesser gentry, yeomen, and husbandmen, though there is a danger of this being inferred from the architecture alone. In the NSLP the standing building survey was part of a wider investigation of the landscape as a whole, and the history of every tenement, with or without a house, was researched. As described in Chapter 6, there are marked local differences in the size and disposition of the landholdings associated with tenements in different areas, and in some cases these can be traced back to the late medieval period. There are also clear examples of one tenement absorbing the lands of another, and some cases of large tenements being broken down into smaller holdings, although overall, broad continuity is the dominant theme until the late 18th–early 19th century.

There were no manor houses within the study area, as Wick and Congresbury Marsh were part of Congresbury Manor, and St Georges, Waywick, and West Wick were part of Banwell Manor, both of which were based on the dryland. The manors of Puxton and Rolstone were held by families who were resident elsewhere (the Paynes in Hutton and the St Loes in Churchill). Three of the farmhouses, however, stand out from the rest in having clear indications of relatively high status, and each was free from the constraints of being a customary tenement. The substantial U-shaped farmhouse at The Grange was built in the mid- to late 17th century, and is recorded in the survey of 1739 as 'the farthest house in the parish, late Averys' held by John Barratt. It appears to have comprised an amalgamation of two customary tenements – the halfyardland called Folletts (42a 3r) and the yardland called Coles (53a) recorded in the survey of 1567 – but which were sold off in the late 16th century (BRO 04241, 04235; PRO PROB 11/62/f239; SRO DD/BK 2(6)8–10); in the tithe survey it comprised 104 acres. Doubleton Farm appears to have originated as a three-room cross-passage house, but developed into a wealthy dwelling in the 16th–17th centuries with the addition of a substantial rear kitchen block and then a further wing to create a building with at least the appearance of a U-shaped house. Unfortunately nothing is known of its early history although in 1812 Bennett described it as a 'capital freehold mansion', and in the tithe survey it held 82 acres of land. The third building of considerable status which had a U-shaped plan with two rear wings by the 17th century is Puxton Moor Farm. It is unfortunately also poorly documented, lying outside the manor of Puxton by the 18th century.

The late medieval/16th-century three-room cross-passage houses were mostly associated with substantial landholdings of around 40 acres (a customary halfyardland) or more. In the tithe survey Brimbleworth Farm held 42 acres, and the earliest reference is in 1661 when a 'messuage, close, one rod Old Auster and 40 acres of land (20 of which were arable) at Puttingworth' was a customary tenement of Banwell manor (WCL 10189, p.17). Landhouse Farm (in 1840) and Laurel Farm (since at least 1642) in Rolstone, and Appleton Farm (since at least 1738), Hippisleys Farm and Hodders Farm (both in 1840) were also associated with landholdings of *c* 40 acres. Larger holdings were seen at Rolstone Court (an amalgamation sometime before 1642 of 'Latches' tenement (31 acres) with the roofless tenement called 'Hatchouse' (27 acres) (WRO 2667/23/44[4]), The Cedars (96 acres from at least 1738), Chestnut Farm (*c* 90 acres in 1567), and Sluice Farm (58 acres from at latest 1777). Boxbush Farm lay outside the manor of Rolstone

Table 8.6 The landholdings associated with standing buildings that have been surveyed

MANOR and tenement	house structure	customary acres				comment
PUXTON		**1840**	**1770**	**1642**	**mid-C16**	
Appletree Cottage	17th-century single-room cottage	1	2	2		customary tenement
Church House	small 17th-century symmetrical two-room central-passage house	1	6	6		customary tenement
Glebe Cottage	late medieval two- or three-room cross-passage house	21	–	22		parsonage
Mays Green Farm	small 17th-century symmetrical two-room central-passage house	7	8			customary tenement
Myrtle Farm	larger 17th-century symmetrical two-room central-passage house	10	28	16	15	customary tenement
Old Chestnut Farm	small 17th-century symmetrical two-room central-passage house	38	9	10	10	customary tenement
Puxton Court	19th-century double pile house	56	48	40½	40½	customary tenement
Puxton Moor Farm	?17th-century U-shaped farmhouse	22	12	59?		formerly part of the demesne?
ROLSTONE		**1840**	**1770**	**1651**		
Boxbush Farm	late medieval–early 16th-century three-room cross-passage house with open hall	33				freehold tenement?
Gout House Farm	late medieval–early 16th-century three-room cross-passage house with open hall	24				freehold tenement?
Land House	late medieval–early 17th-century three-room cross-passage house	40				freehold tenement?
Laurel Farm	?late medieval–early 17th-century three-room cross-passage house	38	44	42		customary tenement
Rolstone Court	late medieval–early 17th-century three-room cross-passage house	101	66	66		customary tenement comprising two earlier tenements
Stuntree Farm	17th-century three-room axial-passage house	22	24	50		customary tenement that was broken up in the 18th century
The Poplars	18th-century symmetrical two-room central-passage house	10				freehold tenement?
BANWELL		**1840**		**1661**		
Brimbleworth Farm	15th-century three-room cross-passage house with open hall	42		40		within manor of Banwell
Doubleton Farm	?late medieval–early 17th-century three-room cross-passage house	82				within manor of Banwell
CONGRESBURY MARSH		**1840**	**1770**	**1739**	**1567**	
Chestnut Farm	late medieval–early 17th-century three-room cross-passage house	140	*	*	90	customary tenement (yardland)
Palmers Elm Farm		38	48	48	48	customary tenement (half yardland)
Pool Farm	17th-century symmetrical two-room central-passage house	39	43	43	41	customary tenement (half yardland)
The Grange	17th-century U-shaped farmhouse	109	*	90	42	customary tenement (half yardland)
The Oaks	17th-century symmetrical two-room central-passage house	48			71	customary tenement (half yardland)

* property identifiable as a fee farm rent, but no acreage given

(table continued)

Table 8.6 (*cont.*) The landholdings associated with standing buildings that have been surveyed

MANOR and tenement	house structure	customary acres				comment
WICK ST LAWRENCE		**1840**	**1770**	**1738**	**1567**	
Appleton Farm	?late medieval–early 17th-century three-room cross-passage house derived from single room structure	42		49	40	customary tenement
Baytree Farm	17th- to 18th-century two-room cottage	38			32	sold off in late 16th century
Castle Cottages	late medieval–early 17th-century three-room cross-passage house	38			21	Dean and Chapter
Gervinia Cottages	17th-century symmetrical two-room central-passage house	8				Dean and Chapter
Icelton Farm	17th-century symmetrical two-room central-passage house	80		97	88	customary tenement
The Cedars	?late medieval–early 17th-century three-room cross-passage house	146		96	85	customary tenement
Sluice Farm	? late medieval–early 17th-century three-room cross-passage house	70	58		?72	sold off in late 16th century
Hippsleys Farm	?late medieval–early 17th-century three-room cross-passage house	40			?16	sold off in late 16th century
Hodders Farm	late medieval–early 17th-century three-room cross-passage house derived from single room structure	41				sold off in late 16th century
Court Farm	19th-century house incorporating earlier fabric	36				sold off in late 16th century
Manor Farm	17th-century three-room axial-passage house	20			?19	sold off in late 16th century
Willow Farm	17th-century three-room axial-passage house	0				sold off in late 16th century

Figure 8.6 Puxton church, from the south

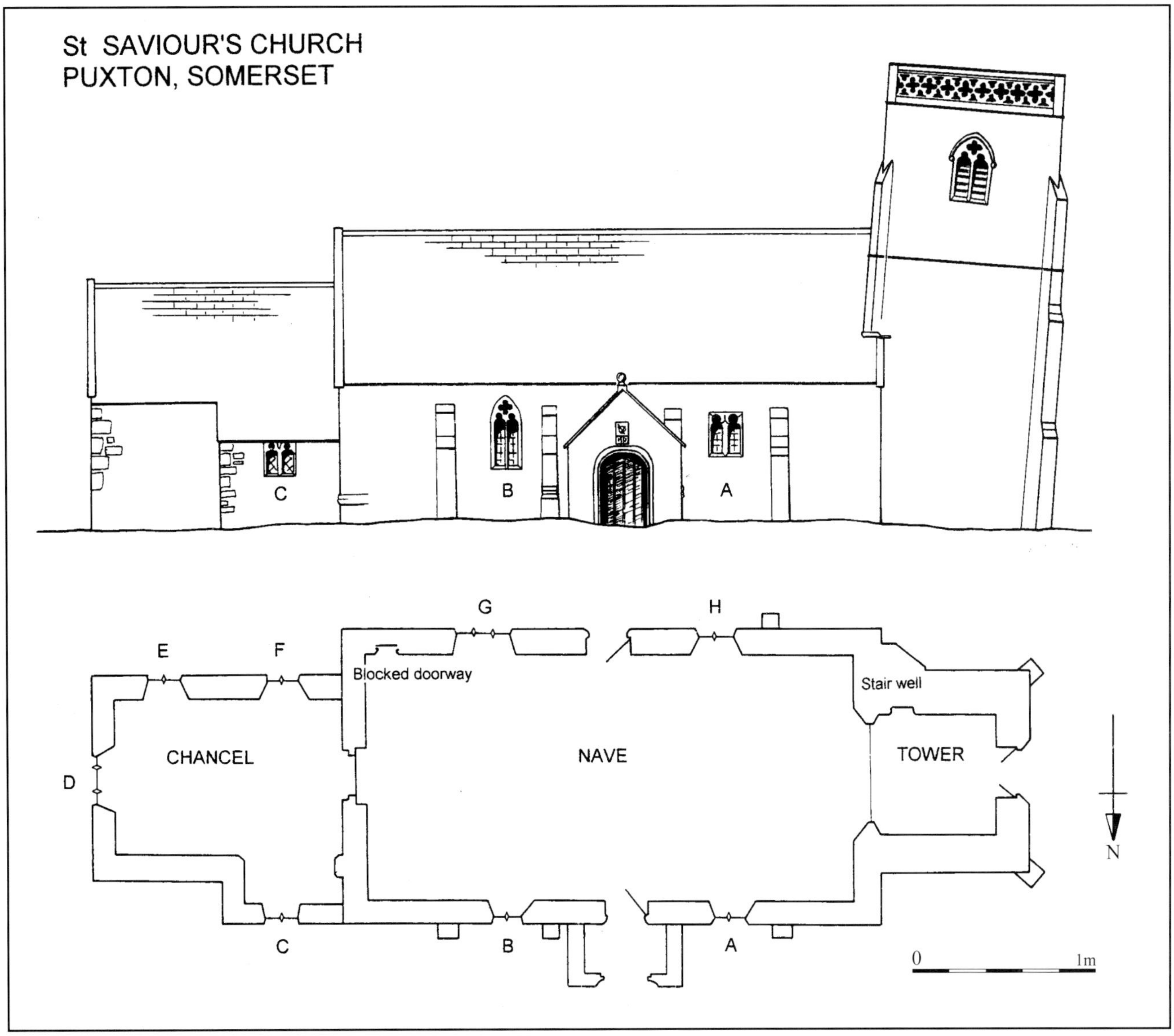

Figure 8.7 Plan and elevation of Puxton church (drawn by Colin Humphreys)

and in the tithe survey held 33 acres, while all that can be said of Gout House Farm is that in the tithe survey it held 24 acres of land.

The 17th-century two- and three-roomed houses (averaging 12 to 14m long) were smaller than their three-roomed cross-passage predecessors (averaging about 17 to 18m in length) though there is some relationship between their size and the extent of the tenement's landholding. Myrtle Farm is at the smaller end of the size range (at 12.2m long) and in 1567 and 1642 held just 15–16 acres (growing to 28 acres by 1755); Pool Farm, with 41 acres in 1567, was also 12.2m long, whereas The Oaks held 71 acres in 1567 and was 13.7m long. It would appear, therefore, that although the new 17th-century houses were significantly smaller than their late medieval predecessors, their size does generally reflect the landed wealth of their occupiers. The smaller two-roomed central-passage houses were certainly associated with far smaller landholdings, such as Old Chestnut Farm which from 1567 to the late 18th century held just 10 acres of land, and Church House which held just 6 acres from at least 1642.

The church of the Holy Saviour, Puxton

The first standing building to be recorded as part of the NSLP was Puxton church (Fig 8.6), with a measured plan and elevation drawn up by Colin Humphreys in 1998 (Fig 8.7). At that time there was no access to the roof space, which was concealed behind a ceiling, though in 2003 the church was declared redundant and taken into the care of the Churches Conservation Trust. During the subsequent repairs, further recording was undertaken by Richard Parker of Exeter Archaeology, and this included the opportunity to examine the roof space.

The documentary evidence

In 1174 x 91 Henry Tortmanus granted his chapel of 'Wringmareis' to Bruton Priory (*Bruton* No. 134; and see *Bruton* No. 135, p.241n), which can almost certainly be identified at Puxton as in *c* 1215 the parson of Congresbury confessed that he had no right in the chapel of 'Pokereleston' and sought a pardon from the Prior of Bruton (*Bruton* No. 135). Puxton was a chapelry of Banwell, whose church was also held by Bruton Priory, and in 1291 the *Taxatio Ecclesiasticus* records the church of Banwell with a chapel as worth £31 6s 8d (and see *Shrewsbury*, No. 599; *Bekynton* Nos 187 and 1522; *Stillington*, No. 128). In 1536 the *Valor Ecclesiasticus* records that William Webbe, vicar of Banwell, with the annexed chapel of Puxton, was owned by Abbey and Convent of Bruton, and was worth £26 6s net annually. In 1539 the church and cemetery at Puxton was consecrated and dedicated to St Saviour, by William Fynch, the first and last bishop of Taunton (*Knyght*, No. 584), but it remained a chapel of Banwell and in 1542 the Crown endowed the Dean and Chapter of Bristol Cathedral with the Rectory of Banwell (with the chapels of Churchill and Puxton with their lands, tithes etc), and it is from this date that the parish registers begin. The Dean and Chapter leased this estate to Edith Payne (of Bristol), including the 'chapel of Puxton and Balls Barn, with all their lands, tithes etc, that were parcel of the rectory of Banwell, at a yearly rent of £12 13s 4d' (PRO REQ2/226/13). In 1654 is it specified that Balls Barn was the tithe barn for Puxton, though curiously it was located in Rolstone in field PxTM 194 (Balls Barn)[11] which, like the Puxton glebe, lay outside the manors of Puxton and Rolstone (PRO E134/1654/Mich 16). In 1772 the parish of Puxton was created out of Banwell (Collinson 1791, 599; Knight 1902, 215).

The standing structure *by Richard Parker*

General description

The church stands in a small churchyard to the south of the main road through Puxton village and is approached from the north. The church is of particular interest as it was only partially restored in the 19th century and the interior retains the character and furnishings typical of a pre-ecclesiological Anglican village church. It is a small three-cell structure consisting of a chancel, nave, and western tower, with a small porch at the centre of the north side of the nave. The nave and the tower are both rendered, except for the dressings of windows and buttresses, and the character of the stonework is obscured. The chancel was thoroughly restored in the 19th century and the stonework of this part of the building has been exposed.

Exterior: chancel

This part of the church is constructed of randomly coursed squared limestone rubble, with dressings of the same material, under a steeply pitched slate roof. On the north side of the chancel an extension has been added in the 19th century for an organ chamber or vestry and much of the medieval north wall has consequently been removed or obscured, though an engraving of 1804 (B G 1804) shows that it originally had a door on the north side. The east window of the chancel is of three lights with cusped trefoil heads and rather crude reticulated tracery with cusps only in the upper sections of the lights. The chamfers of the mullions do not die into the chamfered sill but are abruptly 'stopped' with square blocks at the base. The window may be late medieval in date or, as it is rather clumsy in appearance, it may be a post-Reformation repair replicating an earlier window of similar form. There are two windows in the south wall, both square-headed and of two lights with trefoil heads and sunk spandrels. The eastern window is larger and has been restored in the 19th century, the head of the window having been renewed and a moulded dripstone with pronounced square terminals added. The western of the two windows is smaller and without a dripstone. Its mullions are chamfered and stopped in the same abrupt way as the east window of the chancel. This window may be of 15th- or early 16th-century date. The extension to the north of the chancel is lit by a 19th-century two-light window with dressings of Bath stone.

Exterior: nave

The nave is wider and taller than the chancel, and is covered by a steeply pitched slate roof of 19th- or early 20th-century date, which overlies an earlier roof structure. On the east wall of the nave there are traces of a chamfered plinth and a moulded string-course clasping the east end but, unusually, these are not continued further west. It is possible that the plinth and string-course have been cut back flush with the wall when the nave was rendered, or that the rest of the nave has been rebuilt, retaining only part of the east wall. Unfortunately any evidence for the plinth or string-course is concealed by the presence of the render.

The south side of the nave has a central doorway flanked by two windows. The eastern window has an arched head and three lights with very crude, uncusped reticulated tracery. The tracery incorporates four-centred and round-headed arches with simply chamfered mullions and tracery bars; only one of the mullions is 'stopped' in the manner described above. This window is probably of late 16th- or 17th-century date, though it may replicate an earlier window. The doorway between the windows has a two-centred arch with chamfered dressings and no dripstone. To the west of the doorway is a two-light window with elaborately moulded jambs and

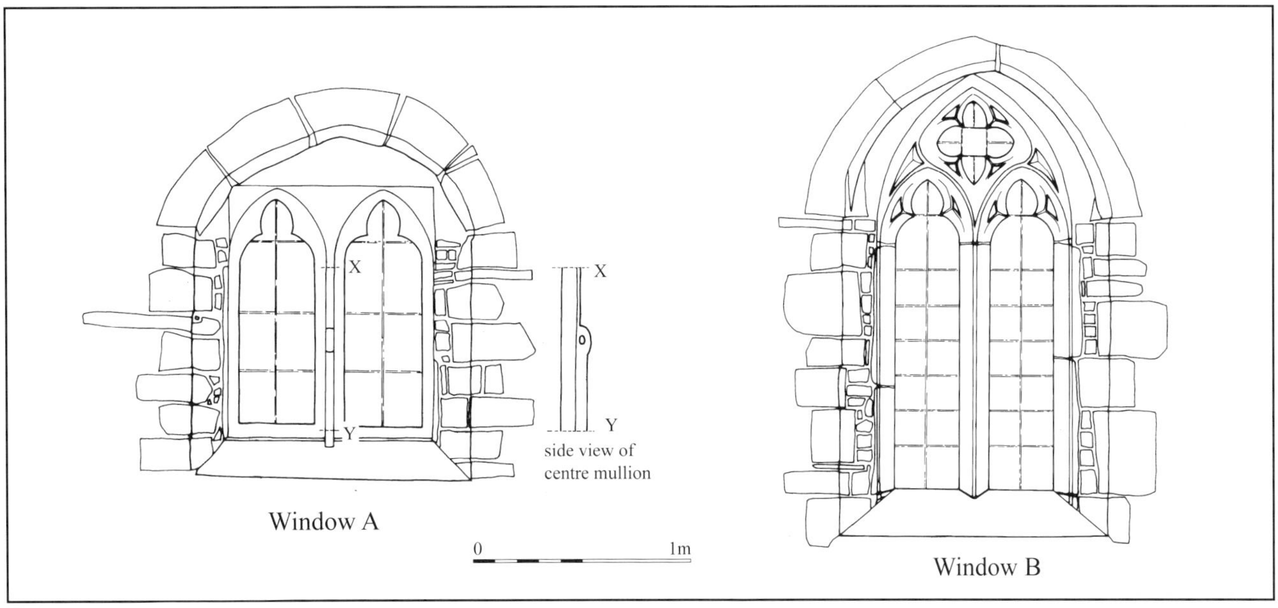

Figure 8.8 Interior views of the two windows in the north wall of the nave (drawn by Colin Humphreys)

mullions, cusped, trefoiled heads to each light and pierced spandrels. The window is square-headed and has a moulded dripstone. Although the mouldings of the mullions are rich and complex these are still stopped at the base like those of the chancel window. This window is of high quality and may date from the 15th or early 16th century. Adjoining this window is a single buttress with two offsets and no plinth.

The north side of the nave has five bays defined by four buttresses, each with two offsets, one of which is now partly embedded in the porch. These buttresses are not identical; the central pair of buttresses has more elaborate offsets and deep mouldings at plinth level, which are entirely absent in the eastern and western buttresses. The mouldings of these plinths do not match those of the east end of the nave and there are no buttresses at the angles. In the second bay from the east is a two-light window with trefoil-headed lights and an ogee quatrefoil above (Fig 8.8, window B). The tracery is flowing and the lights are very slightly ogee in form. The mullions and tracery bars are chamfered, and the mullions die away into the chamfered sill. There is no dripstone over this window, which probably dates from the 14th century. The third bay from the east contains the main doorway. This has a chamfered, triangular-headed four-centred arch and retains an early door. The doorway is covered by a small projecting porch, with benches on either side, and is entered by a richly moulded opening with a true four-centred arch under a gable with copings and a ball finial. The roof of the porch is ceiled and could not be examined. Above the porch doorway is a carved coat of arms, said to be of the St Loe family who held Puxton from the 15th century to 1563 (Knight 1902, 216), and which has been added rather crudely to a second stone bearing the date '1557'. The raised stone frames of these two elements do not match each other and it is possible that one or other has been reused from elsewhere and reset here. This porch covers one of the buttresses and must be a later addition to the church. To the west of the porch, the fourth bay contains a very small two-light window with sharply pointed trefoiled heads to each light (Fig 8.8, window A). This window has no dripstone and the lights are cut in the manner of plate tracery. The window may be of 14th-century date.

Exterior: tower

The tower has a marked and disturbing lean to the west as a result of subsidence. It is a two-stage tower with diagonal buttresses at the corners, each having three offsets. There is a moulded plinth at the base and a string-course defining the belfry stage. On the west elevation is a west door with a moulded two-centred arched head and a dripstone over. Above this is a large, two-light west window with cinquefoil heads to each light and reticulated tracery. This window has a heavy dripstone with head terminals. On the south side of the tower the south-eastern angle is occupied by a polygonal stair turret rising to the roof and lit by small rectangular windows. The tower chamber is also lit by a plain rectangular window in this elevation. On the east face of the tower the tower arch opening to the interior of the church is two-centred and elaborately moulded. Above this arch, within the roof space, are the truncated remains of the weathering of a shallow-pitched roof (see below).

The belfry stage has small two light windows in each face, with trefoil-headed lights surmounted by a cusped quatrefoil, and dripstones with head terminals. The belfry louvres are of oak. The tower is surmounted by an ornamental parapet of pierced, cusped lozenges which varies on each elevation; on the south side the parapet is solid, without

Figure 8.9 Early roof line and graffiti on the eastern side of the church tower, now covered by a steeper pitched roof (and see Fig 8.10 for wider view) (photo by Richard Parker)

ornament, on the east side the quatrefoil centres of each lozenge alone are pierced, the spandrels between each lozenge being carved in the solid. The west side has a central gargoyle draining the roof, and the east side has a grotesque in the same position. Both the southern and eastern parapets may have been rebuilt at different periods. The tower is surmounted by a short, slated spire with a gilded weathercock and historic lead work covered in graffiti. The shallow pitch of the weathering for the nave roof and the Perpendicular character of the tracery in the west and belfry windows suggests that the tower is late medieval, perhaps of 15th-century date.

Interior

The chancel arch is more elaborately moulded than the tower arch and appears to incorporate a low stone wall with an embattled or brattished cornice. This may represent the base of a rood screen. Evidence of a rood stair survives in the form of a blocked doorway in the south wall immediately to the west of the chancel arch and, most unusually, evidence of the supporting beam and parapet wall of the rood loft itself may be observed in the form of timbers embedded in the southern and northern walls.

The chancel was thoroughly restored in the late 19th century. The roof has been entirely renewed with an open roof of common-rafter trusses consisting of A-frames with ashlar pieces and extra braces at the collar, giving the roof a seven-sided form instead of the wagon or cradle shape common in West Country churches. It is unknown whether or not this roof replicates the earlier roof of the chancel. A tie-beam crosses the centre of the chancel and appears to be contemporary with the roof. There is a wide arched opening through the north wall into the extension on the north side and good furnishings of the same period.

The nave roof is currently ceiled just above its junction with the walls in all except the eastern bay, where the ceiling has been removed and replaced at a higher level in order to expose the top of the chancel arch. This modification appears to have been made in the 20th century. The east wall above this ceiling has been stripped, possibly when the modifications to the ceiling were made, removing any evidence of wall paintings. The west wall of the nave, between the tower arch and the weathering of the earlier roof, retains its wall plaster, and this bears traces of graffiti, written in a red pigment in an ornate, curling script. The graffiti appear to consist of a series of initials or personal names (Fig 8.9).

Figure 8.10 Roof structure within Puxton church, now obscured by a ceiling (photo by Richard Parker)

Nave roof

The present roof of the nave replaces an earlier roof with a much shallower pitch, for which the weathering remains on the east wall of the tower (Fig 8.9). The weathering fixes the height of the ridge at a point considerably lower than the present ridge and, most unusually, if the slope of each plane of the roof is continued outwards, it also fixes the height of the eaves of the earlier roof higher than the present eaves level by at least a metre. Until the present roof was constructed, the nave walls therefore seem to have been considerably taller.

The roof is supported by four trusses with chamfered feet that are visible below the level of the later ceiling and are embedded in the wall tops. The trusses divide the nave into five bays which terminate at each end with the east and west walls of the nave; there are no end trusses. This is reflected in the arrangement of the buttresses of the north wall, which may suggest that the wall was extensively rebuilt when the roof was added. Each truss consists of a pair of principal rafters butted together with a vertical joint at the apex. The principal rafters are linked by a cambered collar beam that is tenoned into the principals and secured at each end by two pegs. The principals are chamfered from the point where they emerge from the nave walls to a point just below collar level, where the chamfers end in run-out stops. The collars and principals above this are square-sectioned and without mouldings.

Each principal rafter is pierced with mortices to receive three levels of purlins and there is a diagonally set ridge tree at the apex. The purlins are all chamfered, and at the ends of each purlin the chamfers are stopped with diagonally cut stops. The ends of the purlins are housed in the faces of the principals, and their tenons are staggered within the joint and pegged from above. The lowest, or first, level of purlins serves visually as a wall plate, appearing immediately above the wall top. Between the second and third levels of purlins are pairs of curved, chamfered wind braces rising from sockets in the sides of the principal rafters to meet the third purlin at the centre of each bay. Oddly, the eastern and western bays have only a single wind brace on each side, even though these bays are of similar dimensions. This is perhaps a consequence of the absence of proper trusses against the east and west walls.

Many original common rafters survive on both sides of the roof. These are most interesting, since their lower sections, between the first and second purlins, are heavily marked with nail holes showing that they were formerly concealed by boards or lath and plaster. These nail holes do not continue above the second purlin and the feet of the principals and the lower purlins were unmarked by nails. No evidence of an earlier flat ceiling across the church at this level could be discerned; neither was there any evidence of plastering between the common rafters in the upper parts of the roof. It is evident that, although the lower sections of each bay were either plastered or boarded over, the decorative curved wind braces and the common rafters above this point were exposed. This is a most unusual combination of an open roof with limited ceiling, and may have been designed to display decorative painting on the lower panels. It is possible that some parts of the early ceiling plaster or boards may survive above the present ceiling in the canted areas near the wall tops.

No decorative painting, carpenters' assembly marks or numbering were observed on the roof structure, although these may conceivably have perished due to the decay of the timbers. Many of the roof timbers are so damaged that they have lost their original surfaces and any integrity in their joints, with the result that they are pulling from their sockets. This may be the result of many centuries of beetle damage or water penetration, unchecked because it was invisible from below due to the inserted ceiling. Alternatively it may be due to the quality of the materials employed. Some of the timbers are very pale, almost white in colour, and with a very tortuous pattern to the grain suggesting elm rather than oak. It is possible that a variety of different woods was employed that were not all equally durable.

The roof has been extensively braced and repaired at several different periods. Additional timber collars have been added to the trusses and the common rafters have been doubled up. These repairs may have been carried out at the time the ceiling was inserted, since they imply that the roof structure was no longer visible from within the church. Later repairs have involved the addition of iron straps and ties to support and reinforce failing joints. No. attempt to replace or renew any missing timbers appears to have been made, and the additional ironwork is relatively discreet. The present slate roof rests on additional common rafters forming a second roof overlying the earlier roof timbers but augmenting rather than replacing them. This suggests that the nave was in fact restored in the late 19th or early 20th century, in a manner highly sensitive to the historic structure. One of the nave benches is marked '1907' in paint at the end where it normally butts against the nave wall, which may provide a clue as to the date of this restoration.

Nave ceiling

The present ceiling of the nave is suspended from long, ovolo-moulded beams bolted to the feet of the earlier principal rafters. These beams run across the nave slightly above the level of the lower purlins and are generally fixed to the east side of the principals. In order to clasp the principals from both sides, additional curving timbers or cleats have been added to each beam and all three timbers firmly bolted together. The bolts are secured in a very distinctive way. The rod of each bolt was either pierced or bent round upon itself, to form a slot at the end of the rod. A circular washer was then threaded onto the rod, and a triangular metal wedge driven through the slot, tightening the washer against the face of the timber. It is uncertain whether the cleats are contemporary with the ceiling, or whether they were added at a later date to reinforce the ceiling beams.

The ceiling is supported on large cleft laths nailed to the underside of deep plank joists running from beam to beam and secured in position with large iron nails or spikes. The ends of the joists are staggered in each bay, and are cut in a concave form, reducing the depth of timber through which the spikes are driven. The character of the ovolo mouldings on the underside of the beams and of the iron fastenings of the beams and joists suggests that the ceiling was inserted during the 17th century. It is possible that the ceiling was added in order to permit a painted decorative scheme on the underside of the ceiling.

Bell chamber

The bell chamber is approached by the newel stair within the stair turret at the south-eastern corner of the tower and is at the third level of the tower. The bell chamber has been abandoned, possibly as a result of concern for the safety of the tower, and the only bell now present hangs below the belfry, from a steel girder that was probably added in the 20th century. In 1871 two bells remained. One bore the inscription: 'Johannes O Vocabitur' and may have been medieval (after the Reformation bells ceased to bear the names of saints), while the other was inscribed 'Henrey Hoskens Churchwarden. 1680. I P I P' (Ellacombe 1874, 159). These are said to have been the first and fifth in the original peel of bells (Bennett 1804, 201). It was not possible to inspect the existing bell due to the unstable condition of the floor but it may be either one of these bells, or a later recasting.

The bell frame has escaped modern repair and reinforcement, and survives almost intact. It is designed to hold two bells, and is massively constructed and held together by wooden pegs. The frame consists of three upright trusses, each with a sill beam and a central post jowling outwards slightly at the head on each face. The posts are braced by massive diagonal struts, each notched on the flank to receive a purlin (now missing) that served to keep the three trusses upright and apart. Above the central post in each truss is a horizontal beam that took the bearings for the headstocks. These beams are thickened at the centre by a raised area with curved ends and have a central notch for the bearing. The beams have notched ends and may not originally have run the full width of the belfry; they have been extended by more recent timbers to meet the eastern and western walls of the tower, and there are additional horizontal and diagonal braces.

The bell frame is also buttressed by a diagonal brace on the south side of the tower. The whole structure rests upon four large beams running from north to south over which the three trusses run from east to west. The eastern foot of each truss is linked to the other trusses by a further horizontal beam that rests upon them. It is possible that this bell frame is contemporary with the tower, and it may well have been installed in the 15th century.

Tower roof

The roof of the tower is supported by a beam running from north to south across the tower. From this springs a short spire post that is met by hip rafters from each corner of the tower. On each side four or more common rafters rise to support the boarding over which the lead is laid. The basic structure of this roof may well be medieval.

Discussion

Early medieval

The presence of a circular Norman font (Robinson 1914, 106) and the simple plan of the church suggest that the building is of early medieval origin and may contain at least some fabric of this period. No early features have been identified in the present survey though it is possible that evidence of blocked windows or other potentially datable fabric may survive beneath the render covering the walls of the nave. A possible early origin for the church may perhaps be conjectured from the evidence of the redundant roof line on the east wall of the tower. This shows that the earlier (?15th-century) roof was of much shallower pitch than at present and that the walls of the nave were therefore considerably taller. The nave would thus have been very oddly proportioned for an unaisled building, since the nave did not require such height to allow for a clerestory. Unusually high and narrow proportions are characteristic of the main vessels of Saxon churches, such as Bradford-on-Avon in Wiltshire, Bitton in southern Gloucestershire, and Escomb and Monkwearmouth in Co. Durham (Cox and Bradley Ford 1954, 47; Taylor and Taylor 1965, 74; Smith *et al* 1994, 19). The length of the nave (14.6m, 47.9 feet) at Puxton is also is also just under twice its width (7.8m, 25.6 feet), very similar proportions to the second phase church at Cheddar, for example (Taylor 1978, 1033).

13th and 14th century

The earliest fabric now visible is represented by the north windows of the nave, which may be dated on stylistic grounds to the 14th century. The eastern window in the north wall, for example, has a tall, narrow opening and flowing tracery forms incorporating ogee curves. The western window in this wall consists of a group of small lancets and might even be of late 13th-century date.

15th century

The remaining windows of the nave and chancel include some very richly moulded work of the 15th century and other windows of similar, but plainer, character. The tower also appears to be a 15th-century addition. These elements may have formed part of an extensive remodelling of the church incorporating a new and characteristically late medieval low-pitched roof over the nave. This may provide a context for the insertion of the south-western window of the nave and also those on the south side of the chancel. The great variety of size and detail in these windows may not necessarily suggest that they were added at widely differing periods, but possibly that they were given by different individuals or organisations. The western window in the south wall of the nave is particularly splendid and may have been the gift of a wealthy family or parish guild.

The bell frame, tower roof and the possibly medieval bell which formerly hung in the tower may be contemporary with the tower itself, which is probably of 15th-century date. Unfortunately the addition of the tower appears to have had a disastrous effect on the fabric of the church as it began to subside westwards. The subsidence of the tower must have caused severe structural damage to the south and north walls as the west wall separated from the rest of the building. The result may have been the racking and collapse of the roof structure that perhaps necessitated the complete replacement of the roof and possibly also the rebuilding of the walls of the nave.

16th century

The nave appears to have been extensively reconstructed when the roof was rebuilt. The north wall, in particular may have been entirely taken down; the windows may have been reset and the plinth on the east wall is abruptly discontinued. The provision of four buttresses aligning with the trusses of the replacement roof suggests that the rebuilding of the wall and the roof are contemporary. The eaves level was substantially lowered, perhaps to reduce the weight and increase the stability of the wall. The buttresses flanking the main doorway were given particularly ornate plinths and the main doorway has a flattened, angular head that is probably of 16th-century date. Similar arches were used in the rebuilding of the western range of the cloister at Cleeve Abbey by Abbot Dovell in the 1530s (Gilyard Beer 1990, 11). The porch is clearly a later addition to the nave.

The south wall of the church has only one buttress at its western end and it is possible that more early fabric has survived within this wall. Its eastern end in particular may not have been badly affected by the subsiding tower. However, the eaves were reduced to the same level as on the north side and the lack of a plinth continuing from the east wall may show that the wall has also been disturbed.

The new roof of the church has no arch braces and is based upon simple A-frames, with a diagonally set ridge. The decorative qualities of this roof were provided by curved wind braces and layers of chamfered and stopped purlins. Unusually, the lowest level of each bay appears to have been plastered or boarded over; this seems to have been an original feature, since the wind braces do not spring from the level of the wall tops but from the second level of purlins. There is no evidence of ceiling in any other part of the roof and it is suggested here that these areas were intended as a field to display decorative painting. This may have been an economical substitute for the deep and heavily carved cornices, which appeared as a canted first stage above the wall tops in many late medieval roofs, usually in association with tie-beam or hammer-beam roofs. Examples from Somerset include the refectory at Cleeve Abbey, and St Cuthbert's Church at Wells, where the cornices display carved angels. The lack of any end truss is particularly odd considering the structural instability of the tower. Although the roof is slightly stretched and disjointed, the end purlins still reach very close to the wall of the tower and there is no suggestion that they have been lengthened or replaced. This supports the argument that the roof was reconstructed as a consequence of the subsidence of the tower, and suggests that the tower has not moved westward very far since the roof was constructed.

The dating of the roof is particularly difficult. There is nothing in the character of the carpentry to distinguish it from medieval constructional techniques, and it is only unusual in that it resembles a type of roof more often found in domestic than ecclesiastical contexts. It is probable that the roof dates from the 16th century, though whether before or after the Reformation is difficult to say. On balance, the provision for ceiling in the lower parts of the roof, if these areas were intended for painting, suggests that the roof is pre-Reformation in date. The surviving evidence of the rood loft in the north wall of the nave may also imply that the rebuilding of this wall (and therefore the replacement of the roof) preceded the redundancy of such features at the Reformation.

The porch is clearly an addition to the north side of the church and may well have been added in 1557 as announced on the datestone over the entrance. The four-centred entrance arch would be compatible with this date. The obvious context for this phase of work on the structure was its consecration and dedication to St Saviour in 1539.

17th century

At a later period the nave roof was bridged over with ovolo-moulded beams and a flat ceiling was provided. The character of the mouldings and of the joists suggests the late 17th century, and the work may well have been undertaken as part of a re-edification of the church following the Commonwealth. The ceiling may have been intended to display painted decoration, which had become popular, albeit briefly, in both ecclesiastical and domestic contexts at this period.

The date of the destruction of the rood loft is not known, though the window at the eastern end of the south wall of the nave may have been inserted following the destruction of the rood stair, which possibly projected beyond the south wall in a small turret. This window is crudely Gothic, with a clumsiness of detail and absence of cusping in the tracery, suggesting a 17th-century date. This window may represent either a survival of traditional architectural forms or a conscious attempt to evoke medieval architecture for ideological reasons. Similar uncusped medieval tracery dating from the 1660s survives at St Stephen's Church in Exeter. The date of 1680 on the second bell recorded in the 19th century may indicate a phase of alterations to the church at that date, or possibly the completion of a longer campaign of restoration.

18th century

Little evidence for 18th- and early 19th-century repairs was observed during the survey (though the box pews and a reading desk on the southern side of the nave are probably 18th-century in date: Robinson 1914, 105). Structural alterations to the church seem to have been few. These may include the extra timber cleats added to the beams in the 17th-century nave ceiling, which are secured by unusual metal fixings. It is uncertain whether these cleats are additions, although they are crude in relation to the ovolo-moulded beams. It has not been possible to establish the nature of the earlier fixings and it is unclear whether the existing bolts augment or replace earlier spikes or pegs. Additional collar beams were also added to the roof and the common rafters were augmented with additional timbers, perhaps during an 18th-century campaign of repairs and reroofing.

19th and 20th century

The church was visited in 1825 by the Bishop of Bath and Wells, who ordered repairs which were carried out in the same year (SRO DD/SAS G/1740 1/1/7). Robinson (1914, 106) states that the chancel was rebuilt around 'thirty years ago' (ie in the 1880s), though probably on the same plan (based on an engraving of 1801: Bennett 1804, 201; Robinson 1914, 106). The chancel had been in a bad condition for some time as in 1736 presentments of the churchwardens at the visitations of the Dean and Chapter of the Cathedral Church of Bristol record 'All well saving that we present that the windows of the chancell of the said parish church and all the porch of the parish church are out of repair' (SRO D/D/Pbc 7). The open common-rafter roof and the extension to its north side also date to the late 19th century. Although the initial impression is of a rather heavy handed restoration, close examination shows that the repairs to the windows involved piecemeal repair rather than wholesale replacement, and that no attempt was made to impose a uniform style upon the building or return it to an 'ideal' period. The architect and date of this restoration is not known. It may have been intended to restore the nave also, but this seems to have been delayed, possibly as a result of the cost implications or due to uncertainty over the stability of the tower.

The nave may have been restored in 1907 (as is implied by the date scrawled on the end of a nave pew), by which time fashions had changed, and an appreciation of post-Reformation furnishings such as those surviving at Puxton had developed, inspired by the conservative philosophy of the Society for the Protection of Ancient Buildings. The repairs to the nave roof at this period involved the insertion of iron straps to hold the failing structure together, and the erection of a new roof over and above the original timbers.

Notes

1 In tracing the tenement in Congresbury and Wick the following research by Gill Bedingfield used the surveys of 1567, 1593, 1596, 1646/47, 1656, 1700 and 1738, the rentals of 1748 and 1771, the 'bargain books' (lease books) for 1604–20 and 1634–1789, and miscellaneous deeds.

2 *Acus* may be translated as pen/point (Latham 1980, 6), and a field-named 'Pen' occurs in the tithe survey to the east of the field named Freemans (PxTM 170). Both these fields are shown on the *c* 1770 map as lying outside the manor and in the possession of George Hardwick, and the *c* 1795 rental shows this freehold in the possession of George Hardwick 'late Kings'. In 1718 John and Sarah King held 'all that messuage or tenements wherein John Prattant and Agnes his wife formerly dwelt and wherein one John White as tenant to said John King then dwelt in Puxton with all outhouses buildings courts yards backsides gardens orchards and hereditaments thereto belonging' that amounted to 58 acres and included closes called Axbridge, Chandlers Mead, Ding, and Freemans all of which can be identified in the tithe survey as the land of Villa Farm (SRO DD/SOG 341, 903).

3 'Yadhays' could mean 'Easthays' (PxTM 192); 'Coxe Channders' may be close to Chandlers Mead (PxTM 187) and Chandlers Grove (PxTM 197), both to the west of Ashfield; 'Chonnehyl' may lie adjacent to Chount Lane (PxTM 219–21?).

4 Doubleton Farm in Rolstone, Glebe Cottage in Puxton, Chestnut Farm, The Grange in Congresbury Marsh and Willow Farm in Bourton (SRO DD/V/AXR).

5 Banksea Cottages in Wick, Brimbleworth Farm in St Georges and Myrtle Farm in Puxton (SRO DD/V/AXR.28.1, 3.1 and 24.4).

6 Appletree Cottage, Gout House Farm, Laurel Farm, Manor Farm, Mays Green Farm, The Cedars.

7 Appleton Farm, Baytree Farm, Boxbush Farm, Church House, Doubleton Farm, Gout House, Hippisleys Farm, Icelton Farm, Landhouse, Pool Farm, Rolstone Court, The Oaks, Stuntree Farm.

8 Glebe Cottage, Castle Cottages (both ends), Hodders Farm, Land House, Mays Green Farm, and The Poplars.

9 Yarborough Cottage in Banwell; Mountain Ash Cottage, Old Farm, and possibly April Cottage in Churchill; Park Farm in Congresbury; Firtree Farm in Nailsea; Greenhill Orchard Cottage and Hale Farm in Winscombe; 24 High Street and Home Farm in Yatton.

10 Hillend Farm, Bowman's Batch and Winthill Cottage in Banwell; Iwood, Poplar Farm, Silver Street House and Urchinwood in Congresbury; Causeway House, Macquarie Farm and Well Cottage in Yatton.

11 A slightly raised rectangular platform in the south west corner of the field, adjacent to Balls Barn Lane and the Balls Yeo, produced a scatter of building stone and medieval pottery when fieldwalked.

9 The evolution of a marshland settlement: Puxton – 'summer dike', village and hamlet

Whilst the NSLP explicitly had the whole landscape as its focus, there was also the need for some site-based work in order to date key features in the relict and historic landscapes, and to obtain comparative palaeoenvironmental and palaeoeconomic assemblages from the different periods of its exploitation, modification, and transformation. This required a strategy of carefully targeted excavations that were focused on three Romano-British relict landscapes at Banwell Moor, Kenn Moor, and Puxton Dolemoor (see Chapter 2), and the medieval shrunken settlement at Puxton. This chapter starts with a detailed examination of the village plan based on its 19th-century morphology, integrated with the results of archaeological survey, documentary research, and standing building recording. The results of survey and excavation in the two of the main areas of shrunken settlement earthworks are then described along with the artefact reports. The palaeoenvironmental and palaeoeconomic assemblages are described in Chapter 10.

The settlement plan in the 19th century

We first have a complete plan of the settlement pattern in eastern Puxton in 1840 and the tithe map shows that it contained a number of key elements (Figs 9.1 and 9.2):

- the oval-shaped Church Field, within the original northern boundary of which lay the church of St Saviour and the tofts of two tenements: PxTM 7 (The Bungalow) and PxTM 6 (Church House).
- the village green, immediately north of Church Field, which was the remnant of a broad area of roadside waste upon which was located the Poor House (PxTM 5) and School (PxTM 9a). The rest of the roadside waste had been enclosed by PxTM 4 (Church View) to the east, and two cottages to the west (PxTM 9 and PxTM 10).
- Puxton Lane runs north from the village green past a triangular-shaped field that was a piece of enclosed roadside waste (The Wash) at junction with Mays Lane. Old Chestnut Farm (PxTM 17) and Myrtle Farm (PxTM 15) lay to the west and Glebe Cottage (PxTM 21) to the east.
- Mays Lane runs west from Puxton Lane towards Mays Green, with a cottage (PxTM 12) on its southern side. For the first *c* 250m it runs almost parallel to the edge of the village green *c* 125m to the south.
- Puxton Lane also runs east from the village green around the eastern side of Church Field, past Appletree Cottage (PxTM 30), and then south through the western end of the recently enclosed Puxton Moor past Goose Acre Farm (PxTM 34), Puxton Moor Farm (PxTM 105), and South Farm (PxTM 95), to Sandford.

Archaeological, documentary, and vernacular buildings survey

Each of the pre-1840 farmhouses and cottages within the present hamlet of Puxton was the subject of archaeological, documentary, and standing building recording alongside a programme of earthwork survey, soil chemistry survey, shovel test pitting, and excavation on a series of deserted sites that in many cases can be identified with roofless (ie abandoned) tenements recorded in the 15th- to 16th-century court rolls. The two main areas of shrunken settlement earthworks were also examined through a series of excavations.

Earthwork survey (Fig 9.3.A)

Earthworks suggestive of deserted settlement, notably slightly raised platforms defined by ditches and areas without gripes, were identified at eight locations around the village. Earthworks directly south of the church are suggestive of a main enclosure containing a building platform towards its north-east corner, with a series of small paddocks to the south and east, all bounded by an substantial ditch to the west (excavated in Trench 2 as F.128: Figs 9.4 and 9.5). Other ditched platforms still survive north of the junction of Puxton Lane and Mays Lane (CoTM 112: Home Ground), and to the north of Goose Acre Farm (PxTM 31 Coles), though a fourth set has been destroyed by modern development but appears on aerial photography from the 1940s (PxTM 25/26: Haynes; Fig 6.1.B). Smaller platforms are located immediately south of Mays Lane in PxTM 12 (Joneses) and PxTM 142 (Flemans), and east of Church Field in PxTM 38 (Butts). Slightly raised areas without gripes in PxTM 39 (Oxlease) and PxTM 93 (Sharps) are also suggestive of former houses.

Fieldwalking (Fig 9.3.B)

Relatively few fields in the immediate vicinity of Puxton were ploughed during the course of this project, though these included Church Field which revealed a discrete concentration of pottery, stone, and other occupation debris in the main enclosure

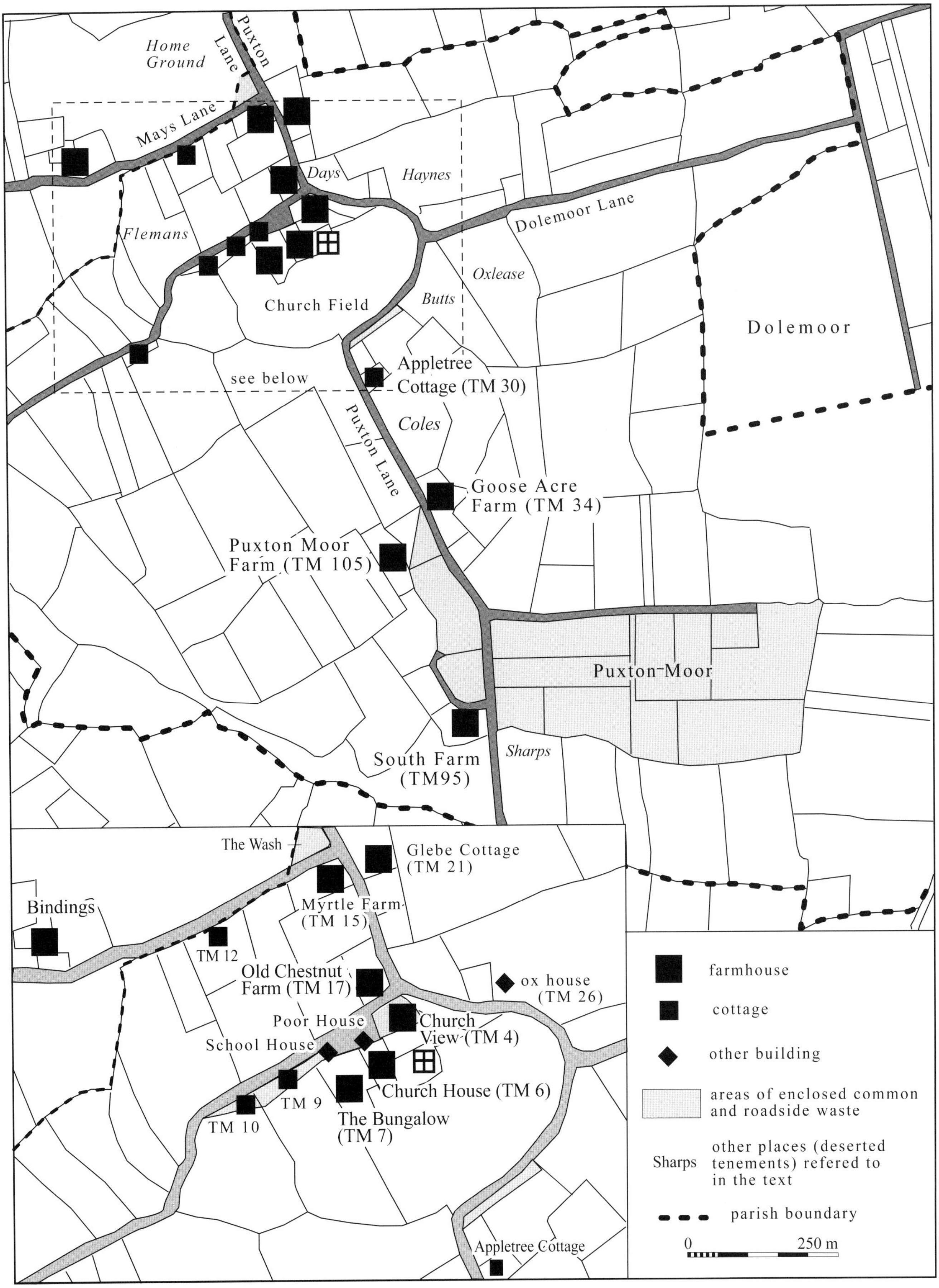

Figure 9.1 Puxton village in 1840 (based on the tithe map), with abandoned tenements (identified through documentary and archaeological research) named in italics

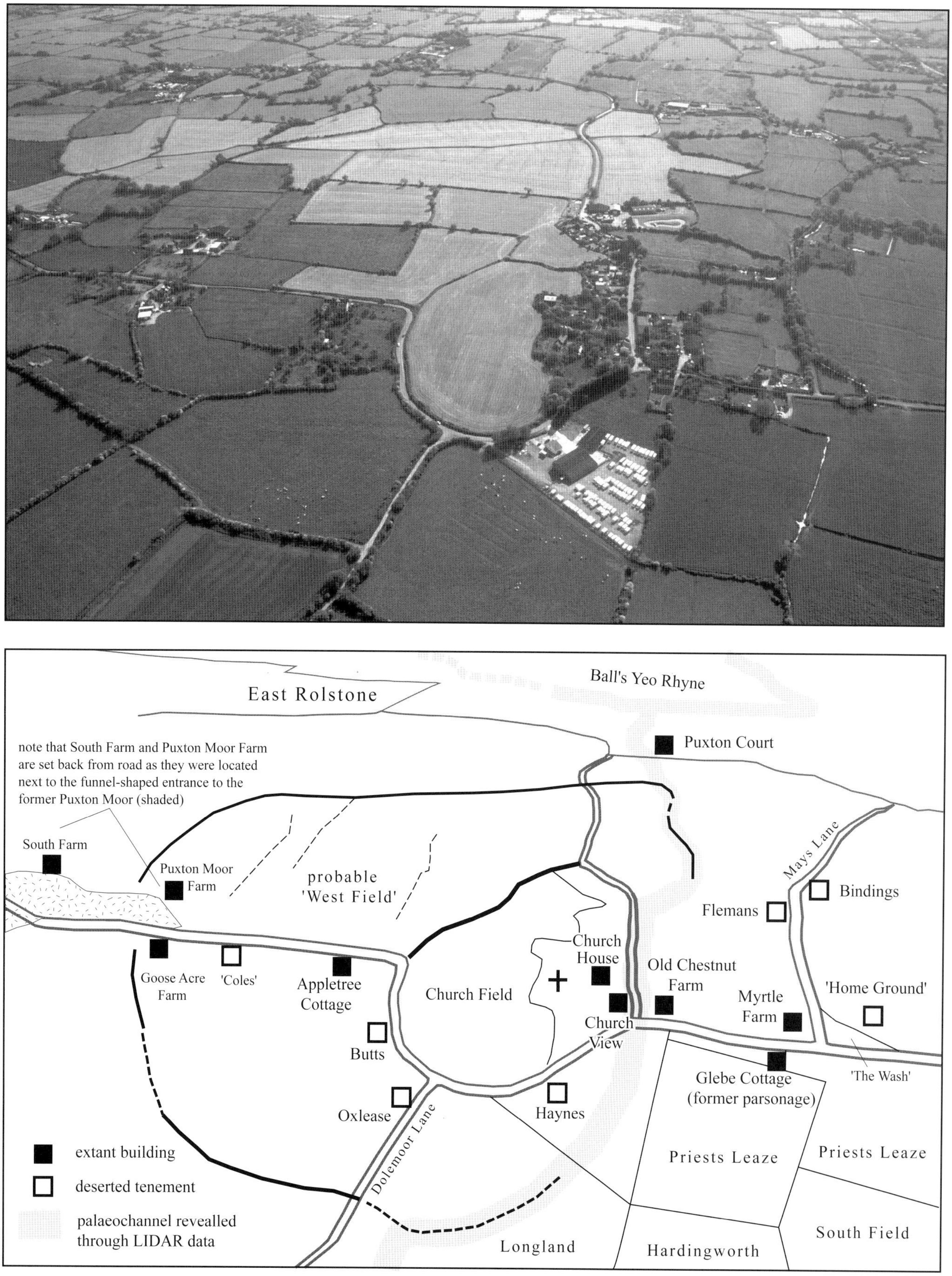

Figure 9.2 Aerial view and interpretation of Puxton from the east, looking towards East Rolstone (top left). A recent LIDAR survey by the Environment Agency reveals that the infield enclosure (Church Field) was constructed to the south of a former creek

immediately south of the church. Several fields down Dolemoor Lane (PxTM 46, 47 and 51), south of Church Field (PxTM 110–11), and to the west of Church Field (PxTM 94, 98–9, 112–14, 116–17, 121–2, 124–7) were also walked and produced nothing more than a manure scatter.

Shovel test pitting (Fig 9.3.B)

A number of fields with potential deserted settlements were under permanent pasture and so alternative means of prospection were required. A series of shovel test pits were excavated in and around suspected deserted farmsteads, confirming medieval occupation on the earthwork platforms at Home Ground (north of Mays Lane), Haynes, Butts, and Coles. Shovel test pits were also dug within the gardens of the recently demolished Bindings Cottage.

Soil chemistry survey (Fig 9.3.B)

A number of fields were subject to soil chemistry survey starting with the deserted sites at Church Field and Home Ground that were used to test the phosphate/heavy metal signature given by areas of known medieval occupation. The methodology and detailed results for Church Field are described in Rippon *et al* 2001. The survey also confirmed abnormally high concentrations on the earthwork platforms in Butts and Oxlease. An extensive survey was also carried out in and around the two fields called Hardingworth (PxTM 43 and 44) because of the suggestion that the '-worth(y)' field-name may be indicative of a deserted settlement (see Chapter 6). A concentration of phosphate and heavy metals was revealed, but upon excavation these proved to be related to a dump of post-medieval debris in the topsoil.

Documentary research

The documentary history of every tenement in Puxton was researched, including those with and without houses as several of the latter proved to be ruinous or roofless tenements, identifiable in the late 15th- to 16th-century court rolls that were later incorporated into other tenements or leased out as accommodation land (Table 9.1).

Standing building recording

In addition to the church, five standing buildings were surveyed as part of the NSLP (Glebe Cottage, Old Chestnut Farm, Church House, Appletree Cottage and Puxton Moor Farm), in addition to Myrtle Farm that had been previously recorded E D H Williams (SRO DD/V/AXR).

The excavations

The programme of earthwork survey, soil chemistry, fieldwalking, and shovel test pitting revealed a series of potential deserted farmsteads, of which a sample was examined through excavation. A key priority was clearly Church Field, as this enclosure appeared to pre-date the formation of the surrounding historic landscape, and also contained the earthworks of a clearly defined enclosure, including a possible building platform, which soil chemistry and fieldwalking suggested contained domestic occupation. Five trenches were therefore positioned across its major elements: Trenches 3 and 11 examined the ditch and bank running around the edge of Church Field, while Trenches 1, 2 and 12 investigated the building platform. The second area selected for excavation was Home Ground to the north of Mays Lane, which, although actually located in Congresbury parish, marks the northernmost expansion of Puxton village. These were by far the best-preserved shrunken settlement earthworks in Puxton, and soil chemistry and shovel test pitting confirmed the presence of domestic occupation that was sectioned in Trenches 4 and 5. The phases of activity were as follows (Phases 1–3 relate to the excavations on Dolemoor):

4 pre-infield enclosure (buried land surface beneath bank around Church Field)
5 construction of bank and ditch around Church Field and features on a different orientation to the historic landscape
6 12th–early 13th century: features within Church Field and Home Ground conforming to the historic landscape (and at Home Ground sealed beneath a later garden soil)
7 later medieval–early post-medieval features related to drainage and agricultural use
8 *c* 17th century: reoccupation of Home Ground
9 *c* 18th–19th century: latest infilling of ditches/gripes at Church Field and Home Ground
10 topsoil.

Excavations in Church Field, 1996 and 1999
(Figs 9.4 to 9.6)

Phases 4 and 5

All of the features excavated at Puxton were cut into estuarine silty clays of the Upper Wentlooge Formation, which also underlay the bank built around the perimeter of Church Field. There is no evidence from the excavations or coring (Fig 3.1) for a bedrock island underlying Puxton. Soil micromorphology in Trench 11 (which sectioned the bank) suggests that it was constructed on the surface of a high intertidal salt marsh (see below).

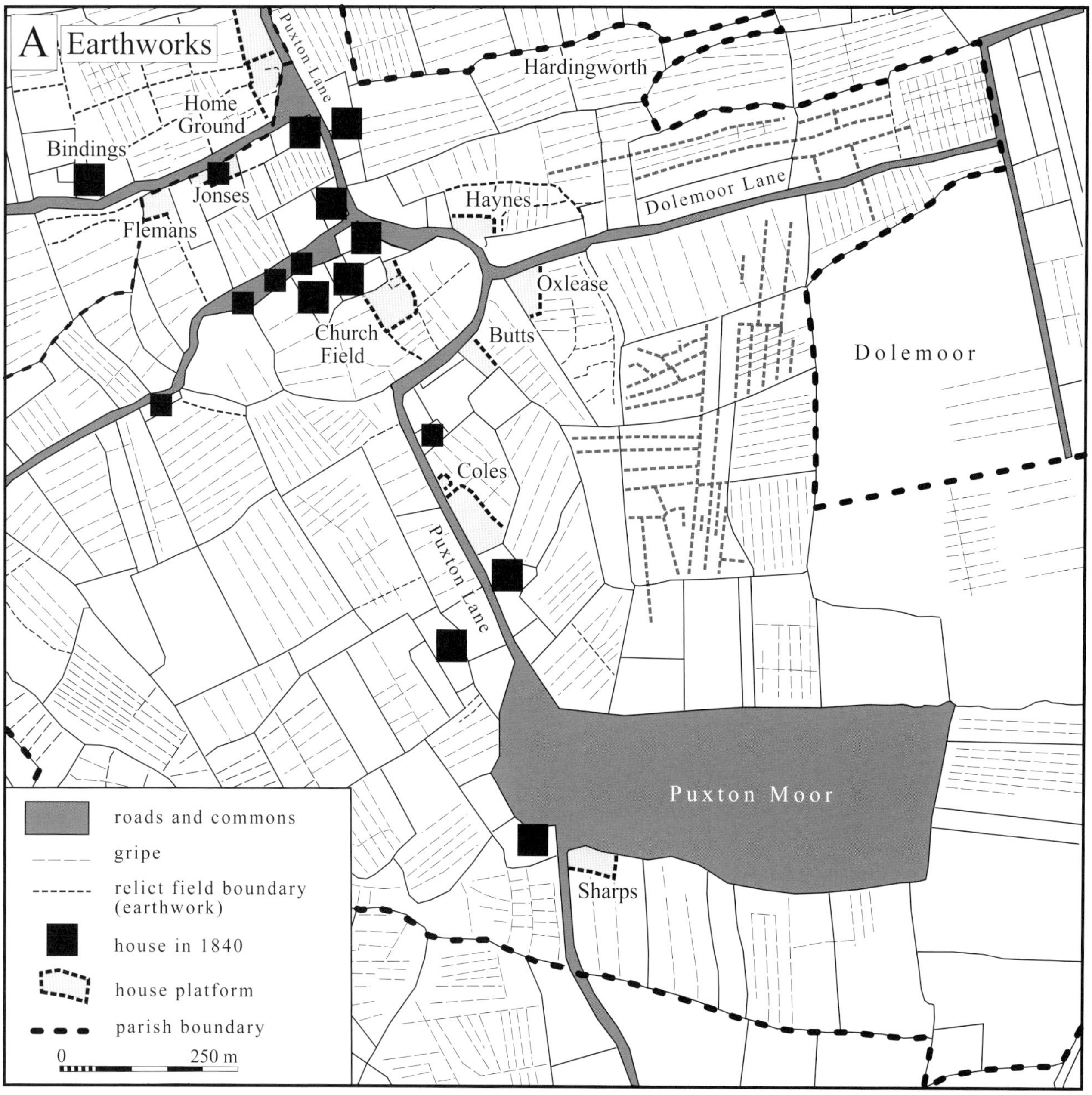

Figure 9.3(A) Archaeological survey around Puxton: earthworks

The enclosure bank (Trench 11)

Historic landscape analysis suggests that the oval-shaped infield enclosure at Church Field is stratigraphically the earliest feature in this area. The earthwork bank that currently runs around the eastern side of Church Field is *c* 11m wide and stands up to 0.4m high, giving a very low, shallow profile. When sectioned in Trench 11 the bank appeared to comprise two components: a *c* 0.25m thick layer of very mottled light blue/brown silty clay (502) overlying a *c* 0.2m thick layer of mottled mid-blue/grey silty clay (503). Layer 503 rested on top of a light blue/grey silty clay with frequent light brown mottles (523), which in the field had the appearance of the natural Upper Wentlooge alluvium, but which soil micromorphology revealed can be sub-divided in two: the upper 0.10m is very similar to 503 and probably represents a zone of mixing between the bank material and the underlying 0.04m of 523 which shows weak horizontal bedding, marked gleying, and some biological reworking indicative of it being the natural Wentlooge alluvium. This in turn overlay a very similar but slightly lighter blue/grey silty clay that microscopically contained even more pronounced bedding and very little biological reworking (context 524). The lower part of 523 appears to represent an immature buried land surface but not a fully developed soil, suggesting that the bank was constructed on the surface of a high salt marsh. Little pollen was preserved, but context 503 produced

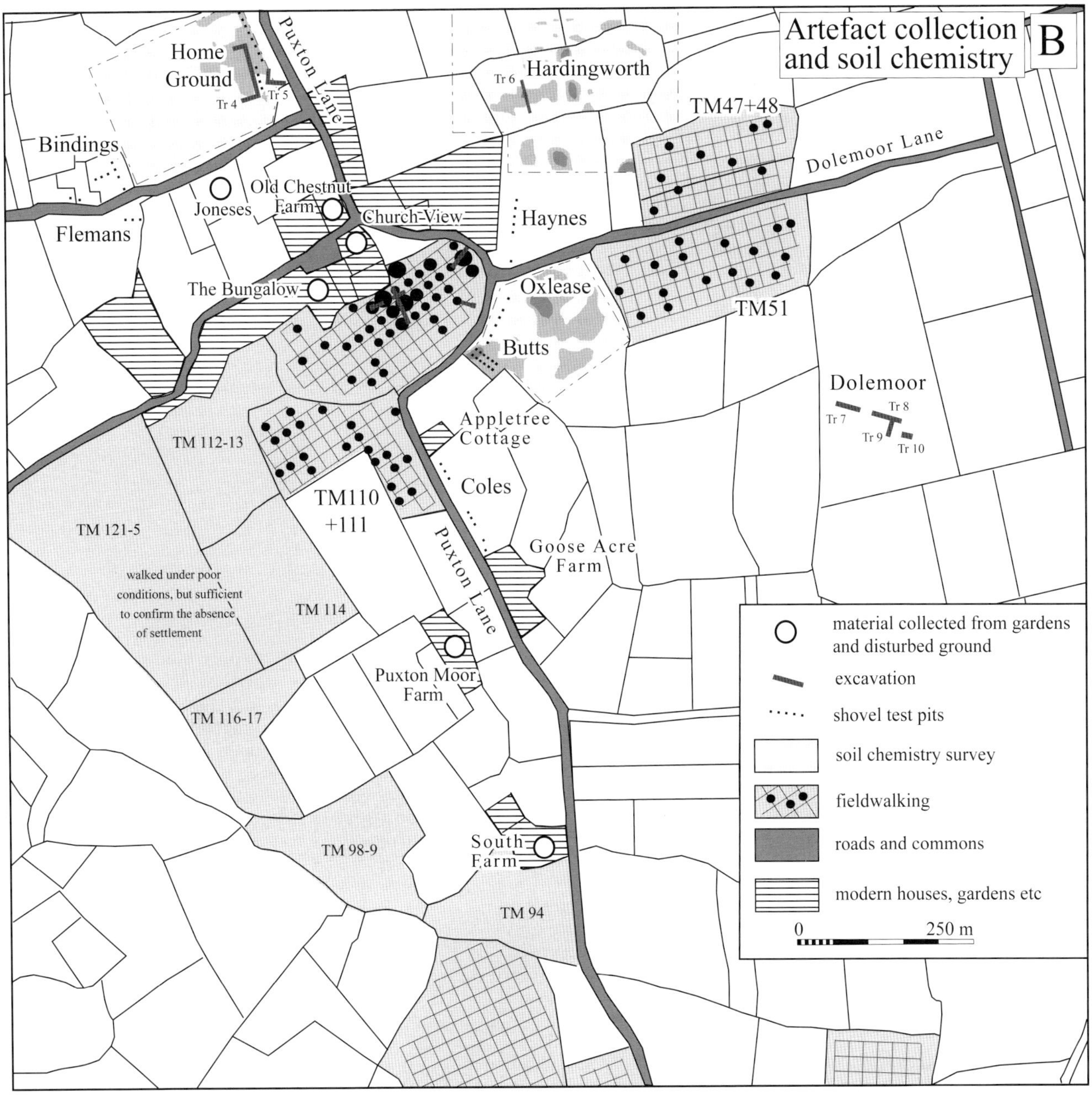

Figure 9.3(B) Archaeological survey around Puxton: fieldwalking, soil chemistry, shovel test pitting, and garden surveys

a small assemblage of plant macrofossils characterised by annual opportunists that are quick to colonise areas of bare ground and include fig-leaved goosefoot (see Jones, Chapter 10).

The only datable material from this trench was a small assemblage of very abraded sherds of Romano-British pottery (see Timby, Chapter 4), and a single late 11th- to 13th-century sherd from the upper (and possibly disturbed) part of the bank (context 502). Fieldwalking in the area, and the topsoil from Trench 11, however, produced a manure scatter of late 11th- to 13th-century pottery and it may be significant that so little of this material came to be incorporated into the bank, suggesting that it was constructed before the manuring of Church Field had commenced.

Soil micromorphology: the buried ground surface beneath the Church Field bank *by J L Heathcote*

At Puxton Church Field a 0.5m monolith sampled the land surface buried beneath the medieval enclosure bank (the methodology is as described in Chapter 3). In the field, the lower make-up of the bank (context 503) did not appear to overlie a buried soil and the principal question was the nature of the local environment at the time the bank was constructed. Two scenarios were possible: that the bank represents an early sea wall or summer dike that was built on the surface of an intertidal marsh, or that it was raised after a sea wall was built elsewhere and represents a land boundary within a landscape that

Table 9.1 Documentary, standing building, and archaeological evidence for farmsteads and cottages in Puxton village

documentary	landholding	standing structure	archaeological	interpretation
Church View (Cambridge's alias Hort's) (PxTM 4)				
customary tenement of *c* 41 acres (Tenement J on map of *c* 1770) that in 1570 was the amalgamation of three tenements, two of which were then roofless ('Coles' and 'Oxlease')	scattered over putative open fields to the west and south of Church Field, along with several closes to the east	very heavily restored (not surveyed in detail): probably 17th/18th-century	13th-century and later pottery was collected from flower-beds	large landholding derived from the consolidation of three tenements, the others probably being at TM 39 'Oxlease' and TM 31 'Coles' (see below); TM 4 itself appears to be an enclosure from the village green
Church House (Barrets) (PxTM 6)				
customary tenement of 6 acres in 1642 (Tenement F on map of *c* 1770)	two parcels in the former common field at Ashfield (TM Nos 205 and 208)	?18th-century two-celled cottage. An inscribed stone just below the chimney bears a date stone inscribed 1786 (Clarke 1980, 2)		house and small landholding carved out of TM 7 (The Bungalow)?
The Bungalow (Simmon's) (PxTM 7)				
customary tenement of 25 acres in *c* 1642 (Tenement K on map of *c* 1770)	the whole of Church Field, part of the putative common field north of Puxton Moor, and a parcel of the putative open field south west of Church Field	demolished (now occupied by modern bungalow)	Clarke (1980, 3) describes occupation debris; pottery includes six sherds of a coarse limestone-tempered fabric (late 10th/11th century?)	typical customary tenement with fields scattered throughout the eastern part of the parish, including the putative open fields
by the Old School House (PxTM 9)				
landless cottage in *c* 1642	none	demolished (site now occupied by modern houses)		landless cottage on area of enclosed roadside waste
north of Babers (PxTM 10)				
post-1642 landless cottage	none	demolished (site now occupied by modern houses)		post-1642 landless cottage on area of enclosed roadside waste
Briarwood (PxTM 123)				
post-*c*1770 cottage, that may lie on the site of a customary tenement of 15 acres deserted after 1569	landless cottage post-*c* 1700; disposition of 15 acres unknown	19th-century cottage (not surveyed)		post-*c* 1770 landless cottage on area of enclosed roadside waste, occupying site of a house that had been deserted between 1569 and *c* 1770
Old Chestnut Farm (PxTM 17)				
customary tenement of 10 acres in 1547 (Tenement M on map of *c* 1770)	scattered over eastern part of Puxton, including in the putative open fields to the west of Puxton church	two-celled house dating from the 17th century, extended to the north and south during the 18th century	large amounts of 12th-/13th-century through to post-medieval pottery collected from flower-beds	typical customary tenement with fields scattered throughout the eastern part of the parish, including the putative open fields

(table continued)

Table 9.1 (*cont.*) Documentary, standing building, and archaeological evidence for farmsteads and cottages in Puxton village

documentary	landholding	standing structure	archaeological	interpretation
Myrtle Farm (Athays) (PxTM 15)				
amalgamation of two tenements: the now deserted 'Haynes', a customary tenement of 15 acres in 1566, and the present Myrtle Farm, a customary tenement with the remaining 12–13 acres that make up 'lt Sam. Athay (Taylors), 28a' in the c1770 Survey (Tenement L)	scattered over eastern part of Puxton, including fields in putative open fields to the west of Puxton church, north of Puxton Moor, and south of Puxton Moor	not surveyed; Listed as 17th-century cross-passage house		amalgamation of two tenements (the present Myrtle Farm and the now deserted 'Haynes')
cottage site immediately west of Myrtle Farm (Averys/Taylors) (PxTM 14)				
landless cottage in 1755 which did not exist in 1642 (roofless Tenement O on map of *c* 1770)	this toft, the field to the south and a detached field east of Hardingworth	site deserted	earthwork platform	post-*c*1642 cottage with small amount of land
cottage site further west of Myrtle (Joneses, late Cheekes) (PxTM 12)				
cottage and five acres in 1642 (Tenement H on map of *c* 1770)	three scattered parcels and rights in common meadow in Dolemoor	site deserted	pronounced earthwork platform; three sherds of 13th- to 15th-century pottery collected from disturbed ground	decayed tenement with several strips in Dolemoor
Flemans/Shalvers? (PxTM 142)				
customary tenement of 19 acres in 1642 (roofless Tenement N on map of *c* 1770)	parcels scattered over the eastern part of Puxton parish, including parcel in putative common field north of Puxton Moor	site deserted	earthwork platform; test pitting in field to west ('Sollards', CoTM 110) revealed large amounts of 12th- to 15th-century pottery	typical Puxton smallholding with lands scattered throughout the eastern part of the parish, including the putative common fields
Bindings Cottage/Bunns (CoTM 106)				
halfyardland of 39 acres in 1567	compact block of closes with detached parcels in former common fields at Dolemoor, Gildenhurst, and Goosey	site deserted: cottage demolished in 20th century	test pitting produced 12th-/13th-century through to post-medieval pottery	typical compact Congresbury-type halfyardland
'Home Ground', north of Home Ground (Co TM 112)				
unnamed 16 acres of pasture in five closes adjoining John Payne's 1567 messuage	compact block of closes	site deserted by time of 1567 Survey	several earthwork platforms with 12th- to 14th-century occupation, and possibly reoccupation in 17th/18th century	typical compact Congresbury-type tenement located on eastern side of small triangular-shaped green ('The Wash': TM 18) at entrance to Mays Lane
Glebe Cottage (formerly the Parsonage) (PxTM 21)				
parsonage first recorded in 1636	compact block of closes adjacent to the parsonage, with parcel in common fields to north of Puxton Moor and in Twindix	two-celled house possibly dating from the 17th century or earlier		parsonage, and glebe that included parcels of several common fields; located on eastern side of 'The Wash' at entrance to Mays Lane

(table continued)

Table 9.1 (*cont.*) Documentary, standing building, and archaeological evidence for farmsteads and cottages in Puxton village

documentary	landholding	standing structure	archaeological	interpretation
Days (?PxTM 25)				
customary holding of 26½ acres that in 1567 comprised the amalgamation of two tenements, one ruinous (roofless Tenement G on map of *c* 1770)	parcels scattered over the eastern part of Puxton parish, including parcel in putative common field south west of Church Field	deserted by *c* 1770; reoccupied in 20th century and now covered in light industrial units		combination of two pre-1642 tenements, one already roofless by that date and the other by *c* 1770; the obvious locations for these two houses are the small plots TM 3 (north of the church) and TM 25 (Ox House and Pen) respectively
(eastern part of PxTM 3)				
customary holding of 26½ acres that in 1567 comprised the amalgamation of two tenements, one ruinous ('Days' see above) along with an orchard of one rood between the church's house called le Churchhowse and the 'domus mancionem'	see 'Days'	deserted by 1567		
The Church House (western part of PxTM3?)				
tenement that can be traced back to 1566 as the Church House		deserted by *c* 1770 and ground amalgamated with 'Days' field TM 3	inaccessible: covered by scrub and a derelict shed	typical location for a Church House on the edge of the cemetery
Haynes (PxTM 26) (and see Myrtle Farm)				
customary tenement (not described as roofless or ruinous) with 15 acres in 1566 (part of roofless Tenement L in *c* 1770)	deserted by *c* 1770 though an ox house survived	deserted	earthwork platforms; test pitting produced a small amount of 12th–15th-century pottery	
Butts (PxTM 38)				
customary tenement of 11 acres in *c* 1642 (roofless tenement W in *c* 1770)		deserted	earthwork platform; test pitting produced three sherds of fabric AA1 (?late 10th- to 11th-century), and large amounts of 12th- to 15th-century pottery	
TM 39 Oxlease				
part of roofless Tenement J on map of *c* 1770 that can be traced back to the three tenements (two ruinous) held by John and Agnes Atwill in 1570 (see Church View above)	see Church View	deserted	soil chemistry indicates an area of occupation in the north west corner of this field. Corresponds to an area without drainage gripes	tenement that may have been absorbed into Church View (Cambridge's alias Hort's) (PxTM 4)

(table continued)

Table 9.1 (*cont.*) Documentary, standing building, and archaeological evidence for farmsteads and cottages in Puxton village

documentary	landholding	standing structure	archaeological	interpretation
Appletree Cottage (North house) (PxTM 29–30)				
cottage with two acres of land in *c* 1642 (Tenement X in *c* 1770)		single-celled 17th-century cottage	test pitting to the south produced large amounts of medieval pottery	cottage with just two acres of land
Coles (TM 31)				
part of roofless Tenement J on map of *c* 1770 that can be traced back to the three tenements (two ruinous) held by John and Agnes Atwill in 1570 (see Church View above)	see Church View	deserted	earthwork platform; test pitting revealed one sherd of fabric AA1 (?late 10th- to 11th-century), and large amounts of medieval pottery	tenement that may have been absorbed into Church View (Cambridge's alias Hort's) (PxTM 4)
Goose Acre Farm ('Millards') (PxTM 34)				
24 acre customary tenement that can be traced back to *c* 1642 (Tenement R in *c* 1770)	small block of fields immediately east of farm and detached fields in the putative open field to the north	early 20th century (not surveyed)		one of three green-side farmsteads on western edge of Puxton Moor
Puxton Moor Farm (PxTM 105)				
tenement of *c* 33 acres of which 21 acres of land lay within the manor in *c* 1770 (Tenement T) and the house and *c* 12 acres lay outside	concentrated immediately west of house forming a small but coherent block	the west wing survives of what was probably a substantial C-shaped 17th-century house; the rest was rebuilt in the early 20th century		one of three green-side farmsteads on western edge of Puxton Moor. Small freehold that acquired an area of demesne (Tenement T)
South Farm (PxTM 95)				
29 acre customary tenement that can be traced back to 1560/62 (Tenement U in *c* 1770)	small block of fields immediately west of farm and detached fields in the putative open field to the north	modern		one of three green-side farmsteads on western edge of Puxton Moor
Sharps (PxTM 93)				
in 1491 the Court Roll refers to four acres of land called Sharps described as *de antiquo astro* ('the ancestral home or hearth') which is typically applied to small pieces of land held by customary tenants; probably a cottage and five acres recorded in 1547; part of roofless Tenement S in *c* 1770	single field	deserted	possible earthwork platform in north west corner of field, next to a pronounced bulge in the northern field boundary (marking the southern edge of Puxton Moor)	cottage established on the edge of Puxton Moor and abandoned

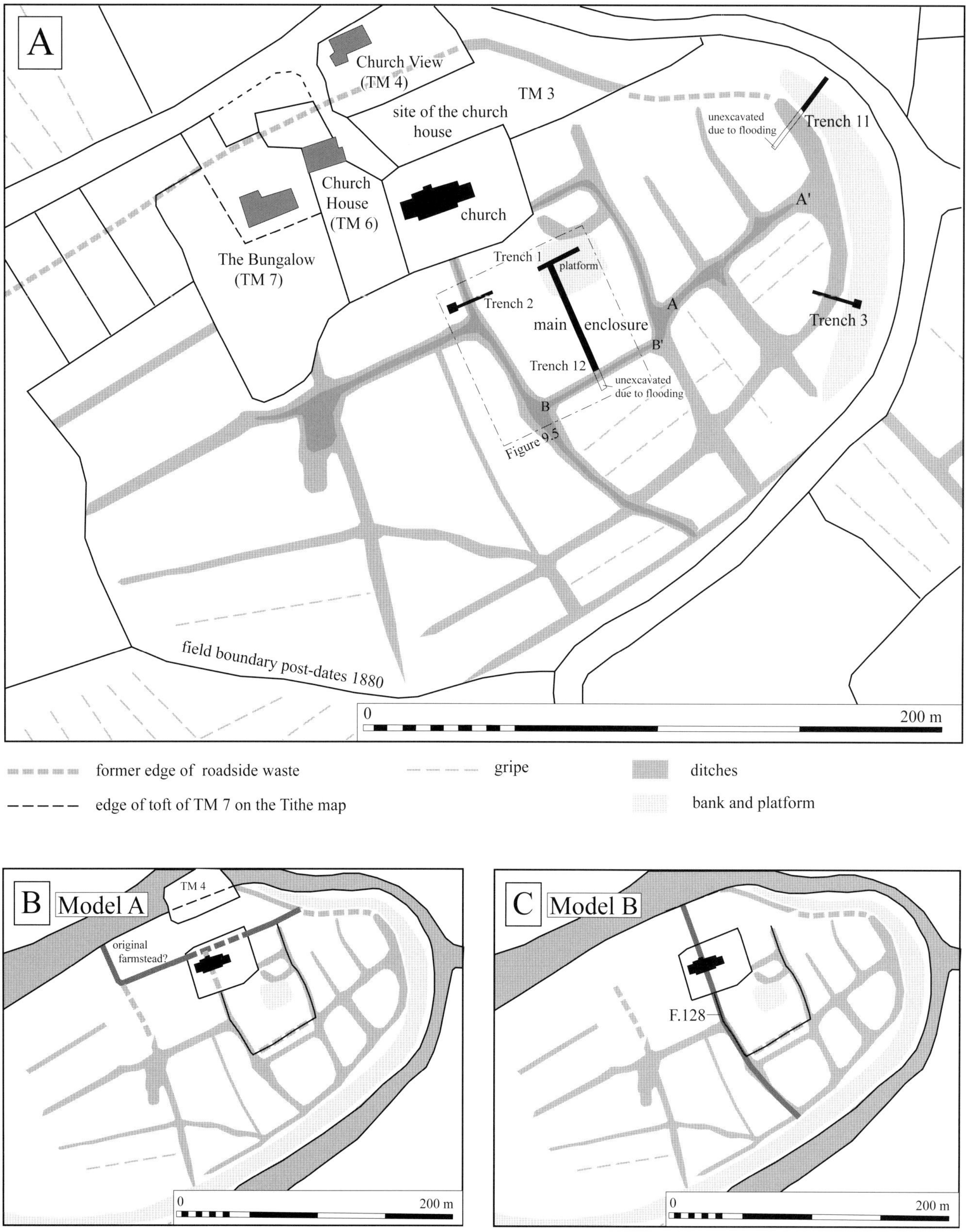

Figure 9.4 The archaeology of Church Field with two possible models for how the earliest phase of settlement may have evolved

was already protected from tidal inundation and so had been subject to soil formation.

The basic composition of the sampled sequence was similar throughout (Table 9.2 CD). All contexts have a silty clay loam texture, are dominated by the mineral component, and have a very low organic matter content that is highly fragmented, strongly decomposed, and randomly distributed throughout the soil fabric. The only variability seen in the organic matter occurs as subtle differences in the colour of the fine organic residues. Although a number of contexts could be differentiated both in the field and in the monolith tin prior to subsampling, it was difficult to recognise these in thin section. Only context 524 (the natural alluvium of the Upper Wentlooge Formation) could be clearly differentiated from the rest of the material, based on its horizontally bedded sediment structure, and the position of other contexts identified in the field had to be identified by measurement. Indeed, what in the field (and macroscopically in the monolith) was recognised as a single context 523 (the potential buried land surface), could be microscopically subdivided into an upper and lower part, the lower 4cm showing weak horizontal bedding. Pedofeatures are present in all contexts and are dominated by gleying features occurring as mottles of iron, manganese, and iron-manganese complexes. Features of bioturbation are also common in all but the lowest context (524) and are found as earthworm passage features, earthworm granules and other soil fauna excrements. The spongy microstructure of contexts 502 and 503 (the bank material) also attests to the fact that the deposit has been biologically reworked.

502 (uppermost surviving part of the bank): this context lacks any internal sediment structure and has a spongy fabric with a porosity of 20% imparted by both channels and irregular pores (vughs). Earthworm passage features comprise material of the same composition as the surrounding soil fabric. These passage features are often reworked by smaller soil fauna, evidenced by the small (100μm), elliptical excrements that are associated with them, that are attributed to Oribatid mites. Elsewhere, these small excrements loosely infill small pores.

503 (lower part of bank make-up): the principal difference between this and the overlying context is the presence of occasional fragments of other sediment fabrics of two types: firstly, rolled aggregates of slightly finer textured material and, secondly, fragments of laminated silty clay and clay. Both types are found embedded in the main fabric and neither has a clear origin. As this context is thought to represent the basal bank sediments (rather than an *in situ* deposit) the fragments of fabric are most likely to have been formed elsewhere and been transported as part of the bank make-up material. Bioturbation is evidenced by the presence of calcareous earthworm granules, earthworm passage features, and Oribatid mite excrements.

523 upper: the boundary between this context and the overlying 503 is very diffuse and its position could only be extrapolated by measurement as the fabric composition and pedofeature content and frequency were very similar to that of context 503.

523 lower: the basal 4cm of context 523 shows weak horizontal bedding comprising fine sand and silty clay couplets. The silty clay units are typically 0.5mm thick and the fine sand beds 1mm thick. Occasional thin channels disrupt the bedding planes, extending vertically downwards. These channels are infilled with brown silty clay that has an internal structure indicating it has been reworked by earthworms. Gleying features are present as mottles of iron and manganese, the latter being particularly strongly developed.

524: the fabric characteristics are dominated by horizontal bedding comprising couplets of pale grey, coarse silt typically 2mm thick and 1mm thick silty clay beds. Gleying features of iron, manganese and iron-manganese complexes are common. Occasional fragments of horizontally bedded, well-oriented clay and silty clay are present, the horizontal alignment suggesting that they have not been strongly reworked from their site of formation. The porosity is low (5%) and the pores are simple channels, generally empty, that suggest biological reworking has been limited.

The thin section analysis has shown that the key context of interest in this sequence, context 523 lying directly beneath the bank, can be sub-divided into two distinct components. The upper part is highly bioturbated and directly comparable to the overlying context 503 (bank make-up material). It is characterised by a mixed silty clay loam textured fabric that lacks internal structure but contains fragments of layered, sediment fabrics that have been reworked from their site of formation. This contrasts with the lower component of 523 which has stronger sedimentary characteristics than soil characteristics, suggesting that although it has experienced a degree of soil forming activity, it is a relatively immature soil. Although context 523 (upper) may represent a zone of mixing (through bioturbation) between the overlying bank material (503) and the buried land-surface (523 lower), the most likely interpretation is that it represents the basal level of bank construction materials, resting on 523 (lower) which represents the original ground surface which lacks evidence for mature soil development. Although bioturbation (through either root action or soil fauna reworking) has occurred, it has only partially disrupted the original sediment bedding structure.

The principal question at this site concerned the nature of the land-surface at the time the bank was constructed, and the consequent implication this has for the reason it was built. Two possible scenarios were proposed: that the bank was built on the surface of an intertidal marsh, or that the bank was raised on reclaimed land. Given the lack of evidence for mature soil development beneath the bank, along with the dominant sedimentary rather than soil characteristics presented by the buried contexts, the former situation appears to be the most likely.

The enclosure ditch (Trench 3)

The ditch F.103 running inside the bank around the eastern side of Church Field was sectioned in Trench 3 (along with several later Romano-British features described in Chapter 4: Figs 9.4 and 9.6). The

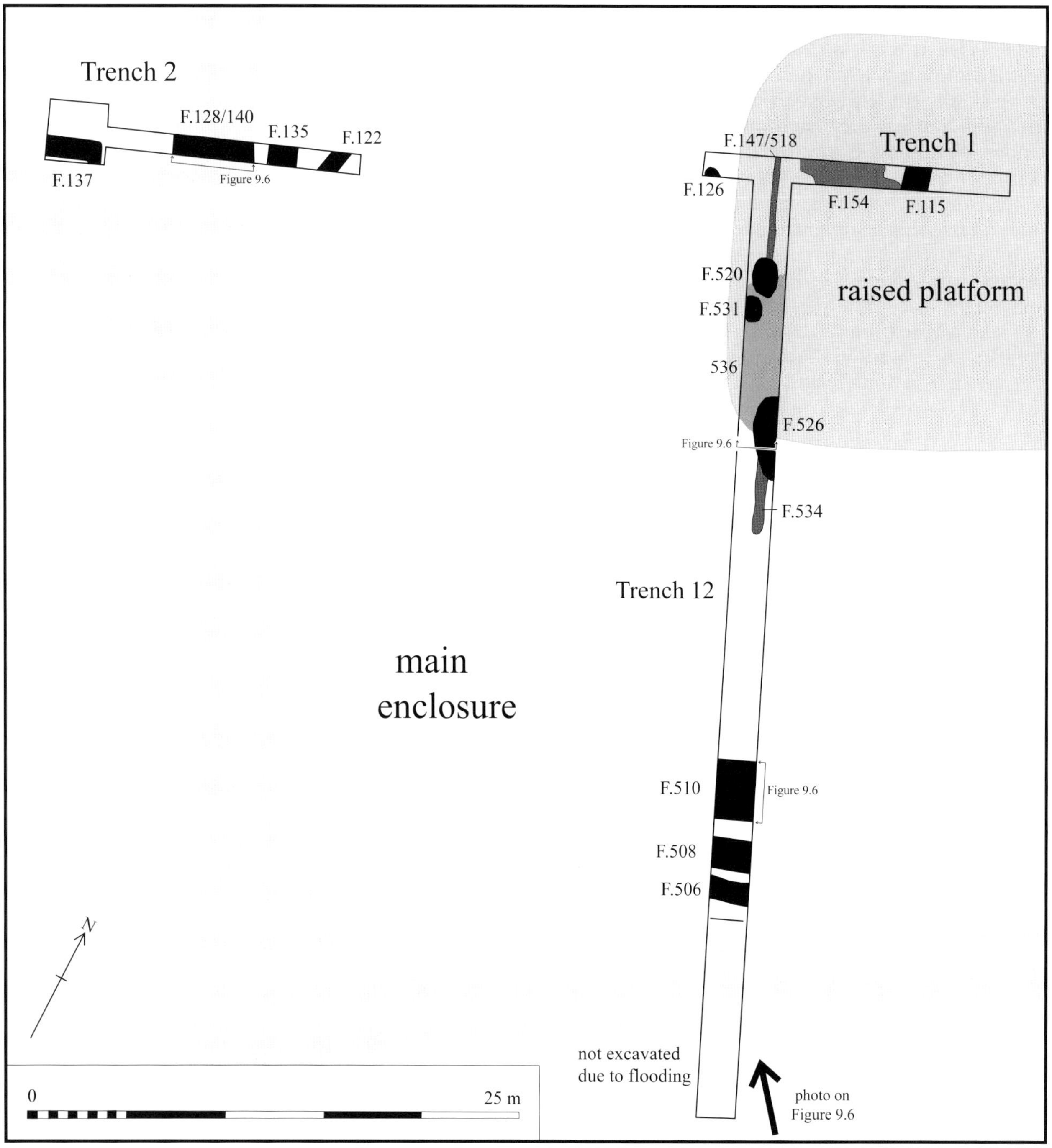

Figure 9.5 Trenches 1, 2, and 12 in Church Field

earliest phase (context 163), heavily truncated by a later recut, comprised a light–mid-blue/grey silty clay, similar to but slightly darker than the natural, and containing occasional flecks of charcoal. There was no dating evidence. The pollen assemblage was characterised by relatively large numbers of willow grains, along with species typical of disturbed ground. Chenopodiaceae were also present but it is impossible to say whether they were weeds of disturbed ground or living on a nearby salt marsh, though the diatoms were wholly freshwater.

F.103 was recut with a U-shaped ditch, *c* 3m wide at the top, *c* 0.8m wide at the base, and 1.35m deep. The basal fill (134) comprised a mid- to dark blue/grey silty clay with occasional flecks of charcoal, small lumps of burnt clay, and three sherds of 12th-century pottery. The plant macrofossil and pollen assemblages included duckweed and bogbean, suggestive of standing water within the ditch, which was fringed with some elder, willow, and rushes along with areas of disturbed ground supporting species such as nettle, dock, chickweed, and fat-hen. The main fill (107) comprised a mid- to light blue/grey silty clay. Occasional marine or marine to brackish diatoms may represent occasional tidal inundation or simply erosion of the natural upper Wentlooge alluvium into which the ditch is cut; unfortunately pollen preservation was very poor and plant macrofossils were absent. The upper fill of F.103 (context 108) comprised a mid- to dark blue/grey silty clay with lumps of lighter brown clay, along with three sherds of 11th- to 12th-century pottery, frequent flecks of charcoal, and lumps of burnt clay, suggestive of a dumped deposit.

Features in the main enclosure

In the centre of Trench 2 lay an irregularly shaped shallow hollow, or area of extensive disturbance (F.154), which was filled with a uniform dark grey/brown silty clay (context 155) that included frequent flecks of charcoal, animal bone, burnt clay, stone, and a handful of late 11th- to 12th-century sherds. This was sealed by a lighter grey/brown silty clay (151) that included a spread of stone rubble.

The hollow F.154 was cut by a small ditch, F.115, *c* 1.2m wide at the top, 0.3m wide at the base, and 0.8m deep, and which did not conform to the predominant north-west/south-east and north-east/south-west orientation of the features within the main enclosure. Its uniform very dark grey/brown fill included large amounts of late 11th- to 12th-century pottery, charcoal, animal bone, marine shellfish (periwinkles and oysters), burnt clay/daub, and stone, and is also suggestive of dumped midden material.

Ditch F.122 similarly did not conform to the predominant orientation of the main enclosure. The profile was heavily truncated by ploughing (only the bottom 0.1m survived) but it appears to have been 0.55m deep (below the modern ground surface), relatively steep sided (perhaps originally 1.2m wide at the top), with a flat bottom 0.75m across. Its single surviving fill was a mid- to dark brown/grey silty clay. There was no dating evidence.

Phase 6 (late 11th to early 13th century): the main period of occupation

The southern boundary ditch of the main enclosure (Trench 12)

Trench 12 extended as far south as the earthworks of the southern boundary ditch of the main enclosure (Fig 9.4, B–B'), though this feature could not be excavated due to flooding. Some 14m to the north, however, lay a series of ditches that continue the line of an extant earthwork to the east (A–A' on Fig 9.4). F.510 comprised a U-shaped ditch *c* 3m wide at the top, *c* 0.6m wide at the base, and 1.0m deep. Its fill was a remarkably uniform mid-blue/grey silty clay with occasional flecks of charcoal, and large amounts of pottery, animal bone, and lumps of burnt clay (dug in arbitrary spits as contexts 511, 517, and 525). Plant macrofossils from the basal fill (525) indicate a freshwater environment with duckweed on the water surface, stands of elder, brambles, and nettles along the ditch sides, and areas of disturbed ground nearby. The large pottery assemblage was dominated by late 11th- to 12th-century fabrics, with a couple of 12th- to 13th-century sherds in the upper fill. The uniformity of this fill, and in particular the lack of a darker, more organically rich basal fill, is suggestive of fairly rapid backfilling, and this ditch is unusual in showing no evidence for recutting (cf F.103, F.128, and F.135). To the south ran F.508, a small, shallow U-shaped ditch 1.5m wide and 0.5m deep, whose uniform fill (509) was very similar to F.510. Just 0.5m further to the south lay a third small boundary ditch/gully (F.506), 0.8m wide, whose upper fill (507) was a slightly darker blue/grey silty clay; it was unexcavated due to flooding.

Features on the platform

To the west of F.154 and running down the centre of the northern part of Trench 12, lay a small rubble-filled gully (F.147 in Trench 1 and F.518 in Trench 12), 0.25–0.3m wide and 0.1m deep. To the west, a shallow depression (F.126) protruding from beneath the section was filled with dark grey/brown silty clay and large amounts of stone rubble and may have been a posthole or the butt end of another gully. In Trench 12, the gully F.518 ran south for 3m before being cut by a pit F.520 (see below). To the south of F.520 gully F.518 could not be traced through a heterogeneous spread of light brown silty clay (536), though 5m to the south a second gully (F.534) was cut by F.526, beyond which it extended a further 5m and then stopped in a rounded butt end.

Pit F.520 was sub-rectangular in plan with steep, almost vertical sides and a flat bottom (1.75m long, 0.8m wide and 0.4m deep). It was filled with a uniform light–mid-brown silty clay (dug in two arbitrary spits: contexts 521 and 533). A similar small sub-rectangular pit (F.531) lay just to the south and appears to have been deliberately backfilled as it contained a highly heterogeneous fill of dumped material (contexts 522 and 532).

A large feature (F.526) on the southern edge of the platform extended from beneath the section of Trench 12. It was at least 1.2m deep and 3.6m across with a U-shaped profile. It was filled with mid-brown silty clay (dug in two arbitrary spits: contexts 527 and 528) with large amounts of charcoal, late 11th- to 12th-century pottery, animal bone, oyster shells, burnt clay, and stone (including a partly dressed block) suggestive of the dumping of midden material.

The western boundary ditch of the main enclosure, F.128 (Trench 2)

Trench 2 was laid across the substantial earthwork ditch (F.128) that marked the western side of the main enclosure south of the church, and that was maintained in a far smaller form into the post-medieval period as a drainage gripe. Two other ditches, F.122 and F.135 were located to the east of

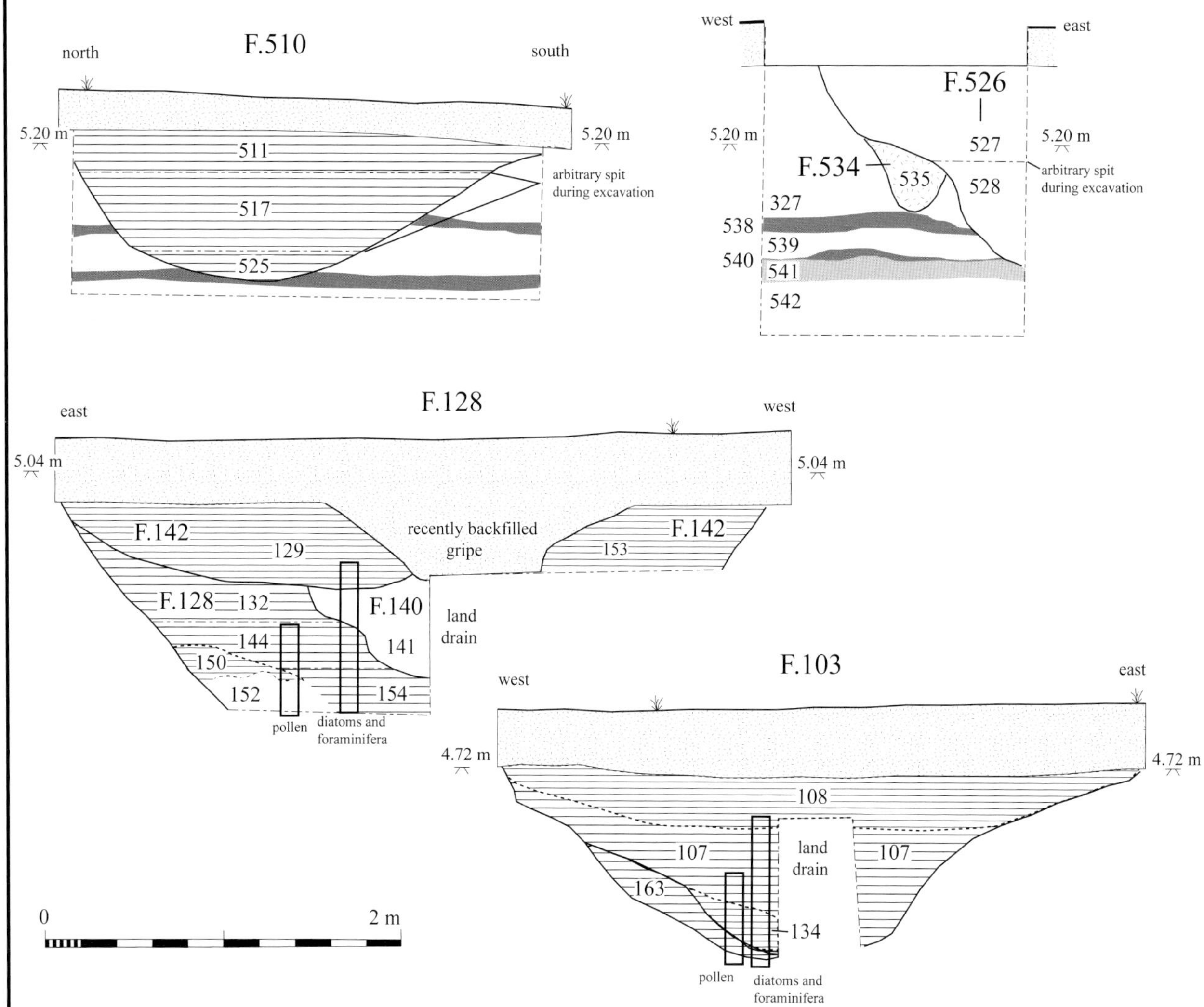

Trench 12 looking north west towards Puxton Church. Wetlands are a difficult environment within which to work and flooding was a problem on several occasions

Figure 9.6 View of Trench 12, and sections across the major features in Church Field

F.128, while to the west there was a shallow ditch/gully (F.137) partly sealed by a substantial spread of stone rubble (context 124).

The earliest cut of F.128 was a relatively steep-sided ditch, *c* 4.5m wide at the top and at least 1.5m deep (it could not be bottomed due to health and safety concerns and the need to maintain an active land drain) (Figs 9.5 and 9.6). The lowest excavated fill (152) was an organic-rich dark grey/brown slightly silty clay with abundant charcoal and waterlogged plant remains, suggestive of a basal fill. This was overlain by light–mid-blue/grey silty clays (dug in three arbitrary spits as contexts 132, 144, and 154) that included occasional flecks of charcoal and waterlogged plant remains particularly lower down. These lower fills contained 12th- to 13th-century pottery. The pollen and plant macrofossils show freshwater conditions within the ditch, and the Mollusca include species both preferring large bodies of well-oxygenated water and poor conditions that are prone to drying out, which may suggest changing conditions over time. The diatom assemblage, along with the very few foraminifera, may suggest very occasional influxes of tidal water, or material eroded out of the natural Upper Wentlooge alluvium into which the ditch was cut (see Cameron and Dobinson, and Kreiser, Chapter 10). The frequency of semi-terrestrial diatoms also suggests that the ditch was prone to drying out. The plant macrofossils, pollen, and Mollusca suggest the ditch edges included damp, well-vegetated habitats with rushes, and also areas of disturbed ground. Elder, bramble, and hazel may have formed a scrubby boundary around the adjacent farmyard whose nutrient rich soils also supported abundant stands of nettles, and which may have provided the habitat for the wood mouse, field vole, and water vole whose bones were recovered from F.128 (see Outram, Chapter 10).

Ditch F.135 (Trench 2)

Ditch F.135 lay 0.8m to the east F.128 and was on the same orientation. It had a shallow, U-shaped profile, being *c* 2m wide at the top, *c* 0.4m wide at the base, and 1.0m deep. The basal fill (145) comprised a light to mid-brown silty clay, with occasional lumps of charcoal and burnt clay. This was sealed by a dark blue/grey silty clay (136) containing abundant charcoal, that merged with a similar layer above (131) containing large amounts of domestic refuse including 12th- to 13th-century pottery, animal bone, marine shellfish (periwinkles, oysters, and a limpet), mortar, and burnt clay/daub. The relatively oxidised fills are indicative of the dryness of this ditch and the poorly preserved non-charred plant macrofossil assemblage was dominated by elder and the weeds of disturbed ground. There was possibly part of an earlier cut on the western side of F.136: context 162 was a light to mid-brown silty clay, similar but slightly darker than the natural. There was no dating evidence.

Ditch F.137 (Trench 2)

To the west of and perpendicular to the major boundary ditch F.128 lay a shallow ditch/gully (F.137), *c* 1.0–1.4m wide and 0.15m deep. Its uniform mid-blue/grey fill was distinct from the more organically rich fills of F.122, F.128, and F.135, and apart from a handful of 12th- to 13th-century sherds it contained little domestic debris suggesting that it lay away from the main focus of occupation. Following its siltation, F.137 was sealed by a structureless spread mainly of Lias limestone stone rubble, with some Carboniferous limestone and Triassic sandstone, with slabs up to 0.5m across (context 124).

Phase 9: recutting of Ditch F.128

Ditch F.128 was recut as F.140, a U-shaped ditch that was itself heavily truncated but originally 1.3m deep and *c* 2m wide. Its single surviving fill comprised a uniform mid- to dark grey brown silty clay that included a sherd of 17th- to 18th-century south Somerset glazed ware. F.140 was in turn recut by F.142, a broad, shallow U-shaped ditch 0.8m deep and originally some 3m wide, filled with a mid-blue grey/brown silty clay (129/153). Finally, F.142 was cut by a recently backfilled modern gripe which itself was cut by the narrow slot within which was inserted a modern ceramic land drain.

Discussion

Earthwork, fieldwalking, and soil chemistry surveys had suggested that Church Field was bounded by a bank and ditch, and contained a series of ditched paddocks or enclosures, the largest of which (immediately to the south of the church) contained an occupation platform. Trenches 3 and 11 confirmed the presence of a substantial bank around the perimeter of Church Field with a ditch on its inside that was recut in the 12th century. Any ditch on its outside will have continued in use as the current field boundary/roadside ditch. The bank does not seal a buried soil (that would have suggested it was built after the area had been reclaimed), but instead appears to have been constructed on the surface of a high intertidal salt marsh some time before the 12th century. Trenches 1, 2, and 12 confirm that the main ditched enclosure was the focus of occupation in the late 11th–12th centuries, with even the stratigraphically earliest features dating from this period. All earlier sherds of the late 10th–11th centuries were found in later contexts and it is impossible to say whether they are residual and represent a pre- to late 11th-century phase of occupation, or the use of these fabrics at the very end of the century alongside pottery from other industries. The overwhelming majority of the pottery is unglazed, though a few sherds of glazed jugs from several features and the topsoil (which contains material ploughed up

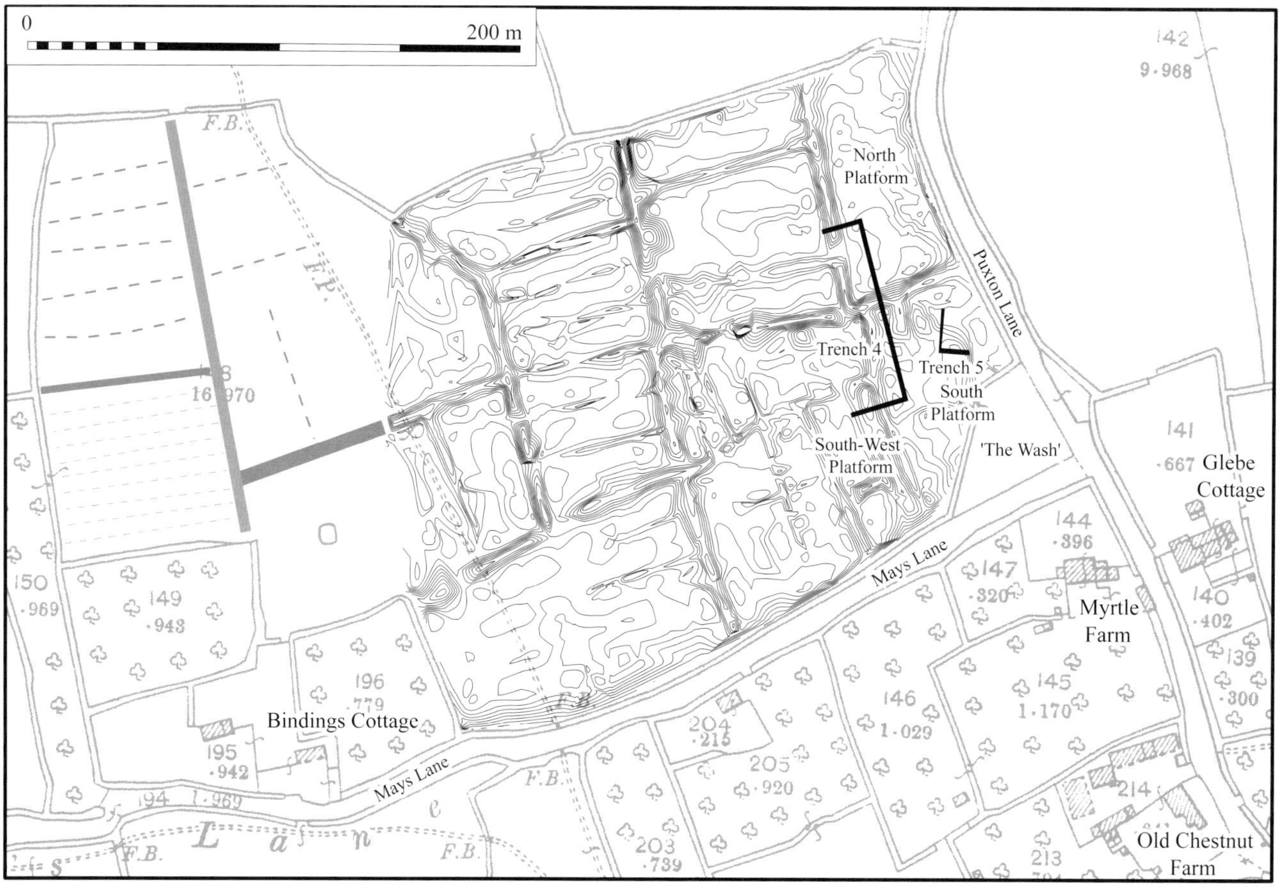

Figure 9.7 Contour survey of shrunken settlement earthworks in Home Ground, north of Mays Lane, and surrounding landscape as depicted on the Second Edition Ordnance Survey 25 inch map (1903)

from the latest occupation horizons) suggests that occupation may have continued into the early 13th century. Palaeoenvironmental material shows freshwater conditions in the ditches, with stands of elder, willow, and nettles along with areas of disturbed ground as would be expected close to a farmstead. There is no evidence of occupation after the early 13th century, though ditch F.128 was recut in the post-medieval period. The small amounts of post-medieval material from the topsoil are indicative simply of manuring and perhaps the dumping of domestic refuse from adjacent occupied tenements to the north.

Excavations at Home Ground north of Mays Lane, 1998

In 1998 two trenches (4 and 5) were excavated in an area of shrunken settlement earthworks in the field north of Mays Lane, known in the Congresbury tithe survey as Sixteen Acres/Home Ground and described in the 1567 survey of Congresbury Manor as '5 closes amounting to 16 acres adjoining Joan Orton's messuage' [Bindings Cottage down Mays Lane] (Fig 9.7). Though tenurially in Congresbury, this deserted tenement was physically a continuation of the village in Puxton and contained the best-preserved shrunken settlement earthworks in the village comprising three platforms, each of which lacked gripes. The South Platform lay just to the north of the triangular-shaped piece of enclosed roadside waste (The Wash) at the junction of Puxton Lane and Mays Lane, and was separated from the larger North Platform by a substantial ditch (F.207 in Trench 4; Fig 9.8). The South-West Platform lay to the west, separated from the South Platform by ditches F.203 and F.205; the lack of domestic refuse from this arm of Trench 4 suggests it was not occupied by a domestic building.

Phase 6: the medieval occupation

The South Platform (Trenches 4 and 5)

Two rectangular drystone structures were recorded in Trench 5 that were probably padstones supporting the timbers of a building. F.351 was 0.95m long, 0.7m wide, and survived to a height of 0.17m, and the partly preserved F.368 was of similar dimensions. The long axes of these well-made stone settings were parallel and oriented north to south, and the distance between them of 5.5m is similar to the width of contemporary medieval peasant houses (the spacing between cruck trusses tending to be rather less: Wrathmell 1989; 2002). This suggests that the building was oriented north–south, roughly parallel

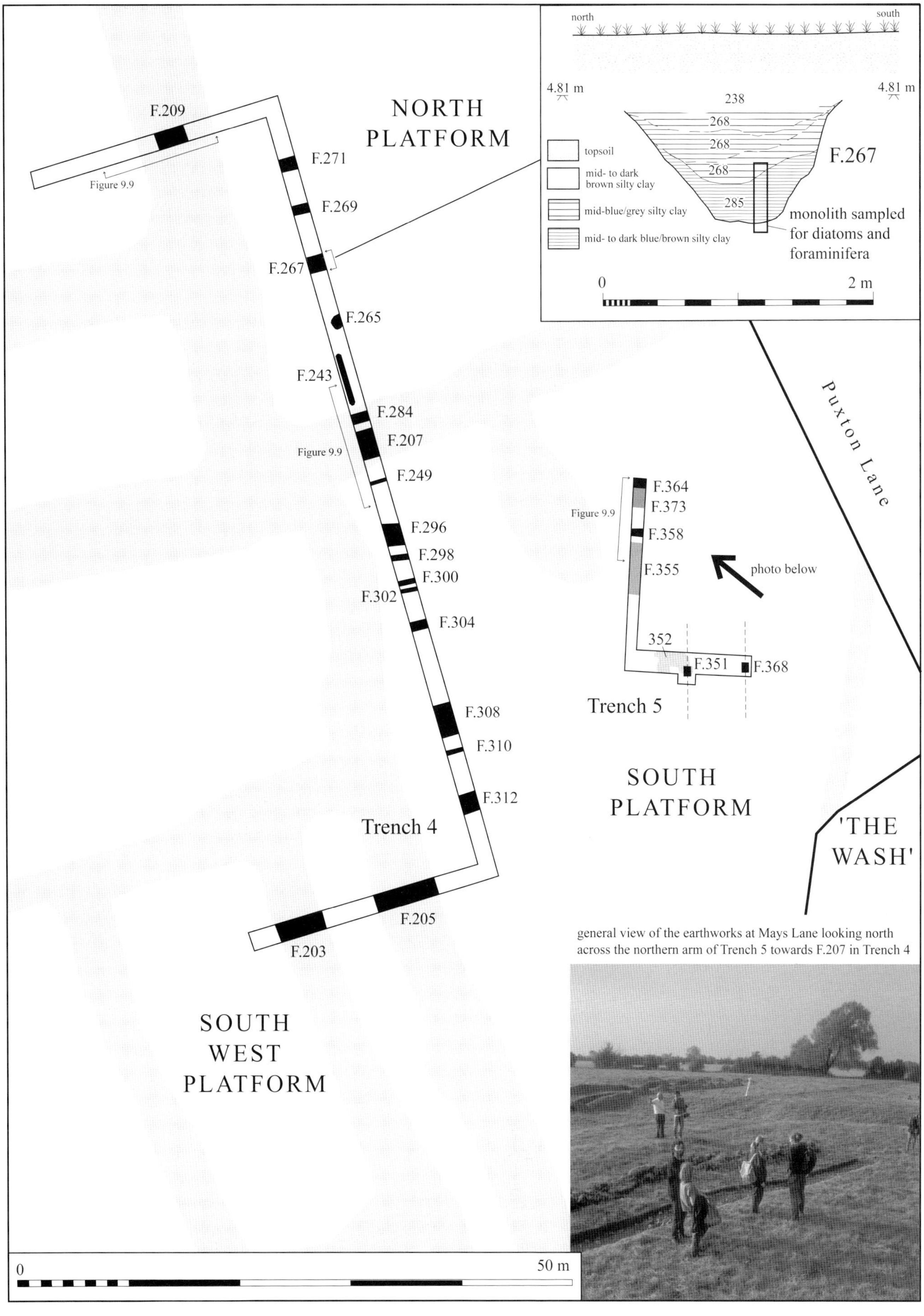

Figure 9.8 Trenches 4 and 5, and section across ditch F.267, in Home Ground, north of Mays Lane, in Puxton

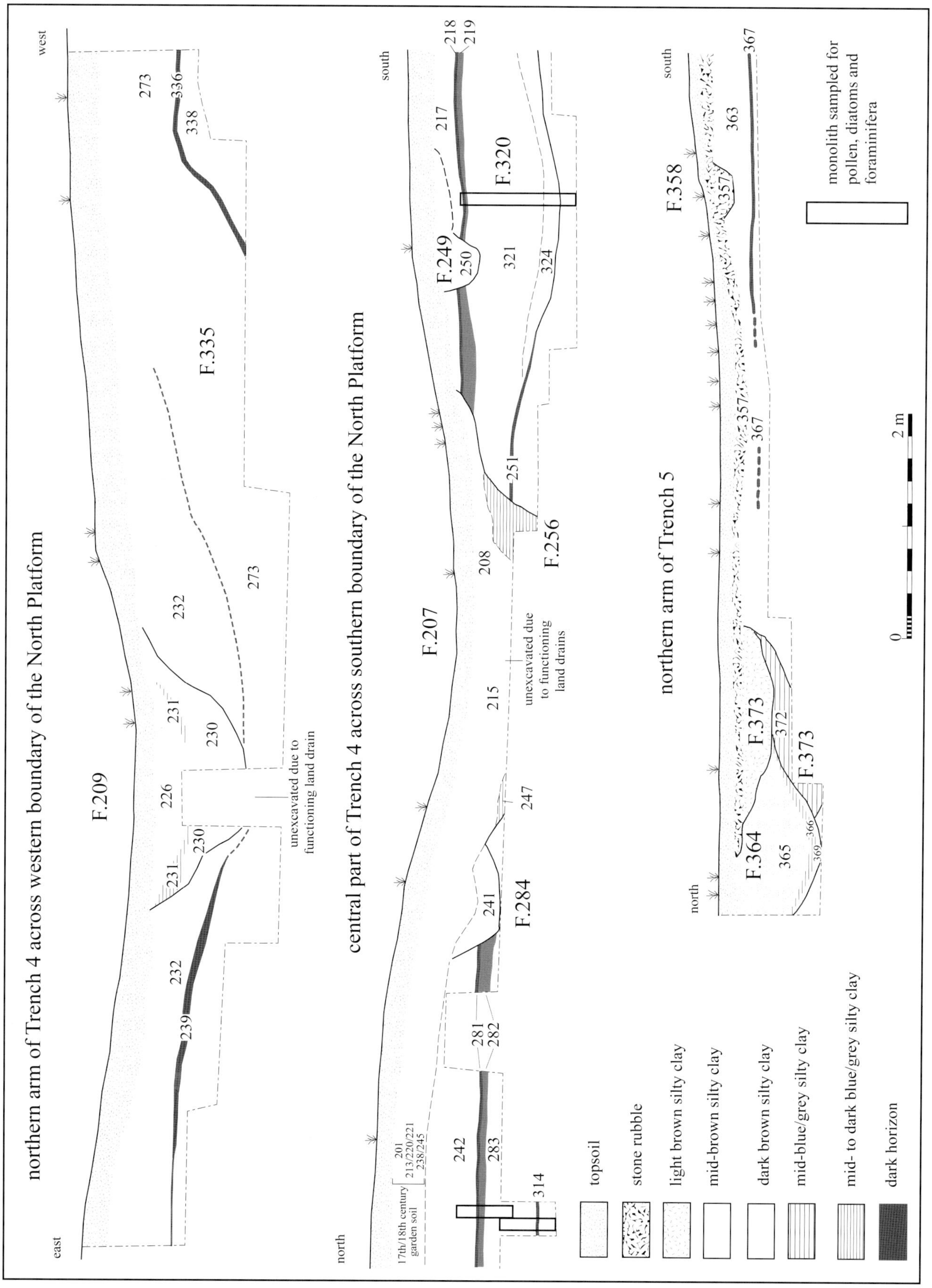

Figure 9.9 Long sections in Home Ground, north of Mays Lane, in Puxton

with the edge of The Wash. This is in contrast to most of the late medieval–17th-century houses on the North Somerset Levels that face south, though Old Chestnut Farm just to the south similarly faces Puxton Lane (Fig 9.7). The two stone settings were set within a heterogeneous light to mid-brown silty clay (354/362/363) that had the appearance of having been dumped/disturbed but not obviously forming a floor surface. A small assemblage of pottery was predominantly late 11th- to 13th-century with two (possibly intrusive) 14th- to 15th-century sherds.

In the northern arm of Trench 5 a shallow U-shaped ditch F.364 was oriented north-west/south-east, perpendicular to the western edge of The Wash (Fig 9.9). The earliest, heavily truncated, cut (F.371) was filled with a mid-grey/brown silty clay (371); the original ditch may have been *c* 2m wide, and *c* 1m deep. The ditch was recut by F.364, which probably had similar dimensions and whose basal fill was a thin layer of mid-brown silty clay (369), sealed by a thin, organic-rich dark blue/grey silty clay (366); the rest of the ditch was filled with a heterogeneous greenish/brown silty clay that may have been dumped (context 365). A third recut (F.373) along this alignment was narrower (1.6m) and shallower (0.3m), and was filled with a heterogeneous light to mid-brown silty clay with frequent flecks of charcoal and lumps of burnt clay/daub (360). Only this latest cut (context 360) produced any datable artefacts: two sherds of late 11th- to 12th-century pottery and a single sherd of late 11th- to 13th-century fabric U4.

The North Platform (Trench 4)

The southern side of the North Platform is marked by the earthworks of a substantial ditch (F.207) some 6m wide (Fig 9.9). Upon excavation in Trench 4 a complex sequence of recuts was revealed of which the earliest were two smaller and heavily truncated features. Ditch F.284 on the very southern edge of the North Platform appears to have had a U-shaped profile that would have been some 2m wide and 1m deep before its truncation by F.207 and was filled with a mid- to dark grey/brown silty clay (241) which contained a few sherds of 12th- to 13th-century pottery. Traces of a heavily truncated ditch (F.256) some 2m to the south are undated. These were cut by a very substantial ditch or sequential recuts of a ditch (F.246/F.253) that could not be fully excavated due to the need to maintain two modern land drains (one of which was leaking and flooding the trench). The upper fill contained large amounts of 17th- to 18th-century pottery.

Several features on the North Platform are suggestive of domestic occupation. A substantial east–west oriented ditch F.267, was 0.8m deep, 1.6m wide at the top, with fairly steep sides and a flat bottom 0.4m wide (Fig 9.8). It contained a fairly uniform basal fill of mid- to dark blue/brown silty clay (285) that became slightly lighter towards the top (context 268). There was a large amount of midden material including 12th- to 13th-century pottery and burnt clay/daub. Palaeoenvironmental evidence is suggestive of a freshwater ditch, prone to drying and fringed by rushes. A small number of estuarine diatoms and foraminifera could have simply been washed from the natural Upper Wentlooge alluvium into which the ditch is cut, or may indicate occasional tidal flooding. To the south a small ditch/gully, F.243, ran north–south across the southern part of the North Platform for *c* 5.4m. It was *c* 0.8–1.0m wide, *c* 0.6–0.8m deep, with a U-shaped profile. It had squared butt ends and was filled with dark brown silty clay rich in midden debris including 12th-century pottery (context 244). Between F.243 and F.267 was a large pit (F.265), around 1.0m square in plan and 0.6m deep. Its lower fill (280) was a distinctive mid- to light green/grey soft clay loam suggestive of cess, which was sealed by a mid- to dark brown silty clay containing midden material including 12th-century pottery (266).

Phase 7: the late medieval/16th-century drainage ditches/gripes

In western part of the South Platform Trench 4 revealed a series of small east–west oriented ditches/gullies, which may have served as drainage gripes and were mostly filled with mid-blue/brown silty clays. In the north-east corner of the South Platform there was a sequence of recut gullies that culminated in F.296. The earliest feature in the sequence, F.332, was a heavily truncated U-shaped feature, originally *c* 1.5m wide and 1.1m deep, whose fill became lighter towards the base (334 merging into 333). This was cut by a shallower, steep-sided but almost flat-bottomed ditch (F.328), which although also truncated may have been *c* 0.9m wide and 0.6m deep, with a similar fill (contexts 329, 330, and 331). This in turn was cut by a larger, almost V-shaped ditch F.296, which was 1.2m wide and 0.8m deep (filled with 297/319). Just 1.8m south of F.296 was a shallow U-shaped gully F.298, which was 1m wide and 0.4m deep (filled with 299). Another 1.8m to the west lay F.300 (filled with 301), a small U-shaped gully 1m wide and 0.7m deep. Just 0.3 m to the south there was another shallow gully F.302, 0.8m wide and 0.5m deep (filled with 303 and 322). Some 1.5m to the south lay F.304, a 1.5m wide feature with an irregular bottom that may have resulted from a series of intercutting ditches similar to F.332, but whose recutting could not be identified due to the similarity in the fills. A further 2.5m to the west lay a substantial ditch F.308 (see below) and beyond that a further two shallow gullies (F.310 and F.312), both *c* 0.8m wide and *c* 0.2m deep, with steep sides and a flat bottom.

Most of these small, regularly spaced ditches/gullies yielded a small number of late 11th- to 13th-century medieval sherds though F.312 produced a large assemblage of 16th-century material (F.302

also produced a 16th-century sherd). The uniformity of their fills and lack of charcoal or other signs of domestic debris suggests that they all post-date the abandonment of the medieval tenement but predate the site's reoccupation in the 17th–18th century (see below).

On the North Platform there were two similar features, F.269 and F.271, both 1.1m wide and 0.5–0.6m deep, and filled with a uniform dark grey/brown silty clay (291 in F.269; 272 in F.271) that became lighter towards the top (270 in F.269). Context 272 produced a small assemblage of 17th- to 18th-century pottery.

Phase 8: the reoccupation of the South Platform in the 17th/18th centuries

Possible post-medieval occupation on the South Platform

A spread of stone rubble, lumps of mortar, and occasional fragments of brick (352/357) within a mid- to dark brown silty clay matrix (353) was recorded across most of Trench 5, also filling a shallow hollow F.355 (fill 356) and gully F.358 (fill 359) that ran along the northern edge of the platform. This spread of debris contained large amounts of 17th- to 18th-century pottery and, while it is possible that the material was dumped from elsewhere, it may represent a demolished post-medieval building.

A substantial ditch F.308, some 3m wide and at least 1m deep, lay towards the western side of the South Platform in Trench 4 and was filled with a mid-brown silty clay (309, 323), rich in midden material and including large amounts of 17th- to 18th-century pottery, animal bone, and marine molluscs (notably mussels and oysters). The plant macrofossils included a range of freshwater species including elder, along with grains of wheat, barley, and oats.

The western edge of the South Platform was marked by the earthworks of another substantial ditch (F.205) some 4m wide. Upon excavation a U-shaped cut was revealed, 1.1m deep, whose basal fill (259) comprised a dark grey/brown silty clay which became lighter with decreasing depth (258). This was sealed by a mid- to dark brown slightly loamy silty clay (206/227) that contained small amounts of 17th- to 18th-century pottery but relatively little other domestic refuse. A large assemblage of small mammal bones is suggestive of a barn owl roost in the trees alongside this boundary (see Kear, Chapter 10).

A possible garden soil on the North Platform

It may have been in the context of this reoccupation of the South Platform that a 0.2–0.3m thick layer of mid- to dark brown slightly loamy silty clay formed across the North Platform, which was excavated in a series of arbitrary spits (213/220/221/238/245/248). There was little differentiation throughout its depth in terms of the material recovered, with 17th- to 18th-century pottery recovered throughout. It is interpreted as a garden soil.

The western boundary ditch of the North Platform (F.209)

The western side of the North Platform was marked by a substantial earthwork ditch F.209, which upon excavation proved to be *c* 2.7m wide at the top, *c* 1.3m deep and with a U-shaped profile (Fig 9.9). It appeared to be cut into a substantial earlier feature associated with the upper dark horizon (239) whose nature could not be determined but which is probably a former tidal creek (F.335). It contained no dating evidence. Ditch F.209 was largely filled with a uniform dark blue/grey silty clay (230), which although organically rich lacked much in the way of charcoal or artefacts. The plant macrofossils and Mollusca suggest a freshwater ditch, prone to drying, with an adjacent hedgerow containing elder, hawthorn, and brambles. The small number of sherds were all post-medieval (the latest being 17th- to 18th-century) and this ditch clearly silted up naturally after the occupation of the platform had ceased.

This basal fill 230 was sealed by a lens of light to mid-brown silty clay (232) that appears to have been washed in both from the east and the west, and so may represent a phase of cultivation (perhaps corresponding to the possible garden soil). This was sealed by further mid-blue/grey silty clay (210/226) that appears to represent the natural siltation of what was by now a shallow earthwork. The pottery was once again 17th- to 18th-century.

South-West Platform

Trench 4 extended across the boundary ditch (F.205) between the South Platform and the South-West Platform (Fig 9.8). The trench was extended across the South-West Platform, to include the earthworks of another north–south oriented ditch (F.203), *c* 2m wide, *c* 1m deep, and with a U-shaped profile. The basal fill comprised a light to mid-blue grey silty clay (279), sealed by a mid-blue/brown silty clay (234, 264) which yielded a single 14th- to 15th-century sherd, and an upper fill of dark blue/brown silty clay (204, 233) which contained three sherds of 16th- to 18th-century pottery. The South-West Platform was otherwise devoid of features and the lack of midden material or other signs of occupation leave its function unclear.

Discussion

The earliest pottery from Home Ground comprised eighteen sherds of late 10th- to 11th-century fabric

AA1 (just 1% of the total, compared to 5% in Church Field, suggesting that this area was occupied slightly later), though all was residual in later contexts. As in Church Field, the earliest stratified features were late 11th–12th century with occupation on both the North and the South Platforms. Unlike in Church Field occupation at Home Ground certainly continued into the 13th century and although small amounts of 14th- to 15th-century pottery were recovered from later contexts, by the 16th century the platforms appear to have been used for agriculture, being drained through a series of small ditches/gullies. In the 17th–18th centuries the South Platform appears to have been reoccupied, with the North Platform cultivated as a garden; domestic rubbish was dumped in the nearby F.308. Very little material was recovered dating to the 19th century and the site was certainly deserted by the time of the tithe survey in 1840.

The medieval and later pottery *by Alejandra Gutiérrez*

Introduction and methodology

An assemblage of 2,883 fragments of pottery weighing some 2.3kg was recovered from the excavations at Puxton (Trenches 1, 2, 3, 4, 5, 11, and 12), mostly derived from ditches and the buried garden soil at Home Ground. The pottery was sorted into fabrics with the aid of a ×20 binocular microscope, and a range of medieval and post-medieval wares were identified. The pottery was then counted and weighed, although in general sherds were too small to allow any calculation of the minimum number of vessels present unless the pottery type was especially distinctive or infrequent; complete profiles were also scarce. Sherds were also examined for cross-fits. Dating has been based on parallels derived from excavations elsewhere in the local area, since the nature of the archaeological stratigraphy and other artefacts from Puxton are unhelpful in providing more specific chronological indicators. The phasing on site is as shown in Table 2.1 and on p 200. Terminology follows the work of Vince (1984) and, where possible, cross-reference has been made between the Puxton assemblage and others from the area, especially the type series from Shapwick (Gutiérrez forthcoming) and Bristol (Ponsford 1998). The fabric types identified are listed and described below.

Medieval fabrics

AA1 ?South Somerset. Late 10th–11th centuries. Usually grey core, grey margins and buff to grey surfaces; soapy texture. Abundant glassy quartz, well sorted <2mm; moderate rounded voids <3mm. A couple of sherds also show sparse white sandstone with glauconite grains < 2.0mm across. Hand made.

AA2 ?Local. ?Late 10th–11th centuries. Usually grey core, grey margins and buff to grey surfaces. Abundant glassy quartz, well sorted <1mm; moderate rounded limestone, well sorted, <3mm; moderate rounded voids <3mm; sub-angular red sandstone <1.5mm. Hand made.

U1 South Somerset. Late 11th–13th centuries. Variety of fabric colours; surfaces are often a different colour to margins and core; usually orange surfaces and light grey core and margins. Chert-tempered fabric with abundant poorly sorted glassy quartz, occasional flint/chert. Hand made. Occasional combing on exterior surface.

PX03 Somerset. Medieval. Brown throughout, sometimes with black surfaces, or grey throughout. Moderate rounded and glassy quartz <1mm; moderate fine-grained red sandstone <1mm; sparse tabular slate <3mm. Hand-made coarsewares.

PX04 Sandstone-rich fabric, probably from North Somerset or from the Bristol region (sandstone is local to North Somerset and the Mendips). ?12th–13th centuries. Moderate inclusions of poorly sorted, sub-angular, red sandstone, usually <1.5mm but larger fragments also found (up to 8mm); moderate poorly sorted, rounded limestone (<2mm) (includes oolite); sparse poorly sorted calcite up to 1mm across; sparse glassy quartz up to 1.5mm across; occasional poorly sorted quartzite, up to 7mm; sparse white sandstone up to 1mm; occasional red/brown clay/ironstsone <2mm; moderate poorly sorted quartz up to 3mm. Sometimes the limestone has burnt out during firing, leaving characteristic voids and pitted surfaces. Hand made.

PX08 Quartz-rich fabric, probably from Avon valley. Late 11th–13th centuries. Characterised by abundant sub-angular quartz, usually 0.3mm but up to 1.5mm, sparse glassy quartz up to 1.0mm across, and occasional clay relicts <3mm. Exterior surface has been smoothed. Hand made. Sherds were found with decoration of stamped circles with a grid.

U4 (Bath A; Vince 1979) Avon Valley/Somerset. Late 11th–13th centuries. Grey core, buff margins and grey surfaces. Abundant mica, rare calcareous inclusions, moderate flint/chert <3mm, clay pellets, moderate glassy quartz <2mm. Smoothed-over surfaces. Hand made. Occasional combing on exterior surface.

PX09 Sandy coarsewares, ?south Somerset. Medieval. Grey core and brown surfaces. Sparse inclusions of sandstone, glassy quartz <1mm, occasional clay relicts up to 6mm, and rare black ?flint. Micaceous clay matrix. Exterior surface has been smoothed over.

PX11 ?Somerset chert-tempered glazed jugs. Medieval. Grey core and red surfaces. Abundant quartz and glassy quartz, poorly sorted, up to 0.5mm; moderate chert/flint <1mm; moderate calcareous inclusions, poorly sorted, <1mm; occasional dark brown clay relicts <3mm. Only one sherd found, belonging to a hand-made, brown-glazed jug, with part of a handle, pierced at the top.

Bristol A-B Very similar components to fabric Bristol A-B (Vince 1984) and Bristol types BPT 1, 3, 7, 20, 115, 176, 190 (Ponsford 1998, 136–7), but it could also be a fabric of local origin. 11th–12th centuries. Dark grey core, brown to yellowish red surfaces. Moderate, well-sorted inclusions of quartz <0.5mm; moderate poorly sorted white sandstone up to 1.0mm; moderate rounded calcareous inclusions up to 1.0mm; occasional chert and sparse angular grey siltstone fragments <1.0mm. Hand made, unglazed.

Proto Ham Green Bristol. 12th–13th centuries. Black to grey, sometimes with a yellowish red skin. Abundant rounded quartz <0.3mm; sparse rounded dark brown ironstone grains <0.3mm; sparse rounded calcareous inclusions <0.3mm. Hand made.

SS Ham Green jugs, Bristol. 12th–13th centuries (Barton 1963; Ponsford 1991). Grey core; buff or white margins;

pink, orange or buff interior surface. Inclusions of well-sorted quartz, limestone and clay pellets. Hand made and finished on low wheel. Green glaze on exterior surface and over the interior of the rim only.

Ham Green cooking pots Bristol. 13th–14th centuries. Black throughout with red surfaces. Abundant sub-angular quartz <0.2mm; moderate rounded mudstone < 1mm, grey, pink or red; sparse calcareous grains <0.5mm. Hand made.

AAA Bristol ware. 13th–15th centuries. Pale yellow throughout, sometimes with a light grey core. Inclusions of quartz and quartzite up to 1.2mm, clay pellets <1mm, occasional sandstone up to 7mm, iron ore 0.2mm across, rounded limestone up to *c* 0.3mm (Vince 1984). Wheel thrown. Green glaze on exterior, sometimes with applied clay strips, or turned grooves. 'Early ware' characterised by thumbed bases, 'late ware' by plain bases.

SR ?Somerset. Medieval. Light orange throughout. Abundant, well-sorted sandstone <3mm; abundant quartz sand; moderate clay pellets < 2mm; in a micaceous clay matrix. Exterior surface smoothed over.

Q Early south Somerset glazed wares. 13th–15th centuries. Red throughout, sometimes with a light grey core. The only visible inclusion is abundant quartz <1mm. Brown, green or clear glaze on exterior surface only; occasional vertical strips of white slip.

Y Sandy ware, probably from south Somerset. 12th century. Grey core and margins, orange surfaces. Inclusions of abundant sub-rounded and glassy quartz, poorly sorted, <3mm. Tripod pitchers with splashes of clear/green glaze on exterior.

XX Chert-tempered fabric, similar in description to Ilchester G25 (Leach 1982). Late 12th–13th centuries. Grey throughout, but orange patches on exterior surface. Sandy fabric with inclusions of very well-sorted quartz <1mm, occasional flint/chert up to 6mm across, occasional calcareous inclusions <1mm. Tripod pitchers with patchy external glaze, mainly green but with orange patches. Sometimes with applied clay strips as decoration.

Stamford ware Stamford, Lincolnshire. 12th century. Fine fabric with quartz and iron grains 0.01mm, ovoid iron-rich clay pellets and ironstone fragments up to 70mm long (Kilmurry 1980, 207). Thin transparent glaze.

SEW South-East Wiltshire tripod pitcher fabric. Late 11th–13th centuries. Black or white core, pink or light brown surfaces. Inclusions: angular quartz up to 1.3mm, sparse brown chert/flint, rounded iron ore up to 0.2mm (Vince 1984; Mepham 2000). Hand made. Clear glaze on the exterior.

Minety glazed ware Minety, Wiltshire. Late 13th–14th centuries. Grey core, white exterior margin, white or pink interior margin, buff or orange interior surface. The main inclusion is abundant oolitic limestone which leaves a characteristic round void when burnt out during firing; occasional chert/flint. All inclusions are ill sorted and mainly <1mm, but also up to 2mm. Wheel-thrown jugs. Exterior green glaze over very rough surfaces; combing decoration on exterior wall.

Worcestershire jugs Worcestershire. Early–mid-13th century. Grey core and margins; orange interior surface. Very dense fabric, with quartz sand and occasional calcareous inclusions, in a micaceous clay matrix. Wheel thrown. Green glaze on exterior surface only; regulating decoration applied to exterior wall.

Altogether 22 medieval fabrics were identified, of which PX04 dominate the assemblage. This fabric alone represents 60% by weight of all the pottery recovered from medieval Phases 5 and 6 together. The inclusions of red sandstone present in the fabric would suggest that it could derive from the local area, perhaps from the edge of the Mendips. Dating has to be by association with other better-known types, such as fabric Bristol A-B, Somerset chert-tempered (fabric U1) (late 11th–13th centuries), and fabric U4 (12th–13th centuries). Fabric PX04 is also dominant in Phase 6, where is found in association with glazed wares from Bristol (SS, AAA) and Somerset (Q) suggesting that it was still current in the 13th century at least.

Fabrics PX03, PX08 and U4 follow in numbers (7%, 6%, 5% respectively, by weight in Phases 5 and 6 together). Of these, fabric U4 is better known, and although referred to as 'Bath A' both the Avon valley in northern Somerset (Vince 1979) and Crockerton in western Wiltshire (Vince 1984) have been suggested as possible places of manufacture. The fabric might simply be part of a wide regional tradition comprising several places of manufacture, sharing similar inclusions and form vessels (Vince 1979, 31). It seems more likely, given the proximity of the source, that vessels found at Puxton might derive from the Avon valley rather than from Wiltshire. This fabric is also common in Bristol (BTP 46) (Ponsford 1998, 137). Fabric PX08 is similar to U4, and it might be a variant of this, but it lacks the flint inclusions and the matrix is less silty.

Fabric PX03 contains red sandstone and slate. Although both tempers are known in wares from north Devon and from west Somerset, near Nether Stowey (Taylor 1999), the presence of polished quartz in PX03 might indicate a source in west Somerset (Alan Vince pers comm). Sandstone-tempered wares of the 12th century found in Bickley, on the hills some 3km north-west of Puxton, have been attributed to the Bridgwater area (Ponsford 2003, type 5).

Fabric AA1 has characteristic inclusions of glassy quartz and a soapy texture. Similar wares have been found at Cheddar (E), Ilchester (A4, A7) and Taunton (41) (Rahtz 1979; Leach 1982; Pearson 1984). This fabric might also represent several places of manufacture in Somerset, although the presence of glauconite in the white sandstone in the fabric of some of the Puxton sherds points to a source in south Somerset at least for those examples. Recent analyses of other medieval wares have proved that similar temper derives from the Blackdown Hills in south-west Somerset (Taylor in Gutiérrez 2004, 108). Although traditionally dated to the late 10th–11th centuries, at Puxton it never appears in isolation but occurs in Phases 5 to 10.

The remainder of the Somerset fabrics appear in significantly fewer numbers. The main group is that from the Bristol area, including early wares (Bristol A-B) of thick walls, Ham Green fabrics (Proto HG, 'cooking pots' and jugs), and later glazed jugs (AAA). The rest of the fabrics represent just a few sherds each and less than 1% by weight of Phases 5 and 6 together. Among these fabrics Y and XX consist entirely of tripod pitchers with patchy exterior glaze. Dating of Ham green-glazed jugs follows the revision published by Ponsford (1991); where diagnostic features are present, Bristol ware jugs have been divided into early (13th century), and late (14th–15th centuries), with plain bases. South Somerset glazed jugs (fabric Q) are similar to Taunton red wares, although no place of manufacture has been identified as yet. Similar wares have been found at Shapwick, near Glastonbury, from contexts dated to the 13th century and into the later medieval period (Gutiérrez forthcoming).

Other regional wares are dominated by glazed jugs, although tripod pitchers from the Salisbury area in Wiltshire (SEW) are also present. Glazed jug products from Minety, Worcester, and Stamford are rare and appear to be residual in the later phases of the site.

Later medieval and post-medieval fabrics

Somerset wares

OO Somerset? 15th–16th century? Light orange throughout, sometimes with a grey core. Fine fabric with abundant sub-angular quartz <0.2mm; occasional fine-grained white sandstone <0.5mm. Open forms with smoothed-over surfaces.

C27 South Somerset, transitional medieval to post-medieval. Orange throughout, but occasionally pinkish or grey core. Sandy texture with no inclusions visible, except for occasional clay pellets. When glaze is present, it only covers the exterior wall of jugs; sometimes with an iron wash.

C28 Somerset? 16th–17th century. Fine, sandy fabric, with well-sorted quartz inclusions. Mainly open forms, such as pancheons. Lead glazed on interior surface. Wheel thrown.

C7 South Somerset post-medieval glazed wares, 17th–18th century. Orange throughout; occasional grey cores. Fine fabric with no visible inclusions, although sometimes there is occasional limestone <1mm, occasional iron oxide <3mm and mica. According to their decoration, the following sub-divisions have been noted:

- **C1**: sgraffito wares, 17th–18th century (white slip sgraffito and amber glaze)
- **C2**: all-over slipwares, 17th–18th century (internal white slip under amber glaze)
- **C3**: trailed slipwares, 17th–18th century
- **C8**: dark brown (iron-rich) glazed wares, 17th–18th century (rich brown colour on internal surface of larger open forms, but on interior and exterior of smaller vessels)
- **C15**: unglazed redwares, mainly flower pots. 18th–19th century.

Regional imports

Malvern Chase ware Malvern Chase, Worcestershire. 16th century. Orange throughout. Occasional inclusions of granite of varying sizes, usually 2–3mm, but up to 8mm across. Iron wash (usually all over) and transparent or brown glaze, sometimes limited to certain areas of the vessel (like bases of puncheons and bowls).

Cistercian-type ware South Gloucestershire. 16th century. Dark red or brown throughout. Moderate to sparse inclusions of quartz and quartzite up to 1mm and rounded iron ore up to 0.4mm. Very thick dark brown/black glaze all over, except on underside of the base, where only a purple wash is visible.

A13 Manganese-powdered tin-glazed. English. Mid-17th century. No inclusions visible. All-over tin glaze; powdered manganese (purple) decoration on exterior surface.

A1 English delftware. 17th–18th century. No inclusions visible. All-over tin glaze; blue decoration.

A55 Anglo-Netherlands tin glazed wares. 17th century. No inclusions visible. Blue decoration on tin glaze on interior surface; yellowish lead-glazed exterior surface.

E North Devon gravel-tempered wares. 17th century. Grey or orange core, grey interior margin and surface, orange exterior margin and surface. Superabundant quartz up to 6mm; abundant milky quartz up to 3mm; sparse limestone up to 2mm; moderate slate <5mm; moderate chert <6mm. Green glaze on interior surface.

KK Staffordshire/Bristol hollow wares. Late 17th–18th century. Buff throughout. Inclusions: moderate iron oxide <0.25mm. Trailed dark brown slip over white slip under amber glaze.

M Staffordshire-type press-moulded flat wares. Late 17th–18th century. Buff throughout. Moderate iron oxide <0.25mm. White/brown slip over brown background slip, all under amber glaze.

B3 Nottingham-type stoneware. End of 17th century–19th century

B19 Press-moulded salt-glazed white stoneware. 18th century.

Foreign pottery

A40 Malling-type jug. Low Countries. 16th century. No. visible inclusions. Interior: clear yellowish lead glaze. Exterior: white tin glaze and powdered blue decoration.

Raeren stoneware Fine dark grey fabric with no inclusions visible. Matt brown glaze exterior.

Frechen stoneware Grey fabric with quartz inclusions. Exterior mottled brown salt glaze.

Late medieval fabrics from Somerset include fine sandy fabrics, usually glazed only on the exterior of closed forms (C27, C28), and coarser unglazed open forms (OO). More refined fabrics, almost free of inclusions, have all been included in fabric C7 which is always lead-glazed and sometimes decorated with trailed slips or sgraffito. In contrast to the glazed vessels of the later medieval period, glazes in fabric C7 cover the whole surface of the vessel or just the interior of open and closed forms. Some variations in the texture of fabrics C7, C1, C2, and C3 may well indicate that they represent several centres of manufacture, and products from several workshops such as Donyatt, Wrangway, Wanstrow, or Nether Stowey may well be included here. As John Allan has demonstrated recently, it is not possible to ascribe wares to individual centres of production on the basis of visual examination alone (Allan 1999a), but the term 'south Somerset' is preferred instead. Techniques of decoration and vessel profiles of lead-glazed wares found at Puxton are well paralleled with the more extensively published products from the Donyatt kilns (Coleman-Smith and Pearson 1981).

Amongst other regional products, Malvernian wares of late medieval date are present in Phases 7–10. These sherds are small but show the characteristic thick, partial glaze and iron wash of the 16th century. Most sherds appear in Phase 9, where they represent 6% by weight, whereas a few sherds in Phases 7 and 8 may represent slightly earlier production, perhaps at the end of the 15th century. Cistercian-type wares from south Gloucestershire have also been identified in Phases 8 and 9, although the majority were found in the topsoil. They consist of cups with grooved walls, covered with a very dark brown, almost black, glaze. Similar looking vessels covered with an iron-rich, dark brown glaze but with a finer and lighter red fabric were also developed in Somerset (fabric C8) and they appear together with the Gloucestershire products, albeit in slightly higher numbers. Small numbers of other 17th- and 18th-century wares were also found in Phases 8 and 9, including just two sherds of North Devon gravel-tempered wares and Bristol/Staffordshire slipwares. The latter have a characteristic buff fabric, clear glaze and brown slips common to both centres and their products cannot be distinguished from one another. Delftware or tin-glazed vessels with either blue decoration (fabric A1) or mottled manganese (A13) also appear in the same phases. Two small sherds with a lead-glazed surface are from an Anglo-Netherlandish source; fine fabrics and similar decoration makes is impossible to distinguish by eye if they are English or imported.

Amongst the pottery of certain foreign origin, there is a single sherd from a 16th-century jug of 'Malling-type' in Phase 9. For many years it was thought that this type of jug was of English manufacture owing to the number of examples found in this country (an early find with a silver mount from West Malling in Kent gave its name to the group as a whole). Recent chemical analysis of finds from London and from the Low Countries have confirmed that these were, however, produced in Antwerp, where they are found in contexts dating to the second half of the 16th century (Hughes and Gaimster 1999, 61–2). Malling jugs are not common finds from excavations, and of the 24 finds identified so far in the south-west of England, most have been found at ports such as Exeter, Totnes, and Plymouth. Their inland distribution, however, is far more limited and seems to be linked to higher-status sites, such as the single example from Bampton Castle in Devon (Allan 1999b, 159) and from the moated site at Shapwick in Somerset (Gerrard 1999; Gutiérrez forthcoming). Five sherds of German stoneware were also recovered. They belong to drinking jugs from Raeren and Frechen (Fig 9.10, no 54), types which were imported to England in large numbers in the 16th and 17th centuries respectively and found widely spread across the country.

Modern wares

Just five sherds of modern wares were found, including four sherds of blue-printed pearlware and a single one of a modern brown English stoneware, all of the 19th century.

Church Field summary by trench

Trench 1

Out of a total of 290 pottery fragments (1,901g) recovered from this trench, almost half (138; 712g) were from the topsoil (context 100). Remarkably, almost all the pottery from the topsoil consisted of medieval wares, with only two fragments of the 17th–18th century and some residual Roman pottery (not included here). Although no joining fragments could be identified, almost all the pottery types present in the topsoil are present in the contexts below, indicating that later activity on site disturbed the medieval contexts, probably in the 17th–18th centuries (Table 9.3 CD).

Pottery from contexts other than the topsoil is all of medieval date, together with three fragments of Roman residual pottery (from contexts 116, 120 and 151). The medieval pottery assemblage is almost exclusively composed of fabrics of local manufacture in the Somerset region, except from a single sherd from a south-east Wiltshire tripod pitcher. These are mostly unglazed wares, except for one fragment from a Bristol jug (context 121) and another from a green-glazed south Somerset jug (context 106).

In the stratigraphically early Phase 5 features, the fill (116) of ditch F.115 contains wares from the late 11th–to 12th centuries, such as those in fabrics AA1, Bristol A-B, U1, and U4, together with local fabric PX04. The pottery assemblage from the spread of occupation debris 151 has a similar composition, but a single Bristol ware sherd (AAA) seems out of context here and may be intrusive. The main group of pottery in Phase 6 derives from the occupation layer 106/118, from which similar fabrics were also recorded in addition to Proto Ham Green coarsewares of the 12th century. Of the glazed wares one is a single sherd from a tripod pitcher of fabric XX, whereas a tiny scrap of a glazed redware (fabric Q) could be intrusive. The absence of any glazed jugs here would suggest an early 12th-century date for the platform. In the same phase, the gully F.119 (120) produced only nine sherds of pottery, including one from an early Bristol ware jug of the 13th century that might indicate a slightly later date for this feature.

Trench 2

This trench yielded 331 fragments (2,274g) of pottery, about a third of which (153 sherds, 1kg) was found in the topsoil (contexts 101 and 109). Although a handful of post-medieval and modern pottery was found here (including pearlware, modern stoneware, lead-glazed wares, delftware and Bristol/Staffordshire slipwares), around 87% by fragment and weight count of all the pottery from this context consisted of medieval wares. As in Trench 1, these derive from the lower levels of the trench, and cross-fits or sherd links across the trench confirm the disturbance of earlier contexts, such as one fragmented vessel in fabric PX09 that was found dispersed in contexts 101, 109 and 124.

Of the Phase 5 contexts excavated here, gully F.122 yielded around a dozen sherds from the late 11th–early 12th centuries (Bristol A-B, U1, U4, PX04, PX03). In Phase 6, ditch F.128 (contexts 130, 131, 132, 144, 150, 152, 153) only yielded coarsewares, of which about half are those in fabrics PX04 and PX08 of possible local origin. Although it is not possible to date the latter very closely, the lack of glazed wares and presence of Proto Ham Green coarsewares would suggest a 12th-century date for the fill of this feature. Ditch F.135 (131, 136, 145, 149) produced coarsewares of fabrics AA1 and Bristol A-B, together with fabric PX04, plus a small sherd of a glazed jug (fabric Q) from context 145. Post-medieval pottery was concentrated in the topsoil (contexts 101 and 109), and only a single fragment of 17th-century lead-glazed ware (fabric C7) was identified from the recut F.140 of ditch F.128 (context 141). The rest of the contexts provided exclusively medieval wares of late 11th- to 13th-century date, although the presence of glazed jugs (Bristol, Ham Green, XX and Early south Somerset), some from the topsoil, point to the end of this date range (12th–13th centuries). The medieval assemblage from this trench is nevertheless dominated by unglazed wares, which make up 98% (by sherd count; 99% by weight) of all those recovered from medieval deposits in Phases 5 and 6.

Trench 3 (the enclosure ditch)

This trench provided only a handful of medieval sherds (eight fragments; 81g), which derive almost exclusively from the fill of ditch F.103. The absence of glazed wares and the chronology of the pottery present suggest a 12th-century (or later) date for the fill, although the assemblage is so small that the dating should be treated with caution.

Trench 11 (the enclosure bank)

Pottery from Trench 11 amounted to seven fragments (31g), all of medieval date and mostly from the topsoil. Only one stratified sherd of chert-tempered ware (U1) was found in the upper part of the bank (context 502).

Trench 12

Trench 12 yielded 972 fragments (8,402g) of pottery. Most of this assemblage is medieval in date, except for a few fragments of 16th- to 17th-century and modern pottery found in the topsoil (context 501), and the intrusive 19th-century pearlware from the platform (context 504). The upper layer of the platform (contexts 501, 504, and 505) also provided a few fragments of residual Roman pottery, and comprised 44% (by sherd count and weight) of all the pottery from this trench. Most of the pottery from the platform can be dated to the 11th–12th centuries, being almost exclusively coarsewares and including fabrics AA1, AA2 and Bristol A-B. Three possible tripod pitchers from south-east Wiltshire and Somerset (XX, Y) were also found here, the latest fragment being from a 13th-century Bristol jug (from context 505), although no other glazed wares were identified.

The rest of the features excavated contained exclusively medieval pottery of the late 11th–12th centuries. Ditch F.510 was the most productive, with 236 fragments (24% of all the fragments from this trench; 16% by weight from the trench). The uppermost layer of this feature (context 511) contained two fragments of early Bristol ware, which it would indicate a possible 13th-century date for at least the upper fill of the feature, although the rest of the sherds are dated predominately to the 12th century, including a Ham Green jug sherd also from context 511.

The same types of pottery are well represented across features in this trench. Sadly, the best-dated fragment, a handle of Stamford ware, was found in the topsoil. If material found here was derived from contexts below, as seems likely, then the Stamford handle's date of *c* 1150–75 might indicate a general date of the end of the 12th to the beginning of the 13th century for the medieval contexts, which would tie in with the dates for the unglazed wares and the presence of early Bristol ware.

Fieldwalking

A fieldwalking survey carried out in Church Field also recovered a high proportion of medieval pottery (112 sherds, 47% of all the pottery collected: Table 9.4 (CD)). Unsurprisingly, fabrics identified are similar to those found during excavation. Proportions, however, are slightly different, and fabrics AA1, U4, U1, and PX08 were found almost in similar numbers to fabric PX04. A handful of glazed jugs were also found. Post-medieval and modern pottery amounted to 125 sherds, some of which are represented in the topsoil of the excavated trenches.

Two sherds from two medieval roof tiles were also recovered from fieldwalking. They probably belong to ridge tiles and are of fabric similar to Bristol products; they are both green glazed on the exterior surface. A sherd of Malvern Chase ridge tile of 16th-century date was also recovered from the topsoil of Trench 2 during surface cleaning (context 101).

Church Field discussion

The pottery assemblage from Church Field shows a clear distinction between two different areas: that from the main enclosure (Trenches 1, 2, and 12) and that across the bank (Trenches 3 and 11). The latter provided only small assemblages of medieval pottery, dominated by the presence of Roman pottery. The assemblages from the area in and around the platform, on the other hand, are dominated by medieval pottery of the late 11th–12th centuries. There are no great differences between the several groups of pottery from Trenches 1, 2, and 12, all having roughly the same types of fabrics in similar proportions. Coarsewares dominate here, making up 98% of all the sherds from medieval contexts. Amongst these, local fabric PX04 accounts for 61% by weight.

Pottery types

There seems to be no pottery earlier than the late 11th century from Church Field. Fabric AA1 (Fig 9.10, Nos 1–7) can be dated to the 10th–11th centuries, but at Puxton it always appears in association with slightly later material. In contexts of Phase 5 (116 and 151) it is associated with Bristol A-B (Fig 9.10, No. 8), chert-tempered wares (U1) and Bath A (U4) of the late 11th–12th centuries. Sadly, it is not possible to confirm whether fabric AA1 is residual in these contexts or simply if its production continued into the 12th century. Certainly, there are no features containing solely pre-11th-century material. Material of the 13th century is very scarce, comprising just fifteen sherds of Bristol ware and one of a glazed Somerset jug. Pottery of the 15th–16th centuries is totally absent, apart from the one fragment of Malvern Chase ware from the topsoil of Trench 12. It is not until the 17th century that there are any signs of activity on site, especially in Trench 2.

The medieval fabrics found in Church Field derive almost exclusively from either local or regional kilns. Together with the possible local fabrics mentioned above, such as PX04 (Fig 9.10, Nos 10–13), other Somerset products dominate, including wares from the Bristol-Bath area, such as fabrics PX08 (Nos 15–18) and U4 (Fig 9.10, Nos 22–5). Bristol workshops provided both unglazed (jars) (Fig 9.10, No. 31) and glazed wares (jugs) (Fig 9.10, No. 32). Imports from further afield are represented by a single handle from a costrel in Stamford ware (Fig 9.10, No. 38). The handle is finely decorated with an applied plait. Stamford fine wares were traded commercially and have a wide distribution across the country, though they are especially concentrated in the central and eastern midlands (Kilmurry 1980, 161). Further south they also appear in Gloucestershire, Bath, and Bristol, although they are not very frequent in Somerset. No foreign imports were present in the assemblage.

Post-medieval pottery from this part of the site is limited in both numbers and range, and includes a selection of typical products of 17th- to 19th-century date, such as English delftware, modern stoneware, Bristol/Staffordshire slipwares, and pearlwares. This material may represent casual dumping or manuring, and strongly suggests a change in the focus of settlement activity between the medieval and post-medieval periods or simply changing practices of rubbish disposal. Post-medieval pottery is probably incorporated into farmyard manures and strewn across the fields, rather than being buried in pits and ditches as seems to be the case in the medieval period.

Vessel forms

As mentioned above, most of the medieval assemblage from Church Field consists of coarsewares; those forms recognised are almost exclusively jars (as defined by MPRG 1998), such as those in fabrics AA1, PX04, PX08, U1, U4 and Proto Ham Green. The most ubiquitous rim profile is everted, sometimes clubbed. Decoration is scarce; parallel or wavy lines appear on some of the Proto Ham Green jars (Fig 9.10, No. 34), incised lines on U1 and U4 jars, and finger impressions along the rim of an AA1 jar (Fig 9.10, No. 2). A tripod pitcher in fabric PX08 was decorated by means of stamping a circular grid (Fig 9.10, No. 18), while the handle (not illustrated) was incised with a wavy line. Other unglazed forms are more difficult to identify among the small sherds, but a pancheon from south Somerset and two tripod pitchers have also been recognised, one each from south-east Wiltshire and from south Somerset (fabric Y). Medieval glazed wares are monotonously represented by jugs (Fig 9.10, No. 32). Typically, among the Bristol and Ham Green products the green glaze is applied on the exterior of the vessel and decoration is limited to incised lines under the glaze, and thumbed bases. In a couple of examples decoration makes use of applied strips of clay under an iron-brown slip, all covered by transparent glaze (contexts 220, 222, 357). In contrast, south Somerset jugs use a transparent glaze, sometimes with green copper drops. The Stamford costrel mentioned above is covered with a very thin transparent glaze.

Home Ground summary by trench

Trench 4

Trench 4 was the largest excavated and provided the biggest assemblage of pottery, consisting of 1,042 fragments (8,572g). Pottery of post-medieval date was more numerous than in Church Field (some 44% of the total weight in Trench 4). On the face of it, the pottery evidence suggests that a number of features might be of early medieval date, although some of the contexts provided very few fragments of pottery (in some cases only one or two sherds). Contexts 241, 244, 266, and 285 all contained 12th-century material; context 268 also had early Bristol ware of the 13th century. A possible late medieval feature is 312, where 16th-century material was abundant, but the presence of residual medieval pottery here suggests this feature disturbed earlier contexts on site. The rest of the features excavated, mainly ditches around the platforms, contained abundant pottery of the 17th and 18th centuries, suggesting the date of their infill. The medieval pottery present in most of them would suggest nevertheless that they were cut/dug through earlier deposits. This is certainly the case for context 309 (feature 308) and for the garden soil (contexts 213, 220–2); in the garden soil, 70% of all the sherds from these four contexts are medieval.

Trench 5

Trench 5 produced 246 fragments (2,399g) of pottery. Their distribution follows a similar trend to Trench 4, with abundant redeposition of medieval pottery in post-medieval contexts, such as 352, 356 and 359. Saxo-Norman pottery (fabric AA1) is present, but is mixed in with later medieval pottery, such as the late Bristol ware of the 14th–15th century (context 354). A high proportion of the better-dated medieval glazed wares are residual in later phases of the site, for example Ham Green, Minety and Worcestershire jugs (in contexts 352, 356, 357, 363).

Home Ground discussion

The assemblage of pottery from Home Ground provides a wider range of fabrics and longer chronological span than that from Church Field. The main characteristic of this assemblage is the frequent redeposition of medieval material in later contexts, pointing to considerable disturbance of the medieval deposits at later dates. The range of fabrics present in the medieval assemblage is very similar to that from Church Field, however, where local and regional types are dominant. Nevertheless, English imports are represented by at least three jugs from Wiltshire (Minety ware) and two from Worcestershire (Fig 9.10, No. 39).

The assemblage contains later medieval wares of 14th- to 15th-century date, represented by Bristol jugs with plain, heavy bases. Most of these later jugs appear mixed in post-medieval contexts, where they are often associated with earlier wares of 12th- to 13th-century date and with sgraffitos, slipwares, and lead-glazed wares of the 17th–18th centuries (contexts 352, 356).

Pottery of 16th-century date is represented by well-known types of this date, especially from south Somerset (fabric C27; Fig 9.10, No. 42), but also from Gloucestershire (Cistercian-type) and Worcestershire (Malvern Chase; Nos 52–3). Imports of German stoneware were also popular in England at this date, and the presence of Raeren and Frechen stoneware is not surprising (Fig 9.10, No. 54). The 'Malling jug' found in Trench 5 is identical in fabric and texture to that found at Shapwick (Gerrard 1999), although the Puxton jug is only decorated in blue. The restricted distribution of this type of ware outside ports hints at the existence of a site of some status, which would allow for access to specialist markets.

Pottery of the 17th–18th centuries is also represented by well-spread types of the period. Products from south Somerset dominated the region's markets at this time, especially slipwares and sgraffito wares. Staffordshire/Bristol slipwares, North Devon gravel-tempered wares, and English delftwares are also to be found among the assemblage.

The range of medieval and later medieval sources of pottery represented in the assemblage from Home Ground is wide for a rural site. It is difficult to find parallels of similar, rural settlements which do not include palaces, castles, manor houses, or abbeys. The best-documented study is that of Shapwick, where both the moated site and village plots were examined. The main difference that existed there between the higher-status plots and those from the village seems to be the presence of pottery coming from a wider range of sources, including London products (Gutiérrez forthcoming). Finds from a 'peasant' house in Bickley, near Puxton, did include only local products from Bristol and other Somerset sources (Ponsford 2003). It is, however, difficult to confirm whether the range of products found at Puxton is genuine and robust evidence of status, or simply of stronger links with Bristol since most of the more non-local wares would have been available there.

Vessel forms

Like the Church Field site discussed above, vessels are very fragmented and identification of forms is difficult when only wall sherds are present and diagnostic sherds are not numerous. Nevertheless, coarseware jars dominated the medieval wares, representing about 70% by weight. A couple of bowls were also recorded in fabric PX08 (Fig 9.10, Nos 20–21) and another one in fabric PX04, this with a bifid rim probably for seating a lid (Fig 9.10, No. 14). Apart from a single tripod pitcher with patchy green glaze (fabric XX), the remaining glazed wares are jugs, among which Ham Green and Bristol products predominate; in a couple of examples decoration makes use of applied strips of clay under an iron-brown slip, all covered by transparent glaze (Fig 9.10, Nos 35–6). A south Somerset jug (fabric Q) shows a thumbed strip around the rim and transparent glaze (Fig 9.10, No. 37). Non-local products include two green-glazed Worcestershire jugs, one of them decorated with a rouletted pattern along the external surface of the wall (Fig 9.10, No. 39). Small sherds of Minety jugs also show green glaze, sometimes with parallel grooving under the glaze cover.

By the 16th century open forms are also found in the Home Ground assemblage, such as bowls/

pancheons from south Somerset, in fabrics OO and C27 (Fig 9.10, Nos 40–2). The range of vessel forms increases notably in the post-medieval period. Together with the flared mugs in Cistercian ware, and the equivalent Somerset types (Fig 9.10, No. 43), there are also several chafing dishes of 16th- to 17th-century date; one of them is a Malvernian ware from the topsoil of Trench 12 (Fig 9.10, No. 53), the rest are all lead-glazed in brown from Trenches 4 and 5. Four delft and Bristol/Staffordshire slipped dishes from Trenches 2 and 4 were found, a blue-decorated delft jar/albarello, and five German stoneware drinking jugs. But the wider repertoire is provided by the typical lead-glazed wares from south Somerset, sometimes with slipped and sgraffito decoration, which includes bowls, jugs, puncheons, mugs, a chafing dish and a colander (Fig 9.10, Nos 44–51).

The medieval pottery from the shovel test pits

A total of 444 sherds (2,227g) were examined from the shovel test pits at five locations around Puxton (Bindings Cottage, Flemans, Haynes, Butts and Coles: Fig 9.3.B). Detailed quantification can be found in Table 9.5 (CD).

Flemans

A small assemblage of pottery was recovered from three shovel test pits west of Flemans. Most of the pottery is of medieval date (12th–13th century; 95% of all the sherds), including mainly coarsewares of local origin and from neighbouring areas, such as Wiltshire (U4); a few Bristol glazed jugs are also present. Interestingly, although the rest of the sherds are of late medieval or post-medieval date, no modern pottery was present (19th century onwards).

Bindings

Shovel test pits from Bindings yielded 103 sherds (587g) of pottery. Almost half is of medieval date (12th–13th century), including green-glazed Bristol jugs (Bristol ware and Ham Green), though most of the medieval sherds belong to unglazed jars. These are represented by local Somerset fabrics (PX03, PX04, PX08, sandy coarseware), and a few sherds of U4 fabric of possible Wiltshire source. A few of the vessels are of later medieval date, including Cistercian ware, Malvern Chase ware and glazed south Somerset jugs (fabric C27). The post-medieval assemblage is of equal size, and it is dominated by plain lead-glazed wares from Somerset; a few decorated wares, such as slipwares both from Somerset (C2) and Bristol/Staffordshire (M/KK), are also present. Modern pottery is sparse (just 11% of the total by count number) comprising mainly plain and decorated pearlwares and a few industrially made redwares (fabric C20).

Haynes

A small selection of sherds, including a few medieval (12th- to 13th-century) and late medieval wares (Malvern Chase, Cistercian ware and unglazed Somerset wares: fabric OO). A few sherds of the 17th–18th centuries and of modern date were also found.

Butts

A sizeable group of pottery was recovered from shovel test pits at Butts. Most of the pottery is of medieval date (12th–13th century; 90% of all sherds recovered), including some early coarsewares (fabric AA1) and Bristol jugs, although the majority of sherds belong to local coarsewares. Just a few late medieval glazed wares (C27 and Malvern Chase ware) are also present, together with some post-medieval lead-glazed vessels, although no decorated vessels were found, such as slipwares of the 18th century. Just four sherds of modern pottery were found; this is a very low number, and includes a sherd from a flower pot (fabric C15).

Coles

More than half of all the sherds provided by shovel test pits at Coles are of medieval date (12th–13th century). The range of fabrics is similar to that found in the other shovel test pits, including local coarsewares and Bristol glazed jugs. A single sherd of earlier medieval date (AA1) was also found here. Just one sherd of 13th- to 15th-century Bristol ware was recovered, along with a handful of post-medieval and modern sherds.

Conclusion

The excavations at Puxton have provided two pottery assemblages of moderate size. That from the Church Field is exclusively of medieval date, whereas that from Home Ground continues well into the post-medieval period. Both assemblages are dominated by products from local workshops and are greatly affected by the location of the site close to Bristol, which must have supplied at least part of the pottery. The medieval assemblage from Church Field consists predominately of coarsewares, but this is probably related to the period of activity which pre-dates the peak in production and distribution of glazed jugs from the Bristol area, rather than having anything to do with the status of the site. Pottery from Home Ground shows a wider range of sources for its medieval and later medieval pottery.

The access to wider markets and contacts could be a pointer to the status of the site. The material from the shovel test pits confirms 12th- to 13th-century occupation on all of the sites, with Haynes occupied into the late medieval period and Bindings through to the 20th century.

Illustrated sherds

1 Fabric AA1. Jar; grey throughout with brown interior surface. Trench 12, context 528, lower fill of F.526.
2 Fabric AA1. Jar; grey throughout with brown surfaces; thumbed rim. Trench 12, context 501, topsoil.
3 Fabric AA1. Jar; grey throughout. Trench 12, context 514, upper layer of platform.
4 Fabric AA1. Jar; grey throughout with brown surfaces. Trench 1, context 100, topsoil.
5 Fabric AA1. Jar; grey throughout with brown surfaces. Trench 1, context 100, topsoil.
6 Fabric AA1. Jar; grey throughout with brown surfaces. Trench 2, context 101, topsoil.
7 Fabric AA1. Small jar; grey throughout with brown surfaces. Trench 1, context 100, topsoil.
8 Fabric Bristol A-B. Jar; grey fabric throughout. Trench 2, context 109.
9 Fabric PX04. Small jar; black throughout. Trench 1, context 118, and Trench 12, context 504.
10 Fabric PX04. Jar; black fabric throughout. Light soot on underside of rim. Trench 2, context 131, ditch F.135.
11 Fabric PX04. Jar; grey fabric throughout. Trench 12, context 504, upper layer of platform.
12 Fabric PX04. Jar; grey fabric with brown surfaces. Trench 12, context 504, upper layer of platform.
13 Fabric PX04. Bowl; grey fabric throughout with interior brown surface. Trench 12, context 501, topsoil.
14 Fabric PX04. Jar with bifid rim; grey fabric throughout. Trench 4, context 220, garden soil on North Platform.
15 Fabric PX08. Jar; grey throughout and light brown exterior surface. Trench 1, context 100, topsoil.
16 Fabric PX08. Jar; grey core and buff/light brown surfaces. Light soot on interior and exterior of rim surfaces. Trench 1, context 118.
17 Fabric PX08. Jar; grey throughout. Trench 2, context 150, basal fill of F.128.
18 Fabric PX08. Tripod pitcher; grey throughout with light brown exterior surface. Unglazed, decorated with impressed stamped decoration. Trench 12, context 511.
19 Fabric PX08. Jar; grey core and buff surfaces. Trench 4, context 309
20 Fabric PX08. Bowl (3 sherds); grey fabric with light brown surfaces on the rim. Light soot on exterior wall. Trench 4, context 309.
21 Fabric PX08. Bowl with wavy rim; grey fabric with light brown surfaces. Trench 4, context 313.
22 Fabric U4. Jar; grey throughout. Trench 2, context 150, basal fill of F.128.
23 Fabric U4. Jar; light brown throughout. Trench 12, context 517, fill of F.510.
24 Fabric U4. Jar; grey fabric throughout, with buff internal surface and light brown exterior. Trench 1, context 106.
25 Fabric U4. Jar; grey with brown surfaces. Trench 12, context 501, topsoil.
26 Fabric U4. Jar; dark grey throughout. Trench 4, context 220, garden soil in North Platform.
27 Fabric U4. Jar; grey throughout with orange internal margin. Trench 4, context 299, gully F.298 on North Platform.
28 Fabric U4. Jar; dark grey fabric with light brown exterior surface. Trench 4, context 268, ditch F.267 on North Platform.
29 Fabric U4. Jar; grey core and brown surfaces. Trench 4, context 221, garden soil in North Platform.
30 Fabric PX09. Bowl (2 sherds); dark grey fabric with light brown surfaces. Trench 2, context 101.
31 Proto Ham Green jar; grey core and brown surfaces. Trench 12, context 533, F520.
32 Ham Green jug with brownish green glaze on exterior surface only; dark grey fabric with pinkish interior surface. Trench 2, context 101, topsoil.
33 Ham Green jug (four sherds) with green glaze on exterior surface and incised decoration of wavy lines; grey fabric throughout. Trench 4, context 285, ditch F.267 on North Platform.
34 Ham Green coarseware jar (three sherds); black fabric and red surfaces. Wavy incised line on interior of rim. Trench 4, context 213.
35 Bristol ware. Jug with green glaze on exterior; dark grey fabric throughout. Trench 4, context 221.
36 Bristol ware. Jug with green glaze exterior; pink fabric throughout. Applied thumbed cordon around the rim; applied strips and pellets in red clay, covered in brown glaze. Trench 4, contexts 220 (wall) and 245 (rim) (probably same vessel).
37 Fabric Q. Jug with applied thumbed cordon around rim. Transparent glaze with green speckles on exterior surface only; grey core and orange surfaces. Trench 5, context 352, rubble.
38 Stamford ware. Handle, probably from a costrel, with plaited band applied; patchy greenish transparent glaze all over; greyish/buff fabric. Trench 12, context 501, topsoil.
39 Worcestershire jug. Green glaze on exterior surface only; rouletted decoration; dark grey fabric. Trench 5, context 357.
40 Fabric OO. Coarseware bowl; brown fabric with grey core. Trench 4, context 221, garden soil in North Platform.
41 Fabric OO. Coarseware bowl; brown fabric throughout with darker brown surfaces. Trench 4, context 309.
42 Fabric C27. Chafing dish with over-all green glaze; part of a hole on the wall near the rim is just visible; orange fabric. Trench 4, context 309.
43 Fabric C8. Cup with over-all very dark brown glaze (except on underside of base). Trench 5, context 356.
44 Fabric C7. Bowl with green glaze on interior surface. Trench 4, context 210.
45 Fabric C7. Bowl (2 sherds) with green glaze on interior surface. Trench 4, context 220.
46 Fabric C7. Pancheon. Trench 4, context 220.
47 Fabric C7. Pancheon with partial brown glaze on interior surface. Trench 4, context 272.
48 Fabric C7. Jar with green glaze on interior surface and with an applied thumbed cordon around rim. Trench 4, context 204.
49 Fabric C7. Jar with thick green glaze on interior surface. Trench 4, context 270.
50 Fabric C7. Handled jar with green glaze on interior surface. Trench 4, context 215.
51 Fabric C7. Pancheon with green glaze on interior and exterior surface, although the rim has been left unglazed. Trench 5, context 356.
52 Malvern Chase bowl. Red wash all over. Trench 4, context 215.
53 Malvern Chase chafing dish. Brown glaze all over. Part of a ?triangular cut on the wall is just visible. Trench 4, context 309.
54 Frechen stoneware. Drinking jug. Mottled brown glaze on interior and exterior surfaces. Trench 4, context 233.

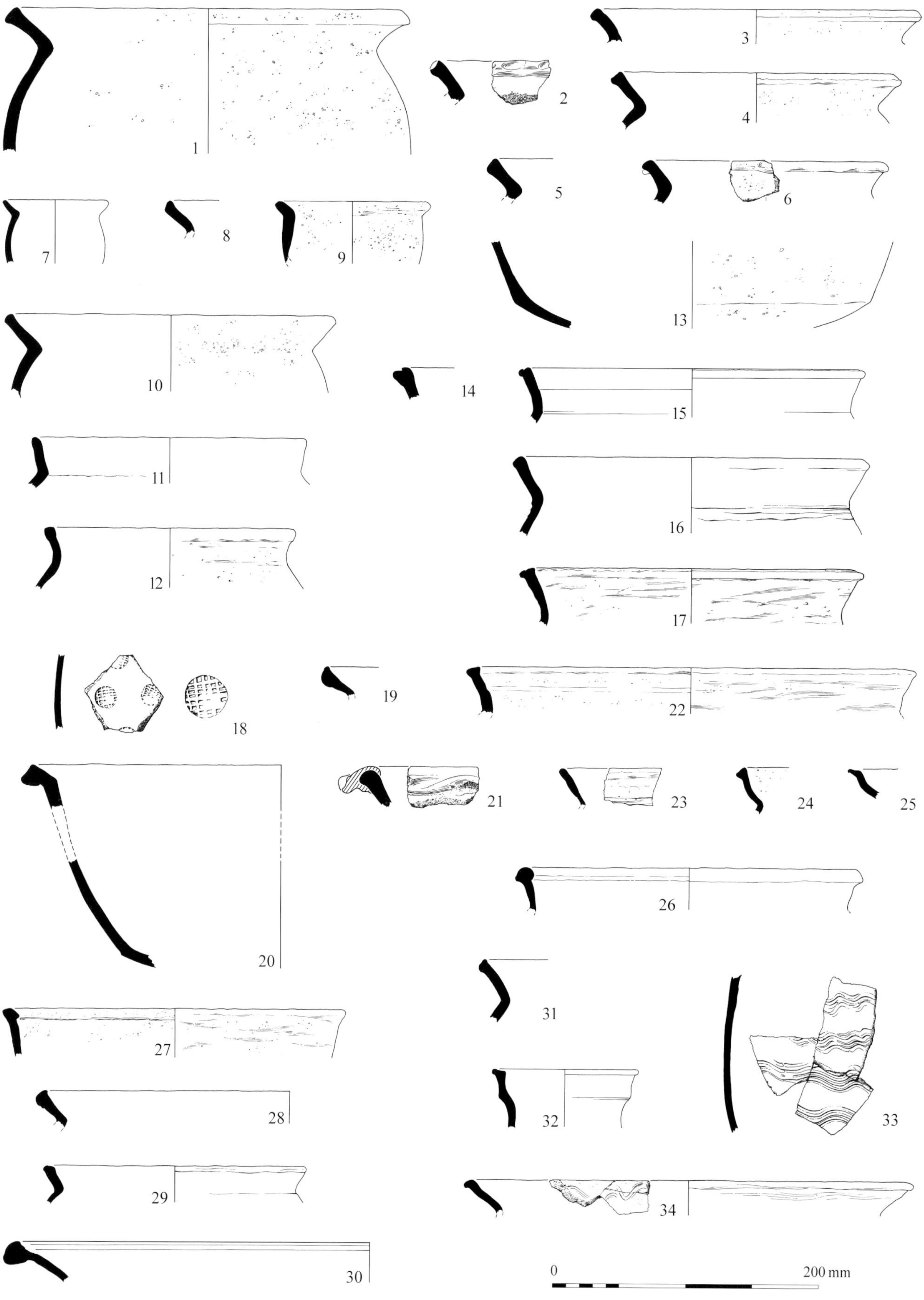

Figure 9.10a Medieval pottery from Puxton (drawing by Mike Rouillard)

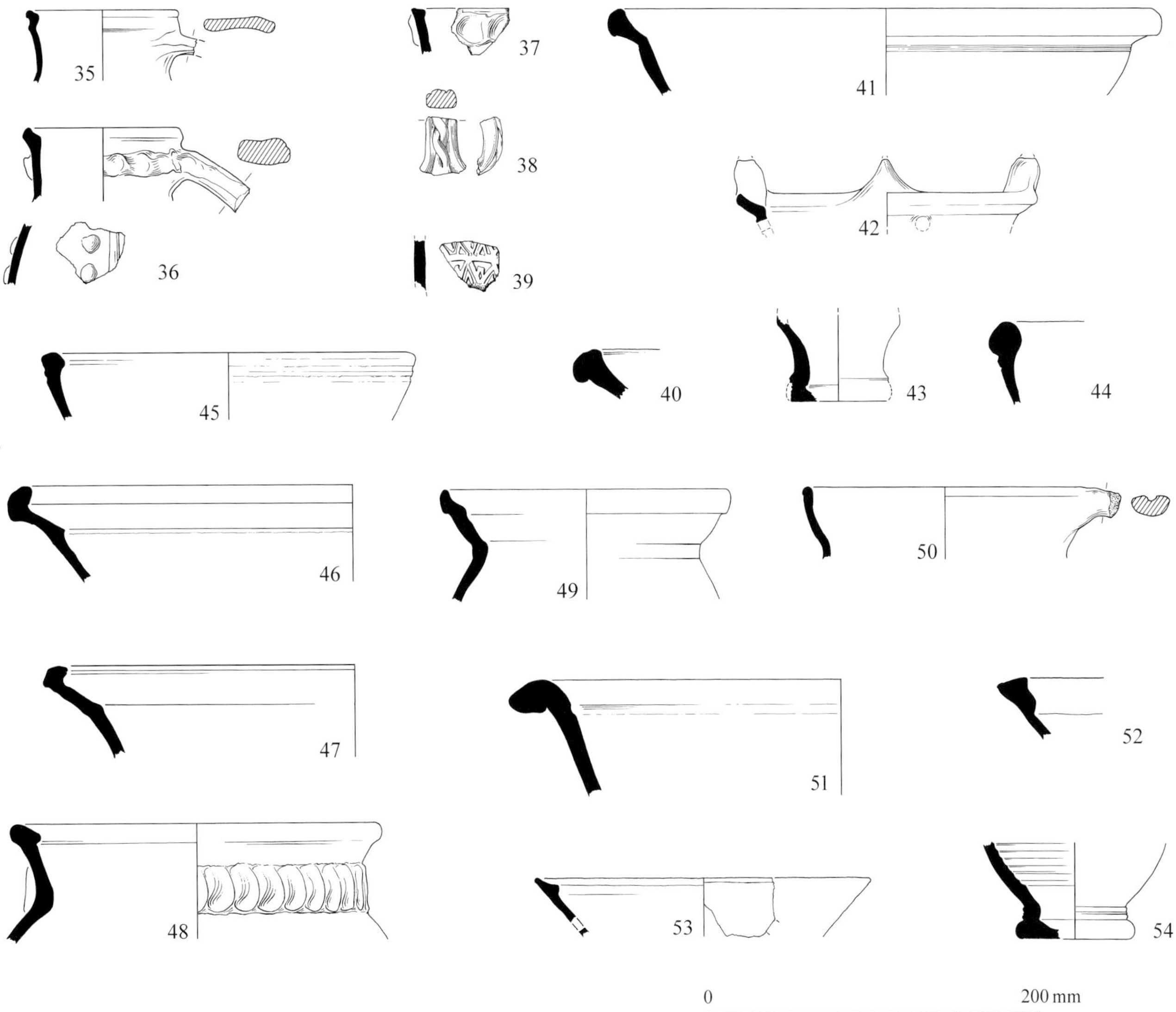

Figure 9.10b Medieval pottery from Puxton (drawing by Mike Rouillard)

Coins

No coins were recovered from the excavations despite extensive bulk sampling and wet sieving, though five medieval coins that had been found by a metal detectorist in Church Field were shown to the author, while two 16th-century coins were recovered from metal detecting the machined-off topsoil at Home Ground.

1 Church Field: Cnut (1016–35), helmet type penny (Seaby and Purvey 1980, No. 1158).
2 Church Field: Henry I (1100–35), quadrilateral on cross fleury type penny (Seaby and Purvey 1980, No. 1276).
3 Church Field: Stephen (1135–54), penny (Seaby and Purvey 1980, Nos 1278–82).
4 Church Field: Henry II, 'Tealby' type cross-and-crosslets penny (1158–80; Seaby and Purvey 1980, types 1337–42).
5 Church Field: Henry II, short cross penny (1180–89; Seaby and Purvey 1980, No. 1344)
6 topsoil Tr 4, Home Ground: hammered silver penny of Elizabeth I (1558–1603)
7 topsoil Tr 5, Home Ground: hammered silver sixpence of Elizabeth I (dated 1594).

Glass

Medieval

1 Fragment of pale blue/green vessel glass, 6mm thick (context 266, upper fill of 12th- to 13th-century pit F.265).

Post-medieval

2 Fragment of flat, pale green glass, 1mm thick (context 227, upper fill of 17th- to 18th-century ditch F.205).
3 Six fragments flat, pale green glass, 1mm thick (context 230, lower fill of 17th- to 18th-century recut in ditch F.205).
4 Fragment of flat mid-green glass, 2mm thick (context 353, 17th- to 18th-century stone scatter in Trench 5).

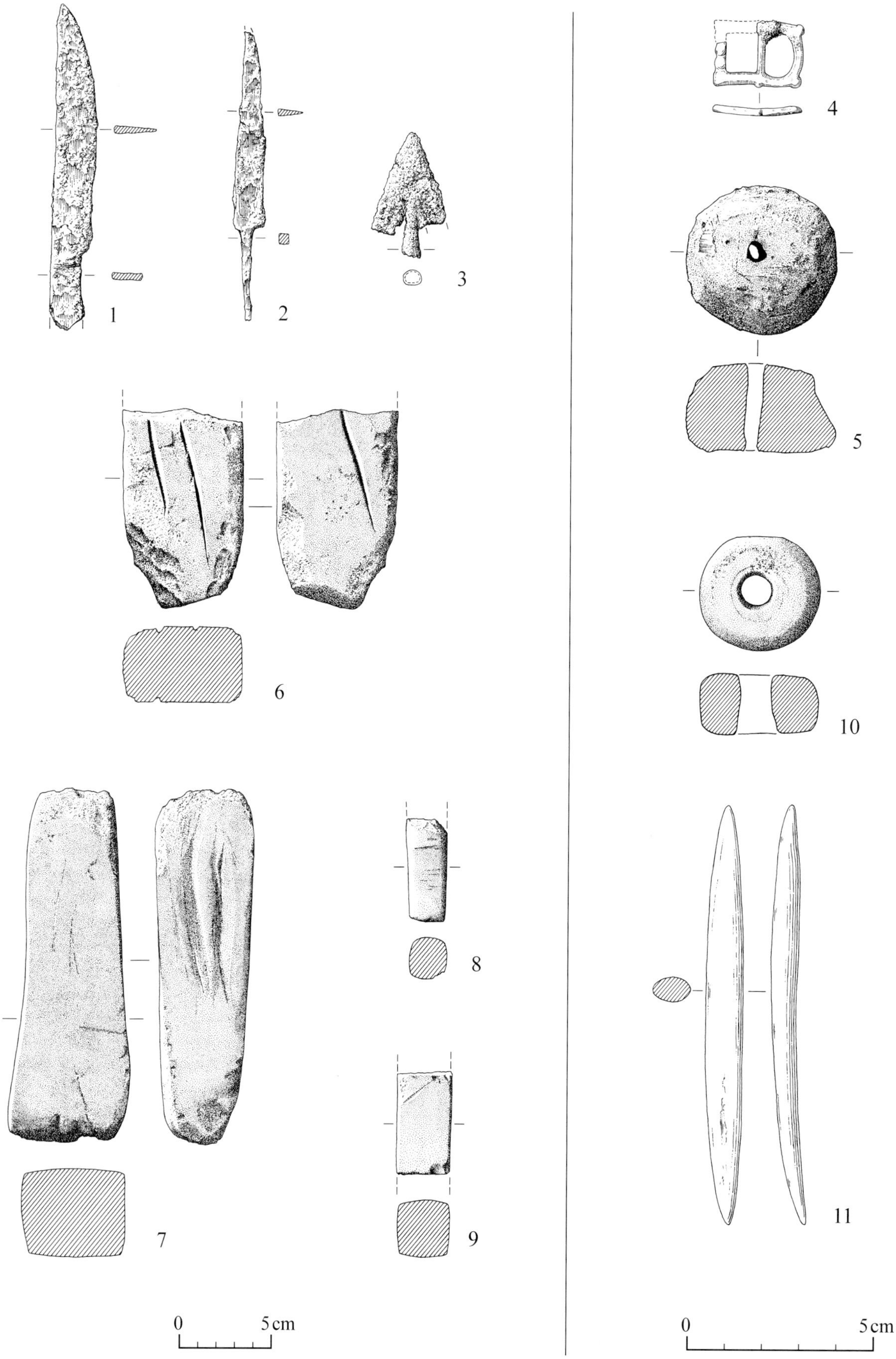

Figure 9.11 Medieval small finds from Puxton (drawing by Mike Rouillard)

Iron smithing slag

Twenty-seven small fragments (473g) of smithing slag were found in Trenches 1 and 12 on the platform in Church Field. Most was recovered from contexts 504–5 along with smaller amounts in features F.115, F.126, F.154, F.510, F.520, F.526, and F.531, all of which also contained domestic refuse. This scatter of material may be indicative of a forge in the vicinity.

Objects of iron *by David Richards*

The small assemblage of iron objects was poorly preserved due to the waterlogged conditions, and was dominated by hand made nails, square or rectangular in section, and with round or squarish heads. There were also a number of small straps and hooks of unknown function. The following items are worthy of note:

Horse and cart fittings

1 Strap. Length 210mm. A rectangular tapering strap widening and curved at one end, which has an oval central hole. The narrow end has a round hole. This seems too large for a curb-bit but may be a cart fitting (context 131, upper fill of ditch F.135).
2 Curb-bit or harness? Length 128mm. A slender rod, with flat, oval terminals with holes at each end (context 221, garden soil on North Platform).
3 Buckle. Length 63mm. A heavy rectangular buckle of which the tongue survives but is detached. From horse or cart harness (context 202, topsoil on South Platform, Trench 4).
4 Horseshoe. Length *c* 110mm. One limb of a wavy-edged shoe with a rolled calwin and six nails a side. The date range of these shoes covers the 10th–13th centuries, but this is probably 12th–13th century (Sparkes 1976, 9) (context 151, fill of hollow F.154).

Domestic objects

5 Knife, length 175mm (Fig 9.11, No. 1). A broad-bladed scale-tang knife, both edges curving upwards towards the tip. The tang is set in line with the blade top, and the shoulder is sloping. Between the first and second rivets there are distinct traces of a shoulder plate (Cowgill *et al* 1986, 9), probably of tin alloy, along with some possible mineralised organic scale material. This was once an elegant ?table knife. Cowgill *et al* (1986, pl 67 No. 265 and pl 68 No. 308) illustrate near parallels from the late 14th century (context 220, garden soil on North Platform).
6 Knife, length 152mm (Fig 9.11, No. 2). A small whittle-tang knife with a slender triangular blade with a thick back. The long tang is set just above the centre line. Cowgill *et al* (1986, pl 60 No. 75) illustrate near parallels from the late 14th century (context 221, garden soil on North Platform).
7 Arrowhead, length 76mm (Fig 9.11, No. 3). A wide, plain, triangular socketed head with most of the socket missing. A common form used in both war and hunting from the 11th–14th centuries (Jessop 1997, type 6) (context 238, garden soil on North Platform).
8 Wall hook. Length 202mm. A tapering, flat spike with a loop forged at the wide end. Would have been driven into a wall or post to hold a ring or chain (context 202, topsoil in South Platform, Trench 4).

Objects of copper alloy *by David Richards*

1 Bronze pin. Length 40mm, with a round solid head. Medieval (Egan and Pritchard 1991, 297) (context 350, topsoil in South Platform, Trench 5).
2 Bronze buckle, length 25mm (Fig 9.11, No. 4). A double-rectangular buckle with two knobs at the curved end. Either silvered or made from silvered alloy. Possibly from a shoe (Egan and Pritchard 1991, fig 54, 384) (context 202, topsoil on South Platform, Trench 4).

Objects of lead

1 Circular lead weight, 38mm diameter at its base reducing to 25mm on top, with a 4mm hole drilled vertically from top to bottom (Fig 9.11, No. 5). Fishing weight? (context 202: dump of stone rubble on South Platform at Home Ground, 19th century).
2 Rectangular fragment of 1.5mm thick sheet lead, 25 × 45mm (context 200: topsoil, Home Ground).
3 Triangular fragment of 1.5mm thick sheet lead, 65mm long, 54mm wide tapering to 6mm (context 213: garden soil on North Platform, Home Ground).
4 Twisted fragment of lead 20mm long and *c* 5mm wide. From window leading? (context 202: dump of stone rubble on South Platform at Home Ground, 19th century).
5 Twisted fragment of lead 25mm long and *c* 5mm wide. From window leading? (context 202: dump of stone rubble on South Platform at Home Ground, 19th century).

Objects of stone

Hones

Four hone stones were recovered from disturbed contexts high in the stratigraphic sequence and so may be post-medieval, though these contexts all contained a considerable amount of residual medieval pottery. The site in Church Field was abandoned during the 13th century, which suggests that No.3 is of medieval date. Nos 3 and 4 are similar, and both are made of the same stone as No. 2, suggesting that they may all be medieval.

1 Broken end of hone stone of fine-grained mid-grey sandstone (Fig 9.11, No. 6). Rectangular in section 40mm × 65mm × 86+mm. Polished on all unbroken surfaces, and with deep point-sharpening grooves on both the broader surfaces (context 202: 19th-century dump of stone rubble on South Platform at Home Ground).
2 Complete hone stone of light pinkish/grey fine-grained sandstone (Fig 9.11, No. 7). Rectangular in section, 185mm long, 50 × 50mm at one end tapering to 35 × 65mm at the other. All longitudinal surfaces polished, and with two point-sharpening groves on one side. Pecked surface at both ends indicates use as a hammer (context 309: 18th- to 19th-century upper fill of ditch F.308 at Home Ground).
3 Broken end of a small hone stone of light pinkish/grey fine-grained sandstone (Fig 9.11, No. 8). Square in section 21 × 22mm. Polish on all longitudinal surfaces. Similar to

Bickley Nos 6 and 7 (Ponsford 2003, fig 33) which have a hole drilled at one end suggesting that they were designed to be hung up (context 101: surface cleaning of stratified contexts in Trench 2, Church Field).

4 Fragment of a small hone stone of light pinkish/grey fine-grained sandstone (Fig 9.11, No. 9). Square in section 31 × 32mm. Polish on all longitudinal surfaces. Broken at both ends. Similar to Bickley Nos 6 and 7 (Ponsford 2003, fig 33) which have a hole drilled at one end suggesting that they were designed to be hung up (context 350: surface cleaning of stratified contexts in Trench 4, Home Ground).

Possible quern fragment

5 Fragment of light pinkish/grey lava, presumably from a quern (context 202, 19th-century dump of stone rubble on South Platform at Home Ground).

'Smoothers' or rubbing stones

6 Oval-shaped cobble *c* 50 × 60 × 100mm, flattened and polished on one side. May have been used to smooth leather, linen, or other fabric (Clark and Gaunt 2000, 109) (context 201: upper part of 18th- to 19th-century garden soil on North Platform).

7 Small naturally rounded pebble *c* 15 × 25 × 38mm with polish at one end (context 527, 12th- to 13th-century ditch F.526).

Spindle whorl

8 Circular stone object, 14mm thick, 32mm in diameter and with an 11mm hole drilled through its centre (Fig 9.11, No. 10). Both sides are of the same size suggesting a post-Conquest date (Clark and Gaunt 2000, 102) (context 131: 12th- to 13th-century upper fill of ditch F.135).

A curiosity

9 Fossil ammonite (context 322, fill of 16th-century gully F.302).

Objects of bone

1 Pin-beater? (Fig 9.11, No. 11). A bone object, 111mm long and 10mm wide, slightly curving (possibly cut from the shaft of a cow tibia: Alan Outram pers comm), and polished on all surfaces. Both ends worked, one with a series of polished facets and the other slightly more rounded perhaps through greater use. Possibly a pin beater (Wade-Martins 1980b, 489; Stamper and Croft 2000, 152) (context 527: 12th–13th-century ditch F.526).

Building materials

Many contexts produced evidence for building materials, with a pronounced difference between the 12th- to 13th-century contexts at Church Field and Home Ground, and the 17th- to 18th-century features at Home Ground. Many medieval contexts produced at least small amounts of small to medium-sized (*c* 5–40mm across) amorphous lumps of burnt clay and although no evidence of wattle impressions were observed most of this material is probably daub from the walls of timber buildings.

Limited amounts of stone were recovered, all of which was readily available in the nearby hills. Lias limestone predominated, with some Carboniferous limestone and Triassic sandstone. Two 12th- to 13th-century contexts in Church Field produced fragments of dressed limestone (context 131 in F.135 and 527 in F.526), which suggests the presence of a well-appointed stone building in the vicinity, perhaps the church which is documented from the late 12th century. A fragment of Malvern Chase ridge tile of 16th-century date was also recovered (context 101, topsoil Trench 2).

The only fragments of brick were recovered from contexts 353 and 357, the spreads of 17th- to 18th-century building rubble in Trench 4. Lumps of mortar were also recovered from these rubble spreads along with the fills of F.308 (context 309) and F.358 (359). Context 222, a dump of soil on the southern edge of the North Platform, contained abundant small flecks and lumps of mortar and may represent the clearance and dumping of soil from next to a collapsed or demolished building. The stone rubble itself was Lias limestone. In Church Field slate was recovered from the topsoil and the post-medieval recuts of F.128 (contexts 109, 140), but was absent from 12th- to 13th-century contexts. Similarly, at Home Ground slate was only found in post-medieval contexts.

Discussion: the evolution of a marshland settlement (Fig 9.12)

The initial occupation at Puxton

Historic landscape analysis had suggested the earliest features on the North Somerset Levels were the oval-shaped infield enclosures of which Puxton was typical, though it was unclear whether they pre- or post-dated the construction of a sea wall along the coast. The sectioning of the bank around the perimeter of Church Field has established that it was constructed on the surface of a high but still intertidal salt marsh, with the low but broad bank probably designed to keep the enclosed area free from the relatively few tides that would have reached this far inland. The infield enclosure appears to have been rooted on the slightly raised banks of a palaeochannel, revealed through the Environment Agency's recent Lidar survey, that branches off the Balls Yeo Rhyne and runs to the south of Puxton Court (Fig 9.2).

The date when the infield enclosure at Puxton was first created, or the site first settled, remains frustratingly unclear. The vast majority of excavated medieval contexts in Church Field and Home Ground date to the late 11th–13th centuries, though the two

Figure 9.12 The development of the settlement of Puxton from its maximum extent c *1220 through its late medieval contraction, to 1840*

earliest pottery fabrics are generally thought to predate these earliest stratified deposits. Fabrics AA1 and AA2 are usually dated in Somerset to the late 10th–early 11th centuries, though at Puxton they are mostly found in association with later fabrics. It is unclear whether this is because AA1 and AA2 actually continued to be made into the later 11th–early 12th century, or because at Puxton they were residual. Only in the basal fill of F.526 (context 528) were four sherds of AA1 found on their own. The distribution of AA1 and AA2 certainly points to Church Field being the earliest area to be occupied as a total of 145 sherds (1,625g, average 11.2g) came from there compared to just nineteen sherds (133g, average 7g) from Home Ground. Clarke (1980, 3) describes occupation debris from the tenement plot now occupied by The Bungalow, and the pottery assemblage includes six sherds of the same coarse limestone-tempered fabric.

Considering the very limited nature of the excavations, the concentration of fabrics AA1 And AA2 in Church Field, and its occurrence in one context on its own, it is argued here that Puxton Church Field was occupied by the 11th century, which supports the tentative Saxon or Saxo-Norman date for the church based on its early roofline and the Norman font (see Chapter 8). The possibility of late 10th-century or earlier occupation cannot be ruled out as there appears to be very little pottery used in Somerset before that date. At the royal palace at Cheddar, for example, contexts dated by coins to the later 9th–early 10th centuries and containing large amounts of domestic refuse produced no pottery (Rahtz 1979, 52–3). On the limited excavations carried out, however, there was no evidence for an aceramic phase of occupation at Puxton.

A retrogressive analysis of the present village plan alongside the results from fieldwalking, earthwork survey, and excavations suggests two possible ways that the settlement in Church Field may have evolved (Fig 9.4). Firstly, the earliest area of occupation may have been in the north-east corner, within an enclosure marked by the southern boundary of PxTM 3 and the southern and western boundary of PxTM 7's toft as depicted on early maps (Fig 9.4.B). Occupation would then have spread south with the creation of the main enclosure in Church Field, and finally the church and its cemetery was superimposed on both these tofts. This hypothesis is logical as the primary settlement focus (PxTM 3–7) lay on the very slightly raised ground of the palaeochannel occupied by the village green, but it is then difficult to see how the main enclosure in Church Field was accessed. The second hypothesis for how the settlement may have evolved is that the primary focus lay in the eastern part of Church Field with the main enclosure and a series of small paddocks etc bounded by ditch F.128 to the west (Fig 9.4.C). This may have developed into the manor house, with Ralph Tortmanus's proprietorial chapel of 'Wringmarsh' in its north-west corner. Following this hypothesis the early occupation in PxTM 7 is a secondary expansion of this settlement.

The expansion of the settlement

Unfortunately, documentary sources shed little light on the growth of Puxton in the 11th–14th centuries as it does not have a separate entry in Domesday or the lay subsidies of 1327 and 1334 (Dickinson 1889; Glasscock 1975). Archaeological evidence, however, enables its expansion to be mapped. The scarcity of pottery fabric AA1 (and the absence of fabric AA2) suggests that the site at Home Ground was occupied later than Church Field, representing an expansion of settlement from its initial focus. Pottery from shovel test pits and garden surveys suggests that during the 12th–13th centuries settlement expanded down Puxton Lane as far as Puxton Moor, though the lack of anything more than a manure scatter in PxTM 47–8 and PxTM 51 shows that there was no expansion east along Dolemoor Lane towards Congresbury, or as far as PxTM 122–6 to the west. It is noticeable that the western end of Mays Lane runs exactly parallel and 160m north of the edge of the village green and it is tempting to see this as a planned extension. Although neither extant field boundaries nor the surviving earthworks shows convincing evidence for tenement plots, in such a small and continuously occupied area any original village plan could easily have been lost.

The status of the Church Field occupants

There are a number of indications that the occupation site in Church Field may have been of some status compared to the Home Ground site. The bird bone assemblage included twenty goshawk bones from a maximum of three birds, and the frequent finds of complete and partial skeletons of such birds in towns is generally taken as evidence of falconry (Hamilton-Dyer, Chapter 10). The pottery assemblages from Church Field and Home Ground are overwhelming from local and regional workshops typical of peasant households in Somerset, though the sherd of a Lincolnshire Stamford ware costrel from Church Field is a rare find for the county (see Gutiérrez, above). There are also indications that the diet of those living at Church Field was of higher status than that of the Home Ground residents. The plant macrofossils included grapes and figs (Jones, Chapter 10), while there were far larger amounts of marine shellfish especially oysters that cannot have lived in the adjacent Estuary and so must have been purchased at market (Chapter 10). The age structure of the cattle bone assemblage at Church Field suggests that its occupants were being supplied with beef, lamb, and pork of prime age (Outram, Chapter 10). The animal bone assemblages from Church Field and Home Ground also differ in a potentially significant way in that roe and fallow deer bones were only recovered from the former. Outram reminds us that while the presence of deer is often taken as a sign of high-status occupation, small quantities of deer did make it onto lower-status tables, but with the usual reminder of the scale of the excavations and size of the assemblages, and taken alongside the presence of goshawks, grapes, figs, Stamford ware, and far larger amounts of shellfish, this consumption of venison may point to the occupation in Church Field being of higher status than Home Ground. Overall, the evidence suggests that Church Field may have been the site of the manor house, located next to the chapel at Holy Saviour.

Village or hamlet?

By the 19th century, the relatively dispersed settlement pattern in the eastern half of Puxton parish would preclude it from being regarded as a village. In the medieval period, however, we have seen that there were not only more occupied farmsteads, but that these were strung out along Puxton Lane all the way from Home Ground to Puxton Moor. Morphologically, Puxton was a nucleated, if largely linear, village reminding us of the dangers of interpreting settlement history simply from 19th-century plans (and see Taylor 1989; Jones and Page forthcoming). In the medieval period this settlement was also at the centre of a landscape showing a considerable degree of communal management with the common meadow at Dolemoor and common pasture of Puxton Moor surviving until 1816. An East Field is documented down Dolemoor Lane (Chapter 6, Fig 2.5), and the field boundary morphology and a highly fragmented pattern of landownership to the south and west of Church Field are also indicative of a former open field, though this was enclosed by *c* 1770. The settlement was also a centre of service provision with a chapel, parsonage, and church house,[1] which in the post-medieval period were joined by the school, poor house, and pound. All in all, the eastern part of the manor and parish of Puxton can be regarded as having a village-based landscape that in the early 13th century probably had around 23 occupied tenements.

The contraction of settlement

The occupation of Church Field ceased in the early 13th century, which is an unlikely date for settlement contraction. In Chapter 7 it was noted that this location, beside the medieval chapel, is an obvious one for the manor house, and that the last occasion when the lords of the manor of Puxton are recorded as living there is in the early 13th century. Taken with the tentative evidence for the occupation here being of a relatively high status, compared to the site at Home Ground, is it tempting to see Church Field as being the site of a small manor house that was abandoned after Puxton came to be perpetually in the same hands as Churchill nearby where the lords were resident (a not uncommon phenomenon: Gardiner in press).

The date when the platforms at Home Ground were abandoned is more difficult to determine as although the stratified medieval features contain nothing later than the 13th century, there are significant amounts of residual 14th- to 16th-century pottery in later contexts. Only the ditch/gully F.302 on the South Platform clearly dates to the late medieval–early post-medieval period, though this appears to have been one of a series of closely spaced drainage ditches that are suggestive of agricultural use rather than domestic occupation.

The late 15th- to 16th-century court rolls record a series of ruinous and roofless tenements in Puxton, whose lands were absorbed by other tenants. Several of these can be located as earthwork platforms suggestive of settlements and in a number of cases this was confirmed by shovel test pits (Table 9.5 (CD)). The pottery assemblages from the deserted sites were dominated by 11th- to 13th-century fabrics (71% by sherd count, 68% by weight), with small amounts of late medieval material (14% by sherd count and 12% by weight) that are comparable to the post-medieval quantities (15% by sherd count and 20% by weight). The small amounts of post-medieval pottery clearly came from the manuring of the fields, as we know from documentary evidence that these sites were deserted by the late 15th–16th century when they are recorded as ruinous and roofless. That the similar amounts of late medieval are similarly derived from manuring, and that the tenements had been abandoned around the 14th century, is confirmed by a comparison with Bindings, which continued to be occupied until the 20th century. At Bindings late medieval fabrics represent 30% by sherd count (38% by weight) of all the medieval pottery, in contrast to three of the deserted sites (Flemans, Butts, and Coles) where it makes up just 14% by sherd count (19% by weight). Haynes is known to have still been occupied in 1566, and the shovel test pits produced an assemblage with roughly equal amounts of 11th- to 13th-century and late medieval pottery. Overall, therefore, the 23 tenements within Puxton village that were occupied in the early 13th century appear to have been reduced to around thirteen by *c* 1500, with Haynes abandoned soon after.

The post-medieval period

During the post-medieval period the population of Puxton appears to have been relatively stable with around fifteen occupied tenements. At Home Ground, to the north of Mays Lane, the rich midden deposit in F.308 and spread of building rubble in Trench 5 suggest that the South Platform was reoccupied during the 17th–18th century perhaps by a cottage whose occupants cultivated the North Platform as a garden. The palaeoenvironmental evidence from the boundary ditches F.205 and F.209 clearly suggests a hedged field boundary (see Jones, Davies, and Kear, Chapter 10), while a turkey bone may suggest that domestic fowl were being kept (see Hamilton-Dyer, Chapter 10). By 1840 this site was abandoned, as was the cottage west of Myrtle Farm (PxTM 14).

Note

1 Church houses are thought to have been a feature of most Somerset parishes from the late medieval period. Though the Puxton example does not survive, those that do consist of a series of ground-floor rooms heated by a large fireplace usually at the gable end and used for baking and brewing, and a single first-floor room open to the roof (Williams 1992). Church houses were built so that the parishioners could have a place for social gatherings away from the church. From the

mid-15th century the authorities were increasingly opposed to to secular activities within the church itself, yet the parishioners were still responsible for maintaining the nave and so needed to raise funds. Church houses were built by the churchwardens, often on pieces of land close to the church acquired from the lord of the manors as a gift or at a peppercorn rent (the latter seems to have been the case in Puxton). They were used for the brewing and sale of ale on certain festival days (Williams 1992, 15). Two examples of church houses surviving close to Puxton, in Yatton and Wick St Lawrence, were both converted to almshouses.

10 The medieval and post-medieval environment and economy of Puxton: palaeoenvironmental reports

The excavations at Church Field and Home Ground produced a series of important palaeoenvironmental assemblages that are described in detail below. A synthesis of this material, and that from the Roman period described in Chapter 4, is presented in Chapter 11.

Pollen *by Heather M Tinsley*

Church Field: buried ground surface sealed beneath the enclosure bank

A section dug through the medieval enclosure bank in Church Field revealed several layers of dumped material the lower of which (context 503), along with the upper part of the underlying buried ground surface (context 523), were sampled by a 50cm monolith tin. Three samples were taken for pollen assessment, from the top (14–15cm) and the centre (21–22cm) of 503, and the uppermost surface of 523 below (26.5–27.5cm). The results from the assessment are shown in Table 10.1 (CD). Very little pollen was recovered from these three samples and the preservation was very poor. Apart from three grains of tree pollen, all pollen was herbaceous, principally Poaceae along with resistant Lactuceae grains which are easily identified, even when partially decayed, because of their spiky morphology. Microscopic charcoal particles >40μm were frequent in all samples. A single egg of the parasite *Ascaris* (intestinal round worm), which occurs in both pigs and humans, was found in the uppermost sample examined. No ecological reconstruction can be made from this pollen data, although both the charcoal and *Ascaris* suggest that there was some human activity in the landscape, prior to construction of the bank.

Church Field: 12th-century enclosure ditch F.103

The enclosure ditch F.103 was sampled in the field using a 50cm monolith tin (Fig 9.6; Table 10.2). This was described in detail prior to sampling for pollen and foraminifera (separate samples were taken in the field for diatom analysis). The results of the assessments from F.103 were disappointing (see Table 10.3 (CD)) as in almost all cases the preservation of pollen was poor (except sample 38–9cm where preservation was classed as poor to moderate). Pollen grains were very thin and many were crumpled. Large numbers were degraded to the extent that they could not be identified. Some pollen has undoubtedly disappeared all together. It is not possible to give a reliable ecological reconstruction from this material, as less robust taxa may well not have been recognised. This must be kept in mind when considering the brief assemblage descriptions and interpretations that are given below.

Context 163, the earliest cut (samples 38–9cm and 32–3cm), is characterised by relatively large numbers of pollen grains of *Salix* (willow) (25 and 14 grains respectively). Willow is insect-pollinated and is usually under-represented in pollen data. It appears that willow trees may have grown alongside, or close to, the ditch. A range of other tree pollen grains is present at very low frequency. The herbaceous pollen is dominated by Poaceae, with some Cyperaceae in the basal sample. A range of taxa typical of disturbed grassland is also present including *Rumex* (docks), *Polygonum* (knotgrasses), and Lactuceae (dandelion and related Asteraceae). One very distinctive feature of this assemblage is the large number of pollen grains of Brassicaceae (cabbage family). Brassicaceae are thick-walled, robust pollen grains, which may be over-represented

Table 10.2 Stratigraphy, pollen and foraminifera samples: Church Field enclosure ditch F.103. Depths are from the top of the monolith tin, which was 0.89m below the present ground surface (5.08m OD)

depth	context	samples	stratigraphy
0–11cm (4.19–4.08m OD)	107	1–2cm 8–9cm	dark grey clay with buff mottles, merging boundary
11–31.5cm (4.08–3.875m OD)	134	13–14cm 28–29cm	lighter dark grey clay with more extensive buff mottles
31.5– 39.5cm (3.875–3.795m OD)	163	32–33cm 38–39cm	dark grey unmottled clay
39.5–50cm (3.795–3.69m OD)	natural		Orange/brown clay with paler patches

Table 10.4 Stratigraphy, pollen and foraminifera samples: Church Field, ditch F.128. Depths are from the top of monolith tin, which was 1.20m below the present ground surface (5.23m OD)

depth	context	samples	stratigraphy
0–24.5cm (4.03–3.785m OD)	144	7.5–8.5cm 17.5–18.5cm	mid-grey clay with pale brown mottles and occasional fine black streaks, merging boundary
24.5–32.0cm (3.785–3.71m OD)	150	28.5–29.5cm	mid-grey clay with pale brown mottles and black streaks, merging boundary
32–50cm (3.71–3.53m OD)	152	36–37cm 47–48cm	becoming darker with increasingly large black streaks and lumps of organic matter

in these sediments as a result, in part, of differential decay of less robust taxa. The Brassicaceae is a large family which includes domestic brassicas such as cabbage, turnip, rape and mustard, and weeds such as *Capsella bursa-pastoris* (shepherd's purse) which could have grown on disturbed ground, cultivated land, pathways or grazed fields. This taxon (Brassicaceae) also includes *Rorippa* (the water-cresses) that could have been growing in the ditch itself. The assemblage from context 134 is also characterised by about 6% cereal-type pollen and a single grain of the distinctive taxon *Centaurea cyanus* (cornflower), a weed associated with cereal cultivation. The cereal-type pollen could have originated from *Glyceria* (sweet grass) growing in or near the ditch, or it could have resulted from local cultivation, processing or disposal of cereals. In view of the small charred cereal assemblage found in F.103 (see Jones, below), disposal of cereal waste in the ditch seems the most likely explanation. A few pollen grains of *Menyanthes* (bogbean) give an indication of the aquatic flora of the ditch; bogbean grows in shallow, fresh water. Chenopodiaceae pollen is present in this assemblage (8 and 10 grains); it is not possible to determine if this represents pollen of disturbance weeds such as fat-hen or of salt marsh taxa.

In the basal fill of the main ditch cut (context 134) the pollen assemblage is essentially the same, apart from a decline in pollen of *Salix,* which could reflect a decrease in the fringing willow trees at the site. The Chenopodiaceae increase somewhat, possibly indicating greater saline influence. In the uppermost sample (context 107) pollen concentration is very low, in addition to preservation being poor. There are high (but variable) concentrations of microscopic charcoal particles >40μm in length suggesting domestic fires in the area during the time the sediments were accumulating.

Church Field 12th- to early 13th-century boundary ditch F.128

The boundary ditch F.128 was sampled in the field using a 50cm monolith tin (Fig 9.6 and Table 10.4). It was described in detail prior to sampling for pollen and foraminifera (separate samples were taken for diatom analysis). The pollen assemblage had similar preservation characteristics to that from F.103 (see above) (Table 10.5 (CD)). The overall character of the assemblage is also similar. Tree pollen values are generally low. F.128 lacks the high values for *Salix* pollen found in F.103; as *Salix* pollen does not usually disperse far, this probably reflects local variation in the distribution of willows. The record for herbaceous taxa is dominated by grasses, with large numbers of Brassicaceae pollen grains and a range of weeds of disturbed ground. Pollen of cereal-type is represented at similar levels to those of F.103. The relatively high Chenopodiaceae values in context 144, at the top of the fill of ditch F.128, could indicate increasing marine influence. High (but variable) concentrations of microscopic charcoal particles were also found in F.103.

Summary Church Field: 12th- to early 13th-century ditches

The pollen preservation in both enclosure ditch F.103 and the boundary ditch F.128 was not good and this is almost certainly a consequence of oxidation in sediments which periodically dried after deposition. Despite this poor preservation, certain features can be identified as common to the pollen assemblages of both ditches and these suggest that the 12th- to 13th-century environment of Church Field was one of anthropogenically disturbed, weedy grassland. Some cereal processing was taking place in the area. The ditches themselves appear to have had a freshwater flora, but in both ditches increased values for Chenopodiaceae pollen towards the top of the sediments suggest some brackish or marine influence.

Plant macrofossil remains *by Julie Jones*

Preservation

Preservation of the plant remains was by anoxic waterlogging, charring, silicification, and mineralisation. Many of the weeds representing the local environment of the features in which they were recovered were preserved by the anaerobic conditions. Certain features can be seen to have had less ideal preservational conditions with much smaller organic floats produced from similar sized original bulk samples, resulting in less abundant, although in many cases similar, assemblages of plant macrofossil remains. Some of the ditch fills included plant matter preserved in a mineralised form, a phenomenon that commonly occurs in cesspits (McCobb *et al* 2001): where there is sufficient moisture present plant tissues are replaced with carbonates and soluble phosphates and although the outer seed cases are often lost, identification of the hard amber-coloured embryo is possible, although sometimes only to genera level. Preservation also occurred by charring, mostly of cereal grain and chaff but also associated weed seeds. Charred material, burned under reducing conditions, in ovens or hearths, is generally more resistant to biological attack, although more prone to mechanical damage. While many of the cereal grains examined were in good condition, many were blistered and pitted with a glassy appearance, likely to have been caused during the charring process, rather than by post-depositional erosion. Poor preservation of some grains has resulted in some samples having relatively high numbers recorded as unidentifiable (indet). The cereal chaff was mostly very fragmentary, but weed seeds were on the whole well preserved. There were also examples in some contexts of silicification of wheat awns, wheat glume tips, and grass culm nodes. Silicification occurs in high-temperature oxidising conditions, which burns out all the carbon leaving the silica skeleton of remains such as those recovered here. Silicified remains have been recovered from other sites from contexts such as corn drier flues and oven or kiln floors (Robinson and Straker 1991).

Church Field (Tables 10.6–10.7 (on CD))

Lowest make-up of bank (context 503)

A bulk sample from the lowest make-up of the bank (503) that surrounds Church Field contained only a very limited assemblage of non charred macrofossils typical of disturbed and waste ground such as common chickweed *(Stellaria media)*, fat-hen, fig-leaved goosefoot, with a few grasses and rush. Charred cereals included two possible wheat grains (cf *Triticum*) and an unidentifiable grain. Although little interpretation can be made from such a limited assemblage many of the weeds found are annual opportunists that would quickly colonise areas of bare ground.

Basal fill of 12th-century enclosure ditch F.103 (context 134)

A sample from the basal fill of the enclosure ditch F.103 produced only a small (35ml) organic float composed of fine roots with many duckweed seeds, mostly in poor condition, but providing the only evidence for the presence of standing water in the ditch. A single bulrush, rushes and fragmented hemlock (*Conium maculatum*) point to the damp nature of the ditch side, hemlock generally occurring on rather heavy soils. Elder, nettle (*Urtica dioica*), and dock are also likely to have formed part of the community along the ditch edge, with areas of bare and disturbed ground supporting annuals such as chickweed (*Cerastium*), orache, fat-hen and fig-leaved goosefoot.

As well as charcoal fragments a small charred cereal assemblage suggests the disposal of cereal waste into the ditch. Low concentrations of wheat, barley, and oat grains occur with a few wheat tough rachis internodes suggesting a free-threshing wheat variety, such as bread wheat. The presence of wheat and barley rachis fragments and oat awns suggest that different components of the cereal ear were present. The charred weed assemblage included some of the same species as found non-charred such as orache, chickweed and fig-leaved goosefoot, but also other typical arable weeds including stinking chamomile (*Anthemis cotula*), bartsia/eyebright (*Odontites / Euphrasia*), and mustard/rape/cole (*Brassica / Sinapis / Raphanus*).

Basal ditch fill of late 11th- to 12th-century boundary ditch F.115 (context 116)

The fill of boundary ditch F.115 contained abundant charcoal, fish scales, and vertebrae, with some egg shell including burnt fragments. The small non-charred assemblage comprises predominantly elder seeds, with a few charred grains, wheat, barley and oat, plus a single wheat tough rachis internode. Charred weed seeds are mostly single occurrences of arable indicators: cleavers (*Galium aparine*), brome, and pale persicaria (*Persicaria lapathifolia*).

Midden deposit at base of 12th- to early 13th-century boundary ditch F.128 (context 152)

Context 152 represents a dump of midden material in the base of ditch F.128. Organic preservation was variable although a large float included abundant small, soft wood fragments. Seed preservation was variable with some individuals fragmented or incomplete. A water-filled ditch is again suggested by the aquatics duckweed, water crowfoot and water plantain, with a bank side community of bulrush, spike-rush, celery-leaved buttercup and greater pond-sedge (*Carex riparia*). Thousands of common nettle seeds suggest the area surrounding the ditch may have supported a rich soil and been colonised by nettles, in association with fig-leaved goosefoot, a plant found in farmyards and manure heaps, that also thrives particularly well on such rich fertile soils. Elder, which also likes nitrogen-rich conditions, can occur in a wide variety of habitats from close to farm buildings to riverbanks and may have formed a shrubby boundary along the ditch side with bramble and hazel also present. Perhaps further away from the ditch bank the local flora is suggested by a mixture of damp pasture and meadow species like buttercup

(*Ranunculus acris / repens / bulbosus*), hemlock, and hairy buttercup with waste or disturbed ground supporting annuals such as chickweed, orache, swinecress (*Coronopus squamatus*) and fat-hen, as with the other ditch fills.

The deposit also included an extensive charred cereal assemblage with abundant charcoal fragments, as well as animal and fish bone and egg shell (some of this was again burnt), suggestive of the disposal of domestic waste. Wheat was by far the most abundant cereal with over 800 well-preserved grains of the short rounded bread wheat form (*Triticum aestivo-compactum* s.l.). In addition to the usual well-preserved tough rachis internodes there were occasional rivet/macaroni wheat (*Triticum turgidum / durum*) rachis fragments showing that both hexaploid and tetraploid forms of wheat were present. The presence of a few spelt wheat spikelet forks suggests that this hulled wheat was also being cultivated. Oat grains were also abundant, with several pedicels of wild oat suggesting that some of the grains were from wild oats although this does not rule out the possibility that oats were also cultivated. Grains of barley, including some hulled grains, and rye (*Secale cereale*), also occurred. Barley chaff was restricted to a few fragmented rachis internode bases. Cultivation of additional field crops is suggested by charred peas (*Pisum sativum*) and celtic beans (*Vicia faba*).

The large charred weed assemblage included many of the same species as occurred in a non-charred form. The most frequent were stinking chamomile, orache, dock, bartsia/eyebright, and grasses (Poaceae) including meadow-grass/cat's-tail (*Poa / Phleum*). Spike-rush, fig-leaved goosefoot and pale persicaria also occurred.

Lower fill of 12th- to early 13th-century boundary ditch F.128 (context 150)

Overlying 152, the waterlogged assemblage from context 150 showed the same suite of macrofossils: freshwater aquatics with bank side and marsh species and a preponderance of nettle seeds with the suggestion of scrubby growth perhaps lining the ditchbank including elder, bramble and hazel, plus birch (*Betula*) and hawthorn (*Crataegus monogyna*). An additional species, unlikely to have formed part of the local community, is fig (*Ficus carica*), probably occurring from chance disposal of food waste. The charred assemblage, although less extensive than in the basal fill, was again predominantly wheat, with chaff from both free-threshing and hulled forms, plus barley and oat grains, accompanied by a small arable weed assemblage.

Fill of 17th- to 18th-century boundary ditch F.140 (recutting F.128) (context 141)

The assemblage from the early post-medieval recut (F.140) of F.128 was very similar to that from the medieval fills with abundant duckweed, water crowfoot and water plantain forming a vegetation cover on the water's surface, with the ditch margins supporting water-cress (*Rorippa nasturtium-aquaticum*), typical of shallow clear freshwater habitats, water mint, species of sedge and rush. There were also abundant water-flea egg cases (*cladoceran ephyppia*), freshwater crustaceans that abound in most stretches of water, forming part of the plankton of ponds and ditches (Clegg 1965).

There is little change in the bank side environment of the ditch, with a community of nettle, elder, bramble and hawthorn, providing a habitat for the scrambling perennial bittersweet (*Solanum dulcamara*). Away from ditch side there is again evidence for damp meadow or pasture supporting species like buttercup, hemlock, and hairy sedge (*Carex hirta*), the latter a plant of various soils, usually in grassy associations such as meadows or hedgebanks but often in hollows where soil moisture accumulates (Jermy *et al* 1982). It would appear that there was little domestic waste disposal into this feature; charred items are restricted to a single wheat grain and one unidentifiable grain with only a small amount of bone noted.

Upper fill of 12th- to early 13th-century boundary ditch F.135 (context 131)

The upper fill of boundary ditch F.135 contained a small non-charred assemblage of predominantly elder, with fig-leaved goosefoot and disturbed ground species fat-hen, chickweed and orache. The only indication of wetland taxa was two duckweed seeds. Less ideal preservation conditions, in this upper fill of a shallow ditch, is likely to be the reason for the small assemblage, rather than any real change in the environment.

Charred preservation included wheat grains, with some better-preserved examples of the rounded form typical of bread wheat, but many were still in poor condition. Tough rachis internodes also suggest a free-threshing form. Barley grains were less abundant, with occasional oat, although there was no distinctive chaff to suggest whether these were a wild or cultivated form. The high percentage of unidentifiable grains is thought to relate to the high temperature at burning. There are also frequent silicified wheat awns and glume tips. The small weed assemblage includes brome (*Bromus*), other grasses, stinking chamomile, and black mustard (*Brassica nigra*), an annual of arable and waste land, but also of stream and ditch banks.

Basal fill of 12th- to early 13th-century ditch F.510 (context 525)

The basal fill of ditch F.510 included waterlogged, charred, and mineralised preservation. Waterlogged preservation included the usual range of taxa of predominantly duckweed, with elder, bramble and annual disturbed ground species. An additional species, not found in the other ditch fills, was flax (*Linum usitatissimum*) found as seeds, capsule and stem fragments. Mineralised preservation includes many of the same species also found waterlogged and charred and includes nettle, elder and mallow (*Malva*), typical of many habitats including field margins, hedgebanks and scrub, all species likely to have originated from the ditch margins. Arable weeds include thorow-wax (*Bupleurum rotundifolium*), bartsia/eyebright and mustard/rape/cole. There are also mineralised concretions containing small stem fragments and some bone, plus remains of flies and their puparia. The presence of grape (*Vitis vinifera*) pips is most likely to come from the disposal of food waste into the ditch and, like the fig, would not have grown locally. Some of these same weeds also occur charred as part of the cereal assemblage, together with poorly preserved grains of wheat, barley, and oat.

Basal fill of 12th-century feature F.526 (context 528)

The lower fill of F.526 contained a similar waterlogged assemblage to the other ditch fills with duckweed, water crowfoot and bulrush forming the ditch community, with elder and nettle lining the ditch. A single flax seed was also noted. Two taxa, pale persicaria and fig-leaved goosefoot show signs of partial mineralisation, with the characteristic hard amber embryos, but still retaining an organic seed coat, perhaps suggesting that mineralisation occurred within the ditch, rather than elsewhere. Other mineralised preservation included a single buttercup (*Ranunculus*) and fly pupae. Charred preservation included grains of wheat, barley, oat, and a limited chaff and weed assemblage.

Middle fill of 12th-century feature F.526 (context 527)

The non-charred assemblage in the middle fill of F.526 is predominantly elder, although a larger group of mineralised seeds includes Chenopodiaceae (goosefoot family), orache, docks, pale persicaria and additional elder. Some cereal grains are also mineralised including examples of rye, barley, and oat including one oat grain with a partial floret still attached. Arable weeds include *Anthemis* sp (probably stinking chamomile) and thorow-wax. Charred preservation includes a similar assemblage to the basal ditch fill, with the addition of the cornfield weed corn marigold (*Chrysanthemum segetum*).

Home Ground (Tables 10.8–10.9 (CD))

Lower fill of 12th- to 13th-century boundary ditch F.267 (context 285)

A fairly small waterlogged assemblage was recovered from the lower fill of ditch F.267, dominated by the aquatics duckweed and water crowfoot, with bulrush and rush forming part of the bank side community, with indications of nettle, orache and buttercup. The charred assemblage is also fairly limited with wheat and barley grains, alongside occasional oats although no chaff to confirm if this was the cultivated form. The weed assemblage includes arable species stinking chamomile, mustard/rape/cole and vetch. Charred celtic bean suggests cultivation of this field crop.

Lower fill of 12th- to 13th-century boundary ditch F.308 (context 323)

The basal fill of ditch F.308 produced a small non-charred assemblage, mostly duckweed, with some water crowfoot, a single pondweed, and occasional rush, buttercup and elder. Charred preservation included grains of wheat, barley, and oat with limited chaff, a few weeds and some silicified wheat/barley awns and wheat glume tips. Occasional mineralised seeds recorded were similar arable weeds as those preserved in a charred form and included clover/medick, sheep's sorrel, mustard/rape/cole, plus a hilum fragment of celtic bean.

Fill of 12th- to 13th-century gully F.243 (context 244)

The fill of a gully F.243 produced a limited non-charred assemblage including duckweed, water crowfoot and bulrush. Disturbed ground species included elder, orache, and fig-leaved goosefoot with grasses, and provide a similar picture to the other features examined. The small charred cereal assemblage includes wheat, barley and oat grains, wheat tough rachis internodes, plus arable weeds stinking chamomile, bartsia/eyebright, greater plantain and dock.

Lower fill of 12th- to 13th-century pit F.265 (context 280)

The lower fill of pit F.265 contained only a few non-charred seeds of rush, duckweed, water crowfoot, buttercup and chickweed. Charred remains were limited to single wheat and barley grains, plus wheat and oat awns. There was no mineralised preservation.

Upper fill of 12th- to 13th-century pit F.265 (context 266)

The upper fill of pit F.265 produced a larger assemblage than the lower fill that again included waterlogged preservation of duckweed, rush, bramble and thistle, with a few charred wheat, barley and oat grains, wheat tough rachis internode, plus a few arable weeds. Mineralised preservation was limited to a single fly pupae.

Lower fill of 17th- to 18th-century recut boundary ditch F.209 (context 230)

The float from the lower fill of the 17th- to 18th-century recut of F.209 contained abundant small soft wood fragments, with a good assemblage of waterlogged plant remains, although preservation was variable with many seeds fragmented. A wet environment around the ditch is shown by the aquatic species duckweed, water plantain and water crowfoot with abundant egg cases of water fleas and the freshwater Bryozoa *Lophopus crystallinus*. Bank side/marsh species include celery-leaved buttercup, water-cress, gipsywort, bulrush, and sedges. Nettles are again common, perhaps growing along the margins of the ditch with elder, bramble and hawthorn, as well as herbaceous species bittersweet, hemlock, hogweed (*Heracleum sphondylium*) and hedge woundwort (*Stachys sylvatica*, a medium to tall perennial of hedgerows and banks mostly in shaded habitats). Other species reflect the grassy local environment with buttercup, silverweed and dock, along with some disturbed ground species, including orache, prickly sow-thistle (*Sonchus asper*) and bristly oxtongue (*Picris echioides*, a plant of stream sides, rough grassy and waste places on heavy calcareous soils). There was no charred preservation in this deposit.

Discussion: the local environment in medieval–early post-medieval Puxton

Most of the samples from Church Field come from ditch fills representing material that had accumulated in them during the 12th–early 13th centuries, along with one upper ditch fill (F.140) dating to the 17th–18th century. The vegetation communities remain fairly stable throughout this period suggesting little change in the local environment. The ditches were clearly water-filled, the aquatic species which occur throughout pointing to still to slow-moving freshwater, although water levels would have fluctuated with changes in the water table throughout the seasons. Duckweed, which is so prominent throughout, floats freely and is not rooted in the mud and could have formed a continuous carpet of green on the water's surface. Similarly water crowfoot can cover the water's surface, while other freshwater species such as water plantain, water-cress, common club-rush, and spike-rush formed part of the community in the swampy margins where there would have been water cover for all but the driest times of the year. The vegetation along the ditch bank also seems fairly consistent: extensive colonies of nettle, perhaps on fairly rich soils also supporting fig-leaved goosefoot, and elder. Elder may also have been a component of scrubby growth along the ditch margins with evidence from different ditch fills for bramble, hazel, hawthorn, and birch.

Away from the immediate vicinity of the ditches weeds of damp pasture or meadow, as well as waste or disturbed ground species, form communities likely to be dominated by grassland. It is interesting that some of these same weeds recovered in a waterlogged state are also present charred in association with the cereal remains. These taxa have been interpreted as forming part of the 'natural' environment, although many vegetation communities have been modified and are in fact man-made or semi-natural habitats, but still retain a rich flora that has adapted to changes in the environment. Cultivation is one such modification to the natural environment, with regular disturbance to the soil, opening up the land and encouraging many annual weeds to gain a roothold over more vigorous perennials. Many of these annuals are quick-growing ephemerals capable of germinating at almost any time of the year and can produce several generations in a year (Blamey and Grey-Wilson 1989). If one examines the list of weeds recovered from Church Field (Table 10.7 (CD)) it will be seen that many of the taxa categorised as belonging to habitats of waste/disturbed/arable ground, dry pasture/rough grassy places/fields, and even bank side and boggy places, were recovered as both charred and waterlogged seeds. The charred examples have therefore been interpreted as forming part of the weed community in field plots growing with the cereals, taking the opportunity given by soil cultivation for them to become established. These would then have been gathered with the crops when they were harvested. Some taxa are particularly associated with cornfields such as thorow-wax, corn marigold, stinking chamomile, and corncockle, and occur in many medieval assemblages. Cleavers (*Galium aparine*) is a twining species which could easily have entangled itself with the cereal stem and been cut with the grain. Other species may have invaded from adjacent unploughed fields, perhaps used for pasture, or have persisted as residual species from before the fields were cultivated. Examples are numerous and include bartsia/eyebright, orache, common chickweed, and dock. Jones (1978) has argued that the common occurrence of charred damp ground species, in particular spike-rush, other sedges and rushes, suggests that some parts of fields used for crops were poorly drained or that marginal land was being used. The important factor at Church Field is to suggest that crop cultivation was local to the settlement and the ditches may not only have served a drainage function but also acted as field boundaries, cultivation stretching on to the poorer drained margins close to these features.

The local environment associated with the enclosure ditches at Home Ground is very similar to Church Field. Apart from the later cut in ditch F.209 dated to the 17th–18th century, organic preservation in the sediments was poor with only limited assemblages of waterlogged plant remains. However, the same suite, albeit in lower concentrations, occurs throughout, with freshwater aquatics, bank side and marsh species suggesting the enclosure ditches were water-filled for at least part of the year. The ditch margins are inhabited by scrubby growth with elder, bramble, and hawthorn as well as herbaceous species, nettle being particularly common. There is little change in the environment away from the ditch side, which shows a similar suite of grassland, disturbed and waste ground species.

Arable cultivation in medieval Puxton

Most of the Church Field ditch fills examined contained some charred plant material as well as animal bone, fish bone, egg shell, and non-organic items such as pottery suggestive of the disposal of domestic waste into these features. The lowest fill of ditch F.128 (context 152) produced the most extensive charred assemblage, with material from the other ditch fills although less abundant, forming a similar pattern. Cereal grain was by far the most abundant component with wheat dominant but also with barley, rye, and oat.

Wheat

The most commonly found cereal was wheat with over 800 grains from the lowest fill of F.128 (context 152), representing 64% of the assemblage. Many of the better-preserved grains from all contexts are of the short-rounded form showing the steep angle of the embryo, characteristic of the hexaploid type (*Triticum aestivocompactum* s.l.). Occasional tail grain was defined as grain less than 4.5mm in length. While it is difficult from grain morphology to distinguish between free-threshing hexaploid and tetraploid wheats, the occurrence of a few examples of tetraploid (rivet/macaroni wheat – *Triticum turgidum/durum*) rachis internodes, showing the characteristic straight sides with swelling under the glume bases, criteria as described by Moffett (1991) and Jacomet (1987), shows that this type was being cultivated. However, the majority of wheat internodes were very fragmentary and have been recorded as of the tough rachis type from a free-threshing wheat, so it seems likely that bread/club wheat (*Triticum aestivum/compactum*), the form most commonly recovered from medieval sites, would also have been cultivated. Bread wheat has a high gluten content which makes it more suitable for bread making than the soft mealy grain of rivet wheat and it may be that both were cultivated for their different qualities. There are also occasional spelt wheat glume bases and spikelet forks, as found in the earlier Roman ditch fills at Dolemoor.

Barley

Barley grains (8%) occur less frequently than wheat, with variable preservation, although some grains have been recorded as hulled barley where traces of the lemma and palaea remained. Barley rachis internodes were few and mostly very fragmented. There was no evidence for sprouted grains, a characteristic which would suggest the grain had germinated possibly as part of the malting process for ale production. However, in addition to malting, barley was also valued as a food grain as a supplement to wheat, or for fodder, although grain used for fodder is less likely to be exposed to fire than grain prepared for human consumption.

Oat

Oat grain was also present in all samples and like barley formed 8% of total cereals, suggesting that in part it represents a crop plant. However, there is also evidence that some oats were crop weeds, as although none of the characteristic floret bases were found identification of a few oat pedicels (stalks) were identified as wild oat (*Avena fatua/ludoviciana*). The lemma bases of wild hexaploid oats appear to detach from the pedicel showing the characteristic reverse scar of the sucker mouth, borne on the lemma base as described by Moffett (1988). Oat awns were also common. Oats were traditionally cultivated as a spring-grown crop, often planted with barley for use as human food or animal fodder, particularly for draught animals due to its high-energy value.

Rye

Charred rye grains occurred in one sample (context 152), forming only 1% of the total assemblage, although there were two mineralised examples in context 525. It may be possible that these also occurred as crop weeds.

Fabaceae

Additional field or garden crops are suggested by the identification of charred seeds of garden pea (*Pisum sativum*) and celtic bean (*Vicia faba*). Preservation of the Fabaceae in a charred form seems to be less common than cereals, as they are less likely to come into contact with fire during cooking preparations. Peas and beans would have been eaten fresh when young, used in soups or pottages, flavoured with herbs or as porreys (stewed vegetables) and as a rich source of protein would have formed an important addition to the diet.

Flax

Flax was found as seeds, capsule and stem fragments in one basal ditch fill (F.510). It was grown for both its fibre, which was made into linen, and its seeds, which are rich in oil (linseed). The separation of fibres from flax stems is a complicated process (Dickson and Dickson 2000) and usually occurs before the seeds are fully ripe, involving soaking in retting pits, so it is perhaps more likely that it was used for its seeds. These may have been pressed for oils, as linseed contains 35–40% oil and does not become rancid like animal oils, or it may have been used as an ingredient in breadmaking. Linseed can also be used as a laxative and the oil-rich seeds retain heat well for poultices.

Due to the small floats obtained from most samples at Home Ground the charred macrofossil assemblages are also fairly limited. However the presence of wheat and barley grains again show utilisation of these crops, perhaps with the addition of oat, although this may be one of the crop weeds. Similar groups of waterlogged and charred seeds are again interpreted as evidence that crop cultivation was local.

Discussion of the charred cereal remains

The charred remains recovered from Church Field have shown a range of cultivated crops, suggesting a mixed crop economy at Puxton during the 12th–early 13th centuries. Out of a total of 2,742 grains, it has been calculated that 64% are wheat, 8% barley, 8% oat, and 1% rye (with 19% unidentifiable), with the possible addition of a garden or field crop of beans and peas. All the samples are from ditch fills and as such represent secondary contexts, which are associated with the general disposal of domestic debris, including animal and fish bone and egg shell at this time. Much emphasis has been placed on the interpretation of crop processing activities from the composition of charred cereal remains recovered from excavations of all periods (Hillman 1981), but these need to be based on samples from primary deposits associated with contexts such as corn driers, storage pits, or granaries. Although it is difficult, therefore, to infer crop processing activities from these assemblages at Puxton, some general statements can be made. Evidence from the remains of wheat show that whole components of the cereal ear are present including primary grain, tail grain, rachis internodes, glume, and awn fragments. The presence of weed seeds also suggests an uncleaned crop. However, as the cereal remains were not from primary contexts, it may be that different elements of crop processing have become remixed following cleaning of hearths or ovens which were then deposited periodically along with other domestic rubbish into these ditches. Certainly the presence of silicified chaff suggests that some of this material originated from the cleaning of ashes from hearths or ovens which is likely to be the result of drying the crops shown to have been utilised at Puxton (wheat, barley, with the possibility of oats and rye), for whatever purpose (animal feed or human consumption). Charred debris could also have accumulated as a result of food preparation from the hearths of individual households.

Mineralised preservation

There was also evidence for mineralised preservation in several of the ditch fills (F.510, context 525; F.526, contexts 527 and 528). Mineralisation is a phenomenon typical of faecal deposits such as cess pits where replacement of the soft cell tissue by carbonates and soluble phosphate occurs. In cess pits the high concentration of organic matter may provide a source of phosphate upon decay. Often in such deposits plant remains recovered are edible species, have been referred to as a 'fruit salad' (Greig 1983) and have been used to interpret diet. Common finds are the undigested remains of apples, figs, strawberries, plums and sloes. This does not, however, seem to be the case at Puxton with the mineralised seeds recovered from Church Field being predominantly those same species recovered waterlogged and charred. The exceptions include grape pips (in 525) and occasional mineralised oat, barley and rye grains (in 525 and 527). Carruthers (2000) suggested that important requirements for mineralisation include a source of soluble phosphates that may be provided by domestic waste and periodically waterlogged conditions which would prevent decay for long enough for fossilisation to occur. It may be possible that the other domestic waste present in the ditch fill may have provided the conditions for decay and that this material does not represent cleanings from the settlement latrines.

Wood charcoal *by Rowena Gale*

A small assemblage of charcoal was recovered from the 12th- to 13th-century contexts in Church Field and Home Ground. The charcoal was mostly firm and well preserved with some fragments measuring up to about 10mm in cross-section. The samples were prepared using standard methods (Gale and Cutler 2000). Anatomical structures were examined using incident light on a Nikon Labophot–2 compound microscope at magnifications up to ×400 and matched to prepared reference slides of modern wood. When possible, the maturity of the wood was assessed (ie heartwood/sapwood) and the stem diameters recorded. It should be noted that during the charring process wood may be reduced in volume by up to 40%.

The taxa identified are presented in Table 10.10 (CD). Classification follows that of *Flora Europaea*

(Tutin and Heywood 1964–80). When a genus is represented by a single species in the British flora, it is named as the most likely origin of the wood, given the provenance and period, but it should be noted that it is rarely possible to name individual species from wood features and exotic species of trees and shrubs were introduced to Britain from an early period (Godwin 1956; Mitchell 1974). The anatomical structure of the charcoal was consistent with the following taxa or groups of taxa:

Aquifoliaceae. *Ilex aquifolium* L., holly
Betulaceae. *Alnus glutinosa* (L.) Gaertner, European alder
Corylaceae. *Corylus avellana* L., hazel
Fagaceae. *Quercus* sp., oak
Oleaceae. *Fraxinus excelsior* L., ash
Rosaceae. Sub-families:
Pomoideae, which includes *Crataegus* sp., hawthorn; *Malus* sp., apple; *Pyrus* sp., pear; *Sorbus* spp., rowan, service tree and whitebeam. These taxa are anatomically similar; one or more taxa may be represented in the charcoal.
Prunoideae. *Prunus spinosa* L., blackthorn.
Tiliaceae. *Tilia* sp., lime

With the exception of alder, the charcoal identified the use of dry land species. The charcoal included both roundwood, for example hazel (diameter 11mm) and the hawthorn group (diameter 5mm), and heartwood, for example ash and oak. The oak consisted of slow-grown wood.

Diatoms *by Nigel Cameron and Simon Dobinson*

Church Field: 12th-century enclosure ditch F.103

Diatoms were preserved in samples taken from both the earliest cut (context 163, sample 115), and the basal fill (context 134, samples 113–14) and the upper fill (context 107, samples 109–11) of the main 12th-century enclosure ditch F.103 (Figs 9.6 and 10.1 (CD)). The lower fill has a wholly freshwater assemblage, and the very occasional polyhalobous taxa of marine or marine–brackish origin in the upper fill may have come directly from the Severn Estuary during a flooding episode, or have been reworked fossil diatoms derived from erosion of the Upper Wentlooge Formation, known from work elsewhere to have been deposited under intertidal conditions (Rippon 2000b, 99), into which the ditch is cut.

Church Field: 12th- to early 13th-century ditch F.128, and 17th- to 18th-century ditch F.140

Diatoms were poorly preserved in samples taken from a column that straddled both the 12th- to early 13th-century boundary ditch F.128 (contexts 144 and 150, samples 120–4) and its 17th- to 18th-century recut (contexts 129 and 141, samples 116–19) (Figs 9.6 and 10.1). Ditch F.128 displays a significantly stronger signal of marine or marine–brackish influence than its post-medieval recut F.140 and indeed the broadly contemporary F.103, though once again these diatoms could have been derived from the erosion of the Upper Wentlooge Formation. In a number of samples, benthic, freshwater taxa, which may better represent the prevailing salinity conditions, are common, such as the oligohabolous indifferent *Achnanthes*, *Cocconeis,* and *Amphora* spp. in the lower fill (context 150, sample 122). Notable amongst the freshwater diatoms is the frequency of aerophilous (semi-terrestrial) species, notably *Hantzschia amphioxys*, along with a number of *Pinnularia* spp. and other taxa such as *Navicula mutica*. The occurrence of diatoms tolerant of desiccation might suggests that the aquatic habitat was subject to drying out, or that these taxa may have been eroded from bank side or soil habitats into the ditch sediments.

Home Ground: 12th- to 13th-century ditch F.267

Diatoms were poorly preserved in samples taken from a column in the 12th- to 13th-century boundary ditch F.267 (contexts 268 and 285, samples 154–7: see Fig 9.8). The upper fill (268) contained *Nitzschia* sp, *Amphora* sp and *Thalassiosira* sp, and only in one sample (156) from the lower fill (285) could the diatoms be identified to species level. In addition to *Nitzschia* sp and *Eunotia* sp, *Paralia sulcata*, a marine planktonic (floating in the water) species, *Tabularia fasciculata*, a brackish-water species, and *Amphora veneta*, a freshwater/halophilous species, were identified in this sample. The marine species is almost certainly allochthonous (transported from elsewhere), being robust and easily transported in tidal waters, though, its presence supports the idea that there was, at least periodically, flooding from the Estuary. Further, the presence of non-planktonic brackish and halophilous taxa suggest that the autochthonous flora was growing in water of elevated salinity compared to freshwater. Overall, despite the poor preservation of diatom valves in this suite of samples, in some of the contexts the presence of marine and brackish water species, particularly in sample 156, provides (unexpected) evidence for contact with the Severn Estuary (a conclusion supported by the presence of brackish water foraminiferan assemblages in ditch F.267: see Kreiser below). Alternatively the presence of these halophilous to marine diatoms could result from the reworking of sediments from earlier strata.

Foraminifera *by Annette Kreiser*

Church Field: 12th-century enclosure ditch F.103

In F.103 all samples contained foraminifera with the exception of 32–3cm (see Fig 9.6 and

Table 10.11 (CD)), though concentrations of tests were low and exceeded ten tests in 10cm^3 of wet sediment in only two samples: 13–14cm and 38–9cm. The assemblages in these samples contain species typical of middle or low marsh environments and tolerant of a wide salinity range. However, the tests are significantly eroded, particularly in the 38–9cm sample, suggesting both poor conditions for preservation and reworking of the tests from the Upper Wentlooge alluvium. The 63μm fractions of all the F.103 samples (except 32–3cm) contain juvenile forms of fully marine genera, such as *Brizalina* and *Spirillina*, along with juveniles of the adult brackish species. The juvenile tests of marine genera are sometimes found transported some distance into brackish waters, probably during storms (Murray 1991), and are unlikely to have survived long in the environment of deposition.

Church Field: 12th- to early 13th-century boundary ditch F.128

In F.128 foraminifera were absent from the 7.5–8.5cm sample and scarce in all other samples (Table 10.12 (CD)), not exceeding three individuals in 10cm^3 wet sediment. The foraminifera found are from the same species as those found in the Church Field F.103 samples. Although sample 47–8cm contains no adult tests, the 63μm fraction contains juvenile tests of the brackish and marine forms found in the F.103 samples. No foraminifera were found in the 63μm fraction of the other samples from F.128.

Home Ground ditch F.267

The results from F.267 are summarised in Table 10.13 (CD) (and see Fig 9.8). Sample 158 from context 268 (the upper fill) contained fewer than ten tests. The species identified were the brackish species *Ammonia beccarii, Haynesina germanica*, and *Elphidium williamsoni* typically found in intertidal environments. Foraminifera were absent in the 63μm fraction. Samples 159, 160 and 161 from the basal fill (context 285) were similar to sample 158. Sample 159 contained occasional tests of *Elphidium williamsoni*, sample 160 contained a few tests of *Haynesina germanica* and *Elphidium williamsoni*, and sample 161 contained *Ammonia beccarii, Haynesina germanica* and an agglutinated species typical of a high marsh environment. The total concentration of forams in 10cm^3 of sediment in each of these ditch samples is less than ten. The 63μm fraction of sample 160 also contained occasional juvenile individuals of the genus *Brizalina*, a marine shelf genus. It is not unusual for small or juvenile forms of *Brizalina* to be found transported into estuaries, particularly following storms (Murray 1991).

Discussion

Most samples from the three medieval ditches contained a very small number of foraminifera and the interpretation of such assemblages is difficult. The sequence from the Church Field enclosure ditch F.103 would appear to show some marine influence. The species present live in middle to low marsh habitats with wide salinity tolerances and the presence of the juvenile marine tests also suggests a greater marine influence. Samples 13–14cm and 38–9cm contain 18 and 29 tests in 10cm^3 of wet sediment respectively, which would normally allow limited environmental interpretation. However, these are relatively small numbers of tests, many of which are heavily etched or eroded, suggesting a degree of post-mortem transport and dissolution. Furthermore, the pollen, plant macrofossil and diatom data all suggest a largely freshwater habitat so it seems probable that the forams in ditch F.103 have been eroded from the Upper Wentlooge alluvium. Foraminifera are either scarce or absent in the samples of Church Field ditch F.128, so the only conclusion one can draw is that those samples containing foraminifera comprise some sediment from a brackish source. All the samples from Home Ground ditch F.267 contain brackish foraminifera commonly found living in salt marsh habitats. However, the concentrations are too low to suggest the probable nature of the brackish environment represented by the samples. It is possible that all the tests are allochthonous (transported from elsewhere) and the presence of small individuals of the marine genus *Brizalina* confirms there is an allochthonous component. The probable source of the tests is the Upper Wentlooge alluvium although occasional inundation by brackish water remains a possibility.

Mollusca by Paul Davies (Table 10.14 (CD))

Church Field

Basal fill of the 12th-century enclosure ditch F.103 (context 134)

In the basal fill of the 12th-century recut of enclosure ditch F.103 (context 134) the aquatic Mollusca are entirely freshwater. The three predominant species (*Lymnaea peregra, Anisus leucostoma*, and *Gyraulus crista*) are representative of a poor freshwater habitat (static and poorly vegetated). Terrestrial species are well represented, suggesting a damp, well-vegetated environment (similar to F.128, context 152). Although there are some shade-loving elements, these most likely indicate long grassland/herbaceous conditions rather than woodland or scrub.

Midden deposit at the base of the 12th- to early 13th-century boundary ditch F.128 (context 152)

Both terrestrial and aquatic Mollusca are well represented in the lower fill of boundary ditch F.128.

The aquatic component contains low numbers of both *Valvata piscinalis* and *Bithynia tentaculata*, both usually indicative of larger and well-oxygenated water bodies. However, the remainder of the aquatics represented are less exacting in their requirements and are typical of small ditches, possibly prone to drying. The presence of *Valvata macrostoma* is noteworthy, the species presently having a very restricted distribution in southern England, typically in floodplain ditches (Kerney 1999). Single individuals of both *Hydrobia ventrosa* and *Ovatella myosotis* are present (comprising 0.7% of the assemblage of 292 individuals). These species are indicative of brackish conditions although, given the small numbers involved, and contemporainity of F.128 with the wholly freshwater enclosure ditch F.103, it is highly likely that the brackish element in 152 was eroded from the natural Upper Wentlooge alluvium into which the ditch is cut.

The terrestrial species represented are, in the main, indicative of a damp, well-vegetated environment. *Carychium tridentatum*, *Discus rotundatus*, *Aegopinella nitidula,* and *Oxychilus cellarius* are all indicative of shade, although the absence of any true woodland component to the assemblage indicates a non-wooded environment. Both *Vallonia costata* and *Vertigo pygmaea* are usually typical of drier, more open habitat, although both can occur in marshes (Kerney and Cameron 1979). Overall, the environment is probably one of long grass/herbs. This may have been growing ditch side, although there is a possibility that the aquatic and terrestrial faunas are temporally separated, with the ditch being filled with water and largely open in the autumn/winter/spring, but dry and well vegetated in the summer. *Cecilioides acicula* is a burrowing species and usually discounted from interpretation.

Upper fill of the 12th- to early 13th-century boundary ditch F.135 (context 131)

Numbers of individuals were low, with only three terrestrial species represented. *Discus rotundatus* may indicate shade (as F.128 above), though numbers are far too low to allow any certainty.

Fill of the 17th- to 18th-century boundary ditch F.140 (recutting F.128) (context 141)

The aquatic assemblage from F.140 is overwhelmingly dominated by *Gyraulus crista* and *Anisus leucostoma*. *Gyraulus crista* is not common in aquatic habitats prone to drying (Kerney 1999), although apart from a single individual of *Valvata piscinalis* there is little indication of favourable conditions for aquatic Mollusca. Indeed, *Lymnaea palustris* is usually indicative of poor conditions. Overall, therefore, one must conclude that there was probably more-or-less permanent water, though not of a particular high quality (static and poorly vegetated). The aquatic assemblage is entirely freshwater.

Terrestrial species are not particularly well represented, with most of the species (*Carychium minimum, Cochlicopa lubrica, Vallonia costata, Nesovitrea hammonis* and *Trichia hispida*) indicative of open, but damp conditions, probably quite short grassland. This is not necessarily indicative of the wider landscape, possibly only representing ditch side conditions. The presence of some *Oxychilus* and a single *Discus* may indicate that at times the vegetation became somewhat longer and offered slightly more shade at ground level.

Home Ground

Lower fill of the 12th- to 13th-century boundary ditch F.308 (context 323)

Overall the numbers of Mollusca from F.308 were not high and any comment must therefore be considered tentative. The aquatic component is mixed, with both *Bithynia tentaculata* and *Valvata piscinalis* usually indicative of good water conditions, but all others represented being tolerant of poorer conditions. *Hydrobia ventrosa* is indicative of brackish conditions, though the two individuals could easily have eroded out from earlier deposits. Numbers of individuals of terrestrial species are low although there are no shade-requiring species present, so conditions are most likely open.

Lower fill of the 12th- to 13th-century boundary ditch F.267 (context 285)

Aquatic numbers are high, although only four species are represented. All four are tolerant of poor freshwater conditions in locations prone to drying, which would therefore seem to be the case here. The terrestrial component contains *Aegopinella nitidula* and *Oxychilus cellarius*, both indicative of a degree of shade. However, there are no 'woodland' species and all of the other terrestrials are typical of open environments. Overall, the indications are of a damp grassy/herbaceous habitat (as for context 152 in Church Field ditch F.128 described above).

Lower fill of the 12th- to 13th-century pit F.265 (context 280)

Overall numbers are low. Most of the shells (13/17) recovered were of *Hydrobia ventrosa*, a species indicative of brackish environments. Without other evidence it is impossible to gauge whether these have been eroded from earlier deposits or are actually representative of brackish conditions at this locality at this time.

Lower fill of the 17th- to 18th-century recut boundary ditch F.209 (context 230)

The aquatic assemblage from the 17th- to 18th-century recut of F.209 is indicative of a ditch environment prone to drying. *Anisus leucostoma, Lymnaea peregra, Lymnaea truncatula* and *Bathyomphalus contortus* are all tolerant of such conditions and *Planorbis planorbis* favours such conditions. The brackish species *Hydrobia ulvae* and *Hydrobia ventrosa* are both present but in very small numbers (2% of the assemblage of 341 individuals) and without corroborative evidence for any tidal influence from the plant macrofossils it would appear likely that they have eroded from earlier deposits. The terrestrial assemblage is diverse, with a considerable shade-indicative component (*Discus, Aegopinella, Oxychilus, Clausilia, Carychium tridentatum*). However, the remaining species are more representative of non-wooded environments and it seems likely that this assemblage represents non-wooded, but highly structured damp grassy/herbaceous conditions. Again, this may be ditch side, although temporal mixing is again a possibility (see above).

Discussion

The medieval and post-medieval features in Church Field and Home Ground have species-rich assemblages indicative of a range of freshwater environments, typically well vegetated but with slowly moving water that was prone to drying out. These conditions mirror those in the late Romano-British reclaimed landscape at Banwell Moor and Kenn Moor. A small number of these medieval contexts contain a very small number of brackish species although in such small numbers (certainly in comparison to the clearly intertidal contexts) these are most likely to have been derived from erosion of the ditch sides (which were cut into this Upper Wentlooge Formation).

Shellfish

A total of 263 marine shellfish were recovered from a variety of contexts spanning the medieval occupation at Church Field through to the post-medieval contexts at Home Ground. As the assemblages in individual contexts were mostly small and fragmented, data for the bivalves in Table 10.15 (CD) is for the minimum number of valves as it was not possible to produce a meaningful calculation for the minimum number of individuals.

Marine shellfish were present, albeit in low numbers, in many contexts in the medieval and post-medieval settlement at Puxton, though they are notably better represented in Church Field than in Home Ground. During the medieval period (11th–13th century) periwinkles (*Littorina littorea*) were most common with 93 individuals (60%) followed by oysters (*Ostrea edulis*) with 54 valves/fragments (36%). There were six (4%) common limpets (*Patella vulgata*). The post-medieval period sees a far greater diversity of species though the virtual disappearance of periwinkles (and those two individuals could easily be residual). Common mussels were now most common with 57 valves (53%), followed by oysters with 43 valves (38%); common limpets, common cockles (*Cardium edule*), and Venus shells (*Venus striatula*) were present in very small numbers.

Limpets and periwinkles can be found in abundance on the nearby rocky shoreline of Brean Down, Worlebury, Middlehope, and the Clevedon to Portishead coast, and they dominate the Bronze Age, Iron Age and Romano-British assemblages at Brean Down (Johnson 1990). Cockles and mussels live on sandy shores, and while they are abundant in the Bristol Channel they have only been recorded very occasionally in the Severn Estuary due to its high suspended sediment load (Boyden and Little 1973, 212; Boyden *et al* 1977, 529–31). There used to be a productive oyster bed at Blue Anchor Bay on the west Somerset coast (between Minehead and Watchet) and odd dead shells have been collected on the south Wales coast, but there is no evidence that they have grown in the Severn Estuary (Boyden *et al* 1977, 530). Indeed, a survey of oyster beds conducted by the Fishmonger's Society in the early 20th century records that the closest beds to Bristol were at the Mumbles on the Gower Peninsula in south Wales (Blockley forthcoming). It is impossible to say whether the oysters at Puxton were cultivated or simply collected from natural beds as the sample size was too small to make metrical analysis worthwhile. In Bristol, however, a larger assemblage showed a considerable variation in size, suggesting they came from a natural population, but that some selection may have taken place during collection (Blockley forthcoming).

As a traded commodity, as opposed to a resource that could be collected locally, the greater abundance of oysters at Church Field, as compared to the contemporary tenement at Home Ground, might suggest a site of higher status. Unfortunately there are few comparable medieval assemblages in the region to test this hypothesis. At Shapwick oysters dominate the assemblages and, while they are present on sites throughout the social spectrum, they were most numerous on the manorial sites; there was also an increased amount of shellfish on early post-medieval sites (Light forthcoming a). Shellfish were either absent or at least not collected/analysed at the contemporary 12th-century farmstead at Bickley on the slopes of the limestone hills to the east of Puxton (Ponsford 2003), and the same appears to be true of many other published urban and rural settlement excavations in Somerset.[1] For the pre-Conquest period, however, a small assemblage from the royal palace at Cheddar contained 53 oyster valves, 26 limpets, 12 periwinkles, and 6 mussel shells (Rahtz 1979). A large assemblage of marine shellfish has been reported from an urban context in Taunton which showed that oysters were present in small numbers during the late medieval period, compared to the 16th century when they became abundant; cockle, limpet, mussel, and whelk, were all present but in very small numbers (Burrow 1988, 161). In Bristol, oysters generally dominate assemblages (Copp 1988; Blockley forthcoming), though at Narrow Quay a change in the pattern of consumption is evident, with mussels and oysters being present in roughly equal numbers in the later 15th century, but oysters coming to dominate in the 16th century (Good 1987, 120–2). At Union Street there is similarly a marked increase in oyster consumption in the 15th to 17th centuries when they appear to have come from cultivated beds (Light forthcoming b). Oysters were also eaten at St Cross nunnery in Compton Martin (Rahtz and Greenfield 1977, 376).

Of the other species seen at Puxton most would have been collected for food, though periwinkles can hardly have had a high calorific value compared to the effort expended on their collection. They could have been cooked up in some form of stew, perhaps have been used as fishing bait (as could limpets), or they could have been brought to the site on seaweed (Coy 1987, 13). Periwinkles can also be used as a source of dye.

The larger mammal bones *by Alan K Outram*

Introduction and methodology

The larger mammal bone assemblage from Puxton is a sizeable one for a rural medieval excavation, though unfortunately once phasing has been carried out and bones from unstratified contexts are excluded, the sample size is significantly reduced. Nonetheless, it is still possible to come to useful conclusions regarding species abundances and, to a certain extent, the age structure of herds. The identification of the faunal remains was carried out by comparison with modern reference material at the Department of Archaeology, University of Exeter. Distinction between sheep and goat was only attempted on those elements that are particularly diagnostic, following the criteria laid down by Boessneck (1969) for the appendicular skeleton and Payne (1985) for teeth.

Not all elements of the mammal skeleton were recorded for the purposes of quantification. The analysis concentrated on those elements that are most informative, identifiable, quantifiable, and have a reasonable rate of survival. The elements included in the analysis were all the long bones, the scapula, the pelvis, the ulna, the calcaneum and astragalus, the atlas and axis, and the phalanges. The head is represented by mandibles, maxilla, occipital condyles, horn cores, and antlers. Vertebral centra and rib fragments have not been included in the main quantification, but were examined for any interesting features, including butchery practices. Abaxial metapodia were also eliminated from quantification.

For long bones, proximal and distal ends were counted separately. The scapula was counted if the glenoid cavity or collum is present. The countable zone on the pelvis was the acetabulum. The assemblage is quantified in terms of a simple Number of Identifiable Specimens (NISP) count (Klein and Cruz-Uribe 1984) with Minimum Number of Element (MNE) and Minimum Number of Animal Units (MAU) (after Binford 1984) also being calculated and presented at the species level. In calculating MNEs, specimens were only discounted if, during analysis, it was clear that two fragments from the same context might derive from the same bone. The MAU count was a modified form of Binford's (1984) method, where it is assumed that a skeleton contains two of each element and elements that differ from that are moderated accordingly (eg the axis count is doubled; bovine phalanges with two per leg, fore and hind, are divided by four).

The ageing of sheep mandibles follows the system of allocating mandibular teeth to wear stage devised by Payne (1973). Cattle mandibular teeth have been aged in a similar way following an adaptation by Halstead (1985) of Payne's (1973) methodology for sheep, using wear patterns observed by Grant (1982). Pig mandible ages are based on tooth eruption data given by Silver (1969). Epiphiseal fusion ages were taken from Silver (1969). Neonatal specimens were identified by virtue of their size, external and internal (where visible) texture, general morphology, and by comparison to reference material. The sexing of pig mandibles was based on the morphology of the canine as given by Schmid (1972) or, in the absence of the canine, on the nature of the canine socket (Halstead pers comm). A selection of useful measurements was taken on each element, as defined by von den Driesch (1976).

Species abundance

Tables 10.16–10.19 (all CD) display identifications by species and element for stratified medieval contexts in Church Field and medieval and post-medieval contexts at Home Ground; the post-medieval phase at Church Field is too small to be worthy of display but Table 10.16, which gives the information for all contexts from Church Field, is included as the majority of topsoil/surface cleaning of the occupation platform will contain overwhelmingly medieval material (see Gutiérrez, Chapter 9). The data by element are given as NISPs, but species totals are also given in the form of MNEs and MAUs. It can be seen that the different forms of quantification have very little impact on the overall pattern that one sees. Whilst sheep and goats have

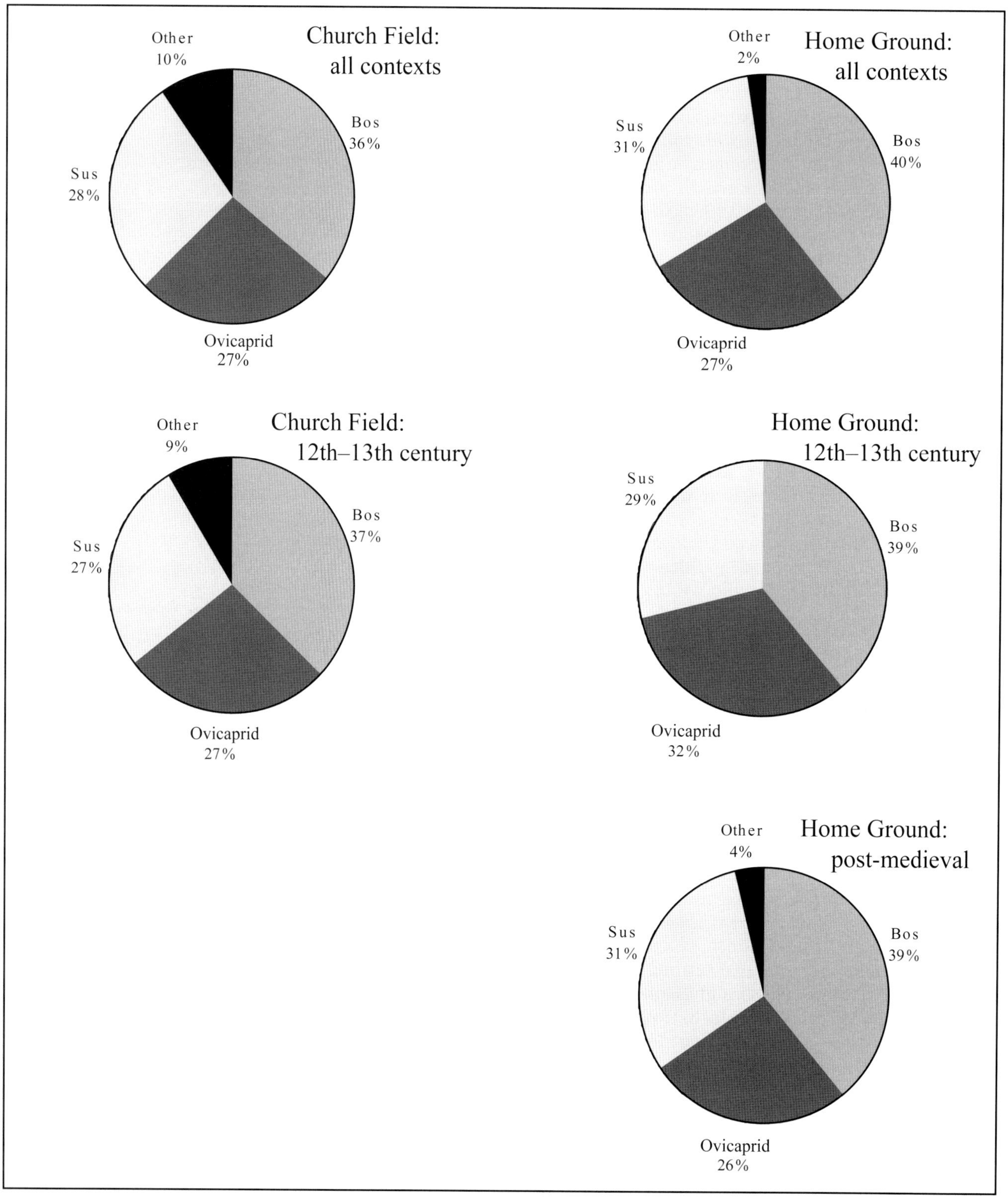

Figure 10.2 Larger mammal species composition at Church Field and Home Ground

been grouped together as ovicaprids, there is no clear evidence for the presence of goats at either of the sites. Where definite speciation of ovicaprids was possible, all were sheep. In Figure 10.2 pie charts of species composition in the two sites, based upon MAU counts, show that in all cases cattle are clearly most numerous, with numbers of pigs and sheep/goats being approximately equal. There does not seem to be any significant difference between species abundances at the two sites or between phases. It is noticeable that other species are less common at Home Ground, but this could easily be a function of sample size. Roe and fallow deer, horse, dog, cat, and hare are all present in small quantities at Puxton. None of these species represents a particular surprise. The presence of deer is often taken as a sign of high-status occupation, since the hunting of deer was the preserve of nobility in the Middle Ages (Grant 1988), though it is clear that small quantities of venison did make it onto the lower-status tables (Grant 2002), and so while the presence of deer at Puxton should be noted, since the quantities are small, not too much should be read into it.

Skeletal part abundances

Tables 10.16–10.19 show that all parts of the skeleton are present at the sites. There is no pattern that is suggestive of any particular activity or bias in the assemblage beyond well-known taphonomic biases (eg the easily destroyed, spongy proximal humerus has depressed values by comparison to more hardy epiphyses). It is clear that both meat-bearing bones and those with little utility are present and it is likely that whole animals were butchered locally, as one might expect for a rural site, rather than meat being supplied from elsewhere.

Age structure

To establish age structures from animal bone assemblages, large sample sizes are required. Age structures can be most accurately ascertained from mandible tooth eruption and wear stages, but unfortunately these sites did not produce sufficient mandibles to make this possible. Bone fusion stages can provide an indication of culling ages up to the point that all bones have fused and because this method collects data from a larger range of elements, such a method can be applied to smaller assemblages. In this case, it was possible to ascertain information on age structures in this way for the medieval phase at Church Field.

Figure 10.3 shows the percentage of animals that are likely to have survived beyond a given bone fusion stage for cattle in the medieval phases in Church Field. One can see that there is little evidence for the culling of animals at a young age (before 18 months), though many animals appear to have died between 2 and 4 years old. Only a very small proportion survived into adulthood. This does not produce a viable, breeding herd structure, so it is clear that the deadstock deposited at Church Field only represents a selection of the livestock from which they derive. It is possible that we are seeing a pattern of killing steers for meat at a time when they have just reached maximum body mass, which could have formed part of a much larger economic strategy that included the keeping of adult cows for milk and breeding, some bulls for breeding, and maybe oxen for labour (see Higham and Message 1969). Unfortunately, there is little evidence regarding sex ratios within this assemblage. All one can say with certainty is that Church Field was being supplied with beef of prime age.

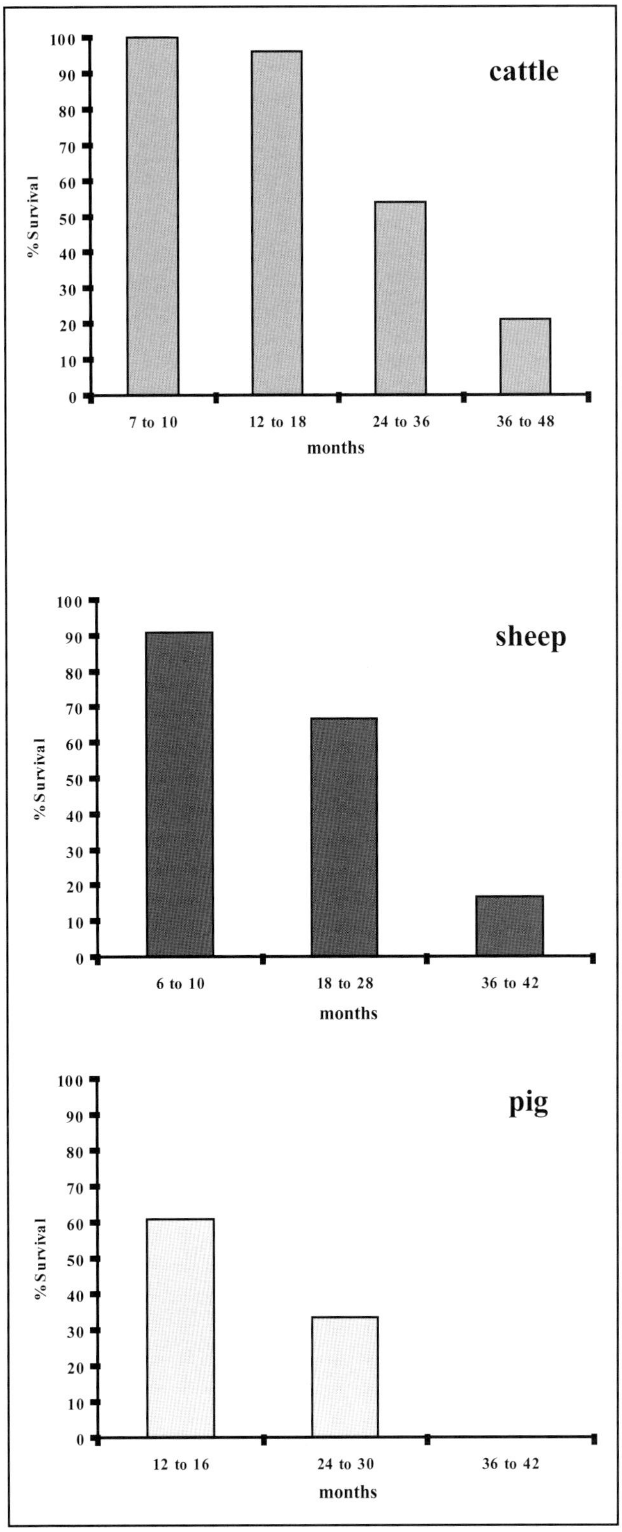

Figure 10.3 Age structure for medieval cattle, sheep, and pig from Church Field

Figure 10.3 also illustrates the fusion data for the medieval sheep/goats at Church Field. The pattern is quite similar to that of cattle and most animals were culled between 2.5 and 3.5 years of age. Once again, very few adult animals are present, suggesting that we are only seeing a selection from the flock. The culling age is again consistent with slaughtering for meat, just as the animal reached full size. Killing at this age is not really compatible with keeping sheep primarily for wool as in an economic regime led by wool production, animals would normally be kept until much older than prime meat culling age in order to continue exploiting their fleeces (Dobney *et al* 1995). Whilst wool production may have been of paramount importance in areas like Lincoln in the 12th–13th centuries (ibid.), this does not appear to have been the case in some other regions. The medieval assemblages at Exeter, like Puxton, show a high proportion of immature animals and Maltby (1979, 46) argues that wool in Devon and Cornwall was not highly regarded at the time. In those counties, wool does not appear to have been of great economic significance until the middle of the 14th century (Maltby 1979, 47).

The same information for pigs is also displayed in Figure 10.3. There are no mature animals and it appears culling occurred between 1 and 3 years of age. This pattern appears to represent the selection of animals for culling at prime meat age. A few pig mandibles could be sexed and both males and females are present.

Sample sizes at Home Ground were too small to carry out a similar analysis, but the data available were consistent with the pattern outlined above. The data available from the ageing of mandibles were also consistent with this pattern.

Butchery

There was little worthy of particular note regarding butchery patterns, but it is worth commenting on two issues. In modern butchery practice, animals are cut into sides down the spine, leaving the vertebrae cut in half down the dorso-ventral plain. This practice occurred as early as the mid-11th century in York (Davis 1987, 189) but was not introduced until the post-medieval period in Exeter (Maltby 1979, 39), for instance. At Puxton there was no evidence for dorso-ventral cleaving of vertebrae in either the medieval or post-medieval contexts. There was, however, evidence of butchery on one horse radius. Pope Gregory III (*c* AD 732) forbade the eating of horse flesh, though it is clear that the ban was never wholly successful (Simoons 1994, 187). There is no evidence, though, for what purpose this particular horse was butchered.

Measurements

Sample sizes are too small to carry out analysis of the metrical data from this site, but these data are provided in Tables 6–15 of the archive report.

Conclusion

The assemblages, at both sites, in both phases, are consistent with domestic debris from the consumption of animals that were principally culled at an age suitable for the provision of meat. Whole carcasses appear to have been present at the site. It is clear that the assemblage only contains a biased selection of the age profile of animals that must have been kept in this region. Cattle appear to have been the most important species. There is evidence that the husbandry regime for sheep in this region was not particularly directed at wool production. It is clear that Puxton, Church Field in particular, was well provisioned with prime meat and the presence of deer could hint at higher-status occupation of the area.

Bird, fish, and amphibian bones

by S Hamilton-Dyer

Bird bone was recovered from the wet sieving of bulk samples from both Church Field and Home Ground. Species identifications were made using the author's modern comparative collections. All fragments were identified to species and element where possible. Recently broken bones were joined and have been counted as single fragments. Measurements follow von den Driesch (1976) and are in millimetres unless otherwise stated. Archive material includes metrical and other data not presented in the text. Just over 200 fragments were submitted for analysis. On examination these totalled 192 individual specimens and included five amphibian bones and a single fish bone. The condition of the bones is generally good, and sometimes excellent, with an ivoried appearance. Most of the bones can be identified to taxon and cut and gnaw marks, though few are clearly visible.

Church Field

Bird bone

At least sixteen species are represented by the 165 bird bones (Table 10.20 (CD)). As expected the majority of the bones identified to taxon are of domestic fowl, comprising 25% of the assemblage. Many of the unidentified fragments are also likely to be of fowl. The fowl bones include at least two attributable to hens and some from immature birds. The bones are typically small in comparison with recent birds. Puncture marks on two bones are likely to have been made by cat. Just three bones, all fowl, from the site offer evidence of butchery and indicate where wing and leg were disjointed. Geese are represented by eleven bones and as it is difficult to separate bones of domestic goose from those of the ancestral wild greylag these have been placed in one group. The remains do, however, include several large and broad bones likely to be from domestic birds. It is similarly difficult to separate the larger duck bones into mallard and domestic and these have also been grouped together, but smaller duck bones could be classed as probably of teal and wigeon. Bones of waders include one of curlew and others comparable with woodcock, lapwing/plover, and jack snipe/dunlin. Another common wetland bird, the heron, is also present. Of note are two bones of crane, an ulna fragment from context 116 (ditch F.115) in Trench 1 and a large carpometacarpus from context 136 (ditch F.135) in Trench 2. The crane is now absent from Britain, and indeed from the near continent, but was once a relatively common breeding bird and winter visitor (Boisseau and Yalden 1998).

There are several bones of corvids including raven, rook/crow and jay. Crow and raven are carrion feeders, raven particularly feeding on dead sheep and afterbirth. Crows and ravens need trees or rocky outcrops for nesting, but will range quite a distance. The rook is a grassland bird, needing tree clumps for nesting. Although an invertebrate feeder, it can be a pest on new seeded crops. The jay is a woodland bird, being reliant on acorns and other seeds for winter. Smaller passerines are represented by two bones only, of thrush and sparrow size from topsoil. Pigeons are represented by a single humerus of an immature bird.

The bones of raptors are almost as frequent as those of fowl, although they do include some partial skeletons. Buzzard occurs in seven contexts, mainly as single bones. One bone attributable to marsh harrier was recovered from occupation material in Trench 12 (context 504) and a further six from a partial skeleton in ditch F.135 in Trench 2. The large size of the bones suggests that this was a female bird. A total of twenty bones of goshawk are present, but are from a maximum of three birds. All are from Trench 2, ten from the upper fill (131) of ditch F.135, one from the disturbed natural nearby (context 133) and a further group of nine from the upper fill of ditch F.128 (context 109). Examination of the bones revealed such similarities that they could be considered the same bird, as none of the elements are repeated side for side, and the measurements of paired bones are extremely close. Whether one bird or more, these measurements are large and, therefore, probably female. The goshawk, especially the larger female, can be used to take animals and birds to the size of hare, partridge and crow. The frequent finds of complete and partial skeletons in towns is generally taken as evidence of falconry (Mulkeen and O'Connor 1997). As a bird of mature woodland, it also seems an unlikely wild resident for the Somerset Levels unless significant areas of cover were available nearby (for which there is no other palaeoenvironmental or documentary evidence).

The other raptor remains are less difficult to interpret. While the goshawk has long been considered a desirable falconer's bird, this does not ever seem to have applied to the buzzard. Remains of this bird are relatively common as it is an adaptable bird of mixed habitat and, while it will take carrion, it was often destroyed as vermin, being perceived as a potential threat to poultry chicks. The marsh harrier is an infrequent find. It is a ground-nesting bird of reed-beds and marshes, hunting low over the fens, and again does not seem to have been used for falconry. Its current rarity is largely due to loss of habitat.

Of considerable interest is the coracoid of a large bird from ditch F.122 (context 123) in Trench 2 which matches *Ciconia* (stork) material in the bird collections of the Natural History Museum at Tring. The two species found in Europe are White, *C. ciconia*, and Black, *C. nigra*, both of which are migratory birds, returning from Africa to breed in Europe during the summer. Although the distinguishing part of this bone is missing and both species have been recorded in Britain, the large size of the Puxton example is most likely to be from a white stork, more commonly seen in Europe especially in the west. The white stork will readily nest on buildings if a suitable platform is present and is encouraged to do so in Germany and Holland. A mixed diet including insects, snakes, frogs, mice and other 'pests' makes the bird a welcome visitor to farming communities. Records of stork from Britain at any period are almost non-existent (Parker 1988; Reid-Henry and Harrison 1988) but it nested in much of Europe in the medieval period and is unmistakably portrayed on page 366 of the Sherborne Missal (Backhouse 2001). There is a celebrated record of a pair of storks nesting in Edinburgh in 1416 (British Ornithologists Union 1971), such a rare event then that it was worthy of note. Whether the bone at Puxton represents a vagrant or the remains of an imported captive cannot be determined.

Fish and amphibian bone

The only identifiable fish bone recovered from the entire site is from midden material (context 527) in Trench 12. This is the dentary of a conger eel of about a metre in length. The conger is an exclusively marine species and must, therefore, have been transported to Puxton from the coast or via a market such as Bristol. Two bones each of frog and toad are also present.

Home Ground

The excavations in Home Ground were less productive of birds, with just 21 bones and only four from medieval contexts (Table 10.21 (CD)). Most of the remains appear to be of domestic poultry, if it is assumed (as seems likely) that the three bones of goose and one of a large duck are of the domesticated forms. In addition to domestic fowl (seven bones) there is a single bone of another non-native member of the Galliformes, a turkey. This species is a native of North America and the post-medieval date for ditch F.209 (context 210) is consistent with the late introduction of this bird. Unlike the

Church Field assemblage only one bone of a raptor is present, a buzzard humerus from gully F.312. There are instead three bones of owl, probably a single tawny owl, from post-medieval fills of ditch F.205. The remaining two bird bones are of a corvid, probably a jay, and a smaller passerine of thrush size. A bone of toad is also present.

Discussion

The bird assemblage from Church Field is exceptionally rich both in terms of species and in the number of remains in comparison with the mammals. Domestic fowl are typically the most common remains but the proportion of wild birds is relatively high and, given the local conditions at this period, the range of wetland species is not unexpected. The presence of several birds needing trees for feeding or nesting implies woodland, or at the very least clumps of trees such as still occur in the vicinity of farmsteads on the Levels. The special features of this assemblage are the raptor remains and the extremely rare find of stork.

The small mammal bones *by Alan K Outram*

The samples and methodology

Small mammal remains were recovered from a variety of 12th- to 13th-century and 17th- to 18th-century contexts at both Church Field and Home Ground. The majority of the material was retrieved by wet sieving, with a few additional specimens having been recovered by hand. Identifications were undertaken using the reference collection in the Department of Archaeology, University of Exeter. Although it is apparent that the full range of skeletal elements was present within the assemblage, identifications concentrated upon the mandibles and maxilla because these elements are most likely to provide accurate identifications to species level, give a good indication of numbers of animals and survive well archaeologically. Minimum Numbers of Individuals (MNIs) have been calculated by taking the most common element (left or right maxilla or mandible) as a minimum for that context and those have been added together to produce the MNIs for phases. This quantification assumes that the same individual is not represented in different contexts. In two cases, quantification was derived from the identification of an appendicular element. These were cases where the identification to species level could be achieved with confidence and the species were not otherwise represented in that context.

Results

Employing the above methodology, 25 specimens were identified and Table 10.22 (CD) shows the MNI counts for each species within the different phases of activity at the two sites. The species identified were house mouse (*Mus musculus*), individuals from the wood mouse genus (*Apodemus* sp., either *Apodemus sylvaticus* or *Apodemus flavicollis*), field vole (*Microtus agrestis*), water vole (*Arvicola terrestis*), common shrew (*Sorex araneus*) and mole (*Talpa europaea*). The sample size is small and no significant trend can be identified between the two main phases of activity. Below are notes on the habitats and behaviour of these species (derived from Corbet and Harris 1991).

- Field voles (*Microtus agrestis*) are ubiquitous throughout the British mainland. They are common in rough grassland but also occur in smaller numbers in woodlands, hedgerows, blanket bogs, dunes, scree and moorlands up to 1300m. They feed mainly on green leaves and grass stems.
- Water voles (*Arvicola terrestis*) tend to live in lowlands on banks near fairly deep, slow-running water (ditches, dykes, rivers, streams, and less commonly ponds). They can, however, live away from water and tend to live mainly below ground in burrows. They feed mainly on grasses, reeds, sedges, and less commonly on some other herbs. Very rarely they eat insects, molluscs and fish.
- House mice (*Mus musculus*) are best known for living in buildings and food stores, but they can live entirely independently from humans. They can live in a wide range of habitats, but prefer there to be cover so they tend to avoid completely open ground. They are not common in woodland, however, probably because of competition with other species. They eat most foodstuffs, but prefer carbohydrate-rich foods to protein and fats.
- Wood mouse genus (*Apodemus* sp.). There are two species of wood mouse that can be found in Britain: wood mouse (*Apodemus sylvaticus*) and the very similar yellow-necked mouse (*Apodemus flavicollis*). The wood mouse is highly adaptable and will live in woodland, arable land, grassland, heather, blanket bog, sand dunes, hedgerows, and gardens. It is rarely found above the tree line and does not like it too wet. The yellow-necked mouse is slightly more restricted to deciduous woodland but will live in hedges, rural gardens and buildings. Both species like to eat seeds, green plants, fruits, worms, and larvae.
- Common shrews (*Sorex araneus*) are commonly found where there is cover from thick grass, scrub, hedgerows and deciduous woodland. They are occasionally found in heather. They feed on insects and other small invertebrates.
- Moles (*Talpa europaea*) are common in deciduous woodland, and agricultural and pasture land. They are uncommon in coniferous forest, sand dunes and moorland. They feed on soil invertebrates.
- Hedgehogs (*Erinaceus europaeus*) are common throughout mainland Britain at the edges of woods or in scrub or hedgerows. Tend to be more scarce

in coniferous woodland and marshy or moorland areas. They feed mainly on invertebrates on the ground, but will also take carrion, birds' eggs and chicks.

Conclusion

The assemblage is consistent with a wide range of environments commonly found in the British Isles, but perhaps most consistent with farmland that provides a certain amount of cover from deciduous woodland, hedgerows or rough scrub. The sample is too small to draw comparisons between phases or the different sites.

Small mammal remains from the upper fill of ditch F.205 at Home Ground *by Amanda Kear*

During the excavation of the 17th- to 18th-century upper fill of ditch F.205 (context 227) at Home Ground, a dense concentration of small mammal remains was found and bulk sampled. The size of this assemblage warranted a more detailed examination than the material from other contexts at Home Ground and in Church Field. For the purposes of calculating this relative abundance in the mammalian skeletal elements, the MNI for each species was added to give a total MNI for mammals. The state of preservation of the bones was assessed by examination under the light microscope. For certain skeletal elements the proportion of intact to damaged bones was counted. The type and patterns of damage were recorded for comparison with material from the literature. Some bones were deliberately broken or subjected to scratching and puncture from forceps and other processing tools. This was in order to compare fresh damage with that already existing on the bones. In these ways it was hoped to distinguish between the various possible causes and timings of damage (pre- and post-mortality, pre- and post-deposition, and pre- and post-excavation) and thus construct a taphonomic history for the bones.

The bone assemblage was in relatively good condition. Table 10.23 (CD) lists the vertebrate species identified from cranial and dental material, while Table 10.24 (CD) records the identifiable skeletal elements and the MNI for each mammal species. The majority of the mammals present were from very small species (under 120mm head and body length). The bulk of the sample proved to be mammal remains, with shrews and microtine rodents (voles) predominating. Isolated examples of three larger species were also recorded: one rat (*Rattus* sp.) was identified from a mandible fragment; one water vole (*Arvicola terrestris*) from a skull, a mandible and isolated teeth; and one mole (*Talpa europaea*) from a single mandible. The common frog (*Rana temporaria*) was also present (as at least fourteen individuals). There were no birds or reptiles.

The total MNI for the mammals is 176. Of this total, 71 individuals were identified from skulls and mandibles as 'unknown vole species'. This is because the molars were missing from the jaws, so a more detailed identification was not possible. Examination of isolated vole teeth confirmed that the 'unidentified' voles were a mixture of field voles (*Microtus agrestis*) and bank voles (*Clethrionomys glareolus*), with the former apparently predominating, but a detailed count of the proportions of each type of tooth was not done. Only a minority of the isolated vole teeth had fully or partially developed roots belonging to sexually mature bank voles.

The most numerous of the murid rodents was *Apodemus* sp., with an MNI of ten. The diagnostic feature for distinguishing the skulls of the wood mouse (*Apodemus sylvaticus*) from those of the yellow-necked field mouse (*Apodemus flavicollis*) is the thickness of the upper incisors (Corbet 1975). As the tools to measure this thickness to the 0.1 to 0.01mm accuracy needed were not available during this study and the incisors were often missing from the skull, these specimens could not be identified beyond genus. The brown rat (*Rattus norvegicus*) reached Britain in the 18th century and then began to displace its predecessor, the black rat (*Rattus rattus*), which is now restricted to localised areas around big rivers, including the mouth of the Severn. With the pottery from the Home Ground ditch giving a 17th- to 18th-century date, it is currently not possible to say if the identified *Rattus* sp. is a black or brown rat.

All the data on the small mammal bones and teeth is consistent with digestion having taken place, making a scat or pellet accumulation the most likely source of the bone specimens from Puxton. It is a common assumption that large quantities of small mammal bones indicate the activities of the barn owl, although other predators catch and accumulate similar faunal assemblages. Comparison of the Puxton material with data from the literature, however, suggests that a barn owl is indeed a prime candidate for creating the assemblage. Barn owls feed almost exclusively on small mammals, with voles, mice and shrews forming 85.9 to 98.6% of their diet (Mikkola 1983). They are not specialists in catching any particular species but stick within the broad category of 'small mammals', taking whatever species are available. Thus the barn owl's diet varies by habitat: they take mostly field voles and common shrews in rough grassland and wetland habitats, whilst wood mice are added to the diet and common shrews are of less importance in woodland habitats (Mikkola 1983). There is a little seasonal variation in its diet, although neither frogs nor birds are of major significance. Barn owls eat more frogs in the spring, when the frogs are migrating towards breeding ponds (Bunn *et al* 1982; Mikkola 1983), whilst birds are more likely to be consumed in January, February and May (Mikkola 1983).

Note

1 **Early medieval sites**: Alcock 1995; Rahtz and Hirst 1974; Rahtz *et al* 1992; **Monastic sites**: Cleeve Abbey: Guy 1999; Glastonbury Abbey: Woods 1995; Glastonbury, The Mound: Carr 1985; Keynsham Abbey: Lowe 1987; Witham Priory: Burrow and Burrow 1990; **rural sites**: Manor Farm Castle Cary: Leach and Ellis 2004; Rockingham Farm, Avonmouth: Locock and Lawler 2000; Stoke sub Hamdon: Montague *et al* 1992; **urban sites**: Bath: Davenport 1991; Bristol: Price and Ponsford 1998; Ilchester: Leach 1982; Taunton: Hutcheson and Andrews 2002; Leach 1984.

Part 4:
Discussion and conclusions

11 Changing environment and economy in the 1st and 2nd millennia AD: synthesis and discussion

By Julie Jones, summarising the reports of Nigel Cameron, Paul Davies, Simon Dobinson, S Hamilton-Dyer, J L Heathcote, Amanda Kear, Annette Kreiser, Alan K Outram, Stephen Rippon, and Heather M Tinsley

Chapters 3, 4, 9, and 10 have included a series of specialist reports on the palaeoenvironmental and palaeoeconomic evidence from the upper part of the alluvial sequence that makes up the North Somerset Levels (the Upper Wentlooge Formation), the Romano-British ditched enclosure system on Puxton Dolemoor and two areas of shrunken settlement earthworks in Puxton itself. This chapter will present a summary and discussion of that evidence, that along with a similar discussion of the late Roman sites at Banwell Moor and Kenn Moor (Rippon 2000b), will explore the changing natural environment over some two millennia and the impact that human modification and transformation had on the landscape.

The upper part of the Upper Wentlooge Formation

The work at Banwell Moor, Kenn Moor, and Puxton Moor has been the first detailed sedimentological and palaeoenvironmental investigation of the upper part of the alluvial sequence in all of the Somerset Levels. As described in Chapter 3, two dark horizons were observed within the upper part of the Upper Wentlooge Formation at Church Field and were investigated in detail in the long section exposed at Home Ground. The upper horizon was also observed and sampled at Hardingworth. At Home Ground the lower horizon (251–314) typically comprised a mottled dark blue/grey silty clay, *c* 20–30mm thick, that in places merged with a darker

Table 11.1 Summary of phasing and broad environmental/landscape conditions at the excavated sites

phase	date	natural environment	cultural landscape
10	modern	freshwater (reclaimed)	• topsoil
9	*c* 18th–19th century	freshwater (reclaimed)	• latest infilling of ditches/gripes at Church Field and Home Ground
8	17th century	freshwater (reclaimed)	• reoccupation at Home Ground
7	14th to 16th century	freshwater (reclaimed)	• agricultural landscape
6	late 11th to 13th century	freshwater (reclaimed)	• occupation in Church Field and Home Ground
5	?*c* late 10th/early 11th century	decrease in inundation?	• 'summer/ring dike' at Church Field • earliest features within Church Field (on a different orientation to the 12th- to 13th-century ditched enclosure)
4	early medieval	intertidal saltmarsh	• alluvium above upper dark horizon
3	late Romano-British	freshwater (reclaimed)	• upper dark horizon (buried soil) at Home Ground and Hardingworth • upper fill of ditched enclosure system at Dolemoor • drainage ditch/gullies beneath later bank in Church Field
2b	early Romano-British	decrease in inundation?	• creation and lower fill of ditched enclosure system at Dolemoor
2a	late Iron Age/ early Romano-British	intertidal saltmarsh	• salt production at Dolemoor • alluvium above the dark horizon at Home Ground
1	middle Iron Age	decrease in inundation	• lower dark horizon at Home Ground
0	pre-middle Iron Age	intertidal saltmarsh	• alluvium below lower dark horizon at Home Ground

brown/black silty clay *c* 40mm thick (326). It was recorded at between + 3.74 and + 4.02m OD and yielded an AMS date in the middle Iron Age of 828–544 cal. BC (2585 ± 50 BP, AA-32358). This lower horizon sealed and was sealed by mid-blue/grey silty clay, with abundant orange/brown mottles, typical of the Upper Wentlooge Formation. Unfortunately problems in the laboratory meant that the samples taken from this lower dark horizon for soil micromorphology could not be examined. This alluvium was sealed by the upper dark horizon comprising a mid-blue/grey silty clay with occasional to frequent darker blue/brown mottling (218/288/367), and which in places sealed a lighter blue/grey silty clay (289). This undulating upper horizon occurred at + 4.8m at Church Field, between + 4.0 and + 4.5m OD (typically + 4.3–4.4m OD) at Home Ground, and + 4.1– 4.3m OD at Hardingworth.

The upper part of the Upper Wentlooge Formation at Home Ground was sampled for diatoms (which were absent from all contexts), foraminifera (both of whose preservation was excellent), pollen (whose preservation was poor), plant macrofossils and Mollusca (whose preservation was variable); detailed reports can be found in Chapter 4. The alluvium (252) below the lower dark horizon was dominated by the brackish, mid- to low marsh foraminifera *Elphidium williamsoni* and *Haynesina germanica*, with the estuary mouth/marine *Ammonia beccarii* suggesting full tidal conditions at this time. A palaeochannel (F.320, context 324) associated with the lower dark horizon (251) contained individuals similar in character to context 252 below, plus a small number of agglutinated tests of high marsh species (agglutinated tests are where the hard shell-like part which surrounds the soft body of the living organism consists of a mass of mineral particles). The alluvium (321) sealing the possible palaeochannel included abundant *Elphidium williamsoni* and *Haynesina germanica,* with some *Nonion depressulus*, a species commonly found in estuary mouth and nearshore sediments, suggesting a greater marine influence for samples in this context. High concentrations of the Mollusca *Hydrobia ventrosa* and *Hydrobia ulvae* clearly indicate that this alluvium is of estuarine or salt marsh origin, while abundant rush (*Juncus*) seeds are also likely to have occurred as part of a salt marsh community. An intertidal mudflat environment is suggested for the overlying clay (219) although in the upper dark horizon (218) only three foraminifera tests were preserved, a high marsh agglutinated species and two individuals of *Haynesina germanica;* the poor preservation makes interpretation difficult.

The only plant macrofossils preserved within the upper dark horizon at Home Ground were a few rush and duckweed (*Lemna*) seeds, though at Hardingworth the upper dark horizon (417) included aquatic communities of duckweed, water crowfoot (*Ranunculus* subg. *Batrachium*), and pondweed (*Potamogeton*), with other marsh species water plantain (*Alisma*), rush (*Juncus*), bulrush (*Typha*), gipsywort (*Lycopus europaeus*), brooklime (*Veronica beccabunga*), and hemp agrimony (*Eupatorium cannabinum*), all indicative of a freshwater environment. Unfortunately, due to poor concentrations and preservation, pollen examined from this same sequence only allowed an assessment count from the upper buried surface where a large proportion of Lactuceae suggests differential preservation resulting in decay of less robust taxa. The overlying alluvium included a few grains of tree pollen taxa, *Pinus*, *Quercus*, *Alnus,* and *Corylus*-type, with the herbaceous pollen dominated by Poaceae with just a few grains of disturbance indicators. Soil micromorphology at Home Ground shows that this upper dark horizon (281) was created following a cessation of tidal inundation and drying out of the ground surface, though there subsequently appears to have been some erosion of the upper few centimetres of the 'A' horizon (topsoil). There is clear evidence of earthworm passage features (bioturbation) and there appears to have been, at least episodically, well-drained conditions.

Overall, this upper dark horizon would appear to indicate that the North Somerset Levels were now free from tidal inundation, which is suggestive of reclamation. At Home Ground it yielded a single sherd of undiagnostic Romano-British pottery and two radiocarbon dates. The first, of 15 cal. BC–cal. AD 230 (1910 ± 45 BP), would appear to be slightly too old as pottery and coins from Banwell Moor, Kenn Moor, Puxton, and Wemberham all suggest a 3rd-century date for reclamation (Timby, Chapter 4; Rippon 2000b). The second radiocarbon date of 1012–826 cal. BC (2775 ± 45 BP, AA-45870) is clearly too old.

In summary, the upper part of the alluvial sequence in and around Puxton comprises the following sequence:

- middle to low salt marsh conditions in the middle Iron Age
- a decrease in the frequency of inundation leading to the formation of the lower dark horizon
- a return to intertidal conditions in the later Iron Age (during which there was an episode of salt production at Dolemoor followed by localised drainage of the marsh surface in the earlier Roman period)
- formation of the upper dark horizon (a buried soil) in a freshwater, reclaimed environment during the later Roman period
- further flooding marked a return to intertidal conditions in the early medieval period.

The Romano-British ditched enclosure system on Dolemoor

A series of ditches forming part of the enclosure system on Dolemoor all showed the same sequence, with an earlier deep steep-sided cut of early Romano-British date and a later shallow-sided recut of medieval or post-medieval date. One ditch, F.365, was extensively sampled for diatoms, foraminifera, pollen, and plant macrofossils, and this suite of environmental indicators shows distinct changes during the period in which the ditch silted up. The pollen data has been placed into three local pollen assemblage zones (Dolemoor 1–3) that illustrate the changes in the dominant taxa at this site (see Tinsley in Chapter 4, Fig 4.8). Pollen zone Dolemoor 3 relates to the medieval–post-medieval recut and is discussed later.

Pollen zone Dolemoor 1 relates to deposition of the lowest silts (384) in the ditch plus the initial formation of a lower organic horizon (383). The herbaceous pollen is characterised by high frequencies of Chenopodiaceae (10–20% TLP) and values of this order are normally interpreted as originating from salt marsh communities. The Chenopodiaceae family includes many halophytic taxa such as *Suaeda* (sea-blite), *Salicornia* (glasswort), and *Atriplex* (oraches) and, with other pollen taxa such as *Solidago virgaurea*-type (which includes daisy and sea aster as well as a range of other related Asteraceae), suggest the source of the pollen is likely to have been from upper salt marsh communities growing on tidal flats beyond the enclosed land, which may have blown or been washed into the ditch by the tide. The local vegetation immediately around the ditch appears to have been a somewhat disturbed community of grasses (Poaceae, forming 11–23% TLP) with ribwort plantain (*Plantago lanceolata*) and mugwort (*Artemisia*-type). Occasional pollen grains of pondweed (*Potamogeton*) indicate the presence of some freshwater in the ditch system even in this early stage of enclosure/drainage. While the earliest silting of the ditch involved the deposition of largely inorganic clay, the later deposition of organic detritus (383) sees a continuity of environment in the pollen assemblage. Diatoms from this initial organic accumulation suggest fully tidal conditions with marine diatoms comprising almost 50% of the assemblage, with over 35% brackish water and almost 10% marine–brackish taxa. Freshwater and even brackish–freshwater diatoms are absent. Foraminifera preservation was poor, with only a few tests of agglutinated forms from vegetated high or middle marsh habitats. Relatively high values for pollen of trees, shrubs, and climbers, include *Quercus* (oak) and *Corylus*-type (hazel), with some *Alnus* (alder), *Pinus* (pine), *Betula* (birch), *Tilia* (lime), and *Ulmus* (elm), although this decreases from 60% TLP at the start of the zone to 32% TLP by the end. The high frequencies of tree pollen are likely to have originated from woodland on higher ground around the margins of the Levels. The presence of pine pollen, which is not likely to have been growing locally, also suggests that tidal water had access to the ditch when it was first silting up, bringing in this allochthonous (transported from elsewhere) element to the pollen assemblage.

Pollen zone Dolemoor 2 comprises several horizons of ditch silting: the upper part of 383, the overlying alluvium (382), the formation of an upper organic-rich horizon (381) and later alluvial (376, 380) silting. Diatoms from the upper levels of the lower organic horizon (383) show a reduction of the marine component to less than 15%, with only a small number of marine planktonic (floating in the water) diatoms such as *Paralia sulcata* and *Cymatosira belgica*, suggesting lower salinity levels, although tidal influence is still evident. Brackish–freshwater diatoms are dominant (over 35%), with freshwater diatoms over 20% of the total. The freshwater taxa include species likely to be from semi-terrestrial habitats such as *Hantzschia amphioxys* and *Pinnularia microstauron*. The pollen evidence also shows a marked change in local conditions, with a fall in Chenopodiaceae at the start of the pollen zone and a corresponding decline in tree pollen and fern spores, suggesting a reduction in tidal influence in the ditch. Halophytic taxa are still present, though at low frequencies suggesting that salt marsh communities remained close to this reclaimed landscape. Colonisation within the ditch is reflected by pollen of freshwater plants such as duckweed and bulrush (*Typha latifolia*), which continues following deposition of the largely inorganic silty clay (382). Macrofossils from 382 suggest a predominantly freshwater environment with aquatics including spiked water-milfoil (*Myriophyllum spicatum*), water crowfoot (*Ranunculus* subg. *Batrachium*), pondweed (*Potamogeton*), and horned pondweed (*Zanichellia palustris*). A few species of water crowfoot and pondweed can tolerate both fresh and brackish water conditions and, with the presence of two further taxa, sea arrow-grass (*Triglochin maritimum*) and annual sea-blite (*Suaeda maritima*), typical of salt marsh habitats, there is a suggestion of at least temporary incursions of brackish water into the ditch. The ditch side would appear to have been lined with reeds and tall herbs, such as common reed (*Phragmites*), common club-rush (*Schoenoplectus lacustris*), great fen-sedge (*Cladium mariscus*), spike-rush (*Eleocharis palustris / uniglumis*), and meadow sweet (*Filipendula*). Away from the ditch side the environment appears to be one of rough grassland, with damp areas suggested by taxa such as silverweed (*Potentilla anserina*) and hairy buttercup (*Ranunculus sardous*), and areas of disturbed ground supporting weeds such as orache (*Atriplex*), docks (*Rumex*), and thistles (*Cirsium / Carduus*).

The ditch appears to have become drier at some point when the organic debris of context 381 accumulated, but this change in sedimentary type is not reflected in the pollen record and the plant communities around the ditch do not appear to have changed. There was no foraminifera preservation in 381, and diatoms show a further decrease in salinity levels with freshwater diatoms now over 45% of the assemblage and less than 1% comprising marine or marine–brackish forms. Brackish water and brackish–freshwater diatoms, however, remain significant. *Synedra tabulata* (10%) and *Synedra pulchella* (7%), for example, are brackish water taxa which grow as epiphytes (plants growing, but not parasitic, on another) on submerged stems and leaves of aquatic macrophytes (higher plants), while other species such as *Surirella ovata* live on the surface of submerged mud. The aquatic environment was, therefore, one of slightly brackish water with aquatic macrophytes, including pondweed and water crowfoot, both abundant here. The increased diatom diversity and development of a planktonic diatom flora may reflect a decrease in the rate of current flow in the channel and the maintenance of a fairly constant water level, the ditch now only infrequently affected by tidal incursions.

This drier phase (381) may have been short-lived and further alluvial sedimentation occurred with the deposition of 380 and 376. Increased pollen concentrations from 376 and above suggest that the rate of sediment accumulation slowed at this point. Towards the end of pollen zone Dolemoor 2 the ditch appears to have been colonised by common club-rush (*Schoenoplectus lacustris*), bur reeds and/or lesser bulrush (*Sparganium emersum*-type), with herbaceous taxa, tubular water-dropwort (*Oenanthe fistulosa*), water mint (*Mentha aquatica*), gipsywort (*Lycopus europaeus*), and celery-leaved buttercup (*Ranunculus sceleratus*). Within the ditch itself, spores of *Spirogyra* and *Mougeotia* (both filamentous green algae) suggest the development of algal mats, while much of the water's surface would have been covered by duckweed and rigid hornwort (*Ceratophyllum demersum*), both taxa suggesting still water conditions. Although once again there is some tolerance in these species to brackish water conditions, other taxa like water plantain (*Alisma plantago-aquatica*) and mare's-tail (*Hippuris vulgaris*) point to a predominantly freshwater environment. Occasional leech cocoons, caddis fly larvae, and statoblasts (overwintering bodies from which new colonies hatch in the spring) of *Lophopus crystallinus*, freshwater bryozoans (moss animals forming colonies in clean fresh water) often found adhering to stems of water plants and duckweed fronds, also indicate freshwater conditions. The overall environment beyond the ditch at this stage was an open one, with very few trees indicated by traces of *Quercus*, *Corylus*-type, and *Alnus* pollen. An increase in the frequency of pollen of taxa indicative of disturbed ground occurs at the start of pollen zone Dolemoor 2. These are particularly types associated with pasture, such as thistles (*Cirsium*-type), sheep's sorrel (*Rumex acetosella*), dandelion (Lactuceae), and ribwort plantain (*Plantago lanceolata*), with macrofossils of orache and red/oak-leaved goosefoot (*Chenopodium rubrum*/*glaucum*), which suggests that weedy pasture was established on the reclaimed marsh. These disturbance herbs decline towards the end of the zone and this could indicate a reduced intensity in the use of the grazing land.

The suite of palaeoenvironmental evidence from the ditched enclosure system on Dolemoor therefore suggests that it initially occupied a high intertidal salt marsh that over time saw a change to predominantly freshwater conditions. The surrounding landscape appears to be lacking in woodland and throughout this period was largely poor-quality grassland, probably used for grazing. The pollen evidence suggests the ditch was originally dug in a salt marsh environment during the early Roman period, the dominance of Chenopodiaceae and taxa such as *Plantago maritima* and *Plantago coronopus* suggestive of a low-species diversity salt marsh close to the strandline. Diatoms show that initially the ditch was exposed to fully tidal/estuarine conditions, with marine and marine–brackish species dominating the assemblage and freshwater species entirely absent.

By the later Roman period marine influences declined and the ditch became a largely freshwater environment. While brackish water elements remain, there is little indication of direct tidal influence. This reduction of direct tidal influence and mean salinity levels resulted in increased stability of the water body shown by the development of an epiphytic diatom flora, brackish–freshwater plankton and an increase in species diversity. Plant macrofossil and pollen evidence suggests the ditch sides would have been well vegetated with reed, rushes, and sedges, and the water's surface covered with a range of freshwater aquatics. Although ditch F.365 failed to reveal any snails, the upper fill of ditch F.311 nearby, which had the same sequence of fills and recut as F.365, produced a low diversity freshwater aquatic assemblage, dominated by Limnaeidae with *Anisus* and *Gyraulus crista*. Together with the low numbers of Succineidae, this would seem indicative of a sluggish but perhaps reasonably vegetated freshwater environment.

Later Romano-British reclamation

All the pottery from Dolemoor was early Romano-British in date, but the palaeoenvironmental succession and analogy with the well-dated sequence at Banwell Moor suggests that these upper silts were deposited following the reclamation of the North Somerset Levels in the later Roman period. The horizon from which these ditches were cut has been lost to ploughing, but it may be that the upper fills of these ditches are contemporary with the buried soil recorded to the west at Hardingworth, Church Field, and Home Ground which also appears to have formed in a reclaimed landscape.

The distribution of residual later Romano-British pottery from fieldwalking and shovel test pitting in and around Puxton suggests that a settlement lies somewhere to the east of Church Field and the only excavated features of this date were recorded in Trench 3 where a number of small gullies were found sealed beneath the medieval bank. A small assemblage of snails recovered from gully F.156 was dominated by Succineidae, a terrestrial, freshwater marsh species that prefers damp places alongside aquatic plants. Much clearer evidence for the nature of the North Somerset Levels during the later Roman period comes from the excavation of two ditched enclosure systems at Banwell and Kenn Moors, where a wide range of well-preserved palaeoenvironmental evidence points to a wholly freshwater landscape in the 3rd–4th centuries (see discussion below and Rippon 2000b).

The (?)late Roman–early medieval return to intertidal conditions

Where preserved, the buried Romano-British soil was sealed by sterile alluvium. Although preservation of palaeoenvironmental indicators at Puxton was poor, at nearby Banwell Moor a suite of indicators shows that this alluvium was deposited in intertidal (high mudflat–salt marsh) conditions. The date when this renewed tidal inundation began is unclear, though the small coin and pottery assemblage from in and around Church Field, along with assemblages at Banwell Moor and Kenn Moor, and the published coin sequence recovered in the 19th century from the villa at Wemberham, contain no indication of occupation after the third quarter of the 4th century.

(?)11th-century reoccupation of the high salt marsh

The embanked and ditched oval-shaped enclosure at Church Field appears to be the earliest feature of the historic (medieval) landscape to survive. A section dug through the enclosure bank was examined by soil micromorphology and showed a sequence representing the original ground surface (523 lower), which appears to be a relatively immature ground surface with an upper zone (523 upper) representing mixing (through bioturbation) of the overlying bank material (503) and the buried land-surface below. Due to the lack of evidence for mature soil development beneath the bank, and the dominant sedimentary rather than soil characteristics presented by the buried contexts, Heathcote (Chapter 10) suggests the bank was built on the surface of an intertidal marsh. The pollen assessment from both the ground surface and bank material showed poor preservation, with mostly herbaceous pollen, principally Poaceae and Lactuceae (dandelion and related Asteraceae), with frequent charcoal particles. A single egg of the parasite *Ascaris*, an intestinal round worm which parasitises pigs and humans, was also found. While ecological reconstruction is not possible from such limited pollen data, the presence of charcoal and *Ascaris* suggest human activity in the landscape prior to the bank's construction. A bulk sample from the lowest make-up of the bank (503) contained a limited assemblage of non-charred macrofossils typical of disturbed and waste ground such as common chickweed *(Stellaria media)*, fat-hen, fig-leaved goosefoot, with a few grasses and rush. Although little interpretation can be made from such a limited assemblage, many of the weeds found are annual opportunists that would quickly colonise areas of bare ground.

Late 11th- to 13th-century occupation in a reclaimed landscape

The ditch (F.103) running around the inside of the Church Field enclosure bank was sectioned in Trench 3. It had been recut during the 12th century, removing most traces of an earlier ditch, and the palaeoenvironmental assemblages therefore relate to the main period of occupation within Church Field, rather than conditions when the enclosure was first constructed. Poor pollen preservation meant that only assessment counts were possible. Although there appears to be a bias towards survival of more resistant types, including Brassicaceae and Lactuceae, making reliable ecological reconstruction difficult, interpretation of the local ditch environment is possible in conjunction with macrofossil and mollusc data. The lowest fill (134) is characterised by relatively large numbers of willow (*Salix*) pollen grains, suggesting that willow may have grown alongside, or close to the ditch. Low frequency of other tree pollen suggests there was little woodland in the area at this time. Terrestrial Mollusca point to a damp, well-vegetated environment, with shade-loving elements present, likely to indicate long grassland or herbaceous conditions rather than woodland or scrub. Plant macrofossils including rush and hemlock (*Conium maculatum*) point to the damp nature of the ditch side, with elder, nettle (*Urtica dioica*), and dock forming part of a community along the ditch edge with areas of bare and disturbed ground supporting annuals such as chickweed (*Cerastium*), orache, fat-hen, and fig-leaved goosefoot. Herbaceous pollen is dominated by Poaceae, with some Cyperaceae and a range of disturbed grassland taxa including *Rumex* (docks), *Polygonum* (knotgrasses), and Lactuceae (dandelion and related Asteraceae). Diatom preservation shows a wholly freshwater assemblage, with a poor freshwater habitat for the ditch (static and poorly vegetated) suggested by Mollusca *Lymnaea peregra*, *Anisus leucostoma*, and *Gyraulus crista*. A cover of duckweed also suggests standing water.

In the upper ditch fill (107) there is little change in the pollen assemblage apart from a decline in *Salix* pollen, which probably reflects a decrease in willow trees. There is a slight increase in Chenopodiaceae pollen and occasional polyhalobous diatom taxa of marine or marine–brackish origin that may have come from a flooding episode, or have been reworked fossil diatoms derived from erosion of the Upper Wentlooge Formation into which the ditch is cut. Significant erosion of foram tests of middle or low marsh environments, also suggests both poor conditions for preservation and reworking from the Upper Wentlooge alluvium.

A series of ditches on and around the main enclosure and building platform south of the church provided similar palaeoenvironmental assemblages, although better preservation in the lowest fill (152) of boundary ditch F.128 allowed more detailed reconstruction of the local ditch environment. Aquatic Mollusca *Valvata piscinalis* and *Bithynia tentaculata* are usually indicative of larger, well-oxygenated water bodies, although other aquatics present are more typical of small ditches, possibly prone to drying. Plant macrofossils point to a water-filled ditch with aquatic taxa including duckweed, water crowfoot, and water plantain, with a bank side community of bulrush, spike-rush, celery-leaved buttercup, and greater pond-sedge (*Carex riparia*). Terrestrial Mollusca show this was a damp, well-vegetated environment, with *Carychium tridentatum*, *Discus rotundatus*, *Aegopinella nitidula*, and *Oxychilus cellarius* all indicative of shade, although the absence of any true woodland component to the assemblage indicates a non-wooded environment. Tree pollen values are low, as in F.103, although F.128 lacks the high values for *Salix* pollen, presumably reflecting local variation in willow distribution, although a shrubby boundary to the ditch side may have been provided by bramble and hazel.

The ditch sides appear to have supported a rich soil colonised by nettles, with achenes present in thousands, and other plants that thrive on rich fertile soils, such as elder and fig-leaved goosefoot. Other taxa present include damp pasture and meadow species, buttercup (*Ranunculus acris / repens / bulbosus*), hemlock, and hairy buttercup; the pollen assemblage is dominated by grasses, while the Mollusca *Vallonia costata* and *Vertigo pygmaea* suggest an environment of long grass/herbs. Annuals of disturbed and waste ground, chickweed, orache, swinecress (*Coronopus squamatus*), and fat-hen also occur, while pollen includes large numbers of Brassicaceae (cabbage family), plus a range of other weeds of disturbed ground. Although there is no change in the vegetation communities shown in the upper fill (150) of F.128, diatoms provide additional evidence for freshwater conditions. Frequent aerophilous (semi-terrestrial) diatoms, notably *Hantzschia amphioxys*, *Pinnularia* spp., and *Navicula mutica*, are all tolerant of desiccation and also suggest the ditch was subject to drying out.

Variable preservation in other fills provides similar assemblages that show that the ditches appear to have been wholly freshwater with no evidence for estuarine water reaching the settlement at this time. The ditch sides appear to have supported nutrient-rich soils, of a similar nature to the fringes of a farmyard, and were well-vegetated by nettles, and fig-leafed goosefoot, with more shrubby growth in different locations around Church Field provided by elder, hazel, bramble, and willow. The adjacent ground appears to have been periodically damp pasture, meadow, and notably arable, with abundant species of disturbed ground which match those found from amongst the charred cereals also present in the ditch fills suggesting that they were indeed grown locally on these heavy clay soils.

The palaeoenvironmental material from Home Ground was less well preserved, though of the same character as that from Church Field. Both the plant macrofossils and Mollusca suggest ditches filled with freshwater, with a damp, grassy environment and some shade provided by elder and bramble. The lower fill (285) of 12th- to 13th-century boundary ditch F.267 included aquatic Mollusca *Anisus leucostoma*, which suggest poor freshwater conditions in the ditch that may have been prone to drying, although a cover of duckweed and water crowfoot would appear to have formed in wetter phases. There is some contradictory evidence from both the foraminifera and diatoms here, although in both cases preservation was poor and counts low. As well as occasional tests of brackish mid- to low marsh foraminifera there were occasional marine, brackish, and freshwater diatoms, although Cameron suggests *Paralia sulcata*, a marine planktonic (floating in the water) species, is almost certainly allochthonous (transported from elsewhere), being robust and easily transported in tidal waters. This, together with the presence of further non-planktonic brackish and halophilous (brackish–freshwater) taxa, suggest that the autochthonous flora was growing in water of elevated salinity compared to freshwater and may suggest the landscape was prone to occasional flooding from the Estuary. Alternatively the presence of these halophilous to marine diatoms could result from the reworking of sediments from earlier strata.

Late 11th- to 13th-century agriculture

Additional palaeoenvironmental evidence is provided from some of the ditch fills, particularly those in Church Field, relating to the local economy of the site from the disposal of domestic waste, which is made all the more significant due to the complete absence of documentary evidence for medieval land use. The basal ditch fill (116) of the boundary ditch F.115 contained predominantly domestic waste including fish scales and vertebrae, and egg shell, some of which was charred. A dump of midden material in the lower ditch fill (152) of F.128 also included animal and fish bone, egg shell, and charcoal, plus a well-preserved charred cereal assemblage, while occasional cereal grains, chaff, and associated arable weed assemblages were recovered from most of the other ditch fills sampled. The most extensive was from the midden deposit in ditch F.128, with over 800 grains of the hexaploid bread wheat (*Triticum aestivocompactum* s.l.). In fact cereal grain was by far the most abundant component found in most ditch fills, with wheat dominant but also barley, rye and oat (an assemblage not dissimilar to Whitegate Farm in Bleadon village, a parish that extends across the limestone hills to the south of the North Somerset Levels and onto the reclaimed wetlands of the Axe Valley: Smith 2003, 2). Well-preserved wheat chaff also shows cultivation of a tetraploid form (rivet/

macaroni wheat – *Triticum turgidum / durum*), with occasional spelt wheat glume bases and spikelet forks, as found in the earlier Roman ditch fills at Dolemoor. Barley, although recorded less frequently than wheat, would also have been a valued food grain as a supplement to wheat and occurred with occasional rye and oat, although the two latter species may have formed part of the crop weed assemblage. Additional field or garden crops include garden pea (*Pisum sativum*) and celtic bean (*Vicia faba*), which as rich sources of protein would have formed an important addition to the diet, as well as being part of the crop rotation system used for improving soil fertility. These crops were also found at Whitegate Farm in Bleadon village (Smith 2003, 2), and Seabank on the North Avon Levels (Insole 1997, 43). Documentary sources suggest that legumes were widely cultivated on the Somerset Levels, and presumably elsewhere on the reclaimed wetlands around the Severn Estuary, where they were an important fodder crop notably for cattle and pigs (Rippon 2004c).

Large numbers of pollen grains of Brassicaceae (cabbage family) were also recovered from enclosure ditch F.103 at Puxton Church Field. This family includes domestic brassicas such as cabbage, turnip, rape, and mustard, as well as weeds like shepherd's purse (*Capsella bursa-pastoris*), and could either suggest additional garden crops or weeds from grazed fields or cultivated land. Seeds, capsule, and stem fragments from flax were recovered from the basal ditch fill of F.510. Flax has many uses and was grown for both its fibre, which is made into linen, and the seeds, which are rich in oil (linseed).

Although the evidence for cereal cultivation has not come from primary contexts, there are indications from some ditch fills for low frequencies of Cereal-type pollen that may indicate local cultivation or processing of cereals (F.103 has about 6% Cereal-type pollen). The presence of different components of the cereal ear from charred remains together with charred arable weed assemblages suggests remixing of different elements from crop processing following cleaning of hearths or ovens which were then deposited periodically along with other domestic rubbish into the ditches around Church Field. Silicified wheat awns and glume tips certainly indicate that some of this material originated from the cleaning of ashes from hearths or ovens which is likely to be the result of drying of the crops cultivated at Puxton. Many of the charred weeds recovered include many of the same species present in a non-charred form and include stinking chamomile (*Anthemis cotula*), orache, dock, bartsia/eyebright (*Odontites / Euphrasia*), and grasses (Poaceae).

In medieval Puxton, cattle (41%) dominated the domesticated livestock at Church Field, with sheep (26%) and pig (33%) also forming a significant part of the diet. Nationally, these figures are comparable to higher-status sites such as castles rather than peasant tenements within villages (Grant 1988, fig 8.2), and can be compared to Bickley, on the limestone hills to the east of the North Somerset Levels where sheep (50%) and cattle (44%) dominated the assemblage and pig (6%) made up a very small part of the diet (Ponsford 2003, 104). The relatively high proportion of pig and cattle at Puxton may in part relate to Church Field being the possible site of the manor house (see Chapter 7). Evidence from the age structure of these cattle bones suggests that many animals were culled between 2 and 4 years for the provision of meat, although it seems likely that these young animals formed only part of a larger herd structure that would have included adult cows for breeding and milk provision. A similar pattern is seen from the sheep bone assemblage, the evidence suggesting that most animals were culled between 2½ and 3½ years, consistent with slaughtering for meat rather than wool provision. There was no evidence for mature pigs and again animals appear to have been culled between 1 and 3 years of age. Small quantities of roe and fallow deer bones suggest some variation in the diet. Additional evidence from some ditch fills shows domestic fowl were kept on the site. Some have been attributed to hens including immature birds, with occasional goose and larger duck bones likely to be from domestic birds. A few bones have butchery marks indicating where wing and leg were disjointed.

The only fish bone was from conger eel associated with other midden material in the fill of ditch F.526, though some contexts also contained limited remains of marine shellfish, notably periwinkles, oysters, and a few common limpets. Shellfish formed part of the diet at Church Field and species such as limpets and periwinkles would have been available locally from the Estuary shores close to Puxton, and were boiled and eaten hot or cold. Oysters would not have been locally available and are likely to have been bought at market, perhaps from Bristol, where oyster remains are ubiquitous in medieval contexts.

The charred macrofossil assemblages recovered from Home Ground are fairly limited, although the presence of wheat and barley grains in many of the ditch fills again show the utilisation of wheat, barley, and possibly oat crops. Similar assemblages of waterlogged and charred seeds are interpreted as evidence that crop cultivation was local. The animal bone evidence is similar to Church Field with cattle, sheep/goat, and pig remains suggesting the slaughtering of young animals for meat, although numbers recovered were fewer. Domestic poultry included goose and duck. Shellfish were less common.

The recutting of the Dolemoor ditches

At Dolemoor all of the excavated early Romano-British ditches were recut, though when this occurred is unclear as the radiocarbon date of 1340 ± 40 (cal AD 642–773) from the basal fill of the recut of F.365 is almost certainly too old (see Chapter 3). Organic sedimentation (375) in the basal fills of the recut ditches marks a hiatus in the pollen diagram, this final phase of sedimentation heralding the beginning of the third pollen zone Dolemoor 3. Sedges (Cyperaceae) and bur reeds or lesser bulrush dominated the pollen assemblage, and bulrush is also abundant in the macrofossil record. The bank side vegetation includes freshwater marsh taxa, water-dropwort (*Oenanthe*), knotweed (*Persicaria maculosa*-type), water plantain (*Alisma*-type), and bogbean (*Menyanthes trifoliata*). Still to slow water conditions in the ditch are again suggested by duckweed, water crowfoot, and pondweed, with green algae colonising the waters surface.

Herbs of disturbed ground are reduced compared with the late Roman phase (Dolemoor 2) and it is possible that use of the surrounding grasslands was less intensive at this stage. There is a suggestion from some herbaceous taxa such as red campion (*Silene dioica*) and carrot family (Apiaceae) for meadow, which fits with the documented use of this area as a common meadow until its enclosure in 1816. An increase in the frequency of microscopic charcoal in the boundary between pollen zones Dolemoor 2 and Dolemoor 3 suggests increased activity at this time.

In the upper part of Dolemoor 3 there is a clearly marked increase in pollen of salt marsh taxa, in particular Chenopodiaceae and *Solidago virgaurea*-type, along with occasional grains of *Limonium* (sea lavender). As a group the halophytes do not reach the levels of the early Roman period (Dolemoor 1), but nevertheless it seems that there was some resurgence in tidal influence at this stage, bringing pollen of salt marsh taxa into what was essentially a freshwater environment. Whilst great care must be taken in relating archaeological evidence to an incomplete historical record, particularly serious tidal flooding is documented around the Severn Estuary in the 14th–15th centuries, 1607, and 1703 (Rippon 1997a, table 10.1). Diatom preservation only allowed assessment counts but showed the presence of marine, marine–brackish and brackish types. In addition, the freshwater/aerophilous diatom *Pinnularia major* is relatively common and, with the presence of chrysophyte stomatocysts, suggests the ditch may have been subject to drying out.

Evidence from this later recutting of the ditch at Dolemoor therefore shows that freshwater conditions still existed at this time although there is evidence to suggest that tidal influences returned to affect the ditch and presumably its associated field system. Although diatom preservation was poor there is a suggestion of both a semi-terrestrial freshwater habitat and a renewal of tidal conditions.

The late-medieval to post-medieval agricultural landscape

By the 14th century farmsteads at both Church Field and Home Ground had been abandoned, though the excavations at both sites have revealed post-medieval features. Church Field at this time was an agricultural field, while in the 17th–18th century the South Platform at Home Ground may have been reoccupied. The plant macrofossil assemblage from the 17th- to 18th-century recut (F.140, context 141) of F.128 in Church Field was very similar to that from the medieval fills with aquatic Mollusca dominated by *Gyraulus crista* (which lives on water plants), abundant cladoceran ephyppia (freshwater crustaceans) and plant macrofossils again suggesting a cover on the water's surface of duckweed, water crowfoot, and water plantain, with water-cress (*Rorippa nasturtium-aquaticum*), typical of shallow clear freshwater habitats, water mint, species of sedge, and rush on the margins. Occasional terrestrial Mollusca, *Carychium minimum, Cochlicopa lubrica, Vallonia costata, Nesovitrea hammonis,* and *Trichia hispida,* suggest open but damp conditions with probably quite short grassland close to the ditch side and some shade provided by stands of nettle, elder, bramble, and hawthorn. Away from the ditch there is again evidence for damp meadow or pasture supporting species like buttercup, hemlock, and hairy sedge (*Carex hirta*). Not surprisingly, it would appear that little domestic waste was dumped into the ditch at this time.

The plant macrofossil assemblage from the lower fill (230) of the 17th- to 18th-century recut of F.209 at Home Ground (the western boundary ditch of the now deserted North Platform) suggests similar conditions to F.140 in Church Field, with freshwater aquatics and the ditch side colonised by sedges, bulrush, and other marsh taxa. There are also some aquatic Mollusca (*Anisus leucostoma, Lymnaea peregra, Lymnaea truncatula*, and *Bathyomphalus contortus*) that are all tolerant of a ditch environment prone to drying. The ditch side environment is similar to Church Field; nettles are again common, perhaps associated along the margins of the ditch with elder, bramble, and hawthorn, with other herbaceous species bittersweet, hemlock, and hogweed (*Heracleum sphondylium*). Hedge woundwort (*Stachys sylvatica*) prefers shaded habitats on banks and hedgerows, providing ideal conditions for the diverse terrestrial mollusc assemblage which includes a considerable shade-indicative component (*Discus, Aegopinella, Oxychilus, Clausilia, Carychium tridentatum*). However, the remaining species are more representative of non-wooded environments, and it seems likely that this assemblage represents non-wooded but highly structured damp grassy/herbaceous conditions. Other species reflect the grassy local environment with buttercup, silverweed, and dock with some disturbed ground species, including orache, prickly sow-thistle (*Sonchus asper*), and bristly oxtongue (*Picris echioides*).

Bringing the story up to date: a review of contemporary landscape management on the Puxton Moor Nature Reserve *by Julie Jones*

A large area to the east of the village at Puxton, including Hardingworth and the Dolemoor, are now managed as a nature reserve by the Avon Wildlife

Trust. The site of 76 acres is designated as a Site of Nature Conservation Interest (SNCI) and a Site of Special Scientific Interest (SSSI) based mainly on the quality of the rhyne system which includes a wide range of wetland species, as well as a Priority Historic Landscape Area recognised as one of the most significant remaining sites in the region due to its relict landscape.

Puxton Moor is characteristic of the North Somerset Levels and Moors, as a historic rural wetland landscape distinguished by low-lying farmland criss-crossed by a network of watercourses originally created as drainage channels and field boundaries or 'wet fences' but which today are prime ecological reservoirs rich in wildlife. The SSSI designation is for both the lowland wet grassland communities and the network of rhynes and ditches that are of high nature conservation interest, for both their botanical interest and range of invertebrate species such as beetles, dragonflies, damselflies, and freshwater snails. Wetter areas of grassland are also vital breeding grounds for increasingly rare wading birds such as the lapwing and snipe. A rotational management regime involves the removal of vegetation from the ditches on a 3–6 year rotation period, which includes coppicing of bank side scrub which limits areas of interest due to the shading it causes, and helps maintain a mosaic of vegetational stages within the ditches across the reserve. Regularly maintained watercourses are the richest in wildlife, supporting more diverse plant communities of up to 30 species. Only small sections of ditch, rather than whole lengths, are cleaned at any one time to maintain diversity and preserve the reservoir of species. In its management as a nature reserve today this diversity of species is of prime concern and contrasts with past activities where the drainage of these grasslands and maintenance of field boundaries to control grazing livestock would have been of more importance.

Surveys of the ditch system at Puxton Moor were carried out in 1991 by Karen Pollack for English Nature when the area was agricultural land before its purchase by the Avon Wildlife Trust. The results show many similarities to the vegetation communities associated with the later Romano-British phase at Dolemoor and medieval activity at Church Field as reconstructed from palaeoenvironmental evidence recovered from ditch fills at these sites. What is not represented in the palaeoenvironmental record are rhynes that are 'closed' by the dominance of hawthorn as the main scrub species but also with bramble, dog rose (*Rosa canina*), blackthorn (*Prunus spinosa*), some elm and willow, either forming a line of continuous hedgerow or as isolated patches of scrub. Where hedgerows grow on one bank of the rhyne aquatic and emergent taxa can survive but where they form on both sides shading of the water in the ditch allows little else to survive. In contrast to 1991 and today, pollen from the later Romano-British ditch fill examined at Dolemoor, Banwell Moor, and Kenn Moor shows that there were very few trees, and traces of alder, hazel, and oak pollen found in the ditches will have come from the surrounding dryland areas. From one of the ditch fills (F.103) in the later 11th- to 13th-century landscape of Church Field it was suggested that relatively high levels of willow pollen originated from willow growing close to the ditch, although low frequencies of other tree pollen suggest little other woodland or scrub cover.

Today, the aquatic and emergent communities vary in different locations across the reserve. Areas of open water are covered with aquatics such as duckweed, rigid hornwort, and soft hornwort (*Ceratophyllum submersum*), horned pondweed, and frogbit (*Hydrocharis morsus-ranae*). Some ditches are dominated by reed, rush, and grasses, others by emergent taxa such as bur-reed, water plantain, water-dropworts, and lesser water-parsnip (*Berula erecta*), and many of those taxa for which evidence was found during the palaeoenvironmental investigations.

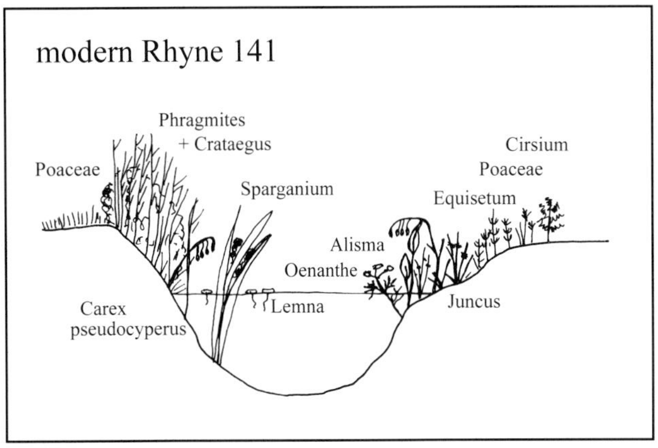

Figure 11.1 Schematic cross-section across modern Rhyne 141 in the Puxton Dolemoor Nature Reserve (drawing by Julie Jones)

A typical example of a modern ditch is Rhyne 141 on the eastern edge of the reserve (Fig 11.1). The ditch is adjacent to semi-improved grassland with low-level cattle grazing which is responsible for some wet poaching of the bank side and has resulted in the formation of a low shelf at the water's edge. The ditch is approximately 2.5m wide with a water depth of 0.9m and silt depth of <0.3m; the bank slope is approximately 30° and the water clear. On one bank of the rhyne hawthorn, blackthorn, dog rose, and bramble with common reed, bur-reed, and cyperus sedge (*Carex pseudocyperus*) occur with lower growing taxa on the more gently sloping opposite bank including rush, water plantain, water-dropwort, and various grasses. There are patches of open water with duckweed (*Lemna gibba*) and frogbit (*Hydrocharis morsus-ranae*). Mollusca recorded from the rhyne include *Lymnaea peregra*, *Bithynia tentaculata*, and *Segmentina complanata*.

So how can studying the modern day landscape be helpful in reconstructing what the environment would have been like in the past? Modern surveys

Table 11.2 Modern plant species associated with poaching and spoil banks beside ditches and rhymes (after Bailey *et al* 1998)

examples of taxa associated with poaching	examples of taxa associated with ditch spoil banks
Bidens tripartita *	*Atriplex (patula)* *
Chenopodium rubrum *	*Cirsium (arvense)* *
Juncus (bufonius) *	*Epilobium hirsutum*
Ranunculus sceleratus *	*Rumex (crispus)* *
Rorippa palustris	*Tripleurospermum inodorum*
Rumex (maritimus) *	*Urtica dioica* *

* taxa also found on Puxton Moor

Table 11.3 The earlier Romano-British landscape and its associated ditched enclosure system at Puxton Dolemoor F.365 (lower cut, basal fills): zonation of plant communities with associated snail faunas

the wider environment			the local environment	
woodland (on higher ground around margins of Severn Estuary)	**marine**	**marine brackish/brackish**	**ditch margin/aquatic**	**disturbed grassland**
Quercus (p)	*Paralia sulcata* (pmd)	*Pseudopodosira westii* (spmd)	*Potamogeton* (p)	Poaceae (p)
Alnus glutinosa (p)	*Rhaphoneis* (md)	*Nitzschia navicularis* (bd)	*Sparganium emersum* type (p)	*Plantago lanceolata* (p)
Corylus type (p)	*Podosira stelligera* (md)	*Caloneis westii* (bd)		*Artemisia* type (p)
Ulmus (p)	*Cymatosira belgica* (md)	*Diploneis interrupta* (bd)		Brassicaceae (p)
Tilia (p)		*Navicula digitoradiata* (bd)		Lactuceae (p)
Pinus (p)		*Nitzschia punctata* (bd)		
Betula (p)	**saltmarsh communities**			
	Chenopodiaceae (p)			
	Solidago virgaurea (p)			
	Plantago maritima (p)			
	Plantago coronopus (p)			

Key: bd = brackish diatoms; md = marine diatoms; p = pollen; pmd = planktonic marine diatoms; spmd = semi-planktonic marine diatoms

have shown the extreme variability between the rhynes on Puxton Moor today which appears to be due to the different types of vegetation cover, algal content, sediment load, substrate type, and levels of disturbance, and the same is likely to have been true during earlier periods of exploitation. This variability, even over relatively small areas of a landscape, not only stresses the value of multiple sampling but also of examining different categories of palaeoenvironmental evidence provided by the micro and macrofossils preserved in archaeological deposits. Palaeoenvironmental sampling will often only give a very local picture, in this instance in the particular ditch fills investigated, and one has to take care in assuming that landscapes over large areas were uniform.

An understanding of the pattern of succession in these wetland environments, where one plant species is gradually replaced by others, eventually leading to the formation of dry woodland communities, is also important in interpreting past communities. This has been studied in the Somerset Levels by Storer (1985, 14), who looked at the changes that occur in a newly cleaned ditch that creates clear areas of open water. Initially there is colonisation by reeds, rushes, sedges, and grasses which spread from the marshy ground surrounding the ditch, gradually encroaching into areas of open water. Aquatic plants and animals are also brought in on water currents, some plants forming an almost continuous cover over the water's surface. With the decay of vegetation, the ditch gradually begins to infill with organic debris and Storer has estimated that within a 4–6 year period a ditch could become completely overgrown – hence the need today to instigate rotational management regimes to maintain diversity on reserves such as Puxton. The same would have been true in the past and regular cleaning would have been needed to preserve these 'wet' field boundaries, which were also a necessary part of drainage of these wetland landscapes. The historical evidence for regular maintenance of ditches in described in Chapter 6.

This research has also shown the effect that cattle

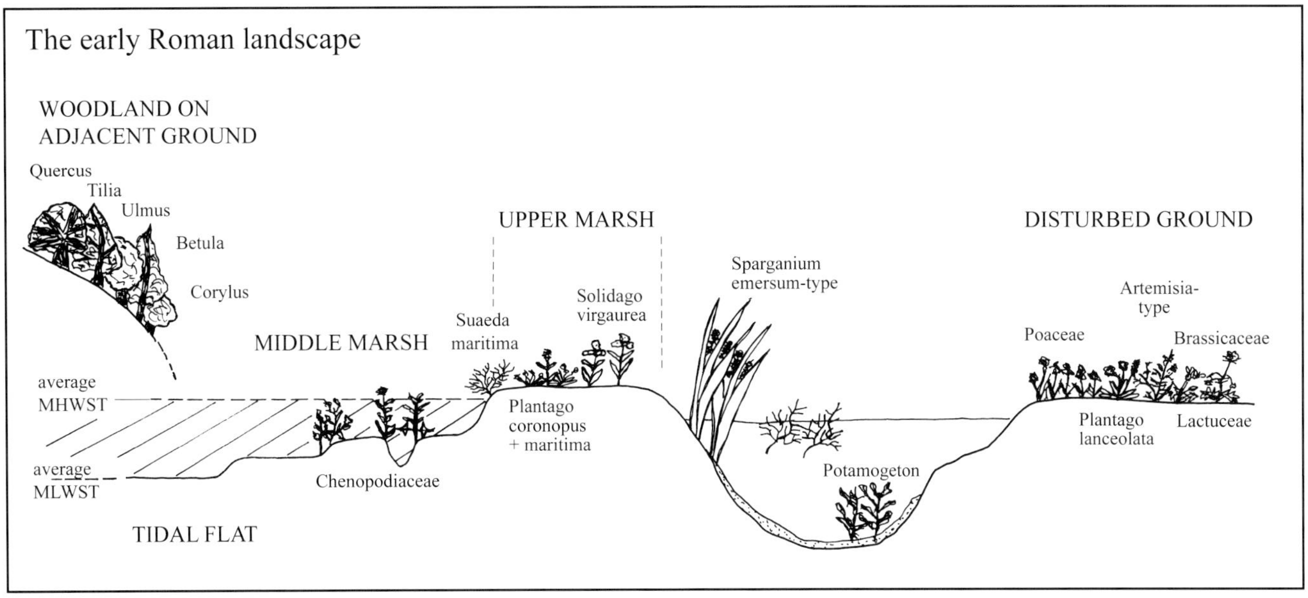

Figure 11.2 Schematic cross-section across the early Roman landscape at Dolemoor (drawing by Julie Jones)

Figure 11.3 A possible modern analogy for an early Roman ditch on the Dolemoor (on the coast at Wick St Lawrence), reflecting the very open landscape with trees restricted to the distant dryland areas

trampling, or 'poaching', has on ditch banks particularly where they are gently graded (<45°) or stepped in order to make access to the water easier (Table 11.3). Poaching tends to provide damp, bare, disturbed ground, more open to light, for annuals or dwarf perennials such as plantains to become established. Grazing of bank vegetation helps to maintain diversity by reducing bank vegetation that would eventually encroach into open water, shading the ditch and forming a closed community. Browsing of tall emergents in the channel itself can also encourage a richer macrophyte flora by enabling more light to reach the waters surface. The effects of the deposition of spoil, excavated as part of the ditch

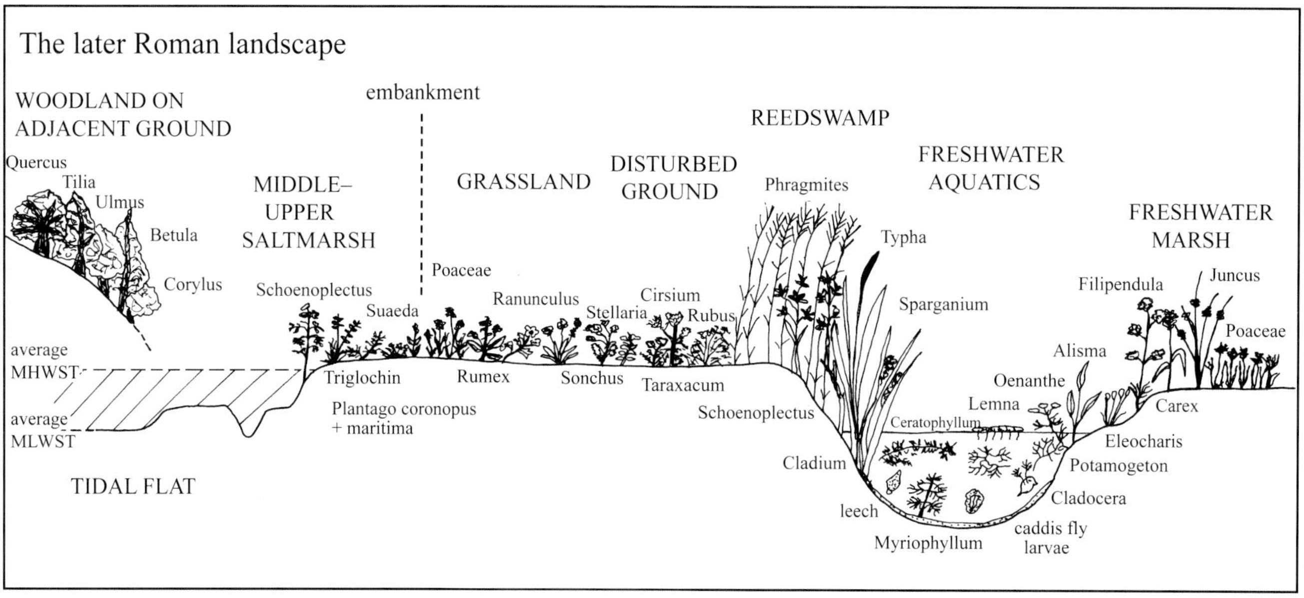

Figure 11.4 Schematic cross-section across the later Roman period at Dolemoor (drawing by Julie Jones)

Figure 11.5 A possible modern analogy for a later Roman ditch on the Dolemoor (Blackstone Rhyne in Puxton)

cleaning process and likely to be dumped fairly close to the ditch side, has also been investigated. This has been seen to provide organically rich sediment that can for several years support its own community of vascular plants (Bailey *et al* 1998). The natural accumulation of dung in these areas where livestock congregate can also enhance species diversity with some areas becoming dominated by rank vegetation such as nettles.

Using these modern analogies, three reconstruction drawings show schematic sections across the landscape suggesting how the environment was modified from the early Roman period (Figs 11.2–11.3 and Table 11.3), when the formation of a ditched enclosure system at

Table 11.4 The later Romano-British landscape and its associated ditched enclosure system at Puxton Dolemoor F.365 (lower cut, middle/upper fills): zonation of plant communities with associated snail faunas

the wider environment			the local environment			
			freshwater indicators			
woodland	**grassland**	**disturbed ground**	**marsh plants**	**swamp plants**	**floating-leaved plants**	**totally submerged rooted plants**
Quercus (p)	*Plantago major* (mp)	Lactuceae (p)	*Filipendula* (p)	*Cladium mariscus* (m)	*Potamogeton* (mp)	*Potamogeton* (mp)
Betula (p)	*Potentilla anserina* (m)	*Atriplex* (m)	*Ranunculus lingua* (m)	*Typha* (mp)	*Hippuris vulgaris* (m)	*Zanichellia palustris* (m)
Pinus (p)	*Rumex acetosella* (p)	*Polygonum aviculare* (m)	*Oenanthe fistulosa* (m)	*A. plantago-aquatica* (m)	*R.nasturtium aquaticum* (m)	*Chara* (m)
Ulmus (p)	*Prunella vulgaris* (m)	*Stellaria media* (m)	*O. pimpinelloides* (m)	*Schoenoplectus lacustris* (m)	*Ranunculus* subg *Batrachium* (m)	*Ceratophyllum demersum* (m)
Corylus type (p)	*Rhinanthus minor* (m)	*C. rubrum / glaucum* (m)	*Lycopus europaeus* (m)	*Phragmites* (m)	*M. spicatum* (m)	**floating plants**
Alnus (p)	*Plantago lanceolata* (p)	*Rubus* sect *Glandulosus* (m)	*Carex* (m) /Cyperaceae (p)	*Menyanthes trifoliata (mp)*		*Lemna* (mp)
Tilia (p)	*Juncus* (m)	Brassicaceae (p)	*Juncus* (m)		**aquatic and water fauna**	
	Carex (m) /Cyperaceae (p)	*Sonchus asper* (m)	*Glyceria* (m)		Cladoceran ephyppia (water flea egg cases)	*Lophopus crystallinus*
		Hyosycamus niger (m)	*Apium nodiflorum* (m)			
	Ranunculus acris-type (p)	*Sambucus niger* (m)	*Mentha aquatica* (m)		Leech cocoons	Caddis fly larvae
	R. sardous (m)	*Sonchus oleraceus* (m)	*Ranunculus sceleratus* (m)		**algae**	
					Spirogyra (s)	*Mougeotia* (s)
	R. acris / repens / bulbosus (m)		*Hydrocotyle vulgaris* (m)			
	Poaceae (p)		*Eleocharis palustris / uniglumis* (m)		**freshwater diatoms**	
	Rumex (m)				*Epithemia turgida* – epiphytes	
	Taraxacum sect *Ruderalia* (m)		*Rumex hydrolapathum* (m)	*S. emersum*-type (p)	*Rhoicosphaenia curvata* epiphytes	
	Cirsium / Carduus (m). *Cirsium arvense* (m)		*Carex vulpina* (m)		*Amphora veneta*	
					Surirella ovata submerged mud	
	Cirsium type (p)					
		brackish indicators				
		saltmarsh	**semi-terrestrial diatoms**		**marine planktonic diatoms**	**brackish water diatoms**
		Solidago virgaurea-type (p)	*Hantzschia amphioxys*		*Paralia sulcata*	*Synedra tabulate* – epiphyte
		Plantago coronopus (p)	*Pinnularia microstauron*		*Cymatosira belgica*	*Synedra pulchella* – epiphyte
		Plantago maritima (p)				
		Suaeda maritima (m)				
		Triglochin maritima (m)				
		S. tabernaemontani (m)				
		Chenopodiaceae (p)				

(m): macrofossils; (p) pollen; (mp) macrofossils and pollen; (s) spores

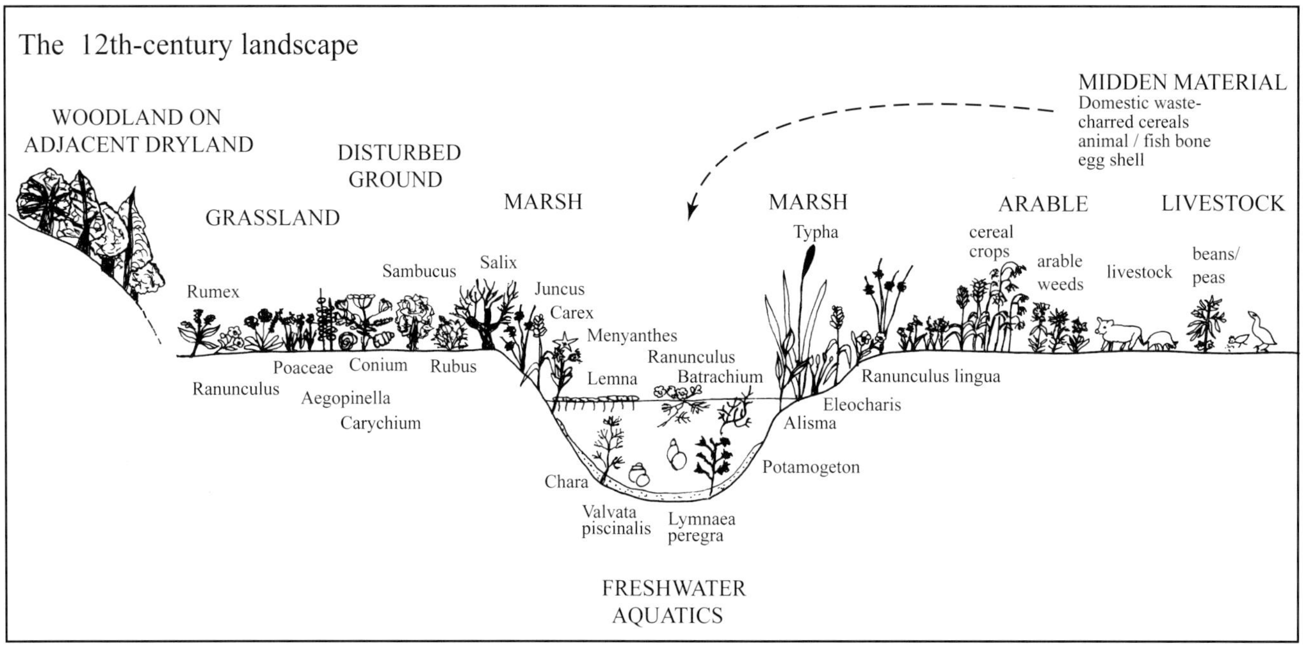

Figure 11.6 Schematic cross-section across the 12th-century landscape at Puxton (drawing by Julie Jones)

Figure 11.7 A possible modern analogy for the medieval landscape at Puxton (Nye Drove in Banwell)

Dolemoor represented an early attempt to drain this wetland landscape, through the later Romano-British episode of reclamation (Figs 11.4–11.5 and Table 11.4), to the medieval period at Church Field, by which time an arable and pastoral economy was in operation (Figs 11.6–11.7 and Table 11.5).

Figure 11.2 illustrates the early Roman landscape at Dolemoor from evidence obtained from the lowest fills of F.365; Figure 11.3 shows a possible analogy (on the coast at Wick St Lawrence). At this time the enclosure system occurred in a high intertidal salt marsh that would have been exposed to fully tidal

Table 11.5 The 11th-/12th-century landscape associated with the ditched enclosure system at Church Field: zonation of plant communities with associated snail faunas

the wider environment			the local environment		
woodland	**grassland**	**disturbed ground**	**marsh plants**	**bankside plants**	**floating plants**
Quercus (p)	*Plantago major* (m)	*Atriplex* (m)	*Ranunculus lingua* (m)	*Carex vulpina* (m)	*Lemna* (mp)
Betula (mp)					
Pinus (p)	*Plantago lanceolata* (p)	*Chenopodium ficifolium* (m)	*Lycopus europaeus* (m)	*Carex riparia* (m)	**floating-leaved plants**
Fagus (p)	Cyperaceae (p)/*Carex* (m)	Chenopodiaceae (p)	Cyperaceae (p)/*Carex* (m)	*A. plantago-aquatica* (m)	*Potamogeton* (mp)
Corylus (mp)	*Juncus* (m)	Lactuceae (p)	*Juncus* (m)	*Typha* (mp)	*R.* subg *Batrachium* (m)
Alnus (p)					
Acer (p)	*Solidago virgaurea* type (p)	*Conium maculatum* (m)	*Eleocharis palustris / uniglumis* (m)		*Menyanthes trifoliata* (p)
Fraxinus (p)	*Ranunculus acris / repens / bulbosus* (m)	*Cerastium* (m)	*Lysimachia* (p)		**totally submerged rooted plants**
Salix (p)	*Ranunculus sardous* (m)	*Stellaria media* (m)	*R. sceleratus* (m)		*Potamogeton* (mp)
	Ranunculus acris type (p)	*Rubus* sect *Glandulosus* (m)			*Chara* (m)
		Brassicaceae (p)	**small mammals/birds**	**aquatic snails**	
	Rumex (mp)		Water Vole	*Valvata piscinalis*	
	Cirsium arvense (m)	*Cirsium vulgare* (m) *Cirsium* (p)	Marsh Harrier	*Lymnaea peregra*	
	Poaceae (mp)		Heron	*Bithynia tentaculata*	
		Sambucus niger (m)		*Aniscus leucostoma*	
		Urtica dioica (m)		*Gyraulus crista*	
		Sonchus asper (m)	**cultivated/of economic importance**		
		Odontites / Euphrasia (m)	**crops**	**food remains**	
		Centaurea cyanus (p)	*Triticum*	Ficus carica	Cattle
		Anthemis cotula (m)	*Avena*	Vitis vinifera	Sheep/Goat
	terrestrial snails		*Hordeum*	Brassicaceae (p)	Pig
	Damp well vegetated/shade	***Drier, more open habitat***	*Secale cereale*	Egg shell	Duck
	Carychium tridentatum	*Vallonia costata*	*Pisum sativum*	Fish scales/vertebrae	Goose
	Discus rotundatus	*Vertigo pygmaea*	*Vicia faba*		Chicken
	Aegopinella nitidula		*Linum usitatissimum*		Roe/Fallow Deer
	Oxychilus cellarius			**rarities**	
	small mammals/birds			Goshawk	
	Wood Mouse	Rook/Crow		(White) Stork	
	Common Shrew	Raven			
	Mole	Jay			
	Hedgehog				
	Field Vole				

conditions. The landscape would have been an open one with predominantly low-growing vegetation, with taxa typical of disturbed grassland with pollen from upper salt marsh plants reaching the ditch. As a newly formed ditch, this would have been fairly open, the only suggested aquatics being pondweeds, with encroachment on the bank side by bur-reeds.

By the later Roman period at Dolemoor, although there were still some brackish elements present, there is little evidence for direct tidal influence in this reclaimed landscape. The area around the ditch has been colonised by common reed, bulrush, common club-rush, and great fen-sedge, but also with lower-growing herbaceous taxa (Figs 11.4–11.5). It is likely that much of the water's surface would have been covered by a range of floating-leaved plants and other freshwater fauna. The landscape remained open with low-growing disturbed and grassland species and there is no evidence for tree cover or hedgerows lining the ditch. The woodland cover suggested from tree pollen evidence is interpreted as representing woodland some distance away, probably on the steeper slopes of the adjacent limestone hills.

By the 12th–13th century the ditched enclosure systems at Church Field show that the landscape was once again a wholly freshwater environment (Figs 11.6–11.7). Much of the plant macrofossil evidence shows a range of freshwater aquatics colonising the water in the ditches, with some taxa like duckweed likely to have formed complete carpets over the water's surface. However, additional evidence provided by snails preserved in some of the fills suggests a variation between different ditches. *Lymnaea peregra, Aniscus leucostoma*, and *Gyraulus crista* in the lowest part of F.103, for example, suggests a static, poorly vegetated ditch, while *Valvata piscinalis* and *Bithynia tentaculata* in the lowest fill of F.128 suggest a larger, well-oxygenated water body. Other snails are typical of small ditches possibly prone to drying. There are no longer the taller swamp taxa as seen in the later Roman ditch at Dolemoor apart from bulrush, and emergents and marsh taxa would have grown along the ditch sides. The disturbed ground taxa include bramble and elder, and there is some evidence for willow so it is likely that there were patches of scrubby growth in some locations, but again no evidence for hedgerows.

The shade-loving elements of the snail assemblage suggest a damp, well-vegetated environment, more akin to long grassland than scrub or hedgerow. The disturbed ground elements of the vegetation, which again point to a largely open landscape, include nutrient-rich taxa and annuals that thrive in bare ground and could be suggestive of poaching and/or clearance of the ditch fills during this phase. Nettle, frequent in several fills, is common where phosphate occurs in the soil and may be suggestive of where spoil has been dumped from ditch clearance. Similarly both fig-leaved goosefoot and elder prefer richer soils and all three taxa may also be indicative of manure-enriched soils. Evidence for cattle poaching is perhaps more difficult to prove, although some of the taxa listed by Bailey *et al* (1998) occur in the Church Field fills. An additional species, celery-leaved buttercup, is also characteristic of nutrient-rich mud at the margins of rivers and ponds, especially where there is some disturbance. It forms a 'character' species in Rodwell's (2000) *Ranunculetum scelerati* (OV 32) community, typical of nitrogen-rich, intermittently wetted and disturbed ground such as heavily manured margins of streams and ponds where livestock water, or silts cleaned out of ditches are deposited. What is clear is that the landscape remained primarily an open one with, as today at Puxton, abundant grassland for a pastoral economy. Much of the animal bone evidence from Church Field comes from cattle, which would have been more tolerant of wet conditions than sheep and would have generally been easier to manage with wet fences in the form of boundary drainage channels.

Overall, there are a number of conclusions that can be drawn from comparing these palaeoenvironmental assemblages with the modern landscape. Firstly, during the Romano-British and medieval periods, the field boundary ditches were more open and lacked the willow trees and hawthorn hedges that are so common today. These more open conditions in the past are closely paralleled on the Puxton Moor Nature Reserve where these hedges are being progressively removed and the ditches regularly cleaned in a more traditional way. Secondly, it may be suggested that a significant part of the palaeoenvironmental flora associated with disturbed ground relate to poaching by cattle of the bank side, and in particular the formation of water side shelves

12 Changing patterns of wetland utilisation in context

The North Somerset Levels Project had as its focus the landscape history of a large tract of reclaimed coastal marshland, and sought to place this in context through a series of wider study areas that embraced the immediately adjacent dryland areas and the wider Severn Estuary region. It has been shown how the development of this one landscape can only be understood by viewing it in its wider context, and that this particular case study can also inform debate about far wider issues (a theme that is discussed further below). From the very start, the NSLP was strongly interdisciplinary in its approach, using a detailed analysis of the historic landscape as a means for integrating research into archaeology, palaeoenvironmental material, documentary archives, field- and place-names, and standing buildings. These different sources of evidence were also used to test hypotheses with regards to how the historic landscape may have evolved. Local variations in the character of settlements, landholdings, and field systems have been traced back into the medieval period, and the overall evolution of these patterns, as suggested by the morphology of the historic landscape, has been confirmed. Although in most cases local variation in landscape character as mapped in the 19th century was found to reflect the situation in the medieval period this was not always the case, as the former village – now dispersed hamlet – of Puxton has shown. In this case, however, there were distinctive signs within the historic landscape that the 19th-century plan of Puxton was not a true reflection of its medieval form, and this becomes even clearer when archaeological and documentary sources are added to the picture (similar results have recently come from the Whittlewood Project in the east midlands: Page and Jones in press). The NSLP also set out to look at the changing patterns of human use of this particular landscape over a long time period – the 1st and 2nd millennia AD – and this has enabled two cycles of exploitation, modification, and transformation to be recognised. It was during the second of these cycles, in the medieval period, that the historic landscape of today evolved.

The origins of local variation in landscape character: working on a cleaned slate

In recent years a series of studies have highlighted fundamental differences in the character of the English landscape, with a 'central province' dominated by large nucleated villages and their former open fields, separating the south-east from the south-west and west of England which have more dispersed settlement patterns and mixed field systems derived from both small common fields and closes held in severalty (eg Rackham 1986; Lewis *et al* 1997; Roberts and Wrathmell 2000; 2002; Williamson 2003; Rippon 2004a). There has been much debate over why the 'central province' saw the emergence of nucleated villages and open fields, with two clear schools of thought emerging: those who see the physical environment and in particular soil conditions as having been the determining factor (eg Williamson 2003), and those who argue that socio-economic factors were the most important (eg Lewis *et al* 1997). There is also considerable debate over whether it was landowners or the local community who were responsible for shaping landscape character (eg Dyer 1985; Harvey 1989).

Reclaimed wetlands can be used as a laboratory within which issues such as these can be addressed. In this study, two of these possible causal factors behind variation in landscape character – the natural environment and antecedent landscapes – cannot have been significant. This reclaimed coastal marshland is physically an almost uniform environment and so any differences in historic landscape character cannot be due to environmental factors. The late and post-Roman flooding also ensured that these areas were used for little more than grazing in the centuries preceding the medieval recolonisation, and in most areas the Romano-British landscape is buried under later alluvium so that there was no antecedent landscape to influence the character of the medieval countryside. Overall, this was a blank sheet upon which medieval communities created an entirely handcrafted landscape. Elsewhere in Somerset lordship was certainly significant in shaping medieval landscape character, notably on the estates of Glastonbury Abbey which seems to have been an enthusiastic exponent of villages and open fields. In this case study, however, significant variation in the character of landscapes created through reclamation is found on estates all held by the same lords – the bishops of Bath and Wells – suggesting that it was their sub-tenants and the local communities who were responsible for shaping the countryside. In the following discussion, therefore, the evidence for how this landscape changed over time is first summarised before a discussion of the context within which these changes occurred.

Exploitation, modification, and transformation of the North Somerset Levels

First time around: the Roman period (Fig 12.1)

Chapter 11 has pulled together the palaeoenvironmental and palaeoeconomic evidence for two

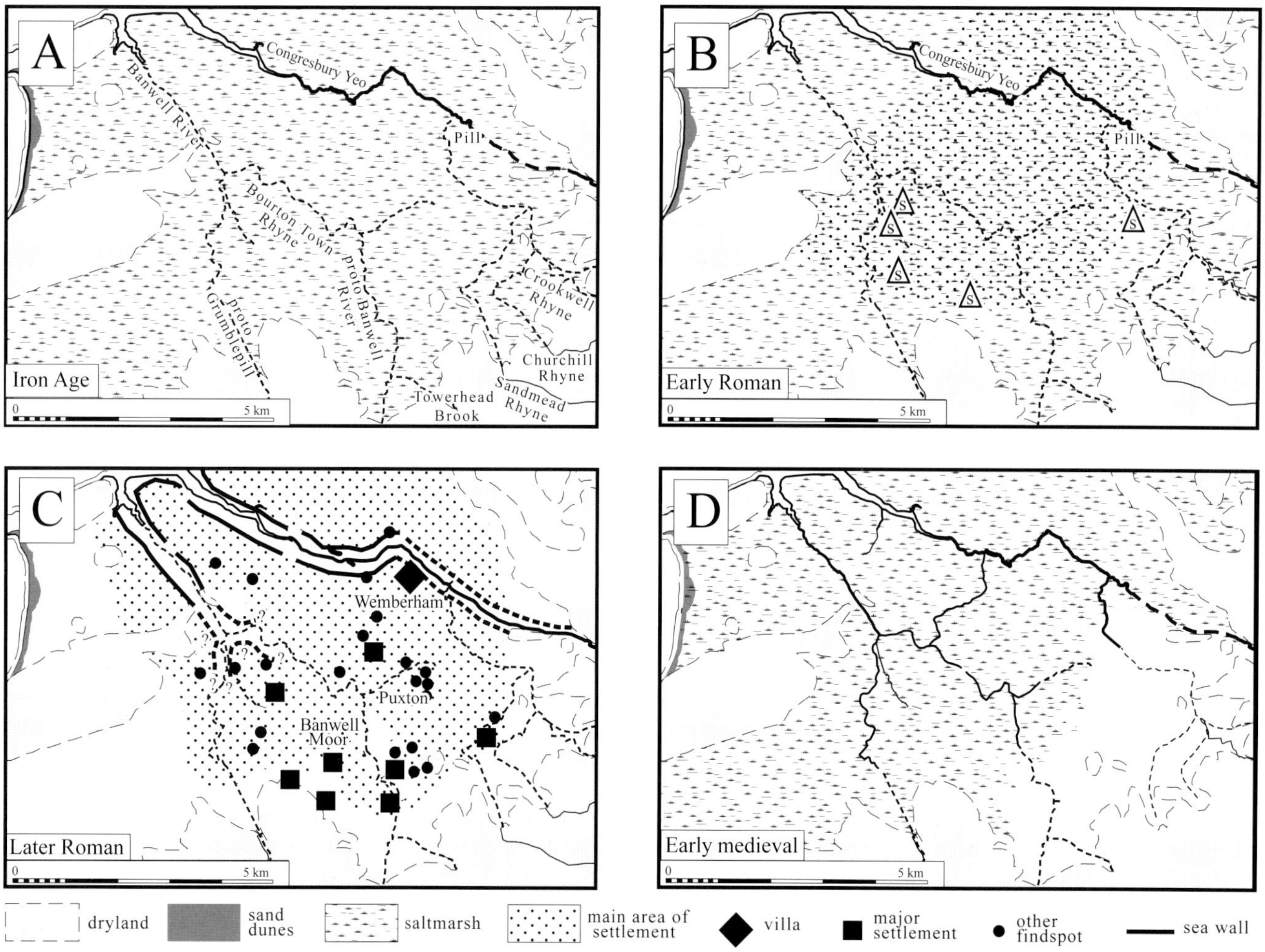

Figure 12.1 A summary of the landscape evolution in the southern part of the North Somerset Levels from the Iron Age to the early medieval period. Note that the exact position of the later Roman sea walls is not known, and the position of the coastline is estimated based on known rates of erosion on the opposite side of the Estuary

periods when human communities changed from simply exploiting the area's rich natural resources to firstly modifying their environment to make it more suited to agriculture, and then ultimately transforming the environment from an intertidal to a freshwater one (through reclamation). Late Iron Age and early Romano-British salt production is now known at several locations on the North Somerset Levels, though somewhat curiously the surviving saltern debris suggests that the means of production, using massive pedestals supporting possibly wooden evaporating vessels, was different to that south of the Mendip Hills in the Brue Valley. It is likely that these marshes were also exploited for their rich grazing land, and the quality of this pasture was subsequently improved through the digging of a ditched enclosure system on Puxton Dolemoor around the later 1st or early 2nd century. Similar field systems are now being recorded at St Georges and West Wick, and are likely to have existed elsewhere on the Levels, for example at Kenn Moor. The palaeoenvironmental evidence clearly shows that this remained an intertidal environment with brackish waters flowing through the ditch system.

Around the mid-3rd century the environment changed from intertidal to freshwater, which was reflected in the palaeoenvironmental sequence in ditch F.365 on Puxton Dolemoor (Chapter 4). A comparison with modern ditch environments suggests that the late Roman landscape was far more open than today, with the field boundaries lacking the willow and hawthorn hedges that commonly grow beside them today. Close analogies can be found in the now traditionally managed Puxton Nature Reserve where the ditches are cleaned out on a six-year rotation (Chapter 11). Because the salt marshes had built up to a point where they were only flooded at the highest of tides, there was probably no need for massive sea walls, only low embankments beneath which the flow of freshwater streams would have been controlled through the construction of dams and sluices (of which the post-medieval structure over Woolaston Pill in Gloucestershire may provide an analogy: Fig 5.5). These flood defences are now buried under later alluvium, or have been lost to coastal erosion, but an ephemeral buried land surface that formed in the years following reclamation, and associated with ditched enclosure systems, are increasingly being recognised right across the North Somerset Levels. This buried landscape is best preserved towards the coast where it is deeply buried under later alluvium, but it is more visible further inland where less frequent post-Roman flooding led to the deposition of less overlying alluvium. In some such areas the late Roman land surface has been destroyed by later ploughing, allowing us to locate settlements and manure scatters through fieldwalking, apart from where it has slumped into the tops of palaeochannels (as at Hardingworth) or is sealed beneath later earthworks (as at Home Ground and Church Field). Elsewhere, in a few special places, these late Roman landscapes survive as earthworks, of which the best preserved, at Banwell Moor, Kenn Moor, and Puxton Dolemoor, have been investigated in this project.

Second time around: exploitation, modification, and transformation in the medieval period

The later Romano-British settlements on the North Somerset Levels and elsewhere around the Severn Estuary appear to have been abandoned in the later 4th century whereupon what had been a freshwater, reclaimed landscape reverted to intertidal salt marshes and mudflats. The use of these marshes for grazing and perhaps fishing probably never ceased, but they were no longer suited to arable cultivation. Towards the end of the 1st millennium, however, human communities once again changed from simply exploiting these rich wetland resources to first modifying the landscape and then transforming it through reclamation. This led to the creation of today's historic landscape that in Chapter 6 was carefully analysed, leading to the identification of a series of character areas. In order to try to understand the different character areas the historic landscape had been disaggregated into its different components, both physical (the drainage and flood defence systems, settlement patterns, field systems, roads and commons) and social (the parochial and manorial structures, and patterns of landholding associated with individual tenements). Whilst this disaggregation makes the consideration of individual components easier, it must always be remembered that this process is a means to an end, not an end in itself. The ultimate aim of this research process is to understand how all the individual components were created alongside each other, and so we must now pull together all the strands of evidence and tell the story of this landscape (Fig 12.2).

Initial colonisation in the late 10th /early 11th centuries (Fig 12.2.A)

By the late 1st millennium AD the North Somerset Levels were probably a mosaic of environments with intertidal mudflats along the coast, higher but still intertidal salt marshes beyond them (which had built up to a height around mean high water spring tide whereby they were flooded only occasionally), and freshwater backfens further inland. One major river crossed the marsh (the Congresbury Yeo), while a series of streams flowed off the adjacent uplands joining the Yeo at Pill (including what became the Crookwell, Churchill, and Sandmead Rhynes). A second series of streams entered the southern side of the Levels, discharging their waters into a small estuary (the modern Banwell River) east of St Thomas' Head, including Grumblepill, the Banwell Yeo, and possibly the Towerhead Brook.

During the early medieval period these marshes lay within large estates that extended from the coastal zone, across the fertile foothills that surround the Levels, and onto the limestone uplands beyond. The marshland grazing would have formed an important part of the economy in what were probably federative estates with a range of dependent and economically specialised settlements in the environmentally marginal areas, perhaps reflected in the origins of Wick as a seasonal dairy farm. Over time, however, perhaps due to rising population, there was a move towards increasing the agricultural productivity of these marshes. Analysis of the historic landscape shows that the stratigraphically earliest features are a series of small, roughly oval-shaped enclosures that probably acted as summer dikes, protecting small areas of marsh from inundation during the growing season of cereals and meadow, with grazing and perhaps more limited cultivation on the marshes beyond. This hypothesis was confirmed at Puxton, as soil micromorphology shows that the infield bank in Church Field was indeed built on the surface of a salt marsh. The distribution of certain and possible infield summer dikes shows a clear preference for the higher ground towards the coast in both the greater Banwell and greater Congresbury estates, but avoiding a zone around 1km wide along the open coast and *c* 500m either side of the major tidal rivers, as presumably these areas were flooded most often. The dating of this initial colonisation is unclear, as two pottery fabrics that are usually dated to the late 10th–early 11th century in Somerset are mostly found in association with later 11th-century pottery at Puxton. A range of other evidence, however, suggests that reclamation of the higher coastal areas was well underway by the mid-11th century. The Domesday survey reveals that there was an extensively settled and cultivated landscape at Kingston Seymour by 1066, Saxo-Norman pottery has also been recovered from St Georges (Prowtings Homes development, Ed McSloy, Cotswold Archaeology, pers comm), and the chapel at Puxton may also have Saxo-Norman origins. As reclamation of the higher coastal areas was clearly well underway by the mid-11th century it is likely that the initial, seasonal, colonisation of these marshes and the construction of the summer dikes took place around the late 10th–early 11th century or earlier.

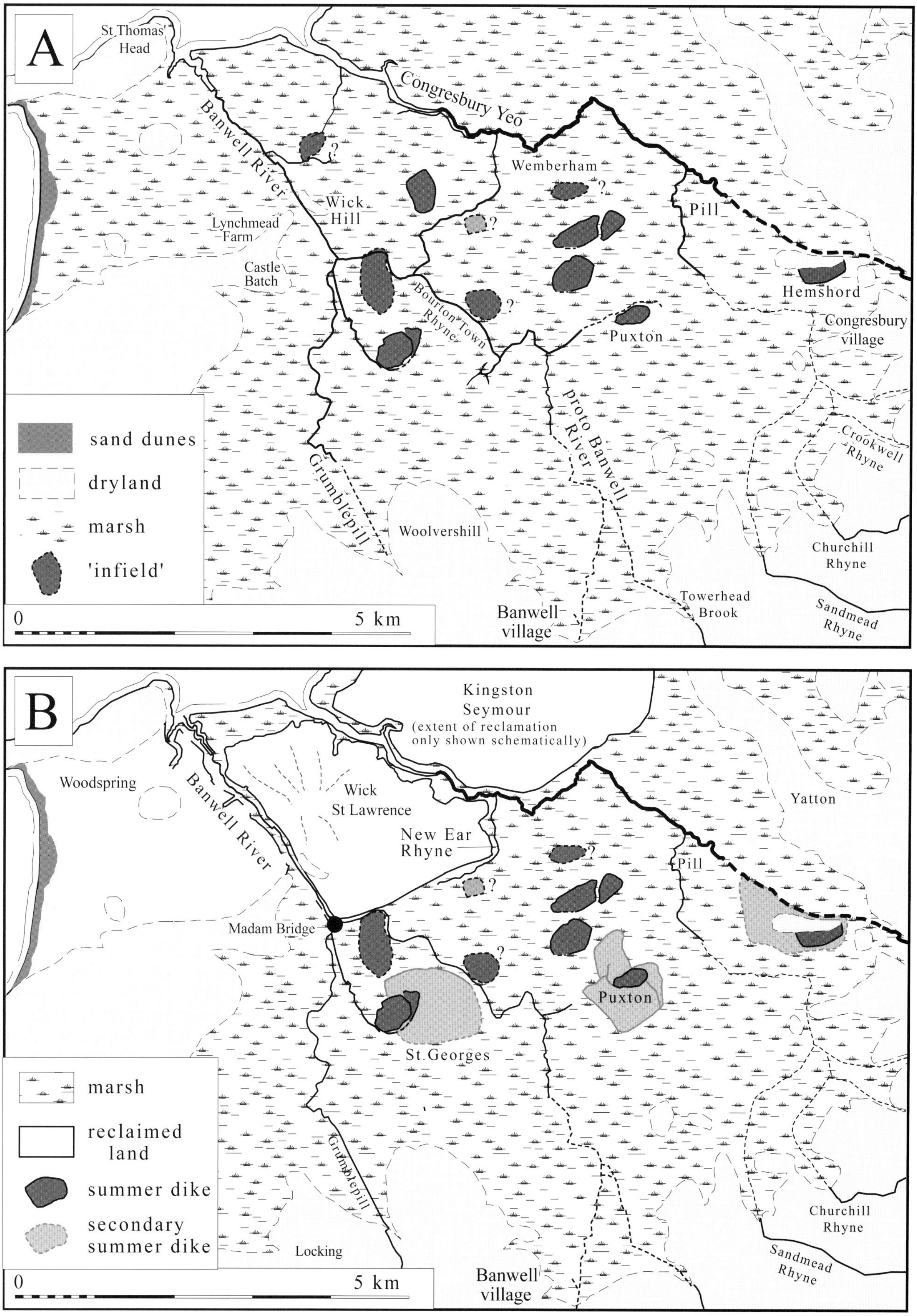

*Figure 12.2 A & B A summary of the landscape evolution in the southern part of the North Somerset Levels in the medieval period. **A**: seasonal 'infield' enclosures on an open intertidal marsh. **B**: further enclosures around the 'infields', and a continuous sea wall around Wick St Lawrence*

The earliest reclamation by the mid-11th century (Fig 12.2.B)

A range of documentary and place-name evidence (presented in Chapter 7) suggests that by the 11th century the great federative estates at Banwell and Congresbury had started to fragment with a series of sub-tenancies and eventually wholly separate manors being created. It may have been in the context of this fragmentation that there was a further intensification in how the marshland landscapes were exploited. Until recently, a sea wall ran from the fen-edge at Congresbury, along the southern bank of the Congresbury Yeo, and then along the open coast to the estuary of the Banwell River and bedrock island at St Thomas' Head. This single embankment protected the whole of the southern half of the North Somerset Levels, and if it had been constructed as a single enterprise it would have been a major undertaking. With the identification of the seasonal summer dikes, such as Puxton Church Field, however, we have seen how the early stages of marshland colonisation was a gradual process, and this also appears to have been the case with reclamation. The identification of a sea wall running down the eastern side of the Banwell River as far as Madam Bridge, and then turning north-east alongside New Ear Rhyne all the way back to the Congresbury Yeo, suggests that what became the manor/parish of Wick St Lawrence (corresponding to the higher coastal marshes within the Congresbury estate, and probably one of its sub-tenancies in Domesday) was once surrounded by its own embankment. The decision had been taken to transform this formerly intertidal landscape into a freshwater environment, while the lower-lying areas inland remained an intertidal environment (although being flooded far less due to the embankment of Wick). At some stage a sea wall was also constructed down the western side of the Banwell River from St Thomas' Head to Lynchmead Farm in order to protect Woodspring from tidal inundation, as this manor also had a sizeable Domesday population of nineteen tenants and six ploughteams (the coastal sand dunes will have provided a natural barrier along the open coast).

In Wick the main settlement focus appears to have been around the later church, where an earlier infield enclosure can be tentatively identified. A set of axial field boundaries radiates from the settlement, and later documentary and field-name evidence shows that this area included open arable fields. Another possible summer dike in Bourton may have provided a second settlement focus whose surrounding field systems have a roughly north-east/south-west trend, also suggesting some degree of planning in the creation of its field systems (including the common field at Dolecroft). In the inland areas there was probably almost no tidal flooding and it may have been in this context that the secondary enclosures at Puxton and St Georges were constructed in order to increase the area of agricultural land.

Expansion inland, and the transfer of Wemberham around the mid- to late 11th century (Fig 12.2.C)

In the mid-11th century we have a well-dated horizon in the creation of the historic landscape. Between 1066 and 1086 a hide of pasture called Wemberham was transferred from the King's manor of Congresbury to the Bishop of Wells's manor of Yatton. This can be identified as Hewish (the extension of Yatton parish south of the Congresbury Yeo), whose southern boundary is marked by the long, straight New Rhyne. This boundary clearly pre-dates the surrounding historic landscape, suggesting that it was created in an area that had not yet been embanked and enclosed. This explains why Wemberham was referred to in Domesday simply as a pasture, in contrast to places like Kingston Seymour and Woodspring that had large numbers of tenants and ploughteams. The more irregular character of the landscape around East Hewish suggests that the initial settlement of Wemberham occurred there, focused around the possible infield enclosure.

By the late 11th–12th century we have clear evidence of extensive occupation at Puxton and St Georges, suggesting that by now these areas had been protected by a sea wall that may have been constructed down the southern side of the New Rhyne. What happened when this embankment reached the Bourton Town Rhyne is unclear though it may have headed north to Madam Bridge as although Banwell to the south was a separate manor, it was also held by the bishops of Wells. The lower-lying backfen areas were open, freshwater, pastures. A comparison of the palaeoenvironmental assemblages from Puxton with the ditches of today suggests that the medieval landscape was far more open, and while some boundaries may have been fringed with occasional willow trees, there were none of the scrubby hawthorn hedges that at ground level can give parts of the Levels a fairly bosky feel.

Key to figures on following pages

Fig 12.2C: the protection of Banwell and Congresbury marshes through the construction of a sea wall along their northern boundaries (Bourton Town Rhyne and New Rhyne)
Fig 12.2D: the protection of Wemberham (Hewish) through the construction of an embankment on the southern side of the Congresbury Yeo, and further enclosure in the backfens
Fig 12.2E: diversion of the Oldbridge River to a new outfall at East Hewish, and continued encroachment on the backfens
Fig 12.2F: diversion of the Oldbridge River to a further new outfall at the New Ear, and maximum extent of encroachment on the backfens

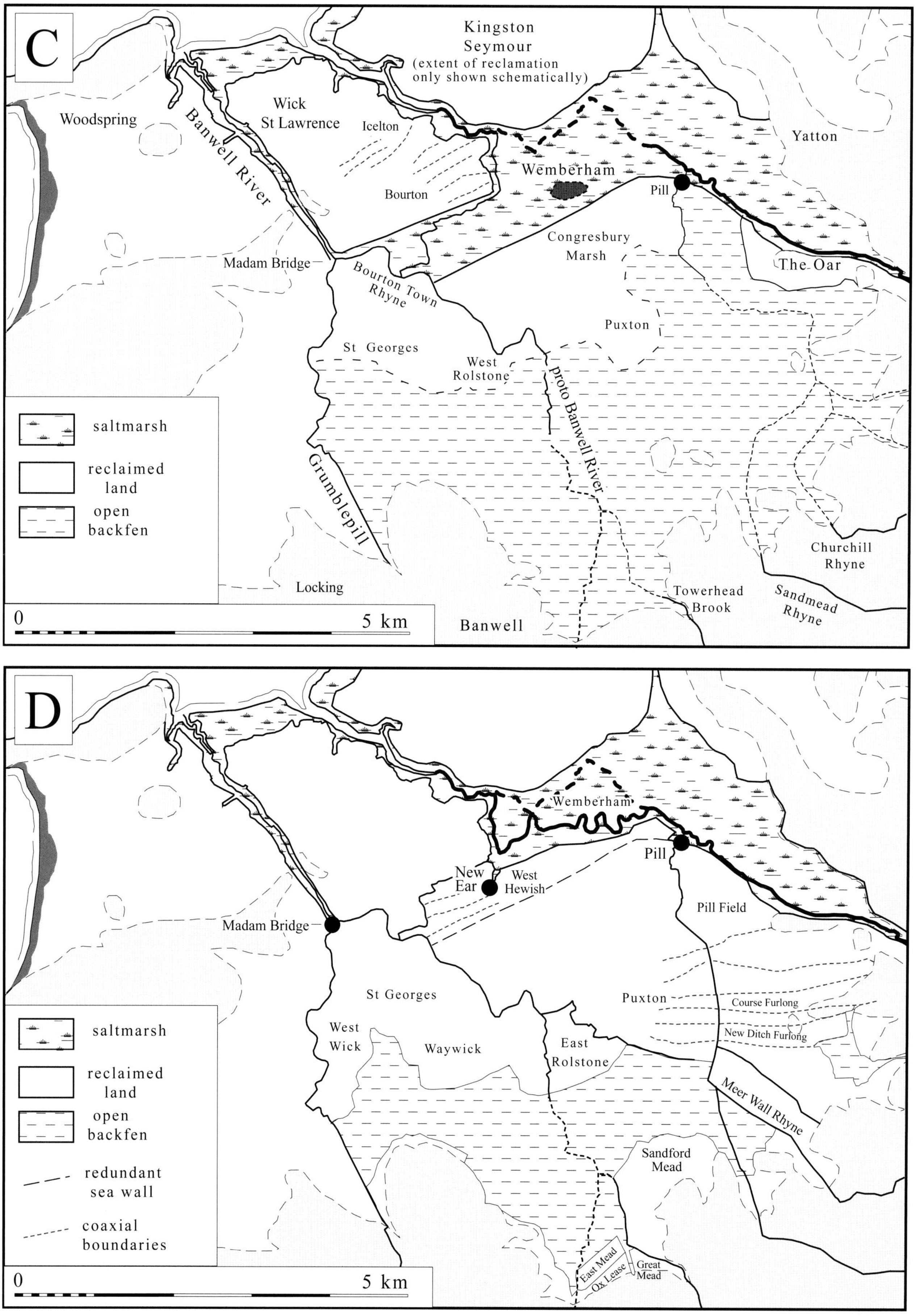

Figure 12.2 C & D A summary of the landscape evolution in the southern part of the North Somerset Levels in the medieval period (see p 274 for explanation)

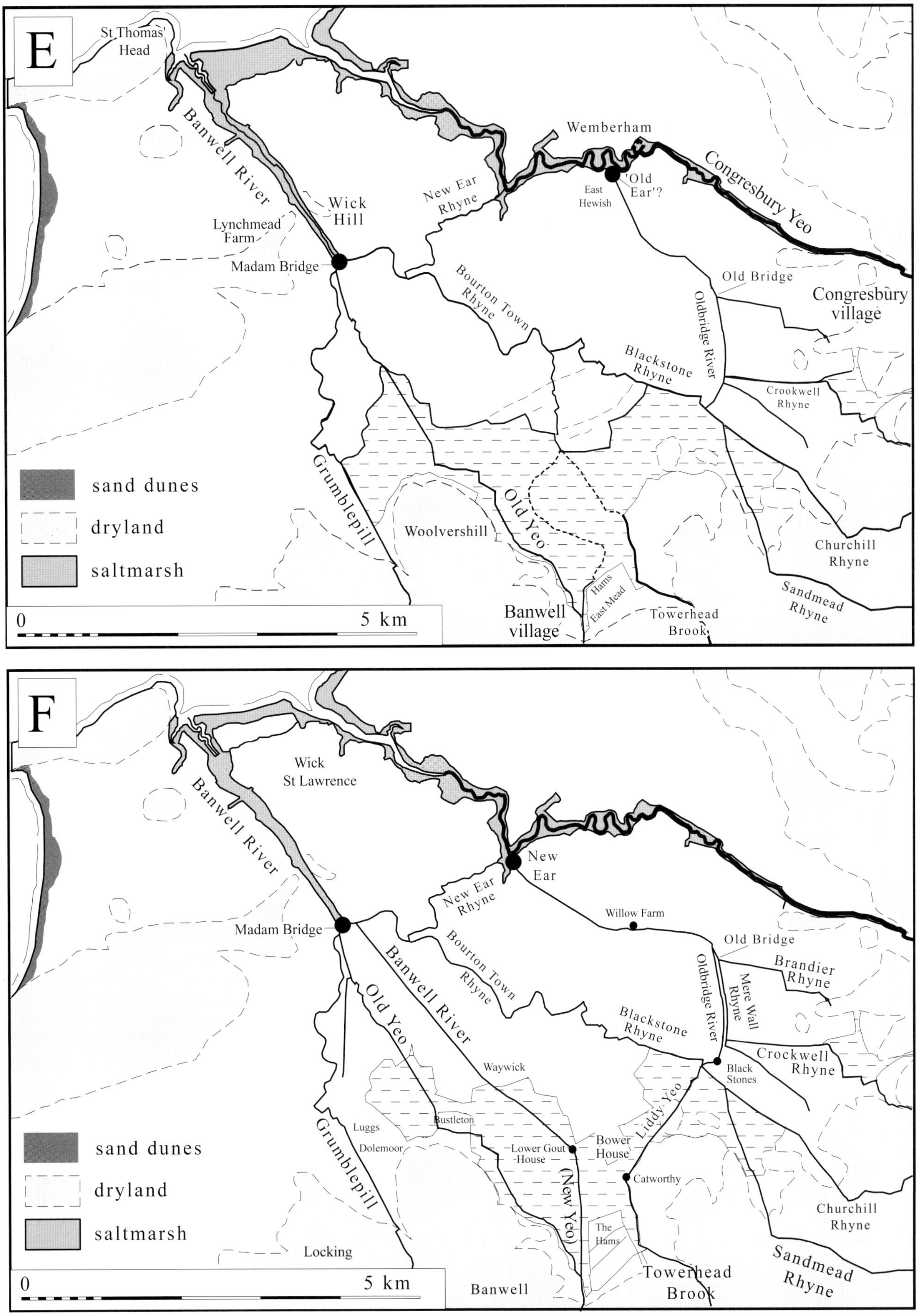

Figure 12.2 E & F A summary of the landscape evolution in the southern part of the North Somerset Levels in the medieval period (see p 274 for explanation)

The embankment of Hewish and expansion into the backfens (Fig 12.2.D)

At some stage Hewish was protected from flooding by building a sea wall along the southern flank of the Congresbury Yeo from Pill to what later became the New Ear in West Hewish. This made the old embankments along New Rhyne redundant, as there was now a continuous sea wall from the fen-edge at Congresbury to St Thomas' Head. The piecemeal way that the embankment of this area now appears to have been created has transformed our understanding of how early medieval reclamation proceeded.

There was further expansion of settlement into the backfens of Banwell with the establishment of settlements at West Wick, Waywick, and Rolstone (none of which are associated with summer ring dikes), though fen-banks were now required to protect these areas from freshwater flooding. The backfen in Congresbury was enclosed and drained through the construction of a series of coaxial walls, rhynes, and droveways, and was managed as a series of common field furlongs within which the tenants of Congresbury, Puxton, and Wick all had rights. At some stage these were cut in two by the construction of the Meer Wall, which may have been built when Puxton was carved out of Congresbury in the late 12th century. The artificial Meer Wall Rhyne was then created to carry the freshwater streams entering the south-eastern part of the Levels through the furlongs, probably initially discharging its water into the Congresbury Yeo at Pill. If the post-medieval manor and parish of Puxton, as mapped in *c* 1770 and 1840 respectively, reflect the estate of Henry Tortmanus and the tithes of his chapel of *Wringmareis*, then they were carved out of a landscape whose settlements and field systems were already well developed, and this is confirmed by later developments such as the construction of the Oldbridge River (see below) that cuts unconformably across the grain of a historic landscape that was already in place.

Further expansion into the backfens, and changes to the drainage system (Fig 12.2.E–F)

At some stage the Meer Wall Rhyne was diverted from its original outfall at Pill to a new sluice at East Hewish. Although its name is not known, it is referred to here as the Old Ear, in contrast to the New Ear at West Hewish that later replaced it. Meanwhile, further expansion in the backfens of Banwell created a sequence of parallel fen-banks in Rolstone, as well as at the Hams extending out from the fen-edge at East Mead. When the limit of enclosure had reached to the south of Waywick, a new artificial watercourse, the New Yeo (now called the Banwell River), was constructed to carry the Banwell stream to the coast. Between the fen-edge and Waywick, the New Yeo cut through open moorland (what became Banwell, Puddy, Castle, Silver, and New Moors) but as it crossed the fen-bank it changed direction slightly and cut across what was already an enclosed landscape. As it crossed the low-lying backfens of Banwell this New Yeo (Banwell River) was embanked and so did not drain the land through which it passed, and this may, therefore, have been the context for the diversion of the Towerhead Brook into a new artificial watercourse, the Liddy Yeo, which becomes the Oldbridge River at Black Stones. From the Old Bridge, the Oldbridge River ran alongside the existing Goosey Drove to Willow Farm, before cutting across what was clearly an already settled and enclosed landscape to its outfall at the New Ear in West Hewish. The Meer Wall Rhyne may have been diverted into the Oldbridge River at this time.

High medieval use of moors

Figure 12.2.F shows the likely maximum extent of settlement and enclosure in the medieval period, based on the surviving historic landscape, but several strands of evidence suggest that there was some agricultural improvement of even the lowest-lying backfen areas in Banwell Moor. The only documentary evidence is a reference to 'Cornemores' (Cormoors) in the Rectory Manor court rolls for 1513–14 which suggests there had been cultivation in that area (SRO T/PH/vch.36). Fieldwalking in Puddy Moor and Silver Moors (enclosed in the 17th–18th centuries), and Twenty Acres (lying within Banwell Moor itself, enclosed in 1797), yielded the very occasional sherd of medieval pottery. This may have been introduced as residual material mixed in with post-medieval manuring, though excavations of the late Romano-British enclosure complex in Twenty Acres also revealed a small ditch, containing several sherds of 12th- to 13th-century green-glazed Ham Green ware, running parallel with West Moor Rhyne which marks the western boundary of Banwell Moor (Rippon 2000b, fig 4).[1]

In the eastern part of Banwell Moor, around Moor Dairy Farm, there is also a relict landscape comprising a series of long straight ditches running parallel to the earthworks of a droveway that continue to the east of Lower Gout House Farm (Rippon 1997b, fig 2; 2000b, fig 3). The regularity of this field system is in sharp contrast to the small and more irregularly arranged clusters of enclosures that make up the late Romano-British relict landscape and several strands of evidence point to a medieval date. Firstly, the droveway continues beyond the edge of Banwell Moor, running east from Lower Gout House Farm to the deserted 12th- to 14th-century farmstead at Bower House where it is aligned with an extant field boundary, suggesting that all were in use at the same time. The earthworks of this trackway and an associated enclosure were sectioned at Moor Dairy. An assessment of the Mollusca by Paul Davies revealed a wholly freshwater assemblage, dominated by *Bithynia tentaculata*, *Lymnaea peregra*, and *Planorbis planorbis*, with some *Valvata piscinalis* and *Anisus vortex*, suggesting flowing clean water.[2] The plant macrofossils similarly show a freshwater environment with abundant water crowfoot (*Ranunculus* subg *Batrachium*), and a few disturbed ground species such as red/oak-leaved goosefoot (*Chenopodium rubrum/glaucum*), nettle (*Urtica dioica*) and bramble (*Robus* sect *Glandulosus*).[3] There was no artefactual dating evidence but a radiocarbon date of 1575 ± 45 BP (cal AD 400–600; AA-50090/GU-10114) was obtained from waterlogged seeds from within the ditch. This is an unlikely date and contradicts evidence from the later Romano-British enclosure complex in Twenty Acres which shows a clear change to intertidal conditions after the area was abandoned in the late 4th century. Like other radiocarbon dates from sites on estuarine alluvium around the Severn Estuary it is likely to be too old (see Chapter 3), and the Moor Dairy relict landscape may be 12th- to 13th-century in date, when expansion into this low-lying area is to be expected. Overall, therefore, it is likely that the Moor Dairy relict landscape relates to a brief period of intensification in the management of the backfens in Banwell during the high Middle Ages, which also saw the creation of Bower House.

The late medieval period

Fieldwalking, excavation, and documentary references to ruinous or roofless tenements, suggest that in the 14th and 15th centuries there was some contraction of settlement, with the shrinkage of villages and hamlets such as Puxton and Bourton. In the low-lying backfens, the isolated farmstead at Bower House was also deserted, and this may similarly account for the abandonment of the relict landscape at Moor Dairy on Banwell Moor. It is significant, however, that in the context of the *c* 100km^2 North Somerset Levels this contraction in the agricultural landscape was very small indeed, and while some nucleated settlements shrank, and the occasional isolated farmstead was deserted, there was no widespread retreat from this physically challenging but agriculturally productive landscape, in contrast to the adjacent uplands where substantial hamlets were deserted in places such as Christon and Wraxall (Rippon 1997a; 2001b).

1607 and all that

The flood of 1607 was clearly a major event in the history of this landscape, which killed a large number of people and livestock. A number of scholars have recently suggested that this flood was caused by a tsunami rather than resulting from a storm surge (Bryant and Haslett 2002; Disney 2005; Haslett and Bryant 2005), though the evidence is far from clear. While some contemporary accounts suggest that the floodwaters came very suddenly, others describe a sustained period of storminess with strong southwesterly winds and a high spring tide. It should also be remembered that such accounts were not necessarily objective descriptions. The title of *God's warning to his people of England*, describing the waters as having arrived on a tranquil day, which would support the tsunami theory, clearly has a strong religious agenda and so should not be read uncritically. Another clear indication of how these early writers were prone to exaggeration is that while plaques around the estuary consistently record how the waters close to the coast were around five feet high, an engraving shows the flood as reaching the eaves of these churches that are typically twice that height (Chapter 1; Fig 1.7).

A high-energy tsunami wave would also be expected to wash marine sediment, flora, and fauna across the flooded landscapes yet no evidence for this has been observed anywhere on the Somerset Levels. Several 16th- to 18th-century ditches were sectioned during the NSLP and no horizon of coarser sediment was identified. Increased pollen associated with salt marsh and coastal habitats was recorded in the undated recut of ditch F.365 on Puxton Dolemoor though there is no way of knowing whether this results from the floods of 1607, 1703, or an undocumented earlier event (see Chapter 4). It is also questionable whether so many late medieval domestic houses, whose stone walls were bonded with little more than mud, would have survived a massive tsunami wave (see Chapter 8).

Whatever the causes of this, the greatest recorded flood to have affected the North Somerset Levels, its long-term impact on the landscape was minimal. Claims have been made that the development of the flooded areas was 'set back more than a century' (Disney 2005) though this does not appear to have been true. The 17th century saw considerable investment in domestic houses, while a series of rentals for Puxton and Rolstone dating to *c* 1630 and 1640 list the same tenements, with the same acreages, and the same rents as in the 16th-century court rolls (Chapter 8). Tenurial continuity and agricultural prosperity are the major themes during the 16th and 17th centuries, in a landscape that may have been costly to maintain, and a risky place to live, but which was an environment with huge potential and which gave a good return on this investment. Fieldwalking has not identified a single site that appears to have been abandoned in the early 17th century, and the vast majority of farmhouses from whose gardens pottery was collected have yielded medieval material suggesting that they continued to be occupied throughout this period. The standing buildings survey has produced evidence for widespread rebuilding of farmhouses in the 17th century; many have produced medieval pottery from their gardens suggesting this was rebuilding not new colonisation. It would appear that this reflects wider patterns of prosperity and investment, not impoverishment. If flooding had been the primary cause of this rebuilding, then it is the north- (coastal-) facing sides of these houses that would have suffered the most damage, yet at Castle Cottages, near the coast in Wick St Lawrence, it was the south-facing front that was rebuilt in the new style. Indeed, there are several socio-economic contexts for this 17th-century investment, perhaps most notably the emergence of the yeoman farmers who had acquired tenements and parcels of the demesne that had been farmed out and eventually sold. Overall, there is little evidence yet published in support of the tsunami theory, and the documentary sources must be read with greater care. Whatever the cause of the flood, and its dramatic short-term effects, its longer-term impact appears to have been negligible.

The finishing touches

During the 17th and 18th centuries there were locally significant changes in the study area, though in the context of the North Somerset Levels as a whole these can be regarded as simply putting the finishing touches to the long process of enclosure: the foundations of the historic landscape – both in terms of its physical fabric and tenurial structures – were laid many centuries before. By the time that the earliest maps were drawn up, in the 18th century, most common fields, both arable and meadow, and large areas of common pasture, had been enclosed (such as New Moor, Silver Moors, and Puddy Moor). The last vestiges of these backfen commons were finally enclosed by Act of Parliament in the late 18th and 19th centuries, along with areas of roadside waste that had characterised the droveways of Congresbury Marsh, Puxton, and Wick. The post-medieval period also saw some changes to the settlement pattern with some farmsteads abandoned as hamlets such as Bourton and Puxton continued to shrink, while new cottages and the occasional farmstead were constructed on areas of former roadside waste.

Having told the story of how this historic landscape was created, we must now explore why it developed such distinctive local variation in its character and in doing so explore how one individual landscape cannot be understood without putting it in its wider context, and how an individual landscape can shed light on far wider issues.

Local and regional variation in landscape character: late Iron Age and Romano-British marshland utilisation

The significance of regional variation in the character of landscape and society – what historians have termed *pays* – is increasingly appreciated by those studying the historic period (eg Thirsk 2000), though it has received far less attention in earlier times. In the Roman period we certainly see the emergence of local and regional variation in the way that the Severn Estuary wetlands were used. On both sides of the Estuary, the early Roman marshlands were modified through the digging of ditched drainage systems, as seen for example at Puxton Dolemoor and Nash Sewage Works (on the Gwent Levels: Meddens and Beasley 2001). These modified marshlands appear to have supported largely pastoral landscapes, and although there was no animal bone recovered from Puxton Dolemoor, on the Avonmouth Levels, north of Bristol, cattle and sheep/goat both appear in significant numbers in the small animal bone assemblages, though with sheep generally dominant (Lawler *et al* 1992; Gardiner *et al* 2002, 12; McGill 2001b, 3–14; Young 1992). In part this may reflect the low status of these settlements with sheep/goat forming *c* 40–60% of an assemblage which is generally typical of less-Romanised settlements (King 1988, fig 6.4), but this dominance of sheep also reflects the prevailing environmental condition, as they are ideally suited to grazing on coastal marshes where the salt helps to prevent foot rot and liver fluke that are common ailments on damp freshwater pastures. At Leigh Beck, on the unreclaimed marshes of Canvey Island in Essex, for example, sheep comprised *c* 95% of the animal bone (Mackley and Faulkner 1994), while the high proportion of sheep (*c* 46% of cattle, sheep and pig) at sites in Fenland (eg Stonea and Grandford: Jackson and Potter 1996, 591–604) on what are clearly very Romanised sites may also reflect the seasonal grazing of sheep on nearby salt marshes.

This dominance of sheep on the unreclaimed marshes is in marked contrast to Nash Sewage Works on the Caldicot Levels where the economy was dominated by cattle (97% of cattle, sheep and pig), presumably reflecting demand from the nearby legionary fortress of Caerleon, a good example of how regional variation in landscape character can be affected by local centres of consumption. In the later Roman period the way in which marshland landscapes around the Severn Estuary were managed diverged even more. The reclamation of wetlands is seen all the way down the English side of the Estuary, with just one area – the Brue Valley in Somerset – left as an unreclaimed salt marsh and used for salt production. It is intriguing to speculate that this may have been a deliberate decision to reserve this area for its rich natural resources in order to supply the Roman military establishment in Wales with salt as it lies next to the transportation route for BB1 pottery from south-east Dorset to the west of Roman Britain (Allen and Fulford 1996; Rippon 1997a). On the Welsh side of the Severn reclamation at this time appears to have been more limited, though on the Wentlooge Level an extensive and carefully planned drainage system, associated with palaeoenvironmental evidence indicative of a freshwater landscape, has been suggested as the work of the Roman legionaries based at Caerleon (Fulford *et al* 1994). On the English side of the Estuary, in contrast, field systems within the embanked wetlands were on a smaller scale and show no sign of overall planning, suggesting a more localised approach to wetland colonisation. Both on the North Somerset Levels at Banwell Moor and Kenn Moor, and the Avonmouth Levels at Crooks Marsh and Oldbury, there is evidence for the keeping of both cattle and sheep, with the former now predominating (Hume 1992; McGill 2001b, 3–14; Masser *et al* 2005), for example forming 54–60 % of the assemblage at Kenn Moor (the higher figure based on the inclusion of cattle-sized and sheep/pig-sized bones in the calculation: Rippon 2000b, table 20). There is also evidence for the cultivation of cereals on most sites, with the best evidence again coming from Kenn Moor where barley (both two-row and six-row) was more abundant than wheat (Rippon 2000b, 122–8), in contrast to the dryland settlement at Catsgore where spelt wheat predominated (Leech 1982b, 137–40).

In at least two cases, Lakehouse Farm near Brent Knoll in the main Somerset Levels, and Wemberham in the North Somerset Levels, there were villas on the reclaimed marshes, while a series of other villas are known close to the fen-edge all the way down the Estuary. In the past it has been unclear whether reclamation was a collaborative venture by these various villa estates, or whether it was the act of single entrepreneurial landowners (such as the residents of Wemberham) who decided to improve an area of unoccupied waste (Rippon 1997a). The latter is now looking less likely for a number of reasons. Firstly, recent work has shown that in the earlier Roman period the marshes were far from an unoccupied wasteland. Secondly, a closer examination of the villas around the North Somerset Levels suggests that although they were of rather varied status, Banwell at least was a substantial structure that must have been supported by a sizeable estate that extended onto the immediately adjacent wetlands (as was the case in the medieval period). Finally, with a better understanding of the likely position of the later Romano-British marshes at the very top of the contemporary tidal frame, and the realisation that low embankments and relatively simple dams and sluices constructed across the tidal creeks could have protected this landscape from tidal inundation, the reclamation of these marshes in the later Roman period now seems a less daunting task than has been assumed in the past.

It would appear, therefore, that reclamation along the eastern side of the Severn Estuary occurred in the context of prosperous villa estates. The significance of this can be seen by looking beyond the Severn region, as nowhere else in Roman Britain is there such clear evidence for the reclamation of marshland. Fenland, for example, remained an intertidal environment with salterns intermixed with settlements, and tidal canals stretching from the coast to the fen-edge (Crowson *et al* 2000; Rippon 2000a). Just as reclamation is not found elsewhere around the coast of Roman Britain, nor are villas spread evenly across the landscape. Some areas, such as the chalk downlands of Salisbury Plain, had very few villas (though a number have recently been discovered in the river valleys: McOmish *et al* 2002; Corney 2000, 35), while in the later Roman period the greatest investment in villas, as reflected for example in the construction of mosaics, is the western *civitates* of the Dobunni and Durotriges (Millett 1990, fig 76). In part this could reflect social factors concerned with the symbolism and status of 'Romanisation', though this same region also sees a variety of other indicators of agricultural investment and innovation. Fowler (2002, 184), for example, has noted that the heavy plough (with a share, coulter, and possibly a mouldboard) was 'used perhaps only on the more advanced estates in the agriculturally richer parts of the province, like the Somerset/Gloucestershire area'. The reclamation of wetlands on the eastern side of the Severn Estuary in the 3rd century AD appears, therefore, to be another reflection of the greater agrarian wealth, investment, and innovation of that region, providing a good example of how an individual landscape can only be understood in its broader context, and how local and regional studies can inform wider discussion of past society.

Medieval marshland reclamation and the origins of villages, hamlets, and farmsteads

All around the Severn Estuary, the late Roman landscape is mostly buried under later alluvium as the flood defences failed and these formerly reclaimed areas reverted to intertidal mudflats and salt marshes. It was the reclamation of these marshes during the medieval period that led to the creation of today's historic landscape. In Kingston Seymour and possibly Wick St Lawrence this was clearly well underway by Domesday. This, along with the widespread occurrence of 11th-century pottery in both Puxton and St Georges, and the possibly Saxo-Norman date for the church at Puxton with its relatively high, narrow nave, suggests that the initial colonisation of these marshes must have occurred by the late 10th/early 11th century, about the same time or slightly after villages and open fields were being created on Glastonbury Abbey's nearby manors on the Polden Hills (Aston and Gerrard 1999). In the adjacent Brue Valley palaeoenvironmental evidence lends some support to the idea that the Glastonbury estates were being exploited more intensively around the 10th century. A pollen sequence from the moors north of Godney shows a marked decline in dryland trees and an increase in clearance herbs (Somerset County Council 1992), which can also be detected in the very top of a sequence from Meare Heath (Beckett and Hibbert 1979, 594). About the same time an increased sedimentation in the palaeochannel of the former River Brue/Sheppey just south of the Panborough-Bleadney Gap is dated to *very approximately* AD 1000 (Aalbersberg 1999, 93),[4] just as increased alluviation is seen in other river valleys in southern England at this time (Robinson 1992, 60). Whilst bearing in mind the limitation of the radiocarbon dating of these palaeoenvironmental sequences, all this evidence points to a general increase in the intensity with which the landscape around the Somerset Levels was exploited and managed at the end of the 1st millennium AD. Indeed, this was a period of general economic expansion that saw an intensification in the exploitation of England's resources both on land and sea, shown, for example, in an expansion of settlement and increased cultivation on the uplands of south-west England at this time (Fyfe *et al* 2003; 2004; Fyfe and Rippon 2004), and a marked increase in marine fishing (notably cod and herring), and the consumption of coastal shellfish, that was concurrent with rise in urbanism and human impact on freshwater ecosystems (O'Connor 1994; Rippon 2000a, 220–5; Barrett *et al* 2004).

In common with the Glastonbury area, some of the hills around the North Somerset Levels also appear to have seen settlement nucleation. As described in Chapter 1, Figure 1.2 shows an analysis of the settlement patterns as depicted on the First Edition Ordnance Survey Six Inch maps. Figure 1.2.A objectively plots all the farmsteads (though at this scale some will be obscured in the tighter nucleations), and Figure 1.2.B interprets this evidence by identifying the larger settlements. In Figure 1.2.C the evidence is interpreted even further. In parishes that are dominated by a village there are usually occasional isolated farmsteads, but these are often towards the edge of the parish, and in locations that suggests they are relatively recent, for example, areas whose field boundary patterns suggest post-medieval enclosure of common or open fields. In Figure 1.2.C these are regarded as landscapes where villages predominate, and settlement nucleations that are associated with the development of seaside resorts (Clevedon and Weston-super-Mare), mining (Nailsea), pottery production (eg south of Weston-super-Mare), and railway junctions (eg south of St Georges in Banwell, and Horsecastle in Yatton), have been omitted. On the basis of this analysis, each parish is attributed to one of four categories of landscape:

- Village-based: a settlement pattern dominated by a single nucleated village though with occasional secondary farmsteads, or hamlets in larger parishes (Portishead, Weston-in-Gordano, and Walton-in-Gordano to the north; Kenn on the Levels; and Uphill, Hutton, Locking and Banwell to the south). Further research has shown that the eastern half of Puxton also had a village-based landscape (see Chapter 9).
- Compact hamlet-based landscapes: a settlement pattern characterised by the presence of several hamlets within a parish and relatively few isolated farmsteads (Backwell, Kewstoke, Puxton, Tickenham, Wick).
- Loosely arranged hamlets and isolated farmstead-based landscapes: a settlement pattern that is dominated by predominantly isolated farmsteads, though with some loosely arranged hamlets (Congresbury Marsh, Kingston Seymour, Rolstone in Banwell on the Levels; Brockley, Chelvey, Cleeve, and Nailsea to the east).
- Mixed settlement patterns characterised by a substantial village but with a number of hamlets and isolated farmsteads (Clevedon, Congresbury, Worle, Wrington, and Yatton), of which three had markets (Clevedon: *CPR 1345–48*, 475; Congresbury: *CChR 1226–57*, 16, Wrington *CChR 1327–41*, 259), though none ever achieved borough status (Beresford and Finberg 1973).

Immediately to the east of the North Somerset Levels, in parishes such as Nailsea and Yatton, the landscape is characterised by largely dispersed settlement patterns, yet on the foothills to the north and south, in landscapes that are physically very similar, there were parishes dominated by a single village. Several of these villages appear to have planned origins, notably Hutton, Weston-in-Gordano, and Portishead (Rippon 1993, fig 3.D.9), and possibly Middletown and West End in Tickenham (Bond 1995, fig 6.4). Earlier cartographic sources show broad similarities in how these village-based landscapes around the fen-edge were managed with open common pasture on the higher limestone hills, woodland cloaking the steeper slopes, open fields covering the gently undulating foothills, small common meadows fringing the fen-edge, and common moors on the low-lying wetlands beyond (eg Hutton: 1759 BRO AC/M8/85/1; Weston-in-Gordano and Portishead: 1741 SRO DD/PN/42). Hutton is particularly well documented. The parish contained two manors in 1066: Hutton assessed as 5 hides and Elborough as 3 hides. Both were held by Glastonbury Abbey, though following the Conquest they were granted to the Bishop of Coutances (*DB Som* 5,10–11, 8,38). No charters survive that name Hutton, though it may have been part of King Ine's grant of 'land at the foot of Mendip' in 705 x 12 (Sawyer 1968, No. 1670; Abrams 1996, 143). A survey in 1309 describes the landscape in great detail (Coward 1978). Hutton and Elborough were now one manor, based at Hutton Court in the village. The manor possessed demesne meadows of its own, as well as parcels in the common meadows along the fen-edge. Hutton Hill was a common pasture 'for the lord and his men'. The lord's arable was partly in closes but largely spread throughout the open fields in a series of named furlongs, which later sources suggest may have been cropped in three fields (East Field, West Field, and North Hills Field).

These landscapes of villages and open fields are directly comparable to those of England's 'central province', but what lay behind their creation and why were they not found in all the adjacent areas? Glastonbury's pre-Conquest ownership of Hutton may be significant as the abbey appears to have been a prime mover in developing and possibly even introducing the concept of village-based landscapes in Somerset. A clear example is on its Polden Hills estate in central Somerset where a series of villages, some clearly planned, were surrounded by regularly arranged two- or three-field systems that covered most of the parish (Aston and Gerrard 1999; Corcos

2002a). This reorganisation of the landscape appears to have occurred within the context of the fragmentation of their 60-hide *Pouelt* estate into a series of 5-hide manors, many of which have place-names of the 'personal name +ington' type (eg Cossington, Edington, and Woolavington). In the rest of Somerset there is a strong correlation between the areas with midland-style villages and open fields, and it may not be a coincidence that one of its outlying estates, at Braunton in Devon, also had an extensive open field, of a type not found elsewhere in northern and western Devon. Glastonbury held Braunton from 855 x 60 (or possibly earlier) to 973, just when it appears to have been reorganising its Somerset estates (Abrams 1996, 66–8; Pearce 2004, 296–7). Returning to North Somerset, Wrington was also acquired by Glastonbury in the 10th century (Sawyer 1968, No. 371), and following its loss of Winscombe to the See of Bath and Wells in the 12th century, it was Glastonbury's only manor north of Mendip (Abrams 1996, 248–9, 251). Wrington also had a substantial nucleated village and a two-field system of agriculture, in an area that otherwise had rather more dispersed settlement patterns and smaller-scale, more irregularly arranged, open fields (*CChR 1327–41*, 259; Keil 1964, table A; Rippon 2004a, 115–31).

While there is a strong tendency for the estates of Glastonbury Abbey in Somerset to see settlement nucleation, this is less evident on manors belonging to the bishops of Wells. Banwell and Congresbury are typical. Both manors were in practice too large to have been exploited from a single village, and while both had a substantial settlement focused on the church associated with common fields, beyond this lay areas of more dispersed settlement and land held in severalty. In Congresbury the common field system lay on the Levels and the low-lying nature of this area makes meadow the most likely land use. Across the rest of the parish, on both the reclaimed wetlands and the drylands, there is no evidence in the surviving documents, field boundary patterns, or the structure of landholding as mapped in the early 18th century for former arable open fields, which is not surprising considering its dispersed settlement pattern in these areas. In contrast, the bishops' manor of Banwell did have had a substantial open field adjacent to a nucleated village, beyond which lay a series of isolated farmsteads and small hamlets associated with land held in severalty. Clearly, in physically very similar environments, there was significant variation in the way that the landscape was managed just as was the case on the reclaimed North Somerset Levels. So why was this the case?

Crucially, because of the nature of this specific landscape – created after marshland reclamation – we can rule out differences in the physical environment. This was about as close to a homogeneous plain as one will find in the British countryside. Earlier – antecedent – cultural landscapes, that may have played a part in shaping England's 'central province', can also be ruled out in this instance, as the Romano-British ground surface is buried under later alluvium. Thanks to the local conditions in this case study, we can clearly identify cultural processes as having been the major factor. In the case of Glastonbury Abbey's estates we can see that lordship was crucial, but on the North Somerset Levels, south of the Congresbury Yeo, this was not the case as the vast majority of the land was part of two great estates – Banwell and Congresbury – that were held together from either the king or the bishops of Wells. Some areas, such as Wick and possibly Puxton, may have become sub-tenancies by the 11th century, but there is no evidence that this was the case in, for example, the Banwell Marsh (St Georges) and Congresbury Marsh districts. All this evidence points to the bishops of Bath and Wells as taking a relatively hands-off approach towards the management of their newly reclaimed lands, and it would appear that it was their sub-tenants and indeed the local marshland communities themselves that were responsible for creating these subtle but important local variations in landscape character.

Notes

1 The possibly medieval ditch is not shown but lay midway along the small extension to Trench II.
2 A copy of the assessment report by Paul Davies can be found in the archive.
3 A copy of the assessment report by Julie Jones can be found in the archive.
4 1531 ± 35 BP, 535–99 cal. AD, a date from shell and so which is expected to be *c* 400–500 years too old due to the carbonate material.

References

Unpublished primary sources

Abbreviations

BodL	Bodleian Library, Oxford
BRO	Bristol Records Office
DRO	Devon Records Office
GRO	Gloucestershire Records Office
LPL	Lambeth Palace Library
PRO	Public Records Office
SMR	North Somerset Sites and Monuments Record
SRO	Somerset Records Office
WCL	Weston-super-Mare Central Library (Local Studies Collection)
WRO	Wiltshire Records Office
WSTM	Weston-super-Mare Museum

General

Register of Electors (SRO Q/RER)
Land Tax Records (SRO Q/REL)

Banwell

Maps

1770	manors of Puxton and Rolstone (SRO DD/X/WI 66)
1772	estate belonging to Richard Taylor [8 individual fields] (SRO DD/CC 14266/2)
1797	Banwell enclosure map (SRO Q/RDe 42)
1826	Congresbury drainage award map (SRO Q/RDE/139)
1827	manors of Puxton and Rolstone (SRO DD/SAS W/528)
1834	tithe map, copied from a parish map of 1834 (SRO D/D/Rt 12)

Manorial and estate: Banwell

1351–52	Banwell hundred court rolls (SRO DD/SAS/C/795)
1513–14	Banwell manor court roll (GRO D547a/M6)
1521–22	Banwell manor court roll (GRO D547a/M6)
1541	dispute over the impounding of cattle in Banwell (PRO REQ2/17/22)
1592	Banwell manorial accounts (PRO SC1/951)
1592–93	Banwell manor court roll (PRO SC2/198/1b)
1695–1743	lease book of manor of Banwell (WCL Acc No 10189)

Manorial and estate: Rectory manor (Banwell Bruton)

1513–14	court rolls (SRO T/PH/vch.36)
1538–39	ministers account of the rectory of Banwell (PRO SC6/HenVIII/3137 m.45)
1573	dispute over tithes (PRO REQ2/257/3)
1603	dispute over copyhold land (PRO REQ2/168/4)
1649	survey of Banwell rectory manor (LPL COMM.XIIa/1)
1654	dispute over tithes (PRO E134/1654/Mich 16)
1712	survey (DRO 2065m add 28/m1)

Manorial and estate: Rolstone

Rentals etc

1430	rental of the manor Rolstone (BRO AC/M8/11; see Coward 1971/72, 31–2)
1482	rental of John Payne of Hutton (incl. property in Rolstone) (BRO AC/M8/14; see Coward 1971/72, 33–4)
1627	rental of the manor of Rolstone (WRO 267/23/38)
1638	rental of the manor of [East] Rolstone (WRO 2667/23/33)
1642	rental of the manor of [East and West] Rolstone (SRO DD/WY box 75)
1645	list of rents in the manor Rolstone not collected (SRO DD/WY box 75)
1650	rental of the manor of Rolstone, in bundle of papers relating to case in Chancery Richard Jennyns vs Wm Wyndham (SRO DD/WY box 75)
1655	rental of East and West Rolstone (WRO 266723/37/7)
1658	rental of the manors of [East and West] Rolstone (SRO DD/WY box 75)

1670–71	list of tenements in hand (WRO 2667/23/37)
1688	list of rents in the manors of East and West Rolstone not collected (WRO 2667/23/38)
1688	rental of East and West Rolstone (WRO 2667/23/33)
1755	rental of the manor Rolstone (SRO DD/WY box 70)
c 1800	list of quit rents in the manors of East and West Rolstone (SRO DD/WY box 75)

Surveys

1648	survey of the manor of East Rolstone (SRO DD/WY box 75)
1649	survey of the manor of East Rolstone (WRO 266723/37)
c 1650	survey of the manor of East Rolstone (WRO 266723/37)
1651	survey of the manor of East Rolstone (WRO 2667/23/38)
1651	survey of the manor of West Rolstone (WRO 2667/23/38)
late C17th	survey of 'Rolstone alias Paynes-barne' (SRO DD/PT box 46)
c 1770	survey of the manors of East and West Rolstone (SRO DD/WY box 70)

Accounts

1653–54	bailiffs accounts (WRO 2667/23/38)
1655–57	Bailiffs accounts (WRO 2667/23/33)
1668–69, 1671, 1677, 1686	Bailiffs accounts (WRO 266723/37/7)

Deeds etc

1570–1647	miscellaneous deeds relating to Great and Little Knights (SRO DD/WY box 75)
1627–49	leases for Land Farm (SRO DD/WY 75)
1632–1795	miscellaneous deeds relating to tenements in Rolstone (SRO DD/WY box 75)
1638–1811	miscellaneous deeds relating to Havadge (SRO DD/WY box 75)
1656–97	lease book for manors of East and West Rolstone (WRO 2667/23/38)
1779–94	contracts book (WRO 2667/23/44)

Poulett estate [formerly Rolstone freehold?]

1700	survey of the estates of Earl Poulett (SRO DD/CN 35/6)
1702–10	court book (SRO DD/PT S/1515)
1721–86	survey and lease record of the estates of Earl Poulett (SRO DD/CN 35/6)

Miscellaneous

1825	George Bennett's *History of Banwell* (SRO DD/SAS G/1740 1/1/7)

Churchill

1826	Congresbury drainage award map (SRO Q/RDE/139)

Congresbury

Maps

1739	maps cut from Book of Surveys of the Manors, Lordships and Estates belonging to the Chamber of Bristol (BRO 33041/BMC/4/PL1/1–4)
1816	Congresbury, Puxton and Wick St Lawrence enclosure map (SRO Q/RDE/133)
1826	Congresbury drainage award map (SRO Q/RDE/139)
1840	tithe map (SRO D/D/Rt 317)

Manorial and estate

Court rolls

1342	Congresbury Hundred court roll (LPL ED 1176 f.22)
1351–52	Congresbury Hundred court rolls (SRO DD/SAS/C/795)
1379	Congresbury Hundred court roll (LPL ED 351 f.1)
1560–70	Congresbury Hundred court rolls (BRO 04235)
1589–91	Congresbury manorial court rolls (BRO 33041 BMC/4/35a, 37)
1653–78	Congresbury manorial court rolls (BRO BMC/4/37b)

Surveys

1567	BRO 04235
1593	BRO 04793
1596	BRO 04793
1646–47	BRO 04236(1–2)
1656	BRO 04241
1700	BRO 33041 BMC/4/18
1739	BRO 33041 BMC/4/20(a)

Bargain books [recording property transfers]

1604–20	BRO 04335(1)
1634–46	BRO 04335(2)
1646–53	BRO 04335(3)

1653–79	BRO 04336(1)
1679–1712	BRO 04336(2)
1712–49	BRO 04336(3)
1751–89	BRO 04336(1)

Rental

1771	BRO 33041 BMC 4/4/14

Deeds

1570	Grange Farm, West Hewish (SRO DD/BK 2(6)8–10)
1737–99	Grange Farm, Mays Green (SRO DD/SOG 341–2)
1595	abstract of title of Queen Elizabeth's Hospital to various fee farm rents (BRO 00576(8))

Kewstoke (including Woodspring Priory)

1410	grant by Robert Pobelowe and John Venables (PRO C143/440/25)
1535	'Declaration of the extent and annual value of all the possessions temporal and spiritual of the several monasteries in the county of Somerset' (SRO DD/SAS/BA7 3)
1840	tithe survey (SRO D/D/Rt 193)

Puxton

Maps

c 1770	map of the manors of Puxton and Rolstone (SRO DD/X/WI 66)
1816	Congresbury, Puxton and Wick St Lawrence enclosure map (SRO Q/RDE/133)
1821	map of estate of Mrs Savadge in Puxton (SRO T/PH/vch 64/3)
1826	Congresbury drainage award map (SRO Q/RDE/139)
1827	manors of Puxton and Rolstone (SRO DD/SAS W/528)
1840	tithe map (SRO D/D/Rt 117)

Manorial and estate

Inquisitions Post Mortem

1432	John Austell (PRO C140/8)
1448	John Sayntlo (PRO C139/131)
1450	William Palton (PRO C130/140)
1462	John Austell (PRO C140/8)
1466	John Kelly (PRO C140/17)
1479	Alice Seyntlowe (PRO C140/70m.28)
1486	Sir Nicholas de Sancto Laudo (PRO C140/70m.28)

Bailiffs Accounts

1472–78	SRO DD/WY box 84
1500–01	BodL Rawlinson B.317
1655	WRO 2667/23/37
1668–69, 1670–74, 1677, 1686	WRO 266723/37/7
1688	WRO 2667/23/33
1750–55	WRO 2667/18/24–6

Court Rolls

1491–1501	BodL Rawlinson B.317
1547–52	BodL Rawlinson B.317
1560–62	WRO 2667/13/452
1562–73	SRO DD/WY W/CR 46/1

Rentals etc

c 1555	BCA Acc. 3938, 3960
c 1630	WRO 2667/23
1642	SRO DD/WY box 75
1645	list of rent in Puxton and Rolstone not collected (SRO DD/WY box 75)
1668	list of rent in Puxton and Rolstone not collected (WRO 2667/23/38)
1670–72	list of tenements in hand (WRO 2667/23/37)
1688	WRO 2667/23/33
1755	SRO DD/WY box 70
c 1795	list of quit rents in the manors of Puxton and East and West Rolstone (SRO DD/WY box 75)

Surveys

c 1770	incomplete (folios 1–2 of 16 [Tenements A–H, excluding E] along with folio 17, a summary of tenants with acreages [SRO DD/WY box 70])

Contract Books etc

1678–82	contract book (WRO 266723/37)
1688–93	contract book (WRO 266723/37)
1749–1787	list of leases (WRO 2667/38)
1779–94	contract book (WRO 2667/23/44)

Deeds

1378–1885	Merton College lands including survey of 1601 (BodL MC 1204–1235)
1482	rental of John Payne of Hutton (incl. property in Puxton) (BRO AC/M8/14; see Coward 1971/72, 33–4)
1535–36	deeds for the manor of Puxton 1535–36 (SRO DD/HI 122)
1535–1654	miscellaneous deeds relating to the manor of Puxton and Rolstone (SRO DD/WY box 75)

1558–59	grant of wardship of William Sentloo (SRO DD/HI 122)
1571–1782	deeds relating to various properties in Puxton (SRO DD/WY box 84)
1603	Longe Mead (SRO DD/WY box 84)
1625–1785	Blackstones (SRO DD/WY boxes 75 and 84)
1655	Twindix (WRO 2667/1/37/22a and 2667/18/25)
1687–1702	Coxes (BRO 08835(9, 10); 08845(1–2); 08840(24)e1)
1687–1892	deeds of Grange Farm, Puxton (relating to Muttleburys in Congresbury, ?Villa Farm in Puxton, and Burnt House in Yatton (SRO DD/SOG 341, 342, 903; SRO DD/BR/U; private ownership)
1625–99	North Twindix (SRO DD/WY box 84)
1712	Waterman's Bow (BRO 08845(9))
1780	Averys (WRO 2667/1/37/24)
1780	Church House (WRO 2667/1/37/25)
1787	North House (WRO 2667/1/37/23)

Glebe and the church

1595	dispute over the lease of the chapel of Puxton and other appurtenances of the Rectory of Banwell (PRO REQ2/226/13)
1636	glebe terrier (BRO DC/E/25)
1649	survey of Puxton Parsonage (LPL COMM.XIIa/1)
1654	dispute over the tithes in Puxton (PRO E134/1654/Mich 16)
1736–1836	presentments of the churchwardens at the visitations of the Dean and Chapter of the Cathedral Church of Wells (SRO D/D/Pbc 7)
1768	particulars of land purchased to augment the curacy of Puxton (BRO DC/E/25/6)

Miscellaneous

1622	lay subsidy (SRO DD/SAS c/275 BK81)
1825	Bennett, G, *Topographical Notices of the Parish of Puxton* (SRO DD/SAS/G/1740 1/1/7)

Wick St Lawrence

Maps

1738	map IX in Book of Surveys of the Manors, Lordships, and Estates belonging to the Chamber of Bristol (BRO 04480)
1812	map of estates of Dean and Chapter of Wells (SRO DD/CC 10877)
1816	Congresbury, Puxton, and Wick St Lawrence enclosure map (SRO Q/RDE/133)
1838	tithe map (SRO D/D/Rt 126)

Manorial and estate

1655	survey of the lands and tenements belonging to the Hospital of Queen Elizabeth … in Bristol (BRO 04237)
1658	list of tenants in Wick St Lawrence (BRO 00572(12)i)
1738	list of tenants in Wick St Lawrence (BRO 00572(12)i)
1751	rental of Congresbury and Wick St Lawrence (BRO 40228)
1762	rental of Congresbury and Wick St Lawrence (BRO BMC/4/12)
1812	survey of the estates of the Dean and Chapter of Wells (SRO DD/CC 10877)

Miscellaneous

1820	drainage board records for the construction of Sampson's Clyce (SRO Q/RDe 139)

Winscombe (including Sandford)

1540	rental (SRO T/PH/VCH 38c/27989)
1792	map and survey (SRO DD/CC 110735)
1826	Congresbury drainage award map (SRO Q/RDE/139)
1840	tithe map (SRO D/D/Rt 195)

Worle

1840	tithe map (SRO D/D/Rt 192)

Yatton (including Hewish)

1700	survey of Huish manor (SRO DD/CN 35/6)
1721–86	survey and lease record for Huish manor (SRO DD/PT 43)
1808	list of persons claiming right of common on Kenn Moor (BRO 16080/11)
1840	tithe map (SRO D/D/Rt 368)

Abbreviations for published primary sources

Asser	*Asser's Life of King Alfred* (Stevenson 1904)
Bath Chartulary	Two Chartularies of the Priory of St Peters at Bath (Hunt 1893)
Bekynton	The Register of Thomas Bekynton Bishop of Bath and Wells 1443–65, volume 1 (Dawes and Maxwell-Lyte 1934)
Bruton	Cartulary of Bruton Priory (Hobhouse *et al* 1894)
Chantries	Survey and Rental of the Chantries in the County of Somerset, 1548 (Green 1888)
Chantry grants	Calendar of Somerset Chantry Grants, 1548–1603 (Woodward 1982)
CChR	Calendars of Charter Rolls
CIM(C)	Calendars of Inquisitions Miscellaneous (Chancery)
CIPM	Calendars of Inquisitions Post Mortem
Cosyn	Dean Cosyn's Manuscript and Wells Cathedral Miscellanea (Watkin 1941)
CPR	Calendar of Patent Rolls
DB Som	*Domesday Book, Somerset* (Thorn and Thorn 1980)
Deeds	Somerset Enrolled Deeds (Bates Harbin 1936)
Drokensford	The Register of Bishop John de Drokensford (Hobhouse 1887)
Fees	Book of Fees (Maxwell Lyte 1920b)
Feudal Aids VI	Inquisitions and Assessments Relating to Feudal Aids with other analogous documents volume VI (Maxwell Lyte 1920a)
Fines II	Pedes Finium Commonly called Feet of Fines for the County of Somerset (Green 1898)
Fines III	Pedes Finium Commonly called Feet of Fines for the County of Somerset (Green 1902)
Fines IV	Pedes Finium Commonly called Feet of Fines for the County of Somerset (Green 1906)
John of Glastonbury	The Chronicle of Glastonbury Abbey (Carley 1985)
Knyght	The Register of William Knyght, Bishop of Bath and Wells, 1541–47 (Maxwell-Lyte 1940)
Leland	The Itinerary of John Leland (Chandler 1993)
Liber Albus I	White Book of Wells (Bird 1907, 1–304)
Liber Albus II	White Book of Wells (Bird 1907, 305–528)
Monington	Glastonbury Feodary (Weaver 1910)
Pleas	Somerset Pleas (Civil and Criminal) from the Rolls of the Itinerant Judges (Chadwyck Healy 1897)
Quarter Sessions	Quarter Sessions Records, James I (Bates 1907)
Red Book	Red Book of the Exchequer (Hall 1896)
Shrewsbury	The Register of Ralph of Shrewsbury, Bishop of Bath and Wells, 1329–63 (Holmes 1896)
Stillington	The Register of Robert Stillington, Bishop of Bath and Wells, 1466–91 (Maxwell-Lyte 1937)
Strachey I	typescript of manuscript notes on the history of Banwell by William Strachey, *c* 1730, part I (Rendell and Rendell 1979)
Strachey III	typescript of manuscript notes on the history of Banwell by William Strachey, *c* 1730, part III (Rendell 1983)
Wards	Sales of Wards in Somerset, 1603–41 (Hawkins 1965)
Wells I	Calendar of the Manuscripts of the Dean and Chapter of Wells (Bird 1907)
Wells II	Calendar of the Manuscripts of the Dean and Chapter of Wells (Bird 1914)
Wells Wills	Medieval Wills from Wells (Shilton and Holsworthy 1925)
Wills	Abstracts of Somersetshire Wills, etc copied from the Manuscript collections of the late Revd Frederick Brown (Brown, nd)
Yatton Churchwardens	Yatton Churchwardens Accounts (Hobhouse 1890)

Bibliography

Aalbersberg, G, 1999 *The Alluvial Fringes of the Somerset Levels*. PhD thesis, Univ of Exeter

Abrams, L, 1996 *Anglo-Saxon Glastonbury: Church and Endowment*. Woodbridge: Boydell Press

Abrams, L, & Carley, J P (eds), 1991 *The Archaeology and History of Glastonbury Abbey*. Woodbridge: Boydell Press

Alcock, L, 1995 *Cadbury Castle Somerset: The Early Medieval Archaeology*. Cardiff: Univ of Wales Press

Alcock, N W, & Hall, L, 1994 *Fixtures and Fittings in Dated Houses 1567–1763*. York: Council for British Archaeology Handbook **11**

Aldhouse-Green, S H R, Whittle, A W R, Allen, J R L, Caseldine, A E, Culver, S J, Day, H, Lundquist, J, & Upton, D, 1992 Prehistoric human footprints from the Severn Estuary at Uskmouth and Magor Pill, Gwent, Wales, *Archaeol Cambrensis*, **141**, 14–55

Allan, J, 1999a Cleeve Abbey: the pottery, *Somerset Archaeol Nat Hist*, **142**, 41–75

Allan, J, 1999b South Netherlands maiolica in South-West England, in D Gaimster (ed) *Maiolica in the North*. London: British Museum Occasional Paper, **122**, 157–66

Allen, J R L, 1991 Salt-marsh accretion and sea-level movement in the Inner Bristol Estuary, southwest Britain: the archaeological and historical contribution, *J Geol Soc London*, **148**, 485–94

Allen J R L, 1997a Geological impacts on coastal wetland landscapes: sea-level rise, with illustrations from the River Banwell, *Proc Som Archaeol Nat Hist Soc*, **141**, 17–34

Allen J R L, 1997b Romano-British and early medieval pottery scatters on the alluvium at Hill and Oldbury, Severn Estuary Levels, *Archaeol in the Severn Estuary*, **8**, 67–84

Allen J R L, 2002a Retreat rates of soft-sediment cliffs: the contribution from dated fishweirs and traps on Holocene coastal outcrops, *Proc Geologists Assoc*, **113**, 1–8

Allen, J R L, 2002b The context and meaning of the Roman Goldcliff Stone, Caldicot Level, *Archaeol in the Severn Estuary*, **13**, 147–54

Allen, J R L, 2004 Chapel (Tump) Farm, Undy, Caldicot Level: an intertidal secondary medieval site and its implications, *Archaeol in the Severn Estuary*, **15**, 71–80

Allen, J R L, & Fulford, M G, 1986 The Wentlooge Level: a Romano-British saltmarsh reclamation in South East Wales, *Britannia*, **17**, 91–117

Allen, J R L, & Fulford, M G, 1987 Romano-British settlement and industry on the wetlands of the Severn Estuary, *Antiq J*, **67(ii)**, 237–89

Allen, J R L, & Fulford, M G, 1990a Romano-British and later reclamations on the Severn salt-marshes in the Elmore area, Gloucestershire, *Trans Bristol Gloucestershire Archaeol Soc*, **108**, 17–32

Allen, J R L, & Fulford, M G, 1990b Romano-British wetland reclamations at Longney, Gloucestershire, and evidence for early settlement of the inner Severn Estuary, *Antiq J*, **70(ii)**, 288–326

Allen, J R L, & Fulford, M G, 1992 Romano-British and later geoarchaeology at Oldbury Flats: reclamation and settlement on the changeable coast of the Severn Estuary, South West Britain, *Archaeol J*, **149**, 81–123

Allen, J R L, & Fulford, M G, 1996 The distribution of South-East Dorset Black Burnished Category 1 pottery in South-West Britain, *Britannia*, **27**, 223–81

Allen, J R L, & Rippon, S, 1995 The historical simplification of coastal flood defences: four case histories from the Severn Estuary Levels, South West Britain, *Trans Bristol Gloucestershire Archaeol Soc*, **113**, 73–88

Allen, J R L, & Rippon, S, 1997a Iron Age to early modern activity and palaeochannels at Magor Pill, Gwent: an exercise in lowland coastal-zone geoarchaeology, *Antiq J*, **77**, 127–70

Allen, J R L, & Rippon, S J, 1997b A Romano-British shaft of dressed stone and the settlement at Oldbury on Severn, County of Avon, *Trans Bristol and Gloucestershire Archaeol Soc*, **115**, 19–27

Andrew, R, 1984 *A Practical Pollen Guide to the British Flora*. Cambridge: Quaternary Res Assoc Technical Guide **1**

Anon, 1762 The 1607 flood, *Gentleman's Magazine*, **32**, 306

Anon, 1922 Additions to the Museum, *Proc Som Archaeol Nat Hist Soc*, **68**, lxxxvi–xciv

Anon, 1986a Historic Buildings Committee – vernacular architecture notes 1986, *Proc Som Archaeol Nat Hist Soc*, **130**, 169–85

Anon, 1986b Historic Buildings Committee – vernacular architecture notes 1987, *Proc Som Archaeol Nat Hist Soc*, **131**, 237–58

Anon, 1988 Historic Buildings Committee – vernacular architecture notes 1988, *Proc Som Archaeol Nat Hist Soc*, **132**, 261–83

Anon, 1989 Historic Buildings Committee – vernacular architecture notes 1989, *Proc Som Archaeol Nat Hist Soc*, **133**, 197–218

Anon, 1990 Historic Buildings Committee – vernacular architecture notes 1990, *Proc Som Archaeol Nat Hist Soc*, **134**, 243–66

Anon, 1991 Historic Buildings Committee – vernacular architecture notes 1991, *Proc Som Archaeol Nat Hist Soc*, **135**, 173–94

Anon, 1992 Historic Buildings Committee – vernacular architecture notes 1993, *Proc Som Archaeol Nat Hist Soc*, **137**, 159–72

Anon, 1993 Historic Buildings Committee – vernacular architecture notes 1992, *Proc Som Archaeol Nat Hist Soc*, **136**, 187–206

ApSimon, A M, 1965 The Roman temple on Brean Down, Somerset, *Proc Univ Bristol Spelaeological Soc*, **10(iii)**, 195–258

Arnold-Forster, F, 1899a *Studies in Church Dedications, volume I*. London: Skeffington

Arnold-Forster, F, 1899b *Studies in Church Dedications, volume II*. London: Skeffington

Astill, G, & Davies, W, 1997 *A Breton Landscape*. London: UCL Press

Aston, M, 1983 Deserted farmsteads on Exmoor and the Lay Subsidy of 1327 in West Somerset, *Proc Som Archaeol Nat Hist Soc*, **127**, 71–104

Aston, M, 1985 *Interpreting the Landscape: Landscape History and Archaeology*. London: Routledge

Aston, M, 1986 Post Roman central places in Somerset, in E Grant (ed) *Central Places, Archaeology and History*. Sheffield: Dept of Archaeol, Univ of Sheffield, 49–77

Aston, M, 2003 Early monasteries in Somerset – models and agendas, in M Ecclestone *et al* (eds) 2003, 36–48

Aston, M, & Gerrard, C, 1999 'Unique, traditional and charming'. The Shapwick Project, Somerset, *Antiq J*, **79**, 1–58

Aston, M, & Gerrard, C, forthcoming *The Shapwick Project*. London, English Heritage

Aston, M, & Iles, R (eds), 1987 *The Archaeology of Avon*. Bristol: Avon County Council

Aston, M, & Lewis, C (eds), 1994 *The Medieval Landscape of Wessex*. Oxford: Oxbow

Aston, M, Austin, D, & Dyer, C (eds), 1989 *The Rural Settlements of Medieval England*. Oxford: Blackwell

Austin, C, & Hall, R de Z, 1970 A cruck-roofed house in North Cadbury, *Proc Som Archaeol Nat Hist Soc*, **114**, 63–8

Austin, C, & Hall, R de Z, 1972 The medieval houses of Stocklinch, *Proc Som Archaeol Nat Hist Soc*, **116**, 86–100

Avery, J R, 1990 *'While we have time ...' 1590–1990: Queen Elizabeth's Hospital's Quarter Centenary*. Bristol

B G, 1804 Topographical account of Puxton, Somersetshire *Gentleman's Magazine*, March 1804, 201

Backhouse, J, 2001 *Medieval Birds in the Sherborne Missal*. London: The British Library

Bailey, K, 1989, The Middle Saxons, in S Bassett (ed) *The Origins of the Anglo-Saxon Kingdoms*. Leicester: Leicester Univ Press, 108–22

Bailey, M, 1989 *A Marginal Economy? East Anglian Breckland in the Later Middle Ages*. Cambridge: Cambridge Univ Press

Bailey, R G, José, P V, & Sherwood, B R, 1998 *United Kingdom Floodplains*. Westbury Academic and Scientific Publishing

Baker, E B, 1884 *A True report of Certain Wonderful Overflowings of Waters ....* Weston-super-Mare

Barber, L, 1998 An early Romano-British salt-working site at Scotney Court, *Archaeologia Cantiana*, **118**, 327–53

Barford, P, 1995 The briquetage from Blackwater Site 11, in T J Wilkinson, & P L Murphy *The Archaeology of the Essex coast, Volume I: The Hullbridge Survey*. East Anglian Archaeology, **71**, 173–80

Barker, G, 1995 *A Mediterranean Valley. Landscape Archaeology and* Annales *History in the Biferno Valley*. London: Leicester Univ Press

Barnes, I, 1993 Second Severn Crossing: English Approaches: an interim statement on the 1992/93 fieldwork, *Archaeol in the Severn Estuary 1993*, 5–29

Barrett, J H, Locker, A M, & Roberts, C M, 2004 The origins of intensive marine fishing in medieval Europe: the English evidence, *Proc Royal Soc B*, **271**, 2417–21

Barton, K, 1963 A medieval pottery kiln at Ham Green, Bristol, *Trans Bristol Gloucestershire Archaeol Soc*, **82–3**, 95–126

Barton, K J, 1964 Star Roman villa, Shipham, Somerset, *Proc Som Archaeol Nat Hist Soc*, **108**, 45–93

Bassett, S, 1989 In search of the origins of Anglo-Saxon kingdoms, in S Bassett (ed) *The Origins of the Anglo-Saxon Kingdoms*. Leicester: Leicester Univ Press, 3–27

Bassett, S, 1997 Continuity and fission in the Anglo-Saxon landscape: the origins of the Rodings (Essex), *Landscape History*, **19**, 25–42

Bates, E H, 1907 *Quarter Session Records for the County of Somerset Vol. I James I*. Somerset Rec Soc, **23**

Bates Harbin, S W, 1936 *Somerset Enrolled Deeds*. Somerset Rec Soc, **51**

Battarbee, R W, 1986 Diatom analysis, in B E Berglund (ed) *Handbook of Holocene Palaeoecology and Palaeohydrology*. Chichester: John Wiley & Sons

Batten, J, 1901 Alhampton, Churchill and Pokerleston (Puxton), *Somerset Dorset Notes Queries*, **7**, 69–72, 103–7

Bayley, J, 2001 Precious metal refining in Roman Exeter, *Proc Devon Archaeol Soc*, **59**, 141–7

Beacham, P, 1989 Rural building 1400–1800, in N Pevsner, & B Cherry *The Buildings of England: Devon*. Penguin Books, London, 62–77

Beagrie, N, 1989 The Romano-British pewter industry, *Britannia*, **20**, 169–92

Beckett, S C, & Hibbert, F A, 1979 Vegetational change and the influence of prehistoric man in the Somerset Levels, *New Phytologist*, **83**, 577–600

Beisly, P, 1996 *The North Marsh of Somerset*. Weston-super-Mare Heritage Centre

Bell, M, 1990 *Brean Down Excavations 1983–87*. London: English Heritage

Bell, M, 2000 Environmental archaeology in the Severn Estuary: progress and prospects, *Archaeol in the Severn Estuary,* **11**, 69–103

Bell, M, Caseldine, A, & Neumann, H, 2000 *Prehistoric Intertidal Archaeology in the Welsh Severn Estuary*. York: Council for British Archaeology Res Rep **120**

Bennett, G, 1804 A topographical account of Puxton, Somersetshire, *Gentlemen's Magazine* for 1894, 201

Bennett, G, 1812 An historical and topographical account of the parish of Banwell in the county of Somerset. Reprinted in several parts, *Search: J Banwell Archaeol Soc*, **4** (1964), 42–54; **5** (1965), 56–70

Bennett, J, 1985 *Sea Mills: The Roman Town of Abonae*. Bristol: City of Bristol Museum and Art Gallery

Bennett, K D, 1994 *Annotated Catalogue of Pollen and Pteridophyte Spores of the British Isles.* Cambridge: Department of Plant Sciences, Univ of Cambridge

Beresford, M W, & Finberg, H P R, 1973 *English Medieval Boroughs: A Handlist*. Newton Abbot: David & Charles

Beresford, M, & Hurst, J, 1990 *The English Heritage book of Wharram Percy deserted medieval village*. London: Batsford

Bettey, J H, 1983 Some major influences on the post-medieval landscape of the Bristol region, *Landscape History,* **5**, 69–77

Binford, L R, 1984 *Faunal Remains from Klasies River Mouth*. New York: Academic Press

Bird, S, 1987 Roman Avon, in M Aston, & R Iles (eds) 1987, 52–71

Bird, W H B, 1907 *Calendar of the Manuscripts of the Dean and Chapter of Wells*, vol. I. London: Historical Manuscripts Commission

Bird, W H B, 1914 *Calendar of the Manuscripts of the Dean and Chapter of Wells*, vol. II. London: Historical Manuscripts Commission

Blair, J, 1991 *Early Medieval Surrey: landholding, church and settlement before 1300*. Stroud: Alan Sutton

Blair, J, 2005 *The Church in Anglo-Saxon Society*. Oxford: Oxford Univ Press

Blamey, M, & Grey-Wilson, C, 1989 *The Illustrated Flora of Britain and Northern Europe.* London: Hodder & Stoughton

Blockley, F, forthcoming Marine molluscs, in K Blockley *Spicers Hall, Bristol: Excavation of a Medieval Merchant's House, 1995*. Bristol: Bristol and Region Archaeol Services

Boessneck, J, 1969 Osteological differences between sheep (*Ovis aries* Linné) and goat (*Capra hircus* Linné), in D Brothwell, & E Higgs (eds) *Science in Archaeology*. London: Thames & Hudson, 331–58

Boisseau, S, & Yalden, D W, 1998 The former status of the Crane Grusgrus in Britain *Ibis*, **140**, 482–500

Bond, J, 1995 Settlement, Land Use and Estate Patterns on the Failand Ridge, North Somerset: A preliminary discussion, in D Hooke, & S Burnell (eds) 1995, 115–52

Bond, J, 2004 *Monastic Landscapes*. Stroud: Tempus

Boon, G C, 1950 The Roman Villa at Kingsweston Park (Lawrence Weston Estate), Gloucestershire, *Trans Bristol Gloucestershire Archaeol Soc* **69**, 5–58

Boon, G C, 1967 Roman pottery from the base of the alluvium at Magor, *Monmouthshire Antiquary,* **2(iii)**, 121–7

Boon, G C, 1972 *Isca: the Roman Legionary Fortress at Caerleon, Monmouthshire.* Cardiff: National Museum of Wales

Boon, G C, 1980 Caerleon and the Gwent Levels in early historic times, in F H Thompson (ed) *Archaeology and Coastal Change*. London: Society of Antiquaries occasional papers **1**, 24–36

Bourne, J, 1988 Kingston place-names, *English Place-Name Soc J,* **20**, 13–37

Bowen, F W E, 1971 *Queen Elizabeth's Hospital, Bristol: The City School*. Clevedon Printing Company

Boyden, C R, & Little, C, 1973 Faunal distributions in soft sediments of the Severn Estuary, *Estuarine and Coastal Marine Science,* **1(iii)**, 203–23

Boyden, C R, Crothers, J H, Little, C, & Mettam, C, 1977 The intertidal invertebrate fauna of the Severn Estuary, *Field Studies,* **4**, 477–554

Bradley, R, 1975 Salt and settlement in the Hampshire Sussex borderland, in K A De Brisay, & K A Evans (eds) 1975, 20–5

Bradley, R, 1992 Roman salt production in Chichester Harbour: rescue excavations at Chidham, West Sussex, *Britannia,* **23**, 27–44

Bramble, 1891 *Proceedings of the Clifton Antiquarian Club*, **2**, 77

Branigan, K, 1976 *The Roman Villa in South-West England*. Bradford on Avon: Moonraker Press

Branigan, K, 1977 *Gatcombe Roman Villa*, BAR Brit Ser **44**. Oxford: British Archaeological Report

Brian, A, 1999 The allocation of strips in Lammas Meadows by the casting of lots, *Landscape History,* **21**, 43–58

British Ornithologists Union, 1971 *The Status of Birds in Britain and Ireland*. London: Blackwell

Bromwich, D, 1984 The manor of Banwell Bruton, *Search: J Banwell Archaeol Soc,* **20**, 24–35

Brooks, N 1989 The creation and early structure of the kingdom of Kent, in S Bassett (ed) *The Origins of the Anglo-Saxon Kingdoms*. Leicester: Leicester Univ Press, 55–74

Broomhead, R A, 1991 *Archaeological Observations on the Lympsham Sewage Treatment Works Elimination Scheme 1991*. Unpubl report. AC Archaeology (copy in Somerset SMR)

Broomhead, R A, 1999 *A Documentary and Archaeological Survey of Two Moorland Sites in Yatton and Congresbury*. Unpubl report for the Yatton and Congresbury Wildlife Action Group

Brown, T, & Foard, G, 1998 The Saxon Landscape: a regional perspective, in P Everson, & T Williamson (eds) *The Archaeology of landscape*. Manchester: Manchester Univ Press, 67–94

Brown, F, nd *Abstracts of Somerset Wills*, 2nd Series

Brunskill, R W, 1978 *Illustrated Handbook of Vernacular Architecture*. London: Faber & Faber

Bryant, E A, & Haslett, S K, 2002 Was the 1607 coastal flooding event in the Severn Estuary and Bristol Channel (UK) due to a tsunami? *Archaeol in the Severn Estuary,* **13**, 163–7

Bulleid, A, 1914 Romano-British potteries in mid Somerset, *Proc Soc Antiq*, **26**, 137–54

Bullock, P, Fedoroff, N, Jongerius, A, Stoops, G, & Tursina, T, 1985 *Handbook for Soil Thin Section Description*. Wolverhampton: Waine Res Publications

Bunn, D S, Warburton, A B, & Wilson, R D S, 1982 *The Barn Owl*. London: T & AD Poyser

Burchill, R, 2000 *Proposed Magistrates Court, St Georges, Banwell, N. Somerset, 1994*. Unpubl archaeological evaluation report BARAS BA/C094; copy in Weston-super-Mare Museum WESTM 2000.30

Burchill, R *et al*, 2001 *The Archaeology of the Pucklechurch to Seabank Pipeline: Volume 3 – appendices to the final report*. Unpubl report. Edinburgh: McGill Archaeological Consultants

Burrow, I, 1981 *Hillfort and Hilltop Settlement in Somerset in the First to Eighth Centuries AD*. BAR Brit Ser, **91**. Oxford: British Archaeological Reports

Burrow, I, 1988 Excavations at 5–8 Fore Street, Taunton 1979, *Proc Som Archaeol Nat Hist Soc,* **132**, 95–164

Burrow, I, & Burrow, C B, 1990 Witham Priory: the first English Carthusian monastery, *Proc Som Archaeol Nat Hist Soc,* **134**, 141–82

Butler, S, 1987 Coastal change since 6000 BP and the presence of man at Kenn Moor, Avon, *Proc Som Archaeol Nat Hist Soc,* **131**, 1–11

Cameron, K, 1996 *English Place-Names*. London: Batsford

Carley, J, 1985 *The Chronicle of Glastonbury Abbey. An Edition, Translation and Study of John of Glastonbury's* Cronica sive Antiquiate Glastoniensis Ecclesie. Woodbridge: The Boydell Press

Carley, J, 1988 *Glastonbury Abbey*. London: Guild Publishing

Carr, J, 1985 Excavations on the Mound, Glastonbury, Somerset, 1971, *Proc Som Archaeol Nat Hist Soc,* **129**, 37–62

Carruthers, W J, 2000 The mineralised plant remains, in A Lawson, & C Gingell (eds) *Potterne 1982–85 – animal husbandry in later Prehistoric Wiltshire.* Wessex Archaeology Report **17**

Carter, S, Jones, J, & McGill, B, 2004 Pucklechurch to Seabank pipeline. Sediment stratigraphic and palaeoenvironmental data from the Avonmouth Levels, *Archaeol in the Severn Estuary,* **14**, 69–86

CAT, 2002a *Land to the South of the Former Grove Farm, St Georges, Worle, Weston-super-Mare, North Somerset, SMR 40841: Archaeological Evaluation*. Unpubl report. Cotswold Archaeology report 01123

CAT, 2002b *Old House, St Georges, Worle, Weston-super-Mare, North Somerset, SMR 40839: Archaeological Evaluation*. Unpubl report. Cotswold Archaeology report 01107

CAT, 2002c *Land at Former Grove Farm, St Georges, Worle, Weston-super-Mare, North Somerset, SMR 40246: Archaeological Evaluation*. Unpubl report. Cotswold Archaeology report 01122

Chadwyck Healy, C E, 1897 *Somerset Pleas (Civil and Criminal) from the Rolls of the Itinerant Judges*. Somerset Rec Soc, **11**

Chandler, J, 1993 *John Leland's Itinerary*. Stroud: Alan Sutton

Churchfield, S, 1988 *Shrews of the British Isles*. Princes Risborough: Shire Publications

Clark, E A, & Gaunt, G D, 2000 Stone objects, in P Stamper, & R A Croft *Wharram: A Study of Settlement on the Yorkshire Wolds VIII: The South Manor Area*. York: York Univ Archaeol Pub **10**, 101–10

Clarke, A, 1998 *Locking Castle Business Park, West Wick, Somerset. Archaeological Watching Brief. North Somerset SMR 40025*. Bristol: Avon Archaeol Unit

Clarke, M, 1976 Bower House on the Moor, *Banwell Soc for Archaeol Newsletter*, October 1976, 1

Clarke, M, 1978 Mays Green, Puxton *Axbridge Archaeol Soc Newsletter*, September 1978

Clarke, M, 1979 The northern levels in Roman times — recent evidence, *Axbridge Archaeol and Local Hist Soc News Sheet* **29**, 2–3

Clarke, M, 1980 Puxton, *Axbridge Archaeol and Local History Soc News Sheet* **38**, 1–4

Clegg, J, 1965 *The Freshwater Life of the British* Isles. London: Frederick Warne & Co Ltd

Coleman-Smith, R, & Pearson, T, 1981 *Donyatt Potteries*, Chichester: Phillimore

Coles, J, 1984 One swallow, one summer? A comment on a wooden stake in Kenn Moor, *Proc Som Archaeol Nat Hist Soc,* **128**, 31

Coles, S D, 1912 *Sea Walls of the Severn*. Bristol

Collingwood, R G, & Wright, R P, 1965 *The Roman Inscriptions of Britain, volume 1: inscriptions on stone*. Oxford: Clarendon Press

Collinson, J, 1791 *History of Somerset, volume III*. Bath: Crutwell

Copp, C, 1988 Mollusc fauna, in B Williams The excavation of medieval and post medieval tenements at 94–102 Temple Street, Bristol, 1975, *Trans Bristol Gloucestershire Archaeol Soc,* **106,** 107–68

Corbet, G B, 1975 *Finding and Identifying Mammals in Britain*. London: British Museum (Natural History) Publications

Corbet, G B, & Harris, S, 1991 *The Handbook of British Mammals, 3rd edition*. Oxford: Blackwell

Corcos, N, 2002a *The Affinities and Antecedents of Medieval Settlement: Topographical Perspectives From Three of the Somerset Hundreds*. BAR Brit Ser **337**. Oxford: British Archaeological Report

Corcos, N, 2002b Bourne and Burrington: a Burnantun estate, *Proc Som Archaeol Nat Hist Soc,* **144**, 117–38

Corney, M, 2000 Characterising the landscape of Roman Britain: a review of the study of Roman Britain 1975–2000, in D Hooke (ed) *Landscape: the richest historical record*. Birmingham: the Society for Landscape Studies, 32–45

Costello, K, & Burley, R, 1997 *Charities on Camera in Edwardian Bristol*. Derby: Breedon Books

Costen, M, 1992a *The Origins of Somerset*. Manchester: Manchester Univ Press

Costen, M, 1992b Huish and Worthy: Old English survivals in a later Landscape, *Anglo-Saxon Studies Archaeol Hist,* **5**, 65–83

Coward, H, 1971/72 Fragments of Banwell's Past, *Search: J Banwell Archaeol Soc,* **11**, 32–4

Coward, H, 1978 The manor of Hutton in 1309, *Search: J Banwell Archaeol Soc,* **14**, 33–50

Coward, H, 1980 The Wowwall: some aspects of government and land-drainage early in the 15th century, *Proc Som Archaeol Nat Hist Soc,* **124**, 151–7

Coward, H, 1981 The Grumblepill: a narrow slice of local history, *Search: J Banwell Archaeol Soc,* **17**, 72–6

Coward, H, nd *The Story of Hutton*, Mid-16th century continued (copy in Weston-super-Mare Central Library)

Cowgill, J, de Neergaard, M, & Griffiths, N, 1986 *Knives and Scabbards: Medieval finds from London*. London: Museum of London

Cox, B, 1976 The place-names of the earliest English records, *J English Place-Names Soc,* **3**, 12–16

Cox, J C, & Bradley Ford, C, 1954 *The Parish Churches of England*. London

Cox, P M, & Hearne, C M, 1991 *Redeemed from the Heath. The Archaeology of the Wytch Farm Oilfield (1987–90)*. Dorchester: Dorset Natural History and Archaeol Soc Monogr, **9**

Cox, P W, & Broomhead, R A, 1993 *The Archaeological Evaluation of the Proposed Accommodation Facilities at Hinkley Point 'C' Power Station, Somerset*. Unpubl report. AC Archaeology (copy on Somerset SMR, PRN 15750)

Cox, S, & Lankstead, D, 2004 St Georges, East Worle, *Bristol and Avon Archaeology,* **19**, 100–1

Coy, J, 1987 Non-domestic faunal resources in south-west England, in N D Balaam, B Levitan, & V Straker *Studies in palaeoeconomy and environment in south west England*. BAR Brit Ser **181**. Oxford: British Archaeological Report, 9–29

Cran, A, 1983 *The Story of Congresbury*. Bristol: Redcliff Press

Crawford, O G S, 1953 *Archaeology in the Field*. London: Dent

Croft, R A, & Mynard, D C, 1993 *The Changing Landscape of Milton Keynes*. Aylesbury: Buckinghamshire Archaeol Soc Monogr, **5**

Crowson, A, Lane, T, & Reeves, J (eds), 2000 *Fenland management project excavations 1991–1995*. Sleaford: Heritage Lincolnshire

Cullen, K, & Cox, S, 2004 *Land at Rose Cottages St Georges, Worle, North Somerset: archaeological evaluation*. Unpubl report. Cotswold Archaeology Report 04141

Cunliffe, B, 1979 *Excavations in Bath 1950–75*. Bristol: Comm for Rescue Excavations in Avon, Gloucestershire and Somerset

Cunliffe, B, 2003 Locating the Dobunni, in M Ecclestone *et al* (eds), 12–16

Dallimore, J, 1995 Lancin Farmhouse, Wambrook, *Proc Som Archaeol Nat Hist Soc,* **138**, 101–9

Dallimore, J, 2001 *Newton St Loe, N E Somerset: a study of the vernacular building survey*. Bath: Bath and North East Somerset Council

Darby, H C 1967 The south-western counties, in H C Darby, & R Welldon Finn (eds) *The Domesday Geography of South-West England*. Cambridge: Cambridge University Press, 348–92

Darby, H C, 1973 Domesday England, in H C Darby (ed) *A New Historical Geography of England*. Cambridge, Cambridge Univ Press, 39–74

Darvill, T, 2003 The land of the Dobunni, in M Ecclestone *et al* (eds) 2003, 2–11

Davenport, P, 1991 *Archaeology in Bath 1976–85*. Oxford: Oxford Univ Comm for Archaeol

Davies, W, & Astill, G, 1994 *The East Brittany Survey. Fieldwork and Field Data*. Aldershot: Scolar Press

Davis, S J M, 1987 *The Archaeology of Animals*. London: Batsford

Davison, A, 1990 *The Evolution of Settlement in Three Norfolk Parishes*. East Anglian Archaeology, **49**

Dawes, M C B, & Maxwell-Lyte, H C, 1934 *The Register of Thomas Bekynton, Bishop of Bath and Wells, 1443–65*. Somerset Rec Soc, **49**

De Brisay, K W, 1978 The Excavation of a Red Hill at Peldon, Essex, with some notes on other sites, *Antiq J,* **58**, 31–60

De Brisay, K A, & Evans, K A, 1975 *Salt: The Study of an Ancient Industry*. Colchester: Colchester Archaeol Group

Defoe, D, 1742 *A Tour Thro' Great Britain, volume II*. Reprinted in 1975 ed S Richardson. London: Garland Publishing

Denys, L, 1992 *A Check List of the Diatoms in the Holocene Deposits of the Western Belgian Coastal Plain with a Survey of their Apparent Ecological Requirements: I. Introduction, Ecological Code and Complete List*. Service Geologique de Belgique, Professional Paper, **246**

Dickinson, F H, 1877 The Banwell charters, *Proc Som Archaeol Nat Hist Soc*, **23**, 49–64

Dickinson, F H, 1889 *Kirbys Quest for Somerset*. Somerset Rec Soc, **3**

Dickson, C, & Dickson, J, 2000 *Plants and People in Ancient Scotland*. Stroud: Tempus

Disney, M, 2005 Britain had its own big waves – 400 years ago, *The Times*, 4 January 2005, 11

Dobney, K M, Jacques, S D, & Irving, B G, 1995 *Of Butchers and Breeds: Report on the Vertebrate Remains from Various Sites in the City of Lincoln*. Lincoln Archaeol Studies, **5**

Draper, S, 2002 Old English *wīc* and *walh*: Britons and Saxons in post-Roman Wiltshire, *Landscape History,* **24**, 30–43

Driesch, A von den, 1976 *A Guide to the Measurement of Animal Bones from Archaeological Sites*, Peabody Museum Bulletin, **1.** Harvard

Ducker, R, 2002a *West Wick Bypass, Weston-super-Mare, North Somerset. Archaeological Monitoring and Recording Programme. North Somerset SMR 42763.* Bristol: Avon Archaeol Unit

Ducker, R, 2002b *Site of Scott Elm Drive, West Wick, Weston-super-Mare. Archaeological Watching Brief Report. North Somerset SMR 42763.* Bristol: Avon Archaeol Unit

Dwelly, E, 1916 *National Records Vol. I: Hearth Tax for Somerset 1664–65.* Fleet, Hampshire

Dyer, C, 1985 Power and conflict in the medieval village, in D Hooke (ed) *Medieval Villages.* Oxford: Oxford Univ Comm Archaeol, 27–32

Dyer, C, 1989 'The retreat from marginal land': the growth and decline of medieval rural settlements, in Aston *et al* (eds) 1989, 45–58

Dyer, C, 1997 Peasants and farmers: rural settlements in an age of transition, in D Gaimster, & P Stamper (eds) *The Age of Transition: The Archaeology of English Culture 1400–1600.* Oxford: Soc Med Archaeol Monogr, **15**, 61–76

Dyer, C, 2002 *Making a Living in the Middle Ages: The People of Britain 850–1520.* New Haven: Yale Univ Press

Ecclestone, M, 1996 *Dairy Production on the Glastonbury Abbey Demesne 1256–1334.* Unpubl MA dissertation, Univ of Bristol

Ecclestone, M, Gardner, K S, Holbrook, N, & Smith, A, 2003 *The Land of the Dobunni.* Comm for Archaeology in Gloucestershire/Council for British Archaeology South West

Edwards, N (ed), 1997 *Landscape and Settlement in Medieval Wales.* Oxford: Oxbow monogr **81**

Egan, G, & Pritchard, F, 1991 *Dress Accessories: Medieval Finds from London 1150–c.1450.* London: Museum of London

Ellacombe, H T, 1874 The church bells in the church towers and turrets of all the parish churches of Somerset, *Trans Exeter Diocesan Architect Soc*, New Ser **3(i)**, 85–188

Evans, J, 1980 *Worlebury: The Story of the Iron Age Hill-fort at Weston-super-Mare.* Weston-super-Mare: Woodspring Museum

Everitt, A, 1986 *Continuity and Colonisation: the evolution of Kentish Settlement.* Leicester: Leicester Univ Press

Everton, A, & Everton, R, 1980 Romano-British occupation at Crooks Marsh Farm, Avonmouth, *Bristol Archaeol Res Group Rev,* **2**, 57–8

Fairclough, G J, 1998 *Historic Landscape Characterisation: the state of the art.* London: English Heritage

Fairclough, G, & Rippon, S, 2002 *Europe's Cultural Landscape: archaeologists and the management of change.* Brussels: Europae Archaeologiae Consilium

Faith, R, 1994 Tidenham, Gloucestershire, and the history of the English manor, *Landscape History,* **16**, 39–51

Farmer, D H, 1987 *The Oxford Dictionary of Saints.* 2nd edn. Oxford: Oxford Univ Press

Farrar, R A H, 1975 Prehistoric and Roman saltworks in Dorset, in K A De Brisay, & K A Evans (eds) 1975, 14–20

Fawn, A J, Evans, K A, McMaster, I, & Davies, G M R, 1990 *The Red Hills of Essex.* Colchester: Colchester Archaeol Group

Field, J, 1972 *English Field-Names: a dictionary.* Newton Abbot: David & Charles

Finberg, H P R, 1955 *Roman and Saxon Withington: A study in continuity.* Leicester: Leicester Univ Press

Finberg, H P R, 1964 *The Early Charters of Wessex.* Leicester: Leicester Univ Press

Findlay, D C, 1965 *The Soils of the Mendip District of Somerset (sheets 279 and 280).* Harpenden: Memoirs of the Soil Survey of Great Britain

Fitter, R, Fitter, A, & Farrer, A, 1987 *Grasses, Sedges, Rushes and Ferns of Britain and Northern Europe.* London: Collins

FitzPatrick, E A, 1993 *Soil Microscopy and Micromophology.* Chichester: John Wiley & Sons

Fleming, A, 1994 Swadal, Swar (and Erechwydd?): early medieval polities in Upper Swaledale, *Landscape History,* **16**, 17–30

Fleming, A, 1998 *Swaledale: Valley of the Wild River.* Edinburgh: Edinburgh Univ Press

Foard, G, 1978 Systematic fieldwalking and the investigation of Saxon settlement in Northants, *World Archaeology,* **9(iii)**, 357–74

Foard, G, & Rippon, S, 1998 Managing the historic landscape: 'The Register of Landscapes of Outstanding Historic Interest in Wales', *Landscape Hist,* **20**, 99–103

Fowler, P J, 1968 Excavation of a Romano-British Settlement at Butcombe, North Somerset, *Proc Univ Bristol Spelaeological Soc,* **11**, 209–35

Fowler, P J, 1975 Continuity in the landscape: some local archaeology in Wiltshire, Somerset and Gloucestershire, in P J Fowler (ed) *Recent Work in Rural Archaeology.* Bradford-on-Avon: Moonraker Press, 121–33

Fowler, P J, 2000 *Landscape plotted and pieced: landscape history and local archaeology in Fyfield and Overton, Wiltshire.* London: Soc of Antiquaries

Fowler, P, 2002 *Farming in the First Millennium AD.* Cambridge: Cambridge Univ Press

Fowler, P J, & Blackwell, I, 1998 *The Land of Lettice Sweetapple: an English Countryside explored.* Stroud: Tempus

Fowler, P J, Gardner, K, & Rahtz, P A, 1970 *Cadbury Congresbury, Somerset 1968*. Bristol

Fox, A, & Ravenhill, W, 1972 The Roman Fort at Nanstallon, Cornwall, *Britannia*, **3**, 56–111

Fulford, M G, 1996 *The Second Augustan Legion in the West of Britain*. Cardiff: National Museum of Wales

Fulford, M G, 2003 The canton of the Dobunni, in M Ecclestone *et al* (eds) 2003, 17–23

Fulford, M G, Allen, J R L, & Rippon, S J, 1994 The settlement and drainage of the Wentlooge Level, Gwent: Excavation and Survey at Rumney Great Wharf 1992, *Britannia*, **25**, 175–210

Fyfe, R M, Brown, A G, & Rippon, S J, 2003 Mid to late-holocene vegetation history of Greater Exmoor, UK: estimating the spatial extent of human-induced vegetation change, *Vegetation History and Archaeobotany*, **12**, 215–32

Fyfe, R M, Brown, A G, & Rippon, S J, 2004 Characterising the late prehistoric, 'Romano-British' and medieval landscape, and dating the emergence of a regionally distinct agricultural system in South West Britain, *J Archaeol Science*, **31**, 1699–714

Fyfe, R M, & Rippon, S J, 2004 A landscape in transition? Palaeoenvironmental evidence for the end of the 'Romano-British' period in South West England, in R Collins, & J Gerrard (eds) *Debating Late Antiquity*. BAR Brit Ser **365**. Oxford: British Archaeological Report, 33–42

Gaffney, C, & Gater, J, 2003 *Revealing the Buried Past: geophysics for archaeologists*. Stroud: Tempus

Gait, P 2001 *Earthwork and geophysical surveys at Riverside Romano-British villa, Banwell, North Somerset*. Unpubl report, North Somerset SMR

Gale, R, & Cutler, D, 2000 *Plants in Archaeology*. Kew: Westbury and Royal Botanic Gardens

Gardiner, J, Allen, M J, Hamilton-Dyer, S, Laidlaw, M, & Scaife, R, 2002 Making the most of it: late prehistoric pastoralism in the Avon Levels, Severn Estuary, *Proc Prehist Soc*, **68**, 1–39

Gardiner, M, in press The origins and persistence of manor houses in England, in M Gardiner, & S Rippon (eds) *Medieval Landscapes in Britain*. Macclesfield: Windgather Press

Gardiner, P, 1996 *The Inter-Conversion of a Post-Medieval farmhouse at Sandford, in the parish of Winscombe, Somerset*. Unpubl dissertation, Dept of Archaeology, Univ Bristol

Gardner, K, 1985 Apples in the landscape: the Puxton Dolmoors, *Bristol and Avon Archaeol*, **4**, 13–20

Gelling, M, 1978 *Signposts to the Past*. Chichester: Phillimore

Gelling, M, & Cole, A, 2000 *The Landscape of Place-Names*. Stamford: Shaun Tyas

Gerrard, C, 1999 A 'Malling' maiolica jug from Shapwick House, Somerset, in D Gaimster (ed) *Maiolica in the North*. London: British Museum Occ Pap **122**, 171–2

Gilbert, P, 1996 The pre-Conquest landscape at Kingston Seymour on the North Somerset Levels: report on fieldwork 1996, *Archaeol in the Severn Estuary*, **7**, 53–8

Gilbertson, D, & Hawkins, A B, 1978 *The Pleistocene Succession at Kenn, Somerset*. London: Bulletin of the Board of the British Geological Survey **66**

Gilbertson, D, & Hawkins, A B, 1983 A prehistoric wooden stake and the alluvial stratigraphy of Kenn Moor, Avon, *Proc Som Archaeol Nat Hist Soc*, **127**, 1–6

Gilson, R G, 1976 South Somerset jointed crucks – some problems, *Proc Som Archaeol Nat Hist Soc*, **120**, 51–5

Gilson, R G, 1985 Three Somerset manor houses, *Proc Som Archaeol Nat Hist Soc*, **129**, 129–39

Gilyard-Beer, R, 1990 *Cleeve Abbey*. London: English Heritage

Glasscock, R E, 1975 *The Lay Subsidy of 1334*. London: The British Academy

Godwin, H, 1956 *The History of the British Flora*, Cambridge: Cambridge Univ Press

Good, L, 1987 The excavation of two docks at Narrow Quay, Bristol, 1978–9, *Post-Med Archaeol*, **21**, 25–126

Grant, A, 1982 The use of tooth wear as a guide to the age of domestic ungulates, in B Wilson, C Grigson, & S Payne (eds) *Ageing and Sexing Animal Bones from Archaeological Sites*. BAR Brit Ser **109**. Oxford: British Archaeological Report, 7–23

Grant, A, 1988 Animal resources, in G Astill, & A Grant (eds), *The Countryside of Medieval England*. Oxford: Blackwell, 149–87

Grant, A, 2002 Food, status and social hierarchy, in P Miracle, & N Milner (eds) *Consuming Passions and Patterns of Consumption*. Cambridge: McDonald Institute, 17–23

Green, E, 1872 On some Somerset chap-books, *Proc Som Archaeol Nat Hist Soc*, **24**, 50–66

Green, E, 1888 *Survey and Rental of the Chantries in the County of Somerset, 1548*. Somerset Rec Soc, **11**

Green, E, 1898 *Pedes Finium commonly called Feet of Fines for the County of Somerset, Edward II to 20 Edward III (1307–46)*. Somerset Rec Soc, **12**

Green, E, 1902 *Pedes Finium commonly called Feet of Fines for the County of Somerset, 21 Edward III to 20 Richard II (1347–99)*. Somerset Rec Soc, **17**

Green, E, 1906 *Pedes Finium commonly called Feet of Fines for the County of Somerset, Henry IV to Henry VI*. Somerset Rec Soc, **22**

Gregson, N, 1985 The multiple estate model: some critical questions, *J Hist Geogr*, **11(iv)**, 339–51

Greig, J, 1983 Plant foods in the past: A review of the evidence from northern Europe, *J Plant Foods*, **5**, 179–214

Griffith, F, & Weddell, P, 1996 Ironworking in the Blackdown Hills: results of recent survey, in P Newman (ed) *The Archaeology of Mining and Metallurgy in South West Britain*. Matlock: Peak

District Mines Historical Soc/Historical Metallurgy Soc, 27–34

Grimm, E, 1990 *Tilia* and *Tilia*.graph: PC spreadsheet and graphics software for pollen data, *INQUA Commission Holocene Working Groups on Data-handling Methods Newsletter*, **4**, 5–7

Grove, J, & Brunning, R, 1998 The Romano-British salt industry in Somerset *Archaeol in the Severn Estuary,* **9**, 61–6

Grundy, G B, 1932 The Saxon charters of Somerset, *Proc Som Archaeol Nat Hist Soc,* **78**, Appendix

Gutiérrez, A, 2004 The medieval pottery, in P Ellis, & P Leach (eds) Roman and medieval remains at Manor Farm, Castle Cary, *Proc Som Archaeol Nat Hist Soc,* **146**, 28–33

Gutiérrez, A, forthcoming Post-Roman pottery, in C Gerrard with M Aston (eds) forthcoming *The Shapwick Project, Somerset: A rural landscape explored,* Soc Med Archaeol Monogr, **35**. Leeds

Guy, C J, 1999 The excavations at the reredorter at Cleeve Abbey, *Proc Som Archaeol Nat Hist Soc,* **142**, 1–40

Hall, D, 1982 *Medieval Fields*. Aylesbury: Shire

Hall, D, 1988 The late Saxon countryside: Villages and their Fields, in D Hooke (ed) 1988, 99–122

Hall, D, 1996 *The Fenland Project, Number 10: Cambridgeshire Survey, Isle of Ely and Wisbech*. East Anglian Archaeology, **79**

Hall, D, & Martin, P W, 1979 Brixworth, Northamptonshire: an intensive field survey, *J Brit Archaeol Assoc,* **132**, 1–6

Hall, H, 1896 *The Red Book of the Exchequer*. London: HMSO

Hall, L J, 1983 *The Rural Houses of North Avon and South Gloucestershire 1400–1720*. Bristol: City of Bristol Museum and Art Gallery Monogr, **6**

Hall, R de Z, 1970 A preliminary catalogue of cruck-roofed buildings in Somerset, *Proc Som Archaeol Nat Hist Soc,* **114**, 48–63

Hall, R de Z, 1973 A further catalogue of Somerset crucks, *Proc Som Archaeol Nat Hist Soc,* **117**, 102–6

Hall, T, 2000 *Minster Churches in the Dorset Landscape*. BAR Brit Ser **304**. Oxford: British Archaeological Report

Hall, T, 2003 The reformation of the British church in the West Country in the 7th century, in M Ecclestone *et al* (eds) 2003, 49–55

Halstead, P, 1985 *A study of mandibular teeth from the Romano-British contexts at Maxey,* East Anglian Archaeology, **27**, 209–14

Harrison, J, 1997 *The Composite Manor of Brent: a study of a large wetland-edge estate up to 1350*. Unpubl PhD thesis, Univ of Leicester

Harten, J D H, & Schuyf, J, 1983 Possible planned medieval villages in the Netherlands, in B Roberts, & R E Glasscock (eds) *Villages, Fields and Frontiers*. BAR Internat Ser **185**. Oxford: British Archaeological Report, 43–59

Harvey, P D A, 1989 Initiative and authority in settlement change, in M Aston *et al* (eds) 1989, 31–43

Haslett, S K, & Bryant, E A, 2005 The AD 1607 coastal flood in the Bristol Channel and Severn Estuary: historical records from Devon and Cornwall, UK, *Archaeol in the Severn Estuary,* **15**, 81–9

Haslett, S K, Davies, P, Curr, R H F, Davies, C F, Kennington, K, & Marhgetts, A J, 1998 Evaluating late Holocene relative sea level change in the Somerset Levels, southwest Britain, *The Holocene,* **8**, 197–207

Haslett, S K, Davies, P, & Strawbridge, F, 1997 Reconstructing Holocene sea-level change in the Severn Estuary and Somerset Levels: the foraminifera connection, *Archaeol in the Severn Estuary,* **8**, 29–40

Haslett, S, Margetts, A, & Williams, H, 2000 Foraminifera, in S Rippon 2000b

Haverfield, F, 1906 Roman Somerset, *Victoria County History of Somerset,* **1**, 207–372

Hawkins, A B, 1971 The Late Weichselian and Flandrian transgression of South West Britain, *Quaternaria,* **14**, 115–30

Hawkins, M J, 1965 *Sales of Wards in Somerset, 1603–41*. Somerset Rec Soc, **67**

Hayes, P P, & Lane, T, 1992 *The Fenland Project, Number 5: Lincolnshire Survey, The South-West Fens*. East Anglian Archaeology, **55**

Healey, R H, 1999 A medieval saltmaking site at Bicker haven, in A Bell, D Gurney, & H Healey (eds) *Lincolnshire Salterns: Excavations at Helpringham, Holbeach St John and Bicker Haven*. East Anglian Archaeology, **89**, 82–101

Heathcote, J, 2000 Soil micromorphology, in Rippon 2000b, 107–12

Hembry, P M, 1967 *The Bishops of Bath and Wells 1540–1640: Social and economic problems*. London: Univ of London Press

Hendey, N I, 1964 *An Introductory Account of the Smaller Algae of British Coastal Waters. Part V. Bacillariophyceae (Diatoms)*. London: Ministry of Agriculture, Fisheries and Food, Series IV

Henig, M, 1993 *Corpus Signorum Imperii Romani. Corpus of Sculpture of the Roman World, Great Britain, Volume 1, Fascicule 7: Roman Sculpture from the Cotswold Region with Devon and Cornwall*. Oxford: Oxford Univ Press

Henig, M, 1995 *The Art of Roman Britain*. London: Batsford

Herring, P, 1998 *Cornwall's Historic Landscape*. Truro: Cornwall County Council

Hey, G, 2004 *Yarnton: Saxon and medieval settlement and landscape. Results of excavations 1990–96*. Oxford: Oxford Archaeology, Thames Valley Archaeol Landscapes Monogr, **20**

Heyworth, A, & Kidson, C, 1982 Sea level changes in Southwest England and Wales, *Proc Geol Assoc,* **93**, 91–111

Higham, C W F, & Message, M A, 1969 An assessment of a prehistoric technique of bovine husbandry, in D Brothwell, & E Higgs (eds) *Science in Archaeology*. London: Thames & Hudson, 315–30

Hillman, G, 1981 Reconstructing crop husbandry

practices from charred remains of crops, in R Mercer (ed) *Farming Practice in British Prehistory*. Edinburgh: Edinburgh Univ Press

Hobhouse, B, 1887 *The Register of Bishop Drokensford, Bishop of Bath and Wells 1309–29*. Somerset Rec Soc, **1**

Hobhouse, B, 1890 *Church-Wardens Accounts of Croscombe, Pitton, Yatton*. Somerset Rec Soc, **4**

Hobhouse, B, Maxwell-Lyte, C H, Hunt, W, Green, E, Horner, J F, & Holmes, T S, 1894 *Two Cartularies of the Augustinian Priory of Bruton and the Cluniac Priory on Montacute*. Somerset Rec Soc, **8**

Hodges, M, 1996 *Churchill: A Brief History of the Area of the Civil Parish*. Churchill: private publication [copy in the Devon and Exeter Institution Library]

Hollinrake, C, & Hollinrake, N, 2003 *An Archaeological Evaluation at the King Alfred's School, Burnham on Sea*. Unpubl report in Somerset SMR

Holmes, T S, 1896 *The Register of Ralph of Shrewsbury, Bishop of Bath and Wells, 1329–63*. Somerset Rec Soc, **9**

Holt, R, 1987 Whose were the profits of milling corn? The abbots of Glastonbury and their tenants 1086–1350, *Past and Present,* **116**, 3–25

Holworthy, R, 1916 *Hearth Tax for Somerset 1664–65*. London: E Dwelly

Homans, G C, 1941 *English Villagers of the Thirteenth Century*. Harvard Univ Press

Hooke, D (ed), 1988 *Anglo-Saxon Settlements*. Oxford: Blackwell

Hooke, D, 1998 *The Landscape of Anglo-Saxon England*. London: Leicester Univ Press

Hooke, D, & Burnell, S (eds), 1995 *Landscape and Settlement in Britain AD 400–1066*. Exeter: Exeter Univ Press

Hoskins, W G, 1953 The rebuilding of rural England, 1560–1640, *Past and Present,* **4**, 44–59

Hoskins, W G, 1955 *The Making of the English Landscape*. London: Hodder & Stoughton

Hughes, M, & Gaimster, D, 1999 Neutron activation analyses of maiolica from London, Norwich, the Low Countries and Italy, in D Gaimster (ed) *Maiolica in the North*. London: British Museum Occasional Paper, **122**, 57–89

Hugo, T, 1859 Taunton Priory, *Proc Som Archaeol Nat Hist Soc,* **9**, 1–128

Hume, L, 1992 *Oldbury on Severn Silt Lagoon, ASMR 8332: Archaeological Salvage Recording*. Unpubl report, Avon Archaeol Unit

Hume, L, 1993 *Archaeological Evaluation of Land at Rust Bridge, Kenn, Avon*. Unpubl report, Avon Archaeol Unit, SMR 9509

Hunt, W, 1893 *Two Chartularies of the Priory of St Peters at Bath*. Somerset Rec Soc, **7**

Hunter, J, 1840 *Ecclesiastical Documents viz A Brief History of the Bishopric of Somerset from its Foundation to the Year 1174*. London: Camden Soc

Hunter, K L, 2002 *An Assessment of the Plant Macrofossils, Other Environmental Remains and Finds from a Site off Scot Elm Drive, West Wick, Weston-super-Mare and an archaeological watching brief at West Wick by-pass.* Unpubl report for Avon Archaeol Unit

Hustedt, F, 1930–66 *Die Kieselalgen Deutschlands, Oesterreichs und der Schweiz unter Berucksichtigung der ubrigen Lander Europas sowie der angrenzenden Meeresgebeite. In Dr. L. Rabenhorsts Kryptogamen-Flora von Deutschland, Oesterrech und der Schweiz,* **7**, Parts 1–3

Hustedt, F, 1953 Die systematik der diatomeen in ihren beziehungen zur geologie und okologie nebst einer revision des halobien-systems, *Sv Bot Tidskr*, **47**, 509–19

Hustedt, F, 1957 Die diatomeenflora des flusssystems der Weser im gebiet der Hansestadt Bremen, *Ab naturw Ver Bremen,* **34**, 181–440

Hutcheson, A, & Andrews, P, 2002 Excavations at the County Hotel, Taunton 1995–96, *Proc Som Archaeol Nat Hist Soc,* **144**, 139–64

Insole, P, 1997 An excavation and auger survey in 1996 at British Gas Seabank, Bristol, on the north Avon Severn Levels, *Bristol and Avon Archaeol,* **14**, 21–47

Ireland, C, 1983, The Roman pottery, in C Heighway, *The East and North Gates of Gloucester*. Bristol: Western Archaeol Trust Monogr, **4**, 96–124

Isles, R, 1978 Avon Archaeology 1977, *Proc Somerset Archaeol Nat Hist Soc,* **122**, 149–52

Jackson, R J P, & Potter, T W, 1996 *Excavations at Stonea, Cambridgeshire 1980–85*. London

Jackson, W, 1877 *Visitors Handbook to Weston-super-Mare and its Vicinity*. London: Hodder & Stoughton

Jacomet, S, 1987 *Prahistorische Getreidefunde: a guide to the identification of prehistoric barley and wheat finds.* Basel: Botanical Institute of the Univ, Dept of Taxonomy and Geobotany

Jennings, J, 1869 *The Dialect of the West of England Particularly Somerset*. London

Jermy, A C, Chater, A O, & David, R W, 1982 *Sedges of the British Isles*. London: Botanical Soc of the British Isles

Jervis, W W, & Jones, S J, 1935 The village of Congresbury: a study in land tenure, *The Somerset Year Book 1935*, 86–91

Jessop, O, 1997 *Medieval Arrowheads*. Finds Res Group Newsheet **22**

Johnson, M, 1990 The Englishman's home and its study, in R Samson (ed) *The social archaeology of houses*. Edinburgh: Edinburgh Univ Press, 245–57

Johnson, M, 1997 Rethinking houses, rethinking transitions: of vernacular architecture, ordinary people and everyday culture, in D Gaimster, & P Stamper (eds) *The Age of Transition: The Archaeology of English Culture 1400–1600*. Oxford: Soc Med Archaeol Monogr, **15**, 145–56

Johnson, S, 1990 Marine Mollusca, in M Bell (ed) 1990, 250–2

Jones, B, & Mattingly, D, 1990 *An Atlas of Roman Britain*. Oxford: Blackwell

Jones, G R J, 1979 Multiple estates and early settlements, in P H Sawyer (ed) *English Medieval Settlement*. London: Edward Arnold, 9–34

Jones, G R J, 1985 Multiple estates perceived, *J Hist Geog,* **11(iv)**, 352–63

Jones, J, 1995 Weston-super-Mare Primary Distributor Road: an assessment of the environmental remains, in G L Smith, & A C Young 1995

Jones, M, 1978 The Plant Remains, in M Parrington (ed) *The excavation of an Iron Age Settlement, Bronze Age Ring Ditches and Roman Features at Ashville Trading Estate, Abingdon, Oxon. 1974–76*. London: Council for British Archaeology Res Rep, **28**, 93–110

Jones, M, 1981 The development of crop husbandry, in M Jones, & G Dimbleby (eds) *The Environment of Man: the Iron Age to the Anglo-Saxon period*. BAR Brit Ser **87**. Oxford: British Archaeological Report, 95–127

Jones, R, & Page, M, 2003 Characterising rural settlement and landscape: Whittlewood Forest in the Middle Ages, *Med Archaeol,* **47**, 53–84

Jones, R, & Page, M, forthcoming *Medieval Villages in an English Landscape: Beginnings and Ends*. Macclesfield: Windgather Press

Jordan, D, 2002 *A Geoarchaeological Evaluation of Deposits from St Georges, Worle*. Unpubl report. Terra Nova

Juggins, S, 1982 *The Geoarchaeology of Hallen Marsh*. Unpubl report in Bristol City SMR

Kain, R J P, 1986 *An Atlas and Index of the Tithe Files of Mid-Nineteenth-Century England and Wales*. Cambridge: Cambridge Univ Press

Kain, R J P, & Oliver, R, 2002 *The historic parishes of England and Wales: an electronic map of boundaries before 1850 with a gazetteer and metadata*. Colchester: History Data Service, UK Data Archive

Keil, I J E, 1964 *The Estates of Glastonbury Abbey in the Later Middle Ages*. Unpubl PhD thesis, Univ of Bristol

Kerney, M P, 1999 *Atlas of the Land and Freshwater Molluscs of Britain and Ireland*. Harley: Colchester

Kerney, M P, & Cameron, R A D, 1979 *A Field Guide to the Land Snails of Britain and North-West Europe*. London: Collins

Keynes, S, & Lapidge, M, 1983 *Alfred the Great: Asser's* Life of King Alfred *and other contemporary sources*. London: Penguin

Kidson, C, & Heyworth, A, 1978 Holocene eustatic sea level change, *Nature,* **273**, 748–50

Kilmurry, K, 1980 *The Pottery Industry of Stamford, Lincs, c AD 850–1250*. BAR Brit Ser **84**. Oxford: British Archaeological Report

King, A, 1988 Villas and animal bones, in K Branigan, & D Miles (eds) *The Economies of Romano-British Villas*. Sheffield: Dept of Archaeology, Univ Sheffield, 51–9

Kissock, J, 1997 'God made nature and men made towns': Post-Conquest and Pre-Conquest villages in Pembrokeshire, in N Edwards (ed) 1997, 123–37

Klein, R G, & Cruz-Uribe, K, 1984 *The Analysis of Animal Bones from Archaeological Sites*. Chicago: Univ of Chicago Press

Knight, J, 1962 The Goldcliff Stone: a reconsideration, *Monmouthshire Antiq*, **1(ii)**, 34–6

Knight, W, 1902 *The Sea-Board of Mendip*. London: J M Dent

Krammer, K, & Lange-Bertalot, H, 1986–91 *Bacillariophyceae*. Stuttgart: Gustav Fisher Verlag

Lane, T, 1993 *The Fenland Project, Number 8: Lincolnshire Survey, the northern fen-edge*. East Anglian Archaeology, **66**

Lane, T, & Morris, E, 2001 *A Millennium of Salt Making: prehistoric and Romano-British Salt Production in the Fenland*. Sleaford: Lincolnshire Archaeol and Heritage Rep Ser **4**

Lankstead, D, 2003 *Grapevine Farm, St Georges, Worle, North Somerset: Archaeological Evaluation and Excavation*. Unpubl report. Cotswold Archaeology report 03047

Latham, R E, 1980 *Revised Medieval Latin Word-List from British and Irish Sources with Supplement*. London: British Academy

Lawler, M, Parkhouse, J, & Straker, V, 1992 *Archaeology of the Second Severn Crossing: Assessment and recommendations for the English Approaches*. Unpubl report. Glamorgan Gwent Archaeol Trust

Leach, M, 1990 *Mice of the British Isles*. Princes Risborough: Shire Publications Ltd

Leach, P, 1982 *Ilchester Volume I: Excavations 1974–75*. Bristol: Western Archaeol Trust

Leach, P, 1984 *The Archaeology of Taunton*. Bristol: Western Archaeol Trust

Leach, P, 2001a *Excavation of a Romano-British roadside settlement in Somerset: Fosse Lane, Shepton Mallet 1990*. London: Britannia Monogr Series, **18**

Leach, P, 2001b *Roman Somerset*. Wimborne: Dovecot Press

Leach, P, & Ellis, P, 2004 Roman and medieval remains at Manor Farm, Castle Cary, *Proc Som Archaeol Nat Hist Soc,* **147**, 80–128

Leech, R H, 1977 Late Iron Age and Romano-British briquetage sites at Quarrylamds Lane, Badgworth, *Proc Som Archaeol Nat Hist Soc,* **121**, 89–96

Leech, R, 1981a The excavation of a Romano-British farmstead and cemetery on Bradley Hill, Somerton, Somerset, *Britannia,* **12**, 177–252

Leech, R, 1981b The Somerset Levels in the Romano-British period, in T Rowley (ed) *The Evolution of Marshland Landscapes*. Oxford: Univ of Oxford Dept of External Studies, 20–51

Leech, R, 1982a The Roman interlude in the South West: the dynamics of economic and social change in Romano-British South Somerset and North Dorset, in D Miles (ed) *The Romano-British Countryside*. BAR Brit Ser **103**. Oxford: British Archaeological Report, 209–67

Leech, R, 1982b *Excavations at Catsgore, 1970–73*. Bristol: Western Archaeol Trust

Leech, R, Bell, M, & Evans, J, 1983 The sectioning of a Romano-British salt-making mound at East Huntspill *Somerset Levels Papers,* **9**, 74–80

Leech, R, & Leach, P, 1982 Roman town and countryside 43–450 AD, in M Aston, & I Burrow (eds) *The Archaeology of Somerset*. Taunton: Somerset County Council, 62–81

Lennard, R, 1955/56 The demesne of Glastonbury Abbey in the eleventh and twelfth centuries, *Econ Hist Rev,* **8**, 255–303

Lennard, R, 1975 The Glastonbury estates: a rejoinder, *Econ Hist Rev,* **28**, 517–23

Letts, J B, 2000 *Smoke Blackened Thatch. A unique source of late medieval plant remains from Southern England*. London: English Heritage

Lewis, C, Mitchell-Fox, P, & Dyer, C, 1997 *Village, Hamlet and Field*. Manchester: Manchester Univ Press

Light, J, forthcoming a Marine molluscs, in M Aston, & C Gerrard (eds) forthcoming

Light, J, forthcoming b The marine and non-marine Mollusca, in *Excavations at Union Street, Bristol*. Oxford: Oxbow Books

Lilly, D, & Usher, G, 1972 Romano-British sites on the North Somerset Levels, *Proc Univ Bristol Spelaeological Soc,* **13(i)**, 37–40

Linnington, R E, & Rogers, G B, *c* 1961 Locking Roman villa, *Locking RAF Station Newsletter*

Little, B, 1976 *Portrait of Somerset, 4th edition*. London: Robert Hale

Lloyd, A T, 1967 The salterns of the Lymington area, *Proc Hampshire Field Club and Archaeol Soc,* **24**, 1–17

Locke, R A, 1806 Survey of Somerset, in M Ward (ed) *Supplement to Collinson's History of Somerset: Richard Locke, 18th century Antiquary, Surveyor and Agriculturalist*. Taunton: Baricotts

Locke, S, 1970–71 The post glacial deposits of the Caldicot Level and some associated archaeological discoveries, *Monmouthshire Antiquary,* **3**, 1–16

Locock, M, 2000 Buried soils of the Wentlooge Formation, *Archaeol in the Severn Estuary,* **10**, 1–10

Locock, M, & Lawler, M, 2000 Moated enclosures on the North Avon Level: survey and excavation at Rockingham Farm, Avonmouth, 1993–97, *Trans Bristol Gloucestershire Archaeol Soc,* **118**, 93–122

Locock, M, & Walker, M, 1998 Hill Farm, Goldcliff: Middle Iron Age drainage on the Caldicot Level, *Archaeol in the Severn Estuary,* **9**, 37–44

Lowe, B J, 1987 Keynsham Abbey: excavations 1961–85, *Proc Som Archaeol Nat Hist Soc,* **131**, 81–156

Machin, R, 1978 *The Houses of Yetminster*. Bristol: Univ Bristol Dept of Extra-Mural Studies

Mackley, M, & Faulkner, N, 1994 *Excavations at the Leigh Beck Marshes 1993*. Rochford Hundred Field Archaeology Group

Maltby, M, 1979 *The Animal Bones from Exeter 1971–75,* Exeter Archaeol Rep, **2**. Sheffield

Manchee, T J, 1831 *The Bristol Charities. Volume 1*. Bristol

Marvell, A, 2004 Roman settlement and economy, in N Nayling, & S McGrail *The Barland's Farm Romano-Celtic Boat*. York: Council for British Archaeology Res Rep, **138**, 99–110

Mason, D J P, 1988 '*Prata Legionis*' in Britain, *Britannia,* **19**, 163–89

Masser, P, Jones, J, & McGill, B, 2005 Romano-British settlement and land-use on the Avonmouth Levels: the evidence of the Pucklechurch to Seabank pipeline project, *Trans Bristol Gloucestershire Archaeol Soc* **123**, 55–86

Maxwell-Lyte, H C, 1920a *Inquisitions and Assessments Relating to Feudal Aids with other analogous documents,* volume IV. London: HMSO

Maxwell-Lyte, H C, 1920b Liber Feodorum. *The Book of Fees commonly called Terra de Nevill, Part 1 1198–1242*. London: HMSO

Maxwell-Lyte, H C, 1937 *The Register of Robert Stillington, Bishop of Bath and Wells, 1466–91*. Somerset Rec Soc, **52**

Maxwell-Lyte, H C, 1940 *The Register of William Knyght, Bishop of Bath and Wells, 1541–47*. Somerset Rec Soc, **55**

McAvoy, F, 1994 Marine salt extraction on salterns at Wainfleet St Mary, Lincolnshire, *Medieval Archaeol,* **38**, 134–63

McCobb, L M E, Briggs, D E G, Evershed, R P, Hall, A R, & Hall, R A, 2001 Preservation of fossil seeds from a 10th century AD cess pit at Coppergate, York, *J Archaeol Science,* **28**, 929–40

McGill, B, 2001a *The Archaeology of the Pucklechurch to Seabank Pipeline: Final Report Volume 2 – Awkley to Crooks Marsh*. Edinburgh: McGill Archaeological Consultants

McGill, B, 2001b *The Archaeology of the Pucklechurch to Seabank Pipeline: Appendices to the final report*. Edinburgh: McGill Archaeological Consultants

McOmish, D, Field, D, & Brown, G, 2002 *The Field Archaeology of the Salisbury Plain Training Area*. Swindon: English Heritage

Meddens, F, 2001 The Roman landscape between Chepstow and Nash and its implications for Roman land management, *Archaeol in the Severn Estuary,* **12**, 1–13

Meddens, F M, & Beasley, M, 2001 Roman seasonal wet pasture exploitation near Nash, on the Caldicot Levels, Wales, *Britannia,* **32**, 141–84

Mepham, L, 2000 The pottery, in M Rawlings Excavations at Ivy Street and Brown Street, Salisbury, 1994, *Wiltshire Archaeol Nat Hist Mag,* **93**, 20–62 (29–37)

Mikkola, H, 1983 *Owls of Europe*. London: T & AD Poyser

Miles, A, 1975 Salt-panning in Romano-British Kent, in K A De Brisay, & K A Evans (eds) 1975, 26–31

Miles, A, 2004 Excavations on the Romano-British industrial site at Broomhey Farm, Cooling, *Archaeologia Cantiana* **124**, 309–42
Millett, M, 1990 *The Romanisation of Britain*. Cambridge: Cambridge Univ Press
Mills, A D, 1991 *A Dictionary of English Place Names*. Oxford: Oxford Univ Press
Mitchell, A, 1974 *A Field Guide to the Trees of Britain and Northern Europe*. London: Collins
Moffett, L, 1988 *The Archaeobotanical Evidence for Saxon and Medieval Agriculture in Central England circa 500AD to 1500AD*. Unpubl MPhil thesis, Univ of Birmingham
Moffett, L, 1991 *The Archaeobotanical Evidence for Free-Threshing Tetraploid Wheat in Britain*. Palaeoethnobotany and Archaeology. International Work-Group for palaeoethnobotany. 8th Symposium, Nitra-Nove Vozokany, 1989. Archaeol Academy of Sciences, Nitra
Montague, R, Hearne, C, & Farwell, D E, 1992 Excavations at North Street, Stoke sub Hamdon, 1992, *Proc Som Archaeol Nat Hist Soc* **136**, 103–15
Moore, P D, Webb, J A, & Collinson, M E, 1991 *Pollen Analysis* 2nd edn. Oxford: Blackwell Scientific Publications
Morgan, O, 1882 *Goldcliff and the Roman Inscribed Stone found there in 1878*. Caerleon and Monmouthshire Antiquarian Soc
Morland, S C, 1963–64 Further notes on Somerset Domesday, *Proc Som Archaeol Nat Hist Soc,* **108**, 94–8
Morris, P, 1979 *Agricultural Buildings in Roman Britain*. BAR Brit Ser **70**. Oxford: British Archaeological Report
MPRG, 1998 *A Guide to the Classification of Medieval Ceramic Forms*, Medieval Pottery Res Group Occasional Paper, **1**
MSRG, 1996 Medieval rural settlement – a policy on their future survey, conservation and excavation, *Med Settlement Res Group Annual Report,* **11**, 5–8
Muir, R, 2001 *Landscape Detective*. Macclesfield: Windgather Press
Mulkeen, S, & O'Connor, T P, 1997 Raptors in towns: towards an ecological model, *International J Osteoarchaeology,* **7 (iv)**, 440–9
Murray, J W, 1973 *Distribution and Ecology of Living Benthic Foraminiferids*. London: Heinemann
Murray, J W, 1979 *British Nearshore Foraminiferids*. London: Academic Press
Murray, J W, 1991 *Ecology and Palaeoecology of Benthic Foraminifera*. London: Longman Scientific
Murray, J W, & Hawkins, A B, 1976 Sediment transport in the Severn Estuary during the past 8000–9000 years, *J Geol Soc London,* **132**, 385–98
Nash, S, 1974 Old Auster, *Somerset and Dorset Notes and Queries,* **28**, 245–7
Nayling, N, & Caseldine, A, 1997 *Excavations at Caldicot, Gwent: Bronze Age palaeochannels in the Lower Nedern Valley*. York: Council for British Archaeology Res Rep, **108**
Nayling, N, & McGrail, S, 2004 *The Barland's Farm Romano-Celtic boat*. York: Council for British Archaeology Res Rep, **138**
Neale, F, 1970 The site of a Roman villa at Havyatt, Somerset, *Proc Univ Bristol Spelaeological Soc,* **12(ii)**, 195–202
Oakes, C M, & Costen, M, 2003 The Congresbury carvings – an eleventh century Saint's shrine, *Antiq J,* **83**, 281–311
O'Connor, T, 1994 Eighth to tenth century economy and environment in York, in J Rackham (ed) *Environment and economy in Anglo-Saxon England*. York: Council for British Archaeology Res Rep, **89**, 136–47
O'Donovan, M A, 1988 *Charters of Sherborne*. Oxford: Oxford Univ Press
Oosthuizen, S, 2002 Medieval greens and moats in the central province: evidence from the Bourne Valley, Cambridgeshire, *Landscape History,* **24**, 73–88
Page, M, & Jones, R, in press Stability and instability in medieval village plans: Case-Studies in Whittlewood, in M Gardiner, & S Rippon (eds) *Medieval Landscapes in Britain*. Macclesfield: Windgather Press
Parker, A J, 1988 The birds of Roman Britain, *J Oxford Archaeol*, **7**, 197–226
Payne, S, 1973 Kill-off patterns in sheep and goat: the mandibles from Asvan Kale, *Anatolian Studies,* **23**, 281–303
Payne, S, 1985 Morphological distinctions between the mandibular teeth of young sheep, *Ovis*, and goats, *Capra, J Archaeol Sci,* **12**, 139–47
Peacock, D P S, 1969 A contribution to the study of Glastonbury Ware from south-western Britain, *Antiq J,* **49**, 41–61
Pearce, S, 2004 *South-western Britain in the Early Middle Ages*. London: Continuum
Pearson, T, 1984 Medieval and post-medieval ceramics in Taunton, in P Leach (ed) 1984, 142–4
Penoyre, J, 1998 Medieval Somerset Roofs, *Proc Som Archaeol Nat Hist Soc,* **141**, 76–89
Penoyre, J, 2005 *Traditional Houses of Somerset*. Taunton: Somerset Books
Penoyre, J, & Penoyre, J, 1999 Somerset dendrochronology project, *Proc Som Archaeol Nat Hist Soc,* **142**, 311–15
Pevsner, N, 1958 *The Buildings of England: North Somerset and Bristol*. London: Penguin Books
Phelps, W, 1836 *The History and Antiquities of Somersetshire*. London
Philip, B, & Willson, J, 1984 Roman site at Scotney Court, Lydd, *Kent Archaeol Rev,* **68**, 156–61
Ponsford, M, 1991 Dendrochronological dates from Dundas Wharf, Bristol and the dating of Ham Green and other medieval pottery, in E Lewis (ed) *Custom and Ceramics*. Wickham, 81–103
Ponsford, M, 1998 Pottery, in R Price, & M Ponsford 1998, 136–55

Ponsford, M, 2003 Excavations at a Saxo-Norman settlement, Bickley, Cleeve, 1982–89, *Proc Som Archaeol Nat Hist Soc,* **146**, 47–112

Poole, E Y, 1885 Remains of an ancient galley found under Grove Terrace, *Weston Mercury,* 4 July 1885, 8

Postan, M, 1952/53 Glastonbury estates in the twelfth century, *Econ Hist Rev,* **5**, 358–66

Postan, M, 1956/57 Glastonbury estates in the twelfth century: a reply, *Econ Hist Rev,* **9**, 106–18

Postan, M, 1972 *The Medieval Economy and Society*. London: Weidenfield & Nicholson

Postan, M, 1975 Glastonbury estates in the twelfth century: a restatement, *Econ Hist Rev,* **28**, 524–7

Powell, D, 1999 The manor book of Banwell, *Search: J Banwell Archaeol Soc,* **23**, 39–41

Price, R, & Ponsford, M, 1998 *St Bartholomew's Hospital Bristol: the excavation of a medieval hospital 1976–78*. York: Council for British Archaeology Res Rep, **110**

Rackham, O, 1986 *A History of the Countryside*. London: Dent

Rackham, O, 1990 *Trees and Woodland in the British Landscape*, 2nd edn. London: Dent

Rahtz, P, 1979 *The Saxon and Medieval Palaces at Cheddar: excavations 1960–62*. BAR Brit Ser **65**. Oxford: British Archaeological Report

Rahtz, P A, & Greenfield, E, 1977 *Excavations at Chew Valley Lake, Somerset*. London: Department of the Environment Archaeol Report **5**

Rahtz, P, & Hirst, S, 1974 *Beckery Chapel Glastonbury 1967–68*. Glastonbury: Glastonbury Antiquarian Soc

Rahtz, P, Hirst, S, & Wright, S M, 2000 *Cannington Cemetery: excavations 1962–63 of prehistoric, Roman, post-Roman and later features at Cannington Park Quarry, near Bridgwater, Somerset*. London: Britannia Monogr, **17**

Rahtz, P, Woodward, A, Burrow, I, Everton, A, Watts, L, Leach, P, Hirst, S, Fowler, P, & Gardiner, K, 1992 *Cadbury Congresbury 1968–73: A Late/Post-Roman Hilltop Settlement in Somerset*. BAR Brit Ser **223**. Oxford: British Archaeological Report

Rahtz, P A, & Watts, L, 1989 Pagan's Hill revisited, *Archaeol J,* **146**, 330–71

Reade, R C, 1885 The Roman villa at Great Wemberham, *Proc Somerset Archaeol Nat Hist Soc,* **31(ii)**, 64–73

Rees, S E, 1979 *Agricultural Implements in Prehistoric and Roman Britain*. BAR Brit Ser **69**. Oxford: British Archaeological Report

Reid-Henry, D, & Harrison, C, 1988 *The History of the Birds of Britain*. London: Collins

Rendell, J N, 1983 Banwell in the early 1700s, *Search: J Banwell Archaeol Soc,* **19**, 77–82

Rendell, J N, 1986/87 Riverside Roman villa, *Search: J Banwell Archaeol Soc,* **22**, 9–12

Rendell, S, 1985/86 The house on the Moor: George Bennett's inheritance, *Search: J Banwell Archaeol Soc,* **21**, 75–7

Rendell, S D, & Rendell, J N, 1979 Banwell in the early 1700s, *Search: J Banwell Archaeol Soc,* **15**, f.A–E

Richter, M, 1976 *Giraldus Cambrensis: the growth of the Welsh nation*. Aberystwyth: The National Library of Wales

Riley, H, & Wilson-North, R, 2001 *The Field Archaeology of Exmoor*. London, English Heritage

Rippon, S, 1993 *Landscape Evolution and Wetland Reclamation Around the Severn Estuary*. Unpubl PhD, Univ of Reading

Rippon, S, 1994a Medieval wetland reclamation in Somerset, in M Aston, & C Lewis 1994, 239–53

Rippon, S, 1994b The Roman settlement and landscape at Kenn Moor. North Somerset: Interim Report on Survey and Excavation in 1993/94, *Archaeology in the Severn Estuary 1994*, 21–34

Rippon, S, 1995a Roman settlement and salt production on the Somerset coast: the work of Sam Nash — a Somerset archaeologist and historian 1913–85, *Proc Som Archaeol Nat Hist Soc,* **139**, 99–117

Rippon, S, 1995b The Roman settlement and landscape at Kenn Moor, Avon: second interim report on survey and excavation, 1994/95, *Archaeol in the Severn Estuary,* **6**, 35–47

Rippon, S, 1996a *Gwent Levels: The Evolution of a Wetland Landscape*. York: Council for British Archaeology Res Rep, **105**

Rippon, S, 1996b *The Gwent Levels Historic Landscape Study: Characterization and Assessment of the Landscape*. Reading: Univ of Reading for Cadw/Countryside Council for Wales

Rippon, S, 1997a *The Severn Estuary: Landscape Evolution and Wetland Reclamation*. London: Leicester Univ Press

Rippon, S, 1997b Roman and medieval settlement on the North Somerset Levels: second season of survey and excavation at Banwell and Puxton, 1997, *Archaeol in the Severn Estuary,* **8**, 41–54

Rippon, S, 1997c Wetland reclamation on the Gwent Levels: dissecting a historic landscape, in N Edwards (ed) 1997, 13–30

Rippon, S, 2000a The *Transformation of Coastal Wetlands: exploitation and management of marshland landscapes in North West Europe during the Roman and Medieval periods*. London: British Academy

Rippon, S, 2000b The Romano-British exploitation of coastal wetlands: survey and excavation on the North Somerset Levels, 1993–97, *Britannia,* **31**, 69–200

Rippon, S, 2000c The historic landscapes of the Severn Estuary Levels, in S Rippon (ed) *Estuarine Archaeology: The Severn and Beyond*. Exeter: Severn Estuary Levels Res Comm, 145–62

Rippon, S, 2001a Reclamation and regional economies of medieval Britain, in B Raftery (ed) *Recent developments in wetland research*. Dublin, 139–58

Rippon, S, 2001b Adaptation to a changing environment: the response of marshland communities to the late medieval 'crisis', *J Wetland Archaeol,* **1**, 15–39

Rippon, S, 2002 Infield and outfield: the early stages of marshland colonisation and the evolution of medieval field systems, in J Coles, & P Lane (eds) *Through Wet and Dry: essays in honour of David Hall.* Sleaford: Heritage Lincolnshire, 54–70

Rippon, S, 2004a *Historic Landscape Analysis*. York: Council for British Archaeology Handbook, **16**

Rippon, S, 2004b A push into the margins? The development of a coastal landscape in North West Somerset during the 1st millennium AD, in J Hines, A Lane, & M Redknap (eds) *Land, Sea and Home*. Leeds: Soc Med Archaeol Monogr, **20**, 359–78

Rippon, S, 2004c Making the most of a bad situation? Glastonbury Abbey and the exploitation of wetland resources in the Somerset Levels, *Med Archaeol,* **48**, 91–130

Rippon, S, 2005 Water and wetlands in medieval estate management: Glastonbury Abbey, Meare and the Somerset Levels in South West England, in J Klápšt (ed) *Ruralia V: proceedings of an international conference, 26 September to 3 October 2003*. Prague, 93–112

Rippon, S, forthcoming a Fields of corn and flocks of sheep: wetland transformation during the medieval period, in Bell, M, & Boardman, J (ed) *Landscape changes over archaeological timescales*

Rippon, S, forthcoming b Waterways and water transport on Reclaimed Coastal Marshlands: the Severn Estuary and Beyond, in J Blair (ed) *Early Medieval Water Management*. Studies in Med Hist and Archaeol. Oxford: Oxford Univ Press

Rippon, S, Fyfe, F M, & Brown, A G, in press Beyond villages and open fields: the origins and development of a historic landscape characterised by dispersed settlement in South West England, *Medieval Archaeol* **50**, 31–70

Rippon, S, Jackson, A, & Martin, M, 2001 The use of soil analysis in the interpretation of an early historic landscape at Puxton in Somerset, *Landscape Hist,* **23**, 27–38

Rivet, A L F, 1966 *Town and Country in Roman Britain* (3rd edn). London: Hutchinson

Roberts, B, 1987 *The Making of the English Village*. London: Longman

Roberts, B K, & Wrathmell, S, 2000 *An Atlas of Rural Settlement in England*. London: English Heritage

Roberts, B K, & Wrathmell, S, 2002 *Region and Place*. London: English Heritage

Robinson, M, 1992 Environmental archaeology of the river gravels: past achievements and future directions, in M Fulford, & E Nichols (eds) *Developing Landscapes of Lowland Britain. The Archaeology of the British Gravels: a Review*. London: Soc Antiq, 47–62

Robinson, M, 1994 Plant macrofossils, in M Fulford *et al* 1994, 202–5

Robinson, M, & Straker, V, 1991 Silica skeletons of macroscopic plant remains from ash, in J Renfrew (ed) *New Light on Early Farming. Recent Developments in Palaeoethnobotany*. Edinburgh: Edinburgh Univ Press

Robinson, W J, 1914 *West County Churches*. Bristol

Rodwell, J S, 2000 *British Plant Communities. Volume 5. Maritime communities and vegetation of open habitats*. Cambridge: Cambridge Univ Press

Rodwell, K A, 1991 Court Farm, Lower Almondsbury, *Trans Bristol Gloucestershire Archaeol Soc,* **109**, 179–94

Rogerson, A, Davison, A, Pritchard, D, & Silvester, R, 1997 *Barton Bendish and Caldecote: Fieldwork in South-West Norfolk*. East Anglian Archaeology, **80**

Rouillard, S E, 1989 The Iron Age pottery from Meare Village East, in J M Coles (ed), *Meare Village East, the excavations of A Bulleid, and H St George Gray 1932–56*. Somerset Levels Papers, **13**, 183–221

Rowlands, I W, 1980 The making of the march: aspects of the Norman settlement of Dyfed, *Anglo-Norman Studies,* **3**, 142–57

Rowley, T, 1981 *The Origins of Open Field Agriculture*. London: Croom Helm

Rudkin, E H, & Owen, D M, 1960 The medieval salt industry on the Lincolnshire marsh, *Lincs Architect and Archaeol Soc Rep Pap* **8**, 76–84

Russett, V, 1989 A Romano-British site at Rooksbridge, *Axbridge Archaeol and Local History Soc J*, 37–89

Rutter, J, 1829 *Delineations of the North Western Division of the Country of Somerset*. London

Rye, G P, 1986/87 Roman villa at Banwell, *Search: J Banwell Archaeol Soc,* **22**, 12–13

Sabin, A, 1968 Old auster: a reply, *Somerset Dorset Notes Queries,* **29**, 191–2

Sawyer, P H, 1968 *Anglo-Saxon Charters: An Annotated List and Bibliography*. London: Royal Historical Soc

Scaife, R G, 1987 Pollen analysis, in N D Balaam, B Levitan, & V Straker, *Studies in palaeoeconomy and environment in south west England*. BAR Brit Ser **181**. Oxford: British Archaeological Report, 223–32

Scaife, R G, 1993 The palynological investigations of the peats and sediments, in S Godbold, & R Turner, *Second Severn Crossing, Archaeological Response: Phase 1, the intertidal zone in Wales*. Cardiff: Cadw, 51–9

Scaife, R G, 1995 Pollen analysis and radiocarbon dating of the intertidal peats at Caldicot Pill, *Archaeol in the Severn Estuary*, **6**, 67–80

Scarth, H, 1885 The Roman villa at Wemberham in Yatton, *Proc Som Archaeol Nat Hist Soc,* **31(ii)**, 1–9

Scarth, H, 1887 On an interment found on Cadbury Hill, *Proc Som Archaeol Nat Hist Soc,* **33(ii)**, 9

Schmid, E, 1972 *Atlas of Animal Bones*. London: Elsevier

Seaby, P, & Purvey, P F, 1980 *Coins of England and the United Kingdom*. London: Seaby

Seagar Smith, R, 2003 *Roman Pottery From the Somerset Levels: material saltern sites held in the collections of Somerset County Museum, Taunton*. Unpubl report. Salisbury, Wessex Archaeology Report 45393

Selkirk, A, 1987 Raunds, *Current Archaeol,* **9**, 323–7

Shaw, M, 1993/94 The discovery of Saxon sites below fieldwalking scatters: settlement evidence at Brixworth and Upton, *Northamptonshire Archaeol,* **25**, 77–92

Shilton, O, & Holsworthy, R, 1925 *Medieval wills from Wells: deposited in the Diocesan Registry, Wells (1543–46 and 1554–56)*. Somerset Rec Soc, **40**

Silver, I, 1969 The ageing and sexing of domestic animals, in D Brothwell, & E Higgs (eds) *Science in Archaeology*. London: Thames & Hudson, 283–302

Silvester, R J, 1988 *The Fenland Project, Number 3: Norfolk Survey, Marshland and Nar Valley*. East Anglian Archaeology, **45**

Silvester, R J, 1993 'The addition of more-or-less undifferentiated dots to a distribution map'? The Fenland Project in Retrospect, in J Gardiner (ed) *Flatlands and Wetlands: current themes in East Anglian archaeology*. East Anglian Archaeology **50**, 24–39

Silvester, R, 1997 Historic settlement surveys in Clywd and Powys, in N Edwards (ed) 1997, 113–21

Simoons, F J, 1994 *Eat Not This Flesh: Food Avoidances from Prehistory to the Present*. Madison: Univ of Wisconsin Press

Skeggs, J, 1992 *Somerset Words: a dialect wordlist particularly relating to agriculture and natural history*. West Buckland: private publication

Smith, E, Hutton, G, & Cook, O, 1994 *English Parish Churches.* London

Smith, G L, 1993 *Broome Manor Nursery, Tickenham, Avon: archaeological watching brief during construction of a wildlife pond and conservation area*. Unpubl report, copy in North Somerset SMR, No 9212. Bristol: Avon Archaeol Unit

Smith, G L, & Young, A C, 1995 *Archaeological Monitoring During the Construction of the Weston-super-Mare Primary Distributor Road*. Unpubl report, Avon Archaeol Unit

Smith, W, 2003 *Medieval Charred Plant Remains from Whitegate Farm, Bleadon, North Somerset*. English Heritage, Centre for Archaeology report 56/2003

Smyth, A P, 1995 *King Alfred the Great*. Oxford: Oxford Univ Press

Somerset County Council, 1992 *A Palaeoenvironmental Investigation of a Field off White's Drove, Godney Moor, Near Wells, Somerset: Interim Report*. Taunton: unpublished report, Somerset County Council Environment Section

Sparkes, I G, 1976 *Old Horseshoes*. Aylesbury: Shire Publications

SSAVBRG, 1982 *Long Load and Knole, Long Sutton: their houses, cottages and farms, settlement and people*. Somerset and South Avon Vernacular Building Res Group

SSAVBRG, 1984 *The Vernacular Buildings of West and Middle Chinnock*. Somerset and South Avon Vernacular Building Res Group

SSAVBRG, 1986 *The Vernacular Houses with Farms and Farmsteads of Alford and Lovington*. Somerset and South Avon Vernacular Building Res Group

SSAVBRG, 1988 *The Vernacular Buildings of Batcombe*. Somerset and South Avon Vernacular Building Res Group

SSAVBRG, 1993 *The Houses, Cottages and Farms of Chiselborough*. Somerset and South Avon Vernacular Building Res Group

SSAVBRG, 1994 *Haselbury Plunknett: evolution and change of Land, Society and Buildings*. Somerset and South Avon Vernacular Building Res Group

Stace, C, 1991 *New Flora of the British Isles*. Cambridge: Cambridge Univ Press

Stacey, N E, 1972 *The Estates of Glastonbury Abbey c 1050–1200*. Unpubl PhD thesis, Univ of Leeds

Stamper, P A, & Croft, R A, 2000 *The South Manor Area*. York: York Univ Archaeol Pubs **10**

Stevenson, W H, 1904 *Asser's Life of King Alfred*. Oxford: Clarendon Press

Stockmarr, J, 1971 Tablets with spores used in absolute pollen analysis, *Pollen et Spores,* **13**, 615

Storer, B, 1985 *The Natural History of the Somerset Levels.* Wimborne: Dovecote Press

SVBRG, 1996 *The Vernacular Buildings of Shapwick*. Somerset Vernacular Building Res Group

SVBRG, 2001 *Vernacular Houses and Farms of Butleigh*. Somerset Vernacular Building Res Group

SVBRG, 2004 *The Traditional Houses and Farms of Compton Dundon*. Somerset Vernacular Building Res Group

Sykes, C M, & Brown, J C, 1960/61 Birdcombe Court Roman Villa, *Proc Som Archaeol Nat Hist Soc,* **105**, 37–51

Taylor, C, 1983 *Village and Farmstead*. London: George Philip

Taylor, C, 1989 Whittlesford: the study of a river edge village, in M Aston *et al* (eds) 1989, 207–30

Taylor, C C, 2002 Nucleated settlement: a view from the frontier, *Landscape Hist,* **24**, 53–72

Taylor, C C, & Fowler, P J, 1978 Roman fields into medieval furlongs? in H C Bowen, & P J Fowler (eds) *Early Land Allotment*. BAR Brit Ser **44**. Oxford: British Archaeological Report, 159–62

Taylor, C S, 1905 Banwell, *Proc Som Archaeol Nat Hist Soc,* **51**, 31–76

Taylor, H M, 1978 *Anglo Saxon Architecture, volume III*. Cambridge: Cambridge Univ Press

Taylor, H M, & Taylor, J, 1965 *Anglo Saxon Architecture, volume 1*. Cambridge: Cambridge Univ Press

Taylor, R, 1999 Appendix 2: petrological study of the temper of the South-West English pottery from Cleeve Abbey, 47–59, in J Allan 'Cleeve Abbey: the pottery', *Proc Som Archaeol Nat Hist Soc,* **142**, 41–75

Thirsk, J (ed), 2000 *The English Rural Landscape*. Oxford: Oxford Univ Press

Thompson, M, 1998 *Medieval Bishops Houses in England and Wales*. Aldershot: Ashgate Press

Thompson, M G, 1997 *The Polden Hill Manors of Glastonbury Abbey: land and people circa 1260 to 1351*. PhD thesis, Univ of Leicester

Thorn, C, & Thorn, F, 1980 *Domesday Book: Somerset*. Chichester: Phillimore

Timby, J, 2000 The pottery, in S Rippon 2000b, 174–83

Timby, J, forthcoming The Roman pottery, in S Rippon Crandon Bridge: A Romano-British port on the Parrett Estuary, Somerset

Tinsley, H M, 2003 *Pollen Analysis of Sediment Samples from Trenches L, A, and H1, Walpole Landfill Site, Pawlett, Somerset*. Unpubl report for Wyvern Waste Services Ltd

Tipping, R, 2002 Climatic variability and 'marginal' settlement in upland British landscapes: a re-evaluation, *Landscapes,* **3(ii)**, 29–37

Tomber, R, & Dore J, 1998, *The National Roman Fabric Reference Collection: a handbook*. London: Museum of London/ English Heritage/British Museum

Toorians, L, 1990 Wizo Flandrensis and the Flemish settlement in Pembrokeshire, *Cambridge Medieval Celtic Studies,* **20**, 99–119

Toorians, L, 1996 Flemish settlements in twelfth-century Scotland, *Revue Belge De Philologie et D'Histoire,* **74**, 659–93

Toorians, L, 2000 Flemish in Wales, in G Proce (ed) *Languages in Britain and Ireland*. Oxford: Blackwell, 184–6

Tutin, T G, & Heywood, V H, 1964–80 *Flora Europaea,* 1–5. Cambridge

Upex, S, 2002 Landscape continuity and fossilization of Roman fields into Saxon and medieval landscapes, *Archaeol J,* **159**, 77–108

Usher, G, 1967 Some observations on the archaeology of the North Somerset Moors, *Clevedon and District Archaeol Soc News Sheet,* **26**, 3–5 [copy in Local Studies Library, Somerset]

Usher, G, & Lilly, D, 1964 A Romano-British pottery site at Venus Street, Congresbury, *Proc Somerset Archaeol Nat Hist Soc,* **108**, 172–4

Van Arsdell, R D, 1994 *The Coinage of the Dobunni*. Oxford

van Hoeve, M L, & Hendrikse M, 1998 *A Study of Non-pollen Objects in Pollen Slides: the Types as Described by Dr Bas van Geel and Colleagues*. Utrecht

Vince, A, 1979 Fabric types, in B Cunliffe (ed) 1979, 27–51.

Vince, A, 1984 *The Medieval Ceramic Industry of the Severn Valley*. Unpubl PhD thesis, Southampton Univ

Wade-Martins, P, 1980a *Village Sites in Launditch Hundred*. East Anglian Archaeology, **10**

Wade-Martins, P, 1980b *Excavations in North Elmham Park 1967–72, volume II*. East Anglian Archaeology, **9**

Walrond, L F J, & Powell, C, 1985 Medieval smoke vents and low room walls in the Severn Plain, *Trans Bristol Gloucestershire Archaeol Soc,* **103**, 163–74

Walker, M J C, Bell, M, Caseldine, A G, Cameron, N G, Hunter, K L, James, J H, Johnson, S, & Smith, D N, 1998 Palaeoecological investigations of middle and late Flandrian buried peats on the Caldicot Levels, Severn Estuary, Wales, *Proc Geologists Assoc,* **109**, 51–78

Warner, P, 1987 *Greens, Commons and Clayland Colonisation: the origins and development of Green-side settlement in East Suffolk*. Leicester: Leicester Univ Press

Warner, P, 1996 *The Origins of Suffolk*. Manchester: Manchester Univ Press

Watkin, D A, 1941 *Dean Cosyn and Wells Cathedral Miscellanea*. Somerset Rec Soc, **56**

Watts, L, & Leach, P, 1996 *Henley Wood, Temples and Cemetery Excavations 1962–69*. York: Council for British Archaeology Res Rep **99**

Watts, V, 2004 *The Cambridge Dictionary of English Place-Names*. Cambridge: Cambridge Univ Press

Weaver, F W, 1905 Worspring Priory, *Proc Som Archaeol Nat Hist Soc,* **51**, 10–30

Weaver, F W, 1910 *A Feodary of Glastonbury Abbey*. Somerset Rec Soc, **26**

Welin, E, Engstrand, L, & Vaczy, S, 1972 Institute of Geological Sciences Radiocarbon Dates II, *Radiocarbon,* **14**, 140–4

Welldon Finn, R, 1964 *Domesday Studies: the* Liber Exoniensis. London: Longmans

West, S E, & McLaughlin, A, 1998 *Towards a landscape history of Walsham le Willows*. East Anglian Archaeology, **85**

Whitelock, D, 1967 *The Genuine Asser*. Reading: Reading Univ

Williams, B, 1853 Additional remarks on the hide of land, and on some ancient manorial customs on Oxfordshire, *Archaeologia,* **35**, 470–2

Williams, E D H, 1977/78 Crucks in Avon., *Proc Som Archaeol Nat Hist Soc,* **122**, 151

Williams, E D H, 1987 Kingston Seymour, Gout Farm, *Proc Somerset Archaeol Nat Hist Soc,* **131**, 256

Williams, E D H, 1991 The building materials of Somerset's vernacular houses, *Proc Som Archaeol Nat Hist Soc,* **135**, 123–34

Williams, E D H, 1992 Church houses in Somerset, *Vernacular Architecture*, **23**, 15–23

Williams, E D H, & Gilson, R G, 1981 Base crucks in Somerset (III) and allied roof forms, *Proc Som Archaeol Nat Hist Soc,* **125**, 45–66

Williams, E H D, & Wilson, R G, 1982 Brick building in Somerset, *Vernacular Architecture,* **13**, 31–4

Williams, M, 1969 The 1801 Crop returns for Somerset, *Proc Som Archaeol Nat Hist Soc,* **113**, 69–85

Williams, M, 1970 *The Draining of the Somerset Levels*, Cambridge: Cambridge Univ Press

Williamson, T, 1987 Early co-axial field systems on the East Anglian boulder clays, *Proc Prehist Soc,* **53**, 419–31

Williamson, T, 2003 *Shaping the Medieval Landscapes*. Macclesfield: Windgather Press

Willis Watson, W G, 1908 *A History of Woodspring Priory, Somerset*. Weston-super-Mare

Wiltshire, P E J, Edwards, K J, & Bond, S, 1994 Microbially derived metallic sulphide spherules, pollen and waterlogging of archaeological sites, *AASP Contributions Series* **29**, 207–21

Woods, H, 1995 Excavations at Glastonbury Abbey 1987–93, *Proc Som Archaeol Nat Hist Soc,* **138**, 7–73

Woodward, G H, 1982 *Calendar of Chantry Grants*, 1548–1603. Somerset Rec Soc, **77**

Wrathmell, S, 1989 *Domestic Settlement 2: Medieval Peasant Farmsteads*. York: Wharram: A Study of Settlement in the Yorkshire Wolds **6**

Wrathmell, S, 2002 Some general hypotheses on English medieval peasant house construction from the 7th to the 17th centuries, in J Klápšt (ed) *The Rural House from the Migration Period to the Oldest Still Standing Buildings*. Prague: Institute of Archaeology, Academy of Sciences of the Czech Republic, 175–86

Wyndham, H A, 1950 *A Family History 1688–1837: The Wyndhams of Somerset, Sussex and Wiltshire*. Oxford: Oxford Univ Press

Yates, A M, Locock, M, & Walker, M J C, forthcoming A Later Bronze Age Coastal Landscape at Cabot Park, Avonmouth, Bristol, *Proc Prehist Soc*

Young, A C, 1992 *Archaeological Observations from Construction Sites in the Avonmouth Levels. Archaeological Report*. Unpubl report. Bristol: Avon Archaeol Unit

Young, A, 2002 *Site of Scott Elm Drive, West Wick, Weston-super-Mare. Archaeological Evaluation Report. North Somerset SMR 42762*. Unpubl report. Bristol: Avon Archaeol Unit

Young, R, & Simmonds, T, 1995 Marginality and the nature of later prehistoric upland settlement in the north of England, *Landscape Hist*, **17**, 5–15

Youngs, F A, 1979 *Guide to the Local Administrative Units of England. Vol.1: Southern England*. London: Royal Historical Society

Index

Page numbers in *italics* denote that the reference is, or includes, an illustration; n – note. All places are in historic Somerset unless specified otherwise.